BRIEF EDITION

THE CHALLENGE OF
DEMOCRACY

FOURTH EDITION

WITH GEORGIA'S CONSTITUTION AND GOVERNMENT

KENNETH JANDA
NORTHWESTERN UNIVERSITY

JEFFREY M. BERRY
TUFTS UNIVERSITY

JERRY GOLDMAN
NORTHWESTERN UNIVERSITY

ABRIDGED BY KEVIN W. HULA

HOUGHTON MIFFLIN COMPANY   Boston New York

Sponsoring Editor: Melissa Mashburn
Senior Associate Editor: Fran Gay
Associate Project Editor: Heather Hubbard
Senior Production/Design Coordinator: Jennifer Meyer Dare
Senior Manufacturing Coordinator: Priscilla Bailey
Marketing Manager Sandra McGuire

Georgia's Constitution and Government, 4th edition, by Arnold Fleischmann and
Carol Pierannunzi is used by permission of The University of Georgia Press.

Credits continue on page C-1, which constitutes an extension of the copyright page.

Custom Publishing Editor: Kyle Henderson
Custom Publishing Production Manager: Kathleen McCourt
Project Coordinator: Kyle Sarofeen

Printed in the United States of America.

ISBN: 0-618-18965-3
N00425

1 2 3 4 5 6 7 8 9 – PP– 04 03 02 01

 **Houghton Mifflin**
Custom Publishing

222 Berkeley Street • Boston, MA 02116

Address all correspondence and order information to the above address.

Contents

3

4

PUBLIC OPINION, POLITICAL SOCIALIZATION, AND THE MEDIA 79

7

8

9

10

11

12

13

Preface

The fourth edition of *The Challenge of Democracy,* Brief Edition, is an abridged and updated version of the very popular sixth edition of *The Challenge of Democracy.* Again, our goal was to streamline the larger text without diminishing any of the qualities that have made it so successful. Additionally, we sought to make the text as current as possible by incorporating examples from events occurring later in 2000 after the publication of the larger text. Among these examples are the results of the November 2000 elections.

Through the process of writing six editions of the larger text, however, what we are most struck by is how enduring our original framework is. *The Challenge of Democracy* is built around two themes that remain as relevant today as they were when we first conceived of this project. The first is the *clash among the values of freedom, order, and equality,* while the second focuses on the *tensions between pluralist and majoritarian visions of democracy.* Knowledge of these conflicts enables citizens to recognize and analyze the difficult choices they face in politics.

Because we wanted to write a book that students would actually read, we sought to discuss politics—a complex subject—in a captivating and understandable way. American politics isn't dull, and its textbooks needn't be either. But equally important, we wanted to produce a book that students would credit for stimulating their thinking about politics. While offering all the essential information about American government and politics, we believed that what was most important was to give students a framework for analyzing politics that they could use long after their studies ended.

Our framework travels well over time, and the past few years are no exception. In our discussion of the impeachment and trial of President Clinton, we explain that this episode was more than just scandal politics or bad judgment on the part of the president. The move to oust Clinton reflects the enduring conflict that emerges when policymakers try to legislate order in society. A few years ago, congressional Republicans claimed a mandate from the voters to enact the Contract with America. Would democracy be enhanced by this kind of majoritarian politics? The continuing fights over affirmative action, discussed in the pages that follow, illustrate the struggle to define equality in a modern, postindustrial society.

Thematic Framework

As noted above, two themes run through our book. One deals with the *conflict among values,* and the other with *alternative models of democracy.* In Chapter 1, we suggest that American politics often reflects conflicts between the values of freedom and order and between the values of freedom and equality. These value conflicts are prominent in contemporary American society, and they help to explain political controversy and consensus in earlier eras.

For instance, in Chapter 2 we argue that the Constitution was designed to promote order, and it virtually ignored issues of political and social equality. Equality was later served, however, by several amendments to the Constitution. In Chapter 12, "Civil Liberties and Civil Rights," we demonstrate that many of this nation's most controversial issues represent conflicts among individuals or groups who hold differing views on the values of freedom, order, and equality. Views on issues such as abortion are not just isolated opinions; they also reflect choices about the philosophy citizens want government to follow. Yet choosing among these values is difficult, sometimes excruciatingly so.

The second theme, also introduced in Chapter 1, asks students to consider two competing models of democratic government. One way that government can make decisions is by means of *majoritarian* principles—that is, by taking the actions desired by a majority of citizens. For instance, in Chapter 8, "Congress," we discuss the Republicans' Contract with America as an effort to move the national government to a more majoritarian system. A contrasting model of government, *pluralism,* is built around the interaction of decision makers in government with groups concerned about issues that affect them. Pluralism is a focus of Chapter 13, "Policymaking and the Budget," which discusses issue networks in the nation's capital.

These models are not mere abstractions; we use them to illustrate the dynamics of the American political system. In Chapter 9, "The Presidency," we discuss the problem of divided government. More often than not over the past forty years, the party that controlled the White House didn't control both houses of Congress. When these two branches of government are divided between the two parties, majoritarian government is difficult. Even when the same party controls both branches, the majoritarian model is not always realized—as Bill Clinton found out during 1993 and 1994.

Throughout the book we stress that students must make their own choices among the competing values and models of government. Although the three of us hold diverse and strong opinions about which choices are best, we do not believe it is our role to tell students our own answers to the broad questions we pose. Instead, we want our readers to learn firsthand that a democracy requires thoughtful choices. That is why we titled our book *The Challenge of Democracy.*

Features of the Fourth Brief Edition

The fourth edition maintains the basic structure of the previous edition while updating the political events of the past few years. We have also drawn on the latest research in political science to make sure that *The Challenge of Democracy* continues to represent the state of the art in our discipline.

To accommodate the major changes and new issues in politics that have occurred since the last edition, every chapter in the text has been thoroughly revised. This edition continues the significant change in Chapter 1 that was introduced in the third edition. Users familiar only with earlier editions should note that we have replaced the term *populist* with *communitarian* in our two-fold typology of political ideologies. In contemporary usage, *populist* is used in many different ways. Journalists, pundits, and social scientists all offer their own definitions of *populist*, while politicians on the left and on the right often lay claim to the label. Worried that these varying uses of the term would confuse students, we replaced it with a less common yet more descriptive term. As explained in Chapter 1, *communitarian* more clearly evokes the political thinking underlying a preference for order and equality.

We cannot inventory all the many changes in this edition, but we can illustrate the thoroughness of our revision with selected examples. In Chapter 3, "Federalism," we examine new restraints on the power of the national government resulting from the Supreme Court's 1997 decision in *United States v. Printz*. Chapter 4, "Public Opinion, Political Socialization, and the Media," has an expanded treatment of the Internet as a medium of group communication. In Chapter 6, "Political Parties, Campaigns, and Elections," we analyze the differences between the two major party platforms in the 2000 presidential campaign. In Chapter 8, "Congress," we do a retrospective assessment of the Contract with America in the context of the majoritarian model of democracy. The effort to impeach and remove the President and the results of the 2000 elections are discussed both in Chapter 8 and Chapter 9 ("The Presidency"). Chapter 9 analyzes the Kosovo crisis and the NATO war against Yugoslavia. Chapter 12, "Civil Liberties and Civil Rights," reports new experimental research tapping American attitudes toward race-preference policies. Chapter 13, "Policymaking and the Budget," has undergone a major rewrite and describes the surprising outcome of a balanced budget during the second term of the Clinton presidency, when balancing the budget seemed impossible during his first term.

As in previous editions, each chapter begins with a vignette. The purpose of each vignette is to draw students into the substance of that chapter, while suggesting one of the themes of the book. Chapters with new or revised vignettes include Chapter 6, "Political Parties, Campaigns, and Elections," which compares Ross Perot's impact on the presidential elections in 1992 and 1996; Chapter 7, "Interest Groups," which describes the setbacks to the tobacco lobby in the halls of Congress; Chapter 8, "Congress," which discusses the House Judiciary Committee's decisions to seek an impeachment of President Clinton; Chapter 9, "The Presidency," which looks at Clinton's decision to pursue a bombing campaign against Milosevic and Yugoslavia; and Chapter 13, "Policymaking and the Budget," which examines the ethical dilemmas brought into the public policy arena by technological innovation—in this case by the cloning of a sheep named Dolly.

This edition continues the series of features, "Politics in a Changing America," designed to illustrate changes over time in the political opportunity, participation, and status of groups such as women, African Americans, youth, Hispanics, and religious fundamentalists. These features allow us to highlight many controversial and complex issues in American society. Some of the original features have been retained, some have been updated, and some are new.

This edition reflects our firm belief that students can better evaluate how our political system works when they compare it with politics in other countries. Once again, several chapters have a boxed feature called "Compared with What?" that treats its topic in a comparative perspective. How much importance do citizens in other parts of the world place on freedom, order, and equality? Do American television reporters color the news with their commentary more than reporters do in other countries?

We have streamlined and enriched the close connection that we initiated in the previous edition between the words in our text and external computer resources. The rich resources of the Internet are featured in several ways. Each chapter concludes with "World Wide Web Resources," a list of World Wide Web sites that includes the URL and a brief description of each site. Another important resource for faculty and student users of our text is *The Challenge of Democracy Web Site* **uspolitics.org** (see below for more details). These advances keep *The Challenge of Democracy* at the leading edge of technology in studying American government.

Each chapter concludes with a brief summary, a list of key terms, a short list of recommended readings, and the World Wide Web Resources feature mentioned above. At the end of the book, we have included a copy of the Declaration of Independence and the Constitution.

The Teaching/Learning Package

When we began writing *The Challenge of Democracy*, we viewed the book as part of a tightly integrated set of instructional materials. We have worked closely with some very talented political scientists and with educational specialists at Houghton Mifflin to produce what we think is a superior set of ancillary materials to help both instructors and students.

For the Instructor: Innovative Teaching Tools

The *Instructor's Resource Manual with Test Items,* written by the authors and Lori Brainard and carefully updated by Kevin Hula of Loyola College in Maryland, provides teachers with material that relates directly to the thematic framework and organization of the book. The *Instructor's Resource Manual* includes learning objectives, chapter synopses, parallel lectures covering the material in each chapter, and suggestions for class projects and activities. The *Test Items* section provides hundreds of identification, multiple-choice, and essay questions.

Software ancillaries available to instructors include the *HMtesting* test generation program in Windows, containing all the items in the printed *Test Items.*

New to this edition is **uspolitics.org**, a companion web site to *The Challenge of Democracy,* developed by the authors. The **uspolitics.org** site offers a variety of teaching aids to instructors who adopt any version of *The Challenge of Democracy* as a textbook for courses in American politics. This site includes chapter summaries, presentation-quality images of data-oriented figures from every chapter, links to key Internet sites, model lectures on chapter topics, and

PowerPoint slides. This free Internet service is available only to faculty members who register as *Challenge* adopters.

Instructors using our site also have access to all of the resources on Houghton Mifflin's American Government home page, which can be accessed through **uspolitics.org** or by clicking on "Political Science" on the Houghton Mifflin web site at **http://college.hmco.com.** There, instructors can use **Political SourceNet**, which contains chapter-by-chapter primary source documents, and Internet assignments that require students to think critically about a document, political web site, or data-oriented map or figure. The American Government home page also features a Faculty Resources section to help political science instructors take full advantage of the unique opportunities the Web offers.

A transparency package, containing thirty full-color overhead transparencies, is available to adopters of the book. For information about a variety of additional visual media products available to adopters of *The Challenge of Democracy,* please contact your Houghton Mifflin sales representative.

For the Student: Effective Learning Aids

The *Study Guide,* written by Melissa Butler of Wabash College and updated by Kevin Hula, is designed to help students master the content of *The Challenge of Democracy,* Brief Edition. The *Study Guide* provides chapter summaries, research topics and resources (both in print and on the World Wide Web), exercises in reading tables and graphs, sample multiple-choice exam questions, and advice on improving study skills, finding internships, and participating in American politics.

The Brief Edition, fourth edition web site offers a wide array of resources for students, including ACE practice tests and links to *IDEAlog,* **uspolitics.org**, and web sites listed in the text.

Students also have access to all of the student resources located on Houghton Mifflin's American Government home page. These include **Political SourceNet**, a collection of chapter-by-chapter primary source documents; additional web links for further exploration; and Internet activities. The American Government home page is accessible from the Brief Edition web site or by clicking on "Political Science" on Houghton Mifflin's College Division site at **http://college.hmco.com**.

A new feature of Political SourceNet is *Crosstabs 4.0.* It allows students to cross-tabulate survey data on the 1996 presidential election and the voting records of members of the 105th Congress (1997–98). The *Crosstabs 4.0 Student Workbook,* which is available separately, shows how to construct and interpret basic cross-tabulations, suggests topics that students might study using the "voters" and "Congress" data sets, and tells how to write an empirical research paper. An *Instructor's Answer Book* is also available.

We invite your questions, suggestions, and criticisms of the teaching/learning package and *The Challenge of Democracy.* You may contact us at our respective institutions, or, if you have access to an electronic mail service, you may contact us through our collective e-mail address <cod@nwu.edu>.

Acknowledgments

In the sixth edition of *The Challenge of Democracy* we acknowledged the contributions of many individuals whose advice and assistance have been of great value. We remain in their debt. They include David Bishop, Stuart Baker, Claire Dougherty, Joe Germuska, Dennis Glenn, Brian Nielsen, Bob Taylor, Diane Petersmarck, Michelle Szumsky, Dennis Chong, Patricia Conley, Kyle Brix, Tony Becker, Brian Oberhauser, Jinney Smith, and Giel Stein (all of Northwestern); Richard Eichenberg, Jim Glaser, Don Klein, Tony Messina, Kent Portney, Pearl Robinson, and Jamie Lynch (of Tufts); Tom Smith, NORC; James Johnson, University of Nebraska, Omaha; Mario Brossard, *The Washington Post;* Ted and Cora Ginsberg; Maureen Roberts Romans; and Melissa Butler.

We would also like to thank reviewers who gave us advice on preparing the fourth edition of *The Challenge of Democracy,* Brief Edition. They are Margaret Ellis, Wichita State University; Monte S. Freidig, Santa Rosa Junior College; Louis Furmanski, University of Central Oklahoma; Michael Hoover, Seminole Community College; and Rogan Kersh, Syracuse University.

K. J.
J. M. B.
J. G.
K. W .H.

The
Challenge
of
Democracy

1

Dilemmas of Democracy

Suppose you are terminally ill and suffer excruciating pain. Do you have a "right" to die in this country? Does the state (that is, the government) have the right—even the duty—to keep you from committing suicide? What about a doctor who helps a doomed and tormented patient to commit suicide?

In the 1990s, Dr. Jack Kevorkian, a retired Michigan pathologist, helped over one hundred gravely ill people kill themselves.[1] Arrested under Michigan's 1992 law against assisted suicide, Kevorkian said, "I have never cared anything about the law."[2] Acquitted by juries in three trials, he evaded prison because his clients triggered their own deaths in each case. Then, in 1998, the TV show "60 Minutes" aired a video of Kevorkian himself giving a lethal injection to Thomas Youk, who was crippled by Lou Gehrig's disease and could not operate the device alone. Viewers heard the suffering and incurable Youk say he wanted to die, and his wife and brother supported his wish. Kevorkian dared the authorities to arrest him, and they did. This time he was convicted of murder. In sentencing the seventy-year-old man to prison for ten to twenty-five years, the judge said, "We are a nation of laws. . . . You may not take the law into your own hands."[3]

What are your views on this controversial issue? Should the government's interest in protecting life outweigh an individual's freedom to end his or her own life? Which is better: to live under a government that allows individuals complete freedom to do whatever they please or to live under one that enforces strict law and order? Which is better: to allow businesses and private clubs to choose their customers and members or to pass laws that require them to admit and serve everyone, regardless of race or sex?

For many people, none of these alternatives is satisfactory. All pose difficult dilemmas. The dilemmas are tied to opposing philosophies that place different values on freedom, order, and equality. This book explains American government and politics in light of these dilemmas. It does more than explain the workings of our government. It encourages you to think about what government should—and should not—do. And it judges the American government against democratic ideals, encouraging you to think about how government should make its decisions. As its title implies, *The Challenge of Democracy* argues that good government often involves difficult choices.

College students frequently say that American government and politics are hard to understand. In fact, many people voice the same complaint. More than 60 percent of a national sample interviewed after the 1996 presidential election agreed with the statement "Politics and government seem so complicated that a person like me can't understand what's going on."[4] With this book, we hope to improve your understanding of "what's going on" by analyzing and evaluating the norms, or values, that people use to judge political events. Our purpose is not to preach what people ought to favor in making policy decisions; it is to teach what values are at stake.

Teaching without preaching is not easy; no one can exclude personal values completely from political analysis. But our approach minimizes this problem by concentrating on the dilemmas that confront governments when they are forced to choose between policies that threaten equally cherished values—such as freedom of speech and personal security.

Every government policy reflects a choice between conflicting values. We want you to understand this idea, to understand that all government policies reinforce certain values (norms) at the expense of others. We want you to interpret policy issues (for example, should assisted suicide go unpunished?) with an understanding of the fundamental values in question (freedom of action versus order and protection of life) and the broader political context (liberal or conservative politics).

By looking beyond the specifics to the underlying normative principles, you should be able to make more sense out of politics. Our framework for analysis does not encompass all the complexities of American government, but it should help your knowledge grow by improving your comprehension of political information. We begin by considering the basic purposes of government.

The Purposes of Government

Most people do not like being told what to do. Fewer still like being coerced into acting a certain way. Yet every day, millions of American motorists dutifully drive on the right-hand side of the street and obediently stop at red lights. Every year, millions of U.S. citizens struggle to complete their income tax forms before midnight, April 15. In both of these examples, the coercive power of government is at work. If people do not like being coerced, why do they submit to it? In other words, why do we have government?

Government may be defined as the legitimate use of force—including imprisonment and execution—within specific geographic boundaries to control human behavior. All governments require their citizens to surrender some freedom as part of being governed. Why do people surrender their freedom to this control? To obtain the benefits of government. Throughout history, government seems to have served two major purposes: maintaining order (preserving life and protecting property) and providing public goods. More recently, some governments have pursued a third and more controversial purpose: promoting equality.

Maintaining Order

Maintaining order is the oldest objective of government. **Order** in this context is rich with meaning. Let's start with "law and order." Maintaining order in this sense means establishing the rule of law to preserve life and to protect property. To the seventeenth-century English philosopher Thomas Hobbes (1588–1679), preserving life was the most important function of government. In his classic philosophical treatise, *Leviathan* (1651), Hobbes described life without government as life in a "state of nature." Without rules, people would live as predators do, stealing and killing for their personal benefit. In Hobbes's classic phrase, life in a state of nature would be "solitary, poor, nasty, brutish, and short." He believed that a single ruler, or sovereign, must possess unquestioned authority to guarantee the safety of the weak to protect them from the attacks of the strong. He believed that complete obedience to the sovereign's strict laws was a small price to pay for the security of living in a civil society.

Most of us can only imagine what a state of nature would be like. But in some parts of the world people actually live in a state of lawlessness. One existed in Somalia in 1992 after the government collapsed, in Haiti in 1994 after the elected president had to flee, and in Bosnia in 1995 after the former Yugoslavia collapsed and Croats, Serbs, and Muslims engaged in ethnic war. Throughout history, authoritarian rulers have used people's fears of civil disorder to justify taking power and becoming the new *established order.*

Hobbes's conception of life in the cruel state of nature led him to view government primarily as a means of guaranteeing people's survival. Other theorists, taking survival for granted, believed that government protected order by preserving private property (goods and land owned by individuals). Foremost among them was John Locke (1632–1704), another English philosopher. In *Two Treatises on Government* (1690), he wrote that the protection of life, liberty, and property was the basic objective of government. His thinking strongly influenced the Declaration of Independence, which identifies "Life, Liberty, and the pursuit of Happiness" as "unalienable Rights" of citizens under government.

Not everyone believes that the protection of private property is a valid objective of government. The German philosopher Karl Marx (1818–1883) rejected the private ownership of property used in the production of goods or services. Marx's ideas form the basis of **communism**, a complex theory that gives ownership of all land and productive facilities to the people—in effect, to the government. In line with communist theory, the 1977 constitution of the former Soviet Union enunciated the following principles of government ownership:

> State property, i.e., the common property of the Soviet people, is the principal form of socialist property. The land, its minerals, waters, and forests are the exclusive property of the state. The state owns the basic means of production in industry, construction, and agriculture; means of transport and communication; the banks; the property of state-run trade organizations and public utilities, and other state-run undertakings; most urban housing; and other property necessary for state purposes.[5]

Even outside the formerly communist societies, the extent to which government protects property is a political issue that sparks much ideological debate.

Providing Public Goods

After governments have established basic order, they can pursue other ends. Using their coercive powers, they can tax citizens to raise funds to spend on **public goods**: benefits and services that are available to everyone—such as education, sanitation, and parks. Public goods benefit all citizens but are not likely to be produced by the voluntary acts of individuals. The government of ancient Rome, for example, built aqueducts to carry fresh water from the mountains to the city. Road building is another public good provided by the governments since ancient times.

Some government enterprises that have been common in other countries—running railroads, operating coal mines, generating electric power—are politically controversial or even unacceptable in the United States. Many Americans believe public goods and services should be provided by private business operating for profit.

Promoting Equality

The promotion of equality has not always been a major objective of government. It gained prominence in the twentieth century, in the aftermath of industrialization and urbanization. Confronted by the contrast of poverty amid plenty, some political leaders in European nations pioneered extensive government programs to improve life for the poor. Under the emerging concept of the welfare state, government's role expanded to provide individuals with medical care, education, and a guaranteed income, "from cradle to grave." Sweden, Britain, and other nations adopted welfare programs aimed at reducing social inequalities. This relatively new purpose of government has been by far the most controversial. People often oppose taxation for public goods (such as building roads and schools) because of its cost alone. They oppose more strongly taxation for government programs to promote economic and social equality on principle.

The key issue here is the government's role in redistributing income, taking from the wealthy to give to the poor. Charity (voluntary giving to the poor) has a strong basis in Western religious traditions; using the power of the state to support the poor does not. Using the state to redistribute income was originally a radical idea, set forth by Marx as the ultimate principle of developed communism: "from each according to his ability, to each according to his needs."[6] This extreme has never been realized in any government, not even in communist states. But over time, taking from the rich to help the needy has become a legitimate function of most governments.

That function is not without controversy, however. For example, after the Republicans won control of Congress in 1994, a fierce partisan battle was waged over the Aid to Families with Dependent Children (AFDC) program, created by the Democrats in 1935. Republicans had long argued that the welfare program to help low-income mothers and their children was inappropriate and ineffective, and in 1996, over the strenuous objection of Democrats, they ended it.

Government can also promote social equality through policies that do not redistribute income. For example, it can regulate social behavior to enforce equality—as it did when the Texas Supreme Court cleared the way for homosexuals to serve in the Dallas police department in 1993. Policies that regulate social behavior, like those that redistribute income, inevitably clash with the value of personal freedom.

A Conceptual Framework
for Analyzing Government

Citizens have very different views on how vigorously they want government to maintain order, provide public goods, and promote equality. Of the three objectives, providing public goods usually is less controversial than maintaining order or promoting equality. After all, government spending for highways, schools, and parks carries benefits for nearly every citizen. Moreover, these services merely cost money. The cost of maintaining order and promoting equality is greater than money; it usually means a tradeoff of basic values.

To understand government and the political process, you must be able to recognize these tradeoffs and identify the basic values they entail. You need to take a broad view, a much broader view than that offered by examining specific political events. You need to use political concepts.

A *concept* is a generalized idea of a class of items or thoughts. It groups various events, objects, or qualities under a common classification or label. The framework that supports this text consists of five concepts that figure prominently in political analysis. We regard these five concepts as especially important to a broad understanding of American politics, and we use them repeatedly. This framework will help you evaluate political events long after you have read this book.

The five concepts that we emphasize relate to (a) what government tries to do and (b) how it decides to do it. The concepts that relate to what government tries to do are *order, freedom,* and *equality.* All governments by definition value order; maintaining order is part of the meaning of government. Most governments at least claim to preserve individual freedom while they maintain order, although they vary widely in the extent to which they succeed. Few governments even profess to guarantee equality, and governments differ greatly in policies that pit equality against freedom. Our conceptual framework should help you evaluate the extent to which the United States pursues all three values through its government.

How government chooses the proper mix of order, freedom, and equality in its policymaking has to do with the process of choice. We evaluate the American governmental process using two models of democratic government: *majoritarian democracy* and *pluralist democracy.* Most governments profess to be democracies. Whether they are or not depends on their (and our) meaning of the term *democracy.* Even countries that Americans agree are democracies— such as the United States and Britain—differ substantially in the type of democracy they practice. We can use our conceptual models of democratic government both to classify the type of democracy practiced in the United States and to evaluate the government's success in fulfilling that model.

Our five concepts can be organized into two groups.

1. Concepts that identify the values pursued by government:
   - Freedom
   - Order
   - Equality

2. Concepts that describe models of democratic government:
   - Majoritarian democracy
   - Pluralist democracy

First we will examine freedom, order, and equality as conflicting values pursued by government. Later in this chapter we will discuss majoritarian democracy and pluralist democracy as alternative institutional models for implementing democratic government.

The Concepts of Freedom, Order, and Equality

These three terms—*freedom, order,* and *equality*—have a range of connotations in American politics. Both *freedom* and *equality* are positive terms that politicians have learned to use to their own advantage. Consequently, *freedom* and *equality* mean different things to different people at different times—depending on the political context in which they are used. *Order,* in contrast, has negative connotations for many people, for it brings to mind government intrusion in private lives. Except during periods of social strife, few politicians in Western democracies call openly for more order. Because all governments infringe on freedom, we examine that concept first.

Freedom *Freedom* can be used in two major senses: freedom *of* and freedom *from.* Franklin Delano Roosevelt used the word in each sense in a speech he made shortly before the United States entered World War II. He described four freedoms—freedom *of* religion, freedom *of* speech, freedom *from* fear, and freedom *from* want.

Freedom of is the absence of constraints on behavior. It is freedom to do something. In this sense, *freedom* is synonymous with *liberty*. **Freedom from** suggests immunity from something undesirable or negative such as fear and want. In the modern political context, *freedom from* often connotes the fight against exploitation and oppression. The cry of the civil rights movement in the 1960s—"Freedom Now!"—conveyed this meaning. If you recognize that *freedom* in the latter sense means immunity from discrimination, you can see that it comes close to the concept of equality.[7] In this book, we avoid using *freedom* to mean "freedom from"; for this sense of the word, we simply use *equality*. When we use *freedom,* we mean "freedom of."

Order When *order* is viewed in the narrow sense of preserving life and protecting property, most citizens would concede the importance of maintaining order and thereby grant the need for government. But when *order* is viewed in the broader sense of preserving the social order, people are more likely to argue that maintaining order is not a legitimate function of government. *Social order* refers to established patterns of authority in society and to traditional modes of behavior. However, it is important to remember that social order can change. Today, perfectly respectable men and women wear bathing suits that would have caused a scandal a hundred years ago.

A government can protect the established order by using its **police power**—its authority to safeguard residents' safety, health, welfare, and morals. The extent to which government should use this authority is a topic of ongoing debate in the United States and is constantly being redefined by the courts. There are those who fear the evolution of a police state—government that uses its power to regulate nearly all aspects of behavior.

Most governments are inherently conservative; they tend to resist social change. But some governments have as a primary objective the restructuring of the social order. Social change is most dramatic when a government is overthrown through force and replaced by a revolutionary government. Societies can also work to change social patterns more gradually through the legal process. Our use of the term *order* in this book includes all three aspects: preserving life, protecting property, and maintaining traditional patterns of social relationships.

Equality Like *freedom* and *order, equality* is used in different senses to support different causes. **Political equality** in elections is easy to define: each citizen has one and only one vote. This basic concept is central to democratic theory—a subject we explore at length later in this chapter. But when some people advocate political equality, they mean more than "one person, one vote." These people contend that an urban ghetto dweller and the chairman of the board of Microsoft are not politically equal despite the fact that each has one vote. Through occupation or wealth, some citizens are more able than others to influence political decisions. For example, wealthy citizens can exert influence by advertising in the mass media or by contacting friends in high places. Lacking great wealth and political connections, most citizens do not have such influence. Thus, some analysts argue that equality in wealth, education, and status—that is, **social equality**—is necessary for true political equality.

There are two routes to achieving social equality: providing equal opportunities and ensuring equal outcomes. **Equality of opportunity** means that each person has the same chance to succeed in life. This idea is deeply ingrained in American culture. The Constitution prohibits titles of nobility, and owning property is not a requirement for holding public office. Public schools and libraries are free to all. For many people, the concept of social equality is satisfied by offering equal opportunities for advancement—it is not essential that people actually end up being equal. For others, true social equality means

I Now Pronounce You . . .
Gay couples renew their vows at Metropolitan Community Church in San Francisco in June 1996. Because few institutions have been more central to society than marriage between a man and a woman, same-sex marriages represent a threat to the social order. Liberals and conservatives usually divide sharply on this issue.

nothing less than **equality of outcome**.[8] They believe that society must see to it that people are equal. According to this view, it is not enough that governments provide people with equal opportunities; they must also design policies to redistribute wealth and status so that economic and social equality are actually achieved.

Some link equality of outcome with the concept of government-supported **rights**—the idea that every citizen is entitled to certain benefits of government, that government should guarantee its citizens adequate (if not equal) housing, employment, medical care, and income. If citizens are entitled to government benefits as a matter of right, government efforts to promote equality of outcome become legitimized.

Clearly, the concept of equality of outcome is very different from that of equality of opportunity, and it requires a much greater degree of government activity. It also clashes more directly with the concept of freedom. By taking from one person to give to another—which is necessary for the redistribution of income and status—the government clearly creates winners and losers. The winners may believe that justice has been served by the redistribution. The losers often feel strongly that their freedom to enjoy their income and status has suffered.

Two Dilemmas of Government

The two major dilemmas facing American government at the beginning of the twenty-first century stem from the oldest and the newest objectives of government—maintaining order and promoting equality. Both order and equality are important social values, but government cannot pursue either without sacrificing a third important value: individual freedom. The clash between freedom and order forms the *original* dilemma of government; the clash between freedom and equality forms the *modern* dilemma of government. Although the dilemmas are very different, each involves trading off some amount of freedom for another value.

The Original Dilemma: Freedom Versus Order The conflict between freedom and order originates in the very meaning of *government* as the legitimate use of force to control human behavior. How much freedom must a citizen surrender to government? This dilemma has occupied philosophers for hundreds of years.

The original purpose of government was to protect life and property, to make citizens safe from violence. How well is the American government doing today in providing law and order to its citizens? Many people living in large cities would say not too well. Surveys indicate that Americans do not trust their urban governments to protect them from crime when they go out alone at night.[9]

When communist governments still ruled in Eastern Europe, the climate of fear in urban America stood in stark contrast with the pervasive sense of personal safety in such cities as Moscow, Warsaw, and Prague. It was common to see old and young strolling late at night along the streets and in the parks of those communist cities. The communist regimes gave their police great powers to control guns, monitor citizens' movements, and arrest and imprison suspicious people, which enabled them to do a better job of maintaining order. Communist governments deliberately chose order over freedom.

In the abstract, people value both freedom and order; in real life, the two values inherently conflict. By definition, any policy that strengthens one value takes away from the other. In a democracy, policy choices hinge on how much citizens value freedom and how much they value order.

The Modern Dilemma: Freedom Versus Equality Popular opinion has it that freedom and equality go hand in hand. In reality, these two values usually clash when governments enact policies to promote social equality. Because social equality is a relatively recent government objective, deciding between policies that promote equality at the expense of freedom, and vice versa, is the modern dilemma of politics. Consider these examples.

During the 1970s, the courts ordered the busing of schoolchildren to achieve equal proportions of blacks and whites in public schools. This action was motivated by concern for educational equality, but it also impaired freedom of choice.

During the 1980s, some states passed legislation that went beyond giving men and women equal pay for equal work to the more radical notion of pay equity—equal pay for comparable work. Women were to be paid at a rate equal to men's even if they had different jobs—providing the women's jobs were of "comparable worth" (meaning the skills and responsibilities were comparable).

In the 1990s, Congress prohibited discrimination in employment, public services, and public accommodations on the basis of physical or mental disabilities. Under the 1990 Americans with Disabilities Act, businesses with twenty-five or more employees could not pass over an otherwise qualified disabled person in employment or promotion, and new buses and trains had to be made accessible to them.

Americans, who think of freedom and equality as complementary rather than conflicting values, often do not notice the clash between those two values. When forced to choose between them, however, Americans are far more likely than people in other countries to choose freedom (see Compared with What? 1.1). The emphasis on equality over freedom was especially strong in the former Soviet Union, which guaranteed its citizens medical care, inexpensive housing, and other social services.

The conflicts among freedom, order, and equality explain a great deal of the political conflict in the United States. The conflicts also underlie the ideologies that people use to structure their understanding of politics.

Ideology and Government

Some people hold an assortment of values and beliefs that produce contradictory opinions on government policies. Others organize their opinions into a **political ideology**—a consistent set of values and beliefs about the proper purpose and scope of government.

How far should government go to maintain order, provide public goods, and promote equality? We can analyze answers to this question by referring to philosophies about the proper scope of government—the range of permissible activities. Imagine a continuum. At one end is the belief that government should do everything; at the other is the belief that government should not exist. These extreme ideologies—from "most government" to "least government"— and those that fall in between are shown in Figure 1.1.

Totalitarianism   **Totalitarianism** is the belief that government should have unlimited power. A totalitarian government controls all sectors of society: business, labor, education, religion, sports, the arts. A true totalitarian favors a network of laws, rules, and regulations that guides every aspect of individual behavior.

Socialism   Whereas totalitarianism refers to government in general, **socialism** pertains to government's role in the economy. Like communism, socialism is an economic system based on Marxist theory. Under socialism (and communism), the scope of government extends to ownership or control of the basic industries that produce goods and services (communications, heavy industry, transportation). Although socialism favors a strong role for government in

MOST
GOVERNMENT

LEAST
GOVERNMENT

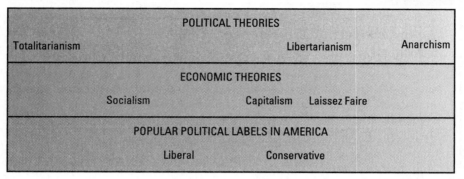

FIGURE 1.1 *Ideology and the Scope of Government*
We can classify political ideologies according to the scope of action that people are willing to allow government in dealing with social and economic problems. In this chart, the three lines map out various philosophical positions along an underlying continuum ranging from "most" to "least" government. Notice that conventional politics in the United States spans only a narrow portion of the theoretical possibilities for government action.

In popular usage, liberals favor a greater scope of government, and conservatives want a narrower scope. But over time, the traditional distinction has eroded and now oversimplifies the differences between liberals and conservatives. See Figure 1.2 for a more discriminating classification of liberals and conservatives.

regulating private industry and directing the economy, it allows more room than communism does for private ownership of productive capacity.

Communism in theory was supposed to result in a "withering away" of the state, but communist governments in practice tended toward totalitarianism, controlling economic, political, and social life through a dominant party organization. Some socialist governments, however, practice **democratic socialism**. They guarantee civil liberties (such as freedom of speech and freedom of religion) and allow their citizens to determine the extent of the government's activity through free elections and competitive political parties. The governments of Britain, Sweden, Germany, and France, among other democracies, have at times been avowedly socialist.

Capitalism Capitalism also relates to the government's role in the economy. In contrast to both socialism and communism, **capitalism** supports free enterprise—private businesses operating without government regulations. Some theorists, most notably economist Milton Friedman, argue that free enterprise is necessary for free politics.[10] Whether this argument is valid depends in part on our understanding of democracy, a subject we discuss later in this chapter.

The United States is decidedly a capitalist country, more so than most other Western nations. But our government does extend its authority into the economic sphere, regulating private businesses and directing the overall

Compared with What? 1.1

The Importance of Freedom and Equality as Political Values

Compared with citizens' views of freedom and equality in fifteen other nations, Americans value freedom more than others do. Respondents in each country were asked which of the following statements came closer to their own opinion:

- "I find that both freedom and equality are important. But if I were to make up my mind for one or the other, I would consider personal freedom more important, that is, everyone can live in freedom and develop without hindrance."
- "Certainly both freedom and equality are important. But if I were to make up my mind for one of the two, I would consider equality more important, that is, that nobody is underprivileged and that social class differences are not so strong."

Americans chose freedom by a ratio of nearly 3 to 1. No other nation showed such a strong preference for freedom, and citizens in four countries favored equality instead. When we look at this finding together with Americans' disdain for order, the importance of freedom as a political concept in the United States is clear.

(continued)

economy. American liberals and conservatives both embrace capitalism, but they differ on the nature and amount of government intervention in the economy that is necessary or desirable.

Libertarianism   **Libertarianism** opposes all government action except that which is necessary to protect life and property. For example, libertarians believe that social programs that provide food, clothing, and shelter are outside the proper scope of government. They also oppose any government intervention in the economy. This kind of economic policy is called **laissez faire**, a French phrase that means "let (people) do (as they please)." Such an extreme policy extends beyond the free enterprise advocated by most capitalists.

Anarchism   Anarchism stands opposite totalitarianism on the political continuum. Anarchists oppose all government, in any form. As a political philosophy, **anarchism** values freedom above all else. Like totalitarianism, anarchism is not a popular philosophy, but it does have adherents on the political fringes. For example, there is a flourishing anarchist culture on the Internet.

Liberals and Conservatives   As shown in Figure 1.1, practical politics in the United States ranges over only the central portion of the continuum. The

Compared with What? 1.1 (continued)

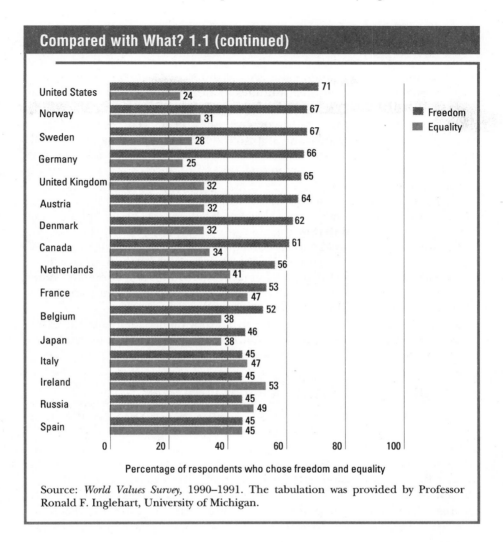

Source: *World Values Survey*, 1990–1991. The tabulation was provided by Professor Ronald F. Inglehart, University of Michigan.

extreme positions—totalitarianism and anarchism—are rarely argued in public debate. And in this era of distrust of "big government," few American politicians would openly advocate socialism. Most debate is limited to a narrow range of political thought. On one side are people commonly called *liberals*; on the other are *conservatives*. In popular usage, liberals favor more government, conservatives less. This distinction is clear when the issue is government spending to provide public goods. **Liberals** favor generous government support for education, wildlife protection, public transportation, and a whole range of social programs. **Conservatives** want smaller government budgets and fewer government programs. They support free enterprise and argue against government job programs, regulation of business, and legislation of working conditions and wage rates.

In other areas, liberal and conservative ideologies are less consistent. The differences no longer hinge on the narrow question of the government's role in providing public goods. Liberals still favor more government and conservatives less, but this is no longer the critical difference between them. Today, that difference stems from their attitudes toward the purpose of government. Conservatives support the original purpose of government—to maintain social order. They are willing to use the coercive power of the state to force citizens to be orderly. But they would not stop with defining, preventing, and punishing crime. They tend to want to preserve traditional patterns of social relations—the domestic role of women and the importance of religion in school and family life, for example.

Liberals are less likely than conservatives to want to use government power to maintain order. Liberals do not shy away from using government coercion, but they use it for a different purpose—to promote equality. They support laws ensuring that homosexuals receive equal treatment in employment, housing, and education; laws that require the busing of schoolchildren to achieve racial equality; laws that force private businesses to hire and promote women and members of minority groups; laws that require public transportation to provide equal access to the disabled.

Conservatives do not oppose equality, but they do not value it to the extent of using the government's power to enforce equality. For liberals, the use of that power to promote equality is both valid and necessary.

A Two-Dimensional Classification of Ideologies

To classify liberal and conservative ideologies more accurately, we have to incorporate the values of freedom, order, and equality into the classification. We can do this using the model in Figure 1.2. It depicts the conflicting values along two separate dimensions, each anchored in maximum freedom at the lower left. One dimension extends horizontally from maximum freedom on the left to maximum order on the right. The other extends vertically from maximum freedom at the bottom to maximum equality at the top. Each box represents a different ideological type: libertarians, liberals, conservatives, and communitarians.*

Libertarians value freedom more than they value order or equality (we will use *libertarian* for people who have libertarian tendencies but may not accept the whole philosophy). In practical terms, libertarians want minimal government intervention in both the economic and the social spheres. For example, they oppose affirmative action laws and laws that restrict transmission of sexually explicit material. Liberals value freedom more than order, but not more than equality. Liberals oppose laws that ban sexually explicit publications but support affirmative action. Conservatives value freedom more than equality

---

*The communitarian category was labeled "populist" in early editions of this book. We have relabeled it for two reasons. First, we believe *communitarian* is more descriptive of the category. Second, we recognize that the term *populist* has been used increasingly to refer to the political styles of Ross Perot and Pat Buchanan. In this sense, a populist appeals to mass resentment against those in power. Though less familiar, the term *communitarian* has fewer connotations.[11]

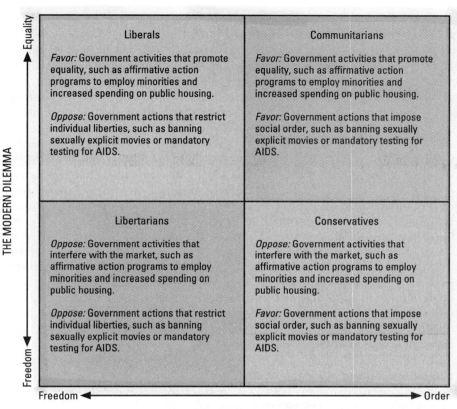

THE MODERN DILEMMA

Equality ↑

Freedom ↓

Liberals

Favor: Government activities that promote equality, such as affirmative action programs to employ minorities and increased spending on public housing.

Oppose: Government actions that restrict individual liberties, such as banning sexually explicit movies or mandatory testing for AIDS.

Communitarians

Favor: Government activities that promote equality, such as affirmative action programs to employ minorities and increased spending on public housing.

Favor: Government actions that impose social order, such as banning sexually explicit movies or mandatory testing for AIDS.

Libertarians

Oppose: Government activities that interfere with the market, such as affirmative action programs to employ minorities and increased spending on public housing.

Oppose: Government actions that restrict individual liberties, such as banning sexually explicit movies or mandatory testing for AIDS.

Conservatives

Oppose: Government activities that interfere with the market, such as affirmative action programs to employ minorities and increased spending on public housing.

Favor: Government actions that impose social order, such as banning sexually explicit movies or mandatory testing for AIDS.

Freedom ◄─────────────────────────► Order

THE ORIGINAL DILEMMA

FIGURE 1.2   Ideologies: A Two-Dimensional Framework
The four ideological types above are defined by the values they favor in resolving the two major dilemmas of government: how much freedom should be sacrificed in pursuit of order and equality, respectively? Test yourself by thinking about the values that are most important to you. Which box in the figure best represents your combination of values?

but would restrict freedom to preserve social order. Conservatives oppose affirmative action but favor laws that restrict pornography.

Finally, at the upper right in Figure 1.2, we have communitarians. This group values both equality and order more than freedom. Its members support both affirmative action laws and laws that restrict pornography. The *Oxford English Dictionary* (1989) defines *communitarian* as "a member of a community formed to put into practice communistic or socialistic theories." The term is used more narrowly in contemporary politics, to reflect the philosophy of the Communitarian Network, a political movement founded by sociologist Amitai Etzioni.[12] This movement rejects both the liberal-conservative classification and the libertarian argument that "individuals should be left on their own to pursue their choices, rights, and self-interests."[13] Like liberals, Etzioni's communitarians believe that there is a role for government in helping the disadvantaged. Like conservatives, they believe that government should be used to promote moral values—preserving the family through more stringent divorce laws, and limiting the dissemination of pornography, for example.[14] However, the Communitarian Network is not dedicated to big government. According to its platform, "The government should step in only to the extent that other social subsystems fail, rather than seek to replace them."[15] Our definition of *communitarian* (small "c") clearly embraces the Communitarian Network's philosophy, but it is broader and more in keeping with the dictionary definition: **communitarians** favor government programs that promote both order and equality, in keeping with socialist theory.

By analyzing political ideologies on two dimensions rather than one, we can explain why people can seem to be liberal on one issue (favoring a broader scope of government action) and conservative on another (favoring less government action). The reason hinges on the purpose of a given government action: which value does it promote: order or equality?

According to our typology, only libertarians and communitarians are consistent in their attitudes toward the scope of government activity, whatever its purpose. Libertarians value freedom so highly that they oppose most government efforts to enforce either order or equality. Communitarians (in our usage) are inclined to trade off freedom for both order and equality. Liberals and conservatives, in contrast, favor or oppose government activity depending on its purpose. As you will learn in Chapter 4, large groups of Americans fall into each of the four ideological categories. Because Americans increasingly choose four different resolutions to the original and modern dilemmas of government, the simple labels *liberal* and *conservative* no longer describe contemporary political ideologies as well as they did in the 1930s, 1940s, and 1950s.

The American Governmental Process: Majoritarian or Pluralist?

When, by a vote of 239 to 173, the House of Representatives passed legislation designed to repeal a ban on assault weapons in March 1996, many Americans were mystified. Only a few years earlier, Congress had passed the ban on assault weapons (military rifles that can fire in very rapid succession), and polls consistently showed that Americans overwhelmingly supported such a ban. Critics of the House vote pointed to the National Rifle Association (NRA), which had pushed hard for lifting the ban. Ban repeal died in the Senate, however. Seeing little public support for the repeal, Senate Majority Leader Bob Dole quickly indicated that he wouldn't bring the bill up for a vote.

The split between the House and Senate reflects a dilemma that legislators often face: an interest group representing a small minority of the population comes to Congress to ask that it enact or defend some policy that the group's members favor, but what is good for that group may not be what is best for the public at large. If the majority is not well mobilized, because it is apathetic about the issue, legislators may be tempted to earn the gratitude of the interest group's followers, who are watching closely to see what Congress will do. Is it democratic for policymakers to favor a vocal minority at the expense of a less-committed majority?

To this point, our discussion of political ideologies has centered on conflicting views about the values government should pursue. We now examine how government should decide what to do. In particular, we set forth criteria for judging whether a government's decision-making process is democratic.

The Theory of Democratic Government

Americans have a simple answer to the question "Who should govern?" It is "The people." Unfortunately, this answer is too simple. It fails to say who *the people* are. Should we include young children? Recent immigrants? Illegal aliens? This answer also fails to indicate how "the people" should do the governing. Should they be assembled in a stadium? Vote by mail? Choose representatives to govern for them? We need to take a close look at what "government by the people" really means.

The word *democracy* originated in Greek writings around the fifth century B.C. *Demos* referred to the common people, the masses; *kratos* meant "power." The ancient Greeks were afraid of **democracy**—rule by rank and file citizens. That fear is evident in the term *demagogue.* We use that term today to refer to a politician who appeals to and often deceives the masses by manipulating their emotions and prejudices.

Many centuries after the Greeks first defined *democracy,* the idea still carried the connotation of mob rule. When George Washington was president, opponents of a new political party disparagingly called it a *democratic* party. No one would do that in politics today. Like *justice* and *decency,* the word *democracy* is used reverently by politicians of all persuasions.

There are two major schools of thought about what constitutes democracy. The first believes democracy is a form of government, and it emphasizes the procedures that enable the people to govern—meeting to discuss issues, voting in elections, running for public office. The second sees democracy in the substance of government policies, in freedom of religion and providing for human needs. The *procedural* approach focuses on how decisions are made; the *substantive* approach is concerned with what government does.

The Procedural View of Democracy **Procedural democratic theory** sets forth principles that describe how government should make decisions. These principles address three distinct questions:

1. *Who* should participate in decision making?
2. *How much* should each participant's vote count?
3. *How many* votes are needed to reach a decision?

According to procedural democratic theory, all adults within the boundaries of the political community should participate in government decision making. We refer to this principle as **universal participation**. How much should each participant's vote count? According to procedural theory, all votes should count equally. This is the principle of **political equality**. Note that universal participation and political equality are two distinct principles. It is not enough for everyone to participate in a decision; all votes must carry equal weight.

Finally, procedural theory prescribes that a group should decide to do what the majority of its participants wants to do. This principle is called **majority rule**. (If participants divide over more than two alternatives and none receives a simple majority, the principle usually defaults to *plurality* rule, in which the group should do what most participants want.)

A Complication: Direct Versus Indirect Democracy   Universal participation, political equality, and majority rule are widely recognized as necessary for democratic decision making. Small, simple societies can achieve all three with direct or **participatory democracy**, in which all members of the group meet to make decisions, observing political equality and majority rule. However, in the United States and nearly all other democracies, participatory democracy is rare. Clearly, all Americans cannot gather at the Capitol in Washington to decide defense policy.

Believing that participatory democracy on the national level was both impossible and undesirable, the framers of the Constitution instituted indirect or **representative democracy**. In such a system, citizens participate in government by electing public officials to make government decisions on their behalf. Within the context of representative democracy, we adhere to the principles of universal participation, political equality, and majority rule to guarantee that elections are democratic. But what happens after the election?

Suppose the elected representatives do not make the decisions the people would have made if they had gathered for the same purpose. To account for this possibility in representative government, procedural theory provides a fourth decision-making principle: **responsiveness**. Elected representatives should follow the general contours of public opinion as they formulate complex pieces of legislation.[16]

We now have four principles of procedural democracy:

- Universal participation
- Political equality
- Majority rule
- Government responsiveness to public opinion

The Substantive View of Democracy   According to procedural theory, the principle of responsiveness is absolute: the government should do what the majority wants, regardless of what that is. At first this seems a reasonable way to protect the rights of citizens in a representative democracy. But what about the rights of minorities? To limit the government's responsiveness to public opinion, we must look outside procedural democratic theory to substantive democratic theory. **Substantive democratic theory** focuses on the substance of government policies, not on the procedures followed in making those policies. It argues

Speak Right Up
At this neighborhood meeting a citizen speaks out about airport noise abatement. Such citizen participation in the democratic process occurs throughout the United States. It may be done directly, as in the town meetings of some small New England villages, or indirectly, as citizens make their views known to elected officials at all levels of government.

that in a democratic government, certain principles must be embodied in government policies. Substantive theorists would reject a law that requires Bible reading in schools because it would violate a substantive principle, the freedom of religion. The core of the substantive principles of American democracy is embedded in the Bill of Rights and other amendments to the Constitution.

In defining the principles that underlie democratic government—and the policies of that government—most substantive theorists agree on a basic criterion: government policies should guarantee *civil liberties* (freedom of behavior such as freedom of religion and freedom of expression) and *civil rights* (powers or privileges that government may not arbitrarily deny to individuals, such as protection against discrimination in employment and housing). But agreement among substantive theorists breaks down when discussion moves from civil rights to *social rights* (adequate health care, quality education, decent housing) and *economic rights* (private property, steady employment). For example, some insist that policies that promote social equality are essential to democratic government.[17] Others restrict the requirements of substantive democracy to those policies that safeguard civil liberties and civil rights.

A theorist's political ideology tends to explain his or her position on what democracy really requires in substantive policies. Conservative theorists have a narrow view of the scope of democratic government and a narrow view of the social and economic rights guaranteed by that government. Liberal theorists believe that a democratic government should guarantee its citizens a much broader spectrum of social and economic rights.

Procedural Democracy Versus Substantive Democracy   The problem with the substantive view of democracy is that it does not provide clear, precise criteria that allow us to determine whether a government is democratic. Substantive theorists are free to promote their pet values—separation of church and state, guaranteed employment, equal rights for women, whatever—under the guise of substantive democracy.

The procedural viewpoint also has a problem. Although it presents specific criteria for democratic government, those criteria can produce undesirable social policies that prey on minorities. This clashes with **minority rights**—the idea that all citizens are entitled to certain rights that cannot be denied by the majority. One way to protect minority rights is to limit the principle of majority rule—by requiring a two-thirds majority or some other extraordinary majority when decisions must be made on certain subjects—or to put the issue in the Constitution, beyond the reach of majority rule.

Clearly, procedural and substantive democracy are not always compatible. In choosing one over the other, we are also choosing to focus on either procedures or policies. As authors of this text, we favor a compromise between the two. On the whole we favor the procedural conception of democracy because it more closely approaches the classical definition of *democracy*—"government by the people." And procedural democracy is founded on clear, well-established rules for decision making. But the theory has a serious drawback: it allows a democratic government to enact policies that can violate the substantive principles of democracy. Thus it is best that pure procedural democracy be diluted so that minority rights and civil liberties are guaranteed as part of the structure of government.

Institutional Models of Democracy

Some democratic theorists favor institutions that tie government decisions closely to the desires of the majority of citizens. If most citizens want laws against the sale of pornography, then the government should outlaw pornography. If citizens want more money spent on defense and less on social welfare (or vice versa), the government should act accordingly. For these theorists, the essence of democratic government is majority rule and responsiveness. Other theorists place less importance on these principles. They do not believe in relying heavily on mass opinion; instead, they favor institutions that allow groups of citizens to defend their interests in the public policymaking process.

Both schools hold a procedural view of democracy but differ in how they interpret "government by the people." We can summarize these theoretical positions using two alternative models of democracy. As a model, each is a hypothetical plan, a blueprint, for achieving democratic government through institutional mechanisms. The *majoritarian* model values participation by the people in general; the *pluralist* model values participation by the people in groups.

The Majoritarian Model of Democracy   The **majoritarian model of democracy** relies on our intuitive notion of what is fair. It interprets "government by the people" as government by the *majority* of the people. To force the government to respond to public opinion, the majoritarian model depends on several mechanisms that allow the people to participate directly.

The popular election of government officials is the primary mechanism for democratic government in the majoritarian model. Citizens are expected to control their representatives' behavior by choosing wisely in the first place and by reelecting or voting out public officials according to their performance.

Majoritarian theorists also see elections as a means for deciding government policies. An election on a policy issue is called a *referendum*. When a policy question is put on the ballot by the action of citizens circulating petitions and gathering a required minimum number of signatures, it is called an *initiative*. Twenty-one states allow their legislatures to put referenda before the voters and give their citizens the right to place initiatives on the ballot. Five other states make provision for one mechanism or the other.[18]

In the United States no provisions exist for referenda at the federal level. However, Americans strongly favor instituting a system of national referenda.[19] The most fervent advocates of majoritarian democracy would like to see modern technology used to maximize the government's responsiveness to the majority. Some have proposed incorporating public opinion polls or using computers for referenda.[20]

The majoritarian model contends that citizens can control their government if they have adequate mechanisms for popular participation. It also assumes that citizens are knowledgeable about government and politics, that they want to participate in the political process, and that they make rational decisions in voting for their elected representatives.

Critics contend that Americans are not knowledgeable enough for majoritarian democracy to work. They point to research that shows that only 22 percent of a national sample of voters said that they "followed what's going on" in government "most of the time." More (40 percent) said that they followed politics "only now and then" or "hardly at all."[21] Some believe that instead of quick and easy mass voting on public policy, what we need is more deliberation by citizens and their elected representatives. Defenders of majoritarian democracy respond that the American public has coherent and stable opinions on the major policy questions.[22]

An Alternative Model: Pluralist Democracy   For years, political scientists struggled valiantly to reconcile the majoritarian model of democracy with polls that showed a widespread ignorance of politics among the American people. When only a little more than half of the adult population bothers to vote in presidential elections, our form of democracy seems to be government by *some* of the people.

The 1950s saw the evolution of an alternative interpretation of democracy, one tailored to the limited knowledge and participation of the real electorate, not the ideal one. It was based on the concept of *pluralism*—that modern society consists of innumerable groups that share economic, religious, ethnic, or cultural interests. Often people with similar interests organize formal groups. When an organized group seeks to influence government policy, it is called an **interest group**. Many interest groups regularly spend a great deal of time and money trying to influence government policy (see Chapter 7). Among them are the American Hospital Association, the National Association of Manufacturers, the National Education Association (NEA), the National Organization for Women (NOW), and, of course, the NRA.

The **pluralist model of democracy** interprets "government by the people" to mean government by people operating through competing interest groups. According to this model, democracy exists when many (plural) organizations operate separately from the government, press their interests on the government, and even challenge the government.[23] Compared with majoritarian thinking, pluralist theory shifts the focus of democratic government from the mass electorate to organized groups. It changes the criterion for democratic government from responsiveness to mass public opinion to responsiveness to organized groups of citizens.

A decentralized, complex government structure offers the access and openness necessary for pluralist democracy. For pluralists, the ideal system is one that divides government authority among numerous institutions with overlapping authority. Under such a system, competing interest groups have alternative points of access to present and argue their claims.

Our Constitution approaches the pluralist ideal in the way it divides authority among the branches of government. When the National Association for the Advancement of Colored People (NAACP) could not get Congress to outlaw segregated schools in the South, it turned to the federal court system, which did what Congress would not do. According to the ideal of pluralist democracy, if all opposing interests are allowed to organize, and if the system can be kept open so that all substantial claims have an opportunity to be heard, the decision will serve the diverse needs of a pluralist society.

The Majoritarian Model Versus the Pluralist Model   In majoritarian democracy, the mass public—not interest groups—controls government actions. The citizenry must be knowledgeable about government and willing to participate in the electoral process. Majoritarian democracy relies on electoral mechanisms that harness the power of the majority to make decisions. Conclusive elections and a centralized structure of government are mechanisms that aid majority rule. Cohesive political parties with well-defined programs also contribute to majoritarian democracy, because they offer voters a clear way to distinguish alternative sets of policies.

Pluralism does not demand much knowledge from citizens in general. It requires specialized knowledge only from groups of citizens, in particular their leaders. In contrast to majoritarian democracy, pluralist democracy seeks to limit majority action so that interest groups can be heard. It relies on strong interest groups and a decentralized government structure—mechanisms that interfere with majority rule, thereby protecting minority interests. We could even say that pluralism allows minorities to rule.

An Undemocratic Model: Elite Theory   If pluralist democracy allows minorities to rule, how does it differ from **elite theory**—the view that a small group of people (a minority) makes most important government decisions? According to elite theory, important government decisions are made by an identifiable and stable minority that shares certain characteristics, usually vast wealth and business connections.[24] Elite theory appeals to many people, especially those who believe that wealth dominates politics.

According to elite theory, the United States is not a democracy but an **oligarchy**, a system in which government power is in the hands of an elite. Although the voters appear to control the government through elections, elite theorists argue that the powerful few in society manage to define the issues and to constrain the outcomes of government decisions to suit their own interests. Clearly, elite theory describes a government that operates in an undemocratic fashion.

Political scientists have conducted numerous studies designed to test the validity of elite theory. Not all of those studies have come to the same conclusion, but the preponderance of available evidence documenting government decisions on many different issues does not generally support elite theory—at least in the sense that an identifiable ruling elite usually gets its way.[25] Not surprisingly, elite theorists reject this view. They argue that studies of decisions made on individual issues do not adequately test the influence of the power elite. Rather, they contend that much of the elite's power comes from its ability to keep things off the political agenda—that is, its power derives from its ability to keep people from questioning fundamental assumptions about American capitalism.[26]

Elite theory remains part of the debate about the nature of American government and is forcefully argued by radical critics of the American political system.[27] Although we do not believe that the scholarly evidence supports elite theory, we do recognize that contemporary American pluralism favors some segments of society over others. The poor are chronically unorganized and are not well represented by interest groups. In contrast, business is better represented than any other sector of the public.[28] Thus, one can endorse pluralist democracy as a more accurate description than elitism in American politics without believing that all groups are equally well represented.

Elite Theory Versus Pluralist Theory   The key difference between elite theory and pluralist theory lies in the durability of the ruling minority. In contrast to elite theory, pluralist theory does not define government conflict in terms of a minority versus the majority; instead, it sees many minorities vying with one another in each policy area. Pluralist democracy makes a virtue of the struggle between competing interests. It argues for government that accommodates this struggle and channels the result into government action. According to pluralist democracy, the public is best served if the government structure provides access for different groups to press their claims in competition with one another.

Note that pluralist democracy does not insist that all groups have equal influence on government decisions. In the political struggle, wealthy, well-organized groups have an inherent advantage over poorer, inadequately organized groups. In fact, unorganized segments of the population may not even get their concerns placed on the agenda for government consideration. This is a critical weakness of pluralism. However, pluralists contend that so long as all groups are able to participate vigorously in the decision-making process, the process is democratic.

American Democracy: More Pluralist Than Majoritarian

It is not idle speculation to ask what kind of democracy is practiced in the United States. The answer to this question can help us understand why our government can be called democratic despite a low level of citizen participation in politics and despite government actions that run contrary to public opinion.

Throughout this book, we probe more deeply to determine how well the United States fits the two alternative models of democracy: majoritarian and pluralist. If our answer is not already apparent, it soon will be. We argue that the political system in the United States rates relatively low according to the majoritarian model of democracy but fulfills the pluralist model very well. Yet the pluralist model is far from a perfect representation of democracy. Its principal drawback is that it favors the well organized, and the poor are the least likely to be members of interest groups. As one advocate of majoritarian democracy once wrote, "The flaw in the pluralist heaven is that the heavenly chorus sings with a strong upper-class accent."[29]

This evaluation of the pluralist nature of American democracy may not mean much to you now. But you will learn that the pluralist model makes the United States look far more democratic than the majoritarian model would. Eventually, you will have to decide the answers to three questions: Is the pluralist model truly an adequate expression of democracy, or is it a perversion of classical ideals designed to portray America as democratic when it is not? Does the majoritarian model result in a "better" type of democracy? If so, could new mechanisms of government be devised to produce a desirable mix of majority rule and minority rights? These questions should play in the back of your mind as you read more about the workings of American government in meeting the challenge of democracy.

Summary

The challenge of democracy lies in making difficult choices—choices that inevitably bring important values into conflict. This chapter has outlined a normative framework for analyzing the policy choices that arise in the pursuit of the purposes of government.

The three major purposes of government are to maintain order, provide public goods, and promote equality. In pursuing these objectives, every government infringes on individual freedom. But the degree of that infringement depends on the government's (and by extension, its citizens') commitment to order and equality. What we have, then, are two dilemmas. The first—the original dilemma—centers on the conflict between freedom and order. The second—the modern dilemma—focuses on the conflict between freedom and equality.

Some people use political ideologies to help them resolve the conflicts that arise in political decision making. These ideologies define the scope and purpose of government. At opposite extremes of the continuum are totalitarianism, which supports government intervention in every aspect of society, and anarchism, which rejects government entirely. An important step back from totalitarianism is socialism. Democratic socialism, an economic system, favors government ownership of basic industries but preserves civil liberties. Capitalism, another economic system, promotes free enterprise. A significant step short of anarchism is libertarianism, which allows government to protect life and property but little else.

In the United States, the terms *liberal* and *conservative* are used to describe a narrow range toward the center of the political continuum. The usage is probably accurate when the scope of government action is being discussed—that is, liberals support a broader role for government than do conservatives. But it is easier to understand the differences among libertarians, liberals, conservatives, and communitarians and their views on the scope of government if the values of freedom, order, and equality are incorporated into the description of their political ideologies. Libertarians choose freedom over both order and equality. Communitarians are willing to sacrifice freedom for both order and equality. Liberals value freedom more than order and equality more than freedom. Conservatives value order more than freedom and freedom more than equality.

Most scholars believe the United States is a democracy. But what kind of democracy is it? The answer depends on the definition of *democracy*. Some believe democracy is procedural; they define democracy as a form of government in which the people govern through certain institutional mechanisms. Others hold to the substantive theory, claiming a government is democratic if its policies promote civil liberties and rights.

In this book, we emphasize the procedural conception of democracy, distinguishing between direct (participatory) and indirect (representative) democracy. In participatory democracy, all citizens gather to govern themselves according to the principles of universal participation, political equality, and majority rule. In an indirect democracy, the citizens elect representatives to govern for them. If a representative government is elected mostly in accordance with the three principles just listed and is also usually responsive to public opinion, then it qualifies as a democracy.

Procedural democratic theory has produced rival institutional models of democratic government. The classical majoritarian model—which depends on majority votes in elections—assumes that people are knowledgeable about government, that they want to participate in the political process, and that they carefully and rationally choose among candidates. The pluralist model of democracy—which depends on interest group interaction with government—argues that democracy in a complex society requires only that government allow private interests to organize and press their competing claims openly in the political arena.

- Which is better: to live under a government that allows individuals complete freedom to do whatever they please or to live under one that enforces strict law and order?

- Which is better: to allow businesses and private clubs to choose their customers and members or to pass laws that require those businesses and clubs to admit and serve everyone, regardless of race or sex?

- Which is better: a government that is highly responsive to public opinion on all matters or one that responds deliberately to organized groups that argue their cases effectively?

Those are enduring questions. The framers of the Constitution dealt with them, and their struggle is the appropriate place to begin our analysis of how these competing models of democracy have animated the debate about the nature of the American political process.

Key Terms

government	anarchism
order	liberals
communism	conservatives
public goods	communitarians
freedom of	democracy
freedom from	procedural democratic theory
police power	universal participation
political equality	political equality
social equality	majority rule
equality of opportunity	participatory democracy
equality of outcome	representative democracy
rights	responsiveness
political ideology	substantive democratic theory
totalitarianism	minority rights
socialism	majoritarian model of democracy
democratic socialism	interest group
capitalism	pluralist model of democracy
libertarianism	elite theory
laissez faire	oligarchy

Selected Readings

Berry, Jeffrey M., Kent E. Portney, and Ken Thomson. *The Rebirth of Urban Democracy.* Washington, D.C.: Brookings Institution, 1993. An examination of neighborhood government in five American cities. The authors conclude that participatory democracy on the local level is a feasible and desirable alternative.

Dahl, Robert A. *Democracy and Its Critics.* New Haven, Conn.: Yale University Press, 1989. The nation's leading expert on pluralist theory examines the basic foundations of democracy. Dahl defends democracy against a variety of criticisms that have focused on its shortcomings.

Ebenstein, William, and Edwin Fogelman. *Today's Isms: Communism, Fascism, Capitalism, Socialism.* 10th ed. Englewood Cliffs, N.J.: Prentice-Hall, 1994. This standard source describes the history of the four major isms and relates each to developments in contemporary politics. It is concise, informative, and readable.

Etzioni, Amitai. *The New Golden Rule: Community and Morality in a Democratic Society.* New York: Basic Books, 1996. Etzioni examines the balance between liberty and morality in government. He argues for basing order on moral commitments rather than on law.

Hudson, William E. *American Democracy in Peril: Seven Challenges to America's Future.* 2d ed. Chatham, N.J.: Chatham House Publishers, 1998. An articulate opponent of pluralism, Hudson makes a compelling case that American institutions are drifting dangerously far from democratic ideals. This highly readable volume tackles a host of issues.

World Wide Web Resources

The World Wide Web (WWW) on the Internet has many sites with information relevant to studying American government and politics. Below are some that are particularly relevant to the ideological typology described in this chapter. The Uniform Resource Locator (URL) needed to find the site is given within angle brackets. Because these addresses may change over time, you may have to search the Web by keywords to locate the site.

The Communitarian Network. This site "is a coalition of individuals and organizations who have come together to shore up the moral, social, and political environment. We are a nonsectarian, nonpartisan, nationwide association." <www.gwu.edu/~ccps>

Libertarian Student Clubs' WWW Network. This site "is a links and updates page for all the libertarian student clubs using the Web. This includes both student affiliates of the Libertarian Party and other student groups seeking to further the cause of libertarianism." <www.mit.edu:8001/activities/libertarians/lscwn.html>

Turn Left. This site bills itself as "the home of liberalism on the Web." It links to authors, politicians, print media, and other sources of liberal ideas. <www.cjnetworks.com/~cubsfan/pnp.html>

The Right Side of the Web. This site calls itself "the most ridiculed, spoofed, *and* imitated site on the Web." It contains a mélange of materials dealing with conservative causes. <www.rtside.com>

Christian Coalition. "A grassroots citizen organization working on behalf of families who want to see less government intrusion in their lives and more family-friendly public policy." <www.cc.org>

2

The Constitution

The midnight burglars made a small mistake. They left a piece of tape over the latch they had tripped to enter the Watergate office and apartment complex in Washington, D.C. A security guard discovered their tampering and called the police, who surprised the burglars in the offices of the Democratic National Committee at 2:30 A.M. The arrests of five men in the early hours of June 17, 1972, triggered a constitutional struggle that eventually involved the president of the United States, the Congress, and the Supreme Court.

The Watergate story unfolded completely only after the landslide reelection of Richard Nixon in November 1972. The five burglars and two men closely connected with the president answered in court for the break-in. The Senate launched its own investigation.

After a stunned nation learned that the president had secretly tape-recorded all of his conversations in the White House, the Senate committee asked for the tapes. Nixon refused, citing the separation of powers between the legislative and the executive branches and claiming that "executive privilege" allowed him to withhold information from Congress. Nixon also resisted subpoenas demanding the White House tapes.

Eventually, the special prosecutor appointed by the attorney general to investigate Watergate brought indictments against Nixon's closest aides. Nixon himself was named an unindicted co-conspirator. Both the special prosecutor and the defendants wanted the White House tapes, but Nixon continued to resist. Finally, on July 24, 1974, the Supreme Court ruled that the president had to hand them over. At almost the same time, the House Judiciary Committee voted to recommend to the full House that Nixon be impeached.

Faced with the collapse of his support and likely impeachment by the full House, Nixon resigned the presidency on August 9, 1974. A month later, acting within his constitutional powers, President Gerald Ford granted private citizen Richard Nixon an unconditional pardon for all crimes that he may have committed. Others were not so fortunate. Three members of the Nixon cabinet (two attorneys general and a secretary of commerce) were convicted and sentenced for their crimes in the Watergate affair.

The Watergate affair posed one of the most serious challenges to the constitutional order of modern American government. The incident ultimately

Starr-gazing
*Independent Counsel Kenneth W. Starr referred grounds for the impeachment of President
Clinton to the House of Representatives in September 1998. Starr presented the House with
abundant evidence of Clinton's sexual affair with intern Monica S. Lewinsky and the
ensuing cover-up. Clinton's defense focused largely on the methods employed by Starr's office
to obtain that evidence. In 1999, after more than two decades and twenty-one investigations
of high-level officials, Congress decided to let the independent counsel law lapse. Critics
argued that the law, born in Watergate's wake, lacked accountability, allowed unchecked
prosecutorial power, and undermined integrity in government.*

developed into a struggle over the rule of law, between the president on the
one hand and Congress and the courts on the other. In the end, the constitutional principle dividing power among the executive, legislative, and judicial
branches prevented the president from controlling the Watergate investigation. The principle of checks and balances allowed Congress to threaten
Nixon with impeachment. The belief that Nixon had violated the Constitution
finally prompted members of both political parties to support impeachment,
leading the president to resign.

The House of Representatives revisited those constitutional issues in 1998
when it voted to impeach President Bill Clinton. Then, in early 1999, voting
mainly along party lines, the Senate declined to convict the president and remove him from office. The Republican senators who voted against impeachment may have believed that Clinton's cover-up of a sexual affair with a White
House intern, although disgraceful, did not constitute an offense for which the
legislative branch should—or could—remove the chief executive from office.
In the words of one analyst, impeachment is a mechanism intended "to shield
the nation against rogue Presidents, not to punish Presidents who are rogues."[1]

Nixon was forced to resign the presidency a little more than a year and a half into his second term. In 1992, 70 percent of Americans still viewed Nixon's actions as having warranted his resignation.[2] In some countries, an irregular change in government leadership provides an opportunity for a palace coup, an armed revolution, or a military dictatorship. But here, significantly, no political violence erupted after Nixon's resignation; in fact, none was expected. Constitutional order in the United States had been put to a test, and it passed with high honors.

This chapter poses some questions about the Constitution. How did it evolve? What form did it take? What values does it reflect? How can it be altered? And which model of democracy—majoritarian or pluralist—does it fit best?

The Revolutionary Roots of the Constitution

The Constitution is just 4,300 words long. But those 4,300 words define the basic structure of our national government. A comprehensive document, it divides the government into three branches and describes the powers of those branches, their relationships, and the interaction between the government and the governed. The Constitution makes itself the supreme law of the land and binds every government official to support it.

Most Americans revere the Constitution as political "scripture." To charge that a political action is unconstitutional is akin to claiming that it is unholy. So the Constitution has taken on symbolic value that has strengthened its authority as the basis of American government. Strong belief in the Constitution has led many politicians to abandon party for principle when constitutional issues are at stake.

The U.S. Constitution, written in 1787 for an agricultural society huddled along the coast of a wild new land, now guides the political life of a massive urban society in the nuclear age. To fully understand the reasons for the stability of the Constitution—and of the political system it created—we must first look at its historical roots, roots that lie in colonial America.

Freedom in Colonial America

Although they were British subjects, the American colonists in the eighteenth century enjoyed a degree of freedom denied most people in the world. In Europe, ancient custom and the relics of feudalism restricted private property, compelled support for established religion, and restricted access to trades and professions; Americans were relatively free of such controls. Also, in America, colonists enjoyed almost complete freedom of speech, press, and assembly.[3]

By 1763; Britain and the colonies had reached a compromise between imperial control and colonial self-government. America's foreign affairs and overseas trade were to be controlled by the king and Parliament (the British legislature); the rest was left to home rule. But the cost of administering the colonies was substantial. Because Americans benefited the most, contended their English countrymen, Americans should bear that cost.

The Road to Revolution

The British believed that taxing the colonies was the obvious way to meet the costs of administering the colonies. The colonists did not agree. They especially did not want to be taxed by a distant government in which they had no representation. During the decade preceding the outbreak of hostilities in 1775, this issue was to convert increasing numbers of colonists from loyal British subjects seeking the rights of Englishmen to revolutionaries seeking the end of British rule over the American colonies.

On the night of December 16, 1773, a group of colonists reacted to a British duty on tea by organizing the Boston Tea Party. A mob boarded three ships and emptied 342 chests of that valuable substance into Boston Harbor. In an attempt to reassert British control over its recalcitrant colonists, Parliament passed the Coercive (or "Intolerable") Acts (1774). One act imposed a blockade on Boston until the tea was paid for; another gave royal governors the power to quarter British soldiers in private homes. Now the taxation issue was secondary; more important was the conflict between British demands for order and American demands for liberty. The Virginia and Massachusetts assemblies summoned a continental congress, an assembly that would speak and act for the people of all the colonies.

The First Continental Congress met in Philadelphia in September 1774. The objective of the assembly was to restore harmony between Great Britain and the American colonies. A leader, called the president, was elected. (The terms *president* and *congress* in American government trace their origins to the First Continental Congress.) In October 1774, the delegates adopted a statement of rights and principles; many of these later found their way into the Declaration of Independence and the Constitution. For example, the congress claimed a right "to life, liberty, and property" and a right "peaceably to assemble, consider of their grievances, and petition the king." Then the congress adjourned, planning to reconvene in May 1775.

Revolutionary Action

By early 1775, however, a movement that the colonists themselves were calling a revolution had already begun. Colonists in Massachusetts were fighting the British at Concord and Lexington. Delegates to the Second Continental Congress, meeting in May, faced a dilemma: should they prepare for war, or should they try to reconcile with Britain? As conditions deteriorated, the Second Continental Congress remained in session, to serve as the government of the colony-states.

On June 7, 1776, the Virginia delegation called on the Continental Congress to resolve "that these United Colonies are, and of right ought to be, free and Independent States, that they are absolved from all allegiance to the British Crown, and that all political connection between them and the State of Great Britain is, and ought to be, totally dissolved." A committee of five men was appointed to prepare a proclamation expressing the colonies' reasons for declaring independence.

Uniquely American Protest
Americans protested the Tea Act (1773) by holding the Boston Tea Party (see background, left) and by using a unique form of painful punishment—tarring and feathering—on the tax collector (see Stamp Act upside-down on the Liberty Tree). An early treatise on the subject offered the following instructions: "First, strip a person naked, then heat the tar until it is thin, and pour upon the naked flesh, or rub it over with a tar brush. After which, sprinkle decently upon the tar, whilst it is yet warm, as many feathers as will stick to it."

The Declaration of Independence

Thomas Jefferson, a young farmer and lawyer from Virginia, drafted the proclamation. Jefferson's document, the **Declaration of Independence**, expressed simply, clearly, and rationally the arguments in support of separation from Great Britain.

The principles underlying the declaration were rooted in the writings of the English philosopher John Locke and had been expressed many times by speakers in congress and in the colonial assemblies. Locke argued that people have God-given, or natural, rights that are inalienable—that is, they cannot be taken away by any government. According to Locke, all legitimate political authority exists to preserve these natural rights and is based on the consent of those who are governed. The idea of consent is derived from **social contract theory**, which states that the people agree to establish rulers for certain purposes and have the right to resist or remove rulers who violate those purposes.[4]

Jefferson used similar arguments in the Declaration of Independence. His simple yet impassioned statement of faith in democracy reverberates to this day: "We hold these truths to be self-evident, that all men are created equal, that they are endowed by their Creator with certain unalienable rights, that among these are life, liberty and the pursuit of happiness."

The First Continental Congress had declared in 1774 that the colonists were entitled to "life, liberty, and property." Jefferson reformulated the objectives as "life, liberty, and the pursuit of happiness." Furthermore, he continued:

> That to secure these rights, Governments are instituted among Men, deriving their just powers from the consent of the governed. That whenever any Form of Government becomes destructive of these ends, it is the Right of the People to alter or to abolish it, and to institute new Government, laying its foundation on such Principles and organizing its Powers in such form, as to them shall seem most likely to effect their Safety and Happiness.

He went on to list the many deliberate acts of the king that had exceeded the legitimate role of government. Finally, Jefferson declared that the colonies were "Free and Independent States," with no political connection to Great Britain.

The major premise of the Declaration of Independence is that the people have a right to revolt if they determine that their government is denying them their legitimate rights. The long list of the king's actions was evidence of such denial. So the people had the right to rebel and form a new government. On July 2, 1776, the Second Continental Congress finally voted for independence. The vote was by state, and the motion carried 11 to 0. (Rhode Island was not present, and the New York delegation, lacking instructions, did not cast its "yea" vote until July 15.) Two days later, on July 4, the Declaration of Independence was approved with few changes.

The War of Independence lasted far longer than anyone expected. It began in a moment of confusion, when a shot rang out as British soldiers approached the town of Lexington on the way to Concord, Massachusetts, on April 19, 1775. The end came six and a half years later with Lord Cornwallis's surrender of his six-thousand-man army at Yorktown, Virginia, on October 19, 1781. It was a costly war: more died and were wounded in relation to the population than in any other conflict except the Civil War.[5]

From Revolution to Confederation

By declaring their independence from England, the colonies left themselves without any real central government. So the revolutionaries proclaimed the creation of a republic. Strictly speaking, a **republic** is a government without a monarch, but the term had come to mean a government based on the consent of the governed, whose power is exercised by representatives who are responsible to them. A republic need not be a democracy, and this was fine with the founders; at that time democracy was associated with mob rule and instability (see Chapter 1). The revolutionaries were less concerned with determining who would control their new government than with limiting the powers of that government. They had revolted in the name of liberty, and now they wanted a government with sharply defined powers. To make sure they got one, they meant to define its structure and powers in writing.

The Articles of Confederation

Barely a week after the Declaration of Independence was signed, the Second Continental Congress received a committee report entitled "Articles of Confederation and Perpetual Union." A **confederation** is a loose association of independent states that agree to cooperate on specified matters. In a confederation, the states retain their sovereignty, which means that each has supreme power within its borders. The central government is weak; it can only coordinate, not control, the actions of its sovereign states.

The **Articles of Confederation**, the compact among the thirteen original colonies that established the United States, was finally adopted on November 15, 1777. The Articles jealously guarded state sovereignty; their provisions clearly reflected the delegates' fears of a strong central government. Under the Articles, each state, regardless of its size, had one vote in the congress. Votes on financing the war and other important issues required the consent of at least nine of the thirteen states.

The common danger—Britain—forced the young republic to function under the Articles, but this first try at a government was inadequate to the task. The delegates had succeeded in crafting a national government that was largely powerless. The Articles failed for at least four reasons: First, they did not give the national government the power to tax. As a result, the congress had to plead for money from the states to pay for the war and to carry on the affairs of the new nation. Second, the Articles made no provision for an independent leadership position to direct the government (the president was merely the presiding officer of the congress). The omission was deliberate—the colonists feared the reestablishment of a monarchy—but it left the nation without a leader. Third, the Articles did not allow the national government to regulate interstate and foreign commerce. (When John Adams proposed that the confederation enter into a commercial treaty with Britain after the war, he was asked, "Would you like one treaty or thirteen, Mr. Adams?").[6] Finally, the Articles could not be amended without the unanimous agreement of the congress and the assent of all the state legislatures; thus, each state had the power to veto any changes to the confederation.

The goal of the delegates who drew up the Articles of Confederation was to retain power in the states. This was consistent with republicanism, which viewed the remote power of a national government as a danger to liberty. In this sense alone, the Articles were a grand success: they completely hobbled the infant government.

Disorder Under the Confederation

Once the Revolution ended and independence was a reality, it became clear that the national government had neither the economic nor the military power to function. Freed from wartime austerity, Americans rushed to purchase goods from abroad. Debt mounted and, for many, bankruptcy followed.

The problem was particularly severe in Massachusetts, where high interest rates and high state taxes were forcing farmers into bankruptcy. In 1786 and 1787, farmers under the leadership of Daniel Shays, a revolutionary war veteran, carried out a series of insurrections to prevent the foreclosure of their farms by creditors. With the congress unable to secure funds from the states to help out, the governor of Massachusetts eventually called out the militia and restored order.[7] Shays's Rebellion demonstrated the impotence of the confederation and the urgent need to suppress insurrection and maintain domestic order.

From Confederation to Constitution

Order, the original purpose of government, was breaking down under the Articles of Confederation. The "league of friendship" envisioned in the Articles was not enough to hold the nation together in peacetime. So in 1786, Virginia invited the states to attend a convention at Annapolis to explore revisions to the Articles of Confederation. Although only five states sent delegates, they seized the opportunity to call for another meeting in Philadelphia the next year. The congress agreed to the convention but limited its mission to "the sole and express purpose of revising the Articles of Confederation."

Shays's Rebellion lent a sense of urgency to the task before the Philadelphia convention. The congress's inability to confront the rebellion was evidence that a stronger national government was necessary to preserve order and property—to protect the states from internal as well as external dangers. "While the Declaration was directed against an excess of authority," remarked Supreme Court Justice Robert H. Jackson some 150 years later, "the Constitution [that followed the Articles of Confederation] was directed against anarchy."[8]

The Constitutional Convention officially opened on May 25, 1787. Although its delegates were authorized only to "revise" the Articles of Confederation, within the first week of debate, Edmund Randolph of Virginia presented a long list of changes, suggested by fellow Virginian James Madison, that would replace the weak confederation of states with a powerful national government. The delegates unanimously agreed to debate Randolph's proposal, which was called the **Virginia Plan**. Almost immediately, then, they rejected the idea of amending the Articles of Confederation, working instead to create an entirely new constitution.

The Virginia Plan

The Virginia Plan dominated the convention's deliberations for the rest of the summer, making several important proposals for a strong central government:

- That the powers of the government be divided among three separate branches: a **legislative branch**, for making laws; an **executive branch**, for enforcing laws; and a **judicial branch**, for interpreting laws.

- That the legislature consist of two houses. The first would be chosen by the people; the second by the members of the first house from among persons nominated by the state legislatures.

- That each state's representation in the legislature be in proportion to taxes paid to the national government, or in proportion to its free population.

- That an executive of unspecified size be selected by the legislature and serve for a single term.

- That the national judiciary include one or more supreme courts and other lower courts, with judges appointed for life by the legislature.

- That the executive and a number of national judges serve as a council of revision, to approve or veto (disapprove) legislative acts. Their veto could be overridden, however, by a vote of both houses of the legislature.

- That the range of powers of all three branches be far greater than that assigned the national government by the Articles of Confederation and include the power of the legislature to override state laws.

By proposing a powerful national legislature that could override state laws, the Virginia Plan clearly advocated a new form of government. It was a mixed structure, with more authority over the states and new authority over the people.

Madison was a monumental force in the ensuing debate on the proposals. However, the constitution that emerged from the convention bore only partial resemblance to the document Madison wanted to create. He endorsed seventy-one specific proposals, but he ended up on the losing side on forty of them.[9] And the parts of the Virginia Plan that were ultimately adopted in the Constitution were not adopted without challenge. Conflict revolved primarily around the basis of representation in the legislature, the method of choosing legislators, and the structure of the executive branch.

The New Jersey Plan

When in 1787 it appeared that much of the Virginia Plan would be approved by the big states, the small states united in opposition. William Paterson of New Jersey introduced an alternative set of resolutions, written to preserve the spirit of the Articles of Confederation by amending rather than replacing them. The **New Jersey Plan** included the following proposals:

- That a single-chamber legislature have the power to raise revenue and regulate commerce.

- That the states have equal representation in the legislature and choose the members of that body.

- That a multiperson executive be elected by the legislature, with powers similar to those listed in the Virginia Plan but without the right to veto legislation.

- That a supreme judiciary be created with a very limited jurisdiction. (There was no provision for a system of national courts.)
- That the acts of the legislature be binding on the states—that is, be regarded as the "supreme law of the respective states," with force used to compel obedience.

The New Jersey Plan was defeated in the first major convention vote, 7–3. However, the small states had enough support to force a compromise on the issue of representation in the legislature.

The Great Compromise

The Virginia Plan's provision for a two-chamber legislature was never seriously challenged, but the idea of representation according to population generated heated debate. The small states demanded equal representation for all states.

A committee was created to resolve the deadlock. It consisted of one delegate from each state, chosen by secret ballot. After working through the Independence Day recess, the committee reported reaching the **Great Compromise** (sometimes called the *Connecticut Compromise*). Representation in the House of Representatives would be apportioned according to the population of each state. Initially, there would be fifty-six members. Revenue-raising acts would originate in the House. Most important, the states would be represented equally in the Senate, by two senators each. Senators would be selected by their state legislatures, not directly by the people.

The delegates accepted the Great Compromise. The smaller states got their equal representation; the larger states, their proportional representation. The small states might dominate the Senate, and the big states might control the House, but because all legislation had to be approved by both chambers, neither group would be able to dominate the other.

Compromise on the Presidency

Contention replaced compromise when the delegates turned to the executive branch. They did agree on a one-person executive—a president—but they disagreed on how the executive would be selected and what the term of office would be. The delegates distrusted the people's judgment; some feared that popular election would arouse public passions. Consequently, the delegates rejected the idea. At the same time, representatives of the small states feared that election by the legislature would allow the larger states to control the executive.

Once again they compromised, creating the *electoral college,* a cumbersome system consisting of a group of electors who are chosen for the sole purpose of selecting the president and vice president. Each state legislature would choose a number of electors equal to the number of its representatives in Congress. Each elector would then vote for two people. The candidate with the most votes would become president, provided that the number of votes constituted a majority; the person with the next greatest number of votes would become vice president. (This procedure was changed in 1804 by the Twelfth Amendment, which mandates separate votes for each office.) If no candidate won a majority, then the House of Representatives would choose a president, with each state casting one vote.

The electoral college compromise eliminated the fear of a popular vote for president. At the same time, it satisfied the small states. If the electoral college failed to produce a president—which the delegates expected would happen—an election by the House would give every state the same voice in the selection process.

Also, the delegates agreed that the president's term of office should be four years and that the president should be eligible for reelection.

The delegates realized that removing a president from office would be a very serious political matter. For that reason, they involved the other two branches of government in the process. The House alone was empowered to charge a president with "Treason, Bribery, or other high Crimes and Misdemeanors," by a majority vote. The Senate was given sole power to try such impeachments. It could convict and thus remove a president only by a two-thirds vote. The chief justice of the United States was required to preside over the Senate trial.

The Final Product

Once the delegates resolved their major disagreements, they dispatched the remaining issues relatively quickly. A committee was appointed to draft a constitution. The Preamble, which was the last section to be drafted, begins with a phrase that would have been impossible to write when the convention opened. This single sentence sets forth the four elements that form the foundation of the American political tradition.[10]

- *It creates a people:* "We the People of the United States" was a dramatic departure from a loose confederation of states.

- *It explains the reason for the Constitution:* "in Order to form a more perfect Union" was an indirect way of saying that the first effort, under the Articles of Confederation, had been inadequate.

- *It articulates goals:* "[to] establish Justice, insure domestic Tranquility, provide for the common defence, promote the general Welfare, and secure the Blessings of Liberty to ourselves and our posterity"—in other words, the government exists to promote order and freedom.

- *It fashions a government:* "do ordain and establish this Constitution for the United States of America."

The Basic Principles

In creating the Constitution, the founders relied on four political principles that together established a revolutionary new political order. These principles were republicanism, federalism, separation of powers, and checks and balances.

Republicanism   **Republicanism** is a form of government in which power resides in the people and is exercised by their elected representatives. The framers were determined to avoid aristocracy (rule by a hereditary class), monarchy (rule by one), and direct democracy (rule by the people). A republic was both new and daring: no people had ever been governed by a republic on so vast a scale. Indeed, the framers themselves were far from sure that their government could be sustained. After the convention ended, Benjamin Franklin was asked what sort of government the new nation would have. "A republic," he replied, "if you can keep it."

Federalism   **Federalism** is the division of power between a central government and regional units. It makes citizens subject to two different bodies of law. A federal system stands between two competing government structures. On the one side is unitary government, in which all power is vested in a central government. On the other side stands confederation, a loose union with powerful states. The Constitution embodied a division of power, but it conferred substantial powers on the national government at the expense of the states.

According to the Constitution, the powers vested in the national and state governments are derived from the people, who remain the ultimate sovereign. National and state governments can exercise their powers over persons and property within their own spheres of authority. But by participating in the electoral process or by amending their governing charters, the people can restrain both the national and the state governments if necessary to preserve liberty.

The Constitution lists the powers of the national government and the powers denied to the states. All other powers remain with the states. However, the Constitution does not clearly describe the spheres of authority within which these powers can be exercised. As we will discuss in Chapter 3, limits on the exercise of power by the national government and the states have evolved as a result of political and military conflict; moreover, the limits have proved changeable.

Separation of Powers   **Separation of powers** is the assignment of the lawmaking, law-enforcing, and law-interpreting functions of government to independent legislative, executive, and judicial branches. Nationally, the lawmaking power resides in Congress, the law-enforcing power resides in the presidency, and the law-interpreting power resides in the courts. Service in one branch prohibits simultaneous service in the others. Separation of powers safeguards liberty by ensuring that all government power does not fall into the hands of a single person or group of people. However, this protection of the people's liberty was tempered with caution. Not only did the separation of powers limit the strength of officeholders, but the methods used to select the officials in each branch were devised to limit the direct influence of the people on that process (see Figure 2.1). In theory, separation of powers means that one branch cannot exercise the powers of the other branches. In practice, however, the separation is far from complete. One scholar has suggested that what we have instead is "separate institutions sharing powers."[11]

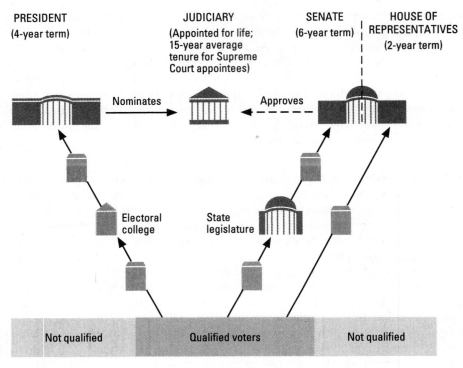

Ballot
box

FIGURE 2.1   ***The Constitution and the Electoral Process***
The framers were afraid of majority rule, and that fear is reflected in the electoral process for
national office described in the Constitution. The people, speaking through the voters, partic-
ipated directly only in the choice of their representatives in the House. The president and
senators were elected indirectly, through the electoral college and state legislatures. (Direct
election of senators did not become law until 1913, when the Seventeenth Amendment was
ratified.) Judicial appointments are, and always have been, far removed from representative
links to the people. Judges are nominated by the president and approved by the Senate.

Checks and Balances   The constitutional system of **checks and balances** is a
means of giving each branch of government some scrutiny of and control over
the other branches. The framers reasoned that checks and balances would
prevent one branch from ignoring or overpowering the others.

Separation of powers and checks and balances are two distinct principles,
but both are necessary to ensure that one branch does not dominate the government. Separation of powers divides government responsibilities among the
legislative, executive, and judicial branches; checks and balances prevent the
exclusive exercise of those powers by any one of the three branches. For example, only Congress can enact laws. But the president (through the power of

the veto) can cancel them, and the Supreme Court (by finding a law in violation of the Constitution) can nullify them. And the process goes on. In a "check on a check," Congress can override a president's veto by an extraordinary (two-thirds) majority in each chamber; and it is empowered to propose amendments to the Constitution, counteracting the Supreme Court's power to find a national law invalid. Figure 2.2 depicts the relationship between separation of powers and checks and balances.

The Articles of the Constitution

In addition to the Preamble, the Constitution includes seven articles. The first three establish the separate branches of government and specify their internal operations and powers. The remaining four define the relationships among the states, explain the process of amendment, declare the supremacy of national law, and explain the procedure for ratifying the Constitution.

Article I: The Legislative Article   In structuring their new government, the framers began with the legislative branch because they thought lawmaking was the most important function of a republican government. Article I is the most detailed and therefore the longest of all the articles. It defines the bicameral (two-chamber) character of the Congress and describes the internal operating procedures of the House of Representatives and the Senate. Section 8 of Article I expresses the principle of **enumerated powers**, which means that Congress can exercise only the powers that the Constitution assigns to it. Eighteen powers are enumerated; the first seventeen are specific powers (for example, the power to regulate interstate commerce).

The last clause in Section 8, known as the **necessary and proper clause** (or the elastic clause), gives Congress the means to execute the enumerated powers (see the Appendix). This clause is the basis of Congress's **implied powers**—those powers that Congress must have in order to execute its enumerated powers. For example, the power to levy and collect taxes (Clause 1) and the power to coin money and regulate its value (Clause 5), when joined with the necessary and proper clause (Clause 18), imply that Congress has the power to charter a bank. Otherwise, the national government would have no means of managing the money it collects through its power to tax. Implied powers clearly expand the enumerated powers conferred on Congress by the Constitution.

Article II: The Executive Article   Article II sets the president's term of office, the procedure for electing a president through the electoral college, the qualifications for becoming president, and the president's duties and powers. The last include acting as commander in chief of the military; making treaties (which must be ratified by a two-thirds vote in the Senate); and appointing government officers, diplomats, and judges (again, with the advice and consent of the Senate).

The president also has legislative powers—part of the constitutional system of checks and balances. For example, the Constitution requires that the

BRANCHES OF GOVERNMENT

	The legislature can:	The executive can:	The judiciary can:
Legislative	• Make laws	• Veto legislation • Recommend legislation	• Review legislative acts
Executive	• Confirm executive appointments (Senate) • Override executive veto • Reject foreign treaties	• Enforce laws	• Review executive acts • Issue injunctions
Judicial	• Impeach • Create or eliminate courts	• Grant pardons • Nominate judges	• Interpret laws

POWERS OF GOVERNMENT

FIGURE 2.2   **Separation of Powers and Checks and Balances**
Separation of powers is the assignment of lawmaking, law-enforcing, and law-interpreting functions to the legislative, executive, and judicial branches. The phenomenon is illustrated by the diagonal from upper left to lower right in the figure. Checks and balances give each branch some power over the other branches. For example, the executive branch possesses some legislative power, and the legislative branch possesses some executive power. These checks and balances are listed outside the diagonal.

president periodically inform the Congress of the "State of the Union" and of the policies and programs that the executive branch intends to advocate in the coming year. Today this is done annually, in the president's State of the Union address. Under special circumstances, the president can also convene or adjourn Congress. Additionally, the duty to "take Care that the Laws be faithfully executed" in Section 3 has provided presidents with a reservoir of power.

Article III: The Judicial Article   The third article was left purposely vague. The Constitution established the Supreme Court as the highest court in the land. But beyond that, the framers were unable to agree on the need for a national judiciary, or its size, its composition, or the procedures it should follow. They left these issues to the Congress, which resolved them by creating a system of federal—that is, national—courts separate from the state courts.

Unless they are impeached, federal judges serve for life. They are appointed to indefinite terms "during good Behavior," and their salaries cannot be lowered while they hold office. These stipulations reinforce the separation of powers; they see to it that judges are independent of the other branches, that they do not have to fear retribution for their exercise of judicial power.

Congress exercises a potential check on the judicial branch through its power to create (and eliminate) lower federal courts. Congress can also restrict the power of the federal courts to decide cases. And, as we have noted, the president appoints—with the advice and consent of the Senate—the justices of the Supreme Court and the judges of the lower federal courts.

Article III does not explicitly give the courts the power of **judicial review**, the authority to invalidate congressional or presidential actions. That power has been inferred from the logic, structure, and theory of the Constitution.

The Remaining Articles   The remaining four articles of the Constitution cover a lot of ground. Article IV requires that the judicial acts and criminal warrants of each state be honored in all other states, and it forbids discrimination against citizens of one state by another state. This provision promotes equality; it keeps the states from treating outsiders differently from their own citizens. The origin of this clause can be traced to the Articles of Confederation. Article IV also allows the addition of new states and stipulates that the national government will protect the states against foreign invasion and domestic violence.

Article V specifies the methods for amending (changing) the Constitution. We will have more to say about this shortly.

An important component of Article VI is the **supremacy clause**, which asserts that, when they conflict with state or local laws, the Constitution, national laws, and treaties take precedence. The stipulation is vital to the operation of federalism. In keeping with the supremacy clause, Article VI also requires that all national and state officials, elected or appointed, take an oath to support the Constitution. The article also mandates that religion cannot be a prerequisite for holding government office.

Article VII describes the ratification process, stipulating that approval by conventions in nine states would be necessary for the Constitution to take effect.

The Framers' Motives

What forces motivated the framers? Surely economic issues were important, but they were not the major issues. The single most important factor leading to the Constitutional Convention was the inability of the national or state governments to maintain order under the loose structure of the Articles of Confederation. Certainly order required the protection of property, but the framers had a view of property that extended beyond their portfolios of government securities. They wanted to protect their homes, their families, and their means of livelihood from impending anarchy.

Although they disagreed bitterly on the structure and mechanics of the national government, the framers agreed on the most vital issues. For example, three crucial features of the Constitution—the power to tax, the necessary and proper clause, and the supremacy clause—were approved unanimously without debate. Indeed, the motivation to create order was so strong, the framers were willing to draft clauses that protected the most undemocratic of all institutions—slavery.

The Slavery Issue

The institution of slavery was well ingrained in American life at the time of the Constitutional Convention, and slavery helped shape the Constitution, although it is mentioned nowhere by name in it. It is doubtful, in fact, that there would have been a Constitution if the delegates had had to resolve the slavery issue.

The question of representation in the House of Representatives brought the issue close to the surface of the debate at the Constitutional Convention and led to the Great Compromise. Representation in the House was to be based on population. But who would be counted in the "population"? Eventually, the delegates agreed unanimously that in apportioning representation in the House and in assessing direct taxes, the population of each state was to be determined by adding "the whole Number of free Persons" and "three fifths of all other Persons" (Article I, Section 2). The phrase "all other Persons" is, of course, a substitute for "slaves."

The three-fifths clause gave states with large slave populations (in the South) greater representation in Congress than states with small slave populations (in the North). The compromise left the South with 47 percent of the House seats, a sizable minority, but in all likelihood a losing one on slavery issues.[12] The overrepresentation resulting from the South's large slave populations translated into greater southern influence in selecting the president as well, because the electoral college was based on the size of the states' congressional delegations. The three-fifths clause also undertaxed states with large slave populations.

Another issue centered around the slave trade. Several southern delegates were uncompromising in their defense of it, while other delegates favored prohibition. The delegates compromised, agreeing that the slave trade could not be ended before twenty years had elapsed (Article I, Section 9). Also, the delegates agreed, without serious challenge, that fugitive slaves be returned to their masters (Article IV, Section 2).

In addressing these points, the framers in essence condoned slavery. Clearly, slavery existed in stark opposition to the idea that "All men are created equal," and though many slaveholders, including Jefferson and Madison, agonized over it, few made serious efforts to free their own slaves. Most Americans seemed indifferent to slavery. Nonetheless, the eradication of slavery proceeded gradually in certain states. By 1787, Connecticut, Massachusetts,

All Were Not Created Equal
This 1845 photograph of Isaac Jefferson, who had been one of Thomas Jefferson's slaves at Monticello, reminds us that the framers of the Constitution did not extend freedom and equality to all. Slavery was widely accepted as a social norm in the eighteenth century.

New Jersey, New York, Pennsylvania, Rhode Island, and Vermont abolished slavery or provided for gradual emancipation. This slow but perceptible shift on the slavery issue in many states masked a volcanic force capable of destroying the Constitutional Convention and the Union.

Selling the Constitution

On September 17, 1787, nearly four months after the Constitutional Convention opened, the delegates convened for the last time, to sign the final version of their handiwork. Because several delegates were unwilling to sign the document, the last paragraph was craftily worded to give the impression of unanimity: "Done in Convention by the Unanimous Consent of the States present."

However, before it could take effect, the Constitution had to be ratified by a minimum of nine state conventions. In each, support was far from "unanimous."

The proponents of the new charter, who wanted a strong national government, called themselves Federalists. The opponents of the Constitution were quickly dubbed Antifederalists. They claimed, however, that they were true federalists because they wanted to protect the states from the tyranny of a strong national government. The viewpoints of the two groups formed the bases of the first American political parties.

The *Federalist* Papers

Beginning in October 1787, an exceptional series of eighty-five newspaper articles defending the Constitution appeared under the title *The Federalist: A Commentary on the Constitution of the United States.* The essays bore the pen name "Publius" and were written primarily by James Madison and Alexander Hamilton, with some assistance from John Jay. Logically and calmly, Publius argued in favor of ratification. Reprinted extensively during the ratification battle, the *Federalist* papers remain the best single commentary we have on the meaning of the Constitution and the political theory it embodies.

Not to be outdone, the Antifederalists offered their own intellectual basis for rejecting the Constitution. In several essays, the most influential authored under the pseudonyms "Brutus" and "Federal Farmer," they attacked the centralization of power in a strong national government, claiming it would obliterate the states, violate the social contract of the Declaration of Independence, and destroy liberty in the process. They defended the status quo, maintaining that the Articles of Confederation established true federal principles.[13]

Of all the *Federalist* papers, the most magnificent and most frequently cited is *Federalist* No. 10, which was written by James Madison. He argued that the proposed constitution was designed "to break and control the violence of faction": "By a faction," Madison wrote, "I understand a number of citizens, whether amounting to a majority or minority of the whole, who are united and actuated by some common impulse of passion, or of interest, adverse to the rights of other citizens, or to the permanent and aggregate interests of the community."

Madison was discussing what we described in Chapter 1 as *pluralism.* What Madison called factions are today called interest groups or even political parties. According to Madison, "The most common and durable source of factions has been the various and unequal distribution of property." Madison was concerned not with reducing inequalities of wealth (which he took for granted) but with controlling the seemingly inevitable conflict that stems from them. The Constitution, he argued, was well constructed for this purpose.

Through the mechanism of representation, wrote Madison, the Constitution would prevent a "tyranny of the majority" (mob rule). The government would not be controlled directly by the people, but would be controlled indirectly, by their elected representatives. And those representatives would have the intelligence and understanding to serve the larger interests of the nation. Moreover, the federal system would require that majorities form first within each state, then organize for effective action at the national level. This and the vastness of the country would make it unlikely that a majority would form that would "invade the rights of other citizens."

The purpose of *Federalist* No. 10 was to demonstrate that the proposed government was not likely to be ruled by any faction. Contrary to conventional wisdom, Madison argued, the key to controlling the evils of faction is to have a large republic—the larger, the better. The more diverse the society, the less likely it is that an unjust majority can form. Madison certainly had no intention of creating a majoritarian democracy; his view of popular government was much more consistent with the model of pluralist democracy discussed in Chapter 1.

Madison pressed his argument from a different angle in *Federalist* No. 51. Asserting that "ambition must be made to counteract ambition," he argued that the separation of powers and checks and balances would control tyranny from any source. If power is distributed equally across the three branches, then each branch has the capacity to counteract the other. In Madison's words, "usurpations are guarded against by a division of the government into distinct and separate departments." Because legislative power tends to predominate in republican governments, legislative authority is divided between the Senate and the House of Representatives, which have different methods of selection and terms of office. Additional protection comes through federalism, which divides power "between two distinct governments"—national and state—and subdivides "the portion allotted to each . . . among distinct and separate departments."

The Antifederalists wanted additional separation of powers and additional checks and balances, which, they maintained, would eliminate the threat of tyranny entirely. The Federalists believed that this would make decisive national action virtually impossible. But to ensure ratification, they agreed to a compromise.

A Concession: The Bill of Rights

Despite the eloquence of the *Federalist* papers, many prominent citizens, including Thomas Jefferson, were unhappy that the Constitution did not list basic civil liberties—the individual freedoms guaranteed to citizens. The omission of a bill of rights was the chief obstacle to the adoption of the Constitution by the states. The colonists had just rebelled against the British government to preserve their basic freedoms. Why didn't the proposed Constitution spell out those freedoms?

The answer was rooted in logic, not politics. Because the national government was limited to those powers that were granted to it and because no power was granted to abridge the people's liberties, a list of guaranteed freedoms was not necessary. In *Federalist* No. 84, Hamilton went even further, arguing that the addition of a bill of rights would be dangerous. Because it is not possible to list all prohibited powers, wrote Hamilton, any attempt to provide a partial list would make the remaining areas vulnerable to government abuse.

But logic was no match for fear. Many states agreed to ratify the Constitution only after George Washington suggested that a list of guarantees be added through the amendment process. Well in excess of one hundred

TABLE 2.1   **The Bill of Rights**
The first ten amendments to the Constitution are known as the Bill of Rights. The
following is a list of those amendments, grouped conceptually. For the actual
order and wording of the Bill of Rights, see the Appendix.

Guarantees	Amendment
Guarantees for Participation in the Political Process	
No government abridgement of speech or press; no government abridgement of peaceable assembly; no government abridgement of petitioning government for redress.	1
Guarantees Respecting Personal Beliefs	
No government establishment of religion; no government prohibition of free religious exercise.	1
Guarantees of Personal Privacy	
Owners' consent necessary to quarter troops in private homes in peacetime; quartering during war must be lawful.	3
Government cannot engage in unreasonable searches and seizures; warrants to search and seize require probable cause.	4
No compulsion to testify against oneself in criminal cases.	5
Guarantees Against Government's Overreaching	
Serious crimes require a grand jury indictment; no repeated prosecution for the same offense; no loss of life, liberty, or property without due process; no taking of property for public use without just compensation.	5
Criminal defendants will have a speedy public trial by impartial local jury; defendants are informed of accusation; defendants may confront witnesses against them; defendants may use judicial process to obtain favorable witnesses; defendants may have legal assistance for their defense.	6
Civil lawsuits can be tried by juries if controversy exceeds $20; in jury trials, fact-finding is a jury function.	7
No excessive bail; no excessive fines; no cruel and unusual punishment.	8
Other Guarantees	
The people have the right to bear arms.	2
No government trespass on unspecified fundamental rights.	9
The states or the people retain all powers not delegated to the national government or denied to the states.	10

amendments were proposed by the states. These were eventually narrowed
down to twelve, which were approved by Congress and sent to the states. Ten
of them became part of the Constitution in 1791, after securing the approval
of the required three-fourths of the states. Collectively, these ten amendments
are known as the **Bill of Rights**. They restrain the national government from
tampering with fundamental rights and civil liberties and emphasize the limited character of the national government's power (see Table 2.1).

Ratification

The Constitution officially took effect upon its ratification by the ninth state, New Hampshire, on June 21, 1788. However, the success of the new government was not ensured until July 1788, by which time the Constitution was ratified by the key states of Virginia and New York after lengthy debate.

The reflection and deliberation that attended the creation and ratification of the Constitution signaled to the world that a new government could be launched peacefully. The French observer Alexis de Tocqueville (1805–1859) later wrote:

> That which is new in the history of societies is to see a great people, warned by its lawgivers that the wheels of government are stopping, turn its attention on itself without haste or fear, sound the depth of the ill, and then wait for two years to find the remedy at leisure, and then finally, when the remedy has been indicated, submit to it voluntarily without its costing humanity a single tear or drop of blood.[14]

Constitutional Change

The founders realized that the Constitution would have to be changed from time to time. To this end, they specified a formal amendment process—a process that was used almost immediately to add the Bill of Rights. With the passage of time, the Constitution also has been altered through judicial interpretation and changes in political practice.

The Formal Amendment Process

The amendment process has two stages: proposal and ratification. Both are necessary for an amendment to become part of the Constitution. The Constitution provides two alternative methods for completing each stage (see Figure 2.3). Amendments can be proposed by a two-thirds vote in both the House of Representatives and the Senate, or by a national convention, summoned by Congress at the request of two-thirds of the state legislatures. All constitutional amendments to date have been proposed by the first method.

A proposed amendment can be ratified by a vote of the legislatures of three-fourths of the states or by a vote of constitutional conventions held in three-fourths of the states. Congress chooses the method of ratification. It has used the state convention method only once, for the Twenty-first Amendment, which repealed the Eighteenth (Prohibition).

Note that the amendment process requires the exercise of **extraordinary majorities** (two-thirds and three-fourths). The framers purposely made it difficult to propose and ratify amendments. They wanted only the most significant issues to lead to constitutional change.

Calling a national convention to propose an amendment has never been tried. Certainly the method raises several thorny questions, the most significant of which concerns what limits, if any, there are on the business of the convention.

PROPOSAL STAGE   RATIFICATION STAGE

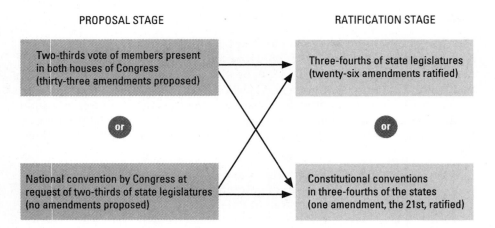

FIGURE 2.3   *Amending the Constitution*
*There are two stages in amending the Constitution: proposal and ratification. Congress has
no control over the proposal stage, but it prescribes the ratification method. Once a state has
ratified an amendment, it cannot retract its action. However, a state may reject an amendment and then reconsider its decision.*

Would a national convention, called to consider a particular amendment, be
within its bounds to rewrite the Constitution? No one really knows.

Most of the Constitution's twenty-seven amendments were adopted to help
keep it abreast of changes in political thinking. The first ten amendments (the
Bill of Rights) were the price of ratification, but they have been fundamental
to our system of government. The last seventeen amendments fall into three
main categories: they make public policy; they correct deficiencies in the government's structure; or they promote equality (see Table 2.2).

Since 1787, about ten thousand constitutional amendments have been
introduced; only a fraction have passed through the proposal stage.
However, once an amendment has been voted by the Congress, chances of
ratification are high. Only six amendments submitted to the states have
failed to be ratified.

Interpretation by the Courts

In *Marbury v. Madison* (1803), the Supreme Court declared that the courts
have the power to nullify government acts when they conflict with the
Constitution. (We will elaborate on judicial review in Chapter 11.) The exercise of judicial review forces the courts to interpret the Constitution. In a way,
this makes a lot of sense. The judiciary is the law-interpreting branch of the
government; as the supreme law of the land, the Constitution is fair game for
judicial interpretation. Judicial review is the courts' main check on the other
branches of government. But in interpreting the Constitution, the courts cannot help but give new meaning to its provisions. This is why judicial interpretation is a principal form of constitutional change.

TABLE 2.2   **Constitutional Amendments: 11 Through 27**

No.	Proposed	Ratified	Intent	Subject
11	1794	1795	G	Prohibits an individual from suing a state in federal court without the state's consent.
12	1803	1804	G	Requires the electoral college to vote separately for president and vice president.
13	1865	1865	E	Prohibits slavery.
14	1866	1868	E	Gives citizenship to all persons born or naturalized in the United States (including former slaves); prevents states from depriving any person of "life, liberty, or property, without due process of law," and declares that no state shall deprive any person of "the equal protection of the laws."
15	1869	1870	E	Guarantees that citizens' right to vote cannot be denied "on account of race, color, or previous condition of servitude."
16	1909	1913	E	Gives Congress the power to collect an income tax.
17	1912	1913	E	Provides for popular election of senators, who were formerly elected by state legislatures.
18	1917	1919	P	Prohibits the making and selling of intoxicating liquors.
19	1919	1920	E	Guarantees that citizens' right to vote cannot be denied "on account of sex."
20	1932	1933	G	Changes the presidential inauguration from March 4 to January 20 and sets January 3 for the opening date of Congress.
21	1933	1933	P	Repeals the Eighteenth Amendment.
22	1947	1951	G	Limits a president to two terms.
23	1960	1961	E	Gives citizens of Washington, D.C., the right to vote for president.
24	1962	1964	E	Prohibits charging citizens a poll tax to vote in presidential or congressional elections.
25	1965	1967	G	Provides for succession in event of death, removal from office, incapacity, or resignation of the president or vice president.
26	1971	1971	E	Lowers the voting age to eighteen.
27	1789	1992	G	Bars immediate pay increases to members of Congress.

P Amendments legislating public policy
G Amendments correcting perceived deficiencies in government structure
E Amendments advancing equality

Political Practice

The Constitution is silent on many issues. It says nothing about political parties or the president's cabinet, for example, yet both have exercised considerable influence in American politics. Some constitutional provisions have fallen

Designated Pourer
The Eighteenth Amendment, which was ratified by the states in 1919, banned the manufac-
ture, sale, or transportation of alcoholic beverages. Banned beverages were destroyed, as
pictured here. The amendment was spurred by moral and social reform groups, such as the
Women's Christian Temperance Union, founded by Evanston, Illinois, resident Frances
Willard in 1874. The amendment proved to be an utter failure. People continued to drink,
but their alcohol came from illegal sources.

out of use. The electors in the electoral college, for example, were supposed
to exercise their own judgment in voting for president and vice president.
Today the electors function simply as a rubber stamp, validating the outcome
of election contests in their states.

Meanwhile, political practice has altered the distribution of power without
changes in the Constitution. The framers intended Congress to be the
strongest branch of government. But the president has come to overshadow
Congress. Presidents like Abraham Lincoln and Franklin Roosevelt used their
powers imaginatively to respond to national crises, and their actions paved the
way for future presidents to further enlarge the powers of the office.

An Evaluation of the Constitution

The U.S. Constitution is one of the world's most praised political documents.
It is the oldest written national constitution and one of the most widely

copied, sometimes word for word. It is also one of the shortest. The brevity of the Constitution may be one of its greatest strengths. The framers simply laid out a structural framework for government; they did not describe relationships and powers in detail. For example, the Constitution gives Congress the power to regulate "Commerce . . . among the several States," but it does not define *interstate commerce*. Such general wording allows interpretation in keeping with contemporary political, social, and technological developments.

The generality of the U.S. Constitution stands in stark contrast to the specificity of most state constitutions. The constitution of California, for example, provides that "fruit and nut-bearing trees under the age of four years from the time of planting in orchard form and grapevines under the age of three years from the time of planting in vineyard form . . . shall be exempt from taxation" (Article XIII, Section 12). Because they are so specific, most state constitutions are much longer than the U.S. Constitution.

Freedom, Order, and Equality in the Constitution

The revolutionaries constructed a new form of government—a *federal* government—that was strong enough to maintain order but not so strong that it could dominate the states or infringe on individual freedoms. In short, the Constitution provided a judicious balance between order and freedom. It paid virtually no attention to equality.

Consider social equality. The Constitution never mentioned *slavery*—a controversial issue even when it was first written. As we have seen, the Constitution implicitly condones slavery in the wording of several articles. Not until ratification of the Thirteenth Amendment in 1865 was slavery prohibited. The Constitution was designed long before social equality was ever thought of as an objective of government. In fact, in *Federalist* No. 10, Madison held that protection of the "diversities in the faculties of men from which the rights of property originate" is "the first object of government."

Over a century later, the Constitution was changed to incorporate a key device for the promotion of social equality—the income tax. The Sixteenth Amendment (1913) gave Congress the power to collect an income tax; it was proposed and ratified to replace a law that had been declared unconstitutional in an 1895 court case. The income tax had long been seen as a means of putting into effect the concept of *progressive taxation*, in which the tax rate increases with income. The Sixteenth Amendment gave progressive taxation a constitutional basis.[15] Progressive taxation promotes social equality through the redistribution of income—that is, high-income people are taxed at high rates to help fund social programs that benefit lower-income people taxed at lower rates.

Social equality itself has never been, and is not now, a prime *constitutional* value. The Constitution has been much more effective in securing order and freedom. Nor did the Constitution take a stand on political equality. It left voting qualifications to the states, specifying only that people who could vote for "the most numerous Branch of the State Legislature" could also vote for representatives to Congress (Article I, Section 2). Most states at that time allowed only taxpaying or property-owning white males to vote. Such inequalities have been rectified by several amendments.

The Constitution and Models of Democracy

Think back to our discussion of the models of democracy in Chapter 1. Which model does the Constitution fit: the pluralist or majoritarian? Actually, it is hard to imagine a government framework better suited to the pluralist model of democracy than the Constitution of the United States. It is also hard to imagine a document more at odds with the majoritarian model. Consider Madison's claim, in *Federalist* No. 10, that government inevitably involves conflicting factions. This concept coincides perfectly with pluralist theory (see Chapter 1). Then recall his description in *Federalist* No. 51 of the Constitution's ability to guard against the concentration of power in the majority through separation of powers and checks and balances. This concept—avoiding a single center of government power that might fall under majority control—also fits perfectly with pluralist democracy.

The delegates to the Constitutional Convention intended to create a republic, a government based on majority consent; they did not intend to create a democracy, which rests on majority rule. They succeeded admirably in creating that republic. In doing so, they also produced a government that developed into a democracy—but a particular type of democracy. The framers neither wanted nor got a democracy that fit the majoritarian model. They may have wanted and they certainly did create a government that conforms to the pluralist model.

Summary

The U.S. Constitution is more than a historic document, an antique curiosity. Although over two hundred years old, it still governs the politics of a mighty modern nation. It still has the power to force from office a president who won reelection by a landslide. It still has the power to see the country through government crises.

The Constitution was the end product of a revolutionary movement aimed at preserving existing liberties. That movement began with the Declaration of Independence, which proclaimed that everyone is entitled to certain rights (among them, life, liberty, and the pursuit of happiness) and that government exists for the good of its citizens. When government denies those rights, the people have the right to rebel.

War with Britain was only part of the process of independence. Some form of government was needed to replace the British monarchy. The Americans chose a republic and defined the structure of that republic in the Articles of Confederation. The Articles were a failure, however. Although they guaranteed the states the independence they coveted, they left the central government too weak to deal with disorder and insurrection.

The Constitution was the second attempt at limited government. It replaced a loose union of powerful states with a strong but still limited national government, incorporating four political principles: republicanism, federalism, separation of powers, and checks and balances. Republicanism is a form of government in which power resides in the people and is exercised by their elected representatives. Federalism is a division of power between the national government and the states. The federalism of the Constitution conferred substantial powers on the national government at the expense of the states. Separation of powers is a further division of the power of the national government into legislative (lawmaking), executive (law-enforcing), and judiciary (law-interpreting) branches. Finally, the Constitution established a system of checks and balances, giving each branch some scrutiny of and control over the others.

When work began on ratification, a major stumbling block proved to be the failure of the Constitution to list the individual liberties the Americans had fought to protect. With the promise to add a bill of rights, the Constitution was ratified. The subsequent ten amendments guaranteed participation in the political process, respect for personal beliefs, and personal privacy. They also contained guarantees against government overreaching in criminal prosecutions. Over the years the Constitution has evolved through the formal amendment process, through the exercise of judicial review, and through political practice.

The Constitution was designed to strike a balance between order and freedom. It was not designed to promote equality; in fact, it had to be amended to redress inequality. The framers had compromised on many issues, including slavery, to ensure the creation of a new and workable government. The framers had not set out to create a democracy. Faith in government by the people was virtually nonexistent two centuries ago. Nevertheless, they produced a democratic form of government. That government, with its separation of powers and checks and balances, is remarkably well suited to the pluralist model of democracy. Simple majority rule, which lies at the heart of the majoritarian model, was precisely what the framers wanted to avoid.

The framers also wanted balance between the powers of the national government and the states. The exact balance was a touchy issue, skirted by the delegates at the Constitutional Convention. Some seventy years later, a civil war was fought over that balance of power. That war and countless political battles before and after it have demonstrated that the national government dominates the state governments in our political system. In the next chapter, we look at how a loose confederation of states has evolved into a "more perfect Union."

Key Terms

Declaration of Independence	republicanism
social contract theory	federalism
republic	separation of powers
confederation	checks and balances
Articles of Confederation	enumerated powers
Virginia Plan	necessary and proper clause
legislative branch	implied powers
executive branch	judicial review
judicial branch	supremacy clause
New Jersey Plan	Bill of Rights
Great Compromise	extraordinary majorities

Selected Readings

Bowen, Catherine Drinker. *Miracle at Philadelphia*. Boston: Atlantic–Little, Brown, 1966. An absorbing, well-written account of the events surrounding the Constitutional Convention.

Kammen, Michael. *A Machine That Would Go of Itself: The Constitution in American Culture*. New York: Alfred A. Knopf, 1986. A remarkable examination of the Constitution's cultural influence. The author argues that Americans' reverence for the Constitution is inconsistent with their ignorance of its content and meaning.

Maier, Pauline. *American Scripture: Making the Declaration of Independence*. New York: Alfred A. Knopf, 1997. An exhilarating piece of historical detective work that tracks the origin of key phrases and ideas in America's most revered document.

Rakove, Jack N. *Original Meanings: Politics and Ideas in the Making of the Constitution*. New York: Alfred A. Knopf, 1996. The meaning, intention, and understanding of the U.S. Constitution from a historian's perspective.

Wood, Gordon S. *The Radicalism of the American Revolution*. New York: Alfred A. Knopf, 1992. Wood argues that the Revolution was not a conservative defense of American rights but a radical revolution that produced a free and democratic society far beyond what was envisioned by the founders.

World Wide Web Resources

The Charters of Freedom. View America's founding documents at the National Archives' virtual exhibit hall. Good graphics, especially of items never exhibited in public.
<www.nara.gov/exhall/charters/charters.html>

Comparing the World's Constitutions. English text and background materials for the world's constitutions. This site contains cross-references for quick comparison of constitutional provisions.
<www.uni-wuerzburg.de/law/index.html>

Federalist Papers Search. Type in keywords to explore what the *Federalist* papers have to say about the issues with this dedicated search engine.
<www.law.emory.edu/pub-cgi/usfedwais>

3

Federalism

The locals called it "our Blood Border." It was a stretch of flat country due east of Beaumont, Texas, down Interstate 10 to the Louisiana state line, where eighteen-year-olds could still drink legally. White crosses dotted the highway alongside the westbound lanes. In 1993, eighty accidents marked by death or injury involved underage drinkers. The crosses were grim reminders of where Texas teenagers, driving home from bars across the Louisiana border, died. Eighteen-year-olds could still drink alcoholic beverages in Louisiana, despite the fact that the minimum drinking age was twenty-one everywhere else in the country. In July 1996, the Louisiana Supreme Court brought the state in line with the rest of the nation.[1]

Our federal system of government explains both Louisiana's lonely stand and the drive toward uniformity. The Constitution divides power between the national and state governments. With only one sobering exception (Prohibition under the Eighteenth Amendment), regulating liquor sales and setting the minimum drinking age have always been the responsibilities of state governments. But over the years, the national government has found ways to extend its influence into areas that are well beyond those originally defined in the Constitution.

Back in 1981, twenty-nine states and the District of Columbia allowed people under twenty-one to purchase and consume some forms of alcoholic beverages. In 1984, however, an action taken in Washington, D.C., marked the beginning of the end of legalized drinking for those under twenty-one. What happened? Did Congress establish a national minimum drinking age? No, at least not directly. Congress simply added a provision to a highway bill. Under that provision, states would lose 5 percent of their federal highway funds in 1986 and 10 percent every year thereafter if they allowed the purchase or consumption of alcohol by those younger than twenty-one. States would have to change their own laws or risk losing federal funds. This was a roundabout method to achieve a national objective. If the national government wanted to set twenty-one as a national drinking age, why not act directly and pass legislation to do so? The plain fact is that the national government lacks the power to act directly in this area.

The national government became concerned about the drinking age because Mothers Against Drunk Driving (MADD) and other interest groups fought hard to increase public awareness of the dangers of driving drunk. These groups argued that a uniform drinking age of twenty-one would reduce highway fatalities. However, campaigning for change on a state-by-state basis would be slow and might even be dangerous. So long as some states allowed teenagers to drink, young people would be able to drive across state lines in order to drink legally. The borders between states would become bloody borders—as the border remained in east Texas—strewn with victims of teenage drinking and driving.

Supporters of the legislation believed that the national government's responsibility to maintain order justified intervention. The lives and safety of people were at stake. Opponents of the plan argued that it constituted age discrimination and infringed on states' rights. They claimed the act was an unwarranted extension of national power, that it limited the freedom of the states and of their citizens.

President Reagan, who had campaigned on a pledge to reduce the size and scope of the national government, strongly opposed replacing state standards with national ones. When confronted with this issue, which pitted order against freedom and national standards against state standards, he first opposed the bill; later, he changed his position. At the signing ceremony, he said:

> This problem is bigger than the individual states. It's a grave national problem and it touches all our lives. With the problem so clear cut and the proven solution at hand we have no misgiving about this judicious use of federal power. I'm convinced that it will help persuade state legislators to act in the national interest.[2]

Several states took the matter to court, hoping to have the provision declared unconstitutional under the Tenth and the Twenty-first Amendments. In June 1987, the Supreme Court reached a decision in *South Dakota v. Dole*. The justices conceded that direct congressional control of the drinking age in the states would be unconstitutional. Nevertheless, the Constitution does not bar the indirect achievement of such objectives. The seven-justice majority argued that far from being an infringement on states' rights, the law was a "relatively mild encouragement to the states to enact higher minimum drinking ages than they otherwise would choose."[3]

These events show how much the role of the national government has changed since the Constitution was adopted. In the early part of the nineteenth century, presidents routinely vetoed bills authorizing roads, canals, and other interstate improvements because they believed these kinds of projects exceeded the constitutional authority of the national government. Eventually, the national government used its authority over interstate commerce to justify creating a role for itself in building roads. Witness the 43,000-mile interstate highway system.

The Highway Act of 1984 and its successor, the 1986 National Minimum Drinking Age Act, show how national and state governments can interact. Congress did not challenge the constitutional power of the states to regulate the minimum drinking age (under the Twenty-first Amendment), but it used its own powers to tax and spend (Article I, Section 8, clause 1) to encourage the states to implement a national standard. Lawmakers in Washington, D.C., believed that few states would pass up highway funds to retain the power to set a minimum drinking age, and they were right.

An important element of federalism was at work here: the respective sovereignties of national and state governments (*sovereignty* is the quality of being supreme in power or authority). Congress acknowledged the sovereignty of the states by not legislating a national drinking age. And the states were willing to barter their sovereignty in this area in exchange for needed revenues. As long as this give-and-take exists, there will be few areas where national power cannot reach.

Sovereignty also affects political leadership. A governor may not be the political equal of a president, but governors have their own sovereignty, apart from the national government. Consequently, presidents rarely command governors; they negotiate, even plead.

In this chapter, we examine American federalism in theory and in practice. Is the division of power between nation and states a matter of constitutional principle or practical politics? How does the balance of power between nation and states relate to the conflicts between freedom and order, and between freedom and equality? Does federalism reflect the pluralist or the majoritarian model of democracy?

Theories of Federalism

The delegates who met in Philadelphia in 1787 tackled the problem of making one nation out of thirteen independent states by inventing a new political form—federal government—which combined features of a confederacy with features of unitary government (see Chapter 2). Under the principle of **federalism**, two or more governments exercise power and authority over the same people and the same territory. For example, the governments of the United States and Pennsylvania share certain powers (the power to tax, for instance), but other powers belong exclusively to one or the other. As James Madison wrote in *Federalist* No. 10, "The federal Constitution forms a happy combination . . . the great and aggregate interests being referred to the national, and the local and particular to state governments." So the power to coin money belongs to the national government, but the power to grant divorces remains a state prerogative. By contrast, authority over state militia may sometimes belong to the national government and sometimes to the states. The history of American federalism reveals that it has not always been easy to draw a line between what is "great and aggregate" and what is "local and particular."*

Nevertheless, federalism offered a solution to citizens' fears that they would be ruled by majorities from different regions and different interests and values. Federalism also provided a new political model. A leading scholar of federalism estimated in 1990 that 40 percent of the world's population lives

---

*The phrase Americans use to refer to their central government—*federal government*—muddies the waters even more. Technically speaking, we have a federal system of government that includes both national and state governments. To avoid confusion from here on, we use the term *national government* rather than *federal government* when we are talking about the central government.

Compared with What? 3.1

The Perpetually Fragmenting Federation of Canada

Federalism tolerates the centrifugal forces (such as different languages and religions) that can sunder a nation and provides the centripetal forces that bind it (such as the powers to raise an army and control a national economy). But federalism is no guarantee that the forces of unity will always overcome those of disunity. Consider the example of Canada.

Canada is a federation of ten provinces. But the Canadian province of Quebec is unique. Eighty percent of its population is French-speaking; almost half speak little or no English. (The vast majority of Canadians outside Quebec speak only English.) Quebec has its own holidays, its own music videos, its own literature. By law, all signs in Quebec must be in French. English is scarcely tolerated.

For decades, Canadians have struggled with the challenge of assimilating yet differentiating Quebec. When Canada drafted a new constitution in 1982, Quebec refused to sign it. Quebecers conditioned their union with the other provinces on a constitutional amendment that would recognize Quebec as a "distinct society" within the country. The amendment had to be approved by all ten provinces. It failed when two provinces refused to ratify the Quebec agreement by the June 1990 deadline.

In October 1992, Canadians rejected another constitutional solution to the Quebec question. The reforms aimed at recognizing Quebec's special status, electing the national senate, and providing self-government for native peoples. Québecois rejected the reforms because they did not go far enough; other provinces rejected them because they went too far.

Repeated threats of secession reached a crescendo in October 1995 when Quebec's voters confronted the latest referendum on independence. The vote was the closest ever: 50.6 percent against independence and 49.4 percent in favor of it. Separatist leaders, taking hope from the substantial movement toward independence, planned for yet another referendum (or *neverendum*, a term coined by some English Canadian wags).

(continued)

under a formal federal constitution, while another 30 percent lives in polities that apply federal principles or practices without formal constitutional acknowledgment of their federalism.[4] (See Compared with What? 3.1.)

Representations of American Federalism

The history of American federalism is full of attempts to capture its true meaning in an adjective or metaphor. By one reckoning, scholars have generated nearly five hundred ways to describe federalism.[5] Let us concentrate on two such representations: dual federalism and cooperative federalism.

Compared with What? 3.1 (continued)

Canadians appeared doomed to endure continued wrangling over the structure of their nation. There is no assurance that they will be able to accommodate Quebec's determined demand for greater autonomy and official recognition of its distinctiveness. Perhaps this perpetual conflict has come to define Canada. While many would say that Canada would not be Canada without Quebec, many might also say that Canada would not be Canada without this perpetual conflict over Quebec's status.

Quebec Demonstration

Sources: Robert C. Vipond, "Seeing Canada Through the Referendum: Still a House Divided," *Publius* 23 (Summer 1993), p. 39; Clyde H. Farnsworth, "For Quebec, the Neverendum," *New York Times,* 5 November 1995, sect. 4, p. 3.

Dual Federalism

The term **dual federalism** sums up a theory about the proper relationship between the national government and the states. This theory has four essential parts. First, the national government rules by enumerated powers only. Second, the national government has a limited set of constitutional purposes. Third, each government unit—nation and state—is sovereign within its sphere. And fourth, the relationship between nation and states is best characterized by tension rather than cooperation.[6]

Dual federalism portrays the states as powerful components of the federal system—in some ways, the equals of the national government. Under dual

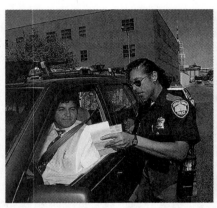

Local Cops, National Cops
Local, state, and national governments share certain powers, such as law enforcement. A San Antonio, Texas, police officer issues a traffic citation (left). A SWAT team from the Federal Bureau of Investigation stands at the ready during a World Cup soccer match in Secaucus, New Jersey (right).

federalism, the functions and responsibilities of the national and state governments are theoretically different and practically separate from each other. Dual federalism sees the Constitution as a compact among sovereign states. Of primary importance in dual federalism are **states' rights**, a concept that reserves to the states all rights not specifically conferred on the national government by the Constitution. Claims of states' rights often come from opponents of a national government policy. Their argument is that the people have not delegated the power to make such policy and thus the power remains in the states or the people. Proponents of states' rights believe that the powers of the national government should be interpreted narrowly. They insist that, despite the elastic clause, which gives Congress the **implied powers** needed to execute its enumerated powers (see Chapter 2), the activities of Congress should be confined to the enumerated powers only. They support their view by quoting the Tenth Amendment: "The powers not delegated to the United States by the Constitution, nor prohibited by it to the States, are reserved to the states respectively, or to the people."

Political scientists use a metaphor to describe dual federalism. They call it *layer-cake federalism*; the powers and functions of national and state governments are as separate as the layers of a cake (see Figure 3.1). Each government is supreme in its own "layer," its own sphere of action; the two layers are distinct; and the dimensions of each layer are fixed by the Constitution.

Dual federalism has been challenged on historical and other grounds. Some critics argue that if the national government is really a creation of the states, it is a creation of only thirteen states, those that ratified the Constitution. The other thirty-seven states were admitted after the national government came into being and were created by that government out of land

Dual Federalism:
The Layer-Cake Metaphor

Citizens cutting into the political system will find clear differences between state and national powers, functions, and responsibilities.

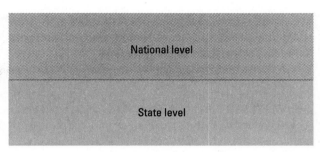

Cooperative Federalism:
The Marble-Cake Metaphor

Citizens cutting into the political system at any point will find national and state powers, functions, and responsibilities mixed and mingled.

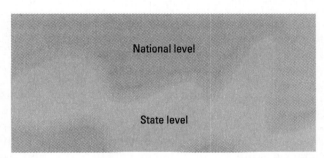

FIGURE 3.1   Metaphors for Federalism
The two views of federalism can be represented graphically.

it had acquired. Another challenge has to do with the ratification process. Remember, special conventions in the original thirteen states, not the states' legislatures, ratified the Constitution. Ratification, then, was an act of the people, not the states. Moreover, the Preamble to the Constitution begins "We the people of the United States," not "We the States." The question of where the people fit into the federal system is not handled well by dual federalism.

Cooperative Federalism

Cooperative federalism, a phrase coined in the 1930s, sums up a different theory of the relationship between national and state governments. This theory acknowledges the increasing overlap in state and national functions and rejects the idea of separate spheres, or layers, for the states and the national government. Cooperative federalism includes three elements. First, national and state agencies typically undertake governmental functions jointly, rather than exclusively. Second, nation and states routinely share power. Third, power is not concentrated at any government level or in any agency; this fragmentation of responsibilities gives people and groups access to many centers of influence.

The bakery metaphor used to describe this kind of federalism is *marble cake.* The national and state governments do not act in separate spheres; they are intermingled. Their functions are mixed in the American federal system.

Critical to cooperative federalism is an expansive view of the Constitution's supremacy clause (Article VI), which specifically subordinates state law to national law and charges every judge to disregard state laws that are inconsistent with the Constitution, national laws, and treaties.

In contrast to dual federalism, cooperative federalism blurs the distinction between national and state powers. Some scholars argue that the layer-cake metaphor has never accurately described the American political structure.[7] The national and state governments have many common objectives and have often cooperated to achieve them. In the nineteenth century, for example, cooperation, not separation, made it possible to develop transportation systems such as canals and to establish state land-grant colleges.

A critical difference between the theories of dual and cooperative federalism is the way they interpret two sections of the Constitution that set out the terms of the relationship between the national and state governments. Article I, Section 8, lists the enumerated powers of Congress, then concludes with the **elastic clause**, which gives Congress the power to "make all Laws which shall be necessary and proper for carrying into Execution the foregoing Powers." The Tenth Amendment reserves for the states or the people "powers" not given to the national government or denied to the states by the Constitution. Dual federalism postulates an inflexible elastic clause and a capacious Tenth Amendment. Cooperative federalism postulates suppleness in the elastic clause and confines the Tenth Amendment to a self-evident, obvious truth.

In their efforts to limit the scope of the national government, conservatives have given much credence to the layer-cake metaphor. In contrast, liberals, believing that one of the functions of the national government is to bring about equality, have argued that the marble-cake metaphor is more desirable.

Conservatives continue to argue that different states have different problems and resources and that returning control to state governments would actually promote diversity. States would be free to experiment with alternative ways to meet their problems. Conservatives also maintain that the national government is too remote, too tied to special interests, and not responsive to the public at large. The national government overregulates and tries to promote too much uniformity. Moreover, the size and complexity of the federal system lead to waste and inefficiency. States, in contrast, are closer to the people and better able to respond to specific local needs. If state governments were revitalized, individuals might believe that they could have a greater influence on decision making, and the quality of political participation would improve.

Furthermore, conservatives believe that shifting power to the states would help them achieve other parts of their political agenda. States would work harder to keep taxes down; they would not be willing to spend a lot of money on social welfare programs; and they would be less likely to pass stiff laws regulating businesses. The 1994 "Republican Revolution" brought a chorus of new conservative voices to Congress calling for a return of power to the states.

What conservatives hope for, liberals fear. They remember that the states' rights model allowed political and social inequalities and supported racism. Blacks and city dwellers were often left virtually unrepresented by white state legislators who disproportionately served rural interests. Liberals believe the states remain unwilling to protect the rights or provide for the needs of their citizens, whether those citizens are consumers seeking protection from business interests, defendants requiring guarantees of due process of law, or poor people seeking a minimum standard of living.

These ideological conceptions of federalism reveal a simple truth. Federalism is not something written or implied in the Constitution; the Constitution is only the starting point in the debate. As one scholar observed, "To understand the condition of federalism, one needs to comprehend the functioning of the whole polity."[8]

The Dynamics of Federalism

Although the Constitution defines a kind of federalism, the actual balance of power between nation and states has always been more a matter of politics than of formal theory. A discussion of federalism, then, must do more than simply list the powers the Constitution assigns the different levels of government. The balance of power has shifted substantially since President Madison agonized over the proper role the national government should play in funding roads. Today, that government has assumed functions never dreamed of in the nineteenth century.

Why has power shifted so dramatically from the states to the national government? The answer lies in historical circumstances, not debates over constitutional theory. By far the greatest test of states' rights came when several southern states attempted to secede from the Union. The threat of secession challenged the supremacy of the national government, a supremacy that northern armies established militarily in the nation's greatest bloodbath, the Civil War.

Some changes in the balance of power were the product of constitutional amendments—for example, the due process and equal protection clauses of the Fourteenth Amendment (1868) and the Seventeenth Amendment's provision for the direct election of senators (1913). Most of the national government's power, however, has come to it through legislation and judicial interpretation. Let us examine these tools of political change.

Legislation and the Elastic Clause

The elastic clause of the Constitution gives Congress the power to make all laws that are "necessary and proper" to carry out its responsibilities. By using this power in combination with its enumerated powers, Congress has been able to increase the scope of the national government tremendously. Change has often come in times of crisis and national emergency—the Civil War, the Great Depression, the world wars. The role of the national government has grown as it has responded to needs and demands that state and local governments were unwilling or unable to meet.

Legislation is one of the prods the national government has used to achieve goals at the state level. The Voting Rights Act of 1965 is a good example.

Section 2 of Article I of the Constitution gives the states the power to specify qualifications for voting. But the Fifteenth Amendment (1870) provides that no person should be denied the right to vote "on account of race, color, or previous condition of servitude." Before the Voting Rights Act, states could not specifically deny blacks the right to vote, but they could require that voters pass literacy tests or pay poll taxes, requirements that virtually disenfranchised blacks in many states. The Voting Rights Act was designed to correct this political inequality (see Chapter 12).

The act gives officials of the national government the power to decide whether individuals are qualified to vote in all elections, including primaries and national, state, and local elections. The constitutional authority for the act rests on the second section of the Fifteenth Amendment, which gives Congress the power to enforce the amendment through "appropriate legislation."

Judicial Interpretation

The Voting Rights Act was not a unanimous hit. Its critics adopted the language of dual federalism and insisted that the Constitution gives the states the power to determine voter qualifications. Its supporters claimed that the Fifteenth Amendment guarantee of voting rights takes precedence over states' rights and gives the national government new responsibilities.

The conflict was ultimately resolved by the Supreme Court, the umpire of the federal system. The Court settles disputes over the powers of the national and state governments by deciding whether the actions of either are unconstitutional (see Chapter 11). In the nineteenth and early twentieth centuries, the Supreme Court often decided in favor of the states. Then for nearly sixty years, from 1937 to 1995, the Court almost always supported the national government in contests involving the balance of power between nation and states. Today, a conservative majority on the Court has started to tip the balance back to the states.

The Commerce Clause: Engine of National Power   The growth of national power has been advanced by the Supreme Court's interpretation of the Constitution's **commerce clause**. The third clause of Article I, Section 8, states that "Congress shall have Power . . . To regulate Commerce . . . among the several States." The Court's interpretation of the clause has varied through the years, but since the middle of the Great Depression, it has generally given Congress wide latitude to exercise legislative power by regulating interstate commerce. However, a shift toward the states occurred in 1995, when the Supreme Court rediscovered constitutional limits on Congress that had been dead and buried for nearly sixty years. The Court's 5–4 ruling in *United States v. Lopez* held that Congress exceeded its authority under the commerce clause when it enacted a law in 1990 banning the possession of a gun in or near a school. A conservative majority, headed by Chief Justice William H. Rehnquist, concluded that having a gun in a school zone "has nothing to do with 'commerce' or any sort of economic enterprise, however broadly one might define those terms."

Whether the ruling will have wide or narrow consequences depends on its subsequent application and interpretation. At a minimum, however, the Court is still the umpire of the federal system.

The Eleventh Amendment: The Umpire Strikes Back   In 1996, the umpire made another dramatic call curtailing congressional power in favor of the states. In a bitterly fought 5–4 ruling, the same five-justice majority bolstered state power by sharply curtailing the authority of Congress to subject states to lawsuits in federal courts. The ruling came in an obscure suit arising from a Seminole tribe's dispute with Florida officials.[9]

A 1988 federal law allowed Indian tribes to sue a state in federal court if the state failed to negotiate in good faith over allowing gambling operations on tribal lands. Many federal laws have provisions that allow people hurt by state violations of such federal laws to sue in federal court. However, the Eleventh Amendment bars such courts from hearing cases in which a state is sued by citizens of another state or country.

The significance of the Supreme Court decision extends far beyond the particular facts; it affects whether individuals or groups can use the federal courts to force states to abide by a variety of national laws. In the majority opinion, the chief justice asserted that "the states, although a union, maintain certain attributes of sovereignty," including immunity from lawsuits.

The Brady Bill and the Limits of National Government Authority   Congress enacted a modest gun-control measure (known as the Brady bill) in 1993. The bill mandated the creation by November 1998 of a national system to check the background of prospective gun buyers, to weed out, among others, convicted felons and the mentally ill. In the meantime, it created a temporary system that called for local law enforcement officials to perform background checks and report their findings to gun dealers in their community. Several sheriffs challenged the law.

The Supreme Court agreed with the sheriffs, delivering a double-barreled blow to the local-enforcement provision in June 1997. In *Printz v. United States,* the Court concluded that Congress could not require local officials to implement a regulatory scheme imposed by the national government. In language that seemingly invoked layer-cake federalism, Justice Antonin Scalia, writing for the five-member conservative majority, argued that locally enforced background checks violated the principle of dual sovereignty by allowing the national government "to impress into its service—and at no cost to itself—the police officers of the 50 States." In addition, the scheme violated the principle of separation of powers, by congressional transfer of the president's responsibility to faithfully execute national laws to local law enforcement officials.[10]

The *Printz* decision generated only muted congressional protest, since the local-enforcement provision was merely temporary. The decision demonstrates, however, that federalism sets real limits on the power of the national government. Nevertheless, Congress retains ample power to secure the cooperation of state governments. Money is its tool.

Grants-in-Aid

Since the 1960s, the national government's use of financial incentives has rivaled its use of legislation and judicial interpretation as a means of shaping relationships between national and state governments. The principal method the national government uses to make money available to the states is grants-in-aid.

A **grant-in-aid** is money paid by one level of government to another level of government, to be spent for a specific purpose. Most grants-in-aid come with standards or requirements prescribed by Congress. Many are awarded on a matching basis: a recipient must make some contribution of its own, which is then matched by the national government. Grants-in-aid take two general forms: categorical grants and block grants.

Categorical grants target specific purposes, and restrictions on their use typically leave the recipient relatively little discretion. Recipients today include state governments, local governments, and public and private nonprofit organizations. There are two kinds of categorical grants: formula grants and project grants. As their name implies, **formula grants** are distributed according to a particular formula, which specifies who is eligible for the grant and how much each eligible applicant will receive. The formulas may weigh such factors as state per capita income, number of school-age children, urban population, and number of families below the poverty line. Most grants, however, are **project grants**—grants awarded on the basis of competitive applications. Recent grants have focused on health (substance abuse and HIV-AIDS programs); natural resources and the environment (asbestos and toxic pollution); and education, training, and employment (for the disabled, the homeless, and the aged).

In contrast to categorical grants, **block grants** are awarded for broad, general purposes. They allow recipient governments considerable freedom in deciding how to allocate money to individual programs. While a categorical grant might be given to promote a very specific activity—say, ethnic heritage studies—a block grant might be earmarked for elementary, secondary, and vocational education. The state or local government receiving the block grant would then choose the specific educational programs to fund with it.

Grants-in-aid are a method of redistributing income. Money is collected by the national government from citizens of all fifty states, then allocated to other citizens, supposedly for worthwhile social purposes. Many grants have worked to remove gross inequalities among states and their citizens. But the formulas used to redistribute this income are not impartial; they are highly political, established through a process of congressional horse trading. Whatever its form or purpose, grant money comes with strings attached. Some strings are there to ensure that the money is used for the purpose for which it was given. Other regulations are designed to evaluate how well the grant is working. Still others are designed to achieve some broad national goal, a goal that is not always closely related to the specific purpose of the grant. For example, as noted earlier, the Highway Act of 1984 reduced the amount of money available to states that allowed those under age twenty-one to drink. The lure of financial aid has proved to be a powerful incentive for states to relinquish the freedom to set their own standards and to accept those set by the national government.

The Developing Concept of Federalism

Federalism scholars have noted that each generation faced with new problems has had to work out its own version of federalism. Succeeding generations have used judicial and congressional power in varying degrees to shift the balance of power back and forth between the national and state governments.

McCulloch v. Maryland

Early in the nineteenth century, the nationalist interpretation of federalism triumphed over states' rights. In 1819, under Chief Justice John Marshall, the Supreme Court expanded the role of the national government in *McCulloch v. Maryland.* The Court was asked to rule whether Congress had the power to establish a national bank and, if so, whether states had the power to tax that bank. In a unanimous opinion written by Marshall, the Court conceded that Congress had only the powers conferred on it by the Constitution, which nowhere mentioned banks. However, Article I granted to Congress the authority to enact all laws "necessary and proper" to the execution of Congress's enumerated powers. Marshall gave a broad interpretation to this elastic clause: "Let the end be legitimate, let it be within the scope of the constitution, and all means which are appropriate, which are plainly adapted to that end, which are not prohibited, consistent with the letter and spirit of the constitution, are constitutional."

The Court clearly agreed that Congress had the power to charter a bank. But did the states (in this case, Maryland) have the power to tax the bank? Arguing that "the power to tax involves the power to destroy," Marshall insisted that states could not tax the national government because the powers of the national government came not from the states but from the people.[11] Marshall was embracing cooperative federalism. To have assumed that the states had the power to tax the national government would have been to give them supremacy over the national government.

States' Rights and Dual Federalism

Many people assume that the Civil War was fought over slavery. It was not. The real issue was the character of the federal union, of federalism itself. At the time of the Civil War, economic and cultural differences between the northern and southern states were considerable. With the southern economy based on labor-intensive agriculture, southerners supported both low tariffs on imported goods and slavery. To protect their manufacturing economy, northerners wanted high tariffs. When they sought national legislation that threatened southern interests, southerners invoked states' rights. They even introduced the theory of **nullification,** the idea that a state could declare a particular action of the national government null and void. The Civil War rendered the idea of nullification null and void but did not settle the balance between national and state power.

Made in the U.S.A.
Young girls working at thread-winder machines in a factory in London, Tennessee (1910).
The U.S. Supreme Court decided in 1918 that Congress had no power to limit the excesses of
child labor. According to the Court, that power belonged to the states, which resisted impos-
ing limits for fear such legislation would drive businesses to other (less restrictive) states.

The New Deal and Its Consequences

The problems of the Great Depression proved too extensive for either state governments or private businesses to handle. So the national government assumed a heavy share of responsibility for providing relief and pursuing economic recovery. Under the New Deal—President Franklin D. Roosevelt's response to the Depression—Congress enacted various emergency relief programs to stimulate economic activity and help the unemployed. Many measures required the cooperation of national and state governments. Through the regulations it attached to funds, the national government extended its power and control over the states.[12]

At first, the Supreme Court's view of the Depression was different from that of the other branches of the national government. In the Court's opinion, the whole structure of federalism was threatened when collections of local troubles were treated as one national problem.

In 1937, however, with no change in personnel, the Court began to alter its course. The Court upheld major New Deal measures. Perhaps the Court had studied the 1936 election returns and was responding to the country's endorsement of the use of national policies to address national problems. Or perhaps the Court sought to defuse the president's threat to enlarge the Court with justices sympathetic to his views. In any event, the Court gave up its effort to set a rigid boundary between national and state power.

Some call the New Deal era revolutionary. There is no doubt that the period was critical in reshaping federalism in the United States. But perhaps the most significant change was in the way Americans thought about their problems and the role of the national government in solving them. Difficulties that at one time had been seen as personal or local problems were now national problems, requiring national solutions. The general welfare, broadly defined, became a legitimate concern of the national government.

In other respects, however, the New Deal was not very revolutionary. For example, Congress did not claim any new powers to address the nation's economic problems. Congress simply used its constitutional powers to suit the circumstances.

From New Federalism to New Age Federalism

In 1969, Richard Nixon advocated giving more power to state and local governments. Nixon wanted to decentralize national policies. He called this plan the *New Federalism*. By contrast, Bill Clinton proposed that the national government act as guru, guiding and encouraging states to experiment with vexing problems. We call this plan *New Age Federalism*.

An Evolving Federalism

Nixon's New Federalism called for combining and reformulating categorical grants into block grants. The shift had dramatic implications for federalism. Block grants were seen as a way to redress the imbalance of power between Washington and the states and localities. New Federalism was nothing more than dual federalism in modern dress.

The perception that the federal system was bloated and out of control began to take hold. In 1976, Jimmy Carter campaigned for president as an outsider who promised to reduce the size and cost of the national government. And he did have some success. As Figure 3.2 shows, after 1978 national government aid to states and localities actually did begin to drop and then level off.

When Ronald Reagan took office in 1981, he promised a "new New Federalism" that would restore a proper constitutional relationship between the federal, state, and local governments. The national government, he said, treated "elected state and local officials as if they were nothing more than administrative agents for federal authority."[13]

Reagan's commitment to reducing federal taxes and spending meant that the states would have to foot an increasing share of the bill for government services (see Figure 3.2). In the mid-1970s, the national government funded 25 percent of all state and local government spending. By 1990, its contribution had declined to 20 percent. With the Democrats in control of both the presidency and Congress, that figure inched up to 22 percent by 1994, but Republican congressional victories in 1994 made increased spending a hard sell.

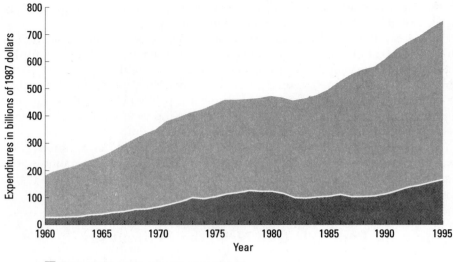

State and local government expenditures

National government grants to state and local government

FIGURE 3.2   ***The National Government's Contribution to State and Local Governments***
*In 1960, the national government contributed less than 15 percent of total state and local
spending. By 1978, the national government had nearly doubled its contribution to state
and local government spending. By 1988, the national government's contribution had
declined to about 18 percent. As the national government's spending remained static or
declined, state and local government spending accelerated, especially for Medicaid, welfare,
prisons, and education. (The slopes of the two figures here indicate the pace of spending
change.) (Source: The Budget for FY 1997: Historical Tables [Washington, D.C.: U.S.
Government Printing Office, 1996], Table 15.2, p. 257.)*

In June 1999, the Supreme Court weighed in with its view of federalism. In
identical 5–4 votes in three separate cases, the Court again embraced the idea
of dual federalism, adjusting the balance of power in favor of the states. The
Court in effect immunized state governments from lawsuits brought by individuals claiming state violations of national laws. "Congress has vast power but
not all power," declared Justice Anthony Kennedy, author of one of the majority opinions. "When Congress legislates in matters affecting the states," continued Kennedy, "it may not treat these sovereign entities as mere prefectures or
corporations. Congress must accord states the esteem due to them as joint participants in a Federal system."[14]

This shift in the balance of power is not secure, however. Congress still retains substantial power to yoke the states.

Preemption: The Instrument of Federalism

Before 1965, increased national power and diminished state power followed
from the growth in categorical grant-in-aid programs—with their attached

conditions—emanating from Washington, D.C. Since 1965, Congress has used its centralizing power in new fields and in novel ways.[15]

Preemption is the power of Congress to enact laws that have the national government assume total or partial responsibility for a state government function. When the national government shoulders a new government function, it restricts the discretionary power of the states. For example, under the Age Discrimination in Employment Act of 1967, the national government stripped the states of their power to establish a compulsory retirement age for their employees.

Mandates and Restraints   Congressional preemption statutes infringe on state powers in two ways, through mandates and restraints. A **mandate** is a requirement that a state undertake an activity or provide a service in keeping with minimum national standards. For example, in 1990, Congress mandated Medicaid coverage for all poor children. As a result, state Medicaid and welfare costs were expected to increase by about 66 percent from 1995 to 1999. To pay for these mandates, state officials faced stark choices: shift scarce resources by reducing or eliminating programs or raise taxes.[16]

In contrast, a **restraint** forbids state government from exercising a certain power. Consider bus regulation. To ensure bus service to small and remote communities, in the past some states would condition the issuance of bus franchises on bus operators' agreeing to serve such communities even if the routes lost money. But in 1982, Congress passed the Bus Regulatory Reform Act, which forbade the states from imposing such conditions. Many states now provide subsidies to bus operators to ensure service to out-of-the-way areas.

Whether preemption takes the form of mandates or restraints, the results are additional costs for state and local government and interference with a fundamental government task: setting priorities. Furthermore, the national government is not obliged to pay for the costs it imposes. As preemption grew in the 1980s, the national government reduced spending in the form of grants to the states, and the states had to pick up the tab.

Constraining Unfunded Mandates   State and local government officials have long voiced strong objections to the national government's practice of imposing requirements on the states without providing the financial support needed to satisfy them. By 1992, more than 170 congressional acts had established partially or wholly unfunded mandates.[17] One of the early results of the Republican-led 104th Congress was the Unfunded Mandates Relief Act of 1995. The legislation requires the Congressional Budget Office to prepare cost estimates of any proposed national legislation that would impose more than $50 million a year in costs on state and local governments or more than $100 million a year in costs on private business. It also requires a cost analysis of the impact of agency regulations.

Other Governments in the Federal System

We have concentrated in this chapter on the roles the national and state governments play in shaping the federal system. Although the Constitution explicitly recognizes only national and state governments, the American federal system has spawned a multitude of local governments as well. A 1992 census counted nearly eighty-seven thousand.[18]

Types of Local Governments

Americans are citizens of both nation and state, but they also come under the jurisdiction of various local government units. These units include **municipal governments**, the governments of cities and towns. Municipalities, in turn, are located in (or may contain or share boundaries with) counties, which are administered by **county governments**. (Sixteen states further divide counties into townships.) Most Americans also live in a **school district**, which is responsible for administering local elementary and secondary educational programs. They also may be served by one or more **special districts**, government units created to perform particular functions, typically when those functions—such as fire protection and water purification and distribution—are best performed across jurisdictional boundaries. All these local governments are created by state governments, either in their constitutions or through legislation.

So Many Governments: Advantages and Disadvantages

In theory, at least, one benefit of localizing government is that it brings government close to the people; it gives them an opportunity to participate in the political process, to have a direct impact on policy. From this perspective, overlapping governments appear compatible with a majoritarian view of democracy.

The reality, however, is somewhat different. Studies have shown that people are much less likely to vote in local elections than in national elections. In fact, voter turnout in local contests tends to be very low, even though the impact of individual votes is much greater. Furthermore, the fragmentation of powers, functions, and responsibilities among national, state, and local governments makes government as a whole seem complicated and hence incomprehensible and inaccessible to ordinary people. In addition, most people have little time to devote to public affairs. These factors tend to discourage individual citizens from pursuing politics and, in turn, enhance the influence of organized groups, which have the resources—time, money, and know-how—to sway policymaking (see Chapter 7). Instead of bringing government closer to the people and reinforcing majoritarian democracy, then, the system's complexity tends to encourage pluralism.

One potential benefit of having many governments is that they enable the country to experiment with new policies on a small scale. New programs or solutions to problems can be tested in one city or state or in a few cities or states. Successful programs can then be adopted by other cities or states or by the nation as a whole. For this reason, states are sometimes called the "laboratories of democracy." These "laboratories" received a boost from Republican-led congressional welfare reforms. By 1997, the national government had abolished its largest welfare program, Aid to Families with Dependent Children (AFDC), and replaced it with a block-grant program. States are eligible for these funds—to be spent as they think fit—provided they follow national job creation guidelines. Most states have completely halted financial assistance to able-bodied persons who are not working, not training for a job, or not seeking a job. Moreover, the national government has imposed a lifetime assistance limit of five years, and many states have imposed shorter periods for the able-bodied to receive assistance.

The large number of governments also makes it possible for government at some level to respond to the diversity of conditions that prevail in different parts of the country. States and cities differ enormously in population, size, economic resources, climate, and other characteristics. Smaller political units are better able to respond to particular local conditions and can generally do so more quickly than larger units. Smaller units, however, may not be able to muster the economic resources to meet some challenges. Consequently, throughout American history, the national government has used its funds to lessen disparities in wealth and development among states.

Contemporary Federalism and the Dilemmas of Democracy

To what extent were conservative hopes and liberal fears realized as federalism developed from the 1980s to the 1990s? Neither were fully realized under the various renditions of federalism. Federalism of the Reagan-Bush variety was used as a tool for cutting the national budget by offering less money to the states. Contrary to the expectations of conservatives and liberals alike, however, states approved tax increases to pay for social services and education. In an era when Washington was less willing to enforce antitrust legislation, civil rights laws, or affirmative action plans, state governments were more likely to do so. At a time when a conservative national government put little emphasis on the value of equality, state governments did more to embrace it.[19]

Conservatives thought that the value of freedom would be emphasized if more matters were left to the states. Traditionally, state governments were relatively small and lacking the wherewithal to limit large corporate interests, for example. But since the 1970s, state governments have become "big governments" themselves. They are better able to tackle problems, and they are not afraid to use their power to promote equality. To the surprise of liberals, who had originally looked to the national government to protect individuals by setting reasonable minimum standards for product safety, welfare payments, and employee benefits, states are now willing to set higher standards than the national government.

When Clinton came to the White House, liberals were delighted. His conservative predecessors, Reagan and Bush, had sought to reinstate layer-cake federalism and dismantle the national government's welfare-state efforts to promote social and political equality. But Clinton's experience as a governor created a strange brew when joined with the Democrats' liberal social welfare policies, and no coherent theory of federalism emerged.[20]

Rain Delay
Melting snow in Minnesota and Wisconsin brought new flooding in 1996 to the people of Davenport, Iowa, who had been devastated by record-breaking floods just three years before. The mighty Mississippi filled John O'Donnell Stadium, home of the River Bandits, a minor league baseball team. Citizens had pitched in to sandbag the field, but to no avail. In disaster areas, the national government aids flood-ravaged states by allocating resources to rebuild or repair vital infrastructure such as roads, water and sewage systems, and schools.

Federalism and Pluralism

Our federal system of government was designed to allay citizens' fears that they might be ruled by a majority in a distant region with whom they did not necessarily agree or share interests. By recognizing the legitimacy of the states as political divisions, the federal system also recognized the importance of diversity. The existence and cultivation of diverse interests are hallmarks of pluralism.

Each of the two competing theories of federalism supports pluralism but in somewhat different ways. Dual federalism aims to decentralize government, to shift power to the states. It recognizes the importance of local rather than national standards and applauds the diversity of those standards. The variety allows the people, if not a direct voice in policymaking, at least a choice of policies under which to live.

In contrast, cooperative federalism is perfectly willing to override local standards for a national standard in the interests of promoting equality. Yet this view of federalism also supports pluralist democracy. It is highly responsive to all manner of group pressures, including pressure at one level from groups unsuccessful at other levels. By blurring the lines of national and state responsibility, this kind of federalism encourages petitioners to try their luck at whichever level of government offers them the best chance of success.

Summary

The government framework outlined in the Constitution was the product of political compromise, an acknowledgment of the original thirteen states' fear of a powerful central government. The division of powers sketched in the Constitution was supposed to turn over "great and aggregate" matters to the national government, leaving "local and particular" concerns to the states. The Constitution does not explain, however, what is great and aggregate and what is local and particular.

Federalism comes in many varieties. Two stand out because they capture valuable differences between the original and modern visions of a federal government. Dual, or layer-cake, federalism wants to retain power in the states and to keep the levels of government separate. Cooperative, or marble-cake, federalism emphasizes the power of the national government and sees national and state governments working together to solve national problems. In its own way, each view supports the pluralist model of democracy.

Over the years, the national government has used both its enumerated and its implied powers to become involved in nearly every area of human activity. The tools of political change include direct legislation, judicial interpretation, and grants-in-aid to states and localities. In the absence of financial incentives, the national government has used its preemptive power, imposing mandates and restraints on the states without necessarily footing the cost.

As its influence grew, so did the national government. Major events, such as the Civil War and the Great Depression, mark major shifts in its growth in size and power. To alter its course, conservatives offered New Federalism and argued for cutting back on the size of the national government, reducing federal spending, and turning programs over to the states in order to solve the problem of unwieldy government. Liberals worried that conservatives, in their haste to decentralize and cut back, would turn over important responsibilities to states that were unwilling or unable to assume them, and that rather than being too responsive, government would be unresponsive. But neither happened in the 1980s. Congressional preemption forced states to meet national standards with or without financial inducements. The states proved ready to tackle some major problems. More than this, they were willing to fund many programs that promoted equality.

The debate over federalism has started to shift in the conservative direction as a result of two forces: the Republican congressional victory in 1994 and the formation of a slender but solid conservative majority in the Supreme Court. One truth emerges from this overview of federalism: the balance of power between the national and state governments will be settled by political means, not by theory.

Key Terms

federalism
dual federalism
states' rights

implied powers
cooperative federalism
elastic clause

commerce clause
grant-in-aid
categorical grant
formula grant
project grant
block grant
nullification

preemption
mandate
restraint
municipal government
county government
school district
special district

Selected Readings

Beer, Samuel H. *To Make a Nation: The Rediscovery of American Federalism.* Cambridge, Mass.: Harvard University Press, 1993. A historical examination of federalism and nationalism in American political philosophy.

Dye, Thomas R. *American Federalism: Competition Among Governments.* Lexington, Mass.: Lexington Books, 1990. Presents a theory of competitive federalism that encourages rivalry among states and local governments, to offer citizens the best array of public services at the lowest cost.

Peterson, Paul E. *The Price of Federalism.* Washington, D.C.: Brookings/A Twentieth Century Fund Book, 1995. Peterson argues that development projects such as roads and buildings are best left to state and local government and that redistributive policies such as welfare and social security are best left to the national government.

Rivlin, Alice. *Reviving the American Dream: The Economy, the States, and the Federal Government.* Washington, D.C.: Brookings Institution, 1992. A lucid examination of economic performance and government performance, resting on a reexamination of the division of responsibilities between the nation and the states.

Zimmerman, Joseph F. *Contemporary American Federalism: The Growth of National Power.* New York: Praeger, 1992. Argues that the expansion of preemption power has altered the allocation of power between nation and states.

World Wide Web Resources

The states have their own organization called the Council for State Government. One of its missions is to promote the sovereignty of the states and their role in the American federal system.
    <www.statesnews.org>

Everything you always wanted to know about the states but were afraid to ask can be found at State-Search. This service of the National Association of State Information Resource Executives is designed to serve as a topical clearinghouse of state government information on the Internet.
    <www.nasire.org/statesearch>

Assessing the New Federalism. This is an "Urban Institute research project to analyze the devolution of responsibility for social programs from the federal government to the states, focusing primarily on health care, income security, job training, and social services."

4

Public Opinion, Political Socialization, and the Media

Fridays are different in Saudi Arabia. After prayers, criminals are paraded in the streets, then punished publicly. Murderers are beheaded; adulterers are flogged; and thieves have their hands chopped off. The Saudi government wants its citizens to get the message: crime will not be tolerated.

What constitutes a crime in Saudi Arabia may not be a crime in the United States, as members of the U.S. armed forces stationed there in 1990 during the Persian Gulf crisis learned. Their mail from home was opened to keep out alcohol and sexually oriented magazines, both of which are illegal in Saudi Arabia. It is also illegal for a woman to drive a car there. Saudi Arabia, which claims the lowest crime rate in the world, is a country that greatly values order.

In contrast, the United States has one of the highest crime rates in the world. Its homicide rate is three to ten times that of most other Western countries. Although no one is proud of this record, the U.S. government would never consider beheading, flogging, or dismembering as a means of lowering the crime rate. The Eighth Amendment to the Constitution forbids "cruel and unusual punishment," and the public would not tolerate such punishment. The public, however, is not squeamish about applying the death penalty (capital punishment) for certain crimes. The Gallup Organization has polled the nation on this issue for fifty years. Except in 1966, most respondents have consistently supported the death penalty for murder. In 2000, 66 percent of all respondents were in favor of the death penalty for murder; only 26 percent opposed it. This is intriguing in view of the fact that only 51 percent of the respondents in the same poll indicated that they believed the death penalty was applied fairly.[1]

Government has been defined as the legitimate use of force to control human behavior. During most of American history, government execution of people threatening the social order was legal. In colonial times, capital punishment was imposed not just for murder but also for antisocial behavior such as denying the "true" God, cursing one's parents, committing adultery, practicing witchcraft, or being a rebellious child.[2] In the late 1700s, some writers, editors, and clergy argued for abolishing the death sentence. The campaign intensified in the 1840s, and again in 1890, when New York State adopted a new "scientific" technique, electrocution, as the means of death. By 1917, twelve states had passed laws against capital punishment. But the outbreak of World War I fed the public's fear of foreigners and radicals, leading to renewed support for the death penalty. Reacting to this shift in public opinion, four states restored it.

The security needs of World War II and postwar fears of Soviet communism fueled continued support for capital punishment. After the anticommunist hysteria subsided in the late 1950s, public opposition to the death penalty increased, but public opinion was neither strong nor stable enough to force state legislatures to outlaw it. In keeping with the pluralist model of democracy, efforts to abolish the death penalty shifted from the legislative arena to the courts.

Opponents argued that the death penalty is cruel and unusual punishment and is therefore unconstitutional. The public in the 1780s had not considered capital punishment either cruel or unusual. But nearly two hundred years later, opponents contended that execution by the state was cruel and unusual by contemporary standards. Their argument had some effect on public opinion. In 1966, a plurality of respondents opposed the death penalty for the first (and only) time since the Gallup Organization began polling the public on the question.

The states responded to this shift in public opinion by reducing the number of executions, until they stopped completely in 1968 in anticipation of a Supreme Court decision. By then, however, public opinion had again reversed in favor of capital punishment. Nevertheless, in 1972, the Court ruled in a 5–4 vote that the death penalty as imposed by existing state laws was unconstitutional.[3] The decision was not well received in many states, and thirty-five state legislatures passed new laws to get around the ruling. Meanwhile, as the nation's homicide rate increased, public approval of the death penalty jumped almost 10 points and continued climbing.

In 1976, the Supreme Court changed its position and upheld three new state laws that let judges consider a defendant's record and the nature of the crime in deciding whether to impose a sentence of death.[4] The Court also rejected the argument that punishment by death itself violates the Constitution, and it noted that public opinion favored the death penalty. Through the end of the 1970s, however, only three criminals were executed. Eventually, the states began to heed public concern about the crime rate. In 1999 alone, ninety-eight murderers were executed, the highest number since 1951.[5]

The history of public thinking on the death penalty reveals several characteristics of public opinion:

1. *The public's attitudes toward a given government policy can vary over time, often dramatically.* Opinions about capital punishment tend to fluctuate with threats to the social order. The public is more likely to favor capital punishment in times of war and when fear of foreign subversion and crime rates are high.

2. *Public opinion places boundaries on allowable types of public policy.* Chopping off a thief's hand is not acceptable to the American public (and surely not to courts interpreting the Constitution), but electrocuting a murderer is.

3. *If asked by pollsters, citizens are willing to register opinions on matters outside their expertise.* People clearly believe execution by lethal injection is more humane than electrocution, asphyxiation in the gas chamber, or hanging. But how can the public know enough about execution to make these judgments?

4. *Governments tend to respond to public opinion.* State laws for and against capital punishment have reflected swings in the public mood. The Supreme Court's 1972 decision against capital punishment came when public opinion on the death penalty was sharply divided; the Court's approval of capital punishment in 1976 coincided with a rise in public approval of the death penalty.

5. *The government sometimes does not do what the people want.* Although public opinion overwhelmingly favors the death penalty for murder, there were only ninety-eight executions in 1999.

The last two conclusions bear on our discussion of the majoritarian and pluralist models of democracy discussed in Chapter 1. Here we probe more deeply into the nature, shape, depth, and formation of public opinion in a democratic government. What is the place of public opinion in a democracy? How do people acquire their opinions? What are the major lines of division in public opinion? How do individuals' ideology and knowledge affect their opinions? What is the relationship between public opinion and ideology?

Public Opinion and the Models of Democracy

Public opinion is simply the collective attitudes of the citizens on a given issue or question. Opinion polling, which involves interviewing a sample of citizens to estimate public opinion as a whole, is such a common feature of contemporary life that we often forget it is a modern invention, dating only from the 1930s (see Figure 4.1). In fact, survey methodology did not develop into a powerful research tool until the advent of computers in the 1950s.

Before polling became an accepted part of the American scene, politicians, journalists, and everyone else could argue about what the people wanted, but no one really knew. Today, sampling methods and opinion polling have altered the debate about the majoritarian and pluralist models of democracy. Now that we know how often government policy runs against majority opinion, it becomes harder to defend the U.S. government as democratic under the majoritarian model. Even at a time when Americans overwhelmingly favored the death penalty for murderers, the Supreme Court decided that existing state laws applying capital punishment were unconstitutional. Even after the Court approved new state laws as constitutional, relatively few murderers were actually executed.

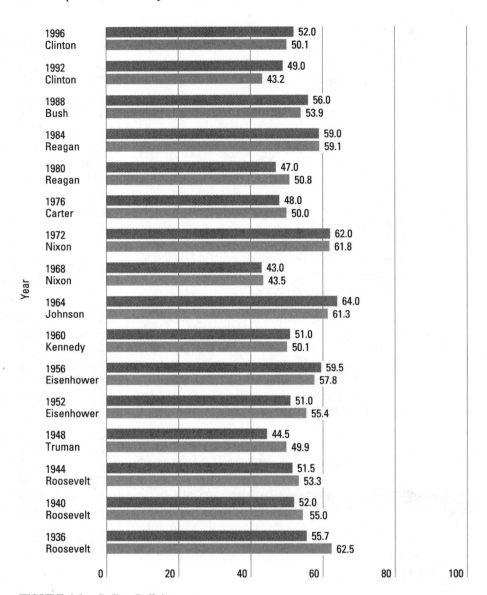

FIGURE 4.1   **Gallup Poll Accuracy**
One of the nation's oldest polls was started by George Gallup in the 1930s. The accuracy of the Gallup Poll in predicting presidential elections over nearly fifty years is charted here. Although not always on the mark, its predictions have been fairly close to election results. The poll was most notably wrong in 1948, when it predicted that Thomas Dewey, the Republican candidate, would defeat the Democratic incumbent, Harry Truman, underestimating Truman's vote by 5.4 percentage points. In 1992, the Gallup Poll was off by an even larger margin, but this time it did identify the winner, Bill Clinton. (Source: The Gallup Organization Web site at <http://www.gallup.com/poll/trends/ptaccuracy.asp>.)

The two models of democracy make different assumptions about public opinion. The majoritarian model assumes that a majority of the people hold clear, consistent opinions on government policy. The pluralist model assumes that the public is often uninformed and ambivalent about specific issues, and opinion polls frequently support that claim. What are the bases of public opinion? What principles, if any, do people use to organize their beliefs and attitudes about politics? Exactly how do individuals form their political opinions? We will look for answers to these questions in this chapter. In later chapters, we assess the effect of public opinion on government policies. The results should help you make up your own mind about the viability of the majoritarian and pluralist models in a functioning democracy.

Political Socialization

Public opinion is grounded in political values. People acquire their values through **political socialization**, a complex process through which individuals become aware of politics, learn political facts, and form political values. Think for a moment about your political socialization. What is your earliest memory of a president? When did you first learn about political parties? If you identify with a party, how did you decide to do so? If you do not, why don't you? Who was the first liberal you ever met? The first conservative? Obviously, the paths to political awareness, knowledge, and values differ among individuals, but most people are exposed to the same influences, or agents of socialization, especially in childhood through young adulthood. These influences are family, school, community, peers, and—of course—television.

Political socialization continues throughout life. As parental and school influences wane in adulthood, peer groups (neighbors, coworkers, club members) assume a greater importance in promoting political awareness and in developing political opinions.[6] Because adults usually learn about political events from the mass media—newspapers, magazines, television, and radio— the media emerge as socialization agents. The role of television is especially important.[7]

Regardless of how people learn about politics, as they grow older, they gain perspective on government. They are likely to measure new candidates (and new ideas) against the old ones they remember. Their values also may change. Finally, political learning comes simply through exposure and familiarity. One example is the act of voting, which people do with increasing regularity as they grow older.

Social Groups and Political Values

No two people are influenced by precisely the same socialization agents in precisely the same way. Still, people with similar backgrounds do share learning experiences; this means they tend to develop similar political opinions. In this

Stop the Presses! Oops, Too Late . . .
*As the 1948 election drew near, few people gave President Harry Truman much of a chance
to defeat his Republican opponent, Thomas E. Dewey. Polling was still new, and nearly all
the early polls showed Dewey far ahead. Most organizations stopped polling weeks before the
election. The* Chicago Daily Tribune *believed the polls and proclaimed Dewey's victory
before the votes were counted. Here, the victorious Truman triumphantly displays the most
embarrassing headline in American politics. Later, it was revealed that the few polls taken
closer to election day showed Truman catching up to Dewey. Clearly, polls estimate the vote
only at the time they are taken.*

section, we examine the ties between people's social backgrounds and their
political values. We examine the ties between background and values by looking at responses to two questions posed by the 1996 National Election Study
administered by the University of Michigan's Center for Political Studies.

The first question deals with abortion. The interviewer said,

There has been some discussion about abortion during recent years. Which
opinion on this page best agrees with your view? You can just tell me the
number of the opinion you choose:

1. By law, abortion should never be permitted. [12 percent agreed.]

2. The law should permit abortion only in case of rape, incest, or when the
   woman's life is in danger. [29 percent]

3. The law should permit abortion for reasons other than rape, incest, or danger to the woman's life, but only after the need for the abortion has been clearly established. [16 percent]

4. By law, a woman should be able to obtain an abortion as a matter of personal choice. [42 percent][8]

Those who chose the last category most clearly valued individual freedom over order imposed by government. Moreover, evidence shows the pro-choice respondents also have concerns about broader issues of social order, such as the role of women and the legitimacy of alternative lifestyles.[9]

The second question pertained to the role of government in guaranteeing employment:

> Some people feel the government in Washington should see to it that every person has a job and a good standard of living. Suppose that these people are at one end of the scale. . . . Others think the government should just let each person get ahead on his own. Suppose these people were at the other end. . . . Where would you put yourself on this scale, or haven't you thought much about this?

Excluding those people who "haven't thought much" about this question, 25 percent of the respondents wanted government to provide every person with a living and 21 percent were undecided. That left 54 percent who wanted the government to leave people alone to "get ahead" on their own. These respondents, who opposed government efforts to promote equality, apparently valued freedom over equality.

Overall, the responses to each of these questions were divided approximately equally. Somewhat less than half the respondents (42 percent) felt that government should not set restrictions on abortion and somewhat more than half (54 percent) thought the government should not guarantee everyone a job and a good standard of living. However, sharp differences in attitudes emerged for both issues when the respondents were grouped by socioeconomic factors—education, income, region, race, religion, and sex. The differences are shown in Figure 4.2 as positive and negative deviations from the national averages for each question. Bars that extend to the right identify groups that are more likely than most Americans to sacrifice freedom for a given value of government, either equality or order. Next, we examine the opinion patterns more closely for each socioeconomic group.

Education

Education increases people's awareness and understanding of political issues. Higher education also promotes tolerance of unpopular opinions and behavior and invites citizens to see issues in terms of civil rights and liberties. This result is clearly shown in the left-hand column of Figure 4.2, which shows that people with more education are more likely to view abortion as a matter of a woman's choice.[10] College-educated individuals

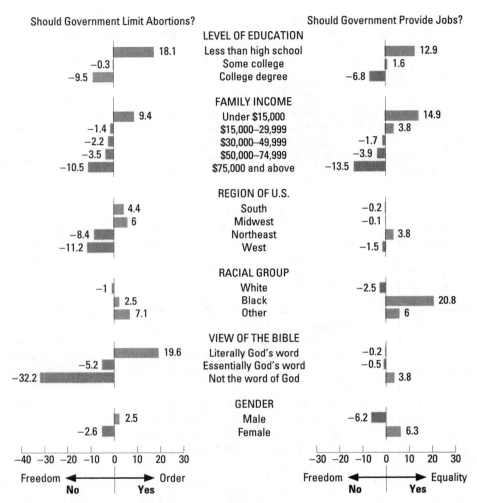

Should Government Limit Abortions?

Should Government Provide Jobs?

LEVEL OF EDUCATION
Less than high school
Some college
College degree

FAMILY INCOME
Under $15,000
$15,000–29,999
$30,000–49,999
$50,000–74,999
$75,000 and above

REGION OF U.S.
South
Midwest
Northeast
West

RACIAL GROUP
White
Black
Other

VIEW OF THE BIBLE
Literally God's word
Essentially God's word
Not the word of God

GENDER
Male
Female

Freedom ◄————► Order
No   Yes

Freedom ◄————► Equality
No   Yes

FIGURE 4.2   Group Deviations from National Opinion on Two Questions
Two questions—one on abortion (representing the dilemma of freedom versus order) and the other on the government's role in guaranteeing employment (freedom versus equality)—were asked of a national sample in 1996. Public opinion for the nation as a whole was sharply divided on each question. These two graphs show how respondents in several social groups deviated from overall public opinion. The longer the bars next to each group, the more its respondents deviated from the expression of opinion for the entire sample. Bars that extend to the left show group opinions that deviate toward freedom. Bars that extend to the right show deviations away from freedom, toward order or equality. (Source: Data from 1996 National Election Study, Center for Political Studies, University of Michigan.)

confronted with a choice between personal freedom and social order tend to choose freedom.

With regard to the role of government in reducing income inequality, the right-hand column in Figure 4.2 shows that people with more education also tend to favor freedom over equality. The higher their level of education, the less likely respondents were to support government-guaranteed jobs and living standards.

Income

In many countries, differences in social class—based on social background and occupation—divide people in their politics.[11] In the United States, we have avoided the ugliest aspects of class conflict, but here wealth sometimes substitutes for class. As Figure 4.2 shows, wealth is consistently linked to opinions favoring a limited government role in promoting order and equality. Wealth and education have a similar impact on opinion: the groups with more education and higher income opt for freedom.

Region

Early in our country's history, regional differences were politically important—important enough to spark a civil war between North and South. For nearly a hundred years after the Civil War, regional differences continued to affect American politics. The moneyed Northeast was thought to control the purse strings of capitalism. The Midwest was long regarded as the stronghold of isolationism in foreign affairs. The South was practically a one-party region, almost completely Democratic. And the individualistic West pioneered its own mixture of progressive politics.

In the past, differences in wealth fed cultural differences between these regions. In recent decades, however, the movement of people and wealth away from the Northeast and Midwest to the Sunbelt states in the South and Southwest has equalized the per capita income of the regions. One product of this equalization is that the "solid South" is no longer solidly Democratic. In fact, the South has tended to vote for Republican candidates for president since 1968.

Figure 4.2 shows more striking differences between the four major regions of the United States on social issues than on economic issues. Respondents in the Northeast and West were more likely to support personal choice than residents of the South and Midwest. People in the Northeast were somewhat more supportive of government efforts to equalize income than were people elsewhere. Despite these differences, regional effects on public opinion are weaker than the effects of most other socioeconomic factors.

The "Old" and "New" Ethnicity: European Origin and Race

In the early twentieth century, the major ethnic groups in America were immigrants from Ireland, Italy, Germany, Poland, and other European countries. They came to the United States in waves during the late 1800s and early 1900s and found themselves in a strange land, usually without money and unable to speak English. Moreover, their religious backgrounds—mainly Catholic and

Jewish—differed from that of the predominantly Protestant earlier settlers. Local politicians saw the newcomers, who were concentrated in urban areas in the Northeast and Midwest, as a new source of votes and soon mobilized them politically. These urban ethnics and their descendants became part of the great coalition of Democratic voters that President Franklin Roosevelt forged in the 1930s. And for years after, the European ethnics supported liberal candidates and causes more strongly than did descendants of the original Anglo-Saxon immigrants.[12] More recent studies of public opinion show the differences are disappearing.[13] But if this **"old" ethnicity**, based on European origin, is giving way to assimilation, a **"new" ethnicity**, based on race, is taking its place.

With the rise of black consciousness and the grassroots civil rights movement in the late 1950s and 1960s, blacks secured genuine voting rights in the South and exercised those rights more vigorously in the North. Although they represented only about 12 percent of the total population, blacks made up sizable voting blocs in southern states and northern cities. Like the European ethnics before them, American blacks were courted for their votes; at long last, their opinions were politically important.

Blacks constitute the largest racial minority in American politics but not the only significant one. Asians, American Indians (Native Americans), and other nonwhites account for another 5 percent of the population. People of Latin American origin are often called Latinos. If they speak Spanish, they are also known as Hispanics. Hispanics make up about 10 percent of the nation's population, but they constitute as much as 28 percent of the population in California and Texas, and 40 percent in New Mexico.[14] Although they are politically strong in some communities, Hispanics have lagged behind blacks in mobilizing across the nation. However, Hispanics are being wooed by non-Hispanic candidates and are increasingly running for public office themselves.

Blacks and members of other minorities display similar political attitudes on questions pertaining to equality. The reasons are twofold.[15] First, racial minorities (excepting second-generation Asians) tend to have low **socioeconomic status**, a combination of education, occupation, status, and income. Second, all racial minorities have been targets of racial prejudice and discrimination and have benefited from government actions in support of equality. The right-hand column in Figure 4.2 clearly shows the effects of race on the freedom-equality issue. Blacks strongly favored government action to improve economic opportunity; other minorities also favored government action but to a lesser degree. The abortion issue produces less difference, although minority groups do favor government restrictions on abortion slightly more than whites do.

Religion

Since the last major wave of European immigration in the 1930s and 1940s, the religious makeup of the United States has remained fairly stable. Today, almost 60 percent of the population is Protestant, about 25 percent is Catholic, only about 2 percent is Jewish, and about 15 percent deny any religious affiliation or choose some other faith.[16] For many years, analysts found strong and consistent differences in the opinions of Protestants, Catholics, and Jews.[17] Protestants were more conservative than Catholics, and Catholics tended to be more conservative than Jews.

Some such differences have remained, especially on the questions of freedom versus order (such as the abortion question), but they are less marked than one might expect. Protestants oppose personal choice on abortion slightly more than Catholics. Nonreligious persons and non-Christians are much more likely to favor personal choice on abortion and are somewhat less inclined toward favoring government job guarantees.

Even greater differences emerge when respondents were classified by their "religiosity," which was measured by their attitude toward the Bible. As Figure 4.2 indicates, religiosity has little effect on attitudes toward economic equality but a powerful influence on attitudes toward social order. Political opinions in the United States do differ sharply according to religious beliefs.

Gender

Differences in sex, which has become known as *gender* in American politics, are often related to political opinions, primarily on the issue of freedom versus equality. As shown in the right-hand column of Figure 4.2, women are much more likely to favor government actions to promote equality. However, men and women usually differ less on issues of freedom versus order, including the abortion issue (see the column on the left of Figure 4.2). Still, on many issues of government policy, the "gender gap" in American politics is wide, with women more supportive than men of government spending for social programs.

From Values to Ideology

We have just seen that differences in groups' responses on two survey questions reflect those groups' value choices between freedom and order and between freedom and equality. But to what degree do people's opinions on specific issues reflect explicit political ideology (the set of values and beliefs that they hold about the purpose and scope of government)? Political scientists generally agree that ideology influences public opinion on specific issues; they have much less consensus on the extent to which people explicitly think in ideological terms.[18] They also agree that the public's ideological thinking cannot be categorized adequately in conventional liberal-conservative terms.[19]

The Degree of Ideological Thinking in Public Opinion

In an early but important study of public opinion, respondents were asked to describe the parties and candidates in the 1956 election.[20] Only about 12 percent of the sample volunteered responses that contained ideological terms (such as *liberal, conservative,* and *capitalism*). Most respondents (42 percent) evaluated the parties and candidates in terms of "benefits to groups" (farmers, workers, or businesspeople, for example). Others (24 percent) spoke more generally about "the nature of the times" (for example, inflation, unemployment, and the threat of war). Finally, a good portion of the sample (22 percent) gave answers that contained no classifiable issue content.

So perhaps we should not make too much of recent findings about the electorate's unfamiliarity with ideology. In a 1996 poll, voters were asked what they thought when someone was described as "liberal" or "conservative."[21] Few responded in explicitly political terms. Rather, most people gave dictionary definitions: "'liberals' are generous (a *liberal* portion). And 'conservatives' are moderate or cautious (a *conservative* estimate)."[22] The two most frequent responses for *conservative* were "fiscally responsible or tight" (17 percent) and "closed-minded" (10 percent). For *liberal* the top two were "open-minded" (14 percent) and "free-spending" (8 percent). Only about 6 percent of the sample mentioned "degree of government involvement" in describing liberals and conservatives. The tendency to respond to questions by using ideological terms grows with increasing education, which helps people understand political issues and relate them to one another. People's personal political socialization can lead them to think ideologically.

The Quality of Ideological Thinking in Public Opinion

What people's ideological self-placement means as the twenty-first century opens is not clear. At one time, the liberal-conservative continuum represented a single dimension: attitudes toward the scope of government activity. Liberals were in favor of more government action to provide public goods, and conservatives were in favor of less. The simple distinction is not as useful today. Many people who call themselves liberals no longer favor government activism in general, and many self-styled conservatives no longer oppose it in principle. As a result, many people have difficulty deciding whether they are liberal or conservative.

Studies of the public's ideological thinking find that two themes run through people's minds when individuals are asked to describe liberals and conservatives. People associate liberals with change and conservatives with tradition. This theme corresponds to the distinction between liberals and conservatives on the exercise of freedom and the maintenance of order.[23]

The other theme has to do with equality. The conflict between freedom and equality was at the heart of President Roosevelt's New Deal economic policies (social security, minimum wage legislation, farm price supports) in the 1930s. The policies expanded the interventionist role of the national government in order to promote greater economic equality, and attitudes toward government intervention in the economy served to distinguish liberals from conservatives for decades afterward.[24] Attitudes toward government interventionism still underlie opinions about domestic economic policies.[25] Liberals support intervention to promote their ideas of economic equality; conservatives favor less government intervention and more individual freedom in economic activities.

In Chapter 1, we proposed an alternative ideological classification based on people's relative evaluations of freedom, order, and equality. We described liberals as people who believe that government should promote equality, even if some freedom is lost in the process, but who oppose surrendering freedom to government-imposed order. Conservatives do not oppose equality in and of itself but put a higher value on freedom than on equality when the two conflict. Yet conservatives are not above restricting freedom when threatened with the loss of order. So both groups value freedom, but one is more willing to trade freedom for equality, and the other is more inclined to trade freedom for order. If you have trouble thinking about these tradeoffs on a single dimension, you are in good company. The liberal-conservative continuum presented to survey respondents takes a two-dimensional concept and squeezes it into a one-dimensional format.[26]

Ideological Types in the United States

Our ideological typology in Chapter 1 (see Figure 1.2) classifies people as liberals if they favor freedom over order and equality over freedom. Conversely, conservatives favor freedom over equality and order over freedom. Libertarians favor freedom over both equality and order—the opposite of communitarians. By cross-tabulating people's answers to the two questions from the 1996 National Election Study about freedom versus order (abortion) and freedom versus equality (government job guarantees), we can classify respondents according to their ideological tendencies. As shown in Figure 4.3, responses of people to the two questions are virtually unrelated to each other. This finding indicates that people do not decide about government activity according to a one-dimensional ideological standard. Figure 4.3 also classifies the sample according to the two dimensions in our ideological typology. Using only two issues to classify people in an ideological framework leaves substantial room for error. Still, if the typology is worthwhile, the results should be meaningful, and they are.

It is striking that the ideological tendencies of the respondents in the 1996 sample depicted in Figure 4.3 are divided almost equally among the four categories of the typology. The sample suggests that more than three-quarters of the electorate favor government action to promote order, increase equality, or both.

The ideological tendencies illustrate important differences among different social groups. Communitarians are prominent among minorities and among people with little education and low income, groups that tend to look favorably on the benefits of government in general. Libertarians are concentrated among people with more education and with higher income, who tend to be suspicious of government interference in their lives. People in the southern states tend to be communitarians, those in the Midwest tend to be conservatives, and those in the Northeast are inclined to be liberals. Men are more likely to be conservative or libertarian than women, who tend to be liberal or communitarian.[27]

This more refined analysis of political ideology explains why even Americans who pay close attention to politics find it difficult to locate themselves on the liberal-conservative continuum. Their problem is that they are

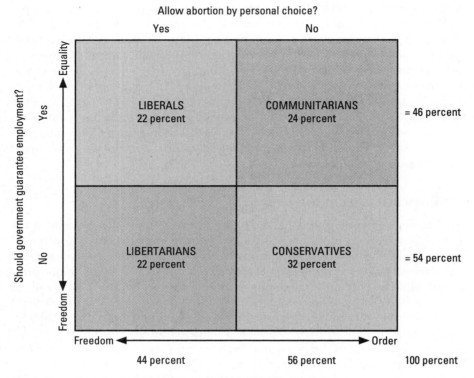

FIGURE 4.3   ***Respondents Classified by Ideological Tendencies***
In the 1996 election survey, respondents were asked whether abortion should be a matter of personal choice or regulated by the government and whether government should guarantee people a job and a good standard of living or people should get ahead on their own. (The questions are given verbatim on pages 84–85.) These two questions presented choices between freedom and order and between freedom and equality. People's responses to the two questions showed no correlation, demonstrating that these value choices cannot be explained by a simple liberal-conservative continuum. Instead, their responses can be more usefully analyzed according to four different ideological types. (Source: 1996 National Election Study, 1996 Center for Political Studies, University of Michigan. Used with permission.)

liberal on some issues and conservative on others. Forced to choose along just one dimension, they opt for the middle category, moderate. However, our analysis also indicates that many people who classify themselves as liberals or conservatives do fit these two categories in our typology. There is value, then, in the liberal-conservative distinction, as long as we understand its limitations.

The Process of Forming Political Opinions

We have seen that people acquire political values through the socialization process and that different social groups develop different sets of political values. We also have learned that some people, but only a minority, think about politics ideologically, holding a consistent set of political attitudes and beliefs. Now let us look at how people form opinions on any particular issue. In particular, how do those who are not ideologues—in other words, most citizens— form political opinions? Four factors—self-interest, political information, opinion schemas, and political leadership—play a part in the process.

Self-Interest

The **self-interest principle** states that people choose what benefits them personally.[28] The principle plays an obvious role in how people form opinions on government economic policies. Taxpayers tend to prefer low taxes to high taxes; farmers tend to favor candidates who promise them more support over those who promise them less. The self-interest principle also applies, but less clearly, to some government policies outside of economics. Members of minority groups tend to see more personal advantage in government policies that promote social equality than do members of majority groups; teenage males are more likely to oppose compulsory military service than are older people of either sex. Group leaders often cue group members, telling them what they should support or oppose.[29]

When a person is not directly affected by a government policy, the self-interest principle plays little or no role. Then people form opinions based on their underlying values.[30] When moral issues are not in question and when people do not benefit directly from a policy, many people have trouble relating to the policy and forming an opinion about it. This tends to be true of the whole subject of foreign policy. Here, many people have no opinion, or their opinions are not firmly held and are likely to change quite easily, given almost any new information.

Political Information

In the United States today, the level of education is high, media coverage of national and international events is extensive, yet the average American displays an astonishing lack of political knowledge.[31] But Americans do not let lack of knowledge stop them from expressing their opinions. They readily offer opinions on issues ranging from capital punishment to nuclear power to the government's handling of the economy. When opinions are based on little knowledge, however, they change easily in the face of new information. The result is a high degree of instability in public opinion poll findings, depending on how questions are worded and on recent events that bear on the issue at hand.

The most recent study of political knowledge was undertaken by Delli Carpini and Keeter.[32] In addition to conducting their own specialized surveys, they collected from existing surveys approximately 3,700 individual items that measured some type of factual knowledge about public affairs. They concluded that enough of the public is "reasonably well informed about politics . . . to meet high standards of good citizenship." They found, "Many of the basic institutions and procedures of government are known to half or more of the public, as are the relative positions of the parties on many major issues."[33] Their analysis also found, however, that political knowledge is not randomly distributed within our society. "In particular, women, African Americans, the poor, and the young tend to be substantially less knowledgeable about politics than are men, whites, the affluent, and older citizens."[34] Education is the strongest single predictor of political knowledge.

Researchers have not found any meaningful relationship between political sophistication and self-placement on the liberal-conservative scale—that is, people with equal knowledge about public affairs and levels of conceptualization are as likely to call themselves liberals as conservatives.[35] Equal levels of political understanding, then, may produce quite different political views as a result of individuals' unique patterns of political socialization.

Opinion Schemas

Even people who do not approach politics from the perspective of a full-blown ideology interpret political issues in terms of some preexisting mental structure. Psychologists refer to the packet of preexisting beliefs that people apply to specific issues as an **opinion schema**—a network of organized knowledge and beliefs that guides the processing of information on a particular subject.[36] The schema concept gives us a more flexible tool for analyzing public opinion than the more rigid concept of ideology. Opinion schemas can pertain to any political figure and to any subject—race, economics, or international relations, for example.[37]

Still, the more encompassing concept of ideology is hard to escape. Researchers have found that people's personal schemas tend to be organized in ways that parallel broader ideological categories. In other words, a conservative's opinion schema about President Bill Clinton may not differ factually from a liberal's, but it will differ considerably in its evaluation of those facts.[38]

Some scholars argue that most citizens, in their attempt to make sense out of politics, pay less attention to the policies pursued by government than to their leaders' "style" in approaching political problems—for instance, whether they are seen as tough, compassionate, honest, or hard working.[39] In this way citizens can relate the complexities of politics to their own personal experiences.

Political Leadership

Public opinion on specific issues is molded by political leaders, journalists, and policy experts. Because of the attention given to the presidency by the media, presidents are uniquely positioned to shape popular attitudes. Consider Ronald Reagan and the issue of nuclear disarmament. In late 1987, President Reagan and Mikhail Gorbachev signed a treaty banning intermediate-range nuclear forces (INFs) from Europe and the Soviet Union. Soon afterward, a national survey found that 82 percent of the sample approved the treaty while 18 percent opposed it. As might be expected, respondents who viewed the

Soviet Union as highly threatening ("hard-liners") were least enthusiastic about the INF treaty. Respondents were then asked to agree or disagree with this statement: "President Reagan is well known for his anticommunism, so if he thinks this is a good deal, it must be." Analysis of the responses showed that "hard-liners" who agreed with the statement were nearly twice as likely to approve the treaty as those who were unmoved by his involvement. The researcher concluded that "a highly conciliatory move by a president known for long-standing opposition to just such an action" can override expected sources of opposition among the public.[40]

The ability of political leaders to affect public opinion has been enhanced enormously by the growth of the broadcast media, especially television.[41] The majoritarian model of democracy assumes that government officials respond to public opinion. But the evidence is substantial that this causal sequence is reversed, that public opinion responds instead to the actions of government officials.[42] If this is true, how much potential is there for public opinion to be manipulated by political leaders through the mass media?

The Media in America

"We never talk anymore" is a common lament of couples who are not getting along very well. In politics, too, citizens and their government need to communicate in order to get along well. *Communication* is the process of transmitting information from one individual or group to another. *Mass* communication is the process by which information is transmitted to large, heterogeneous, widely dispersed audiences. The term **mass media** refers to the means for communicating to these audiences. The mass media are commonly divided into two types. *Print media* (newspapers, magazines) communicate information through the publication of written words and pictures. *Broadcast media* (radio, television) communicate information electronically through sounds and images. Modern politics also utilizes the *fax* (facsimile images sent by telephone) and computers linked over the *Internet*. We refer to these as *group media*, and we consider them separately below.

Our focus here is on the role of the media in promoting communication from government to its citizens and from citizens to their government. In totalitarian governments, information flows more freely in one direction (from government to people) than in the other. In democratic governments, information must flow freely in both directions; a democratic government can respond to public opinion only if its citizens can make their opinions known. Moreover, the electorate can hold government officials accountable for their actions only if voters know what their government has done, is doing, and plans to do. Because the mass media (and increasingly the group media) provide the major channels for this two-way flow of information, they have the dual capability of reflecting and shaping our political views.

The media are not the only means of communication between citizens and government. Agents of socialization (especially schools) function as "linkage mechanisms" that promote such communication. In the next three chapters, we will discuss other major mechanisms for communication: voting, political parties and election campaigns, and interest groups.

Modern Forms of Group Media

The revolution in electronics during the last quarter of the twentieth century produced two new technologies—the fax and the Internet—that have been readily adapted to politics. They are not "mass" media that communicate with the general public, however. They are **group media**—communications technologies used primarily within groups of people with common interests.

Facsimile Transmissions   The fax machine has become standard communications equipment in practical politics. Campaign managers routinely communicate with campaign workers and media representatives by fax, and it is a major medium for communication among political officeholders in Washington.[43] Interest groups frequently rely on automated fax messages concerning issues before Congress—as many as ten thousand a night—sent automatically by computers to sympathizers across the country.[44] Increasingly, recipients of these faxes respond by faxing fervent messages of opposition or support to their congressional representatives, simulating a groundswell of public opinion—despite the fact that less than 10 percent of U.S. homes had fax machines in the mid-1990s (see "High-Tech Lobbying," page 187 in Chapter 7).[45]

The Internet   What we today call the Internet began in 1969 when, with support from the U.S. Defense Department's Advanced Research Projects Agency, computers at four universities were linked to form ARPANET. In its early years, the Internet was used mainly to transmit messages, known as electronic mail, or *e-mail,* among researchers. In 1991, a group of European physicists devised a standardized system for encoding and transmitting a wide range of materials, including graphics and photographs, over the Internet, and the World Wide Web (WWW) was born. In January 1993 there were only fifty Web sites.[46] Today there are millions.

Like the fax, the Internet was soon incorporated into politics, and by 1998 nearly every political organization in the nation had its own Web site. The Internet can even break important stories. Matt Drudge, an Internet "gossip reporter," learned that *Newsweek* had gathered information in early January on a possible sexual relationship between President Clinton and Monica Lewinsky, a White House intern, but was sitting on the story, reluctant to report hearsay about the president's sex life. Drudge, who publishes virtually everything sent to him, posted a report of the story on his Web site, "The Drudge Report," the day Clinton gave his legal deposition in the sexual harassment lawsuit brought against him by Paula Corbin Jones, a former Arkansas state employee. From there the story slithered into Internet newsgroups and then into the mass media with a discussion on ABC's "This Week" the next morning.[47] On September 11, the day after receiving Independent Counsel Kenneth Starr's report on the Lewinsky affair, Congress published it on the

Internet. Within hours, millions read the tawdry details on their computers, as the Web momentarily became a mass medium.[48]

Private Ownership of the Media

In the United States, people take private ownership of the media for granted. In other Western democratic countries, the print media (both newspapers and magazines) are privately owned, but the broadcast media often are not. Private ownership of both print and broadcast media gives the news industry in America more political freedom than any other in the world, but it also makes the media more dependent on advertising revenues. To make a profit, the news operations of the mass media in America must appeal to the audiences they serve. The primary criterion of a story's **newsworthiness** is usually its audience appeal, which is judged according to its potential impact on readers or listeners; its degree of sensationalism (exemplified by violence, conflict, disaster, or scandal); its treatment of familiar people or life situations; its close-to-home character; and its timeliness.[49]

Media owners can make more money either by increasing their audiences or by acquiring additional publications or stations. A decided trend toward concentrated ownership of the media increases the risk that a few major owners could control the news flow to promote their own political interests. In fact, the number of *independent newspapers* has declined as newspaper chains (owners of two or more newspapers in different cities) have acquired more newspapers. Only about four hundred dailies are still independent, and many of these papers are too small and unprofitable to invite acquisition.

As with newspapers, chains sometimes own television stations in different cities, and ownership sometimes extends across different media. When it acquired CBS in 1995, Westinghouse owned TV stations in fourteen major cities and thirty-nine radio stations. In 1996, Westinghouse extended its media empire by purchasing Infinity Broadcasting. The purchase gave Westinghouse a total of eighty-three AM and FM stations, many in the nation's largest markets.[50] Some people fear the concentration of media under a single owner, and government has addressed those fears by regulating media ownership, as well as other aspects of media operation.

Government Regulation of the Media

Although most of the mass media in the United States are privately owned, they do not operate free of government regulation. The broadcast media, however, are subject to more regulations than the print media.

The Federal Communications Act of 1934 created the **Federal Communications Commission** (FCC) to regulate the broadcast and telephone industries. The FCC has five members (no more than three from the same political party) nominated by the president for terms of five years. The commissioners can be removed from office only through impeachment and conviction. Consequently, the FCC is considered an independent regulatory commission: it is insulated from political control by either the president or Congress. (We discuss independent regulatory commissions in Chapter 10.) Today, the FCC is charged with regulating interstate and international communications by radio, television, telephone, telegraph, cable, and satellite.

For six decades—as technological change made television commonplace and brought the invention of computers, fax machines, and satellite transmissions—the communications industry was regulated under the basic framework of the 1934 law that created the FCC. Then, pressured by businesses that wanted to exploit new electronic technologies, Congress, in a bipartisan effort, swept away most existing regulations in the Telecommunications Act of 1996.

The 1996 law relaxed or scrapped limitations on media ownership. For example, broadcasters were previously limited to owning only twelve TV stations and forty radio stations. Now there are no limits on the number of TV stations one company may own, as long as their coverage doesn't extend beyond 35 percent of the market nationwide. The 1996 law set no national limits for radio ownership, and it relaxed local limits. In addition, it lifted rate regulations for cable systems, allowed cross-ownership of cable and telephone companies, and allowed local and long-distance telephone companies to compete with one another and to sell television services. Although even those who wrote the law could not predict its long-range effect, the law quickly spurred even greater concentration of media ownership.

The First Amendment to the Constitution prohibits Congress from abridging the freedom of the press. Over time, *the press* has come to mean all the mass media, and the courts have decided many cases that define how far freedom of the press extends under the law. The most important of these cases are often quite complex. Usually the courts strike down government attempts to restrain the press from publishing or broadcasting the information, reports, or opinions it finds newsworthy. One notable exception concerns strategic information during wartime; the courts have supported censorship of information such as the sailing schedules of troop ships or the planned movements of troops in battle. Otherwise, they have recognized a strong constitutional case against press censorship.

Because the broadcast media are licensed to use the public airwaves, they are subject to additional regulation, beyond that applied to the print media, of the content of their news coverage. The basis for the FCC's regulation of content lies in its charge to ensure that radio and television stations "serve the public interest, convenience, and necessity." With its **equal opportunities rule**, the FCC requires any broadcast station that gives or sells time to a candidate for public office to make an equal amount of time available under the same conditions to all other candidates for that office. The **reasonable access rule** required that stations make their facilities available for the expression of conflicting views or issues from all responsible elements in the community.

Reporting and Following the News

In this section we discuss how the media cover political affairs, and we examine where citizens acquire their political knowledge. We also look at what people learn from the media, and we probe the media's effects on public opinion, the political agenda, and political socialization.

Covering National Politics

Washington, D.C., has by far the biggest press corps of any city in the world—over 6,000 accredited reporters: 2,100 from newspapers, 2,000 from periodicals, and 2,200 from radio and television.[51] However, only about seventy-five "regular" journalists are in the White House press corps.[52] As recently as the Truman administration, reporters enjoyed informal personal relationships with the president. Today, the media's relationship with the president is mediated primarily through the Office of the Press Secretary.

White House correspondents rely heavily on information they receive from the president's staff, each piece carefully crafted in an attempt to control the news report. The most frequent form is the news release—a prepared text distributed to reporters in the hope that they will use it verbatim. A daily news briefing at 11:30 A.M. enables reporters to question the press secretary about news releases. A news conference provides an opportunity to question high-level officials in the executive branch—including the president on occasion. News conferences appear to be freewheeling, but officials tend to carefully rehearse precise answers to anticipated questions.

Occasionally, information is given "on background," which means that reporters can quote the information but cannot identify the source except in a vague reference such as "a senior official says." Information that is disclosed "off the record" cannot even be printed. Journalists who violate these well-known conditions risk losing their welcome at the White House.

Most reporters in the Washington press corps are accredited to sit in the House and Senate press galleries, but only about four hundred cover Congress exclusively.[53] Most news about Congress comes from innumerable press releases issued by its 535 members and from an unending supply of congressional reports.

Congress banned microphones and cameras from its chambers until 1979, when the House permitted live coverage, though it insisted on controlling the shots being televised. To share in the exposure, the Senate began television coverage in 1986. C-SPAN (the Cable Satellite Public Affairs Network) coverage of Congress has become important to professionals in government and politics in Washington. Even members of the Washington press corps watch C-SPAN.

In addition to these recognized sources of news, selected reporters occasionally benefit from leaks of information released by officials who are guaranteed anonymity. Officials may leak news to interfere with others' political plans or to float ideas ("trial balloons") past the public and other political leaders to gauge their reactions. Sometimes a carefully placed leak turns into a gusher of media coverage through the practice of "pack journalism"—the tendency of journalists to adopt similar viewpoints toward the news simply because they hang around together, exchanging information and defining the day's news with one another.

Press Sacks White House Spokesman!
Arriving at his daily briefing of reporters on October 1, 1997, White House spokesman Mike McCurry found on the lectern a paper bag decorated with a face. Without skipping a beat, he donned the bag and announced, "A briefing today from an anonymous source."

Presenting the News

Media executives, news editors, and prominent reporters function as **gate-keepers** in directing the news flow: they decide which events to report and how to handle the elements in those stories. Only a few individuals—no more than twenty-five at the average newspaper or news magazine and fifty at each of the major television networks—qualify as gatekeepers, defining the news for public consumption.[54] They not only select what topics go through the gate but also are expected to uphold standards of careful reporting and principled journalism. In contrast to the print and broadcast media, the Internet has no gatekeepers and thus no constraints on its content.

The established media cannot communicate everything about public affairs. There is neither space in newspapers or magazines nor time on television or radio to do so. Time limitations impose especially severe constraints on television news broadcasting. Each half-hour network news program devotes only about twenty minutes to the news (the rest of the time is taken up by commercials), and there is even less news on local television.

During elections, personification encourages **horse race journalism**, in which media coverage becomes a matter of "who's ahead in the polls, who's raising the most money, who's got TV ads and who's getting endorsed." U.S. television presents elections as contests between individuals rather than as confrontations between representatives of opposing parties and platforms.

Where the Public Gets Its News

Until the early 1960s, most people reported getting more political news from newspapers than from any other source. Television nudged out newspapers as the public's major source of news in the early 1960s. By the mid-1990s, nearly three-fourths of the public cited television as their news source, compared with about two-fifths who named newspapers (some named both). Not only was television the public's most important source of news, but those polled rated television news as more trustworthy than newspaper news by a margin of 2 to 1.[55] But recent studies have found that fewer adults are regularly watching television news, particularly nightly network news (only 42 percent in 1996 versus 60 percent in 1993).[56]

In a recent survey of news media usage, 84 percent of respondents said that they had read or heard the prior day's news through print or broadcast media: newspapers, television, or radio.[57] However, a comparable survey found that only 17 percent of citizens claimed they "follow news of public affairs and government" daily, and almost as many said they did so hardly at all.[58] The 50 percent who said they followed the news either "daily" or "most of the time" were more likely to have some college education. They were also far more likely to be over fifty years old than under thirty (51 versus 11 percent) and much more likely to be men than women (41 versus 28 percent). Race bears little relationship to news attentiveness, once controls for level of education are introduced.[59]

What People Remember and Know

If, as surveys indicate, 84 percent of the public reads or hears the news each day, and if nearly 75 percent regularly watches the news on television, how much political information do these people absorb? By all accounts, not much. A 1997 national survey asked respondents to identify a list of names "in the news." Many more identified Tiger Woods, the young African American golfer (82 percent); Dennis Rodman, the Chicago Bulls basketball rowdy (80 percent); and Ellen DeGeneres, the television comedian who came out as a lesbian (62 percent), than identified Alan Greenspan, chairman of the Federal Reserve Board (20 percent); Kenneth Starr, independent counsel investigating President Clinton (20 percent); and Trent Lott, majority leader of the Senate (15 percent).[60]

Those who are more attentive to news answer more political knowledge questions correctly than those who are less attentive—as expected. Given the enormous improvements in television news coverage and the increasing reliance of the public on TV for news, we might also expect the public to know more than it did twenty years ago.[61] Unfortunately, that is not so. Similar surveys in 1967 and in 1987 asked respondents to name their state governor, representative in the House, and head of the local school district. Only 9 percent failed to name a single official in 1967 compared with 17 percent in 1987. The author of this study attributed the lower performance in 1987 to greater reliance on television for news.[62]

Numerous studies have found that those who rely on television for their news score lower on tests of knowledge about public affairs than those who rely on print media.[63] Among media researchers, this finding has led to the **television hypothesis**—the belief that television is to blame for the low level of citizens' knowledge about public affairs.[64] However, recent research questioned the hypothesis and found that "television was more successful in communicating information about topics that were of low salience [significance] to the audience, while print media were superior in conveying information about topics that had high salience."[65]

Influencing Public Opinion

Americans overwhelmingly believe that the media exert a strong influence on their political institutions, and almost nine out of ten Americans believe that the media strongly influence public opinion.[66] However, measuring the extent of media influence on public opinion is difficult.[67] Because few of us learn about political events except through the media, it could be argued that the media create public opinion simply by reporting events. Consider the dismantling of the Berlin Wall in 1989. Surely the photographs of joyous Berliners demolishing that symbol of oppression affected American public opinion about the reunification of Germany.

The media can have dramatic effects on particular events. Soon after the Lewinsky scandal broke in January 1998, President Clinton had to give his State of the Union address before Congress and a television audience of 50 million. He disappointed any viewers looking for dirt, as he focused on his accomplishments (a robust economy, record low unemployment and inflation, and a virtually balanced budget) and on his proposals for child care, education, and health care. To counter his image as a philandering male, Clinton posed himself as an able president. And his strategy paid off, according to a poll of viewers. Only 33 percent had been "very confident" in his ability to carry out his duties prior to watching, but 48 percent were very confident afterward.[68] The February Gallup Poll found that 70 percent of the public approved of Clinton's job performance—the highest rating of his presidency.

Documenting general effects of media on opinions about general issues in the news is difficult. One study analyzed polls on eighty issues in foreign and domestic affairs at two points in time. For nearly half of these issues, public opinion changed over time by about six percentage points. The researchers compared these changes with policy positions taken by ten different sources of information composed of commentators on television network news, including the president, members of the president's party, members of the opposition party, and members of interest groups. The authors found the news commentators to have the most dramatic effect—they could link a single commentary for or against an issue to a significant corresponding change in opinion (more than four percentage points).[69]

Setting the Political Agenda

Despite the media's potential for influencing public opinion, most scholars believe that the media's greatest impact on politics is found in their power to set the **political agenda**—a list of issues that people identify as needing government attention. Those who set the political agenda define which issues government decision makers should discuss and debate.

The mass media in the United States have traditionally played an important role in defining the political agenda. Television, which brings pictures and sound into almost every home, has enormous potential for setting the political agenda. A careful study designed to isolate and examine television's effects on public opinion concluded, "By attending to some problems and ignoring others, television news shapes the American public's political priorities."[70] Indeed, the farther removed a viewer is from public affairs, "the stronger the agenda-setting power of television news."[71]

One study found varying correlations between media coverage and what the public sees as "the most important problem facing this country today," depending on the type of event. Public opinion was especially responsive to media coverage of recurring problems such as inflation and unemployment.[72] The media's ability to influence public opinion by defining "the news" makes politicians eager to influence media coverage. Politicians attempt to affect not only public opinion but the opinions of other political leaders.[73]

The president receives a daily digest of news and opinion from many sources. In a curious sense, the mass media have become a network for communicating among attentive elites, all trying to influence one another or to assess others' weaknesses and strengths. Suppose the White House is under pressure on some policy matter and is asked to send a representative to appear for fifteen minutes of intense questioning on the "Newshour with Jim Lehrer." The White House might comply as much to influence the thinking of other insiders (who faithfully watch the program) as to influence opinions among the relatively few news sophisticates in the public who watch public television.

Socialization

The mass media act as important agents of political socialization.[74] Young people who rarely follow the news by choice nevertheless acquire political values through the entertainment function of the broadcast media. Years ago, children learned from radio programs; now they learn from television. What children learned from radio was quite different from what they are learning now, however. In the golden days of radio, youngsters listening to popular radio dramas heard repeatedly that "crime does not pay." The message never varied: criminals are bad; the police are good; criminals get caught and are severely punished for their crimes.

Television today does not portray the criminal justice system in the same way, even in police dramas. Consider programs such as "Homicide" and "The X-Files," which have portrayed police and FBI agents as killers. Other series, such as "Law and Order" and "NYPD Blue," sometimes portray a tainted criminal justice system and institutionalized corruption.[75] Certainly, one cannot easily argue that television's entertainment programs help prepare law-abiding citizens.

So the media play contradictory roles in the process of political socialization. On the one hand, they promote popular support for government by joining in the celebration of national holidays, heroes' birthdays, political anniversaries, and civic accomplishments. On the other hand, the media erode public confidence by publicizing citizens' grievances, airing investigative reports of agency malfeasance, and even showing dramas about crooked cops.[76]

Evaluating the Media in Government

Are the media fair or biased in reporting the news? What contributions do the media make to democratic government? What effects do they have on freedom, order, and equality?

Is Reporting Biased?

News reports are presented as objective reality, yet critics of modern journalism contend that news is filtered through the ideological biases of the owners and editors (the gatekeepers) and of the reporters themselves (see Compared with What? 4.1). The argument that news is politically biased has two sides. On the one hand, news reporters are criticized for tilting their stories in a liberal direction, promoting social equality and undercutting social order. On the other hand, wealthy and conservative media owners are suspected of preserving inequalities and reinforcing the existing order by serving a relentless round of entertainment that numbs the public's capacity for critical analysis.

Although the picture is far from clear, available evidence seems to confirm the charge of liberal leanings among reporters in the major news media. In a 1996 survey of over one thousand journalists, 61 percent considered themselves "Democrat or liberal" or leaned that way, compared with only 15 percent who said they were or leaned toward the "Republican or conservative" side.[77] Television coverage in both 1992 and 1996 favored the Democrat Clinton over his Republican opponents, Bush and Dole. In both campaigns, Clinton received more balanced coverage (about 50 percent positive evaluations) than either Republican (only about 30 percent) on the major network news programs.[78]

To some extent, working journalists in the national and local media are at odds with their own editors, who tend to be more conservative.[79] The editors, in their function as gatekeepers, tend to tone down reporters' liberal leanings by editing their stories or not placing them well in the medium. Newspaper publishers are also free to endorse candidates, and almost all daily newspapers

Compared with What? 4.1

Live (and Sometimes Colored): Election News on Television in Three Countries

Compared with television reporters in Britain and Germany, reporters in the United States are more likely to color campaign news through commentary before and after reporting a story. This finding comes from a cross-national study of television coverage of elections in the United States and Britain in 1992 and in Germany in 1990. Stories about the candidates' activities were coded by researchers according to reporters' comments in statements that preceded or followed film of the candidates' appearance. The comments were coded as "deflating," "straight or neutral," "mixed," or "reinforcing." Nearly one-quarter of all U.S. reporters' comments were deflating—nearly three times the incidence in Britain and more than ten times that in Germany. In fact, only about half the comments in the United States were straight or neutral, compared with more than two-thirds in Britain and nearly all in Germany.

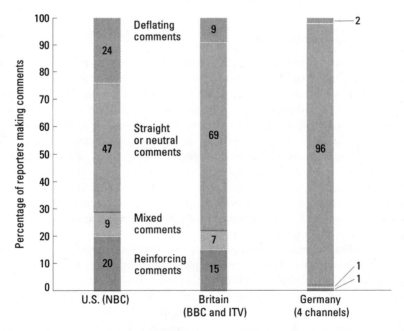

Source: These data were calculated from Table 7 in Holli A. Semetko, "American Election News in Comparative Perspective," paper presented at the annual meeting of the American Political Science Association, Washington, D.C., September 1993.

once openly endorsed one of the two major party candidates for president (usually the Republican candidate). Since the 1970s, daily papers have moved away from making partisan endorsements, and 70 percent made none in

1996—a historic high. Those that did favored Republican Bob Dole nearly two to one, although Clinton was backed by papers with larger circulations and thus he did not trail as much in terms of total circulation.[80]

If media owners and their editors are indeed conservative supporters of the status quo, we might expect them to support officeholders over challengers in elections, regardless of party. However, the evidence tends in the other direction. Let's compare 1980 (when Jimmy Carter, a liberal Democrat, was president and Ronald Reagan, a conservative Republican, was his challenger) with 1984 (when President Reagan faced Walter Mondale, a liberal Democrat). A comparison of television news in 1980 and 1984 found more negative coverage of the incumbent president both times.[81] The researcher concluded that virtually no *continuing* ideological or partisan bias existed on the evening television news. Instead, what was seen as ideological or partisan bias in 1980 and 1984 was actually a bias against presidential *incumbents* and *front-runners* for the presidency.[82] According to this reasoning, if journalists have any pronounced bias, it is against office-holding politicians. When an incumbent runs for reelection, journalists may feel a special responsibility to counteract his or her advantage by putting the opposite partisan spin on the news.[83]

Contributions to Democracy

As noted earlier, in a democracy, communication must move in two directions: from government to citizens and from citizens to government. In fact, political communication in the United States seldom goes directly from government to citizens without passing through the media. The point is important because, as just discussed, news reporters tend to be highly critical of politicians; they consider it their job to search for inaccuracies in fact and weaknesses in argument. Some observers have characterized the news media and the government as adversaries—each mistrusting the other, locked in competition for popular favor while trying to get the record straight. To the extent that this is true, the media serve both the majoritarian and the pluralist models of democracy well by improving the quality of information transmitted to the people about their government.

The mass media transmit information in the opposite direction by reporting citizens' reactions to political events and government actions. The press has traditionally reflected public opinion (and often created it) while defining the news and suggesting courses of government action. But the media's role in reflecting public opinion has become much more refined in the information age. After commercial polls (such as the Gallup and Roper polls) were established in the 1930s, newspapers began to report reliable readings of public opinion. By the 1970s, some news organizations acquired their own survey research divisions. Occasionally, print and electronic media have joined forces to conduct major national surveys. For example, the well-respected *New York Times*/CBS News Poll conducts surveys that are first aired on the "CBS Evening News" and then analyzed at length in the *Times*.

Although polls sometimes create opinions just by asking questions, their net effect has been to generate more accurate knowledge of public opinion and to report that knowledge back to the public. Although widespread knowledge of public opinion does not guarantee government responsiveness to popular demands, such knowledge is necessary if government is to function according to the majoritarian model of democracy.

Effects on Freedom, Order, and Equality

The media in the United States have played an important role in advancing equality, especially racial equality. Throughout the civil rights movement of the 1950s and 1960s, the media gave national coverage to conflict in the South, as black children tried to attend white schools or civil rights workers were beaten and even killed in the effort to register black voters. Partly because of this media coverage, civil rights moved up on the political agenda, and coalitions were formed in Congress to pass new laws promoting racial equality. Women's rights have also been advanced by the media, which have reported instances of blatant sexual discrimination exposed by groups working for sexual equality. In general, the mass media offer spokespersons for any disadvantaged group an opportunity to state their case before a national audience and to work for a place on the political agenda.

Although the media are willing to encourage government action to promote equality at the cost of some personal freedom, they resist government attempts to infringe on freedom of the press to promote order.[84] A 1997 national survey commissioned by the *Chicago Tribune* and published on July 4 showed that the American public does not value freedom of speech and of the press as much as members of the media do. Nearly 60 percent of respondents favored censoring radio hosts who frequently refer to sex; 52 percent would prevent groups from advocating overthrowing the government; 50 percent would restrict material transmitted over the Internet; almost 50 percent would forbid militia or white supremacist groups to demonstrate in their community; and 27 percent actually agreed that the First Amendment goes too far in the rights it guarantees.[85] The *Tribune* responded with an editorial defending the First Amendment and its wording: "Congress shall make no law . . . abridging the freedom of speech, or the press."

The media's ability to report whatever they wish, whenever they wish, certainly erodes efforts to maintain order. For example, sensational media coverage of terrorist acts gives terrorists the publicity they seek; portrayal of brutal killings and rapes on television encourages "copycat" crimes, committed "as seen on TV"; and news stories about the burning of black churches in 1996 spawned "copycat" arsons. Freedom of the press is a noble value and one that has been important to democratic government. But we should not ignore the fact that democracies sometimes pay a price for pursuing it without qualification.

Summary

Public opinion does not rule in America. On most issues, it merely sets general boundaries for government policy. People form their values through the process of political socialization. The most important socialization agents in childhood and young adulthood are family, school, community, and peers. Members of the same social group tend to experience similar socialization processes and thus to adopt similar values. People in different social groups, that hold different values, often express vastly different opinions. Differences in education, race, and religion tend to produce sharper divisions of opinion today on questions of order and equality than do differences in income, region, or ethnicity.

Most people do not think about politics in ideological terms. When asked to do so by pollsters, however, they readily classify themselves along a liberal-conservative continuum. Many respondents choose the middle category, moderate, because the choice is safe. Others choose it because they have liberal views on some issues and conservative views on others. Their political orientation is better captured by a two-dimensional framework that analyzes ideology according to the values of order and equality. Responses to the survey questions we used to establish our ideological typology divide the American electorate almost equally as liberals, conservatives, libertarians, and communitarians. The one-fifth of the public that gave liberal responses—favoring government action to promote equality but not to impose order—was exceeded by the one-third of the public that gave conservative responses to promote order. At almost one-quarter of the public, the communitarians, who wanted government to impose both order and equality, just exceeded the libertarians, who wanted government to do neither.

In addition to ideological orientation, many other factors influence the forming of political opinions. When individuals stand to benefit or suffer from proposed government policies, they usually base their opinions of these policies on self-interest. When citizens lack information on which to base their opinions, they usually respond anyway, which leads to substantial fluctuations in poll results, depending on how questions are worded and on intervening events. The various factors that impinge on the process of forming political opinions can be mapped out within an opinion schema, a network of beliefs and attitudes about a particular topic. People tend to organize their schemas according to broader ideological thinking. In the absence of information, respondents are particularly susceptible to cues of support or opposition from political leaders, communicated through the mass media.

Sometimes the public shows clear and settled opinions on government policy, conforming to the majoritarian model. However, public opinion is often not firmly grounded in knowledge and may be unstable on given issues. Moreover, powerful groups often divide on what they want government to do. This lack of consensus leaves politicians with a great deal of latitude in enacting specific policies, a finding that conforms to the pluralist model. Of course, politicians' actions are under close scrutiny by journalists reporting in the mass media.

The mass media transmit information to large, heterogeneous, and widely dispersed audiences through print and broadcasts. The main function of the mass media is entertainment, but the media also perform the political functions of reporting news, interpreting news, influencing citizens' opinions, setting the political agenda, and socializing citizens about politics. The broadcast media operate under technical, ownership, and content regulations imposed by the government, which tend to promote the equal treatment of political contests on radio and television more than in newspapers and news magazines.

Washington, D.C., hosts the biggest press corps in the world, but only a portion of those correspondents concentrate on the presidency. Because Congress is a more decentralized institution, it is covered in a more decentralized manner. All professional journalists recognize rules for citing sources that guide their reporting. What actually gets reported in the media depends on the media's gatekeepers, the publishers and editors.

Although Americans today get more news from television than from newspapers, newspapers usually do a more thorough job of informing the public about politics. Despite heavy exposure to news in the print and electronic media, the ability of most people to retain much political information is shockingly low. The media's most important effect on public opinion is in setting the country's political agenda. The role of the news media may be more important for affecting interactions among attentive policy elites than in influencing public opinion. The media play more subtle, contradictory roles in political socialization, both promoting and undermining certain political and cultural values. Reporters from the national media tend to be more liberal than the public, as judged by their tendency to vote for Democratic candidates and by their own self-descriptions. However, if the media systematically demonstrate pronounced bias in their news reporting, it tends to work against incumbents and front-runners, regardless of their party, rather than a bias in favor of liberal Democrats.

From the standpoint of majoritarian democracy, one of the most important effects of the media is to facilitate communication from the people to the government through the reporting of public opinion polls. The media zealously defend the freedom of the press, even to the point of encouraging disorder by granting extensive publicity to violent protests, terrorist acts, and other threats to order.

Key Terms

public opinion
political socialization
"old" ethnicity
"new" ethnicity
socioeconomic status
self-interest principle
opinion schema
mass media
group media

newsworthiness
Federal Communications Commission
equal opportunities rule
reasonable access rule
gatekeepers
horse race journalism
television hypothesis
political agenda

Selected Readings

Ansolabehere, Stephen, Roy Behr, and Shanto Iyengar. *The Media Game: American Politics in the Television Age.* New York: Macmillan, 1993. This text on the media's influence in politics explores how the media can filter, alter, distort, or even ignore what politicians have to say.

Craig, Stephen C., and Stephen Earl Bennett, eds. *After the Boom: The Politics of Generation X.* Lanham, Md.: Rowman & Littlefield, 1997. People born in the early 1960s constitute "Generation X." Unlike those born during the Depression and World War II, members of Generation X experienced no comparable historical events when they were growing up in the 1970s and 1980s. This book asks whether Generation X exhibits a distinctive profile and finds little evidence for it.

Delli Carpini, Michael X., and Scott Keeter. *What Americans Know About Politics and Why It Matters.* New Haven, Conn.: Yale University Press, 1996. A comprehensive review and analysis of the public's responses to thousands of factual questions about political processes and institutions, public figures, political parties and groups, and public policies.

Kerbel, Matthew Robert. *Remote and Controlled: Media Politics in a Cynical Age.* Boulder, Colo.: Westview Press, 1995. A historical account of political journalism coverage that draws lessons for today.

Page, Benjamin I. *Who Deliberates: Mass Media in Modern Democracy.* Chicago: University of Chicago Press, 1996. Thoughtfully discusses and analyzes how the public "deliberates" through three specific case studies: the war with Iraq, the Los Angeles riots, and the failed nomination of Zoe Baird for U.S. attorney general.

Stimson, James A. *Public Opinion in America: Mood, Cycles, and Swings.* 2d ed. Boulder, Colo.: Westview Press, 1998. The result of a massive study of more than one thousand survey questions from 1956 to 1996, this book charts the drift of public opinion from liberal in the 1950s to conservative at the end of the 1970s and back toward liberal in the 1990s.

Traugott, Michael W., and Paul J. Lavrakas. *The Voter's Guide to Election Polls.* Chatham, N.J.: Chatham House, 1996. A guide for evaluating election polls, including sampling, interviewing, questionnaires, and data analysis. Done in a question-and-answer format.

World Wide Web Resources

Pew Research Center for The People & The Press. "We are an independent opinion research group, sponsored by the Pew Charitable Trusts, that studies attitudes toward the press, politics, and public policy issues."
<www.people-press.org>

The Gallup Organization World Wide Web Server. George Gallup founded his polling organization in the United States in the 1930s, and the Gallup Poll is now an international institution. This site permits searching the *Gallup Newsletter Archives* for press releases of past surveys. You can also retrieve some results from the latest political polls.
<www.gallup.com>

Roper Center for Public Opinion Research. Located at the University of Connecticut, this center was founded by Elmo Roper, a contemporary of George Gallup. This site offers a powerful question-retrieval system, but you will need access to the Lexis/Nexis subscription service to use it. Some colleges subscribe to that service.
<www.lib.uconn.edu/RoperCenter>

ABC News Reports. This site offers text files to view and news reports in Real-Audio format so that you can listen to contemporary news, old news, Peter Jennings's commentary, and more.
<www.abcnews.com>

CNN Interactive. News and video from a media leader.
<www.cnn.com>

PBS Online. This site provides a gateway to various PBS progams, including a button to the "Online NewsHour," a page based on the comprehensive television

evening news program hosted by Jim Lehrer. The page also covers stories in depth, usually involving interviews with key actors in politics.
<www.pbs.org>

New York Times on the Web. Many people consider the nationally distributed *Times* to be as liberal as the *Wall Street Journal* is conservative. You don't have to subscribe, but you do have to register to use this service.
<www.nytimes.com>

5

Participation and Voting

They seemed like ordinary folks. That's how their suburban neighbors regarded the ten men and two women arrested in Phoenix, Arizona, on July 1, 1996. One worked in a doughnut shop. Another worked for the telephone company. Others painted houses or sold office equipment.[1] One had even run for political office (unsuccessfully). But to the arresting federal agents, they were the Viper Militia, a small, secret paramilitary organization charged with plotting to destroy several public buildings. Indeed, the agents found the suspects' homes stocked with an arsenal of weapons—in addition to the 140 guns, there were hand grenades, rocket launchers, gas masks, silencers, and homemade bombs.[2]

Although it may represent the more extreme paramilitary groups in the United States today, the Viper Militia is but one of hundreds of active militia groups that operate throughout the nation. They communicate through group media: newsletters, faxes, and the Internet.[3] One of the most prominent antimilitia sites on the World Wide Web, "The Militia Watchdog," lists scores of militia sites, including home pages for movements in ten states.[4]

Is involvement in a militia a form of political participation, or is it simply a form of recreation—playing war games in the woods? No doubt, some people are attracted to militias for fun and fellowship, but the militia movement also has a distinct political cast. It views the federal government as a threat to personal freedom. Militia members also see conspiracies against freedom coming from the United Nations, the Council of Foreign Relations (an academically oriented institution that publishes *Foreign Affairs*, a respected journal on international politics), and the Trilateral Commission (a group consisting of business, labor, academic, and media leaders from America, Europe, and Japan). These conspiracies are referenced in a militia movement Web site called "Restoring America." The militia movement is deadly serious in its pledges to defend its view of freedom. Its exaltation of weapons is apparent in the "Minuteman Prayer," seen on a militia Web site:

> God grant me the serenity to accept the things I cannot change; the courage to change the things I can; and the superior firepower to make the difference.[5]

Although most people think of political participation primarily in terms of voting, other forms of political activity are more robust than voting. Have militia members exceeded the boundaries of political participation, or are they simply defending freedom, in the tradition of the minutemen of the American Revolution? How politically active are Americans in general? How do they compare with citizens of other countries? How much and what kind of participation is necessary to sustain the pluralist and majoritarian models of democracy?

In this chapter, we try to answer these and other important questions about popular participation in government. We begin by studying participation in democratic government, distinguishing between conventional and unconventional participation. Then we evaluate the nature and extent of both types of participation in American politics. Next, we study the expansion of voting rights and voting as the major mechanism for mass participation in politics. Finally, we examine the extent to which the various forms of political participation serve the values of freedom, equality, and order and the majoritarian and pluralist models of democracy.

Democracy and Political Participation

Government ought to be run by the people. That is the democratic ideal in a nutshell. But how much and what kind of citizen participation are necessary for democratic government? Champions of direct democracy believe that if citizens do not participate directly in government affairs, making government decisions among themselves, they should give up all pretense of living in a democracy. More practical observers contend that people can govern indirectly through their elected representatives. And they maintain that choosing leaders through elections—formal procedures for voting—is the only workable approach to democracy in a large, complex nation.

Elections are a necessary condition of democracy, but they do not guarantee democratic government. Before the collapse of communism, the former Soviet Union regularly held elections in which more than 90 percent of the electorate turned out to vote, but it certainly did not function as a democracy, because there was only one party. Both the majoritarian and the pluralist models of democracy rely on voting to varying degrees, but both models expect citizens to participate in politics in other ways. For example, they expect citizens to discuss politics, to form interest groups, to contact public officials, to campaign for political parties, to run for office, and even to protest government decisions.

We define **political participation** as "those actions of private citizens by which they seek to influence or to support government and politics."[6] This definition embraces both conventional and unconventional forms of political participation. **Conventional participation** is relatively routine behavior that uses the established institutions of representative government, especially campaigning for candidates and voting in elections. **Unconventional participation**

Things Change
As a nineteen-year-old student at Cornell University, Tom Jones led an armed takeover of the administration building during campus protests against the Vietnam War and for black power in the spring of 1969. Now he is Thomas W. Jones, in his late forties and president and chief executive officer of TIAA-CREF, the college teachers' retirement fund, the world's biggest private pension fund ($115 billion). He is also a member of Cornell's board of trustees. He told the New York Times *that he "made the best decisions I could make under the circumstances, and I will not repudiate that twenty-five years later," but he does regret the incident for its potential for violence. Things change.*

is relatively uncommon behavior that challenges or defies established institutions or the dominant culture (and thus is personally stressful to participants and their opponents).

Voting and writing letters to public officials are examples of conventional political participation; staging sit-down strikes in public buildings and chanting slogans outside officials' windows are examples of unconventional participation. Certainly training with the militia is unconventional; the question is whether the activity is political or not. Experts contend that group participation is often a politicizing experience, developing skills in the individual that transfer to politics.[7] Political demonstrations can be conventional (carrying signs outside an abortion clinic) or unconventional (linking arms to prevent entrance). Various forms of unconventional participation are used by powerless groups to gain political benefits while still working within the system.[8] Militia groups, however, blatantly reject the system. Voting and other methods of conventional participation are important to democratic government. So are unconventional forms of participation. Let us look at both kinds of political participation in the United States.

L.A. Riots, 1992
*At the extremes of unconventional political behavior are activities in which individuals with
a group consciousness protest political actions through personal violence and the destruction
of property. In at least some respects the 1992 riots in Los Angeles can be viewed as such
behavior. In this photo two L.A. residents view the immediate results of that violence. Its
long-term political results are yet to be determined.*

Unconventional Participation

On Sunday, March 7, 1965, a group of about six hundred people attempted to
march 50 miles from Selma, Alabama, to the state capital at Montgomery. The
marchers were demonstrating in favor of voting rights for blacks. At the time,
Selma had fewer than five hundred registered black voters, out of fifteen thousand who were eligible.[9] Alabama governor George Wallace declared the
march illegal and sent state troopers to stop it. The two groups met at the
Edmund Pettus Bridge over the Alabama River at the edge of Selma. The
peaceful marchers were disrupted and beaten by state troopers and deputy
sheriffs—some on horseback—using clubs, bullwhips, and tear gas. The day
became known as Bloody Sunday.

The march from Selma was a form of unconventional political participation. Marching 50 miles in a political protest is certainly not common; moreover, the march challenged the existing institutions that prevented blacks
from participating conventionally—voting in elections—for many decades. In
contrast to some later demonstrations against the Vietnam War, this civil
rights march posed no threat of violence. The brutal response to the marchers

helped the rest of the nation understand the seriousness of the civil rights problem in the South. Unconventional participation is stressful and occasionally violent, but sometimes it is worth the risk.

Support for Unconventional Participation

Unconventional political participation has a long history in the United States. The Boston Tea Party of 1773 was the first in a long line of violent protests against British rule that eventually led to revolution. Yet we know less about unconventional political participation than about conventional participation. The reasons are twofold. First, it is easier to collect data on conventional practices, so they are studied more frequently. Second, political scientists are biased toward institutionalized, or conventional, politics. In fact, some basic works on political participation explicitly exclude any behavior that is "outside the system."[10]

One major study of unconventional political action asked people whether they had engaged in or approved of ten types of political participation outside of voting.[11] Of the five activities shown in Figure 5.1, only signing petitions is clearly regarded as conventional, in the sense that the behavior is widely practiced. The conventionality of two other forms of behavior—lawful demonstrations and boycotts—is questionable. The other two political activities listed in Figure 5.1 are clearly unconventional. In fact, when political activities interfere with people's daily lives (occupying buildings, for example), disapproval is nearly universal.

Americans usually disapprove of unconventional political behavior. When protesters demonstrating against the Vietnam War disrupted the 1968 Democratic national convention in Chicago, they were clubbed by the city's police. Although the national television audience saw graphic footage of the confrontations, most viewers condemned the demonstrators, not the police.

The Effectiveness of Unconventional Participation

Vociferous antiabortion protests discourage many doctors from performing abortions but have not led to the outlawing of abortion. Does unconventional participation ever work (even when it provokes violence)? Yes. Antiwar protesters helped convince President Lyndon Johnson not to seek reelection in 1968, and they heightened public concern over U.S. participation in the Vietnam War. The unconventional activities of civil rights workers also produced notable successes. Dr. Martin Luther King, Jr., led the 1955 Montgomery bus boycott that sparked the civil rights movement. He used **direct action** to challenge specific cases of discrimination, assembling crowds to confront businesses and local governments and demanding equal treatment in public accommodations and government.

Denied the usual opportunities for conventional political participation, members of minorities used unconventional politics to pressure Congress to pass a series of civil rights laws in 1957, 1960, 1964, and 1968—each one in

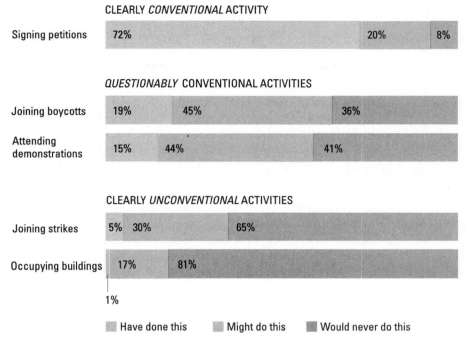

CLEARLY *CONVENTIONAL* ACTIVITY

Signing petitions 72%   20%   8%

QUESTIONABLY CONVENTIONAL ACTIVITIES

Joining boycotts 19%   45%   36%

Attending demonstrations 15%   44%   41%

CLEARLY *UNCONVENTIONAL* ACTIVITIES

Joining strikes 5% 30%   65%

Occupying buildings 17%   81%

1%

Have done this   Might do this   Would never do this

FIGURE 5.1   What Americans Think Is Unconventional Political Behavior
A survey presented Americans with five different forms of political participation outside the electoral process and asked whether they "have done," "might do," or "would never do" any of them. The respondents disapproved of two forms overwhelmingly. Only signing petitions was widely done and rarely ruled out. Even attending demonstrations (a right guaranteed in the Constitution) was disapproved of by 44 percent of the respondents. Boycotting products was less objectionable and more widely practiced. According to this test, attending demonstrations and boycotting products are only marginally conventional forms of political participation. Joining strikes and occupying buildings are clearly unconventional activities for most Americans. (Source: 1990–91 World Values Survey. Data for the United States are available from the Inter-University Consortium for Political and Social Research. The weighted sample size was 1,837.)

some way extending federal protection against discrimination by reason of race, color, religion, or national origin. The 1964 act also prohibited discrimination in employment on the basis of sex. In addition, the Voting Rights Act of 1965 put state electoral procedures under federal supervision, increasing the registration of black voters and the rate of black voter turnout (especially in the South). The civil rights movement shows that social change can occur, even when it is violently opposed at first.

Although direct political action and the politics of confrontation can work, using them takes a special kind of commitment. Studies show that direct action appeals most to those who both (1) distrust the political system and (2) have a strong sense of political efficacy—the feeling that they can do some-thing to affect political decisions.[12] Whether this combination of attitudes pro-duces behavior that challenges the system depends on the extent of organized group activity.[13] The decision to use unconventional behavior also depends on the extent to which individuals develop group consciousness—identification with their group and awareness of its position in society, its objectives, and its intended course of action.[14] These characteristics were present among blacks and young people in the mid-1960s and are strongly present today among blacks and to a lesser degree among women.

Unconventional Participation in America

Although most Americans may disapprove of using certain forms of participa-tion to protest government policies, U.S. citizens are about as likely to take di-rect action in politics as citizens in European democracies. Surveys in Britain, Germany, and France in 1981 found that Americans claim to have participated as much or more than British, German, and French citizens in unconventional actions, such as demonstrations, boycotts, strikes, and occupying buildings.[15] Contrary to the popular view that Americans are apathetic about politics, they are more likely to engage in political protests of various sorts than citizens in other democratic countries.[16]

Is something wrong with our political system if citizens resort to unconven-tional—and widely disapproved—methods of political participation? To an-swer this question, we must first learn how much Americans use conventional methods of participation.

Conventional Participation

A practical test of the democratic nature of any government is whether citizens can affect its policies by acting through its institutions—meeting with public officials, supporting candidates, voting in elections. Citizens should not have to risk their life and property to participate in politics, and they should not have to take direct action to force the government to hear their views. The objective of democratic institutions is to make political participation conven-tional—to allow ordinary citizens to engage in relatively routine, nonthreaten-ing behavior to get the government to heed their opinions, interests, and needs.

In a democracy, a group gathering at a statehouse or city hall to dramatize its position on an issue—say a tax increase—is not unusual. Such a demonstra-tion is a form of conventional participation. The group is not powerless, and its members are not risking their personal safety. But violence can erupt be-tween opposing groups. Circumstances, then, often determine whether orga-nized protest is or is not conventional. Conventional political behaviors fall into two major categories: actions that show support for government policies and those that try to change or *influence* policies.

Supportive Behavior

Supportive behaviors are actions that express allegiance to country and government. When we recite the Pledge of Allegiance or fly the American flag on holidays, we are showing support for the country and, by implication, its political system. Such ceremonial activities usually demand little initiative by citizens. The simple act of turning out to vote is in itself a show of support for the political system. Other supportive behaviors—serving as an election judge in a nonpartisan election or organizing a holiday parade—demand greater initiative.

At times, perceptions of patriotism move people across the line from conventional to unconventional behavior. In their eagerness to support the American system, they break up a meeting or disrupt a rally of a group they believe is radical or somehow "un-American." Radical groups may threaten the political system with wrenching change, but superpatriots pose their own threat. Their misguided excess of allegiance denies nonviolent means of dissent to others. [17]

Influencing Behavior

Citizens use **influencing behaviors** to modify or even reverse government policy to serve political interests. Some forms of influencing behavior seek particular benefits from government; other forms have broad policy objectives.

Particular Benefits   Some citizens try to influence government to obtain benefits for themselves, their immediate families, or their close friends. Serving one's self-interest through the voting process is certainly acceptable in democratic theory. Each individual has only one vote, and no single voter can wangle particular benefits from government through voting unless a majority of the voters agree.

Political actions that require considerable knowledge and initiative are another story. Individuals or small groups who influence government officials to advance their self-interest may secretly benefit without others knowing. Those who quietly obtain particular benefits from government pose a serious challenge to a democracy. Pluralist theory holds that groups ought to be able to make government respond to their special problems and needs. Majoritarian theory holds that government should not do what a majority does not want it to do. A majority of citizens might very well not want the government to do what any particular person or group seeks—if it is costly to other citizens.

What might individual citizens or groups ask of their government, and how might they go about asking for it? Some citizens ask for special services from their local government. Such requests may range from contacting the city forestry department to remove a dead tree in front of a house to calling the county animal control center to deal with a vicious dog in the neighborhood. Studies of such "contacting" behavior find that it tends not to be empirically related to other forms of political activity. Contacting behavior is related to socioeconomic status: people of higher socioeconomic status are more likely to contact public officials.[18]

Americans demand much more of their local government than of the national government. Although many people value self-reliance and individualism in national politics, most people expect local government to solve a wide range of social problems. A study of residents of Kansas City, Missouri, found that more than 90 percent thought it was the city's responsibility to provide services in thirteen areas, including maintaining parks, setting standards for new home construction, demolishing vacant and unsafe buildings, ensuring that property owners clean up trash and weeds, and providing bus service. The researcher noted that "it is difficult to imagine a set of federal government activities about which there would [be] more consensus."[19]

Citizens can also mobilize against a project. The 1980s saw the emergence of the "not-in-my-back-yard," or NIMBY, phenomenon, as citizens pressured local officials to stop undesired projects from being located near their homes. Contributing money to a candidate's campaign is another form of influencing behavior. Here, too, the objective can be particular or broad benefits.

Several points emerge from this review of "particularized" forms of political participation. First, approaching government to serve one's particular interests is consistent with democratic theory, because it encourages input from an active citizenry. Second, particularized contact may be a form of participation unto itself, not necessarily related to other forms of participation. Third, such participation tends to be used more by citizens who are advantaged in knowledge and resources. Fourth, particularized participation may serve private interests to the detriment of the majority.

Broad Policy Objectives   We come now to what many scholars have in mind when they talk about political participation: activities that influence the selection of government personnel and policies. Here, too, we find behaviors that require little initiative (such as voting) and behaviors that require high initiative (attending political meetings, persuading others how to vote). Later in this chapter, we focus on elections as a mechanism for participation. For now, we simply note that voting to influence policy is usually a low-initiative activity. It actually requires more initiative to *register* to vote in the United States than to cast a vote on election day.

Other types of participation to affect broad policies require high initiative. Running for office requires the most (see Chapter 6). Some high-initiative activities, such as attending party meetings and working in campaigns, are associated with the electoral process; others, such as attending legislative hearings and writing letters to Congress, are not. Studies of citizen contacts in the United States show that about two-thirds deal with broad social issues and only one-third are for private gain.[20]

Few people realize that using the court system is a form of political participation, a way for citizens to press for their rights in a democratic society. Although most people use the courts to serve their particular interests, some also use them, as we discuss shortly, to meet broad objectives. Going to court demands high personal initiative.[21] It also requires knowledge of the law or the financial resources to afford a lawyer.

People use the courts for both personal benefit and broad policy objectives. A person or group can bring **class action suits** on behalf of other people in similar circumstances. Lawyers for the National Association for the Advancement of Colored People pioneered this form of litigation in the famous school desegregation case *Brown v. Board of Education* (1954).[22] They succeeded in getting the Supreme Court to outlaw segregation in public schools, not just for Linda Brown, who brought the suit in Topeka, Kansas, but for all others "similarly situated"—that is, for all other black students who wanted to attend desegregated schools. This form of participation has proved to be effective for organized groups, especially those who have been unable to gain their objectives through Congress or the executive branch.

Individual citizens can also try to influence policies at the national level by direct participation in the legislative process. One way is to attend congressional hearings, which are open to the public and occasionally held outside Washington. To facilitate citizen involvement, national government agencies are required to publish all proposed and approved regulations in the daily *Federal Register* and to make government documents available to citizens on request.

Conventional Participation in America

How often do Americans contact government officials and engage in other forms of conventional political participation, compared with citizens in other countries? The most common political behavior reported in a study of five countries was voting to choose candidates. Americans are less likely to vote than citizens in the other four countries studied. But Americans are as likely (or substantially more likely) to engage in all other forms of conventional political participation. As we have seen, the same pattern holds true for unconventional behaviors. Americans, then, are more likely to engage in nearly all forms of unconventional and conventional political participation, except voting.

Other researchers have noted this paradox and written: "If, for example, we concentrate our attention on national elections we will find that the United States is the least participatory of [all] five nations." But looking at the other indicators, they found that "political apathy, by a wide margin, is lowest in the United States. Interestingly, the high levels of overall involvement reflect a rather balanced contribution of both . . . conventional and unconventional politics."[23] Clearly, low voter turnout in the United States constitutes a puzzle, to which we will return.

Participating Through Voting

The heart of democratic government lies in the electoral process. Whether a country holds elections—and if so, what kind—constitutes the critical difference between democratic and nondemocratic government. Elections institutionalize mass participation in democratic government according to the three normative principles of procedural democracy discussed in Chapter 1: electoral rules specify *who* is allowed to vote, *how much* each person's vote counts, and *how many* votes are needed to win.

 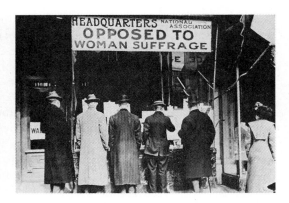

The Fight for Women's Suffrage . . . and Against It
During World War I, militant suffragettes, demanding that President Wilson reverse his opposition to a federal suffrage amendment, stood vigil at the White House and carried banners such as this one comparing the president to Kaiser Wilhelm II of Germany. In the heated patriotic climate of wartime, such tactics met with hostility and sometimes violence and arrests. Suffragettes' gatherings were occasionally disrupted by men—and other women—who opposed extending the right to vote to women.

Again, elections are formal procedures for making group decisions. *Voting* is the act individuals engage in when they choose among alternatives in an election. **Suffrage** and the **franchise** both mean the right to vote. By formalizing political participation through rules for suffrage and for counting ballots, electoral systems allow large numbers of people, who individually have little political power, to wield great power. Electoral systems decide collectively who governs and, in some instances, what government should do. The simple fact of holding elections is less important than the specific rules and circumstances that govern voting. According to democratic theory, everyone should be able to vote. In practice, however, no nation grants universal suffrage. All countries have age requirements for voting, and all disqualify some inhabitants on various grounds: lack of citizenship, criminal record, mental incompetence, and so forth. What is the record of enfranchisement in the United States?

Expansion of Suffrage

The United States was the first country to provide for general elections of representatives through "mass" suffrage, but the franchise was far from universal. When the Constitution was framed, the idea of full adult suffrage was too radical to consider seriously. Instead, the framers left the issue of enfranchisement to the states, stipulating only that individuals who could vote for "the most numerous Branch of the State Legislature" could also vote for their representatives to the U.S. Congress (Article I, Section 2).

Initially, most states established taxpaying or property-holding requirements for voting. Virginia, for example, required ownership of twenty-five acres of settled land or five hundred acres of unsettled land. The original thirteen states began to lift such requirements after 1800. Expansion of the franchise accelerated after 1815 with the admission of new "western" states (Indiana, Illinois, Alabama), where land was more plentiful and widely owned. By the 1850s, the states had eliminated nearly all taxpaying and property-holding requirements, thus allowing the working class—at least its white male members—to vote. Extending the vote to blacks and women took more time.

The Enfranchisement of Blacks The Fifteenth Amendment, adopted shortly after the Civil War, prohibited the states from denying the right to vote "on account of race, color, or previous condition of servitude." However, the states of the old Confederacy worked around the amendment by reestablishing old voting requirements (poll taxes, literacy tests) that worked primarily against blacks. Because the amendment said nothing about voting rights in private organizations, these states denied blacks the right to vote in the "private" Democratic *primary* elections held to choose the party's candidates for the general election. Because the Democratic Party came to dominate politics in the South, the "white primary" effectively disenfranchised blacks despite the Fifteenth Amendment. Also, in many areas of the South, the threat of violence kept blacks from the polls.

The extension of full voting rights to blacks came in two phases, separated by twenty years. In 1944, the Supreme Court decided in *Smith v. Allwright* that laws preventing blacks from voting in primary elections were unconstitutional, holding that party primaries are part of the continuous process of electing public officials.[24] The Voting Rights Act of 1965, which followed Selma's Bloody Sunday by less than five months, suspended discriminatory voting tests. It also authorized federal registrars to register voters in seven southern states, where less than half of the voting-age population had registered to vote in the 1964 election. For good measure, in 1966 the Supreme Court ruled in *Harper v. Virginia State Board of Elections* that state poll taxes are unconstitutional.[25] Although long in coming, these actions by the national government to enforce political equality within the states dramatically increased the registration of southern blacks.

The Enfranchisement of Women Women also had to fight long and hard to win the right to vote. Until 1869, women could not vote anywhere—in the United States or in the rest of the world.[26] Women began to organize to obtain suffrage in the mid-1800s. Known then as *suffragettes,** the early feminists initially had a limited effect on politics. Their first major victory did not come until 1869, when Wyoming, while still a territory, granted women the right to vote. No state followed suit until 1893, when Colorado enfranchised women.

Between 1896 and 1918, twelve other states gave women the vote. Most of these states were in the West, where pioneer women often departed from

---

*The term *suffragist* applied to a person of either sex who advocated extending the vote to women; *suffragette* was reserved primarily for women who did so militantly.

traditional women's roles. Nationally, the women's suffrage movement intensified, often resorting to unconventional political behaviors (marches, demonstrations), which occasionally invited violent attacks from men and even other women. In 1919, Congress finally passed the Nineteenth Amendment, which prohibits states from denying the right to vote "on account of sex." The amendment was ratified in 1920, in time for the November election.

Evaluating the Expansion of Suffrage in America   The last major expansion of suffrage in the United States took place in 1971, when the Twenty-sixth Amendment lowered the voting age to eighteen. For most of its history, the United States has been far from the democratic ideal of universal suffrage. However, compared with other countries, the United States looks pretty democratic.[27] Women did not gain the vote on equal terms with men until 1921 in Norway; 1922 in the Netherlands; 1944 in France; 1946 in Italy, Japan, and Venezuela; 1948 in Belgium; and 1971 in Switzerland. Comparing the enfranchisement of minority racial groups is difficult because most other democratic nations do not have a comparable racial makeup. We should note, however, that the indigenous Maori population in New Zealand won suffrage in 1867, but the aborigines in Australia were not fully enfranchised until 1961. And blacks in South Africa were not allowed to vote freely in elections until 1994. With regard to voting age, nineteen of twenty-seven countries that allow free elections also have a minimum voting age of eighteen. None has a lower age.

Voting on Policies

Disenfranchised groups have struggled to gain voting rights because of the political power that comes with suffrage. Belief in the ability of ordinary citizens to make political decisions and to control government through the power of the ballot box was strongest in the United States during the Progressive era, which began around 1900 and lasted until about 1925. **Progressivism** was a philosophy of political reform that trusted the goodness and wisdom of individual citizens and distrusted "special interests" (railroads, corporations) and political institutions (traditional political parties, legislatures). Such attitudes resurfaced among followers of H. Ross Perot and others who share this populist outlook.

The leaders of the Progressive movement were prominent politicians (former president Theodore Roosevelt, Senator Robert La Follette of Wisconsin) and eminent scholars (historian Frederick Jackson Turner, philosopher John Dewey). Not content to vote for candidates chosen by party leaders, the Progressives championed the **direct primary**—a preliminary election, run by the state governments, in which the voters chose the party's candidates for the general election. Wanting a mechanism to remove elected candidates from office, the Progressives backed the **recall**—a special election initiated by a petition signed by a specified number of voters.

The Progressives also championed the power of the masses to propose and pass laws, approximating the citizen participation in policymaking that is the hallmark of direct democracy. They developed two voting mechanisms for policymaking that are still in use:

- A **referendum** is a direct vote by the people either on a proposed law or on an amendment to a state constitution. The measures subject to popular vote are known as *propositions*. About twenty-five states permit popular referenda on laws, and all but Alabama require a referendum for a constitutional amendment. Most referenda are placed on the ballot by legislatures, not voters.

- The **initiative** is a procedure by which voters can propose an issue to be decided by the legislature or by the people in a referendum. The procedure involves gathering a specified number of signatures from registered voters (usually 5 to 10 percent of the total in the state), then submitting the petition to a designated state agency. About twenty states currently provide for some form of voter initiative.

Over 350 propositions appeared on state ballots in general elections during the 1990s, although fewer than 50 got there by means of initiatives.[28]

What conclusion can we draw about the Progressives' legacy of mechanisms for direct participation in government? One scholar who studied the use of the initiative and referendum paints an unimpressive picture. He notes that an expensive "industry" developed in the 1980s that makes money circulating petitions, then managing the large sums of money needed to run a campaign to approve (or defeat) a referendum.[29]

In 1990, various industries conducted a $10 million campaign to defeat "Big Green," a sweeping California environmental initiative that would have imposed restrictions on offshore drilling, pesticide use, and air pollutants.[30] The money required to mount a statewide campaign has increased the involvement of special interest groups in referendum politics. Moreover, most voters confess they do not know enough about most ballot propositions to vote intelligently on them. One of California's fifteen referenda in the 1996 general election dealt with securities fraud, a technical financial matter beyond most voters' understanding. Because it allowed stockholders to claim fraud and sue corporate officers, under certain conditions, following wide swings in the value of their stocks, the stakes were high. Expenditures on this single campaign were a record-breaking $50 million, with most spent by the proposal's major opponents: a group of securities lawyers, joined by consumer groups. They managed to erase the initial support for the proposition and produce a resounding defeat of the measure.[31]

Clearly, citizens can exercise great power over government policy through the mechanisms of the initiative and referendum. What is not clear is whether these forms of direct democracy improve on the policies made by representatives elected for that purpose.

Voting for Candidates

We saved for last the most visible form of political participation: voting to choose candidates for public office. Voting for candidates serves democratic government in two ways. First, citizens can choose the candidates they think will best serve their interests. Second, voting allows the people to reelect the officials they guessed right about and to kick out those they guessed wrong about. In Chapter 6, we look at the factors that underlie voting choice. Here, we examine Americans' reliance on the electoral process.

In national politics, voters seem content to elect just two executive officers—the president and vice president—and to trust the president to appoint a cabinet to round out his administration. But at the state and local levels, voters insist on selecting all kinds of officials. Every state elects a governor (and forty-two elect a lieutenant governor). Forty states elect an attorney general; thirty-five, a treasurer and a secretary of state; twenty-three, an auditor. The list goes on, down through the superintendent of education, secretary of agriculture, controller, board of education, and public utilities commissioners.[32] Elected county officials commonly include commissioners, a sheriff, a treasurer, a clerk, a superintendent of schools, and a judge (often several). At the local level, voters elect all but about 600 of 15,300 school boards across the nation.[33] Instead of trusting state and local chief executives to appoint lesser administrators (as we do for more important offices at the national level), we expect voters to choose intelligently among scores of candidates they meet for the first time on a complex ballot in the polling booth.

In the American version of democracy, the laws recognize no limit to voters' ability to make informed choices among candidates and thus to control government through voting. The reasoning seems to be that elections are good; therefore, more elections are better, and the most elections are best. By this thinking, the United States clearly has the best and most democratic government in the world because it is the undisputed champion at holding elections. The author of a study that compared elections in the United States with elections in twenty-six other democracies concluded:

> No country can approach the United States in the frequency and variety of elections, and thus in the amount of electoral participation to which its citizens have a right. No other country elects its lower house as often as every two years, or its president as frequently as every four years. No other country popularly elects its state governors and town mayors; no other has as wide a variety of nonrepresentative offices (judges, sheriffs, attorneys general, city treasurers, and so on) subject to election. . . . The average American is entitled to do far more electing—probably by a factor of three or four—than the citizen of any other democracy.[34]

However, we learn from Compared with What? 5.1 that the United States ranks at the bottom of twenty-seven countries in voter turnout! How do we square low voter turnout with Americans' devotion to elections as an instrument of democratic government? To complicate matters further, how do we square low voter turnout with the findings we mentioned earlier, which establish the United States as the leader among five Western democratic nations in both conventional and unconventional political participation, except for voting? Americans seem to participate at high levels in everything except elections.

Compared with What? 5.1

Voter Turnout in Democratic Nations, 1975–1995

Americans participate as much as or more than citizens of other nations in all forms of conventional political behavior except voting. Voter turnout in American presidential elections ranks at the bottom of voting rates for twenty-seven countries with competitive elections. As discussed in the text, the facts are correct, but the comparison is not as damning as it appears.

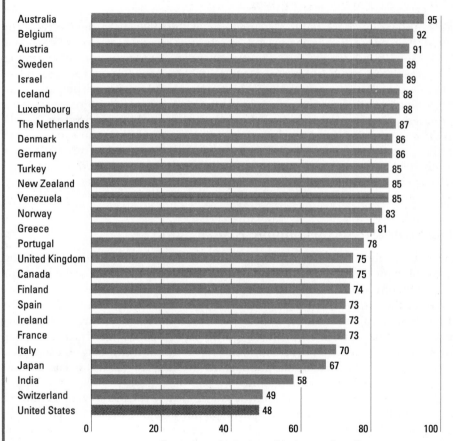

Percentage of voter turnout in democratic nations

Sources: Inter-Parliamentary Union, *Chronicle of Parliamentary Elections and Developments,* Vols. X–XXIX (Geneva: 1975–1995); U.S. Bureau of the Census, Current Population Reports, P20-453 and P20-466, *Voting and Registration in the Election of 1990 [and 1992]* (Washington, D.C.: U.S. Government Printing Office, 1991 [and 1993]), pp. viii, 10. The U.S. data are for all elections from 1976 to 1992, both presidential and nonpresidential election years. The graph shows the percentage of respondents who *said* they voted, which is usually higher than the actual voting turnout.

Explaining Political Participation

As you have seen, political participation can be unconventional or conventional, can require little or much initiative, and can serve to support the government or influence its decisions. This section begins our examination of some factors that affect the most obvious forms of political participation, with particular emphasis on voting. Our first task is to determine how much variation there is in patterns of participation within the United States over time.

Patterns of Participation over Time

Were Americans more politically apathetic in the 1990s than they were in the 1960s? The answer lies in Figure 5.2, which plots several measures of participation from 1952 through 1996. The graph shows a steady pattern of participation over the years (with upward spurts in 1992 because Ross Perot's candidacy added a new dimension to the presidential race). Otherwise, participation varied little across time in the percentage of citizens who worked for candidates, attended party meetings, and tried to persuade people how to vote. *The only line that shows a downward trend is voting in elections.* Not only is voter turnout low in the United States compared with that in other countries, but turnout has basically declined over time. Moreover, while voting has decreased, other forms of participation have remained stable or even increased. What is going on? Who votes? Who does not? Why? And does it really matter?

The Standard Socioeconomic Explanation

Researchers have found that socioeconomic status is a good indicator of most types of conventional political participation. People with more education, higher incomes, and white-collar or professional occupations tend to be more aware of the impact of politics on their lives, to know what can be done to influence government actions, and to have the necessary resources (time and money) to take action. So they are more likely to participate in politics than are people of lower socioeconomic status. This relationship between socioeconomic status and conventional political involvement is called the **standard socioeconomic model** of participation.[35]

Unconventional political behavior is less clearly related to socioeconomic status. Studies of unconventional participation in other countries have found that protest behavior is related to low socioeconomic status and especially to youth.[36] However, scattered studies of unconventional participation in the United States have found that protesters (especially blacks) are often higher in socioeconomic status than those who do not join in protests.[37]

Obviously, socioeconomic status does not account for all the differences in the ways people choose to participate in politics, even for conventional participation. Another important variable is age. As just noted, young people are more likely to take part in political protests, but they are less likely to participate in conventional politics. Voting rates tend to increase as people grow older until about age sixty-five, when physical infirmities begin to lower rates again.[38]

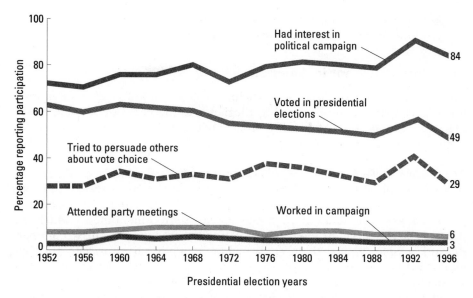

FIGURE 5.2 *Electoral Participation in the United States over Time*
Participation patterns from five decades show that in the 1980s Americans participated in
election campaigns about as much as or more than they did in the 1950s on every indicator
except voting. The turnout rate dropped more than ten percentage points from 1952 to
1996. The decline runs counter to the rise in educational level, a puzzle that is discussed in
the text. (*Source: Reprinted by permission of the publishers from* American National Election
Studies Data Sourcebook, 1952–1978, *Warren E. Miller, Arthur H. Miller, and Edward J.*
Schneider. (Cambridge, Mass.: Harvard University Press). Copyright © 1980 by the President and
Fellows of Harvard College. Data after 1978 comes from subsequent National Election Studies.)

Two other variables—race and gender—have been related to participation in the past, but as times have changed, so have those relationships.
Blacks, who had very low participation rates in the 1950s, now participate at
rates comparable to whites' rates, when differences in socioeconomic status
are taken into account.[39] Women also exhibited low participation rates in
the past, but gender differences in political participation have almost disappeared.[40] (The one exception is in attempting to persuade others how to
vote, which women are less likely to do than men.)[41] Recent research on
the social context of voting behavior has shown that married men and
women are more likely to vote than those of either sex living without a
spouse.[42]

Of all the social and economic variables, education is the strongest single
factor in explaining most types of conventional political participation.[43] The
strong link between education and electoral participation raises questions
about low voter turnout in the United States both over time and relative to
other democracies. The fact is that the proportion of individuals with college
degrees is greater in the United States than in other countries. Moreover, that

proportion has been increasing steadily. Why, then, is voter turnout in elections so low? And why has it dropped over time?

Low Voter Turnout in America

Voting is a low-initiative form of participation that can satisfy all three motives for political participation—showing allegiance to the nation, obtaining particularized benefits, and influencing broad policy. How then do we explain the decline in voter turnout in the United States?

The Decline in Voting over Time   The graph of voter turnout in Figure 5.3 shows that one of the sharpest drops in turnout took place between the 1968 and 1972 elections. It was during this period (in 1971, actually) that Congress proposed and the states ratified the Twenty-sixth Amendment, which expanded the electorate by lowering the voting age from twenty-one to eighteen. Because people younger than twenty-one are much less likely to vote, their eligibility actually reduced the overall national turnout rate (the percentage of those eligible to vote who actually vote). Some observers estimate that the enfranchisement of eighteen-year-olds accounts for about one or two percentage points in the total decline in turnout since 1952, but that still leaves more than ten percentage points to be explained.[44]

Why has voter turnout declined since 1968, while the level of education has increased? Many researchers have tried to solve this puzzle.[45] Some attribute most of the decline to changes in voters' attitudes toward politics. One major factor is the growing belief that government is not responsive to citizens and that voting does no good. Another is a change in attitude toward political parties, along with a decline in the extent and strength of party identification.[46]

U.S. Turnout Versus Turnout in Other Countries   Scholars cite two factors to explain the low voter turnout in the United States compared with that in other countries. First are the differences in voting laws and administrative machinery.[47] In a few countries, voting is compulsory, and, obviously, turnout is extremely high. But other methods can encourage voting—declaring election days to be public holidays, providing a two-day voting period, making it easy to cast absentee ballots. The United States does none of these things.

Furthermore, nearly every other democratic country places the burden of registration on the government rather than on the individual voter. This is important. Voting in the United States is a two-stage process, and the first stage (going to the proper officials to register) requires more initiative than the second stage (going to the polling booth to cast a ballot). In most American states, the registration process is separated from the voting process in both time (usually voters have to register weeks in advance of the election) and geography (often voters have to register at the county courthouse, not the polling place). Moreover, registration procedures often have been obscure, requiring potential voters to call around to find out what to do. Furthermore, people who move (roughly one-third of the U.S. population moves between

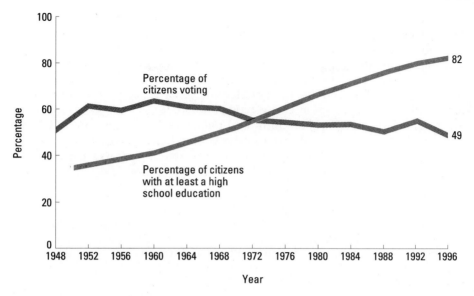

FIGURE 5.3   *The Decline of Voter Turnout: An Unsolved Puzzle*
Level of education is one of the strongest predictors of a person's likelihood of voting in the United States, and the percentage of citizens older than twenty-five with a high school education or more has grown steadily since the end of World War II. Nevertheless, the overall rate of voter turnout has gone down almost steadily in presidential elections since 1960. The phenomenon is recognized as an unsolved puzzle in American voting behavior. (Sources: "Percentage voting" data up to 1988 come from Michael Nelson, ed., Congressional Quarterly's Guide to the Presidency *(Washington, D.C.: Congressional Quarterly, Inc., 1989), p. 170; data since 1988 come from U.S. Bureau of the Census,* Statistical Abstract of the United States, 1997 *(Washington, D.C.: U.S. Government Printing Office, 1997), pp. 289 and 159.)*

presidential elections) have had to reregister. If we compute voter turnout on the basis of those who are registered to vote, about 87 percent of Americans vote—a figure that moves the United States to the middle (but not the top) of all democratic nations.[48] It will take time to assess the impact on registration of the so-called motor-voter law, which, since 1995, has required states to allow citizens to register by mail (similar to renewing drivers' licenses) and at certain agencies that provide public assistance.[49] However, initial indications were not encouraging. A Federal Election Commission study comparing voter registration and turnout for the 1992 and 1996 elections found that, although voter registration was indeed higher in 1996, voter turnout declined from 55 percent to 49 percent of those eligible to vote.[50]

The second factor usually cited to explain low turnout in American elections is the lack of political parties that mobilize the vote of particular social groups, especially lower-income and less-educated people. American parties do make an effort to get out the vote, but neither party is as closely linked to specific groups as are parties in many other countries, where certain parties work hand in hand with ethnic, occupational, or religious groups. Research shows that strong party-group links can significantly increase turnout.[51]

To these explanations for low voter turnout in the United States—the traditional burden of registration and the lack of strong party-group links—we add another. Although the act of voting requires low initiative, the process of learning about the scores of candidates on the ballot in American elections requires a great deal of initiative. Some people undoubtedly fail to vote simply because they feel inadequate to the task of deciding among candidates for the many offices on the ballot in U.S. elections.

Teachers, newspaper columnists, and public affairs groups tend to worry a great deal about low voter turnout in the United States, suggesting that it signifies some sort of political sickness—or at least that it gives us a bad mark for democracy. Others are less concerned.[52] One scholar argues:

> Turnout rates do not indicate the amount of electing—the frequency of occasion, the range of offices and decisions, the "value" of the vote—to which a country's citizens are entitled. . . . Thus, although the turnout rate in the United States is below that of most other democracies, American citizens do not necessarily do less voting than other citizens; most probably, they do more.[53]

Participation and Freedom, Equality, and Order

As we have seen, Americans do participate in government in a variety of ways, and to a reasonable extent, compared with citizens of other countries. What is the relationship of political participation to the values of freedom, equality, and order?

Participation and Freedom

From the standpoint of normative theory, the relationship between participation and freedom is clear. Individuals should be free to participate in government and politics in the way they want and as much as they want. And they should be free not to participate as well. Ideally, all barriers to participation (such as restrictive voting registration and limitations on campaign expenditures) should be abolished—as should any schemes for compulsory voting. In theory, freedom to participate also means that individuals should be able to use their wealth, connections, knowledge, organizational power (including sheer numbers in organized protests), or any other resource to influence government decisions, provided they do so legally. Of all these resources, the individual vote may be the weakest—and the least important—means of exerting political influence. Obviously, then, freedom as a value in political participation favors those with the resources to advance their own political self-interest.

Participation and Equality

The relationship between participation and equality is also clear. Each citizen's ability to influence government should be equal to that of every other

America's Largest Civil Rights Demonstrations
Nation of Islam minister Louis Farrakhan called for a "Million Man March" in Washington, on October 16, 1995, to show that black men were ready to accept their familial and community responsibilities. In response, a crowd of close to a million men gathered in front of the Capitol to share the moving experience. Inspired by that event, a group of black women called for a "Million Woman March" in Philadelphia, on October 25, 1997, to promote a more active role for women in their families and neighborhoods. The organizers, who were not national figures, relied heavily on their Web site to plan the event. They drew hundreds of thousands of women, predominantly black, from across the country in an extraordinary display of grassroots activism. (Source: Ben Schein, "Why the Million Woman March Was Better Than the Million Man March," Peel, an on-line magazine at <www.peelmag.com/million.htm>, 11 February 1998.)

citizen, so that differences in personal resources do not work against the poor or otherwise disadvantaged. Elections, then, serve the ideal of equality better than any other means of political participation. Formal rules for counting ballots—in particular, one person, one vote—cancel differences in resources among individuals.

At the same time, groups of people who have few resources individually can combine their votes to wield political power. Various European ethnic groups exercised this type of power in the late nineteenth and early twentieth centuries, when their votes won them entry to the sociopolitical system and allowed them to share in its benefits (see Chapter 4). More recently, blacks, Hispanics, homosexuals, and the disabled have used their voting power to gain political recognition. However, minorities often have had to use unconventional forms of participation to win the right to vote. As two major scholars of political participation put it, "Protest is the great equalizer, the political action that weights intensity as well as sheer numbers."[54]

Participation and Order

The relationship between participation and order is complicated. Some types of participation (pledging allegiance, voting) promote order and so are encouraged by those who value order; other types promote disorder and so are discouraged. Many citizens—men and women alike—even resisted giving women the right to vote for fear of upsetting the social order by altering the traditional roles of men and women.

Both conventional and unconventional participation can lead to the ouster of government officials, but the regime—the political system itself—is threatened more by unconventional participation. To maintain order, the government has a stake in converting unconventional participation to conventional participation whenever possible. Think about the student unrest on college campuses during the Vietnam War when thousands of protesting students stopped traffic, occupied buildings, destroyed property, and behaved in other unconventional ways. Confronted by such civil strife and disorder, Congress took action. On March 23, 1971, it enacted and sent to the states the proposed Twenty-sixth Amendment, lowering the voting age to eighteen. Three-quarters of the state legislatures had to ratify the amendment before it became part of the Constitution. Astonishingly, thirty-eight states (the required number) complied by July 1, establishing a new speed record for ratification.[55] As one observer argued, the right to vote was extended to eighteen-year-olds not because young people demanded it but because "public officials believed suffrage expansion to be a means of institutionalizing youths' participation in politics, which would, in turn, curb disorder."[56]

Participation and the Models of Democracy

Ostensibly, elections are institutional mechanisms that implement democracy by allowing citizens to choose among candidates or issues. But elections also serve several other important purposes:[57]

- *Elections socialize political activity.* The opportunity to vote for change encourages citizens to refrain from demonstrating in the streets. Elections transform what might otherwise be sporadic citizen-initiated acts into a routine public function. This helps preserve government stability by containing and channeling away potentially disruptive or dangerous forms of mass political activity.

- *Elections institutionalize access to political power.* They allow ordinary citizens to run for political office or to play an important role in selecting political leaders. Working to elect a candidate encourages the campaign worker to identify problems or propose solutions to the newly elected official.

- *Elections bolster the state's power and authority.* The opportunity to participate in elections helps convince citizens that the government is responsive to their needs and wants, which reinforces its legitimacy.

Participation and Majoritarianism

Although the majoritarian model assumes that government responsiveness to popular demands comes through mass participation in politics, majoritarianism views participation rather narrowly. It favors conventional, institutionalized behavior—primarily, voting in elections. Because majoritarianism relies on counting votes to determine what the majority wants, its bias toward equality in political participation is strong. Clearly, better-educated, wealthier citizens are more likely to participate in elections, and get-out-the-vote campaigns cannot counter this distinct bias.[58] Because it favors collective decisions formalized through elections, majoritarianism has little place for motivated, resourceful individuals to exercise private influence over government actions.

Majoritarianism also limits individual freedom in another way: its focus on voting as the major means of mass participation narrows the scope of conventional political behavior by defining which political actions are "orderly" and acceptable. By favoring equality and order in political participation, majoritarianism goes hand in hand with the ideological orientation of communitarianism (see Chapter 1).

Participation and Pluralism

Resourceful citizens who want the government's help with problems find a haven in the pluralist model of democracy. A decentralized and organizationally complex form of government allows many points of access and accommodates various forms of conventional participation in addition to voting. For example, wealthy people and well-funded groups can afford to hire lobbyists to press their interests in Congress. In one view of pluralist democracy, citizens are free to ply and wheedle public officials to further their own selfish visions of the public good. From another viewpoint, pluralism offers citizens the opportunity to be treated as individuals when dealing with the government, to influence policymaking in special circumstances, and to fulfill (insofar as possible in representative government) their social potential through participation in community affairs.

Summary

To have "government by the people," the people must participate in politics. Conventional forms of participation—contacting officials and voting in elections—come most quickly to mind. However, citizens can also participate in politics in unconventional ways—staging sit-down strikes in public buildings, blocking traffic, and so on. Most citizens disapprove of most forms of unconventional political behavior. Yet blacks and women used unconventional tactics to win important political and legal rights, including the right to vote.

People are motivated to participate in politics for various reasons: to show support for their country, to obtain particularized benefits for themselves or their friends, or to influence broad public policy. Their political actions may demand either little political knowledge or personal initiative, or a great deal of both.

The press often paints an unflattering picture of political participation in America. Clearly, the proportion of the electorate that votes in general elections in the United States has dropped and is far below that in other nations. When compared with other nations on a broad range of conventional and unconventional political behavior, however, the United States tends to show as much or more citizen participation in politics. Voter turnout in the United States suffers by comparison with that of other nations because of differences in voter registration requirements. We also lack institutions (especially strong political parties) that increase voter registration and help bring those of lower socioeconomic status to the polls.

People's tendency to participate in politics is strongly related to their socioeconomic status. Education, one component of socioeconomic status, is the single strongest predictor of conventional political participation in the United States. Because of the strong effect of socioeconomic status, the political system is potentially biased toward the interests of higher-status people. Pluralist democracy, which provides many avenues for resourceful citizens to influence government decisions, tends to increase this bias. Majoritarian democracy, which relies heavily on elections and the concept of one person, one vote, offers citizens without great personal resources the opportunity to influence government decisions through elections.

Elections serve to legitimize government simply by involving the masses in government through voting. Whether voting means anything depends on the nature of voters' choices in elections. The range of choices available is a function of the nation's political parties, the topic of the next chapter.

Key Terms

political participation	franchise
conventional participation	progressivism
unconventional participation	direct primary
direct action	recall
supportive behavior	referendum
influencing behavior	initiative
class action suit	standard socioeconomic model
suffrage	

Selected Readings

Browning, Graeme, and Daniel J. Weitzner. *Electronic Democracy: Using the Internet to Influence American Politics.* Wilton, Conn.: On-line, 1996. A modern account of how to use the Internet for grassroots activism.

Conway, M. Margaret, Gertrude A. Steuernagel, and David W. Ahern. *Women and Political Participation.* Washington, D.C.: Congressional Quarterly Press, 1997. A short but comprehensive study of women, American culture, and various forms of women's political activity.

Craig, Stephen C. *The Malevolent Leaders: Popular Discontent in America.* Boulder, Colo.: Westview Press, 1993. The author uses in-depth interviews with citizens and members of Congress to look at the rise of popular discontent with and disengagement from politics.

Dalton, Russell J. *Citizen Politics in Western Democracies.* 2d ed. Chatham, N.J.: Chatham House, 1996. Studies public opinion and behavior in the United States, Britain, Germany (west and east), and France. Two chapters compare conventional citizen action and protest politics in these countries.

Grofman, Bernard, and Chandler Davidson, eds. *Controversies in Minority Voting: The Voting Rights Act in Perspective.* Washington, D.C.: Brookings Institution, 1992. Reviews the aims and accomplishments of the 1965 law that enforced voting rights for blacks in the South and some of its unintended consequences.

World Wide Web Resources

The National Political Index offers information on thirty-two means of accessing government, including contacting federal elected officials, contacting state and local officials, creating state initiatives and referenda, and tracking congressional legislation.
<www.politicalindex.com>

Project Vote Smart is a nonpartisan, nonprofit political information system founded by former presidents Ford and Carter. It includes voting returns, candidate information, campaign finance records, and so on.
<www.vote-smart.org>

California Voter Foundation is "a nonprofit, nonpartisan organization dedicated to applying new technologies to provide the public with access to the information needed to participate in public life in a meaningful way."
<www.webcom.com/cvf>

Corporate Watch pursues "corporate accountability, human rights, social and environmental justice." The site contains information about corporate abuses and efforts to curtail the activities and power of organizations like the World Bank and the International Monetary Fund.

6

Political Parties, Campaigns, and Elections

Would he, or wouldn't he? Would Ross Perot enter the 1996 presidential race, or would he stay out? The two major candidates pondered that question as they prepared their own campaigns. President Bill Clinton, the unchallenged Democratic nominee, hoped Perot would run again. Senator Bob Dole, front-runner for the Republican nomination, hoped Perot would stay out.

In the 1992 presidential election, H. Ross Perot—a businessman with virtu-ally no government experience who had never before run for public office and had no party backing—won nearly 19 percent of the popular vote. That was more than any candidate outside either major party had won since 1912. In his run for president, Perot spent more than $65 million of his personal fortune, mainly for advertising on national television. Although his campaign produced impressive results in the national popular vote, he failed to carry a single state and thus failed to win any votes in the electoral college. Nevertheless, Perot showed that he could affect the outcome. Polls revealed that he drew off more Republican than Democratic votes, in effect helping Clinton win in 1992. Would he be a factor in 1996?

Perot had already discarded the strategy of running for president without a party. In September 1995 he announced on "Larry King Live" that he would create a new political party for independent voters fed up with the two-party system. With Perot's financial backing, an effort was quickly launched to get the Reform Party, as it was known, on the ballot in all fifty states for the 1996 presidential election.

On paper, the Reform Party's chances looked good. Its creator had won al-most 20 million votes in the 1992 presidential election; nearly 60 percent of a 1995 sample had agreed that "we should have a third major political party in this country in addition to the Democrats and Republicans"; and a March 1996 survey estimated that 20 percent of registered voters would prefer some independent or third-party candidate to either Clinton or Dole.[1] Nevertheless, most political analysts predicted that the Reform Party was doomed to fail in 1996, and events proved them right. Perot won only 8 percent of the national vote in his repeat performance. In the 2000 election, Reform Party candidate Patrick J. Buchanan won less than one percent of the national vote, raising questions about the viability of the third party at the national level.

Planning an Expensive Party
A volunteer working for the Reform Party in Naples, Florida, obtains a citizen's signature on a petition to place the party on the state's ballot in 1996. When Perot ran for president as an independent candidate in 1992, he was helped by thousands of volunteers who circulated petitions to get his name on the ballot. Nevertheless, he still had to pay professional petitioners to finish the job. In 1996, with public enthusiasm waning for Perot, volunteers played a smaller role, and his organization had to rely even more on paid workers to register the party on ballots across the country. Perot chose not to run in 2000.

Political analysts discounted the Reform Party's chances because the structure and dynamics of U.S. politics work strongly *against* any third party and *for* the operation of a two-party system. Indeed, the Democratic and Republican parties have dominated national and state politics in the United States for more than 125 years. Their domination is more complete than that of any pair of parties in any other democratic government. Although all democracies have some form of multiparty politics, few have a stable two-party system—Britain and New Zealand being the most notable exceptions.

Why do we have any political parties? What functions do they perform? How did we become a nation of Democrats and Republicans? Do these parties truly differ in their platforms and behavior? Are parties really necessary for democratic government, or do they get in the way of citizens and their government? In this chapter, we will answer these questions by examining political parties, perhaps the most misunderstood element of American politics.

And what of the election campaigns conducted by the two major parties? In this chapter, we also consider how those campaigns have changed over time, how candidates get nominated in the United States, what factors are important in election campaigns, and why voters choose one candidate over another. In addition, we address these important questions: Do election campaigns function more to inform or to confuse voters? How important is money in conducting a winning election campaign? What are the roles of party identification, issues, and candidate attributes in influencing voters' choices and thus election outcomes? How do campaigns, elections, and parties fit into the majoritarian and pluralist models of democracy?

Political Parties and Their Functions

According to democratic theory, the primary means by which citizens control their government is voting in free elections. Most Americans agree that voting is important. Of those surveyed after the 1996 presidential campaign, 87 percent felt that elections made the government "pay attention to what the people think."[2] Americans are not nearly as supportive of the role played by political parties in elections, however. When asked whether Perot should run for president in 1996 as "head of a third party which would also run candidates in state and local races" or "by himself as an independent candidate," 60 percent of a national sample favored his running without a party.[3]

Nevertheless, Americans are quick to condemn as "undemocratic" countries that do not hold elections contested by political parties. In truth, Americans have a love-hate relationship with political parties. They believe that parties are necessary for democratic government; at the same time, they think parties are somehow "obstructionist" and not to be trusted. This distrust is particularly strong among younger voters. To better appreciate the role of political parties in democratic government, we must understand exactly what parties are and what they do.

What Is a Political Party?

A **political party** is an organization that sponsors candidates for political office *under the organization's name.* The italicized part of this definition is important. True political parties select individuals to run for public office through a formal process of **nomination,** which designates them as the parties' official candidates. This activity distinguishes the Democratic and Republican parties from interest groups. The AFL-CIO and the National Association of Manufacturers are interest groups. They often support candidates in various ways, but they do not nominate them to run as their avowed representatives. If they did, they would be transformed into political parties. In short, the sponsoring of candidates designated as representatives of the organization is what defines an organization as a party.

Most democratic theorists agree that a modern nation-state cannot practice democracy without at least two political parties that regularly contest elections. In fact, the link between democracy and political parties is so close that many people define *democratic government* in terms of competitive party politics.

Party Functions

Parties contribute to democratic government through the functions they perform for the **political system**—the interrelated institutions that link people with government. Four of the most important party functions are nominating candidates for election to public office, structuring the voting choice in elections, proposing alternative government programs, and coordinating the actions of government officials.

Nominating Candidates   Without political parties, voters would confront a bewildering array of self-nominated candidates, each seeking votes on the basis of personal friendships, celebrity status, or name. Parties can provide a form of quality control for their nominees through the process of peer review. Party insiders, the nominees' peers, usually know the strengths and faults of potential candidates much better than average voters and thus can judge their suitability for representing the party.

In nominating candidates, parties often do more than pass judgment on potential office seekers. Sometimes they go so far as to recruit talented individuals to become party candidates. In this way, parties help not only to ensure a minimum level of quality among candidates who run for office but also to raise the quality of those candidates.

Structuring the Voting Choice   Political parties also help democratic government by structuring the voting choice—reducing the number of candidates on the ballot to those who have a realistic chance of winning. Established parties—those with experience in contesting elections—acquire a following of loyal voters who guarantee the party's candidates a predictable base of votes. The ability of established parties to mobilize their supporters has the effect of discouraging nonparty candidates from running for office and of discouraging new parties from forming. Consequently, the realistic choice is between candidates offered by the major parties, reducing the amount of new information that voters need in order to make a rational decision.

Proposing Alternative Government Programs   Parties also help voters choose candidates by proposing alternative programs of government action—the general policies their candidates will pursue if they gain office. Even if voters know nothing about the qualities of the parties' candidates, they can vote rationally for candidates of the party that has policies they favor. The specific policies advocated vary from candidate to candidate and from election to election. However, candidates of the same party tend to favor policies that fit their party's underlying political philosophy, or ideology.

In many countries, parties' names—such as "Conservative" and "Socialist"—reflect their political stance. The Democrats and Republicans have issue-neutral names, but many minor parties in the United States have used their names to advertise their policies: the Prohibition Party, the Socialist Party, and even the Reform Party. The neutrality of the two major parties' names suggests that their policies are similar. This is not true. As we shall see, they regularly adopt very different policies in their platforms.

Coordinating the Actions of Government Officials   Finally, party organizations help coordinate the actions of public officials. A government based on the separation of powers, such as that of the United States, divides responsibilities for making public policy. The president and the leaders of the House and Senate are not required to cooperate with one another. Political party organizations are the major means for bridging the separate powers to produce coordinated policies that can govern the country effectively.

A History of U.S. Party Politics

The two major U.S. parties are among the oldest in the world. In fact, the Democratic Party, founded in 1828 but with roots reaching back into the late 1700s, has a strong claim to being the oldest party in existence. Its closest rival is the British Conservative Party, formed in 1832, two decades before the Republican Party was organized, in 1854. Several generations of Americans have supported the Democratic and Republican parties. They have become institutionalized in our political process.

The Emergence of the Party System

Today we think of party activities as normal, even essential, to American politics. It was not always so. The Constitution makes no mention of political parties, and none existed when the Constitution was written in 1787. It was common then to refer to groups pursuing some common political interest as *factions.* Although factions were seen as inevitable in politics, they were also considered dangerous. One argument for adopting the Constitution—proposed in *Federalist* No. 10 (see Chapter 2)—was that its federal system would prevent factional influences from controlling the government.

The debate over ratification of the Constitution produced two factions. Those who backed the Constitution were loosely known as *Federalists,* their opponents as *Antifederalists.* At this stage, the groups could not be called parties because they did not sponsor candidates for election. We can classify George Washington as a Federalist because he supported the Constitution, but he was not a factional leader and actually opposed factional politics. During Washington's administration, however, the political cleavage sharpened between those who favored a stronger national government and those who wanted a less powerful, more decentralized national government.

Members of the first group, led by Alexander Hamilton, proclaimed themselves Federalists. Members of the second group, led by Thomas Jefferson, called themselves Republicans.* Disheartened by the political split in his administration, Washington spoke out against "the baneful effects" of parties in his farewell address in 1796. Nevertheless, parties already existed in the political system. For the most part, from that time to the present, two major political parties have competed for political power.

---

*Although they used the same name, they were not Republicans as we know them today. Indeed, Jefferson's followers were later known as Democratic Republicans, and in 1828 a wing of that party became the Democratic Party.

The Present Party System: Democrats and Republicans

By 1820, the Federalists were no more. In 1828, the Democratic Republican Party split in two. One wing, led by Andrew Jackson, became the Democratic Party. The other later joined forces with several minor parties and formed the Whig Party, which lasted for two decades.

In the early 1850s, antislavery forces (including Whigs and antislavery Democrats) began to organize. They formed a new party, the Republican Party, to oppose the extension of slavery into the Kansas and Nebraska territories. It is this party, founded in 1854, that continues as today's Republican Party. In 1860, the Republicans nominated Abraham Lincoln and successfully confronted a Democratic Party deeply divided over slavery.

The election of 1860 is considered the first of three critical elections under the current party system.[4] A **critical election** is marked by a sharp change in existing patterns of party loyalties among groups of voters. This change, which is called an **electoral realignment**, lasts through several subsequent elections.[5] When one party in a two-party system *regularly* enjoys support from most of the voters, it is called the *majority party*; the other is called the *minority party*.

The 1860 election divided the country between the northern states, which mainly voted Republican, and the southern states, which were overwhelmingly Democratic. The victory of North over South in the Civil War cemented Democratic loyalties in the South, particularly following the withdrawal of federal troops after the 1876 election. For forty years, from 1880 to 1920, no Republican presidential candidate won even one of the eleven states of the Confederacy.

A second critical election, in 1896, transformed the Republican Party into a true majority party when, in opposition to the Democrats' inflationary free silver platform, a link was forged between the Republican Party and business. Voters in the heavily populated Northeast and Midwest surged toward the Republican Party—many of them permanently.

A third critical election occurred in 1932, when Franklin Delano Roosevelt led the Democratic Party to majority party status by uniting southern Democrats, northern urban workers, middle-class liberals, Catholics, Jews, and white ethnic minorities in the "Roosevelt coalition." (The relatively few blacks who voted at that time tended to remain loyal to the Republicans—the "party of Lincoln.") Democrats held control of both houses of Congress in most sessions from 1933 through 1994. In 1994, Republicans gained control of Congress for the first time in forty years. They retained control after the 1996 elections—the first time that Republicans took both houses in successive elections since Herbert Hoover's presidency.

Signs are strong that the coalition of Democratic voters forged by Roosevelt in the 1930s has cracked. Certainly the South is no longer solid for the Democrats. Since 1952, in fact, it has voted more consistently for Republican presidential candidates than for Democrats. The party system in the United States may not be undergoing another realignment; rather, we may be in a period of **electoral dealignment**, in which party loyalties become less important to voters as they cast their ballots. We examine the influence of party loyalty on voting later in this chapter.

The American Two-Party System

The critical election of 1860 established the Democratic and Republican parties as the major parties in our **two-party system**. In a two-party system, most voters are so loyal to one or the other of the major parties that independent candidates or candidates from a third party—which means any minor party— have little chance of winning office. Third-party candidates tend to be most successful at the local or state level. Since the present two-party system was established, relatively few minor-party candidates have won election to the U.S. House; very few have won election to the Senate; and none has won the presidency. However, we should not ignore the special contributions of certain minor parties, among them the Anti-Masonic Party, the Populists, and the Progressives of 1912. In this section, we study the fortunes of minor or third parties in American politics. We also will look at why we have only two major parties, explain how federalism helps the parties survive, and describe voters' loyalty to the two major parties today.

Minor Parties in America

Minor parties have always figured in party politics in America. Most true minor parties in our political history have been of four types:[6]

- *Bolter parties* are formed from factions that split off from one of the major parties. Seven times in thirty-four presidential elections since the Civil War, disgruntled leaders "bolted the ticket" and challenged their former parties. Bolter parties have occasionally won significant proportions of the vote. However, with the exception of Teddy Roosevelt's Progressive Party in 1912 and possibly of George Wallace's American Independent Party in 1968, bolter parties have not affected the outcome of presidential elections.

- *Farmer-labor parties* represent farmers and urban workers who believe that they, the working class, are not getting their share of society's wealth. The People's Party, founded in 1892 and nicknamed the "Populist Party," was a prime example of a farmer-labor party. The Populists won 8.5 percent of the vote in 1892 and became the first third party since 1860 to win any electoral votes. Flushed by success, they endorsed William Jennings Bryan, the Democratic candidate, in 1896. When he lost, the party quickly faded. Farm and labor groups revived many Populist ideas in the Progressive Party in 1924. The party died in 1925.

- *Parties of ideological protest* go further than farmer-labor parties in criticizing the established system. These parties reject prevailing doctrines and propose radically different principles, often favoring more government activism. The Socialist Party has been the most successful party of ideological protest. Even at its high point in 1912, however, it garnered only 6 percent of the vote, and Socialist candidates for president have never won a single state. In recent years, the sound of ideological protest has been heard more from rightist parties, arguing for the radical disengagement of government from society. Such is the program of the Libertarian Party, which stresses freedom over order and equality. The party has run candidates for president in every election since 1972, but it has never won more than 1 percent of votes cast.

* *Single-issue parties* are formed to promote one principle, not a general philosophy of government. The Free Soil Party of the 1840s and 1850s worked to abolish slavery. The Prohibition Party, the most durable example of a single-issue party, opposed the consumption of alcoholic beverages. The party has run candidates in every presidential election since 1884.

Third parties, then, have been formed primarily to express discontent with the choices offered by the major parties and to work for their own objectives within the electoral system.[7] Certainly the Reform Party reflects discontent with existing politics, but otherwise it resists classification. Of the nine principles presented by the Reform Party in 1996, six dealt with government reforms, and only three vaguely addressed substantive policies.[8] Perhaps the Reform Party foreshadows a new type of party, one created from the top by a dynamic leader through a well-funded, mass media–dependent appeal for support from citizens previously uninvolved in partisan politics.[9] Its nominee in 2000, Patrick Buchanan, continued this top-down approach to party leadership by openly rejecting many elements of the party platform.

How have minor parties fared historically? As vote getters, they have not performed well. However, bolter parties have twice won more than 10 percent of the vote. More significantly, the Republican Party originated in 1854 as a single-issue third party opposed to slavery in the nation's new territories; in its first election, in 1856, the party came in second, displacing the Whigs.

As policy advocates, minor parties have a slightly better record. At times, they have had a real effect on the policies adopted by the major parties. Women's suffrage, the graduated income tax, and the direct election of senators all originated in third parties.[10]

Most important, minor parties function as safety valves. They allow those who are unhappy with the status quo to express their discontent within the system, to contribute to the political dialogue. Surely this was the function of Perot's candidacy and of the Reform Party. If minor parties and independent candidates indicate discontent, what should we make of the scores of parties that have sponsored candidates in recent congressional elections or of the several minor parties (Libertarian, Reform, U.S. Taxpayers, Green, Natural Law) that held conventions in the summer of 2000? Not much. The number of third parties that contest elections is much less important than the total number of votes they receive. Despite the presence of numerous minor parties in every presidential election, the two major parties usually collect over 99 percent of the vote. For this reason, Ross Perot's 1992 performance (almost 19 percent of the popular vote) was truly remarkable for a third party candidate. Nevertheless, the two major parties captured all of the electoral votes.

Why a Two-Party System?

The history of party politics in the United States is essentially the story of two parties that have alternating control of the government. With relatively few exceptions, Americans conduct elections at all levels within the two-party system.

This pattern is unusual in democratic countries, where multiparty systems are more common. Why does the United States have only two major parties? The two most convincing answers to this question stem from the electoral system in the United States and the process of political socialization here.

In the typical U.S. election, two or more candidates contest each office, and the winner is the single candidate who collects the most votes, whether those votes constitute a majority or not. When the two principles of *single winners* chosen by a *simple plurality* of votes govern the election of members of a legislature, the system (despite its reliance on pluralities rather than majorities) is known as **majority representation**. Think about how American states choose representatives to Congress. A state entitled to ten representatives is divided into ten congressional districts; each district elects one representative. Majority representation of voters through single-member districts is also a feature of most state legislatures.

Alternatively, a legislature might be chosen through a system of **proportional representation**, which would award legislative seats to a party in proportion to the total number of votes it wins in an election. Under this system, the state might have a single statewide election for all ten seats, with each party presenting a list of ten candidates. Voters could vote for the entire party list they preferred, and the party's candidates would be elected from the top of each list, according to the proportion of votes won by the party. Thus, if a party got 30 percent of the vote in this example, its first three candidates would be elected.

Although this form of election may seem strange, many democratic countries (for example, the Netherlands, Israel, and Denmark) use it. Proportional representation tends to produce (or perpetuate) several parties, because each can win enough seats nationwide to wield some influence in the legislature. In contrast, our system of elections forces interest groups of all sorts to work within the two major parties, for only one candidate in each race stands a chance to be elected under plurality voting. Therefore, the system tends to produce only two parties.

The rules of our electoral system may explain why only two parties tend to form in specific election districts, but why do the same two parties (Democratic and Republican) operate within every state? The contest for the presidency is the key to this question. A candidate can win a presidential election only by amassing a majority of electoral votes from across the entire nation. Presidential candidates try to win votes under the same party label in each state in order to pool their electoral votes in the electoral college. The presidency is a big enough political prize to induce parties to harbor uncomfortable coalitions of voters (southern white Protestants allied with northern Jews and blacks in the Democratic Party, for example) just to win the electoral vote and the presidential election.

The American electoral system may force U.S. politics into a two-party mold, but why do the same two parties reappear from election to election? Why do the Democrats and Republicans persist? This is where political socialization comes into play. These two parties persist simply because they have persisted. After more than one hundred years of political socialization, the two parties today have such a head start in structuring the vote that they discourage challenges from new parties.

Federalism at Work
In November 1998, Reform Party candidate Jesse Ventura was elected governor of
Minnesota in a tight, three-way race. Ventura's surprising election was the most significant
electoral victory won by the Reform Party. This demonstrates the federal structure of the party
system: Reform Party candidates have realized some electoral success at the state and local
level, but the party has not won any national offices. Ventura left the party in February
2000, calling it "hopelessly dysfunctional."

The Federal Basis of the Party System

Focusing on contests for the presidency is a convenient and informative way to
study the history of American parties, but it also oversimplifies party politics to
the point of distortion. Even during its darkest defeats for the presidency, a
party can still claim many victories for state offices. Victories outside the arena
of presidential politics give each party a base of support that keeps its machinery oiled and running for the next contest.[11]

Ronald Reagan's victory in 1980, his 1984 landslide, and George Bush's
convincing win in 1988 might have suggested that the Democrats were
doomed to extinction in presidential politics. Perhaps in an earlier time, when
the existing parties were not so well institutionalized, that would have been so.
However, the Democratic Party not only remained alive but thrived in our federal system. The separation of state politics from national trends affords each

party a chance to lick its wounds after a presidential election debacle and return to campaign optimistically in the next election, as the Republicans did so successfully in the 1994 congressional elections after losing the presidency in 1992.

Party Identification in America

The concept of **party identification** is one of the most important in political science. It signifies a voter's sense of psychological attachment to a party, which is not the same thing as voting for the party in any given election. Scholars measure party identification simply by asking, "Do you usually think of yourself as a Republican, a Democrat, an independent, or what?"[12] Voting is a behavior; identification is a state of mind. For example, millions of southerners voted for Dwight Eisenhower for president in 1952 and 1956 but continued to consider themselves Democrats. The proportions of self-identified Republicans, Democrats, and independents (no party attachment) in the electorate since 1952 are shown in Figure 6.1. Three significant points stand out.

- The number of Republicans and Democrats combined far exceeds the proportion of independents in every year.
- The number of Democrats consistently exceeds that of Republicans.
- The number of Democrats has shrunk over time, to the benefit of both Republicans and independents, and the three groups are now almost equal in size.

Although party identification predisposes citizens to vote for their favorite party, other factors may cause voters to choose the opposition candidate. If they vote against their party often enough, they may rethink their party identification and eventually switch. Apparently, this rethinking has gone on in the minds of many southern Democrats over time. In 1952, about 70 percent of white southerners thought of themselves as Democrats, and fewer than 20 percent thought of themselves as Republicans. By 1996, white southerners were only 33 percent Democratic, 33 percent Republican, and 34 percent independent. Much of the nationwide growth in the proportion of Republicans and independents (and the parallel drop in the number of Democrats) stems from changes in party preferences among white southerners and from the migration of northerners, which translated into substantial gains in the number of registered Republicans by 1996.[13]

Who are the self-identified Democrats and Republicans in the electorate? Figure 6.2 shows party identification by various social groups in 1996. The effects of socioeconomic factors are clear. People who have lower incomes and less education are more likely to think of themselves as Democrats than as Republicans. But the cultural factors of religion and race produce even sharper differences between the parties. Jews are strongly Democratic compared with other religious groups, and African Americans are also overwhelmingly Democratic. Also, American politics has a gender gap: women tend to be more Democratic than men.

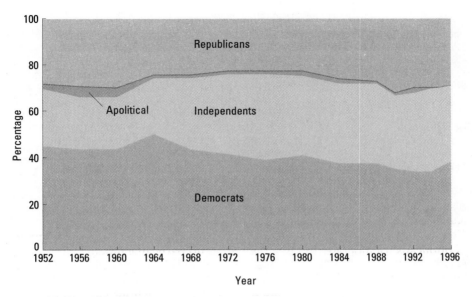

FIGURE 6.1   *Distribution of Party Identification, 1952–1996*
In every presidential election since 1952, voters across the nation have been asked,
"Generally speaking, do you usually think of yourself as a Republican, a Democrat, an
independent, or what?" Most voters think of themselves as either Republicans or Democrats,
but the proportion of those who think of themselves as independents has increased over time.
The size of the Democratic Party's majority has also shrunk. Nevertheless, most Americans
today still identify with one of the two major parties, and Democrats still outnumber
Republicans. (Source: National Election Studies Guide to Public Opinion and Electoral Behavior,
obtained at <www.umich.edu/~nes/nesguide/toptables/tab2a_1.htm>.)

The influence of region on party identification has changed over time. Because of the high proportion of blacks in the South, it is still the most heavily Democratic region, followed closely by the Northeast. The Midwest and West have proportionately more Republicans. Despite the erosion of Democratic strength in the South, we still see elements of Roosevelt's old Democratic coalition in the socioeconomic groups. Perhaps the major change in that coalition has been the replacement of white European ethnic groups by blacks, attracted by the Democrats' backing of civil rights legislation in the 1960s.

Studies show that about half the citizens in the United States adopt their parents' party. But it often takes time for party identification to develop. The youngest group of voters is most likely to be independent, but they have also identified increasingly with Republicans, ever since the Reagan years. The oldest group shows the greatest partisan commitment, reflecting the fact that citizens become more interested in politics as they mature. Also, the youngest age group is most evenly divided between the parties. Some analysts believe this ratio of party identification among today's young voters will persist as they age,

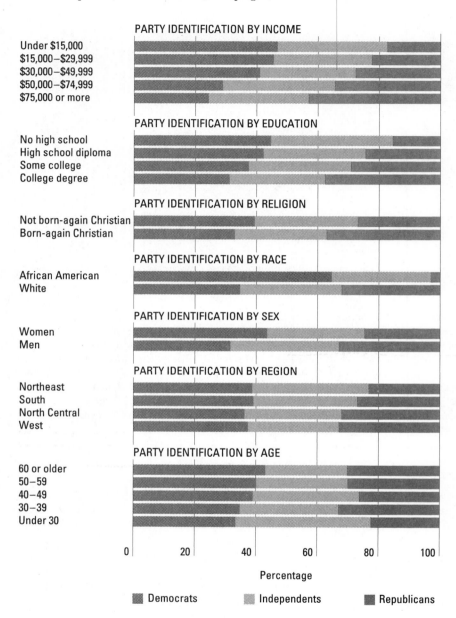

FIGURE 6.2   Party Identification by Social Groups

Respondents to a 1996 survey were grouped by seven different socioeconomic criteria—income, education, religion, race, sex, region, and age—and analyzed according to their self-descriptions as Democrats, independents, or Republicans. Region was found to have the least effect on party identification; religion and race had the greatest effects. (Source: 1996 National Election Study, Center for Political Studies, University of Michigan.)

contributing to further erosion of the Democratic majority and perhaps greater electoral dealignment.

Americans tend to find their political niche and stay there.[14] The enduring party loyalty of American voters tends to structure the vote even before an election is held, even before the candidates are chosen. Later we will examine the extent to which party identification determines voting choice. But first, we will look to see whether the Democratic and Republican parties have any significant differences.

Party Ideology and Organization

George Wallace, a disgruntled Democrat who ran for president in 1968 on the American Independent Party ticket, complained that "there isn't a dime's worth of difference" between the Democrats and Republicans. Humorist Will Rogers said, "I am not a member of any organized political party—I am a Democrat." Wallace's comment was made in disgust; Rogers's in jest. Wallace was wrong; Rogers was close to being right. Here we will dispel the myth that the parties do not differ significantly on issues and explain how they are organized to coordinate the activities of party candidates and officials in government.

Differences in Party Ideology

George Wallace notwithstanding, there is more than a dime's worth of difference between the two parties. In fact, the difference amounts to many billions of dollars, the cost of the different government programs supported by each party. Democrats are more disposed to government spending to advance social welfare (and hence to promote equality) than are Republicans. And social welfare programs cost money, a lot of money. Republicans, however, are not averse to spending billions of dollars for the projects they consider important, among them, national defense. Ronald Reagan portrayed the Democrats as big spenders, but the defense buildup during his first administration alone cost the country over $1 trillion—more precisely, $1,007,900,000,000.[15] The differences in spending patterns reflect some real philosophical differences between the parties.

Voters and Activists   One way to examine the differences is to compare party voters with party activists. When such a comparison was done in 1996, it was found that 16 percent of those who identified themselves as Democrats described themselves as conservatives, compared with 55 percent of those who identified themselves as Republicans. The ideological gap between the parties is even larger among party activists. Only 3 percent of the delegates to the 1996 Democratic convention considered themselves conservatives, compared with 79 percent of the delegates to the Republican convention.[16]

Platforms: Freedom, Order, and Equality   For another test of party philosophy, we can look at the **party platforms**—the statements of policies—adopted in party conventions. Although many people feel that party platforms don't matter very much, several scholars have demonstrated, using different approaches, that winning parties tend to carry out much of their platforms when in office.[17] Party platforms also matter a great deal to the parties' convention delegates. The wording of a platform plank often means the difference between victory and defeat for factions within a party.

The platforms adopted by the Democratic and Republican conventions in 2000 were strikingly different in style and substance. Echoing the New Democrats' move toward the political center, the 2000 Democratic Platform declared that the party had successfully "ended the era of big government." Nevertheless, the party proceeded to promise greater government protection of the environment and new programs to "provide college education, lifelong learning, and ongoing skill development for all Americans." The document also pledged continued support for the Equal Rights Amendment. As befits a conservative party, the 2000 Republican Platform praised the free market system and referred to the glorification of violence, the glamorizing of drugs, and the abuse of women and children as "the pollution of our culture." The platform also called for several amendments to the Constitution. In addition to the Human Life Amendment, it advocated amendments to require a balanced budget, to protect the flag from desecration, and to protect the rights of victims in judicial proceedings.

The difference between the party platforms in 2000 emerged more clearly in their specific proposals. Where the Republicans affirmed that an "unborn child has a fundamental individual right to life," Democrats supported "the right of every woman to choose" between birth and abortion. Republicans opposed national gun registration and federal licensing of gun owners. The Democrats pledged to "require photo license I.D., a full background check, and a gun safety test." While Republicans voiced support for "Right-to-Work laws" and pledged to "stop the involuntary use of union dues for political purposes," Democrats supported legislation to ban "permanent striker replacement workers" and to strengthen the penalties against "employer interference with the right to organize." Republicans affirmed that homosexuality is "incompatible with military service" and urged that sexual preference not be given "special legal protection or standing in law." Democrats pledged to "end workplace discrimination against gay men and lesbians" and to enact special punishment for "hate violence" based on "gender, disability or sexual orientation." The Republicans suggested providing "market-based incentives" to develop environmentally friendly transportation modes, while the Democrats proposed using part of the budget surplus to develop such technologies.

These statements of values clearly distinguish the two parties on the values of freedom, order, and equality that underlie the dilemmas of government discussed in Chapter 1. According to our ideological typology, the Republicans' 2000 platform positions on abortion, homosexual rights, gun control, and labor issues place their party firmly in the conservative category, whereas the Democrats' platform puts their party squarely in the liberal category.

Different but Similar   Democrats and Republicans have very different ideological orientations. Yet many observers claim that the parties are really quite similar in ideology compared to the different parties of other countries. Specifically, both support capitalism—that is, both reject government ownership of the means of production (see Chapter 1). A study of Democratic and Republican positions on four economic issues—ownership of the means of production, the government's role in economic planning, redistribution of wealth, and providing for social welfare—found that Republicans consistently oppose increased government activity. Comparing these findings with data on party positions in thirteen other democracies, the researchers found about as much difference between the American parties as is usual within two-party systems. However, both American parties tend to be more conservative on economic matters than parties in other two-party systems. In most multiparty systems, the presence of strong socialist and antisocialist parties ensures a much greater range of ideological choice than we find in our system, despite genuine differences between Democrats and Republicans.[18]

National Party Organization

American parties parallel our federal system: they have separate national and state organizations (and practically separate local organizations, in many cases). At the national level, each major party has four main organizational components:

- *National convention.* Every four years, each party assembles thousands of delegates from the states and U.S. territories (such as Puerto Rico and Guam) in a **national convention** for the purpose of nominating a candidate for president. This presidential nominating convention is the supreme governing body of the party. It determines party policy through the platform, formulates rules to govern party operations, and designates a national committee, which is empowered to govern the party until the next convention.

- *National committee.* The **national committee,** which governs each party between conventions, is composed of party officials representing the states and territories, including the chairpersons of their party organizations. In 2000, the Republican National Committee (RNC) had about 150 members, and the Democratic National Committee (DNC) had approximately 450 elected and appointed members.[19] The chairperson of each national committee is chosen by the party's presidential nominee, then duly elected by the committee. If the nominee loses the presidential election, the national committee usually replaces the nominee's chairperson.

- *Congressional party conferences.* At the beginning of each session of Congress, Republicans and Democrats in each chamber hold separate **party conferences** (the House Democrats call theirs a *caucus*) to select their party leaders and to decide committee assignments. The party conferences deal only with congressional matters and have no structural relationship to each other and no relationship to the national committee.

- *Congressional campaign committees.* Democrats and Republicans in the House and Senate also maintain separate **congressional campaign committees**, each of which raises its own funds to support its candidates in congressional elections. The separation of these organizations from the national committee tells us that the national party structure is loose; the national committee seldom gets involved with the election of any individual member of Congress. Moreover, even the congressional campaign organizations merely supplement the funds that senators and representatives raise on their own to win reelection.

It is tempting to think of the national party chairperson sitting at the top of a hierarchical party organization that not only controls its members in Congress but also issues orders to the state committees and on down to the local level. Few notions could be more wrong.[20] The national committee has nearly no voice in congressional activity and exercises very little direction of and even less control over state and local campaigns. The main role of a national committee is to support its candidate's personal campaign staff in the effort to win.

For many years, the role of the national committees was essentially limited to planning for the next party convention. The committee would select the site, issue the call to state parties to attend, plan the program, and so on. In the 1970s, however, the roles of the DNC and RNC began to expand—but in different ways.

In response to street rioting during the 1968 Democratic convention, the Democrats created a special commission to introduce party reforms. The McGovern-Fraser Commission formulated guidelines for the selection of delegates to the 1972 Democratic convention. Included in these guidelines was the requirement that state parties take "affirmative action"—that is, see to it that their delegations included women, blacks, and young people "in reasonable relationship to the group's presence in the population of the state."[21] Never before had a national party committee imposed these kinds of rules on a state party organization, but it worked. Although the party has since reduced its emphasis on quotas, the gains by women and blacks have held up fairly well. The representation of young people, however, has declined substantially.

While the Democrats were busy with *procedural* reforms, the Republicans were making *organizational* reforms.[22] Republicans were not inclined to impose quotas on state parties through their national committee. Instead, the RNC strengthened its fundraising, research, and service roles. Republicans acquired their own building and their own computer, and in 1976 they hired the first full-time chairperson of either national party. As RNC chairman, William Brock expanded the party's staff, launched new publications, held seminars, conducted election analyses, and advised candidates—things that national party committees in other countries had been doing for years.

The vast difference between the Democratic and Republican approaches to reforming the national committees shows in the funds raised by the DNC and RNC during election campaigns. During Brock's tenure as chairman of the RNC, the Republicans raised three to four times as much money as the

Democrats. Although the margin has narrowed, Republican party fundraising efforts are still superior. During the 1997–1998 midterm election cycle, the Republicans' national, senatorial, and congressional committees raised $417 million, compared with $253 million raised by the comparable Democratic committees.[23] Also, the Republicans received more of their funds in small contributions (less than $100), mainly through direct-mail solicitation, than the Democrats. In short, the RNC has been raising far more money than the DNC, from many more citizens, as part of its long-term commitment to improving its organizational services. Its efforts have also made a difference at the state and local levels.

State and Local Party Organizations

At one time, both major parties were firmly anchored by strong state and local party organizations. Big-city party organizations, such as the Democrats' Tammany Hall in New York City and the Cook County Central Committee in Chicago, were called *party machines*. A **party machine** was a centralized organization that dominated local politics by controlling elections—sometimes by illegal means, often by providing jobs and social services to urban workers in return for their votes. These patronage and social service functions of party machines were undercut when the government expanded its social services. As a result, most local party organizations lost their ability to deliver votes and thus to determine the outcome of elections.

The individual state and local organizations of both parties vary widely in strength, but recent research has found that "neither the Republican nor Democratic party has a distinct advantage with regard to direct campaign activities."[24] Whereas once both the RNC and the DNC were dependent for their funding on "quotas" paid by state parties, now the funds flow the other way. In addition to money, state parties also receive candidate training, poll data and research, and campaigning instruction.[25]

Decentralized but Growing Stronger

The absence of centralized power has always been the most distinguishing characteristic of American political parties. Moreover, the rise in the proportion of citizens who call themselves "independents" suggests that our already weak parties are in further decline.[26] But there is evidence that our political parties, *as organizations*, are enjoying a period of resurgence. Both parties' national committees have never been better funded or more active in grassroots campaign activities.[27] And more votes in Congress are being decided along party lines. In fact, a specialist in congressional politics has concluded, "When compared to its predecessors of the last half-century, the current majority party leadership is more involved and more decisive in organizing the party and the chamber, setting the policy agenda, shaping legislation, and determining legislative outcomes."[28]

The Model of Responsible Party Government

According to the majoritarian model of democracy, parties are essential to making the government responsive to public opinion. In fact, the ideal role of parties in majoritarian democracy has been formalized in the four principles of **responsible party government**: [29]

1. Parties should present clear and coherent programs to voters.
2. Voters should choose candidates according to the party programs.
3. The winning party should carry out its program once in office.
4. Voters should hold the governing party responsible at the next election for executing its program.

How well do these principles describe American politics? You've learned that the Democratic and Republican platforms are different and that they are much more ideologically consistent than many people believe. So the first principle is being met fairly well. To a lesser extent, so is the third principle: once parties gain power, they usually do what they said they would do. From the standpoint of democratic theory, the real question lies in principles 2 and 4: Do voters really pay attention to party platforms and policies when they cast their ballots? And, if so, do voters hold the governing party responsible at the next election for delivering, or failing to deliver, on its pledges? To answer these questions, we must consider in greater detail the parties' role in nominating candidates and structuring the voters' choice in elections. At the conclusion of this chapter we will return to evaluating the role of political parties in democratic government.

The Evolution of Campaigning

An **election campaign** is an organized effort to persuade voters to choose one candidate over others competing for the same office. An effective campaign requires sufficient resources to acquire and analyze information about voters' interests, to develop a strategy and matching tactics for appealing to these interests, to deliver the candidate's message to the voters, and to get voters to cast their ballots.[30]

In the past, political parties conducted all phases of the election campaign. Today, however, candidates seldom rely much on political parties. How do candidates plan their campaign strategy and tactics now? By hiring political consultants to devise clever "soundbites" (brief, catchy phrases) that catch voters' attention on television, not by consulting party headquarters. How do candidates deliver their messages to voters? By conducting media campaigns, not by counting on party regulars to canvass the neighborhoods.

Increasingly, election campaigns have evolved from being party centered to being candidate centered.[31] Whereas the parties virtually ran election campaigns in the past, now they exist mainly to support candidate-centered campaigns by providing services or funds to their candidates. Nevertheless, we will see that the party label is usually a candidate's prime attribute at election time.

Perhaps the most important change in American elections is that candidates don't campaign just to get elected anymore. It is now necessary to campaign for *nomination* as well. Party organizations once controlled that function. For most important offices today, however, candidates are no longer nominated *by* the party organization but are nominated *within* the party. Party leaders seldom choose candidates themselves; they organize and supervise the election process by which party *voters* choose the candidates. Because almost all aspiring candidates must first win a primary election to gain their party's nomination, those who would campaign for election must first campaign for nomination.

Nominations

The distinguishing feature of the nomination process in American party politics is that it usually involves an election by party voters. Virtually no other political parties in the world nominate candidates to the national legislature through party elections.[32] In more than half the world's parties, local party leaders choose legislative candidates, and their national party organization must usually approve those choices. In fact, in more than one-third of the world's parties, the national organization itself selects the candidates.

Democrats and Republicans nominate their candidates for national and state offices in varying ways across the country because each state is entitled to make its own laws governing the nomination process. (This is significant in itself, for political parties in most other countries are largely free of laws stating how they must select their candidates.) We can classify their nomination practices by the types of party elections held and the level of office sought.

Nomination for Congress and State Offices

In the United States, most aspiring candidates for major offices are nominated through a **primary election**, a preliminary election conducted within the party to select its candidates. Forty-three states use primary elections alone to nominate candidates for all state and national offices, and primaries figure in the nomination process in all the other states.[33] The nomination process, then, is highly decentralized, resting on the decisions of thousands, perhaps millions, of the party rank and file who participate in primary elections.

States hold different types of primary elections for state and congressional offices. The most common type (used by twenty-six states in 2000) is the **closed primary**, in which voters must declare their party affiliation before they are given the primary ballot, which lists the party's potential nominees. Twenty states use the **open primary**, in which voters may choose either party's ballot, listing that party's potential nominees to take into the polling booth. In 2000 four states used variations of the **blanket primary**, in which voters receive one or more ballots listing all parties' potential nominees for each office and can mark their ballots for any candidate, but only one for each office. The top vote getter from each party advances to the general election.

In June 2000, however, the U.S. Supreme Court put the future of blanket primaries in doubt. In *California Democratic Party v. Jones,* the Court ruled that California's blanket primary violated a political party's first amendment right of association.

Nomination for President

The decentralized nature of American parties is readily apparent in candidates' campaigns for the parties' nomination for president. Delegates attending the parties' national conventions held the summer before the presidential election in November nominate presidential candidates. In the past, delegates chose their party's nominee right at the convention, sometimes after repeated balloting over several candidates who divided the vote and kept anyone from getting the majority needed to win the nomination. However, the last time that either party needed more than one ballot to nominate its presidential candidate was in 1952, when the Democrats took three ballots to nominate Adlai E. Stevenson. Since 1972, both parties' nominating conventions have simply ratified the results of the complex process for selecting the convention delegates.

Selecting Convention Delegates   No national legislation specifies how state parties must select delegates to their national conventions. Instead, state legislatures have enacted a bewildering variety of procedures, which often differ for Democrats and Republicans in the same state. The most important distinction in delegate selection is between the presidential primary and the local caucus.

A **presidential primary** is a special primary held to select delegates to attend the party's national nominating convention. In *presidential preference primaries,* party supporters vote directly for the person they favor as their party's nominee for president, and the primary candidates win delegates according to a variety of formulas. In all Democratic primaries, candidates who win at least 15 percent of the vote divide the delegates from that state in proportion to the percentage they won. In almost half the Republican primaries, the winning candidate takes all the state's convention delegates. In *delegate selection primaries,* party voters directly elect convention delegates, who may or may not have declared for a presidential candidate.[34]

Delegate selection by **local caucus** has several stages. It begins with local meetings, or caucuses, of party supporters to choose delegates to attend a larger subsequent meeting, usually at the county level. Most delegates selected in the local caucuses openly back one of the presidential candidates. The county meetings, in turn, select delegates to a higher level. The process culminates in a state convention, which actually selects the delegates to the national convention. Thirteen states used the caucus process in 2000 (a few states combine caucuses with primaries), and Democrats used caucuses more than Republicans did.[35]

Primary elections were first used to select delegates to nominating conventions in 1912. Now parties in more than forty states rely on presidential primaries, which generate more than 80 percent of the delegates.

Who Is Missing from This Photo?
*An assortment of presidential contenders join hands at the first formal gathering of
Republican candidates in New Hampshire on May 2, 1999—nine months before the state's
primary. From the left, the hopefuls are John R. Kasich, Steve Forbes, Alan Keyes, Lamar
Alexander, Elizabeth Dole, and Gary L. Bauer. By July 14, Kasich abandoned all hope for
the nomination and dropped out of the race. On August 16, Lamar Alexander lost hope
after finishing sixth out of nine candidates who had competed in the Iowa "straw poll" two
days earlier. George W. Bush, who won the Iowa poll and eventually the Republican nomination, isn't even pictured with his hand in the pile.*

Campaigning for the Nomination   The process of nominating party candidates
for president is a complex, drawn-out affair that has no parallel in any other
nation. Would-be presidents announce their candidacy and begin campaigning many months before the first convention delegates are selected. Soon after
one election ends, prospective candidates quietly begin lining up political and
financial support for their likely race nearly four years later. By historical accident, two small states—Iowa and New Hampshire—have become the testing
ground of candidates' popularity with party voters. Accordingly, each basks in
the media spotlight once every four years.

The Iowa caucuses and the New Hampshire primary have served different
functions in the presidential nominating process.[36] The contest in Iowa has
traditionally tended to winnow out candidates who are rejected by the party
faithful. The New Hampshire primary, held one week later, tests the Iowa
front-runners' appeal to ordinary party voters, which foreshadows their likely
strength in the general election.

Requiring prospective presidential candidates to campaign before many
millions of party voters in primaries and hundreds of thousands of party activists in caucus states has several consequences:

- The uncertainty of the nomination process attracts a half-dozen or so plausi-
  ble candidates, especially when the party does not have a president seeking
  reelection, as was the case in the early Republican primaries in 2000.

- Candidates favored by most party identifiers usually win their party's nomination. There have been only two exceptions to this rule since 1936, when poll data first became available: Adlai E. Stevenson in 1952 and George McGovern in 1972.[37] Both were Democrats; both lost impressively in the general election.
- Candidates who win the nomination do so largely on their own and owe little or nothing to the national party organization, which usually does not promote a candidate. In fact, Jimmy Carter won the nomination in 1976 against a field of nationally prominent Democrats, although he was a party outsider with few strong connections in the national party leadership.

Although candidates may campaign for the nomination for years before the actual primary season, once the primaries begin the eventual party nominees may emerge quickly from the pack. By March 2000, the major intraparty competition was over, and George W. Bush and Al Gore were clearly going to be selected as the nominees of their parties at the summer conventions.

Elections

By national law, all seats in the House of Representatives and one-third of the seats in the Senate are filled in a **general election** held in early November in even-numbered years. Every state takes advantage of the national election to also fill some of nearly five hundred thousand state and local offices across the country, which makes the election even more "general." When the president is chosen every fourth year, the election year is identified as a *presidential election.* The intervening years are known as *congressional, midterm,* or *off-year elections.*

Presidential Elections

In contrast to almost all other offices in the United States, the presidency does not go automatically to the candidate who wins the most votes. Instead, a two-stage procedure specified in the Constitution decides elections for president; it requires selection of the president by a group (college) of electors representing the states.

The Electoral College   Voters choose the president only indirectly; they actually vote for a slate of little-known electors (their names are usually not even on the ballot) pledged to one of the candidates. Occasionally, electors break their pledges when they cast their written ballots at their state capitols in December. (This happened as recently as 2000.)[38] But usually the electors are faithful. The fundamental principle of the electoral college is that the outcome of the popular vote determines the outcome of the electoral vote. Whether a candidate wins a state by five or five hundred thousand votes, he or she wins all that state's electoral votes.*

---

*The two exceptions are Maine and Nebraska, where two and three of the states' electoral votes, respectively, are awarded by congressional district. The presidential candidate who carries each district wins a single electoral vote, and the statewide winner gets two votes.

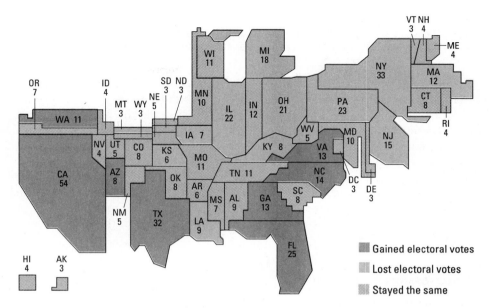

FIGURE 6.3   The Political Geography of the Electoral College
*If the states were sized according to their electoral votes, the nation might resemble this map,
on which the states are drawn according to their population, based on the 1990 census.
Each state has as many electoral votes as its combined representation in the Senate (always
two) and the House (which depends on population). Although New Jersey is much smaller
in area than Montana, it has far more people and is thus bigger in terms of "electoral geography." California, with two senators and fifty-two representatives, has fifty-four electoral
votes—or more than 10 percent of the total of 538. Washington, D.C., has three electoral
votes—equal to the smallest states—although it has no representation in Congress. (Source:
"The 1990 Census: The Changing Shape of the Union," New York Times, 27 December 1990, p.
A10; and Congressional Quarterly Weekly Report, 23 March 1991, p. 765.)*

In the electoral college, each state is accorded one vote for each of its senators (100 votes total) and representatives (435 votes total), adding up to 535
votes. In addition, the Twenty-third Amendment to the Constitution awarded
three electoral votes to the District of Columbia even though it elects no voting members of Congress. So the total number of electoral votes is 538, and a
candidate needs a majority of 270 electoral votes to win the presidency (see
Figure 6.3).*

The most troubling aspect of the electoral college is the possibility that despite winning a plurality or even a majority of popular votes, a candidate could
lose the election in the electoral college. This could happen if one candidate

---

*If no candidate receives a majority when the electoral college votes, the election is thrown into
the House of Representatives. The House votes by state, with each state casting one vote. The candidates in the House election are the top three finishers in the general election. A presidential
election has gone to the House only twice in American history, in 1800 and in 1824, before a stable two-party system had developed.

wins certain states by very wide margins, while the other candidate wins other states by slim margins. Indeed, this happened three times in the nineteenth century (1824, 1876, and 1888) and again in 2000 (see Feature 9.1, p. 232).

Abolish the Electoral College?   Reformers argue that it is wrong to have a system that allows a candidate who receives the most popular votes to lose the election. They favor a purely majoritarian means of choosing the president: direct election by popular vote. Defenders of the electoral college point out that this system, warts and all, has been a stable one. It might be riskier to replace it with a new arrangement that could alter our party system or the way presidential campaigns are conducted. Also, some scholars argue that the electoral college's tendency to magnify the winner's victory margin increases the legitimacy of the president-elect. Reformers may gain some momentum from George W. Bush's 2000 electoral college win over Al Gore, the popular vote winner.

Congressional Elections

The candidates for the presidency are listed at the top of the ballot in a presidential election, followed by the candidates for other national offices and for state and local offices. Voters are said to vote a **straight ticket** when they choose one party's candidates for all the offices. A voter who chooses candidates from different parties is said to vote a **split ticket**. About half of all voters admit to splitting their tickets.[39] A common pattern in the 1970s and 1980s was to elect a Republican as president but send mostly Democrats to Congress, producing divided government (see Chapter 9). This pattern was reversed in the 1994 election, when voters elected a Republican Congress to face a Democratic president. In 2000, Republicans won control of both the presidency and Congress, producing unified government.

Republicans have regularly complained that inequitable districts drawn by Democrat-dominated state legislatures have denied them their fair share of seats. For example, the Republicans won 46 percent of the congressional vote in 1992 but won only 40 percent of the seats.[40] Despite the Republicans' complaint, election specialists point out that this is the inevitable consequence of **first-past-the-post elections**—a British term for elections conducted in single-member districts that award victory to the candidate with the most votes. In all such elections around the world, the party that wins the most votes tends to win more seats than projected by its percentage of the vote. (The same process operates in the electoral college, which, as discussed, generally awards the winner a larger majority in the electoral vote than was won in popular votes.*)

---

*If you have trouble understanding this phenomenon, think of a basketball team that scores, on average, 51 percent of the total points scored in all games that it plays. Such a team usually wins far more than just 51 percent of its games, for it tends to win the close ones.

Campaigns

Barbara Salmore and Stephen Salmore have developed an analytical framework that emphasizes the political context of an election campaign, the financial resources available for conducting the campaign, and the strategies and
tactics that underlie the dissemination of information about the candidate.

The Political Context

The two most important structural factors that face each candidate planning a
campaign are the office the candidate is seeking and whether he or she is the
incumbent (the current officeholder, running for reelection) or the *challenger*
(who seeks to replace the incumbent). Alternatively, the candidate can be running in an **open election**, which lacks an incumbent as a result of resignation
or death. Incumbents usually enjoy great advantages over challengers, especially in elections to Congress.

Every candidate organizing a campaign must also examine the characteristics of the district, including its physical size and the sociological makeup of its
electorate. In general, the bigger and more populous the district and the
more diverse the electorate, the more complicated and costly is the campaign.

The party preference of the electorate is an important factor in the context
of a campaign. It is easier for candidates to get elected when their party
matches the electorate's preference, in part because raising the money
needed to conduct a winning campaign is easier. Finally, significant political
issues—such as economic recession, personal scandals, and war—not only affect a campaign but can dominate it and even negate such positive factors as
incumbency and the normal inclinations of the electorate.

Financing

Former House Speaker Thomas ("Tip") O'Neill once said, "As it is now, there
are four parts to any campaign. The candidate, the issues of the candidate, the
campaign organization, and the money to run the campaign with. Without
money you can forget the other three."[41] Money will buy the best campaign
managers, equipment, transportation, research, and consultants—making the
quality of the organization only a function of money.[42] Although the equation
is not quite that strong, when party sources promise ample campaign funds,
good candidates become available.

Campaign financing is now heavily regulated by national and state governments, and regulations vary according to the level of the office—national,
state, or local. Even at the national level, differences in financing laws for presidential and congressional elections are significant.

Regulating Campaign Financing In 1971, during the period of party reform, Congress passed the Federal Election Campaign Act (FECA), which imposed stringent new rules for full reporting of campaign contributions and expenditures.

FECA has been amended several times since 1971 and usually strengthened. A 1974 amendment created the **Federal Election Commission** (FEC) to implement the law. The FEC now enforces limits on financial contributions to national campaigns and requires full disclosure of campaign spending. The FEC also administers the public financing of presidential campaigns, which began with the 1976 election.

Financing Presidential Campaigns   In 1974, a new campaign finance law made public funds available to presidential primary and general election candidates under certain conditions. Candidates for each party's nomination for president can qualify for federal funding by raising $5,000 (in private contributions no greater than $250 each) in each of twenty states. The FEC then matches these contributions up to one-half of a preset spending limit for the primary election campaign. Originally, under the 1974 law, the FEC limited spending in presidential primary elections to $10 million. But by 2000, cost-of-living provisions were estimated to raise the limit to $33.8 million (plus $6.8 million for fundraising activities).

The presidential nominees of the Democratic and Republican parties receive twice the primary election limit in public funds for the general election campaign (approximately $67.6 million in 2000) provided that they spend only the public funds. Every major candidate since 1976 has accepted public funding. Ross Perot won enough votes in his personally financed 1992 run for president to qualify for $29.2 million in public funds for 1996.

Public funds go directly to each candidate's campaign committee, not to either party. But the FEC also limits what the national committees can spend on behalf of the nominees. In 2000, that limit was $13.7 million.[43] And the FEC limits the amount individuals ($1,000) and organizations ($5,000) can contribute to presidential candidates during the nomination phase and to House and Senate candidates for the primary and general elections. Individuals or organizations are not limited, however, in the amount of *expenses* they can incur to promote candidates of their choice.*

Public funding has had several effects on campaign financing. Obviously, it has limited campaign expenditures. Also, it has helped equalize the amounts spent by major candidates in general elections. And it has strengthened the trend toward "personalized" presidential campaigns because federal funds are given to the candidate, not to the party organization. Also, public funding has forced candidates to spend a great deal of time seeking $1,000 contributions—a limit that has not changed since 1974 despite inflation that has more than doubled the FEC's spending limits. In the 1980s, however, both parties began to exploit a loophole in the law that allowed them to raise a nearly un-

---

*The distinction between *contributions* and *expenses* hinges on whether funds are spent as part of a coordinated campaign (a contribution) or spent independently of the candidate's campaign (an expense). The 1974 amendment to the FECA established limits on both campaign contributions and independent expenditures by interested citizens. In *Buckley v. Valeo* (1976), the Supreme Court struck down the limits on citizens' expenditures as an infringement on the freedom of speech, protected under the First Amendment.

limited amount of so-called "soft money," funds to be spent for the entire ticket on party mailings, voter registration, and get-out-the-vote campaigns. The national committees channel soft money to state and local party commit- tees for registration drives and other activities that are not exclusively devoted to the presidential candidates but nonetheless help them.[44] The net effect of these "coordinated campaigns" is to enhance the role of both national and state parties in presidential campaigns.

You might think that a party's presidential campaign would be closely co- ordinated with the campaigns of its candidates for Congress. But remember that campaign funds go to the presidential candidate, not the party, and that the national party organization does not run the presidential campaign. Presidential candidates may join congressional candidates in public appear- ances for mutual benefit, but presidential campaigns are usually isolated—fi- nancially and otherwise—from congressional campaigns. Both parties spoke piously about rewriting campaign finance laws in the 104th Congress, but leg- islators could not agree on how to reform a system observers said was "in shambles" two decades after the 1974 campaign reform legislation.[45] However, reform efforts continued in the 105th and 106th Congresses.

Strategies and Tactics

In an election campaign, strategy is the broad approach used to persuade citi- zens to vote for a candidate, and tactics determine the content of the messages and the way they are delivered. There are three basic strategies, which cam- paigns may blend in different mixes.[46] A *party-centered strategy* relies heavily on voters' partisan identification as well as on the party's organization to provide the resources necessary to wage the campaign. An *issue-oriented strategy* seeks support from groups that feel strongly about various policies. An *image-oriented strategy* depends on the candidate's perceived personal qualities, such as expe- rience, leadership ability, integrity, independence, and trustworthiness.

The campaign strategy must be tailored to the political context of the elec- tion. Research suggests that a party-centered strategy is best suited to voters with little political knowledge.[47] How do candidates learn what the electorate knows and thinks about politics, and how can they use this information? Candidates today usually turn to pollsters and political consultants, of whom there are hundreds.[48] Professional campaign managers can use information from such sources to settle on a strategy that mixes party affiliation, issues, and images in its messages. In major campaigns, the mass media disseminate these messages to voters in news coverage and advertising.[49]

Making the News   Campaigns value news coverage by the media for two rea- sons: the coverage is free, and it seems objective to the audience. If news sto- ries do nothing more than report a candidate's name, that is important, for name recognition by itself often wins elections. Getting free news coverage is yet another advantage that incumbents enjoy over challengers, for incumbents can command attention simply by announcing political decisions.

Advertising the Candidate   In all elections, the first objective of paid advertising is name recognition. The next is to promote the candidates by extolling their virtues. Campaign advertising also can have a negative objective, to attack one's opponent. But name recognition is the most important. Studies show that many voters cannot recall the names of their U.S. senators or representatives but can recognize those names on a list—as on a ballot. Researchers attribute the high reelection rate for members of Congress mainly to high name recognition (see Chapter 8).

At one time, candidates for national office relied heavily on newspaper advertising; today, they overwhelmingly use the electronic media.[50] After his nomination in 1996, Dole budgeted $45 million of his $62 million in public funds on television to overcome Clinton's lead in the polls.[51]

Using New Media   A major development in campaigning emerged in 1992: the strategic use of new media, including talk shows, entertainment shows, and Perot's half-hour "infomercials." Bill Clinton started the trend in January by appearing on "60 Minutes" to respond to Gennifer Flowers's claim of infidelity. In February, Ross Perot launched his campaign with an appearance on "Larry King Live." Most observers have concluded that these soft-format programs (watched by many people) represent an alternative form of campaigning that provides viewers with important information on candidates' character and policies.

Clinton's successful use of new media in 1992, including a segment on MTV, guaranteed that candidates would again use them in 1996. Sure enough, even seventy-year-old Bob Dole appeared on MTV. In 2000, candidates Al Gore and George W. Bush tried to appear relaxed during appearances on late-night programs with David Letterman and Jay Leno. But the hottest new medium in 2000 was the Internet. Not only did the major and minor parties put up their own home pages, but so did the presidential candidates—including those just seeking nomination.

Explaining Voting Choice

Why do people choose one candidate over another? The answer is not easy to determine, but there are ways to approach the question. Individual voting choices may be viewed as products of both long-term and short-term forces. Long-term forces operate throughout a series of elections, predisposing voters to choose certain types of candidates. Short-term forces are associated with particular elections; they arise from a combination of the candidates and the issues of the time. Party identification is by far the most important long-term force affecting U.S. elections. The most important short-term forces are candidates' attributes and their policy positions.

Despite frequent comments in the media about the decline of partisanship in voting behavior, party identification continues to have a substantial effect on the presidential vote, as Figure 6.4 shows. Typically, the winner holds nearly all the voters who identify with his party. The loser holds most of his fel-

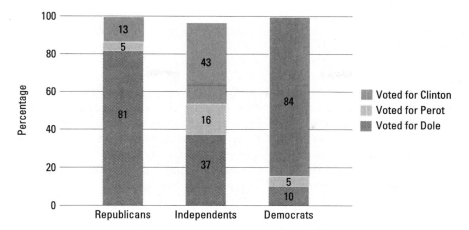

FIGURE 6.4   Effect of Party Identification on the Vote, 1996
The 1996 election showed that party identification still plays a key role in voting behavior—
even with an independent candidate in the contest. The chart shows the results of exit polls
of thousands of voters as they left hundreds of polling places across the nation on Election
Day. Voters were asked what party they identified with and how they voted for president.
Those who identified with one of the two parties voted strongly for their party's candidate,
whereas independent voters divided roughly evenly between Clinton and Dole and were three
times more likely to vote for Perot. (Source: "National Exit Poll Results for Presidential Race,"
distributed by PoliticsNow on the Internet, 6 November 1996.)

low Democrats or Republicans, but some percentage defects to the winner, a
product of short-term forces—the candidates' attributes and the issues—surrounding the election. The winner usually gets most of the independents, who
split disproportionately for him, also because of short-term forces.

Candidates' attributes are especially important to voters who lack good information about a candidate's past performance and policy stands—which
means most of us. Without such information, voters search for clues about the
candidates to try to predict their behavior in office.[52] Some fall back on their
personal beliefs about religion, gender, and race in making political judgments. Such stereotypical thinking accounts for the patterns of opposition and
support met by a Catholic candidate for president (John Kennedy) and a
woman candidate for vice president (Geraldine Ferraro).

Voters who choose between candidates on the basis of their policies are
voting on the issues. Unfortunately for democratic theory, most studies of
presidential elections show that issues are less important than either party
identification or the candidate's attributes when people cast their ballots. Only
in 1972, when voters perceived George McGovern as too liberal for their
tastes, did issue voting exceed party identification in importance.[53]

Although party voting has declined somewhat since the 1950s, the relationship between voters' positions on the issues and their party identification is
clearer today. The more closely party identification is aligned with ideological

orientation, the more sense it makes to vote by party. In the absence of detailed information about candidates' positions on the issues, party labels are a handy indicator of those positions.[54]

If party identification is the most important factor in the voting decision and also is resistant to short-term changes, there are definite limits to the capacity of a campaign to influence the outcome of elections.[55] In a close election, however, just changing a few votes means the difference between victory and defeat, so a campaign can be decisive even if it has little overall effect. But the capacity of image makers and campaign consultants to influence the outcome of presidential elections is minimized because they regularly offset one another by working on both sides. In 2000, both major presidential candidates hired professional campaign consultants and advertising firms.

Campaigns, Elections, and Parties

Election campaigns today tend to be highly personalized, candidate centered, and conducted outside the control of party organizations. The increased use of electronic media, especially television, has encouraged candidates to personalize their campaign messages; at the same time, the decline of party identification has decreased the power of party-related appeals. Although the party affiliations of the candidates and the party identifications of the voters jointly explain a good deal of electoral behavior, party organizations are not central to elections in America, and this has implications for democratic government.

Parties and the Majoritarian Model

According to the majoritarian model of democracy, parties link people with their government by making government responsive to public opinion. The Republican and Democratic parties follow the model in that they formulate different platforms and tend to pursue their announced policies when in office. The weak links in this model of responsible party government have been those that connect candidates to voters through campaigns and elections.

You have not read much about the role of the party platform in nominating candidates, in conducting campaigns, or in explaining voters' choices. Certainly, a presidential candidate who wins enough convention delegates through the primaries will be comfortable with any platform that her or his delegates adopt. But House and Senate nominations are rarely fought over the party platform. And thoughts about party platforms usually are absent from campaigning and from voters' minds when they cast their ballots.

The Republicans' Contract with America was an exception to the rule that party platforms do not matter in elections and in governing. It consisted of ten major proposals that Republican candidates for the House of Representatives promised to bring to a vote if elected in the November 1994 election. The Contract with America became a significant factor in the election campaign and a large part of the Republicans' legislative agenda in the 104th Congress, for Republicans won control not only of the House but also of the Senate in what was called the "Republican Revolution." The Republicans kept their promise by bringing all ten proposals to a vote in the House within one hundred days. Several points in the Contract even became law.

In early 1995, it appeared that the Republicans were following the script of responsible party government and, accordingly, that they would run on the Contract with America in the 1996 election. But later in the 104th Congress, some Republicans (especially in the Senate) failed to follow parts of the script as the public turned against some of their proposals. Before 1995 ended, Republicans stopped talking about the Contract with America. In fact, when Speaker Newt Gingrich addressed the GOP convention in 1996, he did not mention it once, thus seemingly ending this short experiment with responsible party government.[56]

Parties and the Pluralist Model

The way parties in the United States operate is more in keeping with the pluralist model of democracy than with the majoritarian model. Our parties are not the basic mechanism through which citizens control their government; instead, they function as two giant interest groups. The parties' interests lie in electing and reelecting their candidates, in enjoying the benefits of public office. Except in extreme cases, the parties care little about the positions or ideologies favored by their candidates for Congress and statewide offices.

Some scholars believe that stronger parties would strengthen democratic government even if they could not meet all the requirements of the responsible party model. Our parties already perform valuable functions in structuring the vote along partisan lines and in proposing alternative government policies, but stronger parties might also be able to play a more important role in coordinating government policies after elections. At present, the decentralized nature of the nominating process and of campaigning for office offers many opportunities for organized groups outside the party to identify and back candidates who favor their interests. Although this is in keeping with pluralist theory, it is certain to frustrate majority interests on occasion.

Summary

Political parties perform four important functions in a political system: nominating candidates, structuring the voting choice, proposing alternative government programs, and coordinating the activities of government officials. Political parties have been performing these functions longer in the United States than in any other country. The Democratic Party, founded in 1828, is the world's oldest political party. When the Republican Party emerged as a major party after the 1856 election, our present two-party system emerged—the oldest party system in the world.

America's two-party system has experienced three critical elections, each of which realigned the electorate for years and affected the party balance in government. The election of 1860 established the Republicans as the major party in the North and the Democrats as the dominant party in the South. The critical election of 1896 strengthened the link between the Republican Party and business interests in the heavily populated Northeast and Midwest, and it produced a surge in voter support that made the Republicans the majority party nationally for more than three decades. The Great Depression produced conditions that transformed the Democrats into the majority party in the critical election of 1932. Until the Republicans won both houses in the 1994 election, the Democrats enjoyed almost uninterrupted control of Congress for six decades.

Minor parties have not enjoyed much electoral success in America, although they have contributed ideas to the Democratic and Republican platforms. The two-party system is perpetuated in the United States because of the nature of our electoral system and by the political socialization process, which results in most Americans identifying with either the Democratic or the Republican Party. The pattern of party identification has been changing in recent years. As more people are becoming independents and Republicans, the number of Democratic identifiers is dropping. Still, Democrats consistently outnumber Republicans, and together the two parties far outnumber independents.

The two major parties differ in their ideological orientations. Democratic identifiers and activists are more likely to describe themselves as liberal; Republican identifiers and activists tend to be conservative. Organizationally, the Republicans have recently become the stronger party at both the national and the state levels, and both parties are showing signs of resurgence. Nevertheless, both parties are still very decentralized compared with parties in other countries.

Campaigning has evolved from a party-centered to a candidate-centered process. The successful candidate for public office usually must campaign first to win the party nomination, then to win the general election. A major factor in the decentralization of American parties is their reliance on primary elections to nominate candidates. Democratic and Republican nominations for president are no longer actually decided in the parties' national conventions but are determined in advance through the complex process of selecting delegates pledged to particular candidates. Today winners can legitimately say that they captured the nomination through their own efforts and that they owe little to the party organization.

The need to win a majority of votes in the electoral college structures presidential elections. Although a candidate can win a majority of the popular vote but lose in the electoral college, that has not happened in more than one hundred years. In fact, the electoral college typically magnifies the victory margin of the winning candidate.

In the general election, candidates usually retain the same staffs that helped them win the nomination. The dynamics of campaign financing also force candidates to rely mainly on their own resources or—in the case of presidential elections—on public funds. Party organizations now often contribute money to congressional candidates, but the candidates must raise most of the money themselves. Money is essential in running a modern campaign for major office—for conducting polls and advertising the candidate's name, qualifications, and positions on issues through the media. Candidates seek free news coverage whenever possible, but most must rely on paid advertising to get their messages across. Ironically, voters also get most of their campaign information from advertisements. The trend in recent years has been toward negative advertising.

Voting choice is influenced by party identification, candidates' attributes, and policy positions. Party identification is still the most important long-term factor in shaping the voting decision.

Traditionally, major American political parties have followed the model of responsible party government to the extent that they formulate different platforms and tend to translate their platform positions into government policy if elected to power. However, the way that nominations, campaigns, and elections are conducted in America is out of keeping with the ideals of responsible party government that fit the majoritarian model of democracy. In particular, campaigns and elections do not function to link parties strongly to voters as the model posits. The Republicans' Contract with America, however, fulfilled some features of the responsible party model. American parties are better suited to the pluralist model of democracy, which sees them as major interest groups competing with lesser groups to further their own interests. At least political parties aspire to the noble goal of representing the needs and wants of most of the people. As we see in the next chapter, interest groups do not even pretend as much.

Key Terms

political party
nomination
political system
critical election
electoral realignment
electoral dealignment
two-party system
majority representation
proportional representation
party identification
party platform
national convention
national committee
party conference
congressional campaign committee

party machine
responsible party government
election campaign
primary election
closed primary
open primary
blanket primary
presidential primary
local caucus
general election
straight ticket
split ticket
first-past-the-post election
open election
Federal Election Commission

Selected Readings

Ansolabehere, Stephen, and Shanto Iyengar. *Going Negative: How Political Advertisements Shrink and Polarize the Electorate.* New York: Free Press, 1995. The subtitle describes the book's thesis, but in addition the authors contend that political advertising also conveys useful information to citizens about politics.

Beck, Paul Allen. *Party Politics in America.* 8th ed. New York: HarperCollins, 1996. A comprehensive text on political parties.

Issacharpff, Samuel, Pamela S. Karlan, and Richard H. Pildes. *The Law of Democracy: Legal Structures of the Political Process.* Westbury, N.Y.: The Foundation Press, 1998. The authors are lawyers, but don't let that keep you from consulting this rich source on voting rights laws, regulation of political parties, voting systems, and money and politics. The book contains material by political scientists, too.

Mayer, William G., ed. *In Pursuit of the White House: How We Choose Our Presidential Nominees.* Chatham, N.J.: Chatham House, 1996. A valuable set of studies, with plenty of data, on the nomination process, including the problems facing third-party candidates.

Reynolds, David. *Democracy Unbound: Progressive Challenges to the Two-Party System.* Boston: South End Press, 1997. Describes how grassroots activists translate mass discontent into new people-driven parties.

Schattschneider, E. E. *Party Government.* New York: Holt, 1942. A clear and powerful argument for the central role of political parties in a democracy according to the model of responsible party government; a classic book in political science.

Shea, Daniel M., and John C. Green, eds. *The State of the Parties: The Changing Role of Contemporary American Parties.* 2d ed. Lanham, Md.: Rowman & Littlefield, 1996. A valuable collection of empirical studies and theoretical analyses of American parties at the national and state levels. The articles document the increased activity of party organizations in election campaigns.

Wattenberg, Martin P. *The Decline of American Political Parties, 1952–1994.* Cambridge, Mass.: Harvard University Press, 1996. The author argues that the American electorate has lessened its attachment to parties because people now believe that candidates, not parties, solve government problems.

World Wide Web Resources

Democratic National Committee. The DNC home page describes the party's structure, bylaws, platform, and activities.
<www.democrats.org>

Republican National Committee. The RNC home page includes the same kinds of information as the Democrats offer but a bit more of everything.
<www.rnc.org>

The Reform Party Official Website provides not only information about the party, candidates, and platform but also an opportunity to register with the party on-line.
<www.reformparty.org>

The *Federal Election Commission* site contains an extraordinary collection of electoral data, including election results and records of financial contributions and receipts for all national candidates. An extremely helpful resource.
<www.fec.gov>

ELECnet describes itself as "one of the most comprehensive listings of U.S. federal, state, and local elections offices on the Internet," with over four hundred links to election-related sites.
<www.debexar.com/elecnet>

Campaigns & Elections Online. This is the site for the magazine *Campaigns & Elections,* which reports on current campaigns and campaign strategy, methods, products, and so on.
<www.campaignline.com>

AllPolitics. Time and CNN (both owned by Time-Warner) join forces to cover issues, polls, elections, Congress, and virtually everything else in national politics.
<www.allpolitics.com>

7

Interest Groups

"Caution: Cigarette Smoking May Be Hazardous to Your Health." Ever since President Lyndon Johnson signed legislation putting this warning on every pack of cigarettes, antismoking campaigns have become a familiar feature of American culture. However, this pales in comparison with the dramatic announcement on June 20, 1997, that the politically powerful tobacco industry had reached a multibillion-dollar agreement with attorneys general from forty states to partially compensate those states for the social costs of smoking. Led by Michael Moore, Mississippi's attorney general, a coalition of state officials and antismoking organizations such as the Coalition for Tobacco-Free Kids bargained with lawyers from the tobacco companies. Under the $368 billion settlement, the tobacco industry pledged to set up a fund to help states pay the Medicaid costs of sick smokers, accepted a ban on billboard advertising, and agreed to let the Food and Drug Administration regulate nicotine in cigarettes. The deal granted tobacco companies, worried about an onslaught of costly legal battles and falling stock prices, immunity from future lawsuits.[1]

The announcement appeared to signal a remarkable victory for the health interests of all Americans over the economic interests of tobacco manufacturers and growers, but was the tobacco lobby really vanquished? For decades, the tobacco industry has made friends in Washington by contributing millions of dollars to congressional incumbents and their parties. Further strengthening tobacco's clout is the number of senators and representatives who come from tobacco-growing states. Tobacco is raised in twenty states and plays a major role in the economies of Georgia, Kentucky, North Carolina, South Carolina, Tennessee, and Virginia.

The first sign that the tobacco lobby was still influential despite the industry's concessions appeared in August 1997. After President Clinton signed a bill to cut taxes, a barely noticed provision in the bill turned out to reduce cigarette makers' $368 billion costs by $50 billion through some clever financial wizardry. Who slipped this provision into the tax bill? No one stepped forward to take credit. The suspected culprits were the Republican leaders in Congress, especially Senate Majority Leader Trent Lott of Mississippi. Because of the spate of publicity surrounding this sleight of hand, the formerly unnoticed rider was speedily repealed. In the House, Republican leaders allowed a voice vote to rescind the provision, and in the Senate even Majority Leader Lott sided with the overwhelming majority of 95–3.[2]

But other votes also had to make the public wonder who really had won the tobacco wars. Senator Richard Durbin, a Democrat from Illinois, thought the timing seemed right to eliminate federally subsidized crop insurance for tobacco farmers. Not surprisingly, lawmakers from tobacco states saw the issue differently. Representative Edward Whitfield, a Kentucky Republican, vowed that "Those of us who represent tobacco farmers are going to do whatever we can to make sure they can continue to grow their crop."[3] In the end, a coalition of farm states and cigarette manufacturing communities was enough to defeat the Durbin motion, 53–47 in the Senate and 216–209 in the House.

Delayed until 1998 was the vote on whether to accept the pact that Moore and his counterparts in the other states had negotiated. Congressional approval was needed to guarantee the cigarette companies' immunity from future lawsuits. The tobacco industry beefed up its lobbying power by hiring a law firm employing both George Mitchell, the Democrats' former Senate majority leader, and Robert Dole, the Republicans' 1996 presidential candidate and former Senate majority leader. The nation's antitobacco forces, led by the American Lung Association, believed the settlement was not tough enough on big tobacco. Minnesota's attorney general, Hubert H. "Skip" Humphrey III, put together such a persuasive case showing cigarette manufacturers deliberately destroyed research linking smoking with cancer that in May 1998 five tobacco firms settled out of court with Minnesota for $6.5 billion, an amount 50 percent higher than the state would have received under the original agreement negotiated by Moore.[4]

Most Americans recognize that cigarettes are bad for their health and want to alert youths to the dangers of smoking. But the public health concerns of the majority often get drowned out by the more vocal demands of those whose economic well-being depends on tobacco. Although the current trend in American politics appears to favor the antismoking forces over the long haul, tobacco interests, through political contributions and well-organized lobbying, can often outmaneuver the less-organized, less-focused majority.

In this chapter, we look at the central dynamic of pluralist democracy: the interaction of interest groups and government. In analyzing the process by which interest groups and lobbyists come to speak on behalf of different groups, we focus on a number of questions. How do interest groups form? Whom do they represent? What tactics do they use to convince policymakers that their views are best for the nation? Is the interest group system biased to favor certain types of people? If it is, what are the consequences?

Interest Groups and the American Political Tradition

An **interest group** is an organized body of individuals who share some political goals and try to influence public policy decisions. Among the most prominent interest groups in the United States are the AFL-CIO (representing labor union members), the American Farm Bureau Federation (representing farmers), the Business Roundtable (representing big business), and Common Cause (representing citizens concerned with reforming government). Interest groups are also called **lobbies**, and their representatives are referred to as **lobbyists**.

Interest Groups: Good or Evil?

A recurring debate in American politics concerns the role of interest groups in a democratic society. Are interest groups a threat to the well-being of the political system, or do they contribute to its proper functioning? Alexis de Tocqueville, a French visitor to the United States in the early nineteenth century, marveled at the array of organizations he found. He later wrote that "Americans of all ages, all conditions, and all dispositions, constantly form associations."[5] Tocqueville was suggesting that the ease with which we form organizations reflects a strong democratic culture.

Yet other early observers were concerned about the consequences of interest group politics. Writing in the *Federalist* papers, James Madison warned of the dangers of "factions," the major divisions in American society. In *Federalist* No. 10, written in 1787, Madison said that it was inevitable that substantial differences would develop between factions, and that each faction would try to persuade government to adopt policies that favored it at the expense of others.[6] Madison, however, argued against trying to suppress factions. He concluded that they can be eliminated only by removing our freedoms, because "Liberty is to faction what air is to fire."[7]

Madison suggested that relief from the self-interested advocacy of factions should come only through controlling the effects of that advocacy. This relief would be provided by a democratic republic in which government would mediate between opposing factions. The size and diversity of the nation as well as the structure of government would also ensure that even a majority faction could never come to suppress the rights of others.[8]

How we judge interest groups—"good" or "evil"—may depend on how strongly we are committed to freedom or equality (see Chapter 1). A survey of the American public showed that almost two-thirds of those polled regarded lobbying as a threat to American democracy.[9] Yet, as we will demonstrate later, in recent years interest groups have enjoyed unparalleled growth. Apparently, we distrust interest groups as a whole, but we like those that speak on our behalf.

The Roles of Interest Groups

The "evil" side of interest group politics is all too apparent. Each group pushes its own selfish interests, which, despite the group's claims to the contrary, are not always in the best interest of other Americans. The "good" side of interest group advocacy may not be as clear. How do the actions of interest groups benefit our political system?[10]

Politics in a Changing America 7.1

A Political Voice for Christians

New political movements organized in recent years represent diverse interests and constituencies. What their members have in common, however, is a feeling of being marginalized by our political system. Members share a belief that unless they are highly mobilized and aggressive in pursuing their political objectives, policymakers will ignore their concerns. This is certainly the attitude of Christian fundamentalists—Christians whose religious beliefs are based on a literal interpretation of the Bible.

Fundamentalist Christians believe that modern society has turned away from basic moral principles, creating serious social problems. In their eyes, liberal and moderate politicians have mistakenly tried to solve these problems with expensive, wasteful, and counterproductive social programs. Christian fundamentalists feel that what is needed instead is a return to strong family values.

Many groups claim to represent fundamentalists in the political arena, but the Christian Coalition plays a central leadership role. Based in Virginia, this conservative group is closely allied with the Reverend Pat Robertson. Robertson, who ran unsuccessfully for the Republican presidential nomination in 1988, is probably best known for his TV show, "The 700 Club," which is shown around the country on the Christian Broadcasting Network.

The issues that have most animated the Christian Coalition over the years include abortion, homosexuality, prayer in school, and the decline of the nuclear family. In 1997 the Christian Coalition began campaigning for the Religious Freedom Amendment, which would permit school prayer and allow public money to be spent on religious educational institutions.

Under the leadership of executive director Ralph Reed, the Christian Coalition began working on issues less clearly related to its religious roots. For instance, the Christian Coalition lobbied hard for the Contract with America and helped push the $500-per-child tax credit through Congress. In fact, the Christian Coalition became so politicized under Reed that the Federal Election Commission accused it of improperly aiding Republican candidates and the Internal Revenue Service began reviewing its tax-exempt status.

During the summer of 1997, Reed stepped down as executive director to begin his own political consulting firm. Since Reed's departure the Christian Coalition has been hurting financially, and in 1999 Robertson announced that the group would split into two new organizations: the Christian Coalition of America (which would remain tax exempt) and the Christian Coalition International, a not-for-profit (but taxable) organization that would be free to raise money for a Political Action Committee and distribute funds directly to candidates.

Many liberals are antagonistic to the Christian Coalition and other such groups, not simply because they hold competing political views but also because they believe that the Christian right is trying to impose its particular brand of religion on the rest of the country. Although political activism

(continued)

Politics in a Changing America 7.1 (continued)

can also be found in African American churches, synagogues, mainline Protestant congregations, and Catholic parishes, the Christian conservatives are the best organized of all the religious groups in the United States, and churches embracing the beliefs of the Christian right are the most rapidly growing denominations in the country. Pentecostals, an evangelical denomination whose followers are generally sympathetic to Christian conservatism, grew in membership from about 1.9 million in 1960 to 9.9 million in 1990, an increase of 423 percent.

What is especially impressive about the Christian Coalition and other groups associated with the religious right is their success in involving rank-and-file citizens in politics and government. Former senator Nancy Kassebaum of Kansas says of the religious right, "It's a voice that in many ways comes from people who feel that they've never been part of the process." Many Christians who dislike the religious right point out that the Christian Coalition does not speak for all Christians. But for those Christians it does represent, the Christian Coalition is a powerful and passionate advocate.

Sources: Ralph Z. Hallow, "Hodel to Head Christian Coalition, Initially Spurned Robertson Offer," *Washington Times*, 12 June 1997, p. A3; Sam Munger, "Martyrs Before Congress," *The Nation*, 23 June 1997, pp. 5–6; David Shribman, "The Christian Right Regroups," *Fortune*, 8 September 1997, pp. 44, 48; Michael J. Gerson, "Christian Coalition in Unprecedented Crisis," *U.S. News and World Report*, 16 February 1998, pp. 35–36.

Representation Interest groups represent people before their government. Just as a member of Congress represents a particular constituency, so does a lobbyist. A lobbyist for the National Association of Broadcasters, for example, speaks for the interests of radio and television broadcasters when Congress or a government agency is considering a relevant policy decision.

Whatever the political interest—the cement industry, social security, endangered species—it is helpful to have an active lobby operating in Washington. Members of Congress represent a multitude of interests, some of them conflicting, from their own districts and states. Government administrators, too, are pulled in different directions and have their own policy preferences. Interest groups articulate their members' concerns, presenting them directly and forcefully in the political process (see Politics in a Changing America 7.1).

Participation Interest groups are also vehicles for political participation. They provide a means by which like-minded citizens can pool their resources and channel their energies into collective political action. One farmer fighting against a new pesticide proposal in Congress probably will not get very far. Thousands of farmers united in an organization will stand a much better chance of getting policymakers to consider their needs.

Education   As part of their efforts at lobbying and increasing their membership, interest groups try to educate their members, the public at large, and government officials. For example, after Congress proposed significant cutbacks in research money for universities in 1995, the schools and their Washington lobbyists swung into action. To gain the attention of the policymakers they are trying to educate, interest groups need to provide information that is not easily obtained from other sources.[11] Members of Congress were told about a Bank of Boston study that demonstrated that three hundred thousand people in Massachusetts were employed by companies utilizing technology and other resources developed by Massachusetts Institute of Technology researchers. The point was clear: if you cut research funding, you will damage your local economy's chance to grow.[12]

Agenda Building   In a related role, interest groups bring new issues into the political limelight through a process called **agenda building**. American society has many problem areas, but public officials are not addressing all of them. Through their advocacy, interest groups make the government aware of problems, then try to see that something is done to solve them. Women's groups have played a key role in gaining attention for problems—such as unequal pay for women doing similar jobs as men—that were being systematically ignored.[13]

Program Monitoring   Finally, interest groups engage in **program monitoring**. Lobbies follow government programs that are important to their constituents, keeping abreast of developments in Washington and in the communities where the policies are implemented. When a program is not operating as it should, concerned interest groups push administrators to resolve problems in ways that promote the group's goals. They draw attention to agency officials' transgressions and even file suit to stop actions they consider unlawful.

Interest groups do play some positive roles in their pursuit of self-interest. But we should not assume that the positive side of interest groups neatly balances the negative. Questions remain about the overall influence of interest groups on public policymaking. Are the effects of interest group advocacy being controlled, as Madison believed they should be?

Why Interest Groups Form

Do some people form interest groups more easily than others? Are some factions represented while others are not? Pluralists assume that when a political issue arises, interest groups with relevant policy concerns begin to lobby. Policy conflicts are ultimately resolved through bargaining and negotiation between the involved organizations and the government. Unlike Madison, who dwelled on the potential for harm by factions, pluralists believe that interest groups are a good thing, that they further democracy by broadening representation within the system.

An important part of pluralism is the belief that new interest groups form as a matter of course when the need arises. David Truman outlines this idea in his classic work *The Governmental Process*.[14] He says that when individuals are threatened by change they band together in an interest group. For example, if government threatens to regulate a particular industry, the firms that compose that industry will start a trade association to protect their financial well-being. Truman sees a direct cause-and-effect relationship: existing groups stand in equilibrium until some type of disturbance (such as falling wages or declining farm prices) forces new groups to form.

Truman's *disturbance theory* paints an idealized portrait of interest group politics in America. In real life, people do not automatically organize when they are adversely affected by some disturbance. A good example of such "nonorganization" can be found in Herbert Gans's book *The Urban Villagers*.[15] Gans, a sociologist, moved into the West End, a low-income neighborhood in Boston, during the late 1950s. The neighborhood had been targeted for urban redevelopment. This meant that the people living there—primarily poor Italian Americans who very much liked their neighborhood—had to move. The people of the West End barely put up a fight to save their neighborhood. They started an organization, but it attracted little support. Residents remained unorganized. Soon they were moved out, and buildings were demolished.

Disturbance theory fails to explain what happened (or didn't happen) in Boston's West End. An adverse condition or change does not automatically result in the formation of an interest group. What, then, is the missing ingredient? Political scientist Robert Salisbury says that the quality of interest group leadership may be the crucial factor.[16]

Interest Group Entrepreneurs

Salisbury likens the role of an interest group leader to the role of an entrepreneur in the business world. A business entrepreneur is someone who starts new enterprises, usually at considerable personal financial risk. Salisbury says that an **interest group entrepreneur,** or organizer, succeeds or fails for many of the same reasons a business entrepreneur succeeds or fails. The interest group entrepreneur must have something attractive to "market" in order to convince people to join the group.[17] Potential members must be persuaded that the benefits of joining outweigh the costs.

The development of the United Farm Workers shows the importance of leadership in the formation of an interest group. Members of this union are men and women who pick crops in California and other parts of the country. They are predominantly poor, uneducated Mexican Americans. Throughout the twentieth century, various unions tried to organize the pickers, and for many reasons—including distrust of union organizers, intimidation by employers, and lack of money to pay union dues—all failed. Then in 1962, Cesar Chavez, a poor Mexican American, began to crisscross the Central Valley of California, talking to workers and planting the idea of a union.

After a strike against grape growers failed in 1965, Chavez changed his tactics of trying to build a strong union merely by recruiting more and more members. Copying the civil rights movement, Chavez and his followers

FIGURE 7.1   *Social Class and Interest Group Membership*
Membership in interest groups is clearly linked to social class. The higher their total family income, the more likely it is that individuals will belong to at least one political interest group. The data here come from a survey of citizens in five American cities (Birmingham, Alabama; Dayton, Ohio; Portland, Oregon; St. Paul, Minnesota; and San Antonio, Texas). (Source: Based on Jeffrey M. Berry, Kent E. Portney, and Ken Thomson, The Rebirth of Urban Democracy. *Copyright © 1993. Used by permission of Brookings Institution.)*

marched 250 miles to the California state capitol in Sacramento to demand help from the governor. This march and other nonviolent tactics began to draw sympathy from people who had no direct involvement in farming. With his stature increased by that support, Chavez called for a grape boycott, and a small but significant number of Americans stopped buying grapes. The growers, who had bitterly fought the union, were hurt economically. Under this and other economic pressures, they eventually agreed to recognize and bargain with the United Farm Workers.

Who Is Being Organized?

Cesar Chavez's success is a good example of the importance of leadership in the formation of a new interest group. But another important element is at work in the formation of interest groups. The residents of Boston's West End and the farm workers in California were economically poor, uneducated or undereducated, and politically inexperienced—factors that made it extremely difficult to organize them into interest groups. If they had been well-off, well educated, and politically experienced, they probably would have banded together immediately. People who have money, education, and knowledge of how the system operates are more confident that their actions can make a difference (see Figure 7.1).

Every existing interest group has its own history, but the three variables just discussed can help explain why groups may or may not become fully organized. First, a disturbance or adverse change can heighten people's awareness that they need political representation. However, awareness alone does not ensure that an organization will form, and organizations may form in the absence of a disturbance. Second, the quality of leadership is critical to the organization of interest groups. Third, the higher the socioeconomic level of potential members, the more likely they are to know the value of interest groups and to join them.

The question that remains, then, is *how well* are various opposing interests represented. Or, in terms of Madison's premise in *Federalist* No. 10, are the effects of faction—in this case, the advantages of the wealthy and well educated—being controlled? Before we can answer this question, we need to turn our attention to the resources available to interest groups.

Interest Group Resources

The strengths, capabilities, and influence of an interest group depend in large part on its resources. A group's most significant resources are its members, lobbyists, and money, including funds that can be contributed to political candidates. The sheer quantity of a group's resources is important, and so is the wisdom with which its resources are used.

Members

One of the most valuable resources an interest group can have is a large, politically active membership. If a lobbyist is trying to persuade a legislator to support a particular bill, having a large group of members who live in the legislator's home district or state is tremendously helpful. A legislator who has not already taken a firm position on a bill might be swayed by the knowledge that interest groups are keeping voters back home informed of his or her votes on key issues.

Members give an organization not only the political muscle to influence policy but also financial resources. The more money an organization can collect through dues and contributions, the more people it can hire to lobby government officials and monitor policymaking. Greater resources also allow the organization to communicate with its members more and to inform them better. And funding helps the group maintain its membership and attract new members.

Maintaining Membership   To keep the members it already has, an organization must persuade them that it is a strong, effective advocate. Most lobbies use a newsletter to keep members apprised of developments in government that relate to issues of concern and to inform them about steps the organization is taking to protect their interests.

Business, professional, and labor associations generally have an easier time retaining members than do citizen groups—groups whose basis of organization is a concern for issues not directly related to their members' jobs. In many companies, corporate membership in a trade group constitutes only a minor business expense. Labor unions are helped in states that require workers to affiliate with the union that is the bargaining agent with their employer. In contrast, citizen groups base their appeal on members' ideological sentiments. These groups face a difficult challenge: issues can blow hot and cold, and a particularly hot issue one year may not hold the same interest to citizens the next.

Attracting New Members   All membership groups are constantly looking for new members to expand their resources and clout. Groups that rely on ideological appeals have a special problem, because the competition in most policy areas is intense. People concerned about the environment, for example, can join a seemingly infinite number of local, state, and national groups that lobby on environmental issues.

One common method of attracting new members is *direct mail*—letters sent to a selected audience to promote the organization and appeal for contributions. The main drawbacks to direct mail are its expense and low rate of return.

The Free-Rider Problem   The need for aggressive marketing by interest groups suggests that getting people who sympathize with a group's goals to support the group with contributions is difficult. Economists call this difficulty the **free-rider problem**, but we might call it, more colloquially, the "let-George-do-it" problem.[18] Funding for public television stations illustrates this dilemma. Only a fraction of those who watch public television contribute on a regular basis. Why? Because a free rider has the same access to public television as a contributor.

The same problem troubles interest groups. When a lobbying group wins benefits, those benefits are not restricted to members of the organization. For instance, if the American Business Conference wins a tax concession from Congress for capital expenditures, all businesses that fall within the provisions of the law can take advantage of the tax break. Thus, many business executives might not support their firm's joining the American Business Conference, even though they might benefit from the group's efforts; they prefer to let others shoulder the financial burden.

The free-rider problem increases the difficulty of attracting paying members. Nevertheless, millions of Americans contribute to interest groups because they are concerned about an issue or feel a responsibility to help organizations that work on their behalf. Also, many organizations offer membership benefits that have nothing to do with politics or lobbying. **Trade associations**, for example, are a source of information about industry trends and effective management practices; they organize conventions at which members can learn, socialize, and occasionally find new customers or suppliers.

Lobbyists

Interest groups use part of the money they raise to pay lobbyists, who represent the organizations before the government. Lobbyists make sure that people in government know what interest group members want and that groups know what the government is doing.[19] Lobbyists can be full-time employees of an interest group or employees of public relations or law firms hired on retainer. When hiring a lobbyist, an interest group looks for someone who knows his or her way around Washington.

Lobbyists are valued for their experience and their knowledge of how government operates. Often they are people who have served in the legislative or executive branches, people who have firsthand experience with government. Many lobbyists have law degrees and find their legal backgrounds useful in bargaining and negotiating over laws and regulations. Because of their location, many Washington law firms are drawn into lobbying. Corporations without Washington offices rely heavily on these law firms to lobby for them before the national government.

The most common image of a lobbyist is that of someone who spends most of his or her time trying to convince a legislator or administrator to back a certain policy. The stereotype also portrays lobbyists as people of dubious ethics. However, the lobbyist's primary job is not to trade on favors or campaign contributions but to pass on information to policymakers. Lobbyists provide government officials and their staffs with a constant flow of data that support their organizations' policy goals. Lobbyists also try to build a compelling case for their goals, showing that the "facts" dictate that a particular change be made or avoided. What lobbyists are really trying to do, of course, is to convince policymakers that their data deserve more attention and are more accurate than the data presented by other lobbyists.

Political Action Committees

One of the organizational resources that can make a lobbyist's job easier is a **political action committee (PAC)**. PACs pool campaign contributions from group members and donate those funds to candidates for political office (see Figure 7.2). Under federal law, a PAC can give as much as $5,000 to a candidate for Congress for each separate election. A change in campaign finance law in 1974 led to a rapid increase in the number of PACs. The greatest growth came from corporations, most of which had been legally prohibited from operating PACs. There was also rapid growth in the number of nonconnected PACs, largely ideological groups that have no parent lobbying organization and are formed solely for the purpose of raising and channeling campaign funds. Thus a PAC can be the campaign-wing affiliate of an existing interest group or a wholly independent, unaffiliated group.

Why do interest groups form PACs? The chief executive officer of one manufacturing company said his corporation had a PAC because "the PAC gives you access. It makes you a player."[20] Members of Congress and their staffers generally are eager to meet with representatives of their constituencies, but their time is limited. However, a member of Congress or staffer would find it difficult to turn down a lobbyist's request for a meeting if the PAC of the lobbyist's organization had made a significant campaign contribution in the last election.

Typically, PACs, like most other interest groups, are highly pragmatic organizations; pushing a particular political philosophy takes second place to achieving immediate policy goals. As a group, corporate PACs gave 76.4 percent of their contributions to incumbent members of Congress—many of them liberal and moderate Democrats—during the 1993–1994 election cycle.[21] After the Republicans' capture of Congress in 1994, corporations and other business PACs could target more of their money to conservative Republicans.

PAC CONTRIBUTIONS, 1997–1998

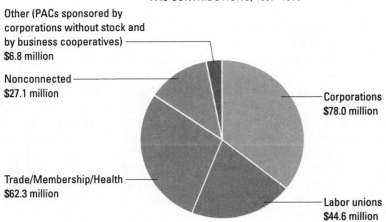

Other (PACs sponsored by corporations without stock and by business cooperatives) — $6.8 million

Nonconnected — $27.1 million

Corporations $78.0 million

Trade/Membership/Health — $62.3 million

Labor unions $44.6 million

*FIGURE 7.2   **PACs Americana***
Most PAC money comes from corporations, business trade groups, and professional associations. Labor unions contribute significantly as well. A much smaller proportion of all PAC contributions comes from citizen PACs, which form the bulk of the "nonconnected" category. Americans at the lower end of the economic spectrum are left out entirely. As Bob Dole once put it, "There aren't any Poor PACs or Food Stamp PACs or Nutrition PACs or Medicare PACs." (Source: "Summary of PAC Contributions to Federal Candidates During 1997–98," Federal Election Commission press release, 8 June 1999.)

The role of PACs in financing congressional campaigns has become the most controversial aspect of interest group politics. Critics charge that members of Congress cannot help but be influenced by the PAC contributions they receive. Political scientists, however, have not been able to document any consistent link between campaign donations and the way members of Congress vote on the floor of the House and Senate. Some recent, sophisticated research does show that PACs have an advantage in the committee process and appear to gain influence because of the additional access they receive.[22]

Whatever the research shows, it is clear that the American public sees PACs as a means of securing privileges for those sectors of society with the resources to purchase additional access to Congress. But in a democracy, influence should not be a function of money; some citizens have little to give, yet their interests need to be protected. From this perspective, the issue is political equality.

Strong arguments can be made for retaining PACs. They offer a means for people to participate in the political system. They allow small givers to pool their resources and to fight the feeling that one person cannot make a difference. Also, PAC defenders point out that prohibiting PACs would amount to a restriction on the freedom of political expression. (We take up the question of PACs and potential reforms at the end of this chapter.)

Lobbying Tactics

Keep in mind that lobbying extends beyond the legislative branch. Groups can seek help from the courts and administrative agencies as well as from Congress. Moreover, interest groups may have to shift their focus from one branch of government to another. After a bill becomes a law, for example, a group that lobbied for the legislation will probably try to influence the administrative agency responsible for implementing the new law. Some policy decisions are left unresolved by legislation and are settled through regulations. Lobbies want to make sure regulatory decisions are as close to the group's preferences as possible.

We discuss three types of lobbying tactics here: those aimed at policymakers and implemented by interest group representatives (direct lobbying); those that involve group members (grassroots lobbying); and those directed toward the public (information campaigns). We also examine the use of new high-tech lobbying tactics as well as cooperative efforts of interest groups to influence government through coalitions.

Direct Lobbying

Direct lobbying relies on personal contact with policymakers. One survey of Washington lobbyists showed that 98 percent use direct contact with government officials to express their group's views.[23] This interaction takes place when a lobbyist meets with a member of Congress, an agency official, or a staff member. In their meetings, lobbyists usually convey their arguments by providing data about a specific issue. If a lobbyist from, for example, a chamber of commerce meets with a member of Congress about a bill the organization backs, the lobbyist does not say (or even suggest), "Vote for this bill, or our people in the district will vote against you in the next election." Instead, the lobbyist might say, "If this bill is passed, we're going to see hundreds of new jobs created back home." The representative has no trouble at all figuring out that a vote for the bill can help in the next election.

Personal lobbying is a day-in, day-out process. Lobbyists must maintain contact with congressional and agency staffers, constantly providing them with pertinent data. One lobbyist described his strategy in personal meetings with policymakers as rather simple and straightforward: "Providing information is the most effective tool. People begin to rely on you."[24]

A tactic related to direct lobbying is testifying at committee hearings when a bill is before Congress. This tactic allows the interest group to put its views on record and to make them widely known when the hearing testimony is published. Although testifying is one of the most visible parts of lobbying, it is generally considered window dressing. Most lobbyists believe that testimony usually does little by itself to persuade members of Congress.

Another direct but somewhat different approach is legal advocacy. Using this tactic, a group tries to achieve its policy goals through litigation. Claiming some violation of law, a group will file a lawsuit and ask that a judge make a ruling that will benefit the organization. When the Food and Drug

An Image That Angered a Nation
Demonstrations by blacks during the early 1960s played a critical role in pushing Congress to pass civil rights legislation. This photo of vicious police dogs attacking demonstrators in Birmingham, Alabama, is typical of scenes shown on network news broadcasts and in newspapers that helped build public support for civil rights legislation.

Administration (FDA) proposed regulations aimed at reducing smoking by minors, cigarette manufacturers counterattacked with a lawsuit filed in federal court. The tobacco industry believed the FDA had exceeded its authority, and it was concerned the agency would take further steps to restrict smoking.[25]

Grassroots Lobbying

Grassroots lobbying involves an interest group's rank-and-file members and may also include people outside the organization who sympathize with its goals. Grassroots tactics, such as letter-writing campaigns and protests, are often used in conjunction with direct lobbying by Washington representatives. Policymakers are more concerned about what a lobbyist says when they know that constituents are really watching their decisions.

If people in government seem unresponsive to conventional lobbying tactics, a group might resort to some form of political protest. A protest or demonstration, such as picketing or marching, is designed to attract media attention to an issue. The main drawback to protesting is that policymaking is a long-term, incremental process but a demonstration is only short-lived. It is difficult to sustain anger and activism among group supporters—to keep large numbers of people involved in protest after protest. A notable exception was the civil rights demonstrations of the 1960s, which were sustained over a long period. The protests were a major factor in stirring public opinion, which in turn hastened passage of the Civil Rights Act of 1964 and the Voting Rights Act of 1965.

Information Campaigns

Interest groups generally feel that public backing strengthens their lobbying efforts. They believe that they will get that backing if they can make the public aware of their position and the evidence supporting it. To this end, interest groups launch **information campaigns**, organized efforts to gain public backing by bringing group views to the public's attention. Various means are used. Some are directed at the larger public, others at smaller audiences with long-standing interest in an issue.

Public relations is one information-campaign tactic. A public relations campaign might send speakers to meetings in various parts of the country, produce pamphlets and handouts, or take out newspaper advertising. During the fight over the Clinton administration's health care reform proposal during 1993 and 1994, the Health Insurance Association of America (HIAA) launched a television ad campaign designed to turn public opinion against the plan. The ads featured a fictional couple named Harry and Louise, who in a series of spots talked conversationally about the plan and pointed out its critical flaws. However, given the costs of televised advertising and the difficulty of truly swaying public opinion with it, few groups rely on paid TV advertising as their primary weapon in advocacy campaigns.

Sponsoring research is another way interest groups press their cases. When a group believes that evidence has not been fully developed in a certain area, it may commission research on the subject. For example, when the Environmental Working Group, a liberal advocacy group, wanted to try to reduce agriculture-related pollution, it initiated tests of water quality in twenty-nine cities located near concentrations of corn farms. The study received a modest amount of press coverage.[26]

High-Tech Lobbying

In recent years, Washington lobbies have added many high-tech tactics to their arsenals. Using such resources as direct mail, e-mail, faxes, polling, and the World Wide Web, lobbies have tried to find ways to expand their reach and increase their impact. The most conspicuous effect of high-tech lobbying is that it speeds up the political process. Using electronic communication, groups can quickly mobilize their constituents, who in turn will quickly contact policymakers about pending decisions. However, it is important to recognize that electronic lobbying isn't all that different from old-fashioned lobbying. Before the computer, interest groups used to telephone their activists and ask them to write letters to policymakers. That approach may have been a little slower, but it still let those in Washington know what their constituents back home wanted.

Although high-tech lobbying tactics facilitate direct communication between citizens and policymakers, which is to be applauded, there is a down side as well. Technology is expensive, so the introduction of such tactics tends to favor those who are already well represented in the political process.[27]

Coalition Building

A final aspect of lobbying strategy is **coalition building**, in which several organizations band together for the purpose of lobbying. Such joint efforts conserve or make more effective use of the resources of groups with similar views. Most coalitions are informal, ad hoc arrangements that exist only for the purpose of lobbying on a single issue.

Coalitions form most often among groups that work in the same policy area and have similar constituencies, such as environmental groups or feminist groups. Yet coalitions often extend beyond organizations with similar constituencies and similar outlooks. Some business groups support the same goals as environmental lobbies, because doing so is in their self-interest. For example, companies in the business of cleaning up toxic waste sites have worked with environmental groups.[28]

Is the System Biased?

As we noted in Chapter 1, our political system is more pluralist than majoritarian. Policymaking is determined more by the interaction of groups with government than by elections. How, then, do we determine whether policy decisions in a pluralist system are fair?

There is no precisely agreed-upon formula, but most people would agree with the following two simple notions. First, all significant interests in the population should be adequately represented by lobbying groups. Second, government should listen to the views of all major interests as it develops policy. We should also recognize that elections inject some of the benefits of majoritarianism into our system, because the party that wins an election will have more say in the making of public policy than its opponent.

Membership Patterns

Those who work in business or in a profession, those with a high level of education, and those with high incomes (recall Figure 7.1) are the most likely to belong to interest groups. Even middle-income people are much more likely to join interest groups than people who are poor.

For example, one-third of those receiving veterans' benefits belong to an organization that works to protect and enhance veterans' benefits. Only about 2 percent of recipients of Aid to Families with Dependent Children (AFDC) were members of welfare rights groups.[29] Clearly, a **membership bias** is part of the pattern of who belongs to interest groups: certain types of people are much more likely than others to belong to interest groups.

The Public Interest Movement

Before we reach the conclusion that the interest group system is biased, we should examine another set of data. The actual population of interest groups in Washington surely reflects a class bias in interest group membership, but that bias may be modified in an important way. Some interest groups derive support from sources other than their membership. Thus, although the Center for Budget and Policy Priorities and the Children's Defense Fund have no welfare recipients among their members, they are highly respected Washington lobbies working on the problems of poor people. Poverty groups gain their financial support from philanthropic foundations, government grants, corporations, and wealthy individuals. Such groups have played an important role in influencing policy on poor people's programs. In short, some bias exists in the representation of the poor, but it is not nearly so bad as membership patterns suggest.

Another part of the problem of membership bias has to do with free riders. The interests that are most affected by free riders are broad societal problems, such as the environment and consumer protection, in which literally everyone can be considered as having a stake in the outcome. The greater the number of potential members of a group, the more likely it is that individuals will decide to be free riders, because they believe that plenty of others can offer financial support to the organization.

Environmental and consumer interests have been chronically underrepresented in the Washington interest group community. In the 1960s, however, a strong public interest movement emerged. **Public interest groups** are citizen groups that have no economic self-interest in the policies they pursue.[30] For example, the members of environmental groups fighting for stricter pollution control requirements receive no financial gain from the enactment of environmental protection policies. The benefits to members are largely ideological and esthetic. In contrast, a corporation fighting the same stringent standards is trying to protect its economic interests. The environmental lobby is a public interest group; the corporation is not.

Today, many public interest groups are important players in Washington politics. Most are environmental and consumer groups, but others work on corporate accountability, good government, poverty, and nutrition. Many conservative public interest groups exist as well, working in areas such as abortion and family values. Overall, the public interest movement has broadened interest group representation in national politics and made the pluralist system more democratic.

Business Mobilization

Because a strong public interest movement has become an integral part of Washington politics, an easy assumption is that the bias in interest group representation in favor of business has been largely overcome. What must be factored in is that business has become increasingly mobilized as well.[31] The 1970s and 1980s saw a vast increase in the number of business lobbies in Washington. Many corporations opened Washington lobbying offices, and many trade associations headquartered elsewhere either moved to Washington or opened branch offices there.

This mobilization was partly a reaction to the success of the liberal public interest movement, which business tended to view as hostile to the free-enterprise system. The reaction of business also reflected the expanded scope of the national government. As the Environmental Protection Agency, the Consumer Product Safety Commission, the Occupational Safety and Health Administration, and other regulatory agencies were created, many more companies found they were affected by federal regulations.

The health care industry is a case in point. As government regulation has become an increasingly important factor in determining health care profits, more and more health care trade associations have opened offices in Washington so that they can make more of an effort to influence the government. In 1981, there were about 250 health care lobbies in Washington. A decade later there were three times that number.[32]

The number of organizations is far from a perfect indicator of interest group strength, however. The AFL-CIO, which represents millions of union members, is more influential than a two-person corporate listening post in Washington. Nevertheless, as a rough indicator of interest group influence, the data show that business has an advantage in this country's interest group system.

Access

The existence of an interest group makes little difference if the government systematically ignores it. Evidence shows that any particular policymaker or office of government can be highly selective in granting access to interest groups. The ideological compatibility between any given interest group and the policymaker it approaches certainly affects the likelihood that the policymaker will grant the group access and listen to what its lobbyists have to say. However, pluralists are convincing when they argue that the national government has many points of access, and virtually all lobbying organizations can find some part of that government to listen to them. If liberal poverty lobbies are shut out of a conservative White House, liberal members of Congress will work with them. All forms of access are not of equal importance, and some organizations have wider access than others. Nevertheless, American government is generally characterized by the broad access it grants to interest groups.

Reform

In an economic system marked by great differences in income, great differences in the degree to which people are organized are inevitable. Moreover, as Madison foresaw, limiting interest group activity is difficult without limiting fundamental freedoms. The First Amendment guarantees Americans the right to petition their government, and lobbying, at its most basic level, is a form of organized petitioning.

Still, if it is felt that the advantages of some groups are so great that they affect the equality of people's opportunity to be heard in the political system, then restrictions on interest group behavior can be justified on the ground that the disadvantaged must be protected. Pluralist democracy is justified on exactly these grounds: all constituencies must have the opportunity to organize, and the competition between groups as they press their case before policymakers must be fair.

Some critics charge that a system of campaign finance that relies so heavily on PACs undermines our democratic system. It is not merely a matter of wealthy interest groups showering incumbents with donations; members of Congress aggressively solicit donations from PACs. Although observers disagree on whether PAC money actually influences policy outcomes, agreement is widespread that PAC donations give donors better access to members of Congress.

The government has placed some restrictions on interest group campaign donations, however. During the 1970s, Congress put some important reforms into effect. Strong disclosure requirements now exist—the source of all significant contributions to candidates for national office is a matter of public record. Legislation also provides for public financing of presidential campaigns; taxpayer money goes in equal amounts to the presidential nominees of the major parties. In 1995, Congress passed additional modest reforms outside the campaign finance area. Lobbyists are now subject to a strict registration requirement and must file reports every six months listing all their clients, the amount they spent on lobbying activities, and how much they were paid.[33] Another reform banned all gifts from lobbyists to legislators (with the exception of gifts of trivial value).[34]

Reformers have called for public financing of congressional elections to reduce the presumed influence of PACs on Congress. Other proposed approaches include reducing the amounts individual PACs can give; limiting the overall amount of money any one candidate can accept from PACs; reducing the costs of campaigning by subsidizing the costs of commercials, printing, and postage; and giving tax incentives to individuals to contribute to candidates. However, incumbents usually find it easier to raise money from PACs than challengers do, so the incentive to leave the status quo intact is strong. And Republicans and Democrats have sharp partisan differences over campaign finance reforms, because each party believes that the other is trying to fashion a system that will somehow handicap the opposing party.

Summary

Interest groups play many important roles in our political process. They are a means by which citizens can participate in politics, and they communicate their members' views to those in government. Interest groups differ greatly in the resources at their disposal and in the tactics they use to influence government.

The number of interest groups has grown sharply in recent years.[35] Despite the growth and change in the nature of interest groups, the fundamental problem identified by Madison more than two hundred years ago endures: in a free and open society, groups form to pursue policies that favor themselves at the expense of the broader national interest. Madison hoped that the solution to the problem would come from the diversity of the population and the structure of our government, and, to a certain extent, Madison's expectations have been borne out. The natural differences between groups have prevented a tyranny of any one faction. Yet the interest group system remains unbalanced, with some segments of society (particularly business, the wealthy, and the educated) considerably better organized than others. The growth of citizen groups has reduced the disparity somewhat, but significant inequalities remain in how well different interests are represented in Washington.

The inequities point to flaws in pluralist theory. There is no mechanism to automatically ensure that interest groups will form to speak for those who need representation. Likewise, when an issue arises and policymakers meet with interest groups that have a stake in the outcome, those groups may not equally represent all the constituencies that the policy changes will affect. The interest group system clearly compromises the principle of political equality stated in the maxim "one person, one vote." Formal political equality is certainly more likely to occur outside interest group politics, in elections between candidates from competing political parties, which better fits the majoritarian model of democracy.

Despite the inequities of the interest group system, little direct effort has been made to restrict interest group activity. Madison's dictum to avoid suppressing political freedoms, even at the expense of permitting interest group activity that promotes the selfish interests of narrow segments of the population, has generally guided public policy. Yet, as the problem of PACs demonstrates, government has had to set some restrictions on interest groups. Permitting PACs to give unlimited amounts to political candidates would undermine confidence in the system. Where to draw the line on PAC activity remains a thorny issue, because there is little consensus on how to balance the conflicting needs of our society.

Congress is one institution that must try to balance our diverse country's conflicting interests. In the next chapter, we will see how difficult this part of Congress's job is.

Key Terms

interest group	political action committee (PAC)
lobby	direct lobbying
lobbyist	grassroots lobbying
agenda building	information campaign
program monitoring	coalition building
interest group entrepreneur	membership bias
free-rider problem	public interest group
trade association	

Selected Readings

Baumgartner, Frank R., and Beth L. Leech. *Basic Interests.* Princeton, N.J.: Princeton University Press, 1998. Offers a critical examination of interest group scholarship and prescribes future directions for the field.

Berry, Jeffrey M. *The New Liberalism.* Washington, D.C.: Brookings Institution Press, 1999. Documents the increasing influence of liberal citizen groups over the congressional agenda.

Cigler, Allan J., and Burdett A. Loomis, eds. *Interest Group Politics.* 5th ed. Washington, D.C.: Congressional Quarterly Press, 1998. This reader includes a selection of essays on lobbying groups.

Costain, Anne N. *Inviting Women's Rebellion.* Baltimore: Johns Hopkins University Press, 1992. A careful and original examination of the origins of the women's movement and its development into a political force.

Hula, Kevin W. *Lobbying Together: Interest Group Coalitions in Legislative Politics.* Washington, D.C.: Georgetown University Press, 1999. Explores why organized interests build coalitions and why they sometimes pursue their policy goals alone.

Wright, John R. *Interest Groups and Congress.* Boston: Allyn & Bacon, 1996. An overview of how lobbies and PACs try to influence Congress.

World Wide Web Resources

U.S. Chamber of Commerce. Find out how interest groups function and the services they provide to their membership. The site lists management training information, a video library, and seminars for business—those in business and those seeking to start a business.
<www.uschamber.org>

AFL-CIO. Read the organization's policy statements, press releases, and "Boycott List." Find information on how to organize a union. A dominant feature of this Web site is information about the AFL-CIO's "Standup Campaign"—a campaign to lobby for good jobs, good wages, and worker protection.
<www.aflcio.org/home.htm>

Sierra Club. Find out how public interest groups work. Visitors to this Web page can read the Sierra Club's magazine as well as *The Planet,* a newsletter for environmental activists. Get information on Sierra Club chapters, politics, and the environment. Follow links to other environmental sites on the Internet.
<www.sierraclub.org>

Electronic Privacy Information Center (EPIC). This public interest group conducts research "to focus public attention on emerging civil liberties issues and to protect privacy, the First Amendment, and constitutional values." The group also participates in lawsuits to pursue its view of the common good.
<www.epic.org>

8

Congress

Henry Hyde, chairman of the House Judiciary Committee, strode from the House side of the Capitol, across the rotunda to the Senate side. Accompanied by other Republican members of the committee, Hyde exhibited a solemn demeanor befitting the gravity of the occasion. He carried with him two articles of impeachment alleging conduct by President William Jefferson Clinton deemed sufficient by the House to remove the president from office. When he reached the office of Secretary of the Senate, Gary Sisco, Sisco was waiting for him. With the articles of impeachment—an indictment, for all intents and purposes—delivered to Sisco, it became the responsibility of the one hundred members of the Senate to sit as jurors in a trial.

Despite the high drama of this moment, the American public remained unconvinced that Congress was doing the right thing in bringing the president to trial. What exactly had Clinton done? Quite simply, he had had a sexual relationship with a young White House intern, Monica Lewinsky, and then he and Lewinsky had tried to cover it up.[1]

The two articles of impeachment had been approved by a majority of the House. Article One said that in testimony before a federal grand jury Clinton had "willfully provided perjurious, false and misleading testimony" concerning his relationship with Ms. Lewinsky. It also asserted that Clinton had given false testimony in a civil suit brought against him by Paula Jones, who claimed that Clinton had crudely propositioned her when he was governor of Arkansas and she was a state employee. Article Two stated that Clinton had engaged in obstruction of justice, including encouraging Ms. Lewinsky to lie in an affidavit in the Jones lawsuit, and had taken actions designed to conceal evidence sought in that civil action.[2]

Months earlier, when revelations about Clinton and Lewinsky first emerged, a Senate trial of the president seemed a distant possibility. Americans did not clamor for Clinton's resignation or for impeachment, and Republicans were not sure how far to take the Lewinsky matter. Three events then propelled the process forward.

First, in September 1998, Independent Counsel Kenneth Starr delivered his report on Clinton to the House. Four years earlier, Starr had been hired to investigate allegations concerning the president's involvement in an Arkansas real estate development called Whitewater. Failing to turn up evidence of criminal wrongdoing in the Whitewater case, Starr refocused his investigation on the Lewinsky matter. The Starr report humiliated the president, making public salacious details taken from Ms. Lewinsky's grand jury testimony.

Second, Republican congressional candidates did relatively poorly in the 1998 elections. Within a matter of days, Newt Gingrich was out as Speaker, and GOP House members quickly coalesced around Louisiana's Bob Livingston as their next Speaker.[3] Understandably, Livingston was hesitant to make impeaching the president his first undertaking as party leader. Into this leadership vacuum jumped Tom DeLay of Texas, who held the third-ranking position in the House party. DeLay pushed and prodded his fellow House members to impeach the president.

Third, Hyde himself became a driving force behind impeachment. Unsure of himself at first, he failed in his efforts to build a bipartisan coalition in the Judiciary Committee.[4] This stood in stark contrast to the committee's response during the Watergate affair, when a minority of the Republicans on the committee voted to recommend impeaching Richard Nixon, a president of their own party. Adding to Hyde's frustration was the fact that the press found out about a lengthy extramarital affair he had carried on in his forties. The Republicans lacked a congressional leader who could be seen as nonpartisan and command the respect necessary to guide the country to remove the president from office. Hyde worked with great diligence with other Republican members of the Judiciary Committee to push through the impeachment charges and to bring them to the floor for a vote by the full House of Representatives.

The party-line votes in the Judiciary Committee were repeated in the full House. By and large, Republicans voted for impeachment and Democrats against it. The House passed two of four counts approved by the Judiciary Committee. Galling to the Republicans, however, was the consistent support for the president expressed in public opinion polls. Just prior to the vote in the Senate, two-thirds of the public approved of Clinton's handling of his job as president while strongly disapproving of both Congress's handling of the impeachment process and of Special Prosecutor Starr.[5] The Senate needed a two-thirds majority to convict the president but could not muster even a simple majority for either count. The Clinton presidency survived.[6]

Hyde and his fellow Republicans believed that they had to act to preserve an appropriate moral code for the presidency. In their minds, Clinton and the Democrats were wrong to place so little value on preserving order. The American public, however, believed that the Republicans went too far and did not apply a punishment proportionate to the crime. In the end, Congress's final decision reflected the majority opinion.

In the pages that follow, we'll examine more closely the relationship between members of Congress and their constituents, as well as the forces (such as political parties) that push legislators toward majoritarianism. We'll also focus on Congress's relations with the executive branch and analyze how the legislative process affects public policy. A starting point is to ask how the framers envisioned Congress.

The Origin and Powers of Congress

The framers of the Constitution wanted to prevent the concentration of power in the hands of a few, but they also wanted to create a union strong enough to overcome the weaknesses of the government created by the Articles of Confederation. They argued passionately about the structure of the new government and in the end produced a legislative body that was as much of an experiment as the new nation's democracy.

The Great Compromise

The U.S. Congress has two separate and powerful chambers: the House of Representatives and the Senate. A bill cannot become law unless it is passed in identical form by both chambers. When drafting the Constitution during the summer of 1787, "the fiercest struggle for power" centered on representation in the legislature.[7] The small states wanted all the states to have equal representation. The more populous states wanted representation based on population; they did not want their power diluted. The Great Compromise broke the deadlock. The small states would receive equal representation in the Senate, but the number of each state's representatives in the House would be based on population, and the House would have the sole right to originate revenue-related legislation.

As the Constitution specifies, each state has two senators, and senators serve six-year terms of office. Terms are staggered, so that one-third of the Senate is elected every two years. When it was ratified, the Constitution directed that senators should be chosen by the state legislatures. However, the Seventeenth Amendment, adopted in 1913, provided for the direct election of senators by popular vote. From the beginning, the people have directly elected members of the House of Representatives. They serve two-year terms, and all House seats are up for election at the same time.

There are 435 members in the House of Representatives. Because each state's representation in the House is in proportion to its population, the Constitution provides for a national census every ten years. Population shifts are handled by the **reapportionment** (redistribution) of seats among the states after each census is taken. Since recent population growth has been centered in the Sunbelt, California, Texas, and Florida have gained seats, and the northeast and midwest states have lost them. Each representative is elected from a particular congressional district within his or her state, and each district elects only one representative. The districts within a state must be roughly equal in population.

Duties of the House and Senate

Although the Great Compromise provided for considerably different schemes of representation for the House and Senate, the Constitution gives them essentially similar legislative tasks. They share many important powers, among them the powers to declare war, raise an army and navy, borrow and coin money, regulate interstate commerce, create federal courts, establish rules for the naturalization of immigrants, and "make all Laws which shall be necessary and proper for carrying into Execution the foregoing Powers."

Of course, the constitutional duties of the two chambers are different in at least a few important ways. As noted earlier, the House alone has the right to originate revenue bills, a right that apparently was coveted at the Constitutional Convention. In practice, this power is of limited consequence because both House and Senate must approve all bills—including revenue bills. The House also has the power of **impeachment**, the power formally to charge the president, vice president, or other "civil Officers" of the national government with "Treason, Bribery, or other high Crimes and Misdemeanors." The Senate is empowered to act as a court to try impeachments; a two-thirds majority vote of the senators present is necessary for conviction. Prior to President Clinton's impeachment, only one president, Andrew Johnson, had been impeached, and in 1868 the Senate came within a single vote of finding him guilty. More recently, the House Judiciary Committee voted to impeach President Richard Nixon for his role in the Watergate scandal, but he resigned (in August 1974) before the full House could vote. A small number of federal judges, however, have been impeached, convicted, and removed from the bench.

The Constitution gives the Senate the power to approve major presidential appointments (such as to federal judgeships, ambassadorships, and cabinet posts) and treaties with foreign nations. The president is empowered to make treaties, but he must submit them to the Senate for approval by a two-thirds majority. Because of this requirement, the executive branch generally considers the Senate's sentiments when it negotiates a treaty.[8]

Despite the long list of congressional powers in the Constitution, the question of what powers are appropriate for Congress has generated substantial controversy. For example, although the Constitution gives Congress the sole power to declare war, many presidents have initiated military action on their own. And at times, the courts have found that congressional actions have usurped the rights of the states.

Electing the Congress

If Americans are not happy with the job Congress is doing, they can use their votes to say so. With a congressional election every two years, the voters have frequent opportunities to express themselves.

The Incumbency Effect

Congressional elections offer voters a chance to show their approval of Congress's performance by reelecting **incumbents** or to demonstrate their disapproval by "throwing the rascals out." The voters seem to do more reelecting than rascal throwing. The reelection rate is astonishingly high; in the majority

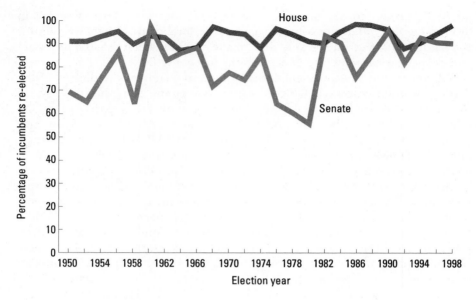

FIGURE 8.1 *Incumbents: Life Is Good*
Despite the public's dissatisfaction with Congress in general, incumbent representatives win reelection at an exceptional rate. Incumbent senators aren't quite as successful but still do well in reelection races. Voters seem to believe that their own representatives and senators don't share the same foibles that they attribute to the other members of Congress. (Sources: Norman J. Ornstein, Thomas E. Mann, and Michael J. Malbin, Vital Statistics on Congress, *1995–1996 [Washington, D.C.: Congressional Quarterly Press, 1996], pp. 60–61. Karen Foerstel, "Voters' Plea for Moderation Unlikely to Be Heeded,"* Congressional Quarterly Weekly Report, *7 November 1998, pp. 2980–2984.)*

of elections since 1950, more than 90 percent of all House incumbents have held on to their seats (see Figure 8.1). Most House elections aren't even close; in recent elections most House incumbents have won at least 60 percent of the vote. Senate elections are more competitive, but incumbents still have a high reelection rate.[9]

These findings may seem surprising, since the public does not hold Congress as a whole in particularly high esteem. Two-thirds of the American public tell pollsters that they disapprove of the job Congress is doing.[10] Close to 60 percent believe that at least half of all members of Congress are personally corrupt, a harsh indictment of the institution.[11] Americans strongly support term limits for members of Congress, to limit the number of years a legislator can serve in the House or Senate.[12] Although term limits have been imposed in many states, in both 1995 and 1997 the House voted against a constitutional amendment for term limits on members of Congress. Although Americans feel disdain for Congress, they tend to distinguish between the institution as a whole and their own representatives. Only 15 percent believe that their own representative is financially corrupt.[13]

Redistricting   One explanation for the incumbency effect centers on redistricting, the way House districts are redrawn by state legislatures after a census-based reapportionment. It is entirely possible for them to draw the new districts to benefit the incumbents of one or both parties. Altering district lines for partisan advantage is commonly called **gerrymandering**.

Name Recognition   Holding office brings with it some important advantages. First, incumbents develop significant name recognition among voters simply by being members of Congress. Congressional press secretaries promote name recognition through their efforts to get publicity for the activities and speeches of their bosses. The primary focus of such publicity seeking is on the local media back in the home district—that's where the votes are.[14] The local press, in turn, is eager to cover what members of Congress are saying about the issues.

Another resource available to members of Congress is the *franking privilege*—the right to send mail free of charge. Mailings work to make constituents aware of their legislators' names, activities, and accomplishments. Periodic newsletters, for example, almost always highlight legislators' success at securing funds and projects for their districts.

Much of the work performed by the large staffs of members of Congress is **casework**—such services for constituents as tracking down a social security check or directing the owner of a small business to the appropriate federal agency. Constituents who are helped in this way usually remember who assisted them.

Campaign Financing   Anyone who wants to challenge an incumbent needs solid financial backing. But here, too, the incumbent has the advantage. Challengers find raising campaign funds difficult because they have to overcome contributors' doubts about whether they can win. PACs show a strong preference for incumbents (see Chapter 7). They tend not to want to risk offending an incumbent by giving money to a long-shot challenger.

Successful Challengers   Clearly the deck is stacked against challengers to incumbents. Yet some challengers do beat incumbents. How? The opposing party and unsympathetic PACs may target incumbents who seem vulnerable because of age, lack of seniority, a scandal, unfavorable redistricting, or other factors.

Senate challengers have a higher success rate than House challengers, in part because they are generally higher-quality candidates. Often they are governors or members of the House who enjoy high name recognition and can attract significant campaign funds because they are regarded as credible candidates.[15]

In 1998, Republicans anticipated making significant gains to their majorities in both House and Senate. The party controlling the White House almost always loses House seats in the midterm election, as voters take out their disappointments with the president on candidates from his party. The president's party usually loses seats in the Senate too. The 1998 election also looked bad for the Democrats because of the Clinton-Lewinsky scandal. But when the votes were counted, the results were stunning. The Democrats actually picked up five seats in the House, and there was no overall change in the Senate.[16] Due to the widespread expectation of Republican gains, the outcome was widely interpreted as a stinging defeat for the GOP.

One reason for this outcome was that the Democrats were viewed as stronger on major issues that concerned voters, especially education, health care, and social security.[17] Ironically, although Republicans were judged to be stronger on matters of ethics and moral values, there was an apparent backlash against the GOP for the impeachment proceedings it had initiated in the House. Still, after the election House Republicans continued with the case and voted to impeach the president. Although there was some concern that Republicans could be hurt in the 2000 elections by their votes on impeachment, GOP strategists believed that the electorate would move on and the focus in the presidential and congressional races would turn to other issues. (see Politics in a Changing America 8.1). As it turned out, they were mostly right—most impeachment participants were re-elected.

In the 2000 Congressional elections, the Democrats gained a few seats in both the House and the Senate, but Republicans remained in control of both chambers by very slim margins. Republicans won 221 House seats to the Democrats' 212 (there are two Independents). The election left each party with 50 Senate seats, but the Republicans remained in control there because Republian Vice President Dick Cheney would break a partisan tie. The most visible Senate race was First Lady Hillary Clinton's victory over Rick Lazio to represent New York.

Whom Do We Elect?

The people we elect (and then reelect) to Congress are not a cross-section of American society. Most members of Congress are professionals—primarily lawyers, businesspeople, and educators.[18] Although nearly a third of the American labor force works in blue-collar jobs, a person employed as a blue-collar worker rarely wins a congressional nomination. Women and minorities also have long been underrepresented in elective office. Yet many women and minorities believe that only members of their own group—people who have experienced what they have experienced—can truly represent their interests. This is a belief in **descriptive representation**, the view that a legislature should resemble the demographic characteristics of the population it represents.[19]

When Congress amended the Voting Rights Act in 1982, it encouraged the states to draw districts that concentrated minorities together so that African Americans and Hispanic Americans would have a better chance of being elected to office. Supreme Court decisions also pushed the states to concentrate minorities in House districts.[20] After the 1990 census, states redrew House boundaries with the intent of creating districts with majority or near-majority minority populations. Some districts were very oddly shaped, snaking through their state to pick up black neighborhoods in various cities but leaving adjacent white neighborhoods to other districts. This effort led to a roughly 50 percent increase in the number of blacks elected to the House. Hispanic representation in the House also increased, from ten to seventeen

Politics in a Changing America 8.1

Was Impeachment the Best Way?

One of the most remarkable aspects of the Clinton impeachment was that all of the major participants got burned. Even though he was eventually acquitted in the Senate, President Clinton was seriously and irreparably wounded by the impeachment; his affair with an intern half his age will forever tarnish his presidency.

Americans also judged Special Prosecutor Kenneth Starr harshly. Starr, a Republican, was never able to persuade the public that he was acting without partisan impulse. His self-righteous persona played poorly, and he seemed overly aggressive in his investigation, especially with tangential figures such as Monica Lewinsky's mother, whom he forced to testify against her daughter before a grand jury.

Leading Republican figures in Congress were hurt as well. Speaker Newt Gingrich resigned a few days after the Republicans' poor performance in the 1998 congressional election, which was widely regarded as a rebuke to the party for its efforts to impeach the president. The party's chosen replacement, Bob Livingston, never actually became Speaker, because shortly after his selection an article indicating that he had been unfaithful to his wife appeared. Livingston quickly resigned from Congress. As noted previously, Henry Hyde was also revealed to be an adulterer. Trent Lott, the Senate majority leader, also received damaging publicity. Several articles noted that he had recently spoken before the Council of Conservative Citizens, a white supremacist organization. Also, the *New Republic,* a liberal magazine, disclosed that House Whip Tom DeLay apparently lied in a court deposition about his role in a pesticide company.

Republicans claim that they were the subject of a witch-hunt by journalists. To many Democrats it seemed like just retribution, given the unrelenting pursuit of Clinton by conservative publications and organizations throughout his presidency. Still, the Republicans were right in arguing that the press probably would have not pursued these stories had there been no GOP effort to impeach Clinton.

The airing of politicians' personal lapses was only part of what contributed to Americans' frustration with the impeachment process. By the time the Senate voted to acquit the president, more than a year had passed since the Lewinsky story first emerged. Most Americans wanted the impeachment to go away—and go away quickly. In fairness, the indictment and trial of a president should proceed not with speed but with all due deliberation, and Congress was right not to expedite the matter.

The broader issue, of course, is whether impeachment was the right instrument to deal with the cover-up of a sexual indiscretion. Republicans were emphatic in pointing out that impeachment is the only tool the Constitution offers Congress for punishing the president. The Constitution lists "Treason, Bribery, or other high Crimes and Misdemeanors" as grounds for impeachment but offers no guidance as to what those terms mean.

(continued)

Politics in a Changing America 8.1 (continued)

We know that the framers were concerned about the abuse of power by the president and understood that it could take various forms. James Madison's account of the Constitutional Convention reports that Edmund Randolph, of Virginia, told fellow delegates that "Guilt wherever found ought to be punished. The Executive will have great opportunity of abusing his power."

The framers were also concerned that the legislature might use its impeachment power unfairly to give it added leverage over the president. Charles Pinckney, of South Carolina, worried that impeachment would be used "as a rod over the Executive" and this could "effectually destroy his independence." In the end, however, the delegates felt that they needed to institute some provision for disciplining presidents who had committed serious crimes.

But if the need for an impeachment process is clear, the circumstances under which it should be set in motion remain murky. Aren't there other ways to discipline a president outside of this constitutional provision? Conviction by the Senate requires that the president be removed from office, an extreme penalty for some transgressions. Many proposed that Congress censure Clinton, thus shaming him for his conduct but stopping short of this more dire punishment. Most Republicans in Congress believed censure was only a slap on the wrist and that legislators needed to do their constitutional duty by voting on impeachment.

Another possibility is to let the courts handle any alleged presidential transgressions that do not warrant impeachment. A related option is to let the courts deal with allegations against a president after he leaves office. However, this means justice will be delayed, as it would have been for Paula Jones, who reached an out-of-court settlement with the president.

The dilemma that troubled the framers seems no easier to resolve today: how do we protect ourselves against presidents' violating the law without giving their opponents the opportunity to cripple them unfairly for political reasons?

members, after redistricting created new districts with large concentrations of Hispanic American voters.

In a decision that surprised many, the Supreme Court ruled in 1993 that states' efforts to increase minority representation through **racial gerrymandering** could violate the rights of whites. In *Shaw v. Reno,* the majority ruled in a split decision that a North Carolina district that meandered 160 miles from Durham to Charlotte was an example of "political apartheid" (see Figure 8.2). In effect, the Court ruled that racial gerrymandering segregated blacks from whites instead of creating districts built around contiguous communities.

In a 1995 case, *Miller v. Johnson,* the Supreme Court went even further in restricting the force of the Voting Rights Act. The Court's majority said that

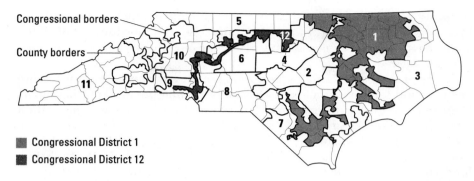

Congressional borders

County borders

■ Congressional District 1
■ Congressional District 12

FIGURE 8.2   "Political Apartheid" or Racial Equality?
To create districts in which African American candidates were likely to win, the boundaries
of two North Carolina congressional districts, 1 and 12, had to weave across the state to
incorporate enough neighborhoods with concentrated minority populations. Justice Sandra
Day O'Connor called these districts examples of "political apartheid." The Shaw v. Reno
and Miller v. Johnson *cases are forcing states to redraw the boundaries of some of these*
oddly shaped districts designed to enhance the representation of minorities in the House of
Representatives. (Source: Shaw v. Reno, *509 U.S. 630 (1993).)*

the states should not draw district boundaries where race is the "predominant factor."[21] In *Abrams v. Johnson* (1997), the Court reaffirmed its position when it blocked the creation of a majority black district in southwest Georgia that it felt could not be drawn without "engaging in racial gerrymandering."[22] Thus it is not merely the shape of the district that is suspect, but the very intent to draw districts to favor an ethnic or racial group. If equality requires descriptive representation, then the Court's direction to states to move away from racial gerrymandering is a retreat from equality in Congress. But, ironically, spreading black and Hispanic voters around more districts, rather than concentrating them in a relatively small number of districts, might actually increase their influence. More representatives will have significant numbers of minority voters in their districts and will have to consider minority views as they contemplate their stands on the issues.

How Issues Get on the Congressional Agenda

The formal legislative process begins when a member of Congress introduces a *bill*, a proposal for a new law. In the House, members drop new bills in the "hopper," a mahogany box near the rostrum where the Speaker presides. Senators give their bills to one of the Senate clerks or introduce them from the floor.[23] But before a bill can be introduced to solve a problem, someone must perceive that a problem exists or that an issue needs to be resolved. In other words, the problem or issue somehow must find its way onto the congressional agenda. *Agenda* has two meanings in the vocabulary of political scientists: (1) a narrow, formal list of things to be done, such as a calendar of bills to be voted on, and (2) the broad, imprecise, and unwritten set of all the issues an institution is considering. Here we use the term in the second, broader sense.

Many of the issues Congress is working on at any one time seem to have been around forever, yet all issues have a beginning point. There has always been violence on TV, for example, but for years it was seen as a matter best left to the private sector to solve. Eventually, though, people began to see the problem as a *political* issue. In 1996, Congress passed legislation requiring new televisions to be equipped with a "V chip," an electronic device that allows parents to lock out all programs they deem unsuitable for their children.

Sometimes a highly visible event focuses national attention on a problem. An explosion in West Virginia mine in 1968 killed seventy-eight miners; Congress promptly went to work on laws to promote miners' safety.[24] Presidential support can also move an issue onto the agenda quickly. Media attention gives the president enormous opportunity to draw the nation's attention to problems he believes need some form of governmental action.

Within Congress, party leaders and committee chairs have the opportunity to influence the political agenda. At times, the efforts of an interest group spark awareness of an issue.

The Dance of Legislation: An Overview

The process of writing bills and getting them passed is relatively simple, in the sense that it follows a series of specific steps. What complicates the process is the many different ways legislation can be treated at each step. Here, we examine the straightforward process by which laws are made. In the next few sections, we discuss some of the complexities of that process.

After a bill is introduced in either house, it is assigned to the committee with jurisdiction over that policy area (see Figure 8.3). A banking bill, for example, is assigned to the Banking and Finance Services Committee in the House or to the Banking, Housing, and Urban Affairs Committee in the Senate. When a committee actively considers a piece of legislation assigned to it, the bill is usually referred to a specialized subcommittee. The subcommittee may hold hearings, and legislative staffers may do research on the bill. The original bill usually is modified or revised. If passed in some form, it is sent to the full committee. A bill approved by the full committee is reported (that is, sent) to the entire membership of the chamber, where it may be debated, amended, and either passed or defeated.

FIGURE 8.3   *The Legislative Process*
The process by which a bill becomes law is subject to much variation. This diagram depicts the typical path a bill might follow. It is important to remember that a bill can fail at any stage because of lack of support.

HOUSE	SENATE
HOUSE	**SENATE**
Bill is introduced and assigned to a committee, which refers it to the appropriate . . .	*Bill is introduced and assigned to a committee, which refers it to the appropriate . . .*

Subcommittee
Subcommittee members study the bill, hold hearings, and debate provisions. If a bill is approved, it goes to the . . .

Subcommittee
Subcommittee members study the bill, hold hearings, and debate provisions. If a bill is approved, it goes to the . . .

Committee
Full committee considers the bill. If the bill is approved in some form, it goes to the . . .

Committee
Full committee considers the bill. If the bill is approved in some form, it goes to the . . .

Rules Committee
Rules Committee issues a rule to govern debate on the floor. Sends it to the . . .

Full House
Full House debates the bill and may amend it. If the bill passes and is in a form different from the Senate version, it must go to a . . .

Full Senate
Full Senate debates the bill and may amend it. If the bill passes and is in a form different from the House version, it must go to a . . .

Conference Committee
Conference committee of senators and representatives meets to reconcile differences between bills. When agreement is reached, a compromise bill is sent back to both the . . .

Full House
House votes on the conference committee bill. If it passes in both houses, it goes to the . . .

Full Senate
Senate votes on the conference committee bill. If it passes in both houses, it goes to the . . .

President
President signs or vetoes the bill. Congress can override a veto by a two-thirds majority vote in both the House and Senate.

Bills coming out of House committees go to the Rules Committee before going before the full House membership. The Rules Committee attaches a rule to the bill that governs the coming floor debate, typically specifying the length of the debate and the types of amendments House members may offer. The Senate does not have a comparable committee, although restrictions on the length of floor debate can be reached through unanimous consent agreements (see the "Rules of Procedure" section later in the chapter).

Even if both houses of Congress pass a bill on the same subject, the Senate and House versions usually differ. In that case, a conference committee, composed of legislators from both houses, works out the differences and develops a compromise version. This version goes back to each house for another floor vote. If both chambers approve the bill, it is then sent to the president for his signature (approval) or **veto** (rejection).

When the president signs a bill, it becomes law. If the president vetoes a bill, it is sent back to Congress with his reasons for rejecting it. The bill becomes law only if Congress overrides the president's veto by a two-thirds vote in each house. If the president neither signs nor vetoes the bill within ten days of receiving it (Sundays excepted), the bill becomes law. But if Congress adjourns within that ten-day period, the president can let the bill die through a **pocket veto**, by not signing it.

In 1996, Congress gave the president a new tool, the **line item veto**. This veto gave the president the authority to strike out specific sections of a bill, invalidating particular items but allowing the rest of the bill to become law. Thus, if the president thought three projects in an appropriations bill were wasteful "pork barrel" spending, he could cross out the lines in the legislation carrying those projects, vetoing the spending for those specific items while leaving the rest of the bill intact.

Although the Supreme Court struck down the line item veto as unconstitutional in 1998 in *Clinton v. City of New York,* what was remarkable about the line item veto was that Congress voluntarily gave away considerable power to the executive branch. Until the Supreme Court intervened, the president had greater authority to direct spending, greater leverage to bargain with Congress, and greater ability to punish uncooperative members of Congress by deleting the projects that legislators cared most about. Congress passed the statute because it believed that the president would use the line item veto to control spending, and thus reduce the budget deficit, better than Congress itself could.[25]

The content of a bill can be changed at any stage of the process, in either house. Lawmaking (and thus policymaking) in Congress has many access points for those who want to influence legislation. This openness tends to fit within the pluralist model of democracy. As a bill moves through the dance of legislation,[26] it is amended again and again, in a search for a consensus that will get it passed and signed into law. The process can be tortuously slow, and it often is fruitless. Derailing legislation is much easier than enacting it. The process gives groups frequent opportunities to voice their preferences and, if necessary, thwart their opponents.

Committees: The Workhorses of Congress

Woodrow Wilson once observed that "Congress in session is Congress on public exhibition, whilst Congress in its committee-rooms is Congress at work."[27] The real nuts and bolts of lawmaking goes on in congressional committees.

The Division of Labor Among Committees

The House and Senate are divided into committees for the same reason that other large organizations are broken into departments or divisions—to develop and use expertise in specific areas. For example, congressional decisions on weapons systems require special knowledge that is of little relevance to decisions on reimbursement formulas for health insurance. It makes sense for some members of Congress to spend more time examining defense issues, becoming increasingly expert as they do so, while others concentrate on health matters.

Eventually, all members of Congress have to vote on each bill that emerges from the committees. Those who are not on a particular committee depend on committee members to examine the issues thoroughly, to make compromises as necessary, and to bring forward a sound piece of legislation that has a good chance of being passed. Each member decides individually on a bill's merits. But once it reaches the House or Senate floor, members may get to vote on only a handful of amendments (if any at all) before they must cast their yea or nay for the entire bill.

Standing Committees   There are several different kinds of congressional committees, but the **standing committee** is predominant. Standing committees are permanent committees that specialize in a particular area of legislation—for example, the House Judiciary Committee or the Senate Environment and Public Works Committee. Most of the day-to-day work of drafting legislation takes place in the eighteen standing Senate committees and twenty standing House committees. Typically from sixteen to twenty senators serve on each standing Senate committee, and on average forty-two members serve on each standing committee in the House. The proportion of Democrats and Republicans on a standing committee generally reflects party proportions in the full Senate or House.

With a few exceptions, standing committees are further broken down into subcommittees. The House Agriculture Committee, for example, has five subcommittees, among them one on specialty crops and another on livestock, dairy, and poultry.

Other Congressional Committees   Members of Congress can also serve on joint, select, and conference committees. **Joint committees** are made up of members of both House and Senate. Like standing committees, joint committees are concerned with particular policy areas. The Joint Economic Committee, for instance, analyzes the country's economic policies. Joint committees are much weaker than standing committees because they are almost always restricted from reporting bills to the House or Senate.

A **select committee** is a temporary committee created for a specific purpose. Congress establishes select committees to deal with special circumstances or with issues that either overlap or fall outside the areas of expertise of standing committees. The Senate committee that investigated the Watergate scandal was a select committee, created for that purpose only.

A **conference committee** is also a temporary committee, created to work out differences between House and Senate versions of a specific piece of legislation. Its members are appointed from the standing committees or subcommittees from each house that originally handled and reported the legislation. Depending on the nature of the differences and the importance of the legislation, a conference committee may meet for hours or for weeks on end. When the conference committee agrees on a compromise, it reports the bill to both houses, which must then either approve or disapprove the compromise; they cannot amend or change it in any way. Only about 15 to 25 percent of all bills that eventually pass Congress go to a conference committee (although nearly all important or controversial bills do).[28] Committee or subcommittee leaders of both houses reconcile differences in other bills through informal negotiation.

Congressional Expertise and Seniority

Once appointed to a committee, a representative or senator has great incentive to remain on it in order to gain increasing expertise and influence. Influence also grows in a more formal way—with **seniority**, or years of consecutive service on a committee. In their quest for expertise and seniority, members tend to stay on the same committees. However, sometimes they switch places when they are offered the opportunity to move to one of the high-prestige committees (such as Ways and Means in the House or Finance in the Senate) or to a committee that handles legislation of vital importance to their constituents.

Within each committee, the senior member of the majority party usually becomes the committee chair. (The majority party in each house controls committee leadership.) Other senior members of the majority party become subcommittee chairs; their counterparts from the minority party gain influence as ranking minority members. The numerous subcommittees in the House and Senate offer multiple opportunities for power and status.

After the Republicans gained control of the House in 1994, Speaker of the House Newt Gingrich made a major break with the seniority system by rejecting three Republicans who were in line to become committee chairs. Gingrich passed over the three to choose committee members who he thought would be especially conservative and aggressive in promoting the Republican program. Speakers had not appointed House committee chairs in this fashion since the first part of the twentieth century, when "Uncle Joe" Cannon ruled the chamber with an iron fist.[29] Gingrich also instituted term limits for committee and subcommittee chairs, restricting their tenure to six years.

The way in which committees and subcommittees are led and organized within Congress is significant because much public policy decision making takes place there. The first step in drafting legislation is to collect information on the issue. Committee staffers research the problem, and hearings may be held to take testimony from witnesses who have special knowledge on the subject.

The meetings at which subcommittees and committees actually debate and amend legislation are called *markup sessions*. The process by which committees reach decisions varies. In many committees, there is a strong tradition of decision by consensus. The chair, the ranking minority member, and others in these committees work hard, in formal committee sessions and in informal negotiations, to find a middle ground on issues that divide committee members. In other committees, members exhibit strong ideological and partisan sentiments. However, committee and subcommittee leaders prefer to find ways to overcome inherent ideological and partisan divisions so that they can build compromise solutions that will appeal to the broader membership of their house. The skill of committee leaders in assembling coalitions that produce legislation that can pass on the floor of their house is critically important.

Oversight: Following Through on Legislation

It is often said in Washington that "knowledge is power." For Congress to retain its influence over the programs it creates, it must be aware of how the agencies responsible for them are administering them. To that end, legislators and their committees engage in **oversight**, the process of reviewing agency operations to determine whether the agency is carrying out policies as Congress intended.

Congress performs its oversight function in a number of different ways. The most visible is the hearing. Hearings may be part of a routine review or the byproduct of information that reveals a major problem with a program or with an agency's administrative practices. Another way Congress keeps track of what departments and agencies are doing is by requesting reports on specific agency practices and operations. Also, a good deal of congressional oversight takes place informally. There is ongoing contact between committee and subcommittee leaders and agency administrators, and between committee staffers and top agency staffers.

Congressional oversight of the executive branch has sharply increased since the early 1970s.[30] A primary reason for this increase was that Congress gave itself the staff necessary to watch over the growing federal government.[31] In addition to significantly expanding the staffs of individual legislators and of House and Senate committees, Congress enhanced its analytical capabilities by creating the Congressional Budget Office and by strengthening the Government Accounting Office (GAO) and the Congressional Research Service of the Library of Congress.

Majoritarian and Pluralist Views of Committees

Government by committee vests a tremendous amount of power in the committees and subcommittees of Congress—and especially in their leaders. This is particularly true of the House, which has more decentralized patterns of influence than the Senate and is more restrictive about letting members amend legislation on the floor. Committee members can bury a bill by not reporting it to the full House or Senate. The influence of committee members extends even further, to the floor debate. Many of them also make up the conference committees charged with developing compromise versions of bills.

In some ways, the committee system enhances the force of pluralism in American politics. Representatives and senators are elected by the voters in particular districts and states, and they tend to seek membership on the committees that make the decisions most important to their constituents. Members from farm areas, for example, want membership on the House and Senate Agriculture Committees. As a result, committees with members who represent constituencies with an unusually strong interest in their policy area are predisposed to write legislation favorable to those constituencies.

The committees have a majoritarian aspect as well. The membership of most committees tends to resemble the general ideological profiles of the two parties' congressional contingents. Even if a committee's views are not in line with the views of the full membership, the committee is constrained in the legislation it writes because bills cannot become law unless they are passed by the parent chamber and by the other house. Consequently, in formulating legislation, committees anticipate what other representatives and senators will accept. The parties within each chamber also have means of rewarding the members who are most loyal to party priorities. Party committees and the party leadership within each chamber make committee assignments and respond to requests for transfers from less prestigious to more prestigious committees. Those whose voting is most in line with the party get the best assignments.[32]

In the Gingrich-led House of Representatives, committee-based pluralism was reduced. First, by violating the seniority norm in selecting chairs, Gingrich served notice on all chairs that they served at his pleasure. Second, on occasion Gingrich publicly sided with other members of a committee when the chair pursued policy goals he opposed. His successor, Dennis Hastert, was much less aggressive as Speaker of the House in his interaction with committees.

Leaders and Followers in Congress

Above the committee chairs is another layer of authority in the organization of the House and Senate. The Democratic and Republican leaders in each house work to maximize the influence of their own party while trying to keep their chamber functioning smoothly and efficiently. The operation of the two houses is also influenced by the rules and norms that each chamber has developed over the years.

The Leadership Task

Each of the two parties elects leaders in each of the two houses. In the House of Representatives, the majority party's leader is the **Speaker of the House**, who, gavel in hand, chairs sessions from the ornate rostrum at the front of the chamber. The Speaker's counterpart in the opposing party is the House *minority leader.* The Speaker is a constitutional officer, but the Constitution does not list the Speaker's duties. The minority leader is not mentioned in the Constitution, but that post has evolved into an important party position in the House.

The Constitution makes the vice president of the United States the president of the Senate. But in practice the vice president rarely visits the Senate chamber unless there is a possibility of a tie vote, in which case he can break the tie. The *president pro tempore* (president "for the time"), elected by the majority party, is supposed to chair the Senate in the vice president's absence, but by custom this constitutional position is entirely honorary. The real power in the Senate resides with the **majority leader**. The top position in the opposing party is Senate *minority leader.* Technically, the majority leader does not preside over Senate sessions (members rotate in the president pro tempore's chair). But the majority leader does schedule legislation in consultation with the minority leader.

Party leaders play a critical role in getting bills through Congress. Their most significant function is steering the bargaining and negotiating over the content of legislation. When an issue divides their party, their house, the two houses, or their house and the White House, the leaders must take the initiative to work out a compromise. Day in and day out, much of what they do is to meet with other members of their house to try to strike deals that will yield a majority on the floor. Beyond trying to engineer tradeoffs that will win votes, the party leaders must persuade others (often powerful committee chairs) that theirs is the best deal possible. After serving his first years as Senate majority leader, Bob Dole said he thought "majority pleader" was a more apt title.[33]

As recently as the 1950s, strong leaders dominated the legislative process. In the contemporary Congress, however, it has been difficult for leaders to control rank-and-file members because they have independent electoral bases in their districts and states and receive the vast bulk of their campaign funds from nonparty sources. Contemporary party leaders are coalition builders, not autocrats. Newt Gingrich, however, was a throwback to an earlier style of leadership. Gingrich won the fierce loyalty and support of rank-and-file Republicans because of his hard work for the party and his dynamic vision for the Republican platform in the 1994 congressional campaign—the Contract with America. Gingrich was successful in getting almost all of the Contract's provisions through the House, gaining acclaim as the most effective Speaker in recent history. But his leadership position was threatened when charges of ethical violations resulted in an unprecedented reprimand by the House and a $300,000 fine. By early 1997 it was reported that ambitious committee chairmen and others were moving to fill the void left by the weakened Speaker.[34]

Gingrich successfully rallied colleagues loyal to him, and the revolt was soon over. But he survived only until the next election. Gingrich resigned soon after the Democrats gained seats in the November 1998 election. His would-be successor, Bob Livingston of Louisiana, resigned only six weeks later after it was reported in the media that he had been unfaithful to his wife. After Livingston resigned, the House Republicans turned to Dennis Hastert of Illinois. Hastert had a conservative voting record in the House, where he built a strong pro-business reputation. The low-key legislator preferred a be-hind-the-scenes style of leadership and, unlike Gingrich, made little effort to influence public opinion. With a slim majority in the 106th Congress, Hastert faced a difficult task in keeping House Republicans unified. As the 2000 election approached, both conservative and moderate House Republicans tried to pull Hastert in their direction.[35] His greatest battles, however, were with House minority leader Dick Gephardt, which were reportedly personal as well as political.

Rules of Procedure

The operations of the House and Senate are structured by both formal rules and informal norms of behavior. Rules in each chamber are mostly matters of parliamentary procedure. For example, they govern the scheduling of legislation, outlining when and how certain types of legislation can be brought to the floor.

As noted earlier, an important difference between the two chambers is the House's use of its Rules Committee to govern floor debate. Lacking a similar committee to act as a "traffic cop" for legislation approaching the floor, the Senate relies on unanimous consent agreements to set the starting time and length of debate. If only one senator objects to an agreement, it does not take effect. Senators do not routinely object to unanimous consent agreements, however, because they know they will need them when bills of their own await scheduling by the leadership.

A senator who wants to stop a bill badly enough may start a **filibuster** and try to talk the bill to death. By historical tradition, the Senate gives its members the right of unlimited debate. The record for holding the floor belongs to Republican senator Strom Thurmond of South Carolina, for a twenty-four-hour, eighteen-minute marathon.[36] In the House, no member is allowed to speak for more than an hour without unanimous consent.

After a 1917 filibuster by a small group of senators killed President Wilson's bill to arm merchant ships—a bill favored by a majority of senators—the Senate finally adopted **cloture**, a means of limiting debate. A petition signed by sixteen senators initiates a cloture vote. It now takes the votes of sixty senators to invoke cloture. Although there is considerable criticism of the filibuster, there is no significant movement within the Senate to reform the rules of debate.

Norms of Behavior

Both houses have codes of behavior that help keep them running. These codes are largely unwritten norms, although some have been formally adopted as rules. Members of Congress recognize that they must eliminate personal conflict, lest Congress dissolve into bickering factions unable to work together. One of the most celebrated norms is that members show respect for their col-

Leaders of the Pack
Because of the system of checks and balances, presidents and members of Congress (of both parties) often must work together to find compromises in order to pass important legislation. This was especially true during the 107th Congress, which was almost evenly divided between Republicans and Democrats. Here, President Bush meets with the leaders of the 107th Congress to discuss education reform proposals. Left to right, the leaders pictured here are House Majority Leader Richard Armey (R-TX), Senate Minority Leader Tom Daschle (D-SD), Senate Majority Leader Trent Lott (R-MS), President Bush, and Speaker of the House Dennis Hastert (R-IL).

leagues in public deliberations. During floor debate, bitter opponents still refer to one another in such terms as "my good friend, the senior senator from . . ." or "my distinguished colleague."

Probably the most important norm of behavior in Congress is that individual members should be willing to bargain with one another. Policymaking is a process of give-and-take; it demands compromise. However, it is important to point out that members of Congress are not expected to violate their consciences on policy issues simply to strike a deal. Rather, they are expected to listen to what others have to say and to make every effort to reach a reasonable compromise. Obviously, if they all stick rigidly to their own views, they will never agree on anything. Moreover, few policy matters are so clear-cut that compromise destroys one's position.

Some important norms have changed in recent years, most notably the notion that junior members of the House and Senate should serve apprenticeships and defer to their party and committee elders during their first couple of years in Congress. The seventy-three new Republicans who entered the House after the GOP sweep in the 1994 elections served notice that they would use their numbers to change the way things were done in Congress, and they did have an impact, most notably in pushing Speaker Gingrich to hold fast on principle in his negotiations with President Clinton. The freshmen thought that there was too much compromise in American politics and that political parties should stand firm for what they believe in.[37]

The Legislative Environment

In this section, we examine the broader legislative environment that affects decision making in Congress. More specifically, we look at the influence on legislators of political parties, the president, constituents, and interest groups. The first two influences push Congress toward majoritarian democracy. The other two are pluralist influences on congressional policymaking.

Political Parties

The national political parties might appear to have limited resources at their disposal to influence lawmakers. They do not control the nominations of House and Senate candidates. Candidates receive the bulk of their funds from individual contributors and political action committees, not from the national parties. Nevertheless, the parties are strong forces in the legislative process. The party leaders and various party committees within each house can help or hinder the efforts of rank-and-file legislators to get on the right committees, get their bills and amendments considered, and climb onto the leadership ladder themselves. Moreover, party members on a committee tend to act as agents of their party as they search for solutions to policy problems.[38]

The most significant reason why the parties are important in Congress is, of course, that Democrats and Republicans have different ideological views. Both parties have diversity, but as Figure 8.4 illustrates, Democrats increasingly tend to vote one way and Republicans the other. The main reason why partisanship has been rising is that each party is becoming increasingly homogeneous.[39] The liberal wing of the Republican Party has practically disappeared, and the party is unified around a conservative agenda for America. Likewise, the conservative wing of the Democratic Party has declined.

As each party has sorted itself out, its ideological wingspan has shrunk. Some applaud this rising partisanship because it is a manifestation of majoritarianism. When congressional parties are more unified, voters have a stronger means of influencing public policy choices through their selection of representatives and senators. Others are skeptical of majoritarianism, believing that Congress is most productive and responsible when it relies on bipartisanship. In their view, parties that cooperate in searching for consensus serve the nation best.

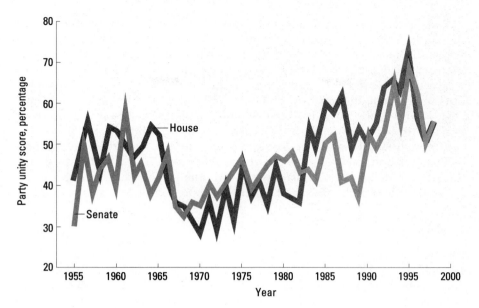

FIGURE 8.4   ***Rising Partisanship***
The lines in this graph show the percentages of representatives and senators who voted with their party on party unity votes (votes in which a majority of one party votes one way and a majority of the other party votes the opposite way). The rising percentage of party unity votes indicates that congressional parties are more frequently at odds with each other. In a true majoritarian system, parties vote against each other on all key issues. (Sources: Norman J. Ornstein, Thomas E. Mann, and Michael J. Malbin, eds., Vital Statistics on Congress, 1995–1996 *[Washington, D.C.: Congressional Quarterly Press, 1994], p. 208; Dan Carney, "As Hostilities Rage on the Hill, Partisan-Vote Rate Soars,"* Congressional Quarterly Weekly Report, *27 January 1996, p. 199; Alan Greenblatt, "Despite Drop in Partisan Votes, Bickering Continued in 1997,"* Congressional Quarterly Weekly Report, *3 January 1998, p. 18; and Alan K. Ota, "Partisan Voting on the Rise,"* CQ Weekly, *9 January 1999, p. 79.)*

The President

Unlike members of Congress, the president is elected by voters across the entire nation. The president has a better claim, then, to representing the nation than does any single member of Congress. But it can also be argued that Congress as a whole has a better claim than the president to representing the majority of voters. Nevertheless, presidents capitalize on their popular election and usually act as though they are speaking for the majority.

During the twentieth century, public expectations of what the president can accomplish in office grew enormously. We now expect the president to be our chief legislator: to introduce legislation on major issues and to use his influence to push bills through Congress.[40] This is much different from our early history, when presidents felt constrained by the constitutional doctrine of separation of powers and had to have members of Congress work confidentially for them during legislative sessions.[41]

Today the White House is openly involved not only in the writing of bills but also in their development as they wind their way through the legislative process. If the White House does not like a bill, it tries to work out a compromise with key legislators in order to have the legislation amended. On issues of the greatest importance, the president himself may meet with individual legislators to persuade them to vote a certain way. To monitor daily congressional activities and lobby for the administration's policies, there are hundreds of legislative liaison personnel who work for the executive branch.

Although members of Congress grant presidents a leadership role in proposing legislation, they jealously guard the power of Congress to debate, shape, and pass or defeat any legislation the president proposes. Congress often clashes sharply with the president when his proposals are seen as ill advised.

Constituents

Constituents are the people who live and vote in a legislator's district or state. As much as members of Congress want to please their party's leadership or the president by going along with their preferences, they have to think about what the voters back home want. If the way members vote displeases enough people, they might lose their seats in the next election.

Constituents' influence contributes to pluralism, because the diversity of America is mirrored in the geographical basis of representation in the House and Senate. A representative from Los Angeles, for instance, may need to be sensitive to issues of particular concern to constituents whose backgrounds are Korean, Vietnamese, Hispanic, African American, or Jewish. A representative from Montana will have few such constituents but must pay particular attention to issues involving minerals and mining. A senator from Nebraska will give higher priority to agricultural issues than to urban issues. Conversely, a senator from New York will be hypersensitive to issues involving the cities. All these constituencies, enthusiastically represented by legislators who want to do a good job for the people back home, push and pull Congress in many different directions.

Interest Groups

As we pointed out in Chapter 7, interest groups offer constituents one way to influence Congress. Because they represent a vast array of vocational, regional, and ideological groupings within our population, interest groups exemplify pluralist politics. Interest groups press members of Congress to take a particular course of action, believing sincerely that what they prefer is also best for the country. Legislators, in turn, are attentive to interest groups because these organizations represent citizens, some of whom live in their home district or state. Lobbies are also sources of useful information and potentially of political support (and, in some instances, campaign contributions) for members of Congress.

Because the four external sources of influence on Congress—parties, the president, constituents, and interest groups—push legislators in both majoritarian and pluralist directions, Congress exhibits aspects of both pluralism and majoritarianism in its operations. We will return to the conflict between pluralism and majoritarianism at the end of this chapter.

The Dilemma of Representation: Trustees or Delegates?

When candidates for the House and Senate campaign for office, they routinely promise to work hard for their district's or state's interests. When they get to Washington, though, they all face a troubling dilemma: what their constituents want may not be what the people across the nation want.

Members of Congress are often criticized for being out of touch with the people they are supposed to represent. This charge does not seem justified. A typical week in the life of a representative means working in Washington, then boarding a plane and flying back to the home district. There the representative spends time meeting with individual constituents and talking to civic groups, church gatherings, business associations, labor unions, and the like. A survey of House members during a nonelection year showed that each made an average of thirty-five trips back to his or her district, spending an average of 138 days there.[42] Legislators work extraordinarily hard at keeping in touch with voters, at finding out what is on their constituents' minds. The problem is how to act on that knowledge.

Are members of Congress bound to vote the way their constituents want them to vote, even if doing so means voting against their consciences? Some say no. They argue that legislators must be free to vote in line with what they think is best. This view is associated with the English political philosopher Edmund Burke (1729–1797). Burke, who served in Parliament, told his constituents in Bristol that "you choose a member, indeed; but when you have chosen him, he is not a member of Bristol, but he is a member of *Parliament.*"[43] Burke reasoned that representatives are sent by their constituents to vote as they think best. As **trustees**, representatives are obligated to consider the views of constituents, but they are not obligated to vote according to those views if they think they are misguided.

Others disagree. They hold that legislators are duty-bound to represent the majority view of their constituents. They maintain that legislators are **delegates** with instructions from the people at home on how to vote on critical issues, and they insist that delegates, unlike trustees, must be prepared to vote against their own policy preferences.

Thus members of Congress are subject to two opposing forces. The interests of their districts encourage them to act as delegates, but their interpretation of the larger national interest calls on them to be trustees. Given these conflicting role definitions, it is not surprising that Congress is not clearly either a body of delegates or a body of trustees. Research has shown, however, that members of Congress are most likely to assume the delegate role on issues that are of great concern to their constituents.[44] But much of the time, what constituents really want is not clear. Many issues are not highly visible back home, they cut across the constituency to affect it in different ways, or constituents only partially understand them. For such issues, no delegate position is obvious.

Pluralism, Majoritarianism, and Democracy

The dilemma that individual members of Congress face in adopting the role of either delegate or trustee has broad implications for the way our country is governed. If legislators tend to act as delegates, congressional policymaking is more pluralistic, and policies reflect the bargaining that goes on among lawmakers who speak for different constituencies. If, instead, legislators tend to act as trustees and vote their consciences, policymaking becomes less tied to the narrower interests of districts and states. But even here there is no guarantee that congressional decision making reflects majority interests,

We end this chapter with a short discussion of pluralism versus majoritarianism in Congress. But first, to establish a frame of reference, we need to take a quick look at a more majoritarian type of legislature—the parliament.

Parliamentary Government

In our system of government, the executive and legislative functions are divided between a president and a congress, each elected separately. Most other democracies—for example, Britain and Japan—have parliamentary governments. In a **parliamentary system**, the chief executive is the legislative leader whose party holds the most seats in the legislature after an election or whose party forms a major part of the ruling coalition. For instance, in Great Britain, voters do not cast a ballot for prime minister. They vote only for their member of Parliament and thus influence the choice of prime minister only indirectly, by voting for the party they favor in the local district election. Parties are unified, and in Parliament legislators vote for their party's position, giving voters a strong and direct means of influencing public policy.

In a parliamentary system, government power is highly concentrated in the legislature, because the leader of the majority party is also the head of the government. Moreover, parliamentary legislatures are usually composed of only one house or have a second chamber that is much weaker than the other. And parliamentary governments usually do not have a court that can invalidate acts of the parliament. Under such a system, the government is in the hands of the party that controls the parliament.

Pluralism Versus Majoritarianism in Congress

The U.S. Congress is often criticized for being too pluralist and not majoritarian enough. The federal budget deficit provides a case in point. Americans were deeply concerned about the big deficits that plagued our national budgets in recent years. And both Democrats and Republicans in Congress repeatedly called for reductions in those deficits. But when spending bills came before Congress, legislators' concern turned to what the bills would or would not do for their district or state. Appropriations bills usually included pork barrel projects that benefited specific districts or states and further added to the deficit.

In a recent transportation bill, Democrat Nita Lowey got a $4.5 million bus facility for Westchester County in New York. Her Republican colleague from New York, James Walsh, got $7 million for buses and transportation projects for Syracuse. Projects such as these get into the budget through bargaining among members. Members of Congress try to win projects and programs that will benefit their constituents and thus help them at election time. To win approval of such projects, members must be willing to vote for other legislators' projects in turn. Such a system obviously promotes pluralism (and spending).

Critics long contended that Congress would have to abandon pluralism before the country would ever achieve a balanced budget. Although legislators have apparently succeeded in eliminating the federal deficit, their success was largely due to a $225 billion windfall in unanticipated tax revenues from a healthy national economy. On May 2, 1997, President Clinton and the Republican leaders of Congress announced that they had reached a compromise agreement to balance the budget by 2002. The president agreed to cut Medicare by $115 billion over five years but saved his pet plan to provide tax credits for college tuition. The Republicans won their $500-per-child tax credit and reductions in the capital gains tax but had to accept several Democratic priorities such as more health care for poor children and more money for education. Both sides agreed to raise taxes sharply on airline tickets and to slash certain domestic programs, including public housing.

The unexpected tax windfall made deeper reductions in popular programs unnecessary and thus helped preserve the pluralistic nature of congressional spending.[45] Whether Congress can maintain the balanced budget (or begin to reduce the monumental national debt) remains to be seen. Yet those who favor pluralism are quick to point out Congress's merits.

Many different constituencies are well served by an appropriations process that allows for pluralism. For the low-income residents of Syracuse and Westchester County, bus service is vital to their livelihood. Middle-class people drive their cars to work and couldn't care less about their local bus system. But dishwashers, maids, and janitors pay taxes to fund the government, too, and they have a right to expect the government to care about the problems they have in getting to work.

Proponents of pluralism also argue that the makeup of Congress generally reflects that of the nation, that different members of Congress represent farm areas, oil and gas areas, low-income inner cities, industrial areas, and so on. They point out that America itself is pluralistic, with a rich diversity of economic, social, religious, and racial groups, and that even if one's own representatives and senators don't represent one's particular viewpoint, it's likely that someone else in Congress does.[46]

The House Republicans' push to enact the Contract with America represented a concerted effort to move the national government toward a more majoritarian system. By presenting the votes in 1994 with a platform of policies they promised to pass, GOP House candidates were emulating candidates running for Parliament in a responsible party system. Majoritarian parties and legislatures give voters more direct control over public policy by allowing citizens a clear means of expressing their preference and of mandating that the majority legislators carry out their platform.

With the 104th Congress (1995–1996) now over, how might this bold experiment be evaluated? What was most impressive was the exceptional unity of House Republicans in voting for the bills that were part of the Contract with America. Almost all of the bills passed with relatively few defections in the Republican ranks. The Republican House candidates kept the promise they made in the 1994 campaign that they would pass the Contract if they won a majority. Yet a good portion of the Contract, including some of its most visible provisions—a balanced budget amendment and term limits for members of Congress—never became law. Furthermore, the $500-per-child tax credit and the capital gains tax cut had to wait for the 105th Congress (and help from a Democratic president) before being passed. Although Republicans could blame Democrat Bill Clinton for vetoing some important parts of the Contract, one of the problems was the Republican majority in the Senate. A number of GOP senators were only nominally committed to the Contract and voted against some of the bills when they reached the Senate. On some items the public actually turned against the Contract (on regulatory reform, for example, because the proposed legislation would have weakened environmental protections).

Although they seemingly embraced majoritarianism with the Contract with America, the Republicans of the 104th Congress did not completely abandon pluralism. Business groups had extraordinary access to GOP leaders and committee chairs, and many bills were put forward to benefit various industries.[47] Majoritarian political systems do not eliminate all traces of interest group politics from the legislative process; nevertheless, interest groups played far too important a role in the 104th Congress for it to be judged an example of majoritarian democracy. Although the Contract with America was an important step in that direction, a true majoritarian democracy would require that both parties put forward platforms they are committed to carrying out, that voters understand what the parties have pledged to do and then vote on that basis, and that the influence of interest groups on policy formulation in Congress be modest. Although strong party unity in legislators' voting and the Contract with America enhanced majoritarianism in Congress, the House and the Senate still remain more pluralistic than majoritarian in nature.

Summary

Congress writes the laws of the land and attempts to oversee their implementation. It helps to educate us about new issues as they appear on the political agenda. Most important, members of Congress represent us, working to see to it that interests from home and from around the country are heard throughout the policy-making process.

We count on Congress to do so much that criticism about how well it does some things is inevitable. However, certain strengths are clear. The committee system fosters expertise; representatives and senators who know the most about particular issues have the most influence over them. And the structure of our electoral system keeps legislators in close touch with their constituents.

Bargaining and compromise play important roles in congressional policymaking. Some find this disquieting. They want less deal making and more adherence to principle. This thinking is in line with the desire for a more majoritarian democracy. Others defend the current system, arguing that the United States is a large, complex nation and the policies that govern it should be developed through bargaining among various interests.

There is no clear-cut answer on whether a majoritarian or a pluralist legislative system provides better representation for voters. Our system is a mix of pluralism and majoritarianism. It serves minority interests that might otherwise be neglected or even harmed by an unthinking or uncaring majority. At the same time, congressional parties work to represent the broader interests of the American people.

Key Terms

reapportionment
impeachment
incumbent
gerrymandering
casework
descriptive representation
racial gerrymandering
veto
pocket veto
line item veto
standing committee
joint committee

select committee
conference committee
seniority
oversight
Speaker of the House
majority leader
filibuster
cloture
constituents
trustee
delegate
parliamentary system

Selected Readings

Fenno, Richard F., Jr. *Home Style*. Boston: Little, Brown, 1978. A classic analysis of how House members interact with constituents during visits to their home districts.

Glaser, James. *Race, Campaign Politics, and the Realignment in the South*. New Haven, Conn.: Yale University Press, 1996. This examination of congressional races in the South looks at how Democratic candidates try to build biracial coalitions.

Herrnson, Paul S. *Congressional Elections*. Washington, D.C.: Congressional Quarterly Press, 1995. Herrnson's study is a comprehensive look at congressional candidates and the electorate.

Mayer, Kenneth R., and David T. Canon. *The Dysfunctional Congress?* Boulder, Colo.: Westview Press, 1999. The authors explore the individual roots of the institutional dilemmas facing the legislative branch.

World Wide Web Resources

Project VoteSmart's CongressTrack. Keep track of your member of Congress. See how members voted on bills, get biographical information, access the *Congressional Record,* and follow links to other congressional information services. Also find the status of current legislation and see how members are evaluated by interest groups.
<www.vote-smart.org/congresstrack>

Library of Congress. View current exhibitions and retrieve current news and events. A highlight of this home page is "American Memory," which contains historical collections (viewable on the Net) for the "National Digital Library."
<www.loc.gov>

House of Representatives. Retrieve information on current and recent legislation and information on members, committees, and other congressional organizations.
<www.house.gov>

Senate. Visitors can get information from and about Senate members, search the member directory, read about Senate history, and search a glossary of Senate terms.
<www.senate.gov>

Thomas. Named after Thomas Jefferson, this is the Library of Congress's congressional service. The site contains the status and full text of bills and laws and a wealth of other information regarding Congress.
<thomas.loc.gov>

9

The Presidency

The greatest political risk to any president is war. Almost by definition, a war brings with it unanticipated consequences. Initial public support can wane quickly when soldiers begin coming home in body bags. The Korean War bedeviled Harry Truman and helped the Republicans capture the White House in 1952. Vietnam sank Lyndon Johnson's presidency.

In January 1999, an ancient conflict in eastern Europe snared President Clinton. Serbia, a nation composed mainly of Eastern Orthodox Christians, was waging war against its own southern province, Kosovo, an area populated almost entirely by ethnic Albanian Muslims. The Serbian leader, Slobodan Milosevic, was also president of what remained of Yugoslavia, a formerly communist nation that had dwindled from six member republics to only two—Serbia and Montenegro. Kosovo had enjoyed considerable political freedom within Yugoslavia until 1989, when Milosevic took away its autonomy because of mistreatment of Serbian residents. The Kosovars resisted and eventually formed a guerrilla movement, the Kosovo Liberation Army (KLA), to counter Serbian forces. Faced with a guerrilla war, Milosevic responded with a brutal campaign of terror against the ethnic Albanians in Kosovo.

As the United States and other Western democracies learned more about what the Serbians were doing in Kosovo, they began to pressure Milosevic to accept a diplomatic solution to the growing crisis. But to Milosevic and many other Serbs, Kosovo was a nonnegotiable issue. It was a historically important region to Serbians, and to permit Kosovo to take even limited steps toward eventual independence was unthinkable. Milosevic's intransigence frustrated the Western allies; they didn't want to go to war against Yugoslavia, but they couldn't stand idly by and let the Serbs continue to slaughter unarmed civilians.

NATO, an alliance of nineteen countries formed after World War II to protect western Europe's democracies from the Soviet bloc, was at a crossroads. Believing that they had no choice, Clinton and the leaders of Britain, France, Germany, Italy, and the other NATO countries began bombing Serbia on March 25. The Serbs responded by forcing ethnic Albanians out of Kosovo. In the following weeks, hundreds of thousands of Kosovar Albanians crossed the border into the neighboring countries of Macedonia and Albania. The exodus of frightened Albanians hardened Western opposition to Serbia's action.

Massive in scope, the NATO bombing inflicted enormous damage not only on Serbia's military but also on its economy. Major factories were destroyed, and the country's infrastructure—its roads, bridges, train tracks, oil refineries, and the like—was decimated by NATO bombs.

Clinton resisted calls to introduce ground troops in Kosovo.[1] The American people supported him, and after six weeks public approval of the war effort was slightly higher than it was when the bombing first started.[2] Clinton knew, however, that if Americans were killed in action, support could quickly vanish. House Republicans voted down a resolution supporting the American effort in Yugoslavia, a stinging rebuke to Clinton. They wanted to make sure the conflict was seen as "Clinton's war."[3] Thus if the war turned out badly, the GOP would be absolved of any responsibility.

Despite increasingly heavy bombardment from the air, the Serbs hung on. Clinton came under criticism for publicly ruling out a ground invasion right from the start. But he said NATO should be patient and stay the course: the bombing would work.

Clinton's instincts proved right. After close to three months of bombing and no sign of NATO's backing down, Milosevic conceded defeat and agreed to withdraw all his troops from Kosovo. NATO peacekeeping troops moved in, and the Albanian Kosovars began returning home. Unfortunately for Clinton, the American public didn't see the conflict as crucial to American interests, and there was no great national celebration when the war ended.[4] For Clinton, the successful outcome was a welcome vindication of his decision to bomb and a rebuke to those who said his presidency had been irreparably crippled by his impeachment.

In this chapter we will analyze presidential leadership, looking at how presidents try to muster majoritarian support for their goals. We'll also focus on a number of other important questions. What are the powers of the presidency? How is the president's advisory system organized? How does the separation of powers between the executive and legislative branches affect public policymaking? Finally, what are the particular issues and problems that presidents face in foreign affairs?

The Constitutional Basis of Presidential Power

When the presidency was created, the thirteen former colonies had just fought a war of independence; their reaction to British domination had focused on the autocratic rule of King George III. Thus delegates to the Constitutional Convention were extremely wary of unchecked power and were determined not to create an all-powerful, dictatorial presidency.

The delegates' fear of a powerful presidency was counterbalanced by their desire for strong leadership. The Articles of Confederation—which did not provide for a single head of state—had failed to bind the states together into a unified nation (see Chapter 2). The delegates knew they had to create some type of effective executive office. Their task was to provide national leadership without allowing any opportunity for tyranny.

Initial Conceptions of the Presidency

Debates over the nature of the office began. Should there be one president or a presidential council or committee? Should the president be chosen by Congress and remain subservient to that body?

The final structure of the presidency reflected the "checks and balances" philosophy that shaped the entire Constitution. The delegates believed they had imposed important limits on the presidency through the powers specifically delegated to Congress and the courts. Those counterbalancing powers would act as checks, or controls, on presidents who might try to expand the office beyond its proper bounds.

The Powers of the President

The requirements for the presidency are set forth in Article II of the Constitution. The president must be a U.S.-born citizen, at least thirty-five years old, who has lived in the United States for a minimum of fourteen years. Article II also sets forth the responsibilities of presidents. In view of the importance of the office, the constitutional description of the president's duties is surprisingly brief and vague. This vagueness has led to repeated conflict about the limits of presidential power.

The major presidential duties and powers listed in the Constitution can be summarized as follows:

- *Serve as administrative head of the nation.* The Constitution gives little guidance on the president's administrative duties. It states merely that "the executive Power shall be vested in a President of the United States of America" and that "he shall take Care that the Laws be faithfully executed." These imprecise directives have been interpreted to mean that the president is to supervise and offer leadership to various departments, agencies, and programs created by Congress. In practice, a chief executive spends much more time making policy decisions for his cabinet departments and agencies than enforcing existing policies.

- *Act as commander in chief of the military.* In essence, the Constitution names the president as the highest-ranking officer in the armed forces. But it gives Congress the power to declare war. The framers no doubt intended Congress to control the president's military power; nevertheless, presidents have initiated military action without the approval of Congress.[5] The entire Vietnam War was fought without a congressional declaration of war.

- *Convene Congress.* The president can call Congress into special session on "extraordinary Occasions," although this has rarely been done. He must also periodically inform Congress of "the State of the Union."

- *Veto legislation.* The president can **veto** (disapprove) any bill or resolution enacted by Congress, with the exception of joint resolutions that propose constitutional amendments. Congress can override a presidential veto with a two-thirds vote in each house.

- *Appoint various officials.* The president has the authority to appoint federal court judges, ambassadors, cabinet members, other key policymakers, and many lesser officials. Many appointments are subject to Senate confirmation.
- *Make treaties.* With the "Advice and Consent" of at least two-thirds of those senators voting at the time, the president can make treaties with foreign powers. The president is also to "receive Ambassadors," a phrase that presidents have interpreted to mean the right to formally recognize other nations.
- *Grant pardons.* The president can grant pardons to individuals who have committed "Offenses against the United States, except in Cases of Impeachment."

The Expansion of Presidential Power

The framers' limited conception of the president's role has given way to a considerably more powerful interpretation. In this section, we look beyond the presidential responsibilities explicitly listed in the Constitution and examine the additional sources of power that presidents have used to expand the authority of the office. First, we look at the claims that presidents make about "inherent" powers implicit in the Constitution. Second, we turn to congressional grants of power to the executive branch. Third, we discuss the influence that comes from a president's political skills. Finally, we analyze how a president's popular support affects his political power.

The Inherent Powers

Several presidents have expanded the power of the office by taking actions that exceeded commonly held notions of the president's proper authority. These men justified what they had done by saying that their actions fell within the **inherent powers** of the presidency. From this broad perspective, presidential power derives not only from those duties clearly outlined in Article II but also from inferences that may be drawn from the Constitution.

When a president claims a power that has not been considered part of the chief executive's authority, he forces Congress and the courts to either acquiesce to his claim or restrict it. In doing so, he runs the risk of suffering a politically damaging rebuff by either body. However, when presidents succeed in claiming a new power, they leave to their successors the legacy of a permanent expansion of presidential authority.

Claims of inherent powers often come at critical points in the nation's history. During the Civil War, for example, Abraham Lincoln issued a number of orders that exceeded the accepted limits of presidential authority and usurped powers constitutionally conferred on Congress. Lincoln said the urgent nature of the South's challenge to the Union forced him to act without waiting for congressional approval. His rationale was simple: "Was it possible to lose the nation and yet preserve the Constitution?"[6] In other words, Lincoln circumvented the Constitution in order to save the nation. Subsequently, Congress and the Supreme Court approved Lincoln's actions. That approval gave added legitimacy to the theory of inherent powers—a theory that over time has transformed the presidency.

Congressional Delegation of Power

Presidential power grows when presidents successfully challenge Congress, but in many instances Congress willingly delegates power to the executive branch. As the American public pressures the national government to solve various problems, Congress, through a process called **delegation of powers**, gives the executive branch more responsibility to administer programs that address those problems. One example of delegation of congressional power occurred in the 1930s, during the Great Depression, when Congress gave Franklin Roosevelt's administration wide latitude to do what it thought was necessary to solve the nation's economic ills.

When Congress concludes that the government needs flexibility in its approach to a problem, the president is often given great freedom in how or when to implement policies. Richard Nixon was given discretionary authority to impose a freeze on wages and prices in an effort to combat escalating inflation. If Congress had been forced to debate the timing of this freeze, merchants and manufacturers would surely have raised their prices in anticipation of it. Instead, Nixon was able to act suddenly, and the freeze was imposed without warning. (We discuss congressional delegation of authority to the executive branch in more detail in Chapter 10.)

However, at other times Congress believes that too much power has accumulated in the executive branch, and it enacts legislation to reassert congressional authority. During the 1970s, many representatives and senators agreed that Congress's role in the American political system was declining, that presidents were exercising power that rightfully belonged to the legislative branch. The most notable reaction was passage of the War Powers Resolution (1973), directed toward ending the president's ability to pursue armed conflict without explicit congressional approval.

The President's Power to Persuade

A president's influence in office comes not only from his assigned responsibilities but also from his political skills and from how effectively he uses the resources of his office. A classic analysis of the use of presidential resources is offered by Richard Neustadt in his book *Presidential Power*, which discusses how presidents gain, lose, or maintain their influence. Neustadt's initial premise is simple: "Presidential power is the power to persuade."[7] Presidents, for all their resources—a skilled staff, extensive media coverage of presidential actions, the great respect the country holds for the office—must depend on others' cooperation to get things done. Harry Truman echoed Neustadt's premise when he said, "I sit here all day trying to persuade people to do the things they ought to have sense enough to do without my persuading them. . . . That's all the powers of the President amount to."[8]

Ability in bargaining, dealing with adversaries, and choosing priorities, according to Neustadt, separates above-average presidents from mediocre ones. A president must make wise choices about which policies to push and which to put aside until he can find more support. He must decide when to accept compromises and when to stand on principles. He must know when to go public and when to work behind the scenes.

A president's political skills can be important in affecting outcomes in Congress. The chief executive cannot intervene in every legislative struggle. He must choose his battles carefully, then try to use the force of his personality and the prestige of his office to forge an agreement among differing factions. In terms of getting members to vote a certain way, presidential influence is best described as taking place "at the margins." Presidents don't have the power to consistently move large numbers of votes one way or the other. They can, however, affect some votes—possibly enough to affect the fate of a closely fought piece of legislation.[9]

Neustadt stresses that a president's influence is related to his professional reputation and prestige. When a president pushes hard for a bill that Congress eventually defeats or emasculates, the president's reputation is hurt. The public perceives him as weak or as showing poor judgment, and Congress becomes even less likely to cooperate with him in the future. Although President Clinton was clearly damaged by his failure to gain passage of his ambitious plan to reform the nation's health care system, he gained considerable respect when he pushed NAFTA (the North American Free Trade Agreement) through Congress.

The President and the Public

Neustadt's analysis suggests that a popular president is more persuasive than an unpopular one. A popular president has more power to persuade because he can use his public support as a resource in the bargaining process.[10] Members of Congress who know that the president is highly popular back home have more incentive to cooperate with the administration.

A familiar aspect of the modern presidency is the effort presidents devote to mobilizing public support for their programs. A president uses televised addresses (and the press coverage surrounding them), remarks to reporters, and public appearances to speak directly to the American people and convince them of the wisdom of his policies. In recent years, presidents have increased their direct communication with the American people. As Figure 9.1 illustrates, the number of public presidential appearances has grown sharply since World War II.

Obviously, modern technology has fostered this growth, but the increase in public appearances and speeches represents something more than increased visibility for the president and his views. The decline of party and congressional leadership hastened the rise of the public president. At the same time, the president's direct communication with the American people made it more difficult for political parties and Congress to reinvigorate themselves.[11]

Presidential popularity is typically at its highest during a president's first year in office. This "honeymoon period" affords the president a particularly

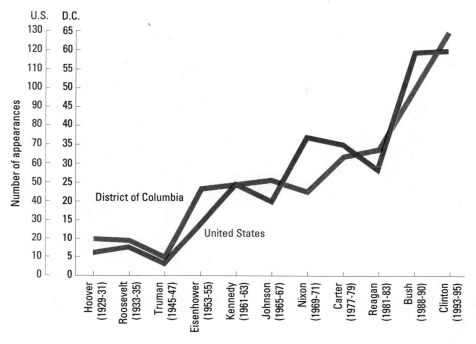

FIGURE 9.1 **Going Public**

This graph depicts the average number of public appearances made in a year by presidents from 1929 to 1990. The increase in presidential public appearances is driven in large part by the efforts of presidents to rally public support for their proposals and policies. Only the first three years of their first terms were examined; the fourth year was not tabulated in order to exclude appearances arranged with an eye toward an upcoming election. Gerald Ford's term is also excluded for this reason. The Bush figures are for his first two years only. (Source: Samuel Kernell, Going Public, *2d ed. [Washington, D.C.: Congressional Quarterly Press, 1993], p. 102. Copyright © 1993 by Congressional Quarterly Press. Used with permission.)*

good opportunity to use public support to get some of his programs through Congress.[12] Several factors generally explain the rise and fall in presidential popularity. First, public approval of the job done by a president is affected by economic conditions, such as inflation and unemployment, as Figure 9.2 shows. Second, a president is affected by unanticipated events of all types that occur during his administration.[13] When American embassy personnel were taken hostage in Teheran by militantly anti-American Iranians, Carter's popularity soared. This "rally 'round the flag" support for the president eventually gave way to frustration with his inability to gain the hostages' release, and Carter's popularity plummeted. The third factor that affects presidential popularity is American involvement in a war. Lyndon Johnson, for example, suffered a loss of popularity during his escalation of the American effort in Vietnam.[14]

Presidents closely monitor their popularity, because it is widely regarded as a basic report card on how well they are performing their duties. A president's

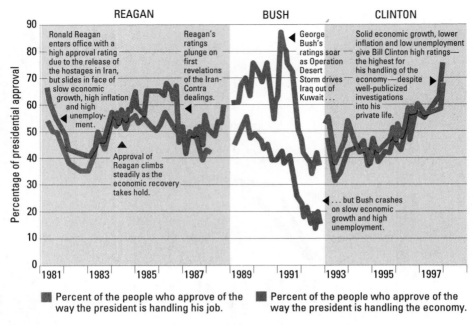

FIGURE 9.2 *Rising and Falling Together: Presidents and the Economy*
Journalists were mystified that President Clinton continued to do well in the polls despite the scandals surrounding his personal life. This chart helps make sense of the public reaction. As these statistics indicate, a president's popularity is closely linked to economic performance. When the economy does well, the public is more willing to forgive a president's peccadilloes, but when a recession threatens, a president's standing can be in jeopardy. (Source: NYT Graphics/NYT Pictures. New York Times/CBS News Poll, New York Times, 1 March 1998. Reprinted by permission.)

popularity can change dramatically during the course of a term. In the aftermath of the Gulf War, roughly nine in ten Americans approved of President Bush's performance in office. A month before the 1992 election, however, fewer than four in ten Americans approved of Bush.

Presidents' obsessive concern with public opinion can be defended as a means of furthering majoritarian democracy: the president tries to gauge what the people want so that he can offer policies that reflect popular preferences. The strategy of leading by courting public opinion, however, poses considerable risks. It is not easy to move public opinion, and presidents who plan to use it as leverage in dealing with Congress are left highly vulnerable if public support for their position does not materialize. When Bill Clinton came into office, he was strongly predisposed toward governing by leading public opinion. His strategy worked poorly, though, because he was frequently unsuccessful in rallying the public to his side on issues crucial to his administration. Communicating with the public is crucial to a modern president's success, but so too is an ability to form bipartisan coalitions in Congress and broad interest group coalitions.

The Electoral Connection

In his farewell address, Jimmy Carter lashed out at the interest groups that had plagued his presidency. Interest groups, he said, "distort our purposes because the national interest is not always the sum of all our single or special interests." Carter noted the president's singular responsibility: "The president is the only elected official charged with representing all the people."[15] Like all other presidents, Carter quickly recognized the dilemma of majoritarianism versus pluralism after he took office. The president must try to please countless separate constituencies while trying to do what is best for the whole country.

It is easy to stand on the sidelines and say that presidents should always try to follow a majoritarian path, pursuing policies that reflect the preferences of most citizens. However, simply by running for office, candidates align themselves with particular segments of the population. As a result of their electoral strategy, their identification with activists in their party, and their own political views, candidates come into office with an interest in pleasing some constituencies more than others.

Each candidate attempts to put together an electoral coalition that will provide at least the minimum 270 (of 538) electoral votes needed to win. Each candidate tries to win votes from different groups of voters through his stand on various issues. Because issue stances can cut both ways—attracting some voters but driving others away—candidates may try to finesse an issue by being deliberately vague. However, a candidate who is noncommittal on too many issues appears wishy-washy. And future presidents do not build their political careers without working strongly for and becoming associated with important issues and constituencies. Moreover, after the election is over, the winning candidate wants to claim that he has been given a **mandate**, or endorsement, by the voters to carry out the policies he campaigned on. New presidents try to make a majoritarian interpretation of the election, claiming that their victory is an expression of the direct will of the people. President Bush was unable to claim a mandate for his policy proposals—including a tax cut and education reform—because he was elected by a razor-thin margin in the electoral college and actually lost the popular vote. He had to pledge cooperation and dialog with Congress instead.

A central reason why it is difficult to read the president's political tea leaves from election results is that the president is elected independently of Congress. Often this leads to **divided government**, with one party controlling the White House and the other party controlling at least one house of Congress. President Clinton, for example, had to work with a Republican-controlled House and Senate throughout six of his eight years in office. This outcome may seem politically schizophrenic, with the electorate saying one thing by electing a president and another by electing a majority in Congress that opposes his policies. But it does not appear to bother the American people. Polls often show that the public feels it is desirable for control of the government to be divided between Republicans and Democrats.[16] As Table 9.1 shows, divided government has become more and more frequent.

Feature 9.1

The 2000 Presidential Election

For five weeks after the 2000 presidential election, Americans waited to find out who their next president would be as numerous lawsuits challenging the results in Florida made their way through the courts. Ultimately, a decision by the United States Supreme Court ended the lawsuits and vote recounts. For the first time since 1888, the winner of the Electoral College—Republican George W. Bush—differed from the winner of the popular vote—Democrat Al Gore. Though Bush won the vote of the Electoral College 271–267, Gore beat him in the popular vote by approximately 540,000 votes in the final tally.

In order to be elected President, a candidate needs to win a combination of states appointing a majority of the Electoral College. With 538 potential votes in the Electoral College, 270 is the magic number (see page 161). Prior to the election on November 7, 2000, pollsters and pundits had been predicting a close outcome, but as the hours flew by on election night with no winner it became apparent just how close the race was going to be. As the polls began to close, it was clear that Vice President Al Gore (the Democratic nominee) was doing very well in large states with significant urban populations, such as New York and California. The Republican candidate, Texas Governor George W. Bush, was meeting his expectations as well, piling up states in the South and the Great Plains with more rural populations. The candidates had expected to fight their most significant battles in the key battleground states of Pennsylvania, Florida, and Michigan. These states, with 23, 25, and 18 Electoral College votes respectively, were too close to predict before the election and large enough to make a big difference in the Electoral College. As the votes came in on election night, it was apparent that most voters in Pennsylvania and Michigan were voting for Gore.

By midnight the race boiled down to the outcome of a single large state. With Bush and Gore neck and neck in the Electoral College, whoever won the 25 electoral votes in Florida would surpass the minimum of 270 required to win the presidency. As the night turned into "the morning after," there was still no clear winner. Bush received frequent updates on the vote count throughout the night from the Republican Governor of Florida, ironically his younger brother, Jeb Bush. Because candidates Bush and Gore were separated by less than 2000 votes in Florida (3/100 of one percent of the vote cast in that state alone), a recount was required by state law. Recounts, first by machine and then by hand in select counties, delayed a clear result in the state for weeks. Furthermore, voting irregularities, "undervotes" (ballots marked in such a way that vote counting machines cannot detect a vote), and a particularly confusing ballot used in Palm Beach County spawned a series of lawsuits challenging the election that ricocheted through both state and federal courts. Finally, more than a month after the election, the U.S. Supreme Court ruled 5–4 that all manual recounts must stop, effectively paving the way for George W. Bush to become the 43rd President of the United States.

TABLE 9.1   Unified and Divided Party Control of Government, 1901–2002
Divided government exists when one party controls the White House and the
other party controls one or both houses of Congress. Early in the twentieth century, divided government was rare. In recent years, it has become common.

Year	President	Senate	House
1901–1903	R	R	R
1903–1905	R	R	R
1905–1907	R	R	R
1907–1909	R	R	R
1909–1911	R	R	R
1911–1913	R	R	D
1913–1915	D	D	D
1915–1917	D	D	D
1917–1919	D	D	D
1919–1921	D	R	R
1921–1923	R	R	R
1923–1925	R	R	R
1925–1927	R	R	R
1927–1929	R	R	R
1929–1931	R	R	R
1931–1933	R	R	D
1933–1935	D	D	D
1935–1937	D	D	D
1937–1939	D	D	D
1939–1941	D	D	D
1941–1943	D	D	D
1943–1945	D	D	D
1945–1947	D	D	D
1947–1949	D	R	R
1949–1951	D	D	D
1951–1953	D	D	D
1953–1955	R	R	R
1955–1957	R	D	D
1957–1959	R	D	D
1959–1961	R	D	D
1961–1963	D	D	D
1963–1965	D	D	D
1965–1967	D	D	D
1967–1969	D	D	D
1969–1971	R	D	D
1971–1973	R	D	D
1973–1975	R	D	D
1975–1977	R	D	D
1977–1979	D	D	D
1979–1981	D	D	D
1981–1983	R	R	D
1983–1985	R	R	D
1985–1987	R	R	D

(continued)

TABLE 9.1   **Unified and Divided Party Control of Government, 1901–2002** *(cont.)*

Year	President	Senate	House
1987–1989	R	D	D
1989–1991	R	D	D
1991–1993	R	D	D
1993–1995	D	D	D
1995–1996	D	R	R
1997–1998	D	R	R
1999–2000	D	R	R
2001–2002	R	R	R

Source: Updated from "An Introduction to Presidential-Congressional Rivalry," in Rivals for Power, *ed. James A. Thurber, pp. 8, 9. Copyright © 1996 by CQ Press.*

Voters appear to use quite different criteria when choosing a president than they do when choosing congressional representatives. As one scholar has noted, "Presidential candidates are evaluated according to their views on national issues and their competence in dealing with national problems. Congressional candidates are evaluated on their personal character and experience and on their devotion to district services and local issues."[17] This congressional independence is another reason why contemporary presidents work so hard to gain public support for their policies.[18]

Scholars are divided as to the impact of divided government. One study showed that just as much significant legislation gets passed and signed into law when there is divided government as when one party controls both the White House and Congress.[19] Using different approaches, other scholars have shown that divided governments are in fact less productive than unified ones.[20] Despite these differences in the scholarly literature, political scientists generally do not believe that divided government produces **gridlock**, a situation in which government is incapable of acting on important policy issues.[21] A strong tradition of bipartisan policymaking in Congress facilitates cooperation when the government is divided. The rising partisanship in Congress (recall Figure 8.4), however, may make divided government more of a problem.

The Executive Branch Establishment

As the president tries to maintain the support of his electoral coalition for the policies he pursues, he draws on the great resources of the executive branch of government. The president has a White House staff that helps him formulate policy. The vice president is another resource; his duties within the administration vary according to his relationship with the president. The president's cabinet secretaries—the heads of the major departments of the national government—play a number of roles, including the critical function of administering the programs that fall within their jurisdictions.

The Executive Office of the President

The president depends heavily on his key aides. They advise him on crucial political choices, devise the general strategies the administration will follow in pursuing congressional and public support, and control access to the president to ensure that he has enough time for his most important tasks. Consequently, he needs to trust and respect these top staffers; many in a president's inner circle of assistants are long-time associates. The president's personal staff constitutes the White House Office.

Presidents typically have a chief of staff, who may be first among equals, or, in some administrations, the unquestioned leader of the staff. There also is a national security adviser to provide daily briefings on foreign and military affairs and longer-range analyses of issues confronting the administration. The Council of Economic Advisers is also located in the White House. Senior domestic policy advisers help determine the administration's basic approach to such areas as health, education, and social services.

Below these top aides are the large staffs that serve them and the president. These staffs are organized around certain specialties. Some staff members work on political matters, such as liaison with interest groups, relations with ethnic and religious minorities, and party affairs. One staff deals exclusively with the media, and a legislative liaison staff lobbies Congress for the administration. The large Office of Management and Budget (OMB) analyzes budget requests, is involved in the policymaking process, and also examines agency management practices. This extended White House executive establishment, including the White House Office, is known as the **Executive Office of the President**. The Executive Office employs close to 1,600 individuals and has an annual budget of over $200 million.[22]

No one agrees about a "right way" for a president to organize his White House staff. However, one factor that influences how a president uses members of his senior staff is the degree to which he delegates authority to them. President Carter immersed himself in policymaking to ensure that he made all the significant decisions himself. When Bill Clinton took over the White House, he instituted a loose staff structure that gave many top staffers direct access to him. Clinton's choice for his chief of staff was Mack McLarty, a friend since childhood and a successful Arkansas businessman who had no Washington experience. This appointment seemed to suggest that Clinton wanted to be his own chief of staff, deeply involved in the nuts and bolts of White House policymaking.

Clinton's undisciplined style and his tendency to take too much on led to considerable criticism of White House operations.[23] In contrast to Clinton, George W. Bush adopted a management style based on the corporate CEO, in which senior advisors were given substantial independent authority to act. Bush's approach was based on the motto "surround yourself with good people, and then let them do their jobs." In particular, his Chief of Staff, former Secretary of Transportation Andrew Card, and Vice President Dick Cheney were given heavy responsibility to oversee elements of the White House office and the EOP. In his heavy use of delegation, Bush's management of the White House resembles the approach taken by President Ronald Reagan during the 1980s.

The Vice President

The vice president's primary function is to be ready and able to take over the presidency if anything happens to the president during his term in office. Traditionally, vice presidents have not been used in any important advisory capacity. Instead, presidents tend to give them political chores—campaigning, fundraising, and "stroking" the party faithful. This is often the case because vice presidential candidates are chosen for reasons that have more to do with the political campaign than with governing the nation. However, Vice President Al Gore's responsibilities extended far beyond such political chores. His high visibility along with his popularity among the party faithful helped him to capture the Democratic nomination for president in 2000. Gore's running mate in 2000 was Sen. Joseph Lieberman, known as a moderate Democrat and a strong moral voice. He was the first Jewish American on a national ticket. Republican George Bush selected former Secretary of Defense Dick Cheney, who brought years of Washington experience to the ticket.

The Cabinet

The president's **cabinet** is composed of the heads of the departments in the executive branch and a small number of other key officials, such as the head of the Office of Management and Budget and the ambassador to the United Nations. The cabinet has expanded greatly since George Washington formed his first cabinet, which included an attorney general and the secretaries of state, treasury, and war. Clearly, the growth of the cabinet to fourteen departments reflects the growth of government responsibility and intervention in areas such as energy, housing, and transportation.

In theory, the members of the cabinet constitute an advisory body that meets with the president to debate major policy decisions. In practice, however, cabinet meetings have been described as "vapid non-events in which there has been a deliberate non-exchange of information as part of a process of mutual non-consultation."[24] Why is this so?

First, the cabinet has become rather large. Counting department heads, other officials of cabinet rank, and presidential aides, it is a body of at least twenty people—a size that many presidents find unwieldy for the give-and-take of political decision making. Second, most cabinet members have limited areas of expertise and simply cannot contribute much to deliberations in policy areas they know little about. The secretary of defense, for example, would probably be a poor choice to help decide important issues of agricultural policy. Third, although cabinet members have impressive backgrounds, they may not be personally close to the president or easy for him to work with. The president often chooses cabinet members because of their reputations, or he may be guided by a need to give his cabinet some racial, ethnic, geographic, sexual, or religious balance.

Finally, modern presidents do not rely on the cabinet to make policy because they have such large White House staffs, which offer most of the advisory support they need. And, in contrast to cabinet secretaries, who may be pulled in different directions by the wishes of the president and the wishes of their clientele groups, staffers in the White House Office are likely to see themselves as being responsible to the president alone. Thus, despite periodic calls for the cabinet to be a collective decision-making body, cabinet meetings seem doomed to be little more than academic exercises. In practice, presidents prefer the flexibility of ad hoc groups, specialized White House staffs, and the advisers and cabinet secretaries with whom they feel most comfortable.

More broadly, presidents use their personal staffs and the large Executive Office of the President to centralize control over the entire executive branch. The vast size of the executive branch and the number and complexity of decisions that must be made each day pose a challenge for the White House. Each president must be careful to appoint to top administrative positions people who are passionate about the president's goals and skillful enough to lead others in the executive branch to fight for the president's program instead of for their own agendas.[25]

The President as National Leader

With an election behind him and the resources of his office at hand, a president is ready to lead the nation. Each president enters office with a general vision of how government should approach policy issues. During his term, a president spends much of his time trying to get Congress to enact legislation that reflects his general philosophy and specific policy preferences.

From Political Values . . .

Presidents differ greatly in their views of the role of government. Lyndon Johnson had a strong liberal ideology concerning domestic affairs. He believed that government has a responsibility to help disadvantaged Americans. In describing his vision of justice in his inaugural address, Johnson used the words *justice* and *injustice* as code words for *equality* and *inequality*. They were used six times in his speech; *freedom* was used only twice. Johnson used his popularity, his skills, and the resources of his office to press for a "just" America—a "Great Society."[26]

To achieve his Great Society, Johnson sent Congress an unprecedented package of liberal legislation. He launched such projects as the Job Corps (which created centers and camps offering vocational training and work experience to youths aged sixteen to twenty-one), Medicare (which provided medical care for the elderly), and the National Teacher Corps (which paid teachers to work in impoverished neighborhoods). Supported by huge Democratic majorities in Congress during 1965 and 1966, he had tremendous success in getting his proposals through. Liberalism was in full swing.

In 1985, exactly twenty years after Johnson's inaugural speech, Ronald Reagan took his oath of office for the second time. Addressing the nation, Reagan reasserted his conservative philosophy. He emphasized *freedom,* using the term fourteen times, and failed to mention justice or equality once. He turned Johnson's philosophy on its head, declaring that "government is not the solution to our problem. Government is the problem." During his presidency, Reagan worked to undo many welfare and social service programs, and he cut funding for such programs as the Job Corps and food stamps. By the end of his term there had been a fundamental shift in federal spending, with sharp increases in defense spending and "decreases in federal social programs [which] served to defund Democratic interests and constituencies."[27]

... To Policy Agenda

The roots of particular policy proposals, then, can be traced to the more general political ideology of the president. Presidential candidates outline that philosophy of government during their campaigns for the White House. But when the hot rhetoric of the presidential campaign meets the cold reality of what is possible in Washington, the newly elected president must make some hard choices about what to push for during the coming term. These choices are reflected in the bills the president submits to Congress, as well as in the degree to which he works for their passage. The president's bills, introduced by his allies in the House and Senate, always receive a good deal of initial attention. In the words of one Washington lobbyist, "When a president sends up a bill, it takes first place in the queue. All other bills take second place."[28]

The president's role in legislative leadership began primarily in the twentieth century. Not until the Budget and Accounting Act of 1921 did executive branch departments and agencies have to clear their proposed budget bills with the White House. Before this, the president did not even coordinate proposals for how much the executive branch would spend on all the programs it administered. Later, Franklin D. Roosevelt required that all major legislative proposals by an agency or department be cleared by the White House. No longer could a department submit a bill without White House support.[29]

Roosevelt's influence on the relationship between the president and Congress went far beyond this new administrative arrangement. With the nation in the midst of the Great Depression, Roosevelt began his first term in 1933 with an ambitious array of legislative proposals. During the first hundred days Congress was in session, it enacted fifteen significant laws, including the Agricultural Adjustment Act, the act creating the Civilian Conservation Corps, and the National Industrial Recovery Act. Never had a president demanded—and received—so much from Congress. Roosevelt's legacy was that the president would henceforth provide aggressive leadership for Congress through his own legislative program.

Chief Lobbyist

When Franklin D. Roosevelt and Harry Truman first became heavily involved in preparing legislative packages, political scientists typically described the process as one in which "the president proposes and Congress disposes." In

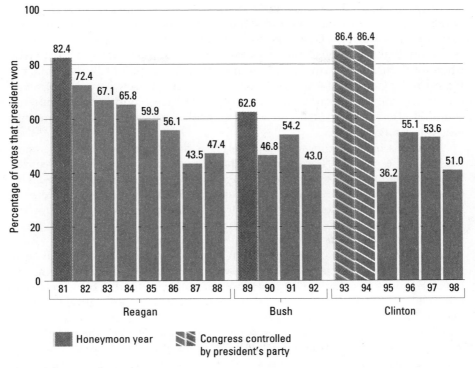

FIGURE 9.3   Legislative Leadership
Presidents vary considerably in their ability to convince Congress to enact the legislation they send to Capitol Hill. Generally, presidents have their greatest success in Congress during their "honeymoon," the period immediately following their inauguration. As this figure demonstrates, Presidents Reagan, Bush, and Clinton all did well during their first year in office. President Clinton fared best, and in a sense he even had an extended honeymoon into his second year, but he was the only one of the three who sent legislation to a Congress controlled by his own party. Note the dramatic changes in Clinton's fortunes in 1995, when he had to cope with a Republican Congress more interested in passing the Contract with America than in considering Clinton's proposals. (Sources: Carroll J. Doherty, "Clinton Finds Support on Hill Despite GOP's Vocal Attacks," Congressional Quarterly Weekly Report, 3 January 1998, p. 14; "Guide to CQ's Voting Analyses," Congressional Quarterly Weekly Report, 3 January 1998, p. 27; David Hosansky, "Clinton's Biggest Prize Was a Frustrated GOP," CQ Weekly, 9 January 1999, p. 75.)

other words, once the president sends his legislation to Capitol Hill, Congress decides on its own what to do with it. Over time, though, presidents have become increasingly active in all stages of the legislative process. The president is expected not only to propose legislation but also to make sure that it passes (see Figure 9.3).

The president's efforts to influence Congress are reinforced by the work of his legislative liaison staff. All departments and major agencies have legislative specialists who work with the White House liaison staff to coordinate the administration's lobbying on major issues. The **legislative liaison staff** is the communications link between the White House and Congress. As a bill slowly makes its way through Congress, liaison staffers advise the president on the problems that emerge. Presidents also depend upon their staff's expertise when lobbying for controversial nominees. In 2001, President Bush's nominee for Attorney General, former Senator John Ashcroft, drew considerable criticism from the left because of his conservative views. Supported by intense White House lobbying, Ashcroft was eventually confirmed despite unusually long and frank hearings.

Decisions on how the administration will respond to such developments must then be reached. For example, when the Reagan White House realized that it was still a few votes short of victory on a budget bill in the House, it reversed its opposition to a sugar price support bill. This attracted the votes of representatives from Louisiana and Florida, two sugar-growing states, for the budget bill. The White House would not call what happened a deal, but it noted that "adjustments and considerations" had been made.[30]

A certain amount of the president's job consists of stereotypical arm-twisting—pushing reluctant legislators to vote a certain way. Yet most day-in, day-out interactions between the White House and Congress tend to be more subtle, with the liaison staff trying to build consensus by working cooperatively with legislators. The White House also works directly with interest groups in its efforts to build support for legislation.[31] Interest groups can quickly reach the constituents who are most concerned about a bill, using their communications network to quickly mobilize members to write, call, or e-mail their members of Congress.

Although much of the liaison staff's work with Congress is done in a cooperative spirit, agreement cannot always be reached. When Congress passes a bill that the president opposes, he may veto it and send it back to Congress. As we noted earlier, Congress can override a veto with a two-thirds majority of those voting in each house. Presidents use their veto power sparingly, but the threat that a president will veto an unacceptable bill increases his bargaining leverage with members of Congress. We have also seen that a president's leverage with Congress is enhanced when he is riding high in the public opinion polls and hindered when the public is critical of his performance.[32]

Party Leader

Part of the president's job is to lead his party. This is very much an informal duty, with no prescribed tasks. In fact, presidents can operate effectively without the help of a national party apparatus. Lyndon Johnson was contemptuous of the Democratic National Committee. He saw to it that the committee's budget was cut. Johnson thought a weak national committee would allow him to control party affairs from the White House. Like other modern presidents, he believed he would be most effective communicating directly with the American people and did not see the need for party officials to be intermediaries in the process of coalition building.[33]

Work with the party may be more important for gaining the presidency than for actually governing. During the 1996 campaign, Vice President Al

Gore campaigned tirelessly for Democratic candidates at all levels and did his best to raise money for the party. Regardless of whether the Clinton-Gore ticket won reelection, he wanted to position himself to make a likely run for the presidency in 2000. Working to shore up support among party activists was a critical step toward gaining the nomination.[34]

The President as World Leader

The president's leadership responsibilities extend beyond Congress and the nation into the international arena. Each administration tries to advance what it sees as the country's best interests in its relations with allies, adversaries, and the developing countries of the world. In this role, the president must be ready to act as diplomat and crisis manager.

Foreign Relations

From the end of World War II to the beginning of the Bush administration, presidents were preoccupied with containing communist expansion around the globe. After the collapse of communism in the Soviet Union and eastern Europe, American presidents entered a new era in international relations. The new presidential job description places much more emphasis on managing economic relations with the rest of the world. Trade relations are an especially difficult problem, because presidents must balance the conflicting interests of foreign countries (many of them U.S. allies), the interests of particular American industries, the overall needs of the American economy, and the demands of the legislative branch.

The decline of communism has not enabled the president to ignore security issues. The world remains a dangerous place, and regional conflicts can still embroil the United States. When Iraq invaded and quickly conquered Kuwait in August 1990, President George Bush responded to protect our economic interests and to stand beside our Arab allies in the area. It was, said one journalist, a "dazzling performance. In roughly four days, Bush organized the world against Saddam Hussein."[35]

Crisis Management

Periodically the president faces a grave situation in which conflict is imminent or a small conflict threatens to explode into a larger war. Handling such episodes is a critical part of the president's job. Thus, voters may make the candidates' personal judgment and intelligence primary considerations in how they cast their ballots.

A president must be able to exercise good judgment and remain cool in crisis situations. John Kennedy's behavior during the Cuban missile crisis of 1962 has become a model of effective crisis management. When the United States learned that the Soviet Union had placed missiles containing nuclear warheads in Cuba, Kennedy sought the advice of a group of senior aides. An armed invasion of Cuba and air strikes against the missiles were two options considered. In the end, Kennedy decided on a less dangerous response: a naval blockade of Cuba. The Soviet Union thought better of prolonging its challenge to the United States and soon agreed to remove its missiles. For a short time, though, the world held its breath over the very real possibility of a nuclear war.

Are there guidelines for what a president should do in times of crisis or at other important decision-making junctures? Drawing on a range of advisers and opinions is certainly one.[36] Not acting in unnecessary haste is another. A third is having a well-designed, formal review process that promotes thorough analysis and open debate.[37] A fourth guideline is rigorously examining the chain of reasoning that has led to the option chosen, to ensure that presumptions have not been subconsciously equated with what is actually known to be true. Still, these are rather general rules and provide no assurance that mistakes will not be made. Each crisis is a unique event.

Presidential Character

How does the public assess which presidential candidate has the best judgment and a character suitable to the office? Americans must make a broad evaluation of the candidates' personalities and leadership styles. The character issue dogged Bill Clinton. During the 1992 campaign, he appeared to tacitly acknowledge marital unfaithfulness when he told an interviewer on CBS's "60 Minutes" that he was responsible for "causing pain in my marriage."[38] Although charges of infidelity threatened to derail his run for the Democratic nomination in 1992, his reckless behavior continued once he was in the White House, when he engaged in a sexual relationship with Monica Lewinsky, an intern half his age.

After becoming president, Clinton faced accusations involving a number of different women. Paula Jones, a former Arkansas state employee, and Kathleen Willey, a former White House volunteer, claimed Clinton made crude, unwanted sexual advances toward them. Clinton vigorously denied both accusations. Jones filed a well-publicized sexual harassment lawsuit against the president, but the case was eventually thrown out of court because there was no evidence that Jones had suffered any adverse repercussions on the job. She appealed the judge's decision to dismiss the case, and in an out-of-court settlement Clinton agreed to pay Jones $850,000 in exchange for her dropping the lawsuit.

Clinton's affair with Lewinsky came to light after Whitewater special prosecutor Kenneth Starr received a tip that Clinton had lied in a deposition in the Paula Jones lawsuit. Starr had been appointed to investigate allegations that both Bill and Hillary Clinton had engaged in wrongdoing some years earlier, when they were members of a small partnership investing in undeveloped property in Arkansas. After four years of investigating the Clintons, Starr had yet to find convincing evidence of any illegality by either of them. When he

Visiting South of the Border
The Canadian border, that is. One of the president's key roles is to act as a diplomat, travel-ing abroad to meet with world leaders and hosting them when they visit the United States, as Canadian Prime Minister Jean Chretien did in February 2001.

told Attorney General Janet Reno of Clinton's possible perjury in the Jones lawsuit, Reno acceded to his request that he be given authority to inquire into this matter as well.

After investigating for over six months, Starr formally recommended that Congress consider impeaching Clinton because, allegedly, he had perjured himself, obstructing justice, and encouraged others to perjure themselves. Clinton's response was twofold. First, he said that he hadn't lied in the Jones deposition when he denied having sex with Lewinsky, because they hadn't en-gaged in sexual intercourse—she had performed oral sex on him. Second, he finally acknowledged that he had had an "inappropriate" relationship with Lewinsky and that it was wrong. He offered a series of apologies both to his family and to the nation.

The American public was appalled by the revelations that their president was engaging in sexual activities with an intern in his private office in the White House, but most people remained unconvinced that his behavior con-stituted an impeachable offense. The buoyant economy and the public's gen-eral satisfaction with Clinton's leadership strongly influenced the country's views. A common opinion was that sex outside of marriage, though immoral, is a private matter and the issue should be left to the president and his wife to resolve between themselves.

Despite his acquittal by the Senate, it seems clear that Clinton had a char-acter flaw that calls into question his fitness for office. Even though Lewinsky was a consensual partner, it was exploitive of Clinton to engage in sex with a young woman who was his employee. It was also reckless and impulsive—hardly desirable qualities in a president. At the same time, Clinton had many admirable qualities, especially his compassion, fairness, and intelligence. His lifelong concern for the disadvantaged made him especially popular with minorities and the poor. Sadly, though, an inappropriate relationship became the defining moment of his presidency.

Summary

When the delegates to the Constitutional Convention met to design the government of this new nation, they had trouble shaping the office of the president. They struggled to find a balance between an office that was powerful enough to provide unified leadership but not so strong that presidents could use their powers to become tyrants or dictators. The initial conceptions of the presidency have slowly been transformed, as presidents have adapted the office to meet the nation's changing needs. The trend has been to expand presidential power. Some of this expansion has come from presidential actions taken under claims of inherent powers. Congress has also delegated a great deal of power to the executive branch, further expanding the role of the president.

Because the president is elected by the entire nation, he can claim to represent all citizens when proposing policy. This broad electoral base equips the presidency to be an institution of majoritarian democracy. Whether the presidency actually operates in a majoritarian manner depends on several factors—the individual president's perception of public opinion on specific issues, the relationship between public opinion and the president's political ideology, and the extent to which the president is committed to pursuing his values through his office.

The executive branch establishment has grown rapidly, and the White House has become a sizable bureaucracy. New responsibilities of the presidency are particularly noticeable in the area of legislative leadership. Now a president is expected to be a policy initiator for Congress, as well as a lobbyist who guides his bills through the legislative process.

The presidential "job description" for foreign policy has also changed considerably. After World War II, presidents were preoccupied with containing the spread of communism. But since the collapse of communism in the Soviet Union and eastern Europe, international economic relations have loomed largest as a priority for presidents. However, national security issues remain important because regional conflicts can directly involve the interests of the United States.

Key Terms

veto
inherent powers
delegation of powers
mandate
divided government

gridlock
Executive Office of the President
cabinet
legislative liaison staff

Selected Readings

Jones, Charles O. *The Presidency in a Separated System.* Washington, D.C.: Brookings Institution, 1994. Jones argues that ours is not a presidency-centered system and that policy initiation in Congress is more independent of the executive branch than most scholars realize.

Neustadt, Richard E. *Presidential Power.* Rev. ed. New York: Wiley, 1980. Neustadt's classic work examines the president's power to persuade.

Patterson, Bradley H., Jr. *The White House Staff.* Washington, D.C.: Brookings Institution, 2000. A comprehensive look at the key positions and staffs that serve the president.

Skowronek, Stephen. *The Politics Presidents Make.* Cambridge, Mass.: Harvard University Press, 1993. A sweeping, magisterial analysis of the cycles of presidential history.

Thurber, James A. *Rivals for Power.* Washington, D.C.: Congressional Quarterly Press, 1996. An excellent collection of essays reviewing the major issues in executive-legislative relations.

World Wide Web Resources

The White House. The highlight of this White House home page is the "interactive citizen handbook." Also available are White House tours and entry into White House "briefing rooms." Enter the briefing rooms to get current information on White House speeches, statements, and press releases as well as current government statistics.
<www.whitehouse.gov.>

Presidential Address. This page is sponsored by the University of Oklahoma Law Center. It allows the visitor to retrieve all State of the Union and inaugural addresses dating back to George Washington. Other historically significant presidential speeches are also available.
<www.law.uoknor.edu/ushist.html>

10

The Bureaucracy

On May 11, 1996, ValuJet flight 592 took off from the Miami airport and headed north. A few minutes later smoke began to fill the cabin, and the pilot turned the plane around to return to Miami. Before it could reach the airport, however, the plane lost power and nose-dived into an alligator-infested swamp in the Everglades. None of the 109 people on board survived.

Plane crashes are shocking, not just because of the carnage but because commercial airline crashes are so rare. Even more shocking than the crash was the revelation that the Federal Aviation Administration (FAA), the regulatory agency charged with setting, monitoring, and enforcing airline safety standards, had documented a poor maintenance record by ValuJet yet had done little to force the airline to improve its repair and record-keeping practices.

The cause of the crash appears to have been some used oxygen canisters, loaded by mistake. Why weren't correct procedures followed? Beyond individual errors in judgment are the financial pressures brought on ValuJet and other airlines by deregulation. Until the late 1970s, airline pricing was oligopolistic, with common fares approved by the government. Today, airlines compete vigorously, and many cut-rate start-ups like ValuJet have taken market share away from major carriers like United, American, and Delta. Many of the new low-cost carriers save money by farming out maintenance work to subcontractors who can do the work more cheaply than the airlines themselves. Indeed, it was a subcontractor who loaded the fatal canisters onto flight 592. This subcontracting has made the FAA's work more difficult, because its work force has not expanded to match the increasing number of companies running or servicing commercial airlines.[1]

Why doesn't the FAA add inspectors and write more regulations to improve its monitoring of carriers and subcontractors? Americans surely want commercial airliners to be as safe as possible. But although Americans want government to reduce the risks of everyday life, there is also great pressure to cut the federal budget, reduce the national debt, and shrink the size of government. Americans want the services big government provides, but they don't want big government.

The controversy over the bureaucracy's role is not just a function of majoritarian opinion that is contradictory; it is also due to the fact that majoritarian-

Flight to Oblivion
After ValuJet flight 592 crashed into the Everglades, the FAA was roundly criticized for failing to do a better job of monitoring airline maintenance and safety standards. After reviewing its own performance, the FAA announced that it was taking steps to improve its supervision of maintenance subcontractors, such as Sabretech, the company that worked for ValuJet at the time of the crash. In September of 1996 ValuJet began flying again on a limited basis.

ism is often pitted against pluralism. One reason why the FAA did not crack down on ValuJet before the crash is that any government rebuke of the carrier would have jeopardized the company's future. (After the crash, the FAA did force the company to suspend service.) More broadly, one of the FAA's responsibilities is to promote the airline industry, and it is thus lobbied heavily on both business and safety issues by large and small carriers alike. Beyond our focus on pluralist and majoritarian dynamics in bureaucratic politics, we will look closely at why Americans dislike government so much. Also, we will discuss reforms that might make government work better.

Organization Matters

A nation's laws and policies are administered, or put into effect, by a variety of departments, agencies, bureaus, offices, and other government units, which together are known as the *bureaucracy*. **Bureaucracy** actually means any large, complex organization in which employees have very specific job responsibilities and work within a hierarchy of authority. The employees of these government units have become known somewhat derisively as **bureaucrats**.

Bureaucracies play a central role in the governments of modern societies. In fact, organizations are a crucial part of any society, no matter how simple. The organization of modern governmental bureaucracies reflects their need to survive. The environment of modern bureaucracies is filled with conflicting political demands and the ever-present threat of budget cuts. The way a given government bureaucracy is organized also reflects the needs of its clients. The bottom line, however, is that the manner in which any bureaucracy is organized affects how well it is able to accomplish its tasks.

Unfortunately, "if organization matters, it is also the case that there is no one best way of organizing."[2] Although greater autonomy may improve the performance of public schools, it may not be a good solution for improving a state social welfare agency, where a primary goal is to treat clients equally and provide the same benefits to people with the same needs and circumstances. The study of bureaucracy, then, centers around finding solutions to the many different kinds of problems faced by large government organizations.

The Development of the Bureaucratic State

A common complaint voiced by Americans is that the national bureaucracy is too big and tries to accomplish too much. To the average citizen, the federal government may seem like an octopus—its long arms reach just about everywhere.

The Growth of the Bureaucratic State

American government seems to have grown unchecked during the twentieth century. As one observer noted wryly, "The assistant administrator for water and hazardous materials of the Environmental Protection Agency presided over a staff larger than Washington's entire first administration."[3] Yet even during George Washington's time, bureaucracies were necessary. No one argued then about the need for a postal service to deliver mail or a treasury department to maintain a system of currency.

However, government at all levels (national, state, and local) grew enormously in the twentieth century.[4] There are a number of major reasons. A principal cause of government expansion is the increasing complexity of society. George Washington did not have an assistant administrator for water and hazardous materials because there was no need for one. A National Aeronautics and Space Administration (NASA) was not necessary until rockets were invented.

Another reason why government has grown is that the public's attitude toward business has changed. Throughout most of the nineteenth century, business was generally autonomous, and government intervention in the economy that might limit that autonomy was considered inappropriate. This attitude began to change toward the end of the nineteenth century, as more Americans became aware that a laissez-faire approach did not always create competitive markets that benefited consumers. Gradually, government intervention came to be accepted as necessary to protect the integrity of markets. And if government was to police unfair business practices effectively, it needed administrative agencies.

During the twentieth century, new bureaucracies were organized to regulate specific industries. Among them are the Securities and Exchange Commission (SEC), which oversees securities trading, and the Food and Drug Administration (FDA), which tries to protect consumers from unsafe food, drugs, and cosmetics. Through bureaucracies such as these, government has become a referee in the marketplace, developing standards of fair trade, setting rates, and licensing individual businesses for operation. As new problem areas have emerged, government has added new agencies, further expanding the scope of its activities.

General attitudes about government's responsibilities in the area of social welfare have changed too. An enduring part of American culture is the belief in self-reliance. People are expected to overcome adversity on their own, to succeed because of their own skills and efforts. Yet certain segments of our population are believed to deserve government support, because we so value their contribution to society or have come to believe that they cannot realistically be expected to overcome adversity on their own.[5] This belief dates back to the nineteenth century. The government provided pensions to Civil War veterans. Later, programs to help mothers and children were developed.[6] In the wake of the Great Depression, the Social Security Act became law, creating a fund that workers pay into and then collect income from during old age. In the 1960s, the government created programs designed to help minorities. As the government made these new commitments, it also created new bureaucracies or expanded existing ones.

Also, government has grown because ambitious, entrepreneurial agency officials have expanded their organizations and staffs to take on added responsibilities. Each new program that is developed leads to new authority. Larger budgets and staffs, in turn, are necessary to support that authority.

Can We Reduce the Size of Government?

When candidates for Congress and the presidency campaign, they typically "run against the government"—even if they are incumbents. Government is unpopular: Americans have little confidence in its capabilities and feel that it wastes money and is out of touch with ordinary people. Americans want a smaller government that costs less and performs better.

If government is to become smaller, bureaucracies will have to be eliminated or reduced in size. Serious budget cuts also require serious reductions in programs. Not surprisingly, presidents and members of Congress face a tough job when they try to cut specific programs. Each government bureaucracy performs a service of value to some sector of society. Farmers want the price supports of the U.S. Department of Agriculture. Builders profit from programs offered by the U.S. Department of Housing and Urban Development. And

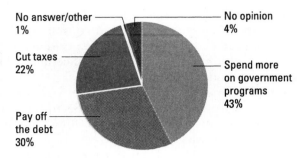

FIGURE 10.1 *Don't Cut Taxes!*
For the first time in decades, policymakers must decide what to do with a budget surplus. Americans may say they do not like big government or paying taxes, but when a recent Gallup Poll asked a random sample of U.S. adults what they would do with a national budget surplus, almost twice as many preferred spending more on government programs to cutting taxes. The favorite areas for additional money were social security, Medicare, and public education. (Source: David W. Moore, "Public Skeptical That Budget Will Be Balanced," Gallup Poll *<www.gallup.com>, 10 January 1998.)*

labor unions want a vigorous Occupational Safety and Health Administration. Interest groups that have a stake in an agency almost always resist efforts to reduce its scope.

As for the public, people's attitudes toward government in general tell only part of the story.[7] When asked about specific programs or functions of government, citizens tend to be highly supportive. As Figure 10.1 shows, the public would rather spend money on government endeavors like social security than cut taxes.

Given interest group and public support, it is rare for the government to abolish a department or agency. But agencies are not immune to change. Major reorganizations, in which programs are consolidated and the size and scope of activities are reduced, are not uncommon.

The tendency for big government to endure reflects the tension between majoritarianism and pluralism. Even when the public as a whole wants a smaller national government, that sentiment can be undermined by the strong desire of different segments of society for government to continue performing some valuable function for them. Lobbies that represent these segments work strenuously to convince Congress and the administration that certain agencies' funding is vital and that any cuts ought to come out of other agencies' budgets.

Bureaus and Bureaucrats

We often think of the bureaucracy as a monolith. In reality, the bureaucracy in Washington is a disjointed collection of departments, agencies, bureaus, offices, and commissions—each a bureaucracy in its own right.

The Organization of Government

By examining the basic types of government organizations, we can better understand how the executive branch operates. In our discussion, we pay particular attention to the relative degree of independence of these organizations and to their relationship with the White House.

Departments   **Departments** are the biggest units of the executive branch, covering broad areas of government responsibility. As noted in Chapter 9, the secretaries (heads) of the departments, along with a few other key officials, form the president's cabinet. The current cabinet departments are State, Treasury, Defense, Interior, Agriculture, Justice, Commerce, Labor, Health and Human Services, Housing and Urban Development, Transportation, Energy, Education, and Veterans Affairs. Each of these massive organizations is broken down into subsidiary agencies, bureaus, offices, and services.

Independent Agencies   Within the executive branch, there are also many **independent agencies** that are not part of any cabinet department. They stand alone and are controlled to varying degrees by the president. Some, among them the CIA, are directly under the president's control. Others, such as the Federal Communications Commission, are structured as **regulatory commissions**. Each commission is run by a small number of commissioners appointed to fixed terms by the president. Some commissions were formed to guard against unfair business practices. Others were formed to protect the public from unsafe products. Although presidents don't have direct control over these regulatory commissions, they can strongly influence their direction through their appointments of new commissioners.

Government Corporations   Congress has created a small number of **government corporations**. In theory, the services these executive branch agencies perform could be provided by the private sector, but Congress has decided that the public will be better served if these organizations have some link with the government. For example, the national government maintains the postal service as a government corporation because it feels that Americans need low-cost, door-to-door service for all kinds of mail, not just for profitable routes or special services. In some instances, the private sector does not have enough financial incentive to provide an essential service. This is the case with the financially troubled Amtrak train line.[8]

The Civil Service

The national bureaucracy is staffed by about 2.8 million civilian employees, who account for about 2 percent of the U.S. work force.[9] Most of those government workers are hired under the requirements of the **civil service**. The civil service was created by the Pendleton Act (1883). The objective of the act was to reduce *patronage*—the practice of filling government positions with the president's political allies or cronies. The civil service fills jobs on the basis of merit and sees to it that workers are not fired for political reasons.

Politics in a Changing America 10.1

Does Gender Make a Difference?

When the U.S. Forest Service was sued for discriminating against women employees, it signed a consent decree pledging to hire enough women at each level of the organization so that its employment mix would be similar to the gender composition of the rest of the American work force. It moved quickly to hire more women in all types of jobs.

It is easy to applaud the Forest Service for tackling discrimination within its ranks in order to create more opportunities for women. Clearly, it makes a difference for women, who can now compete more fairly for better jobs with increased responsibility and better pay. But does employing more women have an impact on the Forest Service's policy decisions? After all, the primary job of the Forest Service is to manage publicly owned forests. Is there a distinctly "feminine" approach to managing trees?

Recent research demonstrates that men and women in the Forest Service differ in important ways. A survey of those working for the agency shows that women are decidedly more concerned about environmental protection. Women in the Forest Service are more likely than men to believe that there are limits to the number of people the earth can support, that the balance of nature is easily upset, that economic growth should be "steady-state," and that humans are abusing the environment.

The Forest Service must balance the needs of consumers for wood products with the desire of Americans to preserve forests for future generations. If a larger percentage of employees entering the Forest Service believes we need to do more to protect the environment, then the balance between development and preservation is likely to shift. Basic policy is set by Congress and by the president's appointees who run the agency. Inevitably, though, a different mix of men and women within the Forest Service is going to affect policy, just as adding a lot more liberals or conservatives to any agency would change it.

The National Forest Products Association, a trade group of businesses that develop or use public forest resources, has warned its members that "the sharp changes in the demographic characteristics of Forest Service employees

(continued)

The vast majority of the national government's workers are employed outside Washington. One reason for this decentralization is to make government offices accessible to the people they serve. Decentralization is also a way to distribute jobs and income across the country. Members of Congress, of course, are only too happy to place some of this "pork" back home, so that their constituents will credit them with the jobs and money that government installations create.

Like most large organizations, the federal government has taken steps to try to make its work force mirror the larger population in terms of race and gender (on gender, see Politics in a Changing America 10.1). Minorities have substan-

Politics in a Changing America 10.1 (continued)

will lead to further deemphasis on commodity production and to increasing emphasis accorded to non-timber resource values." In other words, more women in the agency means a different outlook on how to manage the nation's forests.

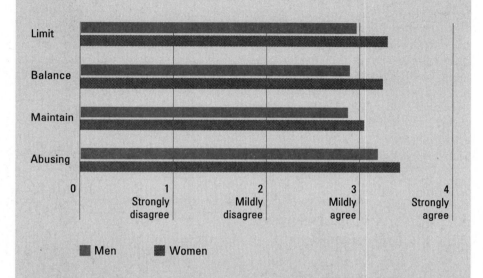

Source: Greg Brown and Charles C. Harris, "The Implications of Work Force Diversification in the U.S. Forest Service," *Administration and Society* 25 (May 1993), pp. 85–113.

Average response based on placement of respondents on a four-point scale:
Limit = We are approaching the limit of the number of people the earth can support.
Balance = The balance of nature is very delicate and easily upset.
Maintain = To maintain a healthy economy we will have to develop a "steady-state" economy, where industrial growth is controlled.
Abusing = Humankind is severely abusing the environment.

tial representation within the federal government's work force, but at the highest level of the civil service, minorities are underrepresented.[10]

Presidential Control over the Bureaucracy

Civil service and other reforms have effectively insulated the vast majority of government workers from party politics. An incoming president can appoint less than 1 percent of all executive branch employees.[11] Still, presidential appointees fill the top policymaking positions in government. Each new president establishes an extensive personnel review process to find appointees who are both politically compatible and qualified in their field. Although the president selects some people from his campaign staff, cabinet secretaries, assistant secretaries, and agency heads tend to be drawn directly from business, universities, and government itself.

Because so few of their own appointees are in each department and agency, presidents often believe that they do not have enough control over the bureaucracy. Presidents find that the bureaucracy is not always as responsive as they might like, for a number of reasons. Principally, pluralism can pull agencies in a direction other than that favored by the president. The Department of Transportation may want to move toward more support for mass transit, but politically it cannot afford to ignore the preferences of highway builders. An agency administrator must often try to broker a compromise between conflicting groups rather than pursue a position that holds fast and true to the president's ideology. Bureaucracies must also follow—at least in general terms—the laws governing the programs they are entrusted with, even if the president doesn't agree with some of those statutes. However, although government bureaucracies may sometimes frustrate the president, by and large their policies move in the direction set by the White House.

Administrative Policymaking: The Formal Processes

Many Americans wonder why agencies sometimes make policy rather than merely carry it out. Administrative agencies are, in fact, authoritative policymaking bodies, and their decisions on substantive issues are legally binding on the citizens of this country.

Administrative Discretion

What are executive agencies set up to do? Cabinet departments, independent agencies, and government corporations are creatures of Congress. Congress creates a new department or agency by enacting a law that describes the organization's mandate, or mission. As part of that mandate, Congress grants to the agency the authority to make certain policy decisions. Congress long ago recognized that it has neither the time nor the technical expertise to make all policy decisions. Ideally, it sets general guidelines for policy and expects agencies to act within those guidelines. The latitude that Congress gives agencies to make policy in the spirit of their legislative mandate is called **administrative discretion**.

Congress often is vague about its intent when setting up a new agency or program. At times a problem is clear-cut but the solution is not, yet Congress is under pressure to act. So Congress creates an agency or program to show that it is concerned and responsive, but it leaves to agency administrators the development of specific solutions. For example, the 1934 enabling legislation that established the FCC recognized a need for regulation in the burgeoning radio industry. But Congress avoided tackling several sticky issues by giving the FCC the ambiguous directive that broadcasters should "serve the public interest, convenience, and necessity."[12] In other cases, a number of obvious solutions to a problem may be available, but lawmakers cannot agree on which one is best. Compromise wording is thus often ambiguous, papering over differences and ensuring conflict over administrative regulations as agencies try to settle lingering policy disputes.

The wide latitude Congress gives administrative agencies often leads to charges that government is out of control, a power unto itself. But such claims are frequently exaggerated. If Congress is unhappy with an agency's actions, it can pass laws invalidating specific policies. This method of control may seem cumbersome, but Congress does have periodic opportunities to amend the original legislation that created an agency or program. Over time, Congress makes increasingly detailed policy decisions, often affirming or modifying agency decisions.[13] Congress can also influence an agency through appropriations legislation.

In general, then, the bureaucracy is not out of control. Congress, however, has chosen to limit its own oversight in one area—domestic and international security. Both the FBI and the CIA have enjoyed a great deal of freedom from formal and informal congressional constraints because of the legitimate need for secrecy in their operations. During the years that J. Edgar Hoover ran the FBI (1924–1972), the organization was something of a rogue elephant, independent of both Congress and the president. The CIA also has abused its need for privacy by engaging in covert operations that should never have been carried out. Congress, however, increased its oversight of the agency and passed legislation designed to force the administration to share more information with Congress.

Rule Making

Agencies make policy through formal administrative procedures, usually **rule making**, the administrative process that results in regulations. **Regulations** are rules that govern the operation of government programs. When an agency issues regulations, it is using the discretionary authority granted to it by Congress to implement a program or policy.

Because regulations are authorized by congressional statutes, they have the effect of law. Regulations are first published as proposals to give all interested parties an opportunity to comment on them and to try to persuade the agency to adopt, alter, or withdraw them. When the FDA issued proposed regulations requiring manufacturers of vitamins and dietary supplements to substantiate the health claims made for their products on the label, the industry fought the regulations vigorously. The manufacturers also asked Congress for relief. Although it was responsible for the legislation authorizing the regulations, Congress passed a one-year moratorium on the proposed rules. Congress

Goring the Bureaucracy
Under the direction of Vice President Gore, the Clinton administration promised to "reinvent government" by streamlining administrative procedures, reducing the number of bureau-crats, and improving service to the public. Evaluations gave mixed reviews to the effort. Critics argue that the reform program focuses too much on short-term savings rather than long-term management issues. On the other hand, the program has been praised for cutting red tape, simplifying rules, and improving procurement practices.

seemed to want to have it both ways, ensuring the integrity of food and drugs while protecting the business interests of industry constituents.

The regulatory process is controversial because regulations often require indi-viduals and corporations to act against their own self-interest. In this case, the producers of vitamins and dietary supplements resented the implication that they were making false claims, and they reminded policymakers that they employ many people to make products that many consumers want. The FDA, however, must balance its desire not to put people out of work through overregulation with its concern that people not be misled or harmed by false labeling.

Administrative Policymaking: Informal Politics

When an agency is considering a new regulation and all the evidence and ar-guments have been presented, how does an administrator reach a decision? Because policy decisions typically address complex problems that lack a single satisfactory solution, they rarely exhibit mathematical precision and efficiency.

The Science of Muddling Through

In his classic analysis of policymaking, "The Science of Muddling Through," Charles Lindblom compared the way policy might be made in the ideal world with the way it is formulated in the real world.[14] The ideal rational decision-making process, according to Lindblom, would begin with an administrator tackling a problem by ranking values and objectives. After the objectives were clarified, the administrator would thoroughly consider all possible solutions to the problem. The administrator would comprehensively analyze alternative solutions, taking all relevant factors into account. Finally, the administrator would choose the alternative that is seen as the most effective means of achieving the desired goal and solving the problem.

Lindblom claims that this "rational-comprehensive" model is unrealistic. To begin with, policymakers have great difficulty defining precise values and goals. Administrators at the U.S. Department of Energy, for example, want to be sure that supplies of home heating oil are sufficient each winter, but at the same time they want to reduce dependence on foreign oil. Obviously, the two goals are not fully compatible. How do administrators decide which is more important? And how do they relate those goals to the other goals of the nation's energy policy?

Real-world decision making parts company with the ideal in another way: the policy selected cannot always be the most effective means to the desired end. Even if a tax at the pump is the most effective way to reduce gasoline consumption during a shortage, motorists' anger would make this theoretically "right" decision politically difficult. The "best" policy is often the one on which most people can agree. However, political compromise may mean that the government is able to solve only part of a problem.

Finally, critics of the rational-comprehensive model point out that policymaking can never be based on truly comprehensive analysis. Time is of the essence, and many problems are too pressing to wait for a complete study.

In short, policymaking tends to be characterized by **incrementalism:** policies and programs change bit by bit, step by step.[15] Decision makers are constrained by competing policy objectives, opposing political forces, incomplete information, and the pressures of time. They choose from a limited number of feasible options that are almost always modifications of existing policies rather than wholesale departures from them. Nevertheless, over time, incremental changes can significantly alter a program.[16]

The Culture of Bureaucracy

How an agency makes decisions and performs its tasks is greatly affected by the people who work there—the bureaucrats. Americans often find their interactions with bureaucrats frustrating because bureaucrats are inflexible (they go by the book) or lack the authority to get things done. Top administrators, too, can also become frustrated with the bureaucrats who work for them.

Why do people act bureaucratically? Individuals who work for large organizations cannot help but be affected by the culture of bureaucracy. Modern bureaucracies develop explicit rules and standards in order to make operations more efficient and to guarantee fair treatment of their clients. Within each organization, **norms** (informal, unwritten rules of behavior) also develop and influence the way people act on the job.

Bureaucracies are often influenced in their selection of policy options by the prevailing customs, attitudes, and expectations of the people working within them. Departments and agencies commonly develop a sense of mission, which emphasizes a particular objective. The Army Corps of Engineers, for example, is dominated by engineers who define the agency's objective as protecting citizens from floods by building dams. There could be other objectives, and there are other methods of achieving flood protection, but the engineers promote the solutions that fit their conception of what the agency should be doing. Agencies with a clear sense of mission are likely to have a strong esprit de corps that adds to the bureaucrats' motivation.

Despite budget cutbacks, adverse public opinion, and other constraints that make their job difficult, most bureaucrats work hard and try to serve the public as best they can. Bureaucrats "go by the book" because "the book" consists of the laws and regulations of this country, as well as internal agency rules and norms. Bureaucratic caution and close adherence to agency rules ensure a measure of consistency. It would be unsettling if government employees interpreted rules as they pleased. Americans expect to be treated equally before the law, and bureaucrats work with that expectation in mind.

Problems in Implementing Policy

The development of policy in Washington marks the end of one phase of the policymaking cycle and the beginning of another. After policies are developed, they must be implemented. **Implementation** is the process of putting specific policies into operation. It is important to study implementation because policies do not always do what they were designed to do.

Implementation may be difficult because the policy to be carried out is not clearly stated. Policy directives to bureaucrats sometimes lack specificity and leave them with too much discretion. When John Frohnmayer headed the National Endowment for the Arts (NEA), he fought legislation intended to prohibit federal funding for "obscene" art. He believed such legislation infringed on artistic freedom. After a bitter fight in Congress, a compromise required that NEA grants be restricted to works falling within "general standards of decency." But what exactly was a "general standard of decency"? It was left to the NEA—with an administrator hostile to the very idea of a decency standard—to figure it out.[17]

Implementation can also be problematic because of the complexity of some government endeavors. Toxic cleanups, for example, pose complicated engineering, political, and financial problems. Inevitably, regional EPA offices and key actors on the local level engage in intense negotiations at each stage of the process.[18] The more organizations and levels of government involved, the more difficult it is to coordinate implementation.

Policymakers can create implementation difficulties by ignoring the administrative capabilities of the agency they have chosen to carry out a program. This happened in 1981 when the Reagan administration and Congress instructed the Social Security Administration to expand its review of citizens receiving disability insurance benefits. The state agencies that carried out the reviews had been handling between 20,000 and 30,000 cases a quarter. The same agencies were ordered to review 100,000 to 150,000 cases a quarter. As the number of people who lost benefits increased, so did legal appeals to reverse the terminations, and the backlog of unresolved cases grew sharply. With the administrative system inundated with more cases than it could handle, the problems with the program reached crisis proportions.

Obstacles to effective implementation can create the impression that nothing the government does succeeds, but programs can and do work. Problems in implementation demonstrate why patience and continual analysis are necessary ingredients of successful policymaking. Implementation is an *incremental* process in which trial and error eventually lead to policies that work.

Reforming the Bureaucracy: More Control or Less?

As we saw at the beginning of this chapter, organization matters. How bureaucracies are designed directly affects how effective they are in accomplishing their tasks.[19] Administrative reforms have taken many different approaches in recent years as the criticism of government has mounted.[20] A central question energizing much of the debate over bureaucratic reform is whether we need to establish more control over the bureaucracy or less.

Deregulation

Many people believe that government is too involved in **regulation**, intervention in the natural workings of business markets to promote some social goal. For example, government might regulate a market to ensure that products pose no danger to consumers. Through **deregulation**, the government reduces its role and lets the natural market forces of supply and demand take over.

Considerable deregulation took place in the 1970s and 1980s, notably in the airline, trucking, financial services, and telecommunications industries. In telecommunications, for example, consumers before 1982 had no choice of long-distance vendors—they could call on AT&T's Bell System or not call at all. After an out-of-court settlement broke up the Bell System in 1982, AT&T was awarded the right to sell the long-distance services that Bell had been providing, but it now had to face competition from other long-distance carriers, such as MCI and Sprint. Consumers have benefited from the competition for long-distance phone calls, and competition has since opened up for local service as well.

Deciding on an appropriate level of deregulation is particularly difficult for health and safety issues. Companies within a particular industry may

The Return of Thalidomide
In the 1960s, ten thousand babies around the world were born without one or more limbs
because their mothers had taken a sedative called thalidomide while pregnant. The United
States was spared this disaster because of the skepticism of Frances Kelsey, a Food and Drug
Administration doctor who refused to allow thalidomide to be prescribed here. In 1997, the
FDA reversed course and decided to permit the use of thalidomide to treat leprosy, but the
dangers to pregnant women remain. To avert a catastrophe, the FDA may include pictures
of thalidomide children with every package of capsules as a stark reminder of the conse-
quences of taking this drug during pregnancy. Shown here is an adult thalidomide victim.

legitimately claim that health and safety regulations are burdensome, making
it difficult for them to earn sufficient profits or compete effectively with foreign manufacturers. But the drug-licensing procedures used by the FDA illustrate the potential danger of deregulating in such policy areas. The thorough
and lengthy process the FDA uses to evaluate drugs has as its ultimate valida-
tion the thalidomide case in the 1960s. Dr. Frances Kelsey, who was assigned
to evaluate the sedative, demanded that all FDA drug-testing requirements be
met, despite the fact that the drug was already in use in other countries.
Before the tests were completed, news came pouring in from Europe that
some women who had taken thalidomide during pregnancy were giving birth
to babies without arms, legs, or ears. Strict adherence to FDA regulation protected Americans from the same tragic consequences.

Nevertheless, the pharmaceutical industry is highly critical of the FDA,
claiming that the licensing procedures are so complex that drugs of great benefit are kept from the marketplace for years and people suffering from dis-

eases are denied access to new treatments. The industry prods the agency to adopt faster procedures. Although the FDA resists doing anything to compromise what it sees as necessary precautions, the AIDS epidemic has brought about some concessions. The FDA has issued new rules expediting the availability of experimental drugs and, more generally, has adopted a somewhat speedier timetable for clinical tests of new drugs.[21]

The conflict over how far to take deregulation reflects the traditional dilemma of choosing between freedom and order. A strong case can be made for deregulated business markets, in which free and unfettered competition benefits consumers and promotes productivity. The strength of capitalist economies comes from the ability of individuals and firms to compete freely in the marketplace, and the regulatory state places restrictions on this freedom. But without regulation, nothing ensures that marketplace participants will act responsibly.

Monitoring, Accountability, and Responsiveness

Bureaucracies must also strive to be responsive to the public, to provide services in an efficient and accessible manner. In the past few years, a management reform program known as **total quality management (TQM)** has increasingly gotten attention. Although initially directed at improving the quality of manufacturing, it is now being adapted to organizations (such as government bureaucracies) that provide services as their "product."

The principles of TQM include listening to the customer, relying on teamwork, focusing on continually improving quality, breaking down barriers between parts of organizations, and engaging in participatory management.[22] Most Americans believe that government has a long way to go toward treating its clients like "customers." But in an era when people are highly antagonistic toward government and budgets are tight, government bureaucrats know they need to improve.

The compelling philosophy behind TQM led the Clinton administration to launch its "reinventing government" initiative, aimed at improving the management of the national government. It had some short-term successes, but there is no shortage of problems with TQM.[23] The single most important rule of TQM is to listen to customers in an effort to serve them better. But who is the customer of a government agency? Are the Department of Agriculture's customers the farmers who want the agency to spend a lot of money providing them with services and subsidies, or are they the taxpayers who want the agency to minimize the amount of money spent by government? TQM does not solve this basic conflict between pluralism and majoritarianism.

Summary

As the scope of government activity grew during the twentieth century, so too did the bureaucracy. The executive branch evolved into a complex set of departments, independent agencies, and government corporations. The way in which these various bureaucracies are organized matters a great deal because the way they are structured affects their ability to carry out their tasks.

Through the administrative discretion granted them by Congress, these bodies make policy decisions through rule making and adjudication that have the force of law. In making policy choices, agency decision makers are influenced by their external environment, especially the White House, Congress, and interest groups. Internal norms and the need to work cooperatively with others both inside and outside their agencies also influence decision makers.

The most serious charge facing the bureaucracy is that it is unresponsive to the will of the people. In fact, the White House, Congress, interest groups, and public opinion act as substantial controls on the bureaucracy. Still, to many Americans, the bureaucracy seems too big, too costly, and too intrusive. Reducing the size and scope of bureaucratic activity is difficult, because pluralism characterizes our political system. The entire executive branch may appear too large, and each of us can point to agencies that we believe should be reduced or eliminated. Yet each bureaucracy has its supporters. Bureaucracies survive because they provide important services to groups of people, and those people—no matter how strong their commitment to shrinking the government—are not willing to sacrifice their own benefits.

Plans for reforming the bureaucracy to make it work better are not in short supply. Proponents of deregulation believe our economy would be more productive if we freed the marketplace from the heavy hand of government supervision. Opponents believe that deregulation involves considerable risk and that we ought to be very careful in determining which markets and business practices can be subjected to less government supervision. To prevent disasters such as the thalidomide episode, government bureaucracies must be able to monitor the behavior of people inside and outside of government and supervise business practices in a wide range of industries. However, most people continue to believe that the overall management of bureaucracies is poor and that government needs to be more customer driven.

Key Terms

bureaucracy	rule making
bureaucrat	regulations
department	incrementalism
independent agency	norms
regulatory commission	implementation
government corporation	regulation
civil service	deregulation
administrative discretion	total quality management (TQM)

Selected Readings

Harris, Richard A., and Sidney M. Milkis. *The Politics of Regulatory Change.* 2d ed. New York: Oxford University Press, 1996. A study of how the regulatory regime of the Reagan years affected policymaking at the Federal Trade Commission and the Environmental Protection Agency.

Howard, Philip K. *The Death of Common Sense.* New York: Warner Books, 1994. A sharp attack on government bureaucracies for being too inflexible and for not giving agency officials more discretion in solving problems.

Kerwin, Cornelius M. *Rulemaking: How Government Agencies Write Law and Make Policy.* Washington, D.C.: Congressional Quarterly Press, 1994. An inside look at how agencies write regulations to carry out the laws they must administer.

Gormley, William T., and David L. Weimer. *Organizational Report Cards.* Cambridge, Mass.: Harvard University Press, 1999. A thoughtful analysis of how to measure an organization's effectiveness and the quality of services it provides.

Light, Paul C. *The True Size of Government.* Washington, D.C.: Brookings Institution, 1999. Light disputes contentions that the federal government has become smaller.

World Wide Web Resources

Fedworld. This site is operated by the National Technical Information Service (of the Department of Commerce). A "central access point" for U.S. government information on-line, it allows you to "locate, order, and have government information delivered to you." It also contains information on federal employment opportunities and abstracts of recent government reports (from all agencies). <www.fedworld.gov>

Federal Communications Commission. This home page provides access to the FCC's Daily Digest, policy agenda, agendas of open meetings, consumer information, and information about developments in the telecommunications industry. <www.fcc.gov>

The *Department of Health and Human Services* site contains links to HHS agencies such as the Food and Drug Administration and the National Institutes of Health, as well as to programs such as Medicare. <www.hhs.gov>

The *Central Intelligence Agency* site provides insight on one of the least understood elements of the executive branch. The site contains declassified intelligence analysis along with unclassified publications, reports, speeches, and testimony presented before Congress. <www.cia.gov>

11

The Courts

"We're going to kill him politically—this little creep. Where did he come from?" asked feminist activist Florence Kennedy.[1] Her target was Judge Clarence Thomas, nominated by President George Bush for a seat on the nation's highest court, the Supreme Court of the United States. Thomas was a staunch conservative. His 1991 appointment, to replace the retiring liberal Justice Thurgood Marshall, would put many liberal decisions at risk.

Thomas endured a determined effort by a range of liberal organizations, including the American Civil Liberties Union and the National Organization for Women, to scuttle his confirmation by the U.S. Senate (a constitutional requirement). He weathered days of questioning from the Senate Judiciary Committee, declining to express his opinions about policies and approaches to constitutional interpretation and thus stymieing his opponents. Thomas's nomination seemed assured until a last-minute witness, Professor Anita Hill, came forward with charges that Thomas had made unwanted advances when she had worked for him ten years earlier. Thomas categorically denied the charges and characterized the process as "a high-tech lynching."[2]

Suddenly, the hearing galvanized the press and the public. A transfixed nation watched the riveting testimony of Hill, Thomas, and a parade of corroborating witnesses. Thomas's critics heaved charges of sexism; his champions leveled charges of racism. The committee failed to unearth convincing proof of Hill's allegations. (National polls at the time showed Americans believed Thomas over Hill by a margin of two to one.) In the end, the Senate voted by a slim margin—52 to 48—to confirm Thomas's nomination.

After taking the oath of office, Thomas withdrew into his work, secure in the knowledge that the Constitution placed him above his detractors. For her part, Anita Hill became a much-sought-after celebrity for liberal and feminist causes. For his part, Thomas knows that he will be serving on the nation's highest court for the rest of his life. "They can say what they want about me," Thomas later remarked to a friend, "but I'm going to be making law for a long time."[3]

The Supreme Court is like a cloister: outsiders find it very difficult to know what transpires within. This is especially true of the events that take place in the conference room where the justices gather twice weekly to cast tentative decisions on cases that have recently been argued before the Court.

"She Said. He Said."
President George Bush nominated forty-three-year-old Clarence Thomas to the nation's highest court in 1991. As Thomas was on the verge of confirmation, Anita Hill, a former Thomas assistant, stepped forward to assert that he had made unwanted advances years earlier. Her charges nearly scuttled Thomas's nomination.

After hearing arguments in two important 1995 cases related to issues of race, Thomas spoke fervently in the conference room of his own struggles with racial segregation and bigotry. (The justices reported these events to their assistants, who spoke without attribution to a reporter.) As Thomas saw it, race-based solutions (such as forcing whites and blacks to attend the same schools or giving African Americans special advantages in securing contracts or employment) are misdirected and harmful because they rest on the patronizing belief that blacks are inherently inferior. The best solution, Thomas averred, would be to ensure equality of opportunity and to remove government from the business of racial classifications. The Constitution, Thomas declared, should be color-blind.[4] He cast his votes accordingly.

A single vote can make a difference. In both 1995 cases, the justices split 5 to 4, with Thomas in the majority. As a result, the Court curtailed the government's power to fashion remedies to racial discrimination in the name of equality and allowed more room for freedom to flourish.[5] These cases and others have signaled a conservative shift in the Court's ideological center—a shift that is largely unaffected by representative institutions or majority rule.

Judges confront conflicting values in the cases brought before them, and in crafting their decisions, judges—especially Supreme Court justices—make policy. Their decisions become the precedents other judges use to rule in similar cases. Judges make public policy to the extent that they influence decisions in other courts. This power of the courts to shape policy creates a difficult problem for democratic theory. According to that theory, the power to make law resides only in the people or their elected representatives. When judges undo the work of elected majorities, they risk depriving the people of the right to make the laws to govern themselves.

Court rulings—especially Supreme Court rulings—extend far beyond any particular case. Judges are students of the law, but they remain human beings. They have their own opinions about the values of freedom, order, and equality. And although all judges are constrained by statutes and precedents from expressing their personal beliefs in their decisions, some judges are more prone than others to interpret laws in light of those beliefs.

America's courts are deeply involved in the life of the country and its people. Some courts, such as the Supreme Court, make fundamental policy decisions vital to the preservation of freedom, order, and equality. Through checks and balances, the elected branches link the courts to democracy, and the courts link the elected branches to the Constitution. But does this arrangement work? Can the courts exercise political power within the pluralist model? Or are judges simply sovereigns in black robes, making decisions independent of popular control? This chapter tries to answer these questions by exploring the role of the judiciary in American political life.

National Judicial Supremacy

Section 1 of Article III of the Constitution creates "one supreme Court." The founders were divided on the need for other national courts, so they deferred to Congress the decision to create a national court system. Those who opposed the creation of national courts believed that such a system would usurp the authority of the state courts.[6] Congress considered the issue in its first session and, in the Judiciary Act of 1789, gave life to a system of federal (that is, national) courts that would coexist with the courts in each state but be independent of them. Federal judges would also be independent of popular influences because the Constitution provided for their virtual lifetime appointment.

In the early years of the Republic, the federal judiciary was not considered a particularly powerful branch of government. It proved especially difficult to recruit and keep Supreme Court justices. They spent much of their time as individual traveling judges ("riding circuit"), and disease and transportation were everyday hazards. The justices met as the Supreme Court for only a few weeks in February and August.[7] John Jay, the first chief justice, refused to resume his duties in 1801 because he concluded that the Court could not muster the "energy, weight, and dignity" to contribute to national affairs.[8] But a period of profound change began in 1801 when President John Adams appointed his secretary of state, John Marshall, to the position of chief justice.

Judicial Review of the Other Branches

Shortly after Marshall's appointment, the Supreme Court confronted a question of fundamental importance to the future of the new republic: if a law enacted by Congress conflicts with the Constitution, which should prevail? The question arose in the case of *Marbury v. Madison* (1803), which involved a controversial series of last-minute political appointments.

The Supreme Court held, in Marshall's forceful argument, that the Constitution was "the fundamental and paramount law of the nation" and that "an act of the legislature repugnant to the constitution is void." In other words, when an act of the legislature conflicts with the Constitution—the nation's highest law—that act is invalid. Marshall's argument vested in the judiciary the power to weigh the validity of congressional acts:

> It is emphatically the province and duty of the judicial department to say what the law is. Those who apply the rule to particular cases, must of necessity expound and interpret that rule. . . . . If a law be in opposition to the constitution, if both the law and the constitution apply to a particular case, so that the court must either decide that case conformably to the law, disregarding the constitution; or conformably to the constitution, disregarding the law; the court must determine which of these conflicting rules governs the case. This is the very essence of judicial duty.[9]

The decision in *Marbury v. Madison* established the Supreme Court's power of **judicial review**—the power to declare congressional acts invalid if they violate the Constitution.* Subsequent cases extended the power to cover presidential acts as well.[10]

Marshall expanded the potential power of the Supreme Court to equal or exceed the power of the other branches of government. Should a congressional act (or, by implication, a presidential act) conflict with the Constitution, the Supreme Court claimed the power to declare the act void. The judiciary would be a check on the legislative and executive branches, consistent with the principle of checks and balances embedded in the Constitution. Judicial review gave the Supreme Court the final word on the meaning of the Constitution.

The exercise of judicial review—an appointed branch's checking of an elected branch in the name of the Constitution—appears to run counter to democratic theory. But, in nearly two hundred years of practice, the Supreme Court has invalidated only about 150 provisions of national law. Only a small number have had great significance for the political system.[11] Moreover, there are mechanisms to override judicial review (constitutional amendment) and to control the excesses of the justices (impeachment). In addition, the Court can respond to the continuing struggle among competing interests (a struggle that is consistent with the pluralist model) by reversing itself.

Judicial Review of State Government

The establishment of judicial review of national laws made the Supreme Court the umpire of the national government. When acts of the national government conflict with the Constitution, the Supreme Court can declare those acts invalid. But suppose state laws conflict with the Constitution, national laws, or federal treaties? Can the U.S. Supreme Court invalidate them as well?

The Court answered in the affirmative in 1796. The case involved a British creditor who was trying to collect a debt from the state of Virginia.[12] Virginia

---

*The Supreme Court had earlier upheld an act of Congress in *Hylton v. United States,* 3 Dallas 171 (1796). *Marbury v. Madison* was the first exercise of the power of a court to invalidate an act of Congress.

law canceled debts owed British subjects, yet the Treaty of Paris (1783), in which Britain formally acknowledged the independence of the colonies, guaranteed that creditors could collect such debts. The Court ruled that the Constitution's supremacy clause (Article VI), which embraces national laws and treaties, nullified the state law.

The states continued to resist the yoke of national supremacy. Advocates of strong states' rights conceded that the supremacy clause obligates state judges to follow the Constitution when state law conflicts with it; however, they maintained that the states were bound only by their own interpretation of the Constitution. The Supreme Court said no, ruling that it had the authority to review state court decisions that called for the interpretation of national law.[13] National supremacy required the Supreme Court to impose uniformity on federal law; otherwise, the Constitution's meaning would vary from state to state. The people, not the states, had ordained the Constitution; and the people had subordinated state power to it in order to establish a viable national government. In time, the Supreme Court would use its judicial review power in nearly 1,200 instances to invalidate state and local laws on issues as diverse as abortion, the death penalty, the rights of the accused, and reapportionment.[14]

The Exercise of Judicial Review

These early cases, coupled with other historic decisions, established the components of judicial review:

- The power of the courts to declare national, state, and local laws invalid if they violate the Constitution
- The supremacy of national laws or treaties when they conflict with state and local laws
- The role of the Supreme Court as the final authority on the meaning of the Constitution

This political might—the power to undo decisions of the representative branches of the national and state governments—lay in the hands of appointed judges, people not accountable to the electorate. Did judicial review square with democratic government?

Alexander Hamilton had foreseen and tackled the problem in *Federalist* No. 78. Writing during the ratification debates surrounding the adoption of the Constitution (see Chapter 2), Hamilton maintained that despite the power of judicial review, the judiciary would be the weakest of the three branches of government because it lacked "the strength of the sword or the purse." The judiciary, wrote Hamilton, had "neither FORCE nor WILL, but only judgment."

Although Hamilton was defending legislative supremacy, he argued that judicial review was an essential barrier to legislative oppression.[15] He recognized that the power to declare government acts void implied the superiority of the courts over the other branches. But this power, he contended, simply reflects the will of the people declared in the Constitution as opposed to the will of the legislature expressed in its statutes. Judicial independence, guaranteed by lifetime tenure and protected salaries, frees judges from executive and legislative control, minimizing the risk of their deviating from the law established in the Constitution. If judges make a mistake, the people or their elected representatives have the means to correct the error, through constitutional amendments and impeachment.

Nevertheless, lifetime tenure does free judges from the direct influence of the president and Congress. And although mechanisms to check judicial power are in place, they require extraordinary majorities and are rarely used. When judges exercise the power of judicial review, then, they can and occasionally do operate counter to majoritarian rule by invalidating the actions of the people's elected representatives (see Compared with What? 11.1 for a discussion of the nature of judicial review in other governments, democratic and nondemocratic).

The Organization of Courts

The American court system is complex, partly as a result of our federal system of government. Each state runs its own court system, and no two states' courts are identical. In addition, we have a system of courts for the national government. The national, or federal, courts coexist with the state courts (see Figure 11.1). Individuals fall under the jurisdiction of both court systems. They can sue or be sued in either system, depending mostly on what their case is about. Litigants file nearly all cases (99 percent) in the state courts.[16]

Some Court Fundamentals

Criminal and Civil Cases   A crime is a violation of a law that forbids or commands an activity. Criminal laws are set forth in each state's penal code, as are punishments for violations. Because crime is a violation of public order, the government prosecutes **criminal cases**. Maintaining public order through the enforcement of criminal law is largely a state and local function. Criminal cases brought by the national government represent only a small fraction of all criminal cases prosecuted in the United States.

Courts decide both criminal and civil cases. **Civil cases** stem from disputed claims to something of value. Disputes arise from accidents, contractual obligations, and divorce, for example. Often the parties disagree over tangible issues (possession of property, custody of children), but civil cases can involve more abstract issues too (the right to equal accommodations, damages for pain and suffering). The government can be a party to civil disputes, called on to defend its actions or to allege wrongdoing.

Procedures and Policymaking   Most civil and criminal cases never go to trial. In a criminal case, a defendant's lawyer and the prosecutor might plea-bargain, which means they negotiate about the severity and number of charges facing the accused. The defendant pleads guilty to a lesser charge in exchange for

Compared with What? 11.1

Judicial Review

The U.S. Constitution does not explicitly give the Supreme Court the power of judicial review. In a controversial interpretation, the Court inferred this power from the text and structure of the Constitution. Other countries, trying to avoid political controversy over the power of their courts to review legislation, explicitly define that power in their constitutions. For example, Japan's constitution, inspired by the American model, went beyond it in providing that "the Supreme Court is the court of last resort with power to determine the constitutionality of any law, order, regulation, or official act."

The basic objection to the American form of judicial review is an unwillingness to place federal judges, who are usually appointed for life, above representatives elected by the people. Some constitutions explicitly deny judicial review. For example, Article 84 of the recently revised Belgian constitution (1994) firmly asserts that "the authoritative interpretation of laws is solely the prerogative of the Legislative authority."

The logical basis of judicial review—that government is responsible to a higher authority—can take interesting forms in other countries. In some, judges can invoke an authority higher than the constitution—God, an ideology, or a code of ethics. For example, both Iran and Pakistan provide for an Islamic review of all legislation (Pakistan also has the American form of judicial review).

By 1992, about seventy countries had adopted some form of judicial review. Australia, Brazil, Canada, India, Japan, and Pakistan give their courts a full measure of judicial review power. Australia and Canada come closest to the American model of judicial review, but the fit is never exact. And wherever courts exercise judicial review, undoing it requires extraordinary effort. For example, in Australia the federal parliament has no recourse after a law is declared unconstitutional by the high court but to redraft the offending act in a manner prescribed by the court. In the United States, overruling judicial review by the Supreme Court would require a constitutional amendment.

Governments with a tradition of judicial review share some common characteristics: stability, competitive political parties, distribution of power (akin to separation of powers), a tradition of judicial independence, and a high degree of political freedom. Is judicial review the cause or the consequence of these characteristics? More likely than not, judicial review contributes to stability, judicial independence, and political freedom; and separation of powers, judicial independence, and political freedom contribute to the effectiveness of judicial review.

Some constitutional courts possess extraordinary power compared with the American model. The German constitutional court has the power to rectify the failure of the nation's lawmakers to act. In 1975, for example, the German constitutional court nullified the legalization of abortion and declared that the government had a duty to protect unborn human life against all threats. The court concluded that the German constitution required the legislature to enact legislation protecting the fetus.

(continued)

Compared with What? 11.1 (continued)

Some judges take their power at face value. South Africa created a constitutional court in 1995 and gave it powers on a par with the legislative and executive branches. In its first major decision, the court's eleven appointed justices abolished the death penalty, a decades-old practice that had placed South Africa among the nations with the highest rate of capital punishment. "Everyone, including the most abominable of human beings, has a right to life, and capital punishment is therefore unconstitutional," declared the court's president.

The Supreme Court of India offers an extreme example of judicial review. In 1967, the court held that the Indian parliament could not change the fundamental rights sections of the country's constitution, even by constitutional amendment. The parliament then amended the constitution to secure its power to amend the constitution. The Supreme Court upheld the amendment but declared that any amendments that attacked the "basic structure" of the constitution would be invalid. In India, the Supreme Court is truly supreme.

Switzerland's Supreme Federal Tribunal is limited by the country's constitution to ruling on the constitutionality of cantonal laws (the Swiss equivalent of our state laws). It lacks the power to nullify laws passed by the national assembly. Through a constitutional initiative or a popular referendum, the Swiss people may exercise the sovereign right to determine the constitutionality of federal law. In Switzerland, the people are truly supreme.

Sources: Henry J. Abraham, *The Judicial Process,* 6th ed. (New York: Oxford University Press, 1993), pp. 270–310; Chester J. Antineau, *Adjudicating Constitutional Issues* (London: Oceana, 1985), pp. 1–6; Jerold L. Waltman and Kenneth M. Holland, *The Political Role of Law Courts in Modern Democracies* (New York: St. Martin's Press, 1988), pp. 46, 99–100; Robert L. Hardgrave, Jr., and Stanley A. Kochanek, *India: Government and Politics in a Developing Nation,* 4th ed. (New York: Harcourt Brace Jovanovich, 1986), p. 93; Howard W. French, "South Africa's Supreme Court Abolishes Death Penalty," *New York Times,* 7 June 1995, p. A3.

the promise of less severe punishment. In a civil case, one side may use a lawsuit as a threat to exact a concession from the other. Often, the parties settle their dispute. When parties do not settle, cases end with *adjudication,* a court judgment resolving the parties' claims and ultimately enforced by the government. When trial judges adjudicate cases, they may offer written reasons to support their decisions. When the issues or circumstances of cases are novel, judges may publish *opinions,* explanations justifying their rulings.

Judges make policy in two different ways. Occasionally, in the absence of legislation, they use rules from prior decisions. We call this body of rules **common**, or **judge-made, law**. The roots of common law lie in the English legal system. Contracts, property, and torts (an injury or wrong to the person or property of another) are common-law domains. The second area of judicial lawmaking involves the application of statutes enacted by legislatures. The

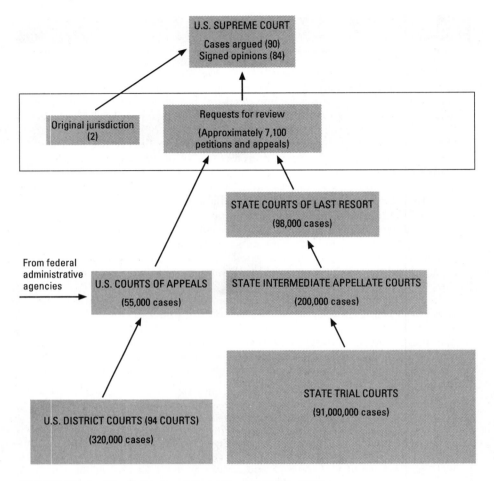

FIGURE 11.1 The Federal and State Court Systems, 1999
The federal courts have three tiers: district courts, courts of appeals, and the Supreme Court.
The Supreme Court was created by the Constitution; all other federal courts were created by
Congress. Most litigation occurs in state courts. The structure of state courts varies from
state to state; usually, there are minor trial courts for less serious cases, major trial courts for
more serious cases, intermediate appellate courts, and supreme courts. State courts were
created by state constitutions. (Sources: Court Statistics Project, State Court Caseload Statistics,
1998 [Williamsburg, Va.: National Center for State Courts, 1999], p. 105; William H. Rehnquist,
"The 1999 Year-End Report on the Federal Judiciary," The Third Branch 32,1 [January 2000],
<http://www.uscourts.gov/ttb/jan00ttb/jan2000.html>.)

judicial interpretation of legislative acts is called *statutory construction.* To determine how a statute should be applied, judges look for the legislature's intent,
reading reports of committee hearings and debates. If these sources do not
clarify the statute's meaning, the court does so. With or without legislation to
guide them, judges look to the relevant opinions of higher courts for authority
to decide the issues before them.

"The Wright Call"
Judge Susan Webber Wright is a federal district court judge in Little Rock, Arkansas. She studied navigation law at the University of Arkansas with (then) Professor Bill Clinton. Wright, a Republican, presided in a civil case brought by Paula Corbin Jones against President Bill Clinton for sexual misconduct when Clinton was Arkansas governor. Wright sided with the president's request to delay the case, but the U.S. Supreme Court overturned her decision. Wright threw the case out entirely in 1998 following a deposition by President Clinton. (Jones and Clinton later settled the matter.) Little more than a year later, Wright found that the president had given intentionally false testimony, tainting the proceedings. She rebuked Clinton, holding him in civil contempt, an ignominious "first" for any American president.

The federal courts are organized in three tiers, as a pyramid. At the bottom of the pyramid are **U.S. district courts**, where litigation begins. In the middle are **U.S. courts of appeals**. At the top is the Supreme Court of the United States. To *appeal* means to take a case to a higher court. The courts of appeals and the Supreme Court are appellate courts; with few exceptions, they only review cases already decided in lower courts.

The U.S. District Courts

There are ninety-four federal district courts in the United States. Each state has at least one district court, and no district straddles more than one state.[17] In 1999, Congress authorized positions for nine new judges in the federal district court system, raising the total to 655. These judges received over 320,000 new criminal and civil cases.[18]

The district courts are the entry point to the federal court system. When trials occur in the federal system, they take place in the federal district courts.

Here is where witnesses testify, lawyers conduct cross-examinations, and judges and juries decide the fate of litigants. More than one judge may sit in each district court, but each case is tried by a single judge, sitting alone. Federal magistrates assist district judges, but they lack independent judicial authority. In 1998, there were 422 full-time magistrates and 77 part-time magistrates.

Sources of Litigation   Today, the authority of U.S. district courts extends to the follwing types of cases:

- Federal criminal cases as defined by national law (for example, robbery of a federally insured bank or interstate transportation of stolen securities)
- Civil cases brought by individuals, groups, or government alleging violation of national law (for example, failure of a municipality to implement pollution-control regulations required by a national agency)
- Civil cases brought against the national government (for example, a vehicle manufacturer sues the motor pool of a government agency for its failure to take delivery of a fleet of new cars)
- Civil cases between citizens of different states when the amount in controversy exceeds $75,000 (for example, when a citizen of New York sues a citizen of Alabama in a U.S. district court in Alabama for damages stemming from an auto accident that occurred in Alabama)

The U.S. Courts of Appeals

All cases resolved in a U.S. district court and all decisions of federal administrative agencies can be appealed to one of the thirteen U.S. courts of appeals. These courts, with a corps of 179 judges, received around fifty-five thousand new cases in 1999.[19] Each appeals court hears cases from a geographic area known as a *circuit*. The United States is divided into twelve circuits.*

Appellate Court Proceedings   Appellate court proceedings are public, but they usually lack courtroom drama. There are no jurors, witnesses, or cross-examinations; these are features of the trial courts. Appeals are based strictly on the rulings made and procedures followed in the trial courts.

Suppose that in the course of a criminal trial a U.S. district judge allows the introduction of evidence that convicts a defendant but was obtained under questionable circumstances. The defendant can appeal on the grounds that the evidence was obtained in the absence of a valid search warrant and so was inadmissible. The issue on appeal is the admissibility of the evidence, not the defendant's guilt or innocence. If the appellate court agrees with the trial judge's decision to admit the evidence, the conviction stands. If the appellate

---

*The thirteenth court, the U.S. Court of Appeals for the Federal Circuit, is not a regional court; it specializes in appeals involving patents, contract claims against the federal government, and federal employment cases.

court disagrees with the trial judge and rules that the evidence is inadmissible, the defendant must be retried without the incriminating evidence or be released.

It is common for litigants to try to settle their dispute while it is on appeal. Occasionally, litigants abandon their appeals for want of resources or resolve. Most of the time, however, appellate courts adjudicate the cases.

The courts of appeals are regional courts. They usually convene in panels of three judges to render judgments. The judges receive written arguments known as *briefs* (which are also sometimes submitted in trial courts). Often the judges hear oral arguments and question the lawyers to probe their arguments. Following review of written briefs and, in many appeals, oral argument, the three-judge panel meets to reach a judgment.

Precedents and Making Decisions

When an appellate opinion is published, its influence can reach well beyond the immediate case. For example, a lawsuit turning on the meaning of the Constitution produces a ruling that serves as a **precedent** for subsequent cases—that is, the decision becomes a basis for deciding similar cases in the same way. At the appellate level, precedent requires that opinions be written.

Making decisions according to precedent is central to the operation of our legal system, providing continuity and predictability. The bias in favor of existing decisions is captured by the Latin expression *stare decisis*, which means "let the decision stand." But the use of precedent and the principle of *stare decisis* do not make lower-court judges cogs in a judicial machine. "If precedent clearly governed," remarked one federal judge, "a case would never get as far as the Court of Appeals: the parties would settle."[20]

Judges on the courts of appeals direct their energies to correcting errors in district court proceedings and interpreting the law (in the course of writing opinions). When judges interpret the law, they often modify existing laws. In effect, they are making policy. Judges are politicians in the sense that they exercise political power, but the black robes that distinguish judges from other politicians signal constraints on their exercise of power.

Uniformity of Law   Decisions by the courts of appeals ensure a measure of uniformity in the application of national law. The courts of appeals harmonize the decisions of district judges within their region so that laws are applied uniformly.

Nevertheless, the regional character of the courts of appeals undermines uniformity somewhat because the courts are not bound by the decisions of other circuits. The percolation of cases up through the federal system of courts practically guarantees that at some point two or more courts of appeals, working with similar sets of facts, are going to interpret the same law differently. However, the problem of conflicting decisions in the intermediate federal courts can be corrected by review in the Supreme Court, where policymaking, not error correction, is the paramount goal.

The Supreme Court

Above the west portico of the Supreme Court Building are inscribed the words EQUAL JUSTICE UNDER LAW. At the opposite end of the building, above the east portico, are the words JUSTICE THE GUARDIAN OF LIBERTY. These mottoes reflect the Court's difficult task: achieving a just balance among the values of freedom, order, and equality. Consider how those values came into conflict in two controversial issues the Court faced in recent years: flag burning and school desegregation.

Flag burning as a form of political protest pits the value of order, or the government's interest in maintaining a peaceful society, against the value of freedom, including the individual's right to vigorous and unbounded political expression. In two flag-burning cases, the Supreme Court affirmed constitutional protection for unbridled political expression, including the emotionally charged act of desecrating a national symbol.[21]

School desegregation pits the value of equality (in this case, equal educational opportunities for minorities) against the value of freedom (the rights of parents to send their children to neighborhood schools). In *Brown v. Board of Education*, the Supreme Court carried the banner of racial equality by striking down state-mandated segregation in public schools. The justices recognized the disorder their decision would create in a society accustomed to racial bias, but in this case equality clearly outweighed freedom. Twenty-four years later, the Court was still embroiled in controversy over equality when it ruled that race could be a factor in university admissions (to diversify the student body), in the *Bakke* case.[22] Having secured equality for blacks, the Court then had to confront the charge that it was denying whites the freedom to compete for admission. The controversy continued in 1995 as a new majority of conservative justices limited race-based preferences in government policies.[23]

The Supreme Court makes national policy. Because its decisions have far-reaching effects on all of us, it is vital that we understand how it reaches those decisions.

Access to the Court

There are rules of access that must be followed to bring a case to the Supreme Court. Also important is sensitivity to the justices' policy and ideological preferences. The notion that anyone can take a case all the way to the Supreme Court is true only in theory, not fact.

The Supreme Court's cases come from two sources. A few arrive under the Court's **original jurisdiction**, conferred by Article III, Section 2, of the Constitution, which gives the Court the power to hear and decide "all Cases affecting Ambassadors, other public Ministers and Consuls, and those in which a State shall be a Party." Cases falling under the Court's original jurisdiction are tried and decided in the Court itself; the cases begin and end there. For example, the Court is the first and only forum in which legal disputes between states are resolved.

The Supreme Court, 2000 Term: The Starting Lineup
The justices of the Supreme Court of the United States, pictured from left to right: Antonin Scalia, Ruth Bader Ginsburg, John Paul Stevens, David Souter, Chief Justice William Rehnquist, Clarence Thomas, Sandra Day O'Connor, Stephen Breyer, and Anthony Kennedy.

Most cases enter the Supreme Court from the U.S. courts of appeals or the state courts of last resort. These cases are within the Court's **appellate jurisdiction**. They have been tried, decided, and reexamined as far as the law permits in other federal or state courts. The Supreme Court exercises judicial power under its appellate jurisdiction because Congress gives it the authority to do so. Congress may change (and, perhaps, eliminate) the Court's appellate jurisdiction. This is a powerful but rarely used weapon in the congressional arsenal of checks and balances.

Litigants in state cases who invoke the Court's appellate jurisdiction must satisfy two conditions. First, the case must reach the end of the line in the state court system. Litigants cannot jump at will from state to federal arenas of justice. Second, the case must raise a **federal question**, an issue covered under the Constitution, federal laws, or national treaties. However, even most cases that meet these conditions do not reach the Supreme Court.

Since 1925, the Court has exercised substantial (today, nearly complete) control over its **docket**, or agenda. The Court selects a handful of cases (less than one hundred) for consideration from the seven thousand or more requests filed each year. These requests take the form of petitions for *certiorari*, in which a litigant seeking review asks the Court "to become informed" of the lower-court proceedings. For the vast majority of cases, the Court denies the petition for *certiorari*, leaving the decision of the lower court undisturbed. No explanations accompany cases that are denied review, so they have little or no value as court rulings.

The Court grants a review only when four or more justices agree that a case warrants full consideration. This unwritten rule is known as the **rule of four**. With advance preparation by their law clerks, who screen petitions and prepare summaries, all nine justices make these judgments at conferences held twice a week.[24]

The Solicitor General

Why does the Court decide to hear certain cases but not others? The best evidence scholars have adduced suggests that agenda setting depends on the individual justices, who vary in their decision-making criteria and on the issues raised by the cases. Occasionally, justices weigh the ultimate outcome of a case when granting or denying review. At other times, justices grant or deny review based on disagreement among the lower courts or because delay in resolving the issues would impose alarming economic or social costs.[25] The solicitor general plays a vital role in the Court's agenda setting.

The **solicitor general** represents the national government before the Supreme Court. Appointed by the president, the solicitor general is the third-highest-ranking official in the U.S. Department of Justice (after the attorney general and the deputy attorney general). The solicitor general's duties include determining whether the government should appeal lower-court decisions; reviewing and modifying, when necessary, the briefs filed in government appeals; and deciding whether the government should file an *amicus curiae* **brief*** in any appellate court.[26] The objective is to create a cohesive program for the executive branch in the federal courts. Solicitors general are a "formidable force" in the setting of the Supreme Court's agenda.[27] Their influence in bringing cases to the Court and arguing them there has earned the solicitor general the informal title of "the tenth justice."

Decision Making

Once the Court grants review, attorneys submit written arguments (briefs). Oral arguments, limited to thirty minutes for each side, usually follow. From October through April, the justices spend four hours a day, five or six days a month hearing arguments. They reach no collective decision at oral argument. A tentative decision is reached only after they have met in conference.

Our knowledge of the dynamics of decision making on the Supreme Court is all secondhand. However, Justice Antonin Scalia, who joined the Court in 1986, remarked that "not much conferencing goes on." By *conferencing*, Scalia meant efforts to persuade others to change their views by debating points of disagreement. "To call our discussion of a case a conference," he said, "is re-

---

* *Amicus curiae* is Latin for "friend of the court." *Amicus* briefs can be filed with permission of the Court. They allow groups and individuals who are not parties to the litigation but have an interest in it to influence the Court's thinking and, perhaps, its decision.

ally something of a misnomer. It's much more a statement of the views of each of the nine Justices, after which the totals are added and the case is assigned" for an opinion.[28] Votes remain tentative until the opinion announcing the Court's judgment is issued.

Judicial Restraint and Judicial Activism How do the justices decide how to vote on a case? According to some scholars, legal doctrines and past decisions explain their votes. This explanation, which is consistent with the majoritarian model, anchors the justices closely to the law and minimizes the contribution of their personal values. This view is embodied in the concept of **judicial restraint**, which maintains that legislators, not judges, should make the laws. Judges are said to exercise judicial restraint when they hew closely to statutes and previous cases in reaching their decisions. Other scholars contend that the value preferences and resulting ideologies of the justices provide a more powerful interpretation of their voting.[29] This view is embodied in the concept of **judicial activism**, which maintains that judges should interpret laws loosely, using their power to promote their preferred social and political goals. Judges are said to exercise judicial activism when they seem to interpret existing laws and rulings with little regard to precedent and to interject their own values into court decisions. Judicial activism, which is consistent with the pluralist model, sees the justices as actively promoting their value preferences.

Judgment and Argument The voting outcome is the **judgment**, the decision on who wins and who loses. The justices often disagree, not only on winners and losers but also on the reasons for their judgments.

After voting, the justices in the majority must draft an opinion setting out the reasons for their decision. The **argument** is the kernel of the opinion—its logical content, as distinct from facts, rhetoric, and procedure. If all justices agree with the judgment and the reasons supporting it, the opinion is unanimous. Agreement with a judgment for reasons different from those set forth in the majority opinion is called **concurrence**. Or a justice can **dissent** if she or he disagrees with a judgment. Both concurring and dissenting opinions may be drafted in addition to the majority opinion.

The Opinion After the conference, the chief justice writes the majority opinion or assigns that responsibility to another justice in the majority. If the chief justice is not in the majority, the writing or assigning responsibility rests with the most senior associate justice in the majority. An opinion may have to be rewritten several times to accommodate colleagues who remain unpersuaded by the draft. Justices can change their votes, and perhaps alter the judgment, at any time before the decision is officially announced.

Justices in the majority frequently try to muffle or stifle dissent in order to encourage institutional cohesion. Since the mid-1940s, however, unity has been more difficult to obtain.[30] Gaining agreement from the justices today is akin to negotiating with nine separate law firms. Nevertheless, the justices must be keenly aware of the slender foundation of their authority, which rests largely on public respect. That respect is tested whenever the Court ventures

Choosing Sides
Justices Ruth Bader Ginsburg (left) and Sandra Day O'Connor (right) are occasional allies on issues of abortion and gender equality. But O'Connor parts company with Ginsburg and tends to side with Chief Justice William Rehnquist (center) on matters dealing with racial equality and federalism. The justices are pictured here in the conference room of the Supreme Court building.

into areas of controversy. Freedom of speech and religion, racial equality, and the right to privacy have led the Court into controversy.

Strategies on the Court

If we start with the assumption that the justices attempt to stamp their own policy views on the cases they review, we should expect typical political behavior from them. Because the justices are grappling with conflict on a daily basis, they probably have well-defined ideologies that reflect their values.

Scholars and journalists have attempted to pierce the veil of secrecy that shrouds the Court from public view and analyze the justices' ideologies.[31] The beliefs of most justices can be located on the two-dimensional model of political values discussed in Chapter 1 (see Figure 1.2). Liberal justices, such as John Paul Stevens and Ruth Bader Ginsburg, choose freedom over order, and equality over freedom. Conservative justices—Antonin Scalia and Clarence Thomas, for example—choose order over freedom, and freedom over equality. These choices translate into policy preferences as the justices struggle to win votes or retain coalitions.

As in any group of people, the justices also vary in intellectual ability, advocacy skills, social graces, temperament, and the like. They argue for the support of their colleagues, offering information in the form of drafts and memoranda to explain the advantages and disadvantages of voting for or against an issue. And the justices make occasional, if not regular, use of friendship, ridicule, and appeals to patriotism to mold their colleagues' views.

The Chief Justice

The chief justice is only one of nine justices, but he has several important functions based on his authority. Apart from his role in forming the docket and directing the Court's conferences, the chief justice can also be a social leader, generating solidarity within the group. Sometimes, a chief justice can embody intellectual leadership. The chief justice also can provide policy leadership, directing the Court toward a general policy position.

When presiding at the conference, the chief justice can control the discussion of issues, although independent-minded justices are not likely to acquiesce to his views. Moreover, justices today rarely engage in a debate of the issues in the conference. Rather, they use their law clerks as ambassadors between justices' chambers and, in effect, "run the Court without talking to one another."[32]

Judicial Recruitment

Neither the Constitution nor national law imposes formal requirements for appointment to the federal courts. Once appointed, district court and appeals judges must reside in the district or circuit to which they are appointed. The president appoints judges to the federal courts, and all nominees must be confirmed by the Senate. Congress sets, but cannot lower, a judge's compensation.

State courts operate somewhat similarly. Governors appoint judges in more than half the states, often in consultation with judicial nominating commissions. In many of these states, voters decide whether judges should be retained in office. In some states, nominees must be confirmed by the state legislature. Contested elections for judgeships are unusual.

The Appointment of Federal Judges

The Constitution states that federal judges hold their commission "during good Behaviour," which in practice means for life.* A president's judicial appointments, then, are likely to survive his administration, providing a kind of political legacy. The appointment power assumes that the president is free to identify candidates and appoint judges who favor his policies.

---

* Only twelve federal judges have been impeached. Of these, seven were convicted in the Senate and removed from office. Three judges were impeached by the Senate in the 1980s. In 1992, Alcee Hastings became the first such judge to serve in Congress.

Judicial vacancies occur when sitting judges resign, retire, or die. Vacancies also arise when Congress creates new judgeships to handle increasing case-loads. In both cases, the president nominates a candidate, who must be confirmed by the Senate. The president has the help of the Justice Department, which screens candidates before the formal nomination, subjecting serious contenders to FBI investigation. The department and the Senate vie for control in the appointment of district and appeals judges.

The "Advice and Consent" of the Senate   For district and appeals vacancies, a practice called **senatorial courtesy** forces presidents to share the nomination power with members of the Senate. The Senate will not confirm a nominee who is opposed by the senior senator from the nominee's state, if that senator is a member of the president's party. The Justice Department searches for acceptable candidates and polls the appropriate senator for her or his reaction to them.

The Senate Judiciary Committee conducts a hearing for each judicial nominee. The chairperson exercises a measure of control in the appointment process that goes beyond senatorial courtesy. If a nominee is objectionable to the chair, he or she can delay a hearing or hold up other appointments until the president and the Justice Department find an alternative. However, committee chairs usually are loathe to place obstacles in a president's path, especially when they may want presidential support for their own policies and constituencies.

The American Bar Association   The American Bar Association (ABA), the biggest organization of lawyers in the United States, was involved in screening candidates for the federal bench from 1946 until 1997.[33] Its role was defined by custom, not law. At the president's behest, the ABA's Standing Committee on the Federal Judiciary routinely rated prospective appointees, using a three-value scale: "well qualified," "qualified" and "not qualified." Presidents did not always agree with the committee's judgment, but the overwhelming majority of appointees to the federal bench had the ABA's blessing. Consultation with the ABA stopped after the organization began to adopt policy positions on controversial issues like abortion and the death penalty.

Recent Presidents and the Federal Judiciary

President Carter wanted to base judicial appointments on merit and make the judiciary more representative of the general population. He appointed substantially more blacks, women, and Hispanics to the federal bench than did any of his predecessors or his immediate successors. Nearly all Carter judges were Democrats.

Clearly, President Reagan did not share Carter's second objective. Only 2 percent of Reagan's appointments were blacks and only 8 percent were women; in contrast, 14 percent of Carter's appointments were blacks and 16 percent were women (see Figure 11.2). Four percent of Reagan judges were

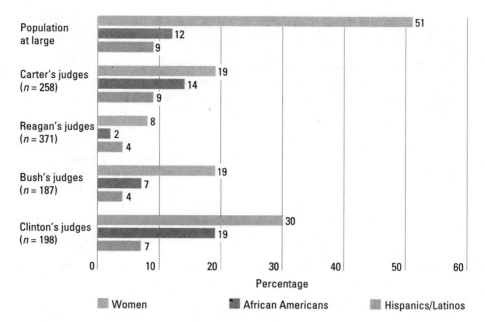

FIGURE 11.2 **Diversity on the Federal Courts**
To what extent should the courts reflect the diverse character of the population? President Carter sought to make the federal courts more representative of the population by appointing more blacks, Hispanics, and women. Reagan's appointments reflected neither the lawyer population nor the population at large. Bush's appointments were somewhat more representative than Reagan's on race and gender criteria. Clinton's nominees represented a dramatic departure in appointments, especially in race and gender. (Sources: Sheldon Goldman and Elliott Slotnick, "Clinton's First Term Judiciary: Many Bridges to Cross,"Judicature, 80 [1997], pp. 254–273; U.S. Bureau of the Census, Statistical Abstract of the United States, 1993 [Washington, D.C.: U.S. Government Printing Office, 1993], Table No. 644.)

Hispanics, compared to 6 percent of Carter judges. President Bush's record on women and minority appointments was better than Reagan's. President Clinton's appointments stood in stark contrast to his conservative predecessors'. For the first time in history, more than half of a president's judicial appointments were women or minorities.

It seems clear that political ideology, not demographics, lies at the heart of judicial appointments. The Reagan-Bush legacy is considerable. Reagan and Bush appointed nearly two-thirds of all judges sitting today.[34] They sought nominees with particular policy preferences in order to leave their stamp on the judiciary well into the twenty-first century. Clinton was animated by the same goal.

Appointment to the Supreme Court

The president is not shackled by senatorial courtesy when it comes to nominating a Supreme Court justice. However, appointments to the Court attract more intense public scrutiny than do lower-level appointments, effectively narrowing the president's options and focusing attention on the Senate's advice and consent.

Of the 146 men and 2 women nominated to the Court, 28—or about 1 in 5—have failed to receive Senate confirmation. The most important factor in the rejection of a nominee is partisan politics. The most recent nominee to be rejected on partisan and ideological grounds was Judge Robert H. Bork.

Sixteen of the twenty-two Supreme Court nominees since 1950 have had prior judicial experience in federal or state courts. This tendency toward "promotion" from within the judiciary may be based on the idea that judges' previous opinions are good predictors of their future opinions on the Supreme Court. After all, a president is handing out a powerful lifetime appointment; it makes sense to want an individual who is sympathetic to his views.

The resignation of Chief Justice Warren Burger in 1986 gave Reagan the chance to elevate Associate Justice William H. Rehnquist to the position of chief justice. Rehnquist faced stern questioning from critics during his Senate confirmation hearings. (Testimony from Supreme Court nominees is a relatively recent phenomenon; it began in 1925.) Reagan then nominated Antonin Scalia, a judge in a federal court of appeals, as Rehnquist's replacement. Rehnquist and Scalia did not try to defend their judicial records; they argued that judicial independence meant that they could not be called to account for their decisions before the Senate. Both judges also ducked discussing issues that might come to the Court for fear of compromising their impartiality. Both were confirmed by the Republican-controlled Senate.[35]

In 1987, when Justice Lewis F. Powell, Jr., resigned, Reagan had an opportunity to shift the ideological balance on the Court toward a more conservative consensus. He nominated Judge Robert Bork, a conservative, to fill the vacancy. Although Bork advocated judicial restraint, some of his critics maintained that he was really a judicial activist draped in the robes of judicial restraint. Bork's critics charged that his true purpose, spelled out in his prodigious writings, was to advance his conservative ideology from the Supreme Court.

The hearings concluded after several days of televised testimony from Judge Bork and a parade of witnesses. Liberals formed a temporary anti-Bork coalition of feminist, labor, environmental, senior citizen, abortion rights, and civil rights groups. They put aside their disagreements and mounted a massive campaign to defeat the nomination, overwhelming conservative efforts to buttress Bork. By the time the hearings ended, public opinion had shifted against him. Although his defeat was a certainty, Bork insisted that the Senate vote on his nomination, hoping for a sober discussion of his record. But the rancor never abated. Bork was defeated by a vote of 58 to 42, the biggest vote margin by which the Senate has ever rejected a Supreme Court nominee.

The rules of the game for appointment to the Supreme Court appeared to have changed in 1990 when President Bush plucked David H. Souter from relative obscurity to replace liberal justice William J. Brennan, Jr. Souter fit the model of other nominees. He had extensive judicial experience as a justice on the New Hampshire Supreme Court and recently had been appointed to the federal court of appeals. But his views on provocative topics were undetectable because he had written little and spoken less on privacy, abortion, religious liberty, and equal protection. Furthermore, during Senate confirmation hearings, he successfully avoided or deflected the most controversial topics. Souter was confirmed by the Senate, 90–9.

Recall from the beginning of this chapter that George Bush left an additional stamp on the Supreme Court when he nominated a conservative black judge, Clarence Thomas, to replace Thurgood Marshall.[36] Thomas has proved a strong ally for other conservatives on the Court.

President Clinton made his mark on the Court in 1993 when Associate Justice Byron R. White announced his retirement. Clinton chose Ruth Bader Ginsburg for the vacancy; she had been an active civil rights litigator, a law professor, and a federal judge. Some Court watchers described her as the Thurgood Marshall of women's rights because of her tireless efforts to alter the legal status of women. Ginsburg's Senate confirmation hearing revealed little of the constitutional philosophy beyond her public record. Ginsburg declined to reveal her constitutional value preferences. She cruised through a 96–3 confirmation vote in the Senate.

Justice Harry Blackmun's resignation in 1994 gave Clinton a second opportunity to leave his imprint on the Court. After six weeks of deliberation, Clinton chose federal appeals judge Stephen G. Breyer for the appointment. Breyer's moderate pragmatic views made him a consensus candidate. He sailed through tame confirmation hearings to become the 108th justice.

The Consequences of Judicial Decisions

Of all the lawsuits begun in the United States, the overwhelming majority end without a court judgment. Many civil cases are settled, or the parties give up, or the courts dismiss the suits because they are beyond the legitimate bounds of judicial resolution. Most criminal cases end with a **plea bargain**, the defendant's admission of guilt in exchange for a less severe punishment. Only about 10 percent of criminal cases in the federal district courts are tried; an equally small percentage of civil cases are adjudicated.

Furthermore, the fact that a judge sentences a criminal defendant to ten years in prison or a court holds a company liable for $11 billion in damages does not guarantee that the defendant will lose his or her freedom or the company will give up any assets. In the cases of criminal defendants, the road of appeal following trial and conviction is well traveled, and, if it accomplishes nothing else, an appeal delays the day when a defendant must go to prison. In civil cases as well, an appeal may be filed to delay the day of reckoning.

Supreme Court Rulings: Implementation and Impact

When the Supreme Court makes a decision, it relies on others to implement it, to translate policy into action. How a judgment is implemented rests in good measure on how it was crafted. Remember that the justices, in preparing their opinions, must work to hold their majorities together, to gain greater, if not unanimous support for their arguments. This forces them to compromise in their opinions, to moderate their arguments, and it introduces ambiguity into many of the policies they articulate. Ambiguous opinions affect the implementation of policy. For example, when the Supreme Court issued its order in 1955 to desegregate public school facilities "with all deliberate speed,"[37] judges who opposed the Court's policy dragged their feet in implementing it.

Because the Supreme Court confronts issues freighted with deeply felt social values or fundamental political beliefs, its decisions have impact beyond the immediate parties in a dispute. The Court's decision in *Roe v. Wade* legalizing abortion generated heated public reaction. Groups opposing abortion vowed to overturn the decision; groups favoring the freedom to obtain an abortion moved to protect the right they had won. Within eight months of the decision, more than two dozen constitutional amendments had been introduced in Congress, although none managed to carry the extraordinary majority required for passage.

Public Opinion and the Supreme Court

Democratic theorists have a difficult time reconciling a commitment to representative democracy with a judiciary that is not accountable to the electorate yet has the power to undo legislative and executive acts. This difficulty may simply be a problem for theorists, however. Policies coming from the Supreme Court, though lagging years behind public opinion, rarely seem out of line with the public's ideological choices.[38] Surveys in several controversial areas reveal that the Court seldom departs from majority sentiment or trends.[39] The evidence squarely supports the view that the Supreme Court reflects public opinion at least as often as other elected institutions do.[40]

There are at least three explanations for the Court's reflecting majority sentiment. First, the modern Court has shown deference to national laws and policies, which typically echo national public opinion. Second, the Court moves closer to public opinion during periods of crisis. Third, rulings that reflect the public view are subject to fewer changes than rulings that depart from public opinion.

The evidence also supports the view that the Court seldom influences public opinion. The Court enjoys only moderate popularity, and its decisions are not much noticed by the public. With few exceptions, there is no evidence of shifting public opinion after a Supreme Court ruling.[41]

The Courts and Models of Democracy

How far should judges stray from existing statutes and precedents? Supporters of the majoritarian model argue that judges must refrain from injecting their own values into their decisions. If the law places too much (or not enough) emphasis on equality or order, the elected legislature, not the courts, can change the law. In contrast, those who support the pluralist model maintain that the courts are a policymaking branch of government. It is thus legitimate for the individual values and interests of judges to mirror group interests and preferences and for judges to consciously attempt to advance group interests as they see fit.

The argument that our judicial system fits the pluralist model gains support from a legal procedure called a **class action**. A class action is a device for assembling the claims or defenses of similarly situated individuals so that they can be tried in a single lawsuit. A class action makes it possible for people with small individual claims and limited financial resources to aggregate their claims and resources in order to make a lawsuit viable. Since the 1940s, class action suits have been the vehicles through which groups have asserted claims involving civil rights, legislative apportionment, and environmental problems. For example, schoolchildren have sued (through their parents) under the banner of class action to rectify claimed racial discrimination by school authorities, as in *Brown v. Board of Education.*

Abetting the class action is the resurgence of state supreme courts' fashioning policies consistent with group preferences. State courts may serve as the staging areas for legal campaigns to change the law in the nation's highest court. They also exercise substantial influence over policies that affect citizens daily, including the rights and liberties enshrined in their state constitutions, statutes, and common law.[42]

Furthermore, a state court can avoid review by the U.S. Supreme Court by basing its decision solely on state law or by plainly stating that its decision rests on both state and federal law. If the U.S. Supreme Court is likely to render a restrictive view of a constitutional right, and the judges of a state court are inclined toward a more expansive view, the state judges can use the state ground to avoid Supreme Court review. In a period when the nation's highest court is moving in a decidedly conservative direction, some state courts have become safe havens for liberal values.

When judges reach decisions, they pay attention to the views of other courts, and not just courts above them in the judicial hierarchy. State and federal court opinions are the legal storehouse from which judges regularly draw their ideas. Often the issues that affect individual lives—property, family, contracts—are grist for state courts, not federal courts. State courts have become arenas for political conflict with litigants—individually or in groups—vying for their preferred policies. The multiplicity of the nation's court system, with overlapping state and federal responsibilities, provides alternative points of access for individuals and groups to present and argue their claims. This description of the courts fits the pluralist model of government.

Summary

The power of judicial review, claimed by the Supreme Court in 1803, placed the judiciary on equal footing with Congress and the president. The principle of checks and balances can restrain judicial power through several means, such as constitutional amendments and impeachment. But restrictions have been infrequent, and the federal courts exercise considerable influence through judicial review and statutory construction.

The federal court system has three tiers. At the bottom are district courts, where litigation begins and most disputes end. In the middle are courts of appeals. At the top is the Supreme Court. The ability of judges to make policy increases as they move up the pyramid from trial courts to appellate courts to the Supreme Court.

The Supreme Court, free to draft its agenda through the discretionary control of its docket, harmonizes conflicting interpretations of national law and articulates constitutional rights. It is helped at this crucial stage by the solicitor general, who represents the executive branch of government before the Court. The solicitor general's influence affects the justices' choice of cases to review.

Political allegiance and complementary values are necessary conditions for appointment by the president to the coveted position of judge. The president and senators from the president's party share the power of appointment of federal district and appellate judges. The president has more leeway in the nomination of Supreme Court justices, although all nominees must be confirmed by the Senate.

Courts inevitably fashion policy for each of the states and for the nation. They provide multiple points of access for individuals to pursue their preferences and so fit the pluralist model of democracy. Furthermore, the class action enables people with small individual claims and limited financial resources to pursue their goals in court, reinforcing the pluralist model.

Judges confront both the original and the modern dilemmas of government. The impact of their decisions can extend well beyond a single case. Some democratic theorists are troubled by the expansion of judicial power. But today's courts fit within the pluralist model and usually are in step with what the public wants.

As the U.S. Supreme Court heads in a more moderate direction, some state supreme courts have become safe havens for liberal policies on civil rights and civil liberties. State court systems have overlapping state and national responsibilities, offering groups and individuals many access points to present and argue their claims.

Key Terms

judicial review	rule of four
criminal case	solicitor general
civil case	*amicus curiae* brief
common (judge-made) law	judicial restraint
U.S. district courts	judicial activism
U.S. courts of appeals	judgment
precedent	argument
stare decisis	concurrence
original jurisdiction	dissent
appellate jurisdiction	senatorial courtesy
federal question	plea bargain
docket	class action

Selected Readings

Baum, Lawrence. *American Courts: Process and Policy.* 3d ed. Boston: Houghton Mifflin, 1994. A comprehensive review of trial and appellate courts in the United States that addresses their activities, describes their procedures, and explores the processes that affect them.

Coffin, Frank M. *On Appeal: Court, Lawyering, and Judging.* New York: Norton, 1994. A close look at the workings of a federal appellate court and the ways in which its chief judge reaches decisions.

Friedman, Lawrence M. *American Law: An Introduction.* 2d ed. New York: Norton, 1998. A clear introduction to the bewildering complexity of the law. Explains how law is made and administered.

Goldman, Sheldon. *Picking Federal Judges: Lower Court Selection from Roosevelt Through Reagan.* New Haven, Conn.: Yale University Press, 1997. A historically rich account of how Presidents Roosevelt through Reagan selected federal district and appellate court judges. A wealth of data and illuminating interviews with key actors describe not only the process of selection, and how it has changed over time, but also what types of judges, demographically and ideologically, each president sought to appoint.

World Wide Web Resources

OYEZ. The U.S. Supreme Court has recorded its public proceedings from 1955 to the present. "Oyez. Oyez. Oyez."—a Web site developed at Northwestern University—contains an archive of the most important arguments and decisions. Download and install the free player from RealAudio (www.realaudio .com). Navigate to the OYEZ site, and the audio files will stream in real time to your desktop.
<oyez.nwu.edu>

The *Federal Judiciary Homepage* is designed "to function as a clearinghouse for information from and about the Judicial Branch of the U.S. Government." It contains extensive information about the history and work of the judicial branch, reports on court-approved wiretaps, and key statistics on the work of American courts.
<www.uscourts.gov>

The *Supreme Court* Web site, established in 2000, contains the calenders and docket of the Court, information on arguments, and guidelines for attorneys.
<www.supremecourtus.gov>

FINDLAW is a premier, all-in-one archive of current legal news stories and an authoritative repository of court opinions for federal and state courts. Supreme Court opinions go back to 1891 and are paginated to the official *U.S. Reports.*
<www.findlaw.com>

The Legal Information Institute, Cornell University. The institute maintains a megasite of law-related materials including a searchable database of Supreme Court opinions since 1990.
<www.law.cornell.edu>

12

Civil Liberties and Civil Rights

University of Michigan student Jake Baker posted shockingly explicit sex stories to an electronic bulletin board, one of the thousands of news groups that form the worldwide collection of networked information called Usenet. Baker wrote fictional fantasies that frequently included rape and violence to women and girls. In one story in which Baker graphically described the torture, rape, and murder of a woman, he gave the victim the name of a classmate at the University of Michigan.[1]

Baker's stories could be read by millions of people every day. Some read them and moved on. Others were appalled and complained. Eventually, university officials acted. Baker admitted writing the stories, waived his right to an attorney, and provided his e-mail password so officials could read his electronic mail. Shortly thereafter, the university president suspended Baker without a hearing. He was told to pack his bags and leave the university immediately.[2]

Had Baker committed a crime? If so, what was it? Writing fiction is not a crime, even when it describes harmful acts. However, after reading his private e-mail, prosecutors decided to charge Baker with making threats to kill or kidnap in electronic messages transmitted by the Internet to a correspondent in Canada. U.S. commerce law prohibits the interstate or international transmission of threats to injure or kidnap a victim. Baker became the first person charged with making e-mail threats over the Internet. The law carries a penalty of up to five years of imprisonment.

The government prosecuted Baker to maintain order—that is, to ensure the peace and safety of the community. The government viewed Baker's private correspondence as evidence of a threat of imminent harm. Baker's attorney, joined by the American Civil Liberties Union, urged dismissal of the government's case. They maintained that the free-speech clause of the First Amendment protected Baker from government action. A federal judge, Avern Cohn, sat at the center of the controversy, holding in the balance Baker's freedom and the community's demand for order. He held that, in the absence of an actual threat to act, Baker's communications were protected by the First Amendment.[3]

Order, of course, is not the only value held by the public. Colorado contractor Randy Pech believed that free competition meant that the lowest bidder would get the job when his company, Adarand Constructors, bid for work installing highway guardrails in Colorado. However, of the five companies that constructed and maintained the state's guardrails, Adarand Constructors was the only one owned by a white person, and each of the other four companies had been designated a "Disadvantaged Business Enterprise," or DBE. The government's objective in designating some businesses as DBEs was to promote affirmative action.

Affirmative action is a commitment by a business, employer, school, or other public or private institution to expand opportunities for women, blacks, Hispanic Americans, and members of other minority groups. Affirmative action embraces a wide range of policies, from special recruitment efforts to numerical goals and quotas.

In 1987, Congress passed a law requiring the U.S. Department of Transportation to set aside at least 10 percent of its highway construction funds for businesses owned by women or members of designated racial minorities. The set-aside policy restricts free competition in order to give DBEs business. This meant that in Colorado a DBE did not have to submit the lowest bid to win the guardrail contract if Randy Pech's company was the lowest bidder.

In 1989, Pech submitted the lowest bid for a guardrail job, but the general contractor awarded the contract to Gonzales Construction, a DBE. Pech challenged the law, claiming that it unconstitutionally discriminated on the basis of race.[4] Pech believed that the government's actions violated his constitutional right to equal protection.

The Fourteenth Amendment declares that no *state* shall deny any person equal protection. Although there is no equivalent constitutional provision compelling the national government to treat persons equally, the Supreme Court has held that the Fifth Amendment's due process guarantee embraces the equal protection principle. Was the national government's affirmative action policy consistent with the Supreme Court's conception of equal protection? We will explore the Court's answer later in this chapter.

In the case of Randy Pech, the government acted to promote equality, but the government's policy to advance minority- and women-owned businesses disrupted the free competition of the marketplace and thereby imposed an unequal burden on Randy Pech. As we shall see later in this chapter, the conflict intensifies when we recognize that Americans advocate competing conceptions of equality.

How well do the courts respond to clashes that pit freedom against order in some cases and freedom against equality in others? Are freedom, order, or equality ever unconditional? In this chapter, we explore some value conflicts that the judiciary has resolved. You will be able to judge from the decisions in these cases whether American government has met the challenge of democracy by finding the appropriate balance between freedom and order and between freedom and equality.

The value conflicts described in this chapter revolve around claims or entitlements that rest on law. Although we concentrate here on conflicts over constitutional issues, the Constitution is not the only source of people's rights. Government at all levels can—and does—create rights through laws written by legislatures and regulations issued by bureaucracies.

We begin this chapter with the Bill of Rights and the freedoms it protects. Then we take a closer look at the role of the First Amendment in the original conflict between freedom and order. Next we explore how the Bill of Rights applies to the states under the Fourteenth Amendment. Then we examine the Ninth Amendment and its relationship to issues of personal autonomy. We then introduce two conceptions of equality and use these conceptions to explore segregation, the civil rights movement, gender equality, and affirmative action.

The Bill of Rights

You may remember from Chapter 2 that the omission of a bill of rights was the most important obstacle to the adoption of the Constitution by the states. Eventually, the First Congress approved twelve amendments and sent them to the states for ratification. In 1791, ten were ratified, and the nation had a bill of rights.

The Bill of Rights imposed limits on the national government but not on the state governments.* During the next seventy-seven years, litigants pressed the Supreme Court to extend the amendments' restraints to the states, but the Court refused until well after the adoption of the Fourteenth Amendment in 1868. Before then, protection from repressive state government had to come from state bills of rights.

The U.S. Constitution guarantees Americans numerous liberties and rights. In this chapter we explore a number of them. We will define and distinguish between *civil liberties* and *civil rights* (although on some occasions, we use the terms interchangeably). **Civil liberties** are freedoms that are guaranteed to the individual. The guarantees take the form of restraints on government. For example, the First Amendment declares that "Congress shall make no law . . . abridging the freedom of speech." Civil liberties declare what the government cannot do. In contrast, civil rights declare what the government must do or provide.

Civil rights are powers or privileges that are guaranteed to the individual and protected against arbitrary removal at the hands of the government or other individuals. The right to vote and the right to a jury trial in criminal cases are civil rights embedded in the Constitution. Today, civil rights also embrace laws that further certain values. The Civil Rights Act of 1964, for example, furthered the value of equality by establishing the right to nondiscrimination in places of public accommodations and the right to equal employment opportunity.

The Bill of Rights lists both civil liberties and civil rights. When we refer to the "rights and liberties" guaranteed by the Constitution, we mean the protections enshrined in the Bill of Rights and in the first section of the Fourteenth

---

* Congress considered more than one hundred amendments in its first session. One that was not approved would have limited the power of the states to infringe on the rights of conscience, speech, press, and jury trial in criminal cases. James Madison thought this amendment was the "most valuable" of the list, but it failed to muster a two-thirds vote in the Senate.

Amendment.[5] The list includes freedom of religion, freedom of speech and of the press, the right to assemble peaceably and to petition the government, the right to bear arms, the rights of the criminally accused, the requirement of due process, and the equal protection of the laws.

Freedom of Religion

> Congress shall make no law respecting an establishment of religion, or prohibiting the free exercise thereof.

Religious freedom was very important to the colonies, and later to the states. That importance is reflected in its position in the Bill of Rights, in the very first amendment. The First Amendment guarantees freedom of religion in two clauses: the **establishment clause** prohibits laws establishing religion; the **free-exercise clause** prevents the government from interfering with the exercise of religion. Together they ensure that the government can neither promote nor inhibit religious beliefs or practices.

At the time of the Constitutional Convention, many Americans, especially in New England, maintained that government could and should foster religion, specifically Protestantism. However, many more Americans agreed that this was an issue for state governments, that the national government had no authority to meddle in religious affairs. The religion clauses were drafted in this spirit.[6]

The Supreme Court has refused to interpret the religion clauses definitively. The result is an amalgam of rulings, the cumulative effect of which is the idea that freedom to believe is unlimited but freedom to practice a belief can be limited. Religion cannot benefit directly from government actions (for example, government cannot make contributions to churches or synagogues), but it can benefit indirectly from government actions (for example, government can supply books on secular subjects for use in all schools—public, private, and parochial).

The Establishment Clause

The provision that "Congress shall make no law respecting an establishment of religion" bars government sponsorship or support of religious activity. The Supreme Court has consistently held that the establishment clause requires government to maintain a position of neutrality toward religions and to maintain that position in cases that involve choices between religion and nonreligion. However, the Court never has interpreted the clause as barring all assistance that incidentally aids religious institutions.

Government Support of Religion   In 1879, the Supreme Court contended, quoting Thomas Jefferson, that the establishment clause erected "a wall of separation between church and state."[7] That wall was breached somewhat in 1947, when the justices upheld a local government program that provided free transportation to parochial school students.[8] The breach seemed to widen in 1968, when the Court held constitutional a government program in which parochial school students borrowed state-purchased textbooks.[9] The objective of the program, reasoned the majority, was to further educational opportunity. The students, not the schools, borrowed the books, and the parents, not the church, realized the benefits.

But in 1971, in **Lemon v. Kurtzman**, the Court struck down a state program that would have helped pay the salaries of teachers hired by parochial schools to give instruction in secular subjects.[10] The justices proposed a three-pronged test for determining the constitutionality of government programs and laws under the establishment clause:

• They must have a secular purpose (such as lending books to parochial school students).

• Their primary effect must not be to advance or inhibit religion.

• They must not entangle the government excessively with religion.

A program or law missing any prong would be unconstitutional.

The program at issue in *Lemon* failed on the last ground. To be sure that the secular teachers did not include religious instruction in their lessons, the government would have needed to constantly monitor them. However, in a 1997 test of the establishment clause, the Court held that "A federally funded program providing supplemental, remedial instruction to disadvantaged children on a neutral basis is not invalid under the Establishment Clause when such instruction is given on the premises of sectarian schools by government employees pursuant to a program containing safeguards" such as that of a New York program that, in the eyes of the Court, did not "run afoul of the three primary criteria" cited in *Lemon*.[11]

School Prayer   The Supreme Court has consistently equated prayer in public schools with government support of religion. In 1962, it struck down the daily reading of this twenty-two-word nondenominational prayer in New York's public schools: "Almighty God, we acknowledge our dependence upon Thee, and we beg Thy blessings upon us, our parents, our teachers, and our country."[12]

In the years since that decision, new challenges on the issue of school prayer have continued to find their way to the Supreme Court. In 1985, the Court struck down a series of Alabama statutes requiring a moment of silence for meditation or voluntary prayer in elementary schools.[13] In 1992, the Court ruled, 5 to 4, that public schools may not include nondenominational prayers in graduation ceremonies.[14]

The establishment clause creates a problem for government. Support for all religions at the expense of nonreligion seems to pose the least risk to social order. Tolerance of the dominant religion at the expense of other religions risks minority discontent, but support for no religion (neutrality between religion and nonreligion) risks majority discontent.

The Free-Exercise Clause

The free-exercise clause of the First Amendment states that "Congress shall make no law . . . prohibiting the free exercise [of religion]." The Supreme Court has struggled to avoid absolute interpretations of this restriction so as not to violate its complement, the establishment clause. An example: Suppose Congress grants exemptions from military service to individuals who have religious scruples against war. These exemptions could be construed as a violation of the establishment clause because they favor some religious groups over others. But if Congress forces conscientious objectors to fight—to violate their religious beliefs—the government would run afoul of the free-exercise clause. In fact, Congress has granted military draftees such exemptions. But the Supreme Court has avoided a conflict between the establishment and free-exercise clauses by equating religious objection to war with any deeply held humanistic opposition to it.[15]

In the free-exercise cases, the justices have distinguished religious beliefs from actions based on those beliefs. Beliefs are inviolate, beyond the reach of government control. But the First Amendment does not protect antisocial actions. Consider conflicting values about working on the Sabbath and using drugs in religious sacraments.

Working on the Sabbath   The modern era of free-exercise thinking begins with ***Sherbert v. Verner*** (1963). Adeil Sherbert was a Seventh-Day Adventist who was disqualified from receiving unemployment benefits after declining a job that required working on Saturday, which is the Adventist Sabbath. In a 7–2 decision, the Supreme Court ruled that the disqualification imposed an impermissible burden on Sherbert's free exercise of religion. The First Amendment, declared the majority, protected observance as well as belief. A neutral law that burdens the free exercise of religion is subject to **strict scrutiny**. This means the law may be upheld only if the government can demonstrate that the law is justified by a "compelling governmental interest" and is the least restrictive means for achieving that interest.[16]

Using Drugs as Religious Sacraments   Partaking of illegal substances as part of a religious sacrament forces believers to violate the law. For example, Rastafarians and members of the Ethiopian Zion Coptic Church smoke marijuana in the belief that it is the body and blood of Christ. Obviously, taking to an extreme the freedom to practice religion can result in license to engage in illegal conduct. And even when such conduct stems from deeply held convictions, government resistance to it is understandable. The inevitable result is a clash between religious freedom and social order.

The courts used the compelling-government-interest test for many years and on that basis invalidated most laws restricting free exercise. But in 1990, the Supreme Court abruptly and unexpectedly rejected its long-standing rule, tipping the balance in favor of social order. In *Employment Division v. Smith,* two members of the Native American Church sought an exemption from an Oregon law that made the possession or use of peyote a crime.[17] (Peyote is a cactus that contains the hallucinogen mescaline. Native Americans have used it for centuries in their religious ceremonies.) Oregon rejected the two church members' applications for unemployment benefits after they were dismissed from their drug-counseling jobs for using peyote. Oregon believed it had a compelling interest in proscribing the use of certain drugs according to its own drug laws.

Justice Antonin Scalia, writing for the 6–3 majority, examined the conflict between freedom and order through the lens of majoritarian democratic thought. He observed that the Court has never held that an individual's religious beliefs excuse him or her from compliance with an otherwise valid law prohibiting conduct that government is free to regulate. Allowing exceptions to every state law or regulation affecting religion "would open the prospect of constitutionally required exemptions from civic obligations of almost every conceivable kind." Scalia cited as examples compulsory military service, payment of taxes, vaccination requirements, and child-neglect laws. Laws that indirectly restrict religious practices are acceptable; only laws aimed at religious groups are constitutionally prohibited.

The political response to *Employment Division v. Smith* was an example of pluralism in action. An unusual coalition of religious and nonreligious groups (including the National Association of Evangelicals, the American Civil Liberties Union, the National Islamic Prison Foundation, and B'nai B'rith) organized to restore the more restrictive strict scrutiny test. The alliance regained in Congress what it had lost in the Supreme Court. In 1993, President Bill Clinton signed into law the Religious Freedom Restoration Act (RFRA). The law once again required government to satisfy the strict-scrutiny standard before it could institute measures that interfere with religious practices. However, the Supreme Court struck back in 1997, declaring the act unconstitutional in *City of Boerne v. Flores*. In the 6–3 decision the Supreme Court declared that Congress lacked the power to change the meaning of the Constitution's free-exercise clause when it enacted the RFRA.[18]

Freedom of Expression

> Congress shall make no law . . . abridging the freedom of speech, or of the press; or the right of the people peaceably to assemble, and to petition the government for a redress of grievances.

James Madison introduced the initial versions of the speech clause and the press clause of the First Amendment in the House of Representatives in June 1789. One was merged with the religion and peaceable assembly clauses to yield the First Amendment.

The sparse language of the First Amendment seems perfectly clear: "Congress shall make no law . . . abridging the freedom of speech, or of the press." Yet a majority of the Supreme Court has never agreed that this "most majestic guarantee" is absolutely inviolable.[19] Historians have long debated the framers' intentions regarding these **free-expression clauses**. The dominant view is that the clauses confer the right to unrestricted discussion of public affairs.[20] Other scholars, examining much the same evidence, conclude that few, if any, of the framers clearly understood the clause; moreover, they insist that the First Amendment does not rule out prosecution for seditious statements (statements inciting insurrection).[21]

Careful analysis of the records of the period supports the view that the press clause prohibited only the imposition of **prior restraint**—censorship before publication. Publishers could not claim protection from punishment if works that had already been published were later deemed improper, mischievous, or illegal. Today, however, the clauses are deemed to bar not only most forms of prior restraint but also after-the-fact prosecution for political and other discourse.

The Supreme Court has evolved two approaches to the resolution of claims based on the free-expression clauses. First, government can regulate or punish the advocacy of ideas, but only if it can prove an intent to promote lawless action and demonstrate that a high probability exists that such action will occur. Second, government may impose reasonable restrictions on the means for communicating ideas, which can incidentally discourage free expression.

Suppose that a political party advocates nonpayment of personal income taxes. Government cannot regulate or punish that party for advocating nonpayment, because the standards of proof—that the act be directed to inciting or producing imminent lawless action and that the act be judged likely to produce such action—do not apply. But government can impose restrictions on the way the party's candidates communicate what they are advocating. Government can bar them from blaring messages from loudspeakers in residential neighborhoods at 3:00 A.M.

Freedom of Speech

The starting point for any modern analysis of free speech is the **clear and present danger test** formulated by Justice Oliver Wendell Holmes in the Supreme Court's unanimous decision in *Schenck v. United States* (1919). Charles T. Schenck and his fellow defendants were convicted under a federal criminal statute for attempting to disrupt World War I military recruitment by distributing leaflets claiming that conscription was unconstitutional. The government believed this behavior threatened the public order. At the core of the Court's opinion, as Holmes wrote, was the view that

> the character of every act depends upon the circumstances in which it is done. . . . The most stringent protection of free speech would not protect a man in falsely shouting fire in a theatre and causing a panic. . . . The question in every case is whether the words used are used in such circumstances and are of such a nature as to create a *clear and present danger* that they will bring about the substantive evils that Congress has a right to prevent. It is a question of proximity and degree. When a nation is at war many things that might be said in time of peace are such a hindrance to its effort that their utterance will not be endured so long as men fight and that no Court could regard them as protected by any constitutional right. [Emphasis added.][22]

Because the actions of the defendants in *Schenck* were deemed to create a clear and present danger to the United States at that time, the Supreme Court upheld the defendants' convictions. The clear and present danger test helps to distinguish the advocacy of ideas, which is protected, from incitement, which is not.

In 1925 the Court issued a landmark decision in *Gitlow v. New York*.[23] Benjamin Gitlow was arrested for distributing copies of a "left-wing manifesto" that called for the establishment of socialism through strikes and class action of any form. Gitlow was convicted under a state criminal anarchy law; Schenck had been convicted under a federal law. For the first time, the Court assumed that the First Amendment speech and press provisions applied to the states through the due process clause of the Fourteenth Amendment. Still, a majority of the justices affirmed Gitlow's conviction.

The protection of advocacy faced yet another challenge in 1948, when eleven members of the Communist Party were charged with violating the Smith Act—a federal law making the advocacy of force or violence against the United States a criminal offense. The leaders were convicted, although the government introduced no evidence that they actually had urged people to commit specific violent acts. The Supreme Court mustered a majority for its decision to uphold the convictions under the Smith Act, but it could not get a majority to agree on the reasons in support of that decision. Four justices announced the plurality opinion in 1951, arguing that the government's interest was substantial enough to warrant criminal penalties.[24] The justices interpreted the threat to government to be the gravity of the advocated action "discounted by its improbability." In other words, a single soap-box orator advocating revolution stands a low chance of success, and a well-organized, highly disciplined political movement advocating revolution in the tinderbox of unstable political conditions stands a greater chance of success. In broadening the meaning of "clear and present danger," the Court held that the government was justified in acting preventively rather than waiting until revolution was about to occur.

By 1969, the pendulum had swung back in the other direction. That year, in ***Brandenburg v. Ohio***, a unanimous decision extended the freedom of speech to new limits.[25] Clarence Brandenburg, the leader of the Ohio Ku Klux Klan, had been convicted under a state law for advocating racial strife at a Klan rally. His comments, filmed by a television crew, included threats against government officials. The Court reversed Brandenburg's conviction because the government had failed to prove that the danger was real. The Court went even further and declared that threatening speech is protected by the First Amendment unless the government can prove that such advocacy is "directed to inciting or producing imminent lawless action and is likely to produce such action."

Symbolic Expression   Symbolic expression, or nonverbal communication, generally receives less protection than pure speech. But the courts have upheld certain types of symbolic expression. ***Tinker v. Des Moines Independent County School District*** (1969) involved three public school students who wore black arm bands to school to protest the Vietnam War. Principals in their school district had prohibited the wearing of arm bands on the grounds that such conduct would provoke a disturbance; the district suspended the students. The Supreme Court overturned the suspensions. Justice Abe Fortas declared for the majority that the principals had failed to show that the forbidden conduct would substantially interfere with appropriate school discipline:

> Undifferentiated fear or apprehension is not enough to overcome the right to freedom of expression. Any departure from absolute regimentation may cause trouble. Any variation from the majority's opinion may inspire fear. Any word spoken, in class, in the lunchroom, or on the campus, that deviates from the views of another person may start an argument or cause a disturbance. But our Constitution says we must take this risk.[26]

The flag is an object of deep veneration in our society, yet its desecration is also a form of symbolic expression protected by the First Amendment. In 1989, a divided Supreme Court struck down a Texas law that barred the desecration of venerated objects. Congress then enacted the Flag Protection Act of 1989 in an attempt to overcome the constitutional flaws of the Texas decision.

The Supreme Court nullified that federal flag-burning statute in *United States v. Eichman* (1990). By a vote of 5 to 4, the justices reaffirmed First Amendment protection for all expressions of political ideas. The vote was identical to the vote in the Texas case, with conservative justices Scalia and Kennedy joining with the liberal wing to forge an unusual majority. The majority placed the same emphasis on freedom that it had in the Texas case, including a quotation from its earlier opinion: "'If there is a bedrock principle underlying the First Amendment, it is that the Government may not prohibit the expression of an idea simply because society finds the idea itself offensive or disagreeable.' Punishing desecration of the flag dilutes the very freedom that makes this emblem so revered, and worth revering."[27]

In that opinion, the Court majority relied on the *substantive* conception of democratic theory, which embodies the principle of freedom of speech. Yet a May 1990 poll revealed that most people wanted to outlaw flag burning as a means of expressing political opinions and that a clear majority favored a constitutional amendment to that end.[28] The *procedural* conception of democratic theory states that government should do what the people want, and in the case of flag burning, the people are willing to abandon the freedom-of-speech principle embodied in the substantive view of democracy.

Free Speech Versus Order: Obscenity The Supreme Court has always viewed obscene material—words, music, books, magazines, films—as outside the bounds of constitutional protection, which means that states may regulate or even ban obscenity. However, difficulties arise in determining what is obscene and what is not.

In *Miller v. California* (1973), its most recent major attempt to clarify constitutional standards governing obscenity, the Court declared that a work—play, film, or book—is obscene and may be regulated by government if (1) the work taken as a whole appeals to prurient interest ("prurient" means having a tendency to excite lustful thoughts); (2) the work portrays sexual conduct in a patently offensive way; and (3) the work taken as a whole lacks serious literary, artistic, political, or scientific value.[29] Local community standards govern application of the first and second prongs of the *Miller* test.

In 1996, Congress passed the Communications Decency Act, which made it a crime for a person knowingly to circulate "patently offensive" sexual material to Internet sites accessible to those under eighteen years old. Is this an acceptable way to protect children from offensive material (perhaps like Jake Baker's stories), or is it a muzzle on free speech? A federal court quickly declared the act unconstitutional. In an opinion of over two hundred pages, the court observed that "just as the strength of the Internet is chaos, so the strength of our liberty depends on the chaos and cacophony of the unfettered speech the First Amendment protects."[30]

The Supreme Court upheld the lower court's ruling in June 1997 in *Reno v. ACLU.*[31] The Court's nearly unanimous opinion was a broad affirmation of free-speech rights in cyberspace, arguing that the Internet was more analogous to print media than to television, and thus even indecent material on the Internet was entitled to First Amendment protection.

Feminism, Free Expression, and Equality   Traditionally, civil liberties conflict with demands for social order. However, civil liberties can also conflict with demands for equality. In the 1980s, city officials in Indianapolis, Indiana, influenced by feminist theorists, invoked equality principles to justify legislation restricting freedom of expression. Specifically, they argued that pornography is sex discrimination.[32] The ordinance banned pornographic material according to the following argument: Government interest in equality outweighs any First Amendment interest in communication. Pornography affects thoughts; it conditions society to subordinate women. An ordinance regulating expression will regulate and control the resulting unacceptable conduct.

United States District Court judge Sarah Evans Barker confronted the tradeoff between equality and freedom in a pluralist democracy. Judge Barker declared the ordinance unconstitutional, stating that it went beyond the categories of unprotected expression (such as child pornography) to suppress otherwise protected expression.

Interest groups that use the democratic process to carve exceptions to the First Amendment benefit at the expense of everyone's rights. Although efforts to restrict behavior that leads to humiliation and degradation of women may be necessary and desirable, "free speech, rather than being the enemy," wrote Judge Barker, "is a long-tested and worthy ally. To deny free speech in order to engineer social change in the name of accomplishing a greater good for one sector of our society erodes the freedom of all."[33] In this recasting of a freedom-versus-order issue into a freedom-versus-equality framework, Judge Barker's tradeoff protected freedom. Her judgment was affirmed by the U.S. Court of Appeals in 1985 and affirmed without argument by the Supreme Court in 1986. However, in the next confrontation— in a pluralist democracy there will surely be others—equality may prove the victor.

Freedom of the Press

The First Amendment guarantees that government "shall make no law . . . abridging the freedom . . . of the press." Although it originally was adopted as a restriction on the national government, since 1931 the Supreme Court has held the free-press guarantee to apply to state and local governments as well.

The ability to collect and report information without government interference was (and still is) thought to be essential to a free society. The print media continue to use and defend the freedom conferred on them by the framers. However, the electronic media have had to accept some government regulation stemming from the scarcity of broadcast frequencies (see Chapter 4).

Defamation of Character Libel is the written defamation of character.* A person who believes his or her name and character have been harmed by false statements in a publication can institute a lawsuit against the publication and seek monetary compensation for the damage. Such a lawsuit can impose limits on freedom of expression; at the same time, false statements impinge on the rights of individuals. In a landmark decision in ***New York Times v. Sullivan*** (1964), the Supreme Court declared that freedom of the press takes precedence—at least when the defamed individual is a public official.[34] The Court unanimously agreed that the First Amendment protects the publication of all statements—even false ones—about the conduct of public officials except when statements are made with actual malice (with knowledge that they are false or in reckless disregard of their truth or falsity). Citing John Stuart Mill's 1859 treatise *On Liberty*, the Court declared that "even a false statement may be deemed to make a valuable contribution to public debate, since it brings about the clearer perception and livelier impression of truth, produced by its collision with error."

Three years later, the Court extended this protection to apply to suits brought by any public figures, whether a government official or not. **Public figures** are people who assume roles of prominence in the affairs of society or who thrust themselves to the forefront of public controversy—officials, actors, writers, television personalities, and others. These people must show actual malice on the part of the publisher that prints false statements about them. Because the burden of proof is so great, few plaintiffs prevail.

Prior Restraint and the Press In the United States, freedom of the press has primarily meant protection from prior restraint, or censorship. The Supreme Court's first encounter with a law imposing prior restraint on a newspaper was in *Near v. Minnesota* (1931).[35] In Minneapolis Jay Near published a scandal sheet in which he attacked local officials, charging that they were in league with gangsters.[36] Minnesota officials obtained an injunction to prevent Near from publishing his newspaper under a state law that allowed such action against periodicals deemed "malicious, scandalous, and defamatory."

---

*Slander is the oral defamation of character. The durability of the written word usually means that libel is a more serious accusation than slander.

The Supreme Court struck down the law, declaring that prior restraint is a special burden on a free press. Chief Justice Charles Evans Hughes forcefully articulated the need for a vigilant, unrestrained press: "The fact that the liberty of the press may be abused by miscreant purveyors of scandal does not make any the less necessary the immunity of the press from previous restraint in dealing with official misconduct." Although the Court acknowledged that prior restraint may be permissible in exceptional circumstances, it did not specify those circumstances, nor has it yet done so.

Consider another case, which occurred during a war, a time when the tension between government-imposed order and individual freedom is often at a peak. In 1971, Daniel Ellsberg, a special assistant in the Pentagon, delivered portions of a classified U.S. Department of Defense study to the *New York Times* and the *Washington Post*. By making the documents public, he hoped to discredit the Vietnam War and thereby end it. The U.S. Department of Justice sought to restrain the *Times* and the *Post* from publishing the documents, contending that publication would prolong the war and embarrass the government. The case was quickly brought before the Supreme Court.

Three days later, in a 6–3 decision in **New York Times v. United States** (1971), the Court concluded that the government had not met the heavy burden of proving that immediate, inevitable, and irreparable harm would follow publication.[37] The majority expressed its view in a brief unsigned opinion; individual and collective concurring and dissenting views added nine opinions to the decision. Two justices maintained that the First Amendment offers absolute protection against government censorship, no matter what the situation. But the other justices left the door ajar for the imposition of prior restraint in the most extreme and compelling of circumstances.

Freedom of Expression Versus Maintaining Order   The courts have consistently held that freedom of the press does not override the requirements of law enforcement. A grand jury called a Louisville, Kentucky, reporter, who had researched and written an article about drug-related activities, and asked him to identify people he had seen in possession of marijuana or in the act of processing it. The reporter refused to testify, maintaining that freedom of the press shielded him from inquiry. In a closely divided decision, the Supreme Court in 1972 rejected this position.[38] The Court declared that no exception exists to the rule that all citizens have a duty to give their government whatever testimony they are capable of giving.

The Supreme Court again confronted the conflict between free expression and order in 1988.[39] The principal of a St. Louis high school had deleted articles on divorce and teenage pregnancy from the school's newspaper on the grounds that the articles invaded the privacy of the individuals who were the focus of the stories. Three student editors claimed that the principal's censorship interfered with the newspaper's function as a public forum, a role protected by the First Amendment. The principal maintained that the newspaper was an extension of classroom instruction and was thus not protected by the First Amendment.

In a 5–3 decision, the Court upheld the principal's actions in sweeping terms. Educators may limit speech within the confines of the school curriculum and speech that might seem to bear the approval of the school, provided their actions serve a "valid educational purpose."

The Rights to Assemble Peaceably and to Petition the Government

The final clause of the First Amendment states that "Congress shall make no law . . . abridging . . . the right of the people peaceably to assemble, and to petition the Government for a redress of grievances." The framers meant that the people have the right to assemble peaceably *in order to* petition the government. Today, however, the right to assemble peaceably is equated with the right of free speech and a free press, independent of whether or not the government is petitioned. Precedent has merged these rights and made them equally indivisible.[40] Government cannot prohibit peaceful political meetings and cannot brand as criminals those who organize, lead, and attend such meetings.[41]

The Right to Bear Arms

The Second Amendment declares

> A well-regulated militia being necessary to the security of a free State, the right of the people to keep and bear arms shall not be infringed.

Gun-control advocates assert that the amendment protects the right of the states to maintain *collective* militias. Gun-use advocates assert that the amendment protects the right of *individuals* to own and use guns. There are good arguments on both sides.

Federal firearms regulations did not come into being until Prohibition, so the Supreme Court had little to say on the matter. In 1939, however, a unanimous Court upheld a 1934 federal law requiring the taxation and registration of machine guns and sawed-off shotguns. The Court held that the Second Amendment protects a citizen's right to own ordinary militia weapons; sawed-off shotguns did not qualify for protection.[42] Restrictions on gun ownership (for example, registration and licensing) have passed constitutional muster. However, outright prohibitions on gun ownership (for example, a ban on handguns) might run afoul of the amendment.

Applying the Bill of Rights to the States

The major purpose of the Constitution was to structure the division of power between the national government and the state governments. Even before it was amended, the Constitution set some limits on both the nation and the states with regard to citizens' rights. It barred both governments from passing **bills of attainder**, laws that make an individual guilty of a crime without a trial. Both were also prohibited from enacting **ex post facto laws**, laws that declare an action a crime after it has been performed. And it barred both nation and states from impairing the **obligation of contracts**, the obligation of the parties in a contract to carry out its terms.

Although initially the Bill of Rights seemed to apply only to the national government, various litigants pressed the claim that its guarantees also applied to the states. In response to one such claim, Chief Justice John Marshall affirmed that the provisions of the Bill of Rights served only to limit national authority. "Had the framers of these amendments intended them to be limitations on the powers of the state governments," wrote Marshall, "they would have . . . expressed that intention."[43]

Change came with the Fourteenth Amendment, which was adopted in 1868. The due process clause of that amendment is the linchpin that holds the states to the provisions of the Bill of Rights.

The Fourteenth Amendment: Due Process of Law

Section 1 . . . No State shall make or enforce any law which shall abridge the privileges or immunities of citizens of the United States; nor shall any State deprive any person of life, liberty, or property, without due process of law. . . .

Most freedoms protected in the Bill of Rights today apply as limitations on the states. And many of the standards that limit the national government serve equally to limit state governments. These changes have been achieved through the Supreme Court's interpretation of the due process clause of the Fourteenth Amendment: "nor shall any State deprive any person of life, liberty, or property, without due process of law." The clause has two central meanings. First, it requires the government to adhere to appropriate procedures. Second, it forbids unreasonable government action. The Supreme Court has used the first meaning of the due process clause as a sponge, absorbing or incorporating the procedural specifics of the Bill of Rights and spreading or applying them to the states.

The Fundamental Freedoms

In 1897, the Supreme Court declared that the states are limited by the Fifth Amendment's prohibition on taking private property without providing just compensation.[44] The Court accomplished its goal by absorbing that prohibition into the due process clause of the Fourteenth Amendment, which applies to the states. Thus, one Bill of Rights protection—but only that one—applied to both the states and the national government, as illustrated in Figure 12.1. In 1925, the Court assumed that the due process clause protected the First Amendment speech and press liberties from impairment by the states.[45]

The inclusion of other Bill of Rights guarantees within the due process clause faced a critical test in **Palko v. Connecticut** (1937).[46] Frank Palko had been charged with homicide in the first degree. He was convicted of second degree murder, however, and sentenced to life imprisonment. The state of Connecticut appealed and won a new trial; this time Palko was found guilty of first-degree

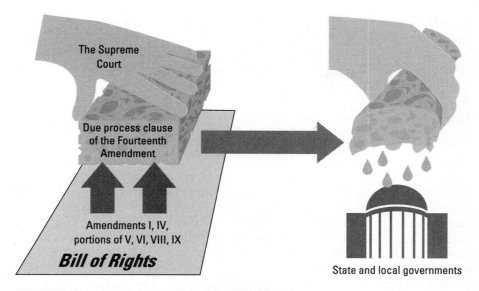

The Supreme Court

Due process clause of the Fourteenth Amendment

Amendments I, IV, portions of V, VI, VIII, IX

Bill of Rights

State and local governments

FIGURE 12.1   The Incorporation of the Bill of Rights
The Supreme Court has used the due process clause of the Fourteenth Amendment as a sponge, absorbing most—but not all—of the provisions in the Bill of Rights and applying them to state and local governments. All provisions in the Bill of Rights apply to the national government.

murder and sentenced to death. Palko appealed the second conviction on the grounds that it violated the protection against double jeopardy guaranteed to him by the Fifth Amendment. This protection applied to the states, he contended, because of the Fourteenth Amendment's due process clause.

The Supreme Court upheld Palko's second conviction. Justice Benjamin N. Cardozo, in his opinion for the majority, formulated principles that were to direct the Court's actions for the next three decades. He noted that some Bill of Rights guarantees—such as freedom of thought and speech—are fundamental, and that these fundamental rights are absorbed by the Fourteenth Amendment's due process clause and are therefore applicable to the states. These rights are essential, argued Cardozo, because "neither liberty nor justice would exist if they were sacrificed." Trial by jury and other rights, though valuable and important, are not essential to liberty and justice and therefore are not absorbed by the due process clause. "Few would be so narrow or provincial," Cardozo claimed, "as to maintain that a fair and enlightened system of justice would be impossible" without these other rights. In other words, only some provisions of the Bill of Rights—the "fundamental" provisions—were absorbed into the due process clause and made applicable to the states. Because protection against double jeopardy was not one of them, Palko died in Connecticut's gas chamber in April 1938.

The next thirty years saw slow but perceptible change in the standard for determining whether a Bill of Rights guarantee was fundamental. The reference point changed from the idealized "fair and enlightened system of justice" in *Palko* to the more realistic "American scheme of justice" thirty years later.[47] Case after case tested various guarantees that the Court found to be fundamental. By 1969, when *Palko* was finally overturned, the Court had found most of the Bill of Rights applicable to the states.

Criminal Procedure: The Meaning of Constitutional Guarantees

"The history of liberty," remarked Justice Felix Frankfurter, "has largely been the history of observance of procedural safeguards."[48] The safeguards embodied in the Fourth through Eighth Amendments to the Constitution specify how government must behave in criminal proceedings. Their application to the states has reshaped American criminal justice in the last four decades in two steps. The first step is the judgment that a guarantee asserted in the Bill of Rights also applies to the states. The second step requires that the judiciary give specific meaning to the guarantee. If the rights are fundamental, their meaning cannot vary from state to state. But life is not quite so simple under the U.S. Constitution. The concept of federalism is sewn into the constitutional fabric, and the Supreme Court recognizes that there may be more than one way to prosecute the accused while heeding fundamental rights.

Consider, for example, the right to a jury trial in criminal cases, which is guaranteed by the Sixth Amendment. This right was made obligatory on the states in *Duncan v. Louisiana* (1968). The Supreme Court later held that the right applied to all nonpetty criminal cases—those in which the penalty for conviction was more than six months' imprisonment.[49] But the Court did not require that state juries have twelve members, the number required for federal criminal proceedings. The Court permits jury size to vary from state to state, although it set the minimum number at six. Furthermore, it has not imposed on the states the federal requirement of a unanimous jury verdict.

In contrast, the Court left no room for variation in its definition of the fundamental right to an attorney, also guaranteed by the Sixth Amendment. Clarence Earl Gideon was a penniless vagrant accused of breaking into and robbing a pool hall. Because Gideon could not afford a lawyer, he asked the state to provide him with legal counsel for his trial. The state refused, and Gideon was subsequently convicted and sentenced to five years in the Florida State Penitentiary. From his cell, Gideon appealed to the U.S. Supreme Court, claiming that his conviction should be struck down because the state had denied him his Sixth Amendment right to counsel. Gideon was also without counsel in this appeal; he filed a hand-lettered "pauper's petition" with the Court, after studying law texts in the prison library. When the Court agreed to consider his case, he was assigned a prominent Washington attorney, Abe Fortas, who later became a Supreme Court justice.[50]

In its landmark decision in ***Gideon v. Wainwright*** (1963), the Court set aside Gideon's conviction and extended to the states the Sixth Amendment right to counsel.[51] The state retried Gideon, who this time had the assistance of a lawyer, and the court found him not guilty. In subsequent rulings that stretched over more than a decade, the Court specified at what points in the course of criminal proceedings a defendant is entitled to a lawyer (from arrest to trial, appeal, and beyond). These pronouncements are binding on all states.

During this period the Court also came to grips with another procedural issue: informing suspects of their constitutional rights. Ernesto Miranda was arrested in Arizona in connection with the kidnapping and rape of an eighteen-year-old woman. After the police questioned him for two hours and the woman identified him, Miranda confessed to the crime. An Arizona court convicted him on the basis of that confession—although he was never told he had the right to counsel and the right not to incriminate himself. Miranda appealed his conviction, which was overturned by the Supreme Court in 1966.[52]

The Court based its decision in *Miranda v. Arizona* on the Fifth Amendment privilege against self-incrimination. According to the Court, warnings are necessary to dispel the coercion that is inherent in custodial interrogation without counsel. The Court does not require warnings if a person is only in custody without questioning or subject to questioning without arrest. But in *Miranda* the Court found the combination of custody and interrogation sufficiently intimidating to require warnings before questioning. These statements are known today as the *Miranda* **warnings**. Among them:

- You have the right to remain silent.
- Anything you say can be used against you in court.
- You have the right to talk to a lawyer of your own choice before questioning.
- If you cannot afford to hire a lawyer, a lawyer will be provided without charge.

The Fourth Amendment guarantees that "the right of the people to be secure in their persons, houses, papers, and effects, against unreasonable searches and seizures, shall not be violated." The Court made this right applicable to the states in *Wolf v. Colorado* (1949).[53] But, although the Court found that protection from illegal searches by state and local government was a fundamental right, it refused to apply to the states the **exclusionary rule** that evidence obtained from an illegal search and seizure cannot be used in a trial.

The justices considered the exclusionary rule again in *Mapp v. Ohio* (1961).[54] An Ohio court had found Dolree Mapp guilty of possessing obscene materials after an admittedly illegal search of her home for a fugitive. The Ohio Supreme Court affirmed her conviction, and she appealed to the U.S. Supreme Court. In a 6–3 decision, the Court declared that "all evidence obtained by searches and seizures in violation of the Constitution is, by [the Fourth Amendment], inadmissible in a state court." The decision was historic. It placed the exclusionary rule within the confines of the Fourth Amendment and required all levels of government to operate according to the provisions of that amendment.

The struggle over the exclusionary rule took a new turn in 1984, when the Court reviewed *United States v. Leon.*[55] In this case, a judge had issued a search warrant without "probable cause" having been firmly established. The police, relying on the warrant, found large quantities of illegal drugs. The Court, by a vote of 6 to 3, established the **good faith exception** to the exclusionary rule. The justices held that the state could introduce at trial evidence seized on the basis of a mistakenly issued search warrant. The exclusionary rule, argued the majority, is not a right but a remedy justified by its ability to deter illegal police conduct. Such a deterrent effect was not a factor in *Leon:* The police acted in good faith. Hence, the Court decided, there is a need for an exception to the rule.

The exclusionary rule continues to divide the Supreme Court. In 1990, the justices again reaffirmed the rule, but only by a bare 5–4 majority.[56] The current Supreme Court line-up has a more conservative bent, which suggests that the battle over the exclusionary rule has not ended.

The Ninth Amendment and Personal Autonomy

> The enumeration in the Constitution, of certain rights, shall not be construed to deny or disparage others retained by the people.

The wording and history of the Ninth Amendment remain an enigma; the evidence supports two different views. The amendment may protect rights that are not enumerated, or it may simply protect state governments against the assumption of power by the national government.[57] The meaning of the amendment was not an issue until 1965, when the Supreme Court used it to protect privacy, a right that is not enumerated in the Constitution.

Controversy: From Privacy to Abortion

In *Griswold v. Connecticut* (1965), the Court struck down, by a vote of 7 to 2, a seldom-used Connecticut statute that made the use of birth-control devices a crime.[58] Justice William Douglas, writing for the majority, asserted that the "specific guarantees in the Bill of Rights have penumbras [partially illuminated regions surrounding fully lit areas]" that give "life and substance" to broad, unspecified protections in the Bill of Rights. Several specific guarantees in the First, Third, Fourth, and Fifth Amendments create a zone of privacy, Douglas argued, and this zone is protected by the Ninth Amendment and is applicable to the states by the due process clause of the Fourteenth Amendment.

Griswold established a zone of personal autonomy, protected by the Constitution, which was the basis of a 1973 case that sought to invalidate state antiabortion laws. In *Roe v. Wade* (1973), the Court in a 7–2 decision declared unconstitutional a Texas law making it a crime to obtain an abortion except for the purpose of saving the woman's life.[59]

Justice Harry A. Blackmun, who authored the majority opinion, based the decision on the right to privacy protected by the due process clause of the Fourteenth Amendment. The Court declared that in the first three months of pregnancy, the abortion decision must be left to the woman and her physician. In the interest of protecting the woman's health, states may restrict but not prohibit abortions in the second three months of pregnancy. Finally, in the last three months of pregnancy, states may regulate or even prohibit abortions to protect the life of the fetus except when medical judgment determines that an abortion is necessary to save the woman's life. In all, the Court's ruling affected the laws of forty-six states.

The dissenters—Justices Byron White and William Rehnquist—were quick to assert what critics have frequently repeated since the decision: the Court's judgment was directed by its own dislikes, not by any constitutional compass. In the absence of guiding principles, they asserted, the majority justices simply substituted their views for the views of the state legislatures whose abortion regulations they invalidated.[60]

The composition of the Court shifted under President Ronald Reagan. His elevation of Rehnquist to chief justice in 1986 and his appointments of Antonin Scalia in 1986 and Anthony Kennedy in 1988 raised new hope among abortion foes and old fears among advocates of choice.

A perceptible shift away from abortion rights materialized in *Webster v. Reproductive Health Services* (1989). In *Webster*, the Court upheld the constitutionality of a Missouri law that denied the use of public employees or publicly funded facilities in the performance of an abortion unless the woman's life was in danger.[61] Furthermore, the law required doctors to perform tests to determine whether fetuses twenty weeks old and older could survive outside the womb. This was the first time the Court upheld significant government restrictions on abortion.

The Court has since moved cautiously down the road toward greater government control of abortion. In 1990, the justices split on two state parental notification laws. Since then, a new coalition—forged by Reagan and Bush appointees Sandra Day O'Connor, David Souter, and Anthony Kennedy—has reaffirmed *Roe* yet tolerates additional restrictions on abortion. In *Planned Parenthood v. Casey* (1992), the Court opted for O'Connor's test that restrictions must not place "an undue burden" on a woman's ability to choose an abortion. The Court remains deeply and bitterly divided on abortion.[62]

The abortion issue pits freedom against order. The decision to bear or beget children should be free from government control. Yet government has a legitimate interest in protecting and preserving life, including fetal life, as part of its responsibility to maintain an orderly society. Rather than choose between freedom and order, the majority on the Court has loosened constitutional protection on abortion rights and cast the politically divisive issue into the state legislative process, where elected representatives can thrash out the conflict.

Personal Autonomy and Sexual Orientation

The right-to-privacy cases may have opened a Pandora's box of divisive social issues. Does the right to privacy embrace private homosexual acts between consenting adults? Consider the case of Michael Hardwick, who was arrested in 1982 in his Atlanta bedroom while having sex with another man. In a standard approach to prosecuting homosexuals, Georgia charged him under a state criminal statute with the crime of sodomy, which means oral or anal intercourse. Hardwick sued to challenge the law's constitutionality. He won in the lower courts. However, in a bitterly divided ruling in 1986, the Supreme Court held in **Bowers v. Hardwick** that the Constitution does not protect homosexual relations between consenting adults, even in the privacy of their own homes.[63]

The appointments of conservatives to replace liberals on the Court places freedom-preferring policies such as gay rights in continued jeopardy. However, Clinton's appointments of Ruth Bader Ginsburg and Stephen Breyer signaled movement toward a liberal view. That the Court will soon reverse course on matters of personal autonomy is unlikely. It would take several more liberal Court appointments and the right cases to create the conditions for a change in direction.

Issues around sexual orientation have shifted toward the states, where various groups continue to assert their political power. State courts and state legislatures have demonstrated their receptivity to positions that are probably untenable in the federal courts.

Two Conceptions of Equality

Most Americans support **equality of opportunity**, the idea that people should have an equal chance to develop their talents and that effort and ability should be rewarded equitably. This form of equality glorifies personal achievement and free competition, and it allows everyone to play on a level field where the same rules apply to all. Special recruitment efforts aimed at identifying qualified minority or female job applicants, for example, ensure that everyone has the same chance starting out. Low-bid contracting illustrates equality of opportunity, because every bidder has the same chance to compete for work.

Americans are far less committed to **equality of outcome**, which means greater uniformity in social, economic, and political power among different social groups. Equality of outcome can occur only with restrictions on the free competition that is the basis of equality of opportunity. For example, schools and businesses aim at equality of outcome when they allocate admissions or jobs on the basis of race, gender, or disability—factors that are unrelated to ability. Some observers refer to these allocations as *quotas;* others call them *goals*. The difference is subtle. A quota *requires* that a specified, proportional share of some benefit go to a favored group. A goal *aims* for a proportional allocation of benefits, without requiring it. The government seeks equality of outcome when it adjusts the rules to handicap some bidders and favor others. The vast majority of Americans, however, consistently favor low-bid contracting and merit-based admissions and employment over preferential treatment.[64] Quota- or goal-based policies muster only modest support (see Politics in a Changing America 12.1).

Quota policies generate the most opposition because they confine competition. Quotas limit advancement for some individuals and ensure advancement for others by taking into account factors unrelated to ability. Quotas seem to be at odds with individual initiative. In other words, equality clashes with freedom. To understand the ways government resolves this conflict, we have to understand the evolution of civil rights in this country. The struggle of blacks has been a beacon lighting the way for Native Americans, Hispanic Americans, women, and the disabled. Each of these groups has confronted **invidious discrimination.** Discrimination is simply the act of making or recognizing distinctions. When making distinctions among people, discrimination may be benign (that is, harmless) or invidious (harmful).

The Civil War Amendments

The Civil War amendments were adopted to provide freedom and equality to black Americans. The Thirteenth Amendment, ratified in 1865, provided that

> neither slavery nor involuntary servitude . . . shall exist within the United States, or any place subject to their jurisdiction.

The Fourteenth Amendment, adopted three years later, provides first that freed slaves are citizens:

> All persons born or naturalized in the United States, and subject to the jurisdiction thereof, are citizens of the United States and of the State wherein they reside.

As we saw earlier in this chapter, it also prohibits the states from abridging the "privileges or immunities of citizens of the United States" or depriving "any person of life, liberty, or property, without due process of law." The Fourteenth Amendment then goes on to protect equality under the law, declaring that no state shall

> deny to any person within its jurisdiction the equal protection of the laws.

The Fifteenth Amendment, adopted in 1870, added a measure of political equality:

> The right of citizens of the United States to vote shall not be denied or abridged by the United States or by any State on account of race, color, or previous condition of servitude.

American blacks were thus free and politically equal—at least according to the Constitution. But for many years the courts sometimes thwarted the efforts of other branches to protect these constitutional rights.

Congress and the Supreme Court: Lawmaking Versus Law Interpreting

In the years after the Civil War, Congress went to work to protect the rights of black citizens. In 1866, lawmakers passed a civil rights act that granted all citizens—white and black—the right to make and enforce contracts, sue or be

Politics in a Changing America 12.1

Preferences Out, Extra Effort In

Americans are divided over affirmative action. But what is the source of the divide? Some critics of affirmative action suggest that it is rooted in objections to preferences. Some defenders of affirmative action claim that objections to the use of preferences mask deep-seated racial prejudice.

To unlock these questions, Professor James H. Kuklinski and six colleagues used a novel experiment in a 1991 national survey of white Americans' racial attitudes. The respondents were randomly divided into two groups. Respondents in each group were then asked slightly different versions of the same question:

1. Some people say that because of past discrimination, qualified blacks should be given *preference* in university admissions. Others say that this is wrong because it discriminates against whites. How do you feel—are you in favor of or opposed to giving qualified blacks preference in admission to colleges and universities?
2. Some people say that because of past discrimination, an *extra effort* should be made to make sure that qualified blacks are considered for university admissions. Others say that this is wrong because it discriminates against whites. How do you feel—are you in favor of or opposed to making an extra effort to make sure qualified blacks are considered for admission to colleges and universities?

The first question mentions *preference;* the second question substitutes *extra effort.* If whites' objections to affirmative action are rooted in a lack of concern for blacks or outright prejudice, then there should be little difference in the responses to the two different questions. Alternatively, if the element of *preference* is crucial, then responses should differ across the two questions.

(continued)

sued, give evidence, and inherit, purchase, lease, sell, hold, or convey property. Later, in the Civil Rights Act of 1875, Congress attempted to guarantee blacks equal access to public accommodations (streetcars, inns, parks, theaters, and the like).

Athough Congress enacted laws to protect the civil rights of black citizens, the Supreme Court weakened some of those rights. In 1873, the Court ruled that the Civil War amendments had not changed the relationship between the state and national governments.[65] State citizenship and national citizenship remained separate and distinct. According to the Court, the Fourteenth Amendment did not obligate the states to honor the rights guaranteed by U.S. citizenship. In effect, the Court stripped the amendment of its power to secure for black citizens the freedoms guaranteed by the Bill of Rights.

In 1883, the Court struck down the public accommodations section of the Civil Rights Act of 1875.[66] The justices declared that the national government

Politics in a Changing America 12.1 (continued)

The pair of bar graphs reveal that only 25 percent of white Americans favor preferential treatment, but 60 percent endorse extra effort. In other words, U.S. whites overwhelmingly reject affirmative action if it involves preferences, but a clear majority of them support going the extra mile to ensure that all blacks meriting assistance receive it.

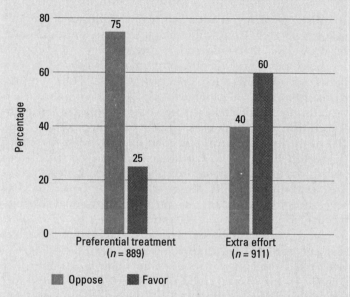

Source: James H. Kuklinski et al., "Racial Prejudice and Attitudes Toward Affirmative Action," *American Journal of Political Science,* 41 (April 1997), pp. 402–419.

could prohibit only government action that discriminated against blacks. Private acts of discrimination or acts of omission by a state, they maintained, were beyond the reach of the national government. The Court refused to see racial discrimination as an act that the national government could prohibit. By tolerating racial discrimination, the justices abetted **racism**, the belief that there are inherent differences among the races that determine people's achievement and that one's own race is superior to, and thus has a right to dominate, others.

The Court's decisions gave the states ample room to maneuver around civil rights laws. In the matter of voting rights, for example, states that wanted to bar black men from the polls simply used nonracial means to do so. One popular tool was the **poll tax**, first imposed by Georgia in 1877. This was a tax of $1 or $2 on every citizen who wanted to vote. The tax was not a burden for most whites. But many blacks were tenant farmers who did not have any extra money for voting. Other bars to black suffrage included literacy tests, minimum education requirements, and a grandfather clause that restricted suffrage to men who could establish that their grandfathers were eligible to vote before 1867 (three years before the Fifteenth Amendment declared that race could not be used to deny individuals the right to vote).[67] Intimidation and violence were also used to keep blacks from the polls.

The Roots of Racial Segregation

Well before the Civil War, **racial segregation** was a way of life in the South: blacks lived and worked separately from whites. After the war, southern states began to enact Jim Crow laws that enforced segregation (*Jim Crow* was a derogatory term for a black person). Once the Supreme Court took the teeth out of the Civil Rights Act of 1875, such laws proliferated. They required blacks to live in separate (generally inferior) areas and restricted them to separate sections of hospitals, separate cemeteries, separate schools, and separate sections of streetcars, trains, jails, and parks. Each day, in countless ways, blacks were reminded of the inferior status accorded them by white society.

In 1892, Homer Adolph Plessy—who was seven-eighths Caucasian—took a seat in a "whites only" car of a Louisiana train. He refused to move to the car reserved for blacks and was arrested. Plessy argued that Louisiana's law mandating racial segregation on its trains was an unconstitutional infringement on the privileges and immunities guaranteed by the Fourteenth Amendment and its equal protection clause. The Supreme Court disagreed. The majority in *Plessy v. Ferguson* (1896) upheld state-imposed racial segregation.[68] They based their decision on the **separate-but-equal doctrine**, which held that separate facilities for blacks and whites satisfied the Fourteenth Amendment so long as they were equal. The lone dissenter, John Marshall Harlan, who envisioned a "color-blind Constitution," wrote this in his dissenting opinion:

> We boast of the freedom enjoyed by our people above all other peoples. But it is difficult to reconcile that boast with a state of the law which, practically, puts the brand of servitude and degradation upon a large class of our fellow citizens—our equals before the law. The thin disguise of "equal" accommodations for passengers in railroad coaches will not mislead any one, nor atone for the wrong this day done.[69]

Three years later, the Supreme Court extended the separate-but-equal doctrine to the schools.[70] The justices ignored the fact that black educational facilities (and most other "colored only" facilities) were far from equal to those reserved for whites.

By the end of the nineteenth century, racial segregation was firmly and legally entrenched in the American South. Although constitutional amendments and national laws to protect equality under the law were in place, the Supreme Court's interpretation of those amendments and laws rendered them ineffective. Several decades passed before any change was discernible.

The Dismantling of School Segregation

By the middle of the twentieth century, public attitudes toward race relations were slowly changing. Black troops had fought with honor—albeit in segregated military units—in World War II. Blacks and whites were working together in unions and in service and religious organizations. Social change and court decisions suggested that government-imposed segregation was vulnerable.

President Harry S Truman risked his political future with his strong support of blacks' civil rights. In 1947, he established the President's Committee on Civil Rights. The committee's report, issued later that year, became the agenda for the civil rights movement over the next two decades. It called for national laws prohibiting racially motivated poll taxes, segregation, and brutality against minorities, and for guarantees of voting rights and equal employment opportunity. In 1948, Truman ordered the **desegregation** (the dismantling of authorized racial segregation) of the armed forces.

In 1947, the U.S. Department of Justice had begun to submit briefs to the courts in support of civil rights. Perhaps the department's most important intervention came in ***Brown v. Board of Education.***[71] This case was the culmination of twenty years of planning and litigation by the National Association for the Advancement of Colored People (NAACP) to invalidate racial segregation in public schools.

Linda Brown was a black child whose father tried to enroll her in a white public school in Topeka, Kansas. Brown's request was refused because of Linda's race. A federal district court found that the black public school was, in all major respects, equal in quality to the white school; therefore, according to the *Plessy* doctrine, Linda was required to go to the black public school. Brown appealed the decision.

Brown v. Board of Education reached the Supreme Court in late 1951. The justices delayed argument on the sensitive race issue, placing the case beyond the 1952 national election. *Brown* was merged with four similar cases into a class action (see Chapter 11). The class action was supported by the NAACP and coordinated by Thurgood Marshall, who later became the first black justice to sit on the Supreme Court. The five cases squarely challenged the separate-but-equal doctrine. By all tangible measures (standards for teacher licensing, teacher-pupil ratios, library facilities), the two school systems in each case—one white, the other black—were equal. The issue was legal separation of the races.

On May 17, 1954, Chief Justice Earl Warren, who had recently joined the Court, delivered a single opinion covering four of the cases. Warren spoke for a unanimous Court when he declared that "in the field of public education the doctrine of 'separate but equal' has no place. Separate educational facilities are inherently unequal,"[72] depriving the plaintiffs of the equal protection of the laws. Segregated facilities generate in black children "a feeling of inferiority . . . that may affect their hearts and minds in a way unlikely ever to be undone."[73] In short, the nation's highest court found that state-imposed public school segregation violated the equal protection clause of the Fourteenth Amendment.

The Court deferred implementation of the school desegregation decisions until 1955. Then, in **Brown v. Board of Education II**, it ruled that school systems must desegregate "with all deliberate speed," and it assigned the process of supervising desegregation to the lower federal courts.[74]

Some states quietly complied with the *Brown* decree. Others did little to desegregate their schools. Many communities in the South defied the Court, sometimes violently. This resistance, along with the Supreme Court's "all deliberate speed" order, placed a heavy burden on federal judges to dismantle what was the fundamental social order in many communities.[75] Gradual desegregation under *Brown* was in some cases no desegregation at all. By 1969, a unanimous Supreme Court ordered that the operation of segregated school systems must stop "at once."[76]

Two years later, the Court approved several remedies to achieve integration, including busing, racial quotas, and the pairing or grouping of noncontiguous school zones. But these remedies applied only to **de jure segregation**, government-imposed segregation (for example, government assignment of whites to one school and blacks to another within the same community). Court-imposed remedies did not apply to **de facto segregation**, segregation that is not the result of government influence (for example, racial segregation resulting from residential patterns).

Public opinion strongly opposed the busing approach, and Congress sought limits on busing as a remedy. In 1974, a closely divided Court ruled that lower courts could not order busing across school district boundaries unless each district had practiced racial discrimination or unless school district lines had been deliberately drawn to achieve racial segregation.[77]

The Civil Rights Movement

The NAACP concentrated on school desegregation but made headway in other areas as well. The Supreme Court responded to NAACP efforts in the late 1940s by outlawing the whites-only primary elections in the South, declaring them to be in violation of the Fifteenth Amendment. The Court also declared segregation on interstate bus routes to be unconstitutional, and it desegregated restaurants and hotels in the District of Columbia. Despite these and other decisions that chipped away at existing barriers to equality, the realization of equality required the political mobilization of the people—black and white—into what is now known as the **civil rights movement**.

Civil Disobedience

Rosa Parks, a black woman living in Montgomery, Alabama, sounded the first call to action. That city's Jim Crow ordinances required blacks to sit in the back of the bus and empowered drivers to order blacks to vacate an entire row of seats to make room for one white or to order blacks to stand even when some seats were vacant. In December 1955, Parks boarded a city bus on her way home from work and took an available seat in the front of the bus. She

A Modern-Day Moses
Martin Luther King, Jr., was a Baptist minister who believed in the principles of nonviolent protest practiced by India's Mohandas ("Mahatma") Gandhi. This photograph, taken in 1963 in Baltimore, captures the crowd's affection for King, the man many thought would lead them to a new Canaan of racial equality. King, who won the Nobel Peace Prize in 1964, was assassinated in 1968 in Memphis, Tennessee.

refused to give up her seat when the driver asked her to do so and was arrested and fined $10 for violating the city ordinance.

Under the leadership of a charismatic twenty-six-year-old Baptist minister named Martin Luther King, Jr., Montgomery's black community responded to Parks's arrest with a boycott of the city's bus system. A **boycott** is a refusal to do business with a company or individual, as an expression of disapproval or a means of coercion. A year after the boycott began, the federal courts ruled that segregated transportation systems violated the equal protection clause of the Constitution.

In 1957, King helped organize the Southern Christian Leadership Council (SCLC) to coordinate civil rights activities. King was totally committed to nonviolent action to bring racial issues into the light. To that end, he advocated **civil disobedience**, the willful but nonviolent breach of unjust laws.

Martin Luther King, Jr., had risen to worldwide prominence by August, 1963, when he organized and led "A March for Jobs and Freedom," in Washington, D.C. More than 250,000 people, black and white, gathered peaceably at the Lincoln Memorial to hear King speak. "I have a dream," he told them, "that my little children will one day live in a nation where they will not be judged by the color of their skin but by the content of their character."[78]

The Civil Rights Act of 1964

President Lyndon B. Johnson considered civil rights his top legislative priority. Within months after he assumed office, Congress passed the Civil Rights Act of 1964, the most comprehensive legislative attempt ever to erase racial discrimination in the United States. Among its many provisions, the act

- Entitled all persons to "the full and equal enjoyment" of goods, services, and privileges in places of public accommodation without discrimination on the grounds of race, color, religion, or national origin
- Established the right to equality in employment opportunities
- Strengthened voting rights legislation
- Created the Equal Employment Opportunity Commission (EEOC) and charged it with hearing and investigating complaints of job discrimination*
- Provided that funds could be withheld from federally assisted programs that were administered in a discriminatory manner

President Johnson's goal was a "great society." Soon a constitutional amendment and a series of civil rights laws were in place to help him meet his goal:

- The Twenty-fourth Amendment, ratified in 1964, banned poll taxes in primary and general elections for national office.
- The Economic Opportunity Act of 1964 focused on education and training to combat poverty.
- The Voting Rights Act of 1965 empowered the attorney general to send voter registration supervisors to areas in which fewer than half the eligible minority voters had been registered. This act has been credited with doubling black voter registration in the South in only five years.[79]
- The Fair Housing Act of 1968 banned discrimination in the rental or sale of most housing.

The Continuing Struggle over Civil Rights

However, civil rights laws on the books do not ensure civil rights in action. While Congress has tried to restore and expand civil rights enforcement, in recent years the Supreme Court has weakened it. The Court restricted minority contractor set-asides of state public works funds, an arrangement it had approved in 1980. (Recall that a set-aside is a purchasing or contracting provision that reserves a certain percentage of funds for minority-owned

---

*Since 1972, the EEOC has had the power to institute legal proceedings on behalf of employees who allege that they have been victims of illegal discrimination.

contractors.) The five-person majority held that past societal discrimination alone cannot serve as the basis for rigid quotas.[80]

Buttressed by Republican appointees, the Supreme Court continued to narrow the scope of national civil rights protections in a string of decisions that suggested the ascendancy of a new conservative majority concerned more with freedom than with equality.[81] To counter the Court's changing interpretations of civil rights laws, liberals turned to Congress to restore and enlarge earlier Court decisions by writing them into law. The result was a comprehensive new civil rights bill. The Civil Rights Act of 1991 reversed or altered twelve Court decisions that had narrowed civil rights protections. The new law clarified and expanded earlier legislation and increased the costs to employers for intentional, illegal discrimination. Continued resentment generated by equal outcomes policies moved the battle back to the courts, however.

Civil Rights for Other Minorities

Recent civil rights laws and court decisions protect members of all minority groups. The Supreme Court underscored the breadth of this protection in an important decision in 1987.[82] The justices ruled unanimously that the Civil Rights Act of 1866 (known today as "Section 1981") offered broad protection against discrimination to all minorities. Previously, members of white ethnic groups could not invoke the law in bias suits. The 1987 decision allows members of *any* ethnic group—Italian, Iranian, Norwegian, or Chinese, for example—to recover money damages if they prove they were denied a job, excluded from rental housing, or subjected to another form of discrimination prohibited by the law. The 1964 Civil Rights Act offers similar protections but specifies strict procedures for filing suits that tend to discourage litigation.

Clearly the civil rights movement has had an effect on all minorities. Here we examine the civil rights struggles of three groups—Native Americans, Hispanic Americans, and the disabled.

Native Americans

In 1924, Indians received U.S. citizenship. Until that time, they were considered members of tribal nations whose relations with the U.S. government were determined by treaties. The agencies responsible for administering Indian reservations kept Native Americans poor and dependent on the national government. And Indian lands continued to shrink through the 1950s and into the 1960s—despite signed treaties and the religious significance of portions of the lands they lost.

Anger bred of poverty, unemployment, and frustration with an uncaring government exploded into militant action in November 1969, when several Indians seized Alcatraz Island, an abandoned island in San Francisco Bay. The group cited an 1868 Sioux treaty that entitled them to unused federal lands; they remained on the island for a year and a half. In 1973, armed members of the American Indian Movement seized eleven hostages at Wounded Knee,

Righting a Wrong
*During World War II, Congress authorized the quarantine of Japanese residents in the
western United States. The Supreme Court upheld the congressional action in 1944. More
than 110,000 men, women, and children—including native-born U.S. citizens—were
incarcerated simply because they were of Japanese ancestry. The men pictured here were
confined to the Japanese Evacuation Colony at Manzanar, California. In 1988, Congress
passed legislation that offered apologies and a $20,000 tax-free reparation to each surviving
internee. The cost to the government: $1.25 billion.*

South Dakota—the site of an 1890 massacre of two hundred Sioux (Lakota) by
U.S. cavalry troops. They remained there, occasionally exchanging gunfire
with federal marshals, for seventy-one days until the government agreed to examine the treaty rights of the Oglala Sioux.[83]

In 1946, Congress enacted legislation establishing an Indian claims commission to compensate Native Americans for land that had been taken from
them. In the 1970s, the Native American Rights Fund and other groups used
that legislation to win important victories in the courts. The tribes won the return of lands in the Midwest and in the states of Oklahoma, New Mexico, and
Washington. In 1980, the Supreme Court ordered the national government to
pay the Sioux $117 million plus interest for the Black Hills of South Dakota,
which had been stolen from them a century before. Other cases, involving
land from coast to coast, are still pending.

The special status accorded Indian tribes in the Constitution has proved attractive to a new breed of Indian leaders. Some of the 557 recognized tribes
have successfully instituted casino gambling on their reservations, even in the

face of state opposition. Congress allows these developments provided that the tribes spend their profits on Indian assistance programs. The wealth created by casino gambling and other ventures funded with gambling profits may prove to be Native Americans' most effective weapon for retaining and regaining their heritage.

Hispanic Americans

Many Hispanic Americans have a rich and deep-rooted heritage in America, but until the 1920s that heritage was largely confined to the southwestern states and California. Then, unprecedented numbers of Mexican and Puerto Rican immigrants came to the United States in search of employment and a better life. Like blacks who had migrated to northern cities, most of them found poverty and discrimination.

World War II gave rise to another influx of Mexicans, this time primarily courted to work on farms in California. But by the late 1950s, most farm workers—blacks, whites, and Hispanics—were living in poverty. Hispanic Americans who lived in cities fared little better. Yet millions of Mexicans continued to cross the border into the United States, both legally and illegally. The effect was to depress the value of farm labor in California and the Southwest.

The Hispanic American population continues to grow. The 20 million Hispanics living in the United States in the 1970s were still mainly Puerto Rican and Mexican American, but they were joined by immigrants from the Dominican Republic, Colombia, Cuba, Ecuador, and elsewhere. Although civil rights legislation helped them to an extent, they are among the poorest and least-educated groups in the United States.

Voter registration and voter turnout among Hispanics are lower than among other groups. Also, voter turnout depends on effective political advertising, and Hispanics are not targeted as often as other groups with political messages that they can understand. But despite these stumbling blocks, Latinos have started to exercise a measure of political power.

Hispanics occupy positions of power in national and local arenas. The 106th Congress (1999–2001) convened with a diverse group of eighteen Hispanic House members. They form the Congressional Hispanic Caucus, an informal bipartisan group dedicated to voicing and advancing issues affecting Hispanic Americans. The National Hispanic Caucus of State Legislators, which has 250 members, has a similar mission. Latinos have won the mayoralties of San Antonio, San Diego, Denver, and Miami. President Clinton appointed two Hispanics to his first cabinet.

Disabled Americans

Forty-three million disabled Americans gained recognition in 1990 as a protected minority with the enactment of the Americans with Disabilities Act (ADA). The law extends the protections embodied in the Civil Rights Act of 1964 to people with physical or mental disabilities, including people with

AIDS and recovering alcoholics, and drug abusers. It guarantees them access to employment, transportation, public accommodations, and communication services.

Advocates for the disabled found a ready model in the existing civil rights laws. Opponents argued that the changes mandated by the 1990 law (such as access for those confined to wheelchairs) could cost billions of dollars, but supporters replied that the costs would be offset by an equal or greater reduction in federal aid to disabled people, who would rather be working.

A change in the law, no matter how welcome, does not ensure a change in attitudes. Laws that end racial discrimination do not extinguish racism, and laws that ban biased treatment of the disabled cannot mandate their acceptance. But civil rights advocates predict that bias against the disabled, like similar attitudes toward other minorities, will wither away as they become full participants in society.

Gender and Equal Rights: The Women's Movement

The Supreme Court has expanded the array of legal weapons available to all minorities to help them achieve social equality. Women, too, have benefited from this change.

Protectionism

Until the early 1970s, laws that affected the civil rights of women were based on traditional views of the relationship between men and women. At the heart of these laws was **protectionism**—the notion that women must be sheltered from life's harsh realities. And protected they were, through laws that discriminated against them in employment and other areas. With few exceptions, women were also "protected" from voting until early in the twentieth century.

Protectionism reached a peak in 1908, when the Court upheld an Oregon law limiting the number of hours women could work.[84] Rife with assumptions about the nature and role of women, the decision gave wide latitude to laws that "protected" the "weaker sex." However, in 1991, the Supreme Court clearly moved away from protectionism by striking down an employer's policy excluding women capable of bearing children from jobs that involve exposure to toxic substances that could harm a developing fetus. Relying on amendments to the 1964 Civil Rights Act, the Court declared that "women as capable of doing their jobs as their male counterparts may not be forced to choose between having a child and having a job."[85]

Political Equality for Women

In 1878, Susan B. Anthony, a women's rights activist, persuaded a U.S. senator from California to introduce a constitutional amendment requiring that "the right of citizens of the United States to vote shall not be denied or abridged by the United States or by any State on account of sex." The amendment was introduced and voted down a number of times over the next twenty years. Meanwhile, a number of states—primarily in the Midwest and West—did grant limited suffrage to women.

By the early 1900s the movement for women's suffrage had became a political battle to amend the Constitution. The battle was won in 1920, when the **Nineteenth Amendment** gave women the right to vote in the wording first suggested by Anthony.

Prohibiting Sex-Based Discrimination

The movement to provide equal rights to women advanced a step with the passage of the Equal Pay Act of 1963. That act requires equal pay for men and women doing similar work. However, to remove the restrictions of protectionism, women needed equal opportunity for employment. They got it in the Civil Rights Act of 1964 and later legislation. The EEOC, which had been created by that law, was empowered to act on behalf of victims of invidious sex discrimination, or **sexism**.

Stereotypes Under Scrutiny

After nearly a century of protectionism, the Supreme Court began to take a closer look at gender-based distinctions. In 1971, it struck down a state law that gave men preference over women in administering the estate of a person who died without naming an administrator.[86] Two years later, the justices declared that paternalism operated to "put women not on a pedestal, but in a cage."[87] They then proceeded to strike down several gender-based laws that either prevented or discouraged departures from "proper" sex roles. In 1976, the Court finally developed a workable standard for reviewing these kinds of laws. Gender-based distinctions are justified only if they serve some important government purpose.[88]

The courts have not been reluctant to extend to women the *constitutional* guarantees won by blacks. In 1994, the Supreme Court extended the Constitution's equal protection guarantee by forbidding the exclusion of potential jurors on the basis of their sex.[89] The 1994 decision completed a constitutional revolution in jury selection that began in 1986 with a bar against juror exclusions based on race.

In 1996, the Court spoke with uncommon clarity when it declared that the men-only admissions policy of the Virginia Military Institute (VMI), a state-supported military college, violated the equal protection clause of the Fourteenth Amendment. In an effort to meet women's demands to enter VMI—and to stave off continued legal challenges—Virginia had established a separate-but-equal institution called the Virginia Women's Institute for Leadership (VWIL). Writing for a six-member majority in *United States v. Virginia,* Justice Ruth Bader Ginsburg applied a demanding test she labeled "skeptical scrutiny" to official acts that deny individuals rights or responsibilities based on their sex. "Parties who seek to defend gender-based government action," she wrote, "must demonstrate an 'exceedingly persuasive justification' for that action." Ginsburg declared that "women seeking and fit for a VMI-quality education cannot be offered anything less, under the State's obligation to afford them genuinely equal protection."[90] The upshot is that distinctions based on sex are almost as suspect as distinctions based on race.

The Equal Rights Amendment

Policies protecting women, based largely on sexual stereotypes, have been woven into the legal fabric of American life. This protectionism has limited the freedom of women to compete with men socially and economically on an equal footing. However, the Supreme Court has been hesitant to extend the principles of the Fourteenth Amendment beyond issues of race. If constitutional interpretation imposes such a limit, then only a constitutional amendment can overcome it.

The **Equal Rights Amendment (ERA)** was first introduced in 1923. The ERA declared that "equality of rights under the law shall not be denied or abridged by the United States or any State on account of sex." A national coalition of women's rights advocates generated enough support to get the ERA through Congress in 1972. However, the amendment died on July 1, 1982, still three states short of adoption.

Despite its failure, some scholars argue that for practical purposes, the Supreme Court has implemented the ERA through its decisions. It has struck down distinctions based on sex and held that stereotyped generalizations of sexual differences must fall.[91] In recent rulings, the Court has held that states may require employers to guarantee job reinstatement to women returning from maternity leave, that sexual harassment in the workplace is illegal, and that a hostile work environment will be judged by a reasonable perception of abuse rather than a demonstration of psychological injury.[92]

Affirmative Action: Equal Opportunity or Equal Outcome?

In his vision of the Great Society, President Johnson linked economic rights with civil rights, and equality of outcome with equality of opportunity. "Equal opportunity is essential, but not enough," he declared. "We seek not just legal equity but human ability, not just equality as a right and a theory but equality as a fact and equality as a result."[93] This commitment led to affirmative action programs to expand opportunities for women, minorities, and the disabled.

Affirmative action embraces a range of public and private programs, policies, and procedures, including special recruitment, preferential treatment,

Civil Rights Groups Dodge Teacher's Bullet
*Sharon Taxman, a Piscataway, New Jersey, high school teacher, sued her school board in
1989 when, in a downsizing choice between two equally qualified teachers, it invoked "diversity" as the reason to lay her off in favor of a black teacher. The lower courts sided with
Taxman, but the school board, supported by the Clinton administration, appealed to the
Supreme Court, which granted review. Fearing a precedent-setting judgment that would
further curtail the use of racial preferences, the Black Leadership Forum—a hastily devised
coalition of twenty-one black civic, fraternal, and civil rights groups—pitched in with a
generous financial settlement in late 1997, offering Taxman an inflation-adjusted deal she
could not refuse.*

and quotas in job training and professional education, employment, and the
awarding of government contracts. The point of these programs is to move beyond equality of opportunity to equality of outcome.

Arguments for affirmative action programs (from increased recruitment
efforts to quotas) tend to use the following reasoning. Certain groups have
historically suffered invidious discrimination, denying them educational and
economic opportunities. To eliminate the lasting effects of such discrimination, the public and private sectors must take steps to provide access to good
education and jobs. If the majority once used discrimination to hold groups
back, discriminating to benefit those groups is fair. Therefore, quotas are a legitimate means to provide a place on the ladder of success.[94]

Affirmative action opponents maintain that quotas for designated groups
necessarily create invidious discrimination (in the form of reverse discrimination) against individuals who are themselves blameless. Moreover, they say,

Compared with What? 12.1

How Other Nations Struggle with Affirmative Action

Americans are not alone in their disagreements over affirmative action. Controversies, and even bloodshed, have been the order of the day in countries where certain groups receive government-sanctioned preferences over others.

One study found several common patterns among countries that had enacted preferential policies. Though begun as temporary measures, preferential policies tended to persist and even to expand to include more groups. Although the policies usually sought to improve the situation of disadvantaged groups as a whole, they often benefited the better-off members of such groups more so than the worse-off members. Finally, preferential policies tended to increase antagonisms among different groups within a country.

As in the United States, preferential policies in Canada and Australia are called "affirmative action" measures. In India, however, such policies carry the label "positive discrimination." But that isn't the only way India differs from the United States when it comes to preferential policies.

Although India is the world's largest democracy, its society is rigidly stratified into groups called castes. Members of the lower castes (the lowest being the "untouchables") were historically restricted to the least prestigious and lowest paying jobs. To improve their status, India has set aside government jobs for the lower castes, who make up half of India's population of 1 billion. India now reserves 27 percent of government jobs for the lower castes and an additional 23 percent for untouchables and remote tribe members. Gender equality has also improved since a 1993 constitutional amendment that set aside one-third of all seats in local government councils for women. Even the country's 15 million eunuchs, who work as prostitutes or as dancing partners

(continued)

quotas lead to admission, hiring, or promotion of the less qualified at the expense of the well qualified. In the name of equality, such policies thwart individuals' freedom to succeed. Do preferential policies in other nations offer lessons for us? See Compared with What? 12.1 to learn the answer.

Reverse Discrimination

The Supreme Court confronted an affirmative action quota program for the first time in *Regents of the University of California v. Bakke*.[95] Allan Bakke, a thirty-five-year-old white man, had twice applied for admission to the University of California Medical School at Davis. He was rejected both times. The school had reserved sixteen places in each entering class of one hundred for qualified minority applicants, as part of the university's affirmative action program. Bakke's qualifications (college grade point average and test scores) exceeded those of any of the minority students admitted in the two years his applications were re-

Compared with What? 12.1 (continued)

or guards for Moslem women, may soon have government jobs set aside for them. (In late 1997, activists began legal proceedings to force the government to set job quotas for eunuchs.)

Positive discrimination in India has intensified tensions between the lower and upper castes. In 1990, soon after the new quotas were established, scores of young upper-caste men and women set themselves ablaze in protest. And when Indian courts issued a temporary injunction against the positive discrimination policies, lower-caste terrorists bombed a train and killed dozens of people. Political conflict continues to this day as India's upper-caste members grow increasingly bitter about losing their once-exclusive access to well-paying government jobs in an economy that is not expanding rapidly enough to satisfy its citizenry.

India's experience with positive discrimination has implications for majoritarian and pluralist models of democracy. All governments broker conflict to varying degrees. Under a majoritarian model, group demands could lead quickly to conflict and instability, because majority rule leaves little room for compromise. A pluralist model allows different groups to get a piece of the pie. By parceling out benefits, pluralism mitigates disorder in the short term. But in the long term, repeated demands for increased benefits can spark instability. A vigorous pluralist system should provide acceptable mechanisms (legislative, executive, bureaucratic, judicial) to vent such frustrations and yield new allocations of benefits.

Sources: Trudy Rubin, "Will Democracy Survive in India?" *The Record* (New Jersey), 19 January 1998, p. A12; Alex Spillius, "India's Old Warriors to Launch Rights Fight," *The Daily Telegraph*, 20 October 1997, p. 12; Robin Wright, "World's Leaders: Men, 187, Women, 4," *Los Angeles Times*, 30 September 1997, p. A1; "Indian Eunuchs Demand Government Job Quotas," *Agence France Presse*, 22 October 1997.

jected. Bakke contended, first in the California courts, then in the Supreme Court, that he was excluded from admission solely on the basis of race. He argued that the equal protection clause of the Fourteenth Amendment and the Civil Rights Act of 1964 prohibited this reverse discrimination.

The Court's decision in *Bakke* contained six opinions and spanned 154 pages. But even after careful analysis of the decision, discerning what the Court had decided was difficult. No opinion had a majority. One bloc of four justices opposed the medical school's plan; a second bloc of four justices supported the plan. Justice Lewis F. Powell, Jr., agreed with parts of both arguments. With the first bloc, he argued that the school's rigid use of racial quotas violated the equal protection clause of the Fourteenth Amendment. With the second bloc, he contended that the use of race was permissible as one of several admissions criteria. Powell cast the deciding vote ordering the medical school to admit Bakke. Despite the confusing multiple opinions, the Court signaled its approval of affirmative action programs in education that use race as a *plus* factor (one of many such factors) but not as *the* factor (one that alone determines the outcome).

Other cases followed. In 1979, the Court upheld a voluntary affirmative action plan that gave preferences to blacks in an employee training program.[96] Five years later, however, the Court held that affirmative action did not exempt minorities (typically the most recently hired employees) from traditional work rules, which generally specify that the last hired are the first fired. Layoffs must proceed by seniority, declared the Court, unless minority employees can demonstrate that they are actual victims of their employer's discrimination.[97]

In 1995, the Supreme Court struck a sharp blow to the legal foundations of government policies that award benefits on the basis of race, signaling an end to equal outcomes policies. Recall Randy Pech's lawsuit challenging a government set-aside program for minority contractors. Writing for a 5–4 majority in *Adarand Constructors v. Peña,* Justice Sandra Day O'Connor declared that such programs must be subject to the most searching judicial inquiry ("strict scrutiny") and must be "narrowly tailored" to achieve a "compelling government interest."[98] Few, if any, programs can satisfy the Court's stringent requirements for constitutionality. (The Court sent the *Adarand* case back to the trial court so that it could evaluate the facts in light of the strict scrutiny standard.)

Quota policies are now under serious threat from several quarters. In 1996, a federal appeals court, relying on the *Adarand* case, rejected the use of race or ethnicity as the determining factor in law school admissions. Meanwhile, the governing board of the University of California voted to scrap its race-based admissions policy. And legislative movements in more than a dozen states took steps to curtail or eliminate racial preferences in educational admissions and financial aid. Colorado, for example, began to offer college scholarships on the basis of need rather than race.[99] The biggest showdown to date over the future of affirmative action occurred during the 1996 elections. California voters were asked to approve or reject a ballot initiative to amend the state constitution as follows:

> Neither the State of California, nor any of its political subdivisions or agents, shall use race, sex, color, ethnicity or national origin as a criterion for either discriminating against, or granting preferential treatment to, any individual or group in the operation of the State's system of public employment, public education or public contracting.

The initiative passed with 54 percent of the vote.

The Politics of Affirmative Action

A comprehensive review of nationwide surveys conducted over the past twenty years reveals an unsurprising truth: blacks favor affirmative action programs, and whites do not. Women and men do not differ on this issue. The gulf between the races was wider in the 1970s than it is today, but the moderation results from shifts among blacks, not whites. Perhaps the most important finding is that "whites' views have remained essentially unchanged over 20 years."[100]

How do we account for the persistence of equal outcomes policies? A majority of Americans have consistently rejected explicit race or gender preferences for the awarding of contracts, employment decisions, and college admissions, regardless of the groups such preferences benefit. Nevertheless, preference policies have survived and thrived under both Democrats and Republicans. The list of protected groups has expanded beyond African Americans to include Hispanic Americans, Native Americans, Asian Pacific Americans, Subcontinental Asian Americans, and women. Politicians have a powerful motive—votes—to expand the number of protected groups and the benefits such policies provide.

The conflict between freedom and equality will continue as other individuals and groups press their demands through litigation and legislation. The choice the country makes will depend on whether and to what extent Americans are prepared to change their minds on these thorny issues.

Summary

When the states and the people established the new government of the United States, they compelled the framers, through the Bill of Rights, to protect their freedoms. In their interpretation of the first ten amendments, the courts, especially the Supreme Court, have taken on the task of balancing freedom and order.

The First Amendment protects several freedoms: freedom of religion, freedom of speech and of the press, and the freedom to assemble peaceably and petition the government. The establishment clause demands government neutrality toward religions and between the religious and the nonreligious. According to judicial interpretations of the free-exercise clause, religious beliefs are inviolable, but the Constitution does not protect antisocial actions in the name of religion. Extreme interpretations of the religion clauses could bring the clauses into conflict with each other.

Freedom of expression encompasses freedom of speech, freedom of the press, and the right to assemble peaceably and petition the government. Freedom of speech and freedom of the press have never been held to be absolute, but the courts have ruled that the Bill of Rights gives them far greater protection than other freedoms. Exceptions to free-speech protections include some forms of symbolic expression, and obscenity. Press freedom has had broad constitutional protection because a free society depends on the ability to collect and report information without government interference. The rights to assemble peaceably and to petition the government stem from the guarantees of freedom of speech and of the press. Each freedom is equally fundamental, but the right to exercise them is not absolute.

The adoption of the Fourteenth Amendment in 1868 extended the guarantees of the Bill of Rights to the states. The due process clause became the vehicle for applying specific provisions of the Bill of Rights—one at a time, case after case—to the states. The designation of a right as fundamental also called for a definition of that right. The Supreme Court has tolerated some variation from state to state in the meaning of certain constitutional rights. The Court has also imposed a duty on governments to inform citizens of their rights so that they are equipped to exercise them.

As it has fashioned new fundamental rights from the Constitution, the Supreme Court has become embroiled in controversy. The right to privacy served as the basis for the right of women to terminate a pregnancy, which in turn suggested a right to personal autonomy. The abortion controversy is still raging, and the justices have called a halt to the extension of personal privacy in the name of the Constitution.

Americans want equality, but they disagree on the extent to which government should guarantee it. At the heart of this conflict is the distinction between equal opportunities and equal outcomes.

Congress enacted the Civil War amendments—the Thirteenth, Fourteenth, and Fifteenth Amendments—to provide full civil rights to black Americans. In the late nineteenth century, the Supreme Court interpreted the amendments very narrowly, declaring that they did not restrain individuals from denying civil rights to blacks and that they did not apply to powers that were reserved for the states. The Court's rulings had the effect of denying the vote to most blacks and of institutionalizing racism, making racial segregation a fact of daily life.

Through a series of court cases spanning two decades, the Court slowly dismantled segregation in the schools. The battle for desegregation culminated in the *Brown* cases in 1954 and 1955, in which a now-supportive Supreme Court declared segregated schools to be inherently unequal and therefore unconstitutional. The Court also ordered the desegregation of all schools and upheld the use of busing to do so.

Gains in other civil rights areas came more slowly. The motivating force was the civil rights movement, led by Martin Luther King, Jr., until his assassination in 1968. King believed strongly in civil disobedience and nonviolence, strategies that helped secure for blacks equality in voting rights, public accommodations, higher education, housing, and employment opportunity.

Civil rights activism and the civil rights movement worked to the benefit of all minority groups; in fact, they benefited all Americans. Native Americans obtained some redress for past injustices. Hispanic Americans came to recognize the importance of group action to achieve economic and political equality. Disabled Americans won civil rights protections enjoyed by African Americans and others. And civil rights legislation removed the protectionism that was, in effect, legalized discrimination against women in education and employment.

Despite legislative advances in the area of women's rights, the states did not ratify the Equal Rights Amendment. Still, the struggle for ratification produced several positive results, heightening awareness of women's roles in society and mobilizing their political power. And legislation and judicial rulings implemented much of the amendment's provisions in practice. The Supreme Court now judges sex-based classification with "skeptical scrutiny," meaning that distinctions based on sex are almost as suspect as distinctions based on race.

Government and business instituted affirmative action programs to counteract the results of past discrimination. These provide preferential treatment for women, minorities, and the disabled in a number of areas that affect individuals' economic opportunity and well-being. In effect, such programs discriminate to remedy earlier discrimination. When programs make race the determining factor in awarding contracts, offering employment, or granting admission to educational institutions, the courts will be skeptical of their validity. Notwithstanding congressional efforts to reverse some Supreme Court decisions, a conservative majority on the Court has emerged to roll back the equality-preferring policies of the more liberal bench that held sway through the 1980s.

Many of the civil liberties and civil rights that Americans enjoy today were defined by the courts. This raises a basic issue. By offering constitutional protection to certain public policies, the courts may be threatening the democratic process, the process that gives the people a say in government through their elected representatives. One thing is certain, however. The challenge of democracy requires the constant balancing of freedom, order, and equality.

Key Terms

affirmative action
civil liberties
civil rights
establishment clause
free-exercise clause
strict scrutiny
free-expression clauses
prior restraint
clear and present danger test
public figures
bill of attainder
ex post facto law
obligation of contracts
Miranda warnings
exclusionary rule
good faith exception
equality of opportunity

equality of outcome
invidious discrimination
racism
poll tax
racial segregation
separate-but-equal doctrine
desegregation
de jure segregation
de facto segregation
civil rights movement
boycott
civil disobedience
protectionism
Nineteenth Amendment
sexism
Equal Rights Amendment (ERA)

Key Cases

Lemon v. Kurtzman
Sherbert v. Verner
Brandenburg v. Ohio
Tinker v. Des Moines Independent County School District
Miller v. California
New York Times v. Sullivan
New York Times v. United States
Palko v. Connecticut
Gideon v. Wainwright
Griswold v. Connecticut
Roe v. Wade
Bowers v. Hardwick
Plessy v. Ferguson
Brown v. Board of Education
Brown v. Board of Education II
United States v. Virginia
Regents of the University of California v. Bakke
Adarand Constructors v. Peña

Selected Readings

Branch, Taylor. *Parting the Waters: America in the King Years, 1954–1963.* New York: Simon & Schuster, 1988. A riveting, Pulitzer Prize–winning narrative history and biography of the King years.

Branch, Taylor. *Pillar of Fire: America in the King Years, 1963–65.* New York: Simon & Schuster, 1998. The second volume of Branch's prize-winning narrative.

Browning, Rufus P., Dale Rogers Marshall, and David H. Tabb. *Racial Politics in American Cities.* New York: Longman, 1990. This collection of essays documents the continuing struggle for minority access to political power in cities across the United States.

Carter, Stephen L. *The Culture of Disbelief: How American Law and Politics Trivialize Religious Devotion.* New York: Basic Books, 1993. In this wide-ranging, thoughtful work, Carter argues that Americans can simultaneously preserve separation of church and state, embrace American spirituality, and avoid treating believers with disdain.

Garrow, David. *Liberty and Sexuality: The Right to Privacy and the Making of* Roe *v.* Wade. New York: Macmillan, 1994. This is a comprehensive, historical narrative of the fundamental right to sexual privacy.

Levy, Leonard W. *The Establishment Clause: Religion and the First Amendment.* New York: Macmillan, 1986. This searching study of the establishment clause claims that the view that government can assist all religions is historically groundless. Levy argues that it is unconstitutional for government to provide aid to any religion.

Lewis, Anthony. *Make No Law: The Sullivan Case and the First Amendment.* New York: Random House, 1991. This is an enlightening study of a great constitutional decision. Lewis illuminates the history and evolution of the First Amendment guarantees of free expression and free press.

Smolla, Rodney A. *Free Speech in an Open Society.* New York: Alfred A. Knopf, 1993. A lucid examination covering a wide range of contemporary problems in free speech, such as flag burning.

Sniderman, Paul M., and Thomas Piazza. *The Scar of Race.* Cambridge, Mass.: Belknap Press of Harvard University Press, 1993. The authors of this insightful study argue that the problems of race cannot be reduced to racism. On many racial issues, white Americans are open to argument and persuasion, even though they disagree on racial policies.

Verba, Sidney, and Gary R. Orren. *Equality in America: The View from the Top.* Cambridge, Mass.: Harvard University Press, 1985. Two political scientists isolate different meanings of equality, then analyze the opinions of American leaders on the application of equality of opportunity across a range of policy areas.

World Wide Web Resources

American Civil Liberties Union Freedom Network. Check out this site to get up-to-the-minute reports on the state of civil liberties around the nation.
   <www.aclu.org>

The Newseum bills itself as an interactive museum devoted to First Amendment issues. The site includes programs broadcast via RealAudio.
   <www.freedomforum.org>

The Flag Burning Page confronts the core American values of order versus freedom. The site takes a libertarian approach, neither encouraging nor discouraging flag burning. Its single mission is to prevent any constitutional ban on flag desecration. There's a link to a virtual flag burning, if that's your cup of tea. <www.esquilax.com/flag>

Native American Resources. A wealth of links to issues related to native peoples. <www.cowboy.net/native>

Americans with Disabilities Act (ADA) Document Center Web site contains a treasury of information about the ADA and its application to a long list of issues. <janweb.icdi.wvu.edu/kinder>

The Asia Society is a good source for content and links to Web sites concerned with fostering a better understanding of Asia and with improved communication between Americans and the people of Asia. <www.asiasociety.org>

US Latino Web Sites. An excellent source of content links addressing the concerns of Spanish-speaking people. The webmaster notes that "only Web sites that are reflective of US Latino realities were considered." <www.public.iastate.edu/~savega/reclst.html>

The National Gay and Lesbian Task Force was founded in 1973. The organization is an interest group that fights for gay rights. <www.ngltf.org>

National Association for the Advancement of Colored People (NAACP). Extensive web site produced by the nation's largest civil rights organization. <www.naacp.org>

The National Organization for Women (NOW) Home Page. A very useful home page that provides access to NOW policy statements, press releases, and research, as well as links to women's resources on the Internet. <www.now.org>

13

Policymaking and the Budget

"Hello Dolly!" heralded the newspaper headlines, announcing a most unusual birth. In February 1997, Scottish scientists stunned the world with the news that they had cloned a sheep. The clone—named Dolly—was an exact replica of its mother. While Dolly placidly munched her dinner, religious, government, and academic leaders were thrown into turmoil as they pondered the implications of this first cloning of a mammal and speculated about potential human cloning.

Thirty years earlier, Joshua Lederberg, an American Nobel laureate in genetics, had broached the subject of human cloning. He thought the idea was exciting. Humankind would be able to clone its best and brightest people for all time. Also, the human genetics pool could be made predictable, with undesirable traits weeded out. Lederberg suggested other uses for human cloning as well. If a child were brain damaged in an accident, the parents could have a replacement made of their beloved offspring. Or if someone needed a bone marrow transplant to win a fight against leukemia, an identical infant could be reproduced to save the original.[1]

Critics of cloning wonder whether creating a replica of another individual would truly be possible. Even if a Thomas Jefferson or a Mother Teresa were genetically reproduced, would the copy really be the same as the original?

Another concern is that the diversity of the human gene pool could be lost over time. What is popular and desirable in one era of human history may be unpopular and out of fashion in another era. Ancient China valued Mandarins, scholars who served as bureaucrats, but Nazi Germany prized blond, blue-eyed warriors. And individuals of historical renown have sometimes been more admired by later generations than by their contemporaries. Recall the fates of Socrates, Joan of Arc, and Gandhi.

Additionally, human cloning could threaten the philosophical underpinnings of democracy. Americans believe that every individual is unique and possesses inalienable rights bestowed by his or her creator. Each person's distinctive genetic makeup bolsters this individuality and our belief in the preciousness of a single life.

Informed of Dolly's arrival, President Clinton began hammering out a policy to deal with this revolutionary advance in technology. First, he issued an executive order forbidding the use of federal money for cloning research; then he handed the task of debating the legal and ethical ramifications of cloning to the National Bioethics Commission. Panel chairman Harold Shapiro, president of Princeton University, thought the issues involved were remarkably difficult, because they "go to the very nature of what it means to be human."[2] In response to the commission's recommendations, President Clinton appealed for a five-year moratorium on all attempts to duplicate a human being. Over sixty-four thousand scientists agreed to honor the president's request, but in December 1997, Dr. Richard Seed stated that he would defy the voluntary ban and try to produce the first human clone. In reaction to this announcement, President Clinton declared human cloning to be an affront "to our cherished concepts of faith and humanity" and urged Congress to outlaw it in the United States.[3]

The president's remarks touched a responsive chord with the public and politicians alike, as most Americans appeared to share the president's deep distaste for cloning. According to one public opinion poll, over 90 percent of Americans would not want to clone themselves, and almost three-quarters thought human cloning violated God's will.[4] In Congress there also seemed to be growing interest in addressing this issue. Not only were members concerned about the ramifications of a full-fledged human clone, but Representative Vernon Ehlers, a Republican from Michigan, also wanted to prohibit the creation of human embryos that would briefly be used for medical research and then allowed to die. The FDA got into the act by warning Dr. Seed that his laboratory would be closed if he proceeded without the agency's permission.

The case of Dolly illustrates how rapid technological change can suddenly thrust a new issue onto the public agenda. Of course, many other factors can also push an issue forward: a heinous crime, the courageous determination of an individual, a miscarriage of justice, Mother Nature—the list of possibilities is more or less endless. How do policy issues arise, and what happens to them once they catch the public's attention?

Previous chapters have focused on individual institutions of government. Here we focus on government more broadly and ask how policymaking takes place across institutions. We first identify different types of public policies and then analyze the stages in the policymaking process. We then examine how policy is made when many competing interest groups are trying to influence the outcome and how relationships between those groups, and between such groups and different parts of government, structure the policymaking process. Finally, we take a closer look at budgeting and policies relating to the economy.

Government Purposes and Public Policies

In Chapter 1, we noted that nearly all citizens are willing to accept limitations on their personal freedom in return for various benefits of government. We defined the major purposes of government as maintaining order, providing public benefits, and promoting equality. Different governments place different values on each broad purpose, and those differences are reflected in their public policies. A **public policy** is a general plan of action adopted by a government to solve a social problem, counter a threat, or pursue an objective.

Whatever their form and effectiveness, all policies have this in common: they are the means by which government pursues certain goals in specific situations. People disagree about public policies because they disagree about one or more of the following elements: the goals that government should have, the means it should use to achieve goals, and the perception of the situation at hand.

How do policymakers attempt to achieve their goals? As a starting point, we will divide government policies into four broad types: public policies that prohibit, protect, promote, or provide.

Some policies are intended to *prohibit* behaviors that endanger society. All governments outlaw murder, robbery, and rape. Governments that emphasize order tend to favor policies of prohibition, which instruct people in what they must not do (drink liquor, have abortions, use illegal drugs).

Some policies are intended to *protect* certain activities, business markets, or special groups of citizens. For example, taxes were once levied on colored margarine (a butter substitute) to reduce its sales and protect the dairy industry from competition. Regulations affecting the testing of new drugs are intended to protect citizens from harmful side effects. Although governments argue that these kinds of regulations serve the public good, some people believe that most protective legislation is unwarranted government interference.

Some policies are intended to *promote* social activities that the government considers important. For instance, our government has used advertising to urge people to buy bonds or to join the army. To promote railroad construction in the 1860s, Congress granted railroad companies huge tracts of public land as rights-of-way through western states.

The government also promotes activities through favorable tax treatment. Because tax breaks result in a loss of government revenue, the technical term for this form of government promotion is *tax expenditure.* For example, the government encourages people to buy their own homes by allowing homeowners to deduct from their taxable income the interest they pay on their mortgages.

Finally, some policies are intended to *provide* benefits directly to citizens, either collectively or selectively. Collective benefits are facilities or services that all residents share (mail service, roads, schools, street lighting, libraries, parks). Selective benefits go to certain groups of citizens (poor people, farmers, veterans, college students). Collective benefits can be more difficult to deliver because either the construction of facilities (roads, dams, sewer systems) or the creation of organizations (transportation agencies, power companies, sanitation departments) is necessary to provide them. Many selective benefits are simply payments to individuals in the form of food stamps, subsidies, pensions, and loans. The payments are made because the recipients are particularly needy, powerful, or both.

We distinguish government policies according to their approach not simply to create an inventory of problem-solving methods but also to emphasize the relationship between policy and process. By *process* we mean the configuration of participants involved, the procedures used for decision making, and the degree of cooperation or conflict usually present.

Our premise is simple: different kinds of policies affect the political process in different ways. If a policy proposal affects a well-organized constituency adversely, that constituency will fight it aggressively. When the Clinton administration proposed legislation to raise grazing fees on federal land, western ranchers who wanted to maintain the relatively low rates they were paying resisted bitterly. Other policies pit well-organized groups against each other. Action for Children's Television and other organizations promoting educational programming for children have long pressured the Federal Communications Commission (FCC) to require broadcasters to air more high-quality shows for young viewers. The National Association for Broadcasters, representing 1,400 local TV stations, opposes such rules.

The Policymaking Process: A Model

We can separate the policymaking process into four stages: agenda setting, policy formulation, implementation, and policy evaluation.[5] Figure 13.1 shows the four stages in sequence. As the figure indicates, policymaking is a circular process: the end of one phase is the beginning of another.

Agenda Setting

Agenda setting is the stage in which problems are defined as political issues. Many problems confront Americans in their daily lives, but government is not actively working to solve them all. For example, the problem of poverty among the elderly did not suddenly arise during the 1930s, but that is when inadequate income for the elderly was defined as a political problem. When the government begins to consider acting on an issue it has previously ignored, we say that the issue has become part of the political agenda.

Why does an existing social problem become redefined as a political problem? There is no single reason; many factors can stimulate new thinking about a problem. Sometimes, highly visible events or developments push issues onto the agenda. Issues may also reach the agenda through the efforts of scholars and activists to get more people to pay attention to a condition about which the general public seems unaware. The likelihood that a certain problem will move onto the agenda is also affected by who controls the government and by broad ideological shifts. Agenda building also may involve redefining old issues so that people look at them in different ways.[6]

Policy Formulation

Policy formulation is the stage of the policymaking process in which formal policy proposals are developed and officials decide whether to adopt them. The most obvious kind of policy formulation is the proposal of a measure by the president or the development of legislation by Congress. Administrative

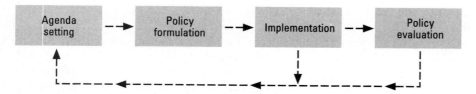

FIGURE 13.1   The Policymaking Process
This model, one of many possible ways to depict the policymaking process, shows four stages. Feedback on program operations and on performance from the last two stages stimulates new cycles of the process.

agencies also formulate policy through the regulatory process. Courts, too, formulate policy when their decisions establish new interpretations of the law.

Implementation

Policies are not self-executing; **implementation** is the stage in which they are carried out. When agencies in Washington issue regulations, some government bodies must put those policies into effect. Consider the case of the 1990 Americans with Disabilities Act. The owners of office buildings not in compliance probably would not have repositioned their water fountains simply because Washington had published new regulations. Administrative bodies at the regional, state, or local level had to inform them of the rules, give them a timetable for compliance, communicate the penalties for noncompliance, answer questions, and report to Washington on how well the regulations were working.

As pointed out in Chapter 10, one of the biggest problems at the implementation stage of policymaking is coordination. After officials in Washington enact a law and write the new regulations, people outside Washington typically are designated to implement the policy. The agents may be local officials, state administrators, or federal bureaucrats headquartered in regional offices around the country. Although implementation may sound highly technical, it is very much a political process calling for a great deal of bargaining and negotiation among different groups of people in and out of government.

Policy Evaluation

Policy evaluation is the analysis of how well a policy is working. Evaluation tends to draw heavily on approaches used by academics, including cost-effectiveness analysis and statistical methods designed to provide quantitative measurements of program outcomes. Technical studies can be quite influential in decisions about whether to continue, expand, alter, reduce, or eliminate programs.

One interesting example of policy evaluation involves weaponry used in the Persian Gulf War. In that conflict, the United States for the first time made extensive use of "smart bombs"—bombs that are electronically guided to their targets. During the war the Pentagon touted the effectiveness of these weapons, showing the American public dramatic videotapes of smart bombs hitting targets in Iraq. Later, a thorough and dispassionate study by Congress's General Accounting Office compared the very expensive smart bombs and the far cheaper "dumb bombs" and showed no difference in their accuracy. This is the kind of policy evaluation that is most useful: directly comparing different ways of achieving the same goal and determining the relative effectiveness and efficiency of each approach.

Evaluation is part of the policymaking process because it helps to identify problems and issues arising from current policy. In other words, evaluation studies provide **feedback** about program performance. (The dotted line in Figure 13.1 represents a feedback loop. Problems that emerge during the implementation stage also provide feedback to policymakers.) By drawing attention to emerging problems, policy evaluation influences the political agenda. Thus, we come full circle. The end of the process—evaluating whether the policy is being implemented as it was envisioned when it was formulated— marks the beginning of a new cycle of public policymaking.

Issue Networks

Within any issue area, a number—often a very large number—of interest groups try to influence policy decisions. Representatives from these organizations interact with each other and with government officials on a recurring basis. The ongoing interaction produces both conflict and cooperation.

The various individuals and organizations that work in a particular policy area form a loosely knit community. More specifically, those "who share expertise in a policy domain and who frequently interact constitute an issue network."[7] The boundaries and membership of an **issue network** are hardly precise, but in general terms networks include members of Congress, committee staffers, agency officials, lawyers, lobbyists, consultants, scholars, and public relations specialists.

Government by Policy Area:
The Case of Telecommunications

Political scientists have long analyzed policymaking by issue area. The issue network framework, however, is a relatively new tool. In the 1950s, policy communities were typically smaller, consisting of the chairmen of a few key committees or subcommittees, a top agency official, and a couple of lobbyists from the principal trade groups, who negotiated behind the scenes to settle important policy questions. Political scientists used to call such small, tightly knit policy communities *iron triangles*. Iron triangles were thought to be relatively autonomous and to operate by consensus.

The explosion in the number of interest groups and the growth of government and overlapping jurisdictions brought an end to iron triangles. Issue networks, today's policy area communities, are much more open and much more conflictual. The telecommunications industry provides a useful illustration of the changing nature of politics in Washington. Once a harmonious iron triangle, telecommunications today is a large issue network filled with conflict.

For many years, the telecommunications industry was dominated by American Telephone & Telegraph (AT&T), which, with its affiliated Bell System telephone companies around the country, constituted a monopoly.[8] Customers had no choice but to use the phone lines and phone equipment of "Ma Bell." Within the telecommunications iron triangle—a policymaking community made up of some key members of Congress, the Federal Communications Commission, and AT&T—policymaking was usually consensual and uncontroversial. Then, in 1974, the U.S. Department of Justice filed a lawsuit against the corporation, charging it with illegal monopolistic behavior in the telecommunications industry.

The eventual outcome of the suit, in 1982, was an out-of-court settlement that required AT&T to give up control over local operating service. The Bell System was broken up into seven independent regional telephone companies (the "Baby Bells"). AT&T was allowed to retain its long-distance service, but it would have to compete against other long-distance carriers. The giant telephone company had fallen victim to a growing belief among academics and policymakers that government regulation was hampering the economy by restricting competition and lessening the incentives for innovation, as well as limiting the price and product choices available to consumers. Thus, telecommunications was deregulated.[9]

Today, policymaking in telecommunications bears no resemblance to an iron triangle. After the AT&T divestiture, competition among businesses selling communications services and equipment intensified. Many new companies joined the highly fractious issue network. Much of the political conflict that ensued involved fights between the Baby Bells and long-distance carriers, each side wanting to expand into new markets while protecting current markets from encroachment by would-be competitors.

Three important developments in telecommunications forced the government to abandon the regulatory framework of 1982. One is technological innovations, such as cellular phones and other forms of wireless communication, that were either not anticipated by the consent decree or excluded from it. Another is the pivotal convergence of various technologies. Telephone lines, for example, became critically important to computer users as the electronic transmission of data and digital communications became more feasible. The third development is entrepreneurs' perception of the future as a period in which the strongest companies—or at least those that survived the tumultuous changes in the marketplace—would be the ones that were alliances of many different businesses with expertise in individual products. Such alliances could offer an array of services to customers through integrated technology.

Those three developments forced the government to move toward a truly deregulated market with legislation passed in 1996. Telecommunications firms can now enter almost any business and package these services together. Local phone companies can offer long-distance services, and long-distance companies can offer local service.[10]

As Figure 13.2 shows, changes in the industry have created an issue network characterized not so much by political alliances as by business alliances.

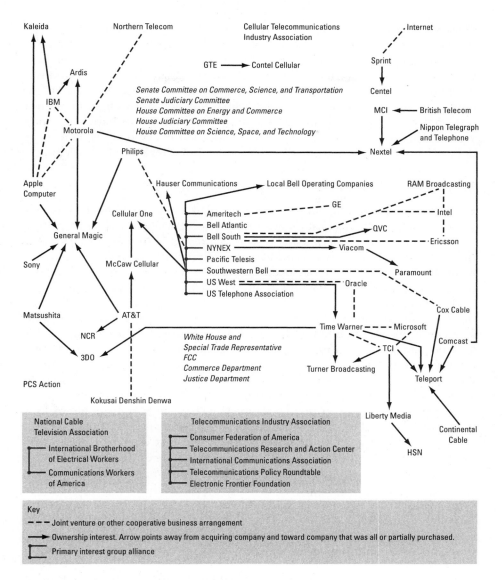

FIGURE 13.2   The Telecommunications Issue Network
There is no one way to draw an issue network. This graphic illustrates the different types of relationships among the different private sector groups involved in the telecommunications industry. Recent trends in the industry are toward more and more mergers and acquisitions as companies try to expand into integrated, large-scale entities that can provide a range of services that will be popular in the future. The congressional committees and units of the executive branch specified in this figure are those with primary responsibility for telecommunications policymaking. (Source: Jeffrey M. Berry, "The Dynamic Qualities of Issue Networks," paper delivered at the annual meeting of the American Political Science Association, New York City, September 1994.)

Mergers, acquisitions, joint ventures, and cross-ownership arrangements have spawned many firms with far-reaching interests.[11] (The figure depicts the industry in the spring of 1994; since then, the changes have accelerated.) Generally though, issue network politics is characterized by rapidly changing coalitions as partners on one issue become opponents on the next. Conflict within the telecommunications issue network is chronic. No one controls telecommunications policymaking, but many organizations and individuals have a say in it. With hundreds of lobbies active in many important policy areas, issue network politics has come to characterize contemporary policymaking in Washington.

Issue Networks and Democracy

For many years, political scientists have described American democracy as a system in which different constituencies work energetically to influence policies of concern to them. Policymaking is seen as a response to these groups rather than to majority will. This is a considerably different conception of democracy from the more traditional perspective, that policies reflect what most people want. It is a pluralist, not a majoritarian, view of American government.

In a number of ways, issue networks promote pluralist democracy. They are open systems, populated by a wide range of interest groups. Decision making is not centralized in the hands of a few key players; policies are formulated in a participatory fashion. But there is still no guarantee that all relevant interests are represented, and those with the greatest financial resources have an advantage. Nevertheless, issue networks provide access to government for a diverse set of competing interests and thus further the pluralist ideal.[12]

Those who prefer majoritarian democracy, however, see issue networks as an obstacle to achieving their vision of how government should operate. The technical complexity of contemporary issues makes it especially difficult for the public at large to exert control over policy outcomes. However, although issue networks promote pluralism, keep in mind that majoritarian influences on policymaking are still significant. The broad contours of public opinion can be a dominant force on highly visible issues. Elections, too, send messages to policymakers about the most widely discussed campaign issues. What issue networks have done, however, is facilitate pluralist politics in policy areas in which majoritarian influences are weak.

Economic Policy and the Budget

Economic Theory

Keynesian theory, developed by John Maynard Keynes, a British economist, holds that government can stabilize the economy through a combination of fiscal and monetary policies. **Fiscal policies**, which are enacted by the president and Congress, involve changes in government spending and taxing. When demand for goods and services is too low, according to Keynes, government should either spend more itself—hiring people and thus giving them money—or cut taxes, giving people more of their own money to spend. When demand is too great, the government should either spend less or raise taxes, giving people less money to spend. **Monetary policies**, which are largely determined by the Federal Reserve Board, involve changes in the money supply and operate less directly on the economy. Increasing the amount of money in circulation increases demand and thus increases price inflation. Decreasing the money supply decreases aggregate demand and inflationary pressures.

Despite some problems with the assumptions of Keynesian theory, capitalist countries have widely adopted it in some form.[13] At one time or another, nearly all have used the Keynesian technique of **deficit financing**—spending in excess of tax revenues—to combat an economic slump. The objective of deficit financing is to inject extra money into the economy to stimulate aggregate demand.

In 1946, the year Keynes died, Congress passed an employment act establishing "the continuing responsibility of the national government to . . . promote maximum employment, production and purchasing power." It also created the **Council of Economic Advisors** (CEA) within the Executive Office of the President to advise the president on maintaining a stable economy.

Although most economists accept Keynesian theory in its broad outlines, they deprecate its political utility. Some argue that government spending programs take too long to enact in Congress and to implement through the bureaucracy. As a result, jobs are created not when they are needed but years later, when the crisis may have passed and government spending needs to be reduced. Also, government spending is easier to start than to stop, because the groups that benefit from spending programs tend to defend them even when they are no longer needed. A similar criticism applies to tax policies. Politically, it is much easier to cut taxes than to raise them.

Recognizing these limitations of fiscal policies, **monetarists** argue that government can control the economy's performance effectively only by controlling the nation's money supply. Monetarists favor a long-range policy of small but steady growth in the amount of money in circulation rather than frequent manipulation of monetary policies.

Monetary policies in the United States are under the control of the **Federal Reserve System**, which acts as the country's central bank. At the top of the system is the board of governors, seven members appointed by the president for staggered terms of fourteen years. The president designates one member of the board to be its chairperson, serving a four-year term that extends beyond the president's term of office.

When Ronald Reagan came to office in 1981, he embraced a school of thought called **supply-side economics** to deal with the double-digit inflation that the nation was experiencing. Keynesian theory argues that inflation results when consumers, businesses, and governments have more money to spend than there are goods and services to buy. The standard Keynesian solution is to reduce demand (for example, by increasing taxes). Supply-siders argue that inflation can be lowered more effectively by increasing the supply of goods (that is, they stress the supply side of the economic equation). Specifically, they favor tax cuts to stimulate investment (which, in turn, leads to the production of more goods) and less government regulation of business (again, to increase productivity—which they hold will yield more, not less, government revenue). Supply-siders believe that government interferes too much with the efforts of individuals to work, save, and invest.

Budgeting for Public Policy

To most people—college students included—the national budget is B-O-R-I-N-G. To national politicians, it is an exciting script for high drama. The numbers, categories, and percentages that numb normal minds cause politicians' nostrils to flare and their hearts to pound. The budget is a battlefield on which politicians wage war over the programs they support.

Today, the president prepares the budget, and Congress approves it. This was not always the case. Before 1921, Congress prepared the budget under its constitutional authority to raise taxes and appropriate funds. The budget was formed piecemeal by enacting a series of laws that originated in the many committees involved in the highly decentralized process of raising revenue, authorizing expenditures, and appropriating funds.

Congressional budgeting (such as it was) worked well enough for a nation of farmers but not for an industrialized nation with a growing population and an increasingly active government. Soon after World War I, Congress realized that the budget-making process needed to be centralized. With the Budget and Accounting Act of 1921, it thrust the responsibility for preparing the budget onto the president. The act established the Bureau of the Budget to help the president write "his" budget, which had to be submitted to Congress each January. Congress retained its constitutional authority to raise and spend funds, but now Congress would begin its work with the president's budget as its starting point. And all executive agencies' budget requests had to be funneled for review through the Bureau of the Budget (which became the Office of Management and Budget in 1970); requests that were consistent with the president's overall economic and legislative program were incorporated into the president's budget.

The Nature of the Budget

The national budget is complex. But its basic elements are not beyond understanding. We begin with some definitions. The *Budget of the United States Government* is the annual financial plan that the president is required to submit to Congress at the start of each year. It applies to the next **fiscal year (FY),** the interval the government uses for accounting purposes. Currently, the fiscal year runs from October 1 to September 30. The budget is named for the year in which it *ends,* so the FY 2001 budget applies to the twelve months from October 1, 2000, to September 30, 2001.

Broadly, the budget defines **budget authority** (how much government agencies are authorized to spend on programs); **budget outlays**, or expenditures (how much agencies are expected to spend); and **receipts** (how much is expected in taxes and other revenues). Figure 13.3 diagrams the relationship of authority to outlays. President Clinton's FY 2001 budget contained authority for expenditures of $1,885 billion, but it provided for outlays of "only" $1,835 bil-

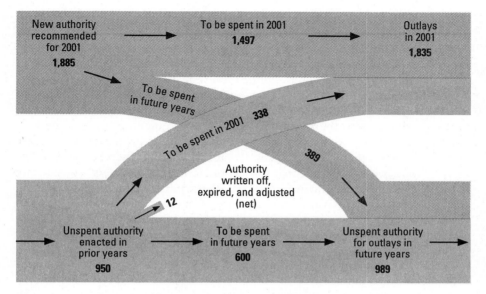

FIGURE 13.3 Relationship of Budget Authority to Budget Outlays
*The national budget is a complicated document. One source of confusion for people studying
the budget for the first time is the relationship of budget authority to budget outlays. These
two amounts differ because of sums that are carried over from previous years and reserved
for future years. This diagram helps explain the relationship (all amounts are in billions of
dollars). (Source: Executive Office of the President,* Budget of the United States Government,
Fiscal Year 2001: Analytical Perspectives *[Washington, D.C.: U.S. Government Printing Office,
2001], p. 374.) Some numbers do not sum due to rounding.*

lion. His budget also anticipated receipts of $2,019 billion, leaving an estimated
surplus of $184 billon—the difference between receipts and outlays.

Clinton's FY 2001 budget, with appendices, was thousands of pages long
and weighed several pounds. (The president's budget document contains
more than numbers. It also explains individual spending programs in terms of
national needs and agency objectives, and it analyzes proposed taxes and
other receipts.) Each year, the publication of the president's budget is anx-
iously awaited by reporters, lobbyists, and political analysts eager to learn his
plans for government spending in the coming year.

Preparing the President's Budget

The budget that the president submits to Congress each winter is the end
product of a process that begins the previous spring under the supervision of
the **Office of Management and Budget (OMB)**. OMB is located within the
Executive Office of the President and is headed by a director appointed by the
president with the approval of the Senate. The OMB, with a staff of more than
five hundred, is the most powerful domestic agency in the bureaucracy, and its

director, who attends meetings of the president's cabinet, is one of the most powerful figures in government.

The OMB initiates the budget process each spring by meeting with the president to discuss the economic situation and his budgetary priorities. It then sends broad budgeting guidelines to every government agency and requests their initial projection of how much money they will need for the next fiscal year. The OMB assembles this information and makes recommendations to the president, who then develops more precise guidelines describing how much each is likely to get. By summer, the agencies are asked to prepare budgets based on the new guidelines. By fall, they submit their formal budgets to the OMB, where budget analysts scrutinize agency requests, considering both their costs and their consistency with the president's legislative program. A lot of politicking goes on at this stage as agency heads try to circumvent the OMB by pleading for their pet projects with presidential advisers and perhaps even with the president himself. Unlike presidents Reagan and Bush, who basically delegated economic policy to others in their administrations, Clinton was more involved in the process and made more of the big decisions himself.

Political negotiations over the budget may extend into the early winter— often until it goes to the printer. The voluminous document looks very much like a finished product, but the figures it contains are not final.

Passing the Congressional Budget

The president's budget must be approved by Congress. Its process for doing so is a creaky conglomeration of traditional procedures overlaid with structural reforms from the 1970s, external constraints from the 1980s, and changes introduced by the 1990 Budget Enforcement Act. The cumbersome process has had difficulty producing a budget according to Congress's own timetable.

The Traditional Procedure: The Committee Structure   Traditionally, the tasks of budget making were divided among a number of committees—a process that has been retained. Three types of committees are involved in budgeting:

- **Tax committees** are responsible for raising the revenues to run the government. The Ways and Means Committee in the House and the Finance Committee in the Senate consider all proposals for taxes, tariffs, and other receipts contained in the president's budget.

- **Authorization committees** (such as the House Armed Services Committee and the Senate Banking, Housing, and Urban Affairs Committee) have jurisdiction over particular legislative subjects. The House has about twenty committees that can authorize spending, and the Senate about fifteen. Each pores over the portions of the budget that pertain to its area of responsibility. However, in recent years power has shifted from the authorization committees to the appropriations committees.

- **Appropriations committees** decide which of the programs approved by the authorization committees will actually be funded (that is, given money to spend). For example, the House Armed Services Committee might propose building a new line of tanks for the army, and it might succeed in getting this proposal enacted into law. But the tanks will never be built unless the appropriations committees appropriate funds for that purpose. Thirteen distinct appropriations bills are supposed to be enacted each year to fund the nation's spending.

Two serious problems are inherent in a budgeting process that involves three distinct kinds of congressional committees. First, the two-step spending process (first authorization, then appropriation) is complex; it offers wonderful opportunities for interest groups to get into the budgeting act in the spirit of pluralist democracy. Second, because one group of legislators in each house plans for revenues and many other groups plan for spending, no one is responsible for the budget as a whole.

Reforms of the 1970s: The Budget Committee Structure The Budget and Impoundment Control Act of 1974 fashioned a typically political solution to the problems of wounded egos and competing jurisdictions that had frustrated previous attempts to change the budget-making process. All the tax and appropriations committees (and chairpersons) were retained, but new House and Senate budget committees were superimposed over the old committee structure. The **budget committees** supervise a comprehensive budget review process, aided by the Congressional Budget Office. The **Congressional Budget Office (CBO),** with a staff of more than two hundred, has acquired a budgetary expertise equal to that of the president's OMB, so it can prepare credible alternative budgets for Congress.

At the heart of the 1974 reforms was a timetable for the congressional budgeting process. The budget committees are supposed to propose an initial budget resolution that sets overall revenue and spending levels, broken down into twenty-one different "budget functions," such as national defense, agriculture, and health. By April 15, both houses are supposed to have agreed on a single budget resolution to guide their work on the budget during the summer. The appropriations committees are supposed to begin drafting the thirteen appropriations bills by May 15 and complete them by June 30. Throughout, the levels of spending set by majority vote in the budget resolution are supposed to constrain pressures by special interests to increase spending.

Congress implemented this basic process in 1975, and it worked reasonably well for the first few years. But the process broke down during the Reagan administration, when the president submitted annual budgets with huge deficits. The Democratic Congress adjusted Reagan's spending priorities away from the military and toward social programs, but it refused to propose a tax increase to reduce the deficit without the president's cooperation. At loggerheads with the president, Congress encountered increasing difficulty in enacting its budget resolutions according to its own timetable.

Lessons of the 1980s: Gramm-Rudman Alarmed by the huge deficits in Reagan's budgets, frustrated by his refusal to raise taxes, and stymied by their own inability to cut the deficit, members of Congress were ready to try almost anything. Republican senators Phil Gramm of Texas and Warren Rudman of New Hampshire were joined by Democrat Ernest Hollings of South Carolina in a drastic proposal to force a balanced budget by gradually eliminating the deficit. Soon known simply as **Gramm-Rudman**, this 1985 act mandated that the budget deficit be lowered to a specified level each year until the budget was balanced by FY 1991. If Congress did not meet the deficit level in any year, the act would trigger across-the-board budget cuts.

Unable to make the deficit meet the law in 1986 or 1987, Congress and the president simply changed the law to match the deficit. Gramm-Rudman showed that Congress lacked the will to force itself to balance the budget by an orderly plan of deficit reduction.

Progress in the 1990s   When the 1990 recession threatened another huge deficit for FY 1991, Congress and President Bush agreed on a new package of reforms and deficit targets in the **Budget Enforcement Act (BEA)** of 1990. Instead of defining annual deficit targets, the BEA defined two types of spending: **mandatory spending** and **discretionary spending**. Spending is mandatory for **entitlement programs** (such as social security and veterans' pensions) that provide benefits to individuals legally entitled to them and cannot be reduced without changing the law. This is not true of discretionary spending, which is expenditures authorized by annual appropriations, such as for the military. For the first time, the law established **pay-as-you-go restrictions** on mandatory spending: any proposed expansion of an entitlement program must be offset by cuts to another program or by a tax increase. Similarly, any tax cut must be offset by a tax increase somewhere else or by spending cuts.[14] Also for the first time, the law imposed limits, or "caps," on discretionary spending.

To get the Democratic Congress to pass the BEA, Bush accepted some modest tax increases. Just two years earlier, however, Bush had accepted his party's nomination for president with the vow, "Read my lips: no new taxes." Consequently, he faced a rebellion from members of his own party in Congress, who bitterly opposed the tax increase. Indeed, the tax hike may have cost him reelection in 1992.

Although Bush paid a heavy price for the BEA, the 1990 law did limit discretionary spending and slowed unfinanced entitlements and tax cuts. Clinton's 1993 budget deal, which barely squeaked by Congress, made even more progress in reducing the deficit. It retained the limits on discretionary spending and the pay-as-you-go rules from the 1990 act and combined spending cuts and higher revenues to cut the accumulated deficits from 1994 to 1998 by $500 billion. The 1993 law worked better than expected, and the deficit declined to $22 billion in 1997.[15]

The 1990 and 1993 budget agreements, both of which encountered strong opposition in Congress, helped pave the way for the historic **Balanced Budget Act (BBA)** that President Clinton and Congress negotiated in 1997. The BBA accomplished what most observers thought was beyond political possibility. It not only led to the balanced budget it promised but actually produced a budget surplus ahead of schedule—the first surplus since 1969. The BBA had something for both sides. President Clinton achieved his greatest legislative victory and a place in history for having successfully balanced the budget—a goal that had eluded presidents Nixon, Ford, Carter, Reagan, and Bush. He

Arguing About the Refund Check
President Bush made "tax relief" one of the centerpieces of his first 100 days in office, propos-
ing to spend much of the budget surplus on a $1.6 trillion tax cut. Tax reform proposals
often raise conflicts of freedom versus equality. In this case, Republicans argued that the cut
would give surplus tax money back to the people so they could spend it how they chose, while
Democrats argued that Bush's tax cut plan was too unequal because wealthier Americans
would benefit more than poorer ones.

and the Democrats also managed to extend the scope of the child tax credit to
low-income families, to launch a new children's health initiative, to restore
welfare benefits for disabled legal immigrants, and to strengthen or restore
other programs dear to Democrats. The Republican Congress achieved two of
its most important goals: a balanced budget and the first broad-based tax cut
since the Reagan days of 1981. In fact, the agreement took away much of the
conflict between the parties over fiscal issues.[16]

Taxing and Spending Decisions

Tax Policies   Tax policy is designed to provide a continuous flow of income. A
major text on government finance says that tax policy is sometimes changed to
accomplish one or more of several objectives:

- To adjust overall revenue to meet budget outlays
- To make the tax burden more equitable for taxpayers
- To help control the economy by raising taxes (thus decreasing demand) or
  by lowering taxes (thus increasing demand)[17]

In 1986 Congress passed one of the most sweeping tax reform laws in history. The new policy reclaimed a great deal of revenue by eliminating many deductions for corporations and wealthy citizens. By eliminating many tax brackets, the new tax policy approached the idea of a flat tax—one that requires everyone to pay at the same rate. A flat tax has the appeal of simplicity, but it violates the principle of **progressive taxation**, under which the rich pay proportionately higher taxes than the poor. Governments can rely on progressive taxation to redistribute wealth and thus promote economic equality.

After the 1986 tax reform there were only two tax rates—15 and 28 percent. In 1990 Bush was forced to violate his pledge of "no new taxes" by creating a third tax rate, 31 percent. Clinton created a fourth level, 40 percent in 1993, moving toward a more progressive tax structure.

Spending Policies   The national government spends hundreds of billions of dollars every year. Where does the money go? To understand current expenditures, it is a good idea to examine national expenditures over time, as in Figure 13.4. The effect of World War II is clear. Spending for national defense rose sharply after 1940, peaked at about 90 percent of the budget in 1945, and fell to about 30 percent in peacetime. The percentage allocated to defense rose again in the early 1950s, reflecting rearmament during the Cold War with the Soviet Union. Thereafter, the share of the budget devoted to defense decreased steadily (except for the bump during the Vietnam War in the late 1960s), until the trend was reversed by the Carter administration in the 1970s and shot upward during the Reagan presidency. Defense spending significantly decreased under Bush and continued to go down under Clinton.

Government payments to individuals (social security checks) consistently consumed less of the budget than national defense until 1971. Since then, payments to individuals have accounted for the largest portion of the national budget, and they have been increasing. Net interest payments have also increased substantially in recent years, reflecting the rapid growth of the national debt. Pressure from payments for national defense, individuals, and interest on the national debt has squeezed all other government outlays.

National spending has increased from about 15 percent of gross domestic product (GDP) soon after World War II to over 20 percent, for many years at the price of a growing national deficit. There are two major explanations for this steady increase in government spending. One is bureaucratic, the other political.

The bureaucratic explanation for spending increases involves **incremental budgeting**. When compiling their funding requests for the coming year, bureaucrats traditionally ask for the amount they got in the current year, plus some increment to fund new projects. Because Congress already approved the agency's budget for the current year, it pays little attention to the agency's current size (the largest part of its budget) and focuses instead on the extra money (the increment) requested for the next year. As a result, few agencies are ever cut back, and spending continually goes up.

Concern in the 1990s over the budget deficit substantially checked the practice of incremental budgeting. When the Republicans took over control of Congress in 1995, they largely disregarded Clinton's FY 1996 budget and

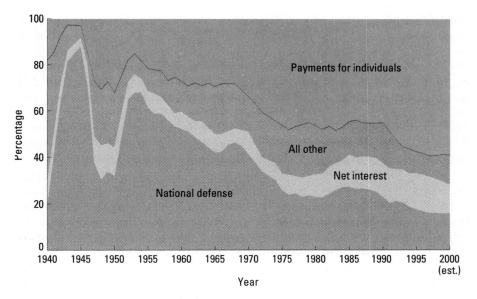

FIGURE 13.4   National Government Outlays over Time
This chart plots the percentage of the annual budget devoted to four major expense categories
over time. It shows that significant changes have occurred in national spending since 1940.
During World War II, defense spending consumed more than 80 percent of the national
budget. Defense again accounted for most national expenditures during the Cold War of the
1950s. Since then, the military's share of expenditures has declined, while payments to
individuals (mostly in the form of social security benefits) have increased dramatically. Also,
as the graph shows, the proportion of the budget paid in interest on the national debt has
increased substantially since the 1970s. (Source: Executive Office of the President, Budget of the
United States Government, Fiscal Year 2001: Historical Tables *[Washington, D.C.: U.S.*
Government Printing Office, 2000], pp. 103–109.)

proceeded to slash government programs. Only after Clinton vetoed five appropriations bills and the government experienced two historic shutdowns did
the president and Congress compromise on spending.[18] Nevertheless, the final
spending bill for FY 1996 was judged by an outside expert to be "one of the
most significant reversals in the course of government since World War II."[19]

Certain government programs are effectively immune to budget reductions, because they have been enacted into law and enshrined in politics. For
example, social security legislation guarantees certain benefits to program participants when they retire. Medicare and veterans' benefits also entitle citizens
to certain payments. Because these payments have to be made under existing
law, they represent uncontrollable outlays. In Clinton's FY 2001 budget, about
two-thirds of all budget outlays were uncontrollable or relatively uncontrollable—mainly payments to individuals under social security, Medicare, and
public assistance; interest on the national debt; and farm price supports. To
be sure, Congress could change the laws to abolish such entitlement payments. But politics argues against large-scale reductions. The Republicans in

Congress drew public criticism for "reducing" spending on health care, even though they took pains to explain that their program actually allowed for increased spending and they were only "cutting the rate of increase."[20]

What spending cuts would be acceptable to or even popular with the public? At the most general level, voters favor cutting government spending, but they tend to favor maintaining "government programs that help needy people and deal with important national problems."[21] A perplexed Congress, trying to avoid a budget deficit, faces a public that favors funding programs at even higher levels than those favored by most lawmakers.[22] Moreover, spending for the most expensive of these programs—social security and Medicare—is uncontrollable.

Social Security   **Social security** is social insurance that provides economic assistance to people faced with unemployment, disability, or old age; it is financed by taxes on employers and employees. Initially, social security benefits were distributed only to the aged, the unemployed, and surviving spouses—most of whom were widows—with dependent children. Today, social security also provides medical care for the elderly and income support for the disabled.

The social security taxes collected today pay the benefits of today's retirees. Thus, social security (and social insurance in general) is not a form of savings; it is a pay-as-you-go tax system. Today's workers support today's elderly. For that reason the solvency of the social security program will soon be tested. As the baby boomer generation retires, beginning about 2010, politicians will face an inevitable dilemma: whether to lower benefits and generate the ire of retirees or to raise taxes and generate the ire of taxpayers. As a group, older Americans exercise enormous political power. People at or near retirement age now make up almost 30 percent of the potential electorate, and voter turnout among older Americans is reported to be about twice that of younger people.[23]

Medicare   On July 30, 1965, President Johnson signed a bill that provided a number of health benefits to the elderly and the poor. The **Social Security Act** was amended to provide **Medicare**, health care for all people aged sixty-five or older. Fearful of the power of the American Medical Association (AMA), which then opposed any form of government-provided medical care, the Democrats confined their efforts to a compulsory hospitalization-insurance plan for the elderly (this is known today as Part A of Medicare). In addition, the bill contained a version of an alternative Republican plan, which called for voluntary government-subsidized insurance to cover physicians' fees (this is known today as Part B of Medicare). A third program, added a year later, is called *Medicaid*; it provides medical aid to the poor through federally assisted state health programs. Medicaid is a need-based comprehensive medical and hospitalization program: if you are very poor, you qualify.

Summary

Government tries to solve problems through a variety of approaches. Some public policies prohibit, some protect, some promote, and some provide. The approach chosen can significantly affect the policymaking process.

Although there is much variation in the policymaking process, we can conceive of it as consisting of four stages. The first stage is agenda setting, the process by which problems become defined as political issues worthy of government attention. Once people in government feel that they should be doing something about a problem, an attempt at policy formulation will follow. All three branches of the national government formulate policy. Once policies have been formulated and ratified, administrative units of government must implement them. Finally, once policies are being carried out, they need to be evaluated. Implementation and program evaluation influence agenda building, because program shortcomings become evident during these stages. Thus, the process is really circular, with the end often marking the beginning of a new round of policymaking.

Policymaking in many areas can be viewed as an ongoing process of interaction within issue networks composed of actors inside and outside government. Each network offers a way to communicate and exchange information and ideas about a particular policy area. In a network, lobbying coalitions form easily and dissolve rapidly as new issues arise. Issue networks place a high premium on expertise as public policy problems grow ever more complex.

Keynesian theory holds that the government should take an active role in dealing with inflation and unemployment, using fiscal and monetary policies to control aggregate demand. Monetarists believe fiscal policies are unreliable; they opt instead to use the money supply to affect aggregate demand. Supply-side economists focus on controlling the supply of goods and services rather than the demand for them.

Congress alone prepared the budget until 1921, when it thrust the responsibility onto the president. Later, Congress restructured the process under the House and Senate budget committees. The new process worked well until it confronted the huge budget deficits of the 1980s. Because so much of the budget involves military spending and uncontrollable payments to individuals, balancing the budget by reducing what remains—mainly spending for nonentitlement domestic programs—was regarded as impossible. Unwilling to accept responsibility for passing a tax increase, Congress passed the Gramm-Rudman deficit-reduction law in 1985. The deficit problem proved so intractable, however, that Congress had to amend the law in 1987 to extend the deadline to 1993—and the budget still wasn't balanced. When the Republicans gained control of Congress in 1995, they abandoned the informal policy of incremental budgeting and drastically cut spending on discretionary programs.

Although President Bush promised "no new taxes" when he was campaigning for office in 1988, he had to acknowledge the need for revenue increases to cut the deficit and was forced to accept the Budget Enforcement Act of 1990, which raised the income tax. This act modified the budgeting procedure and made it easier to meet the Gramm-Rudman targets. In 1993, President Clinton narrowly won approval of a fourth income tax bracket, at 40 percent. Responding to increased revenue and a hold on spending, the deficit declined. Aided by a growth economy, Clinton engineered taxing and spending changes in 1997 that produced a budget surplus in FY 1998—the first surplus since 1969.

Often, disagreements about public policy are disagreements about values. Some of the oldest and most costly domestic policies, such as social security and Medicare, pose choices between freedom and equality. Gradually, programs to aid the elderly and the poor have been transformed into entitlements. These government programs have reduced poverty among some groups, especially the elderly. However, there are significant concerns about the long-term economic viability of these programs as the American public ages.

Key Terms

public policy
agenda setting
policy formulation
implementation
policy evaluation
feedback
issue network
Keynesian theory
fiscal policies
monetary policies
deficit financing
Council of Economic Advisers
monetarists
Federal Reserve System
supply-side economics
fiscal year (FY)
budget authority
budget outlays
receipts

Office of Management and Budget (OMB)
tax committees
authorization committees
appropriations committees
budget committees
Congressional Budget Office (CBO)
Gramm-Rudman
Budget Enforcement Act (BEA)
mandatory spending
discretionary spending
entitlement program
pay-as-you-go restrictions
Balanced Budget Act (BBA)
progressive taxation
incremental budgeting
social security
Social Security Act
Medicare

Selected Readings

Anderson, James E. *Public Policymaking*. 2d ed. Boston: Houghton Mifflin, 1994. A brief overview of the policymaking system.

Axelrod, Donald. *Budgeting for Modern Government*. 2d ed. New York: St. Martin's Press, 1995. A thorough explanation of the process of public budgeting, from agency requests to the finished budget. Excellent in evaluating criticisms and proposing reforms.

Eisner, Robert. *The Great Deficit Scares: The Federal Budget, Trade, and Social Security*. New York: Century Foundation Press, 1997. Eisner is one of the few prominent economists who think that a budget deficit is not as serious a problem as the public has been led to believe. He argues that the deficit is calculated improperly, not allowing for capital assets.

Penny, Timothy J., and Steven E. Schier. *Payment Due: A Nation in Debt, a Generation in Trouble*. Boulder, Colo.: Westview Press, 1996. A former member of Congress (Penny) and a scholar collaborate in analyzing the problems in reducing the deficit and the consequences for America if we do not.

Pierson, Paul. *Dismantling the Welfare State*. New York: Cambridge University Press, 1994. The decline of support for welfare in the United States and Britain during the 1980s is viewed through a comparative lens.

Schick, Allen, with Felix Lostracco. *The Federal Budget: Politics, Policy, and Process*. Washington, D.C.: Brookings Institution, 2000. Explains not only the budgetary process, but also the implication of the return to surplus at the end of the twentieth century.

Stein, Herbert. *On the Other Hand . . . Reflections on Economics, Economists, and Politics*. Washington, D.C.: American Enterprise Institute, 1995. The chairman of

President Nixon's Council of Economic Advisers examines controversies over economic growth, employment, taxes, and deficits, and the ideas of economists whose theories have influenced economic practice.

World Wide Web Resources

The Heritage Foundation. This is the home page for this conservative public policy think tank. In addition to "this week's top ten facts," visitors interested in public policy jobs can access the foundation's job bank. This page also provides its "Candidate Education Guide," the latest news on current issues (such as tax reform) and various foundation publications, including current and back issues of the foundation's magazine, *Policy Review: Journal of American Citizenship.* <www.heritage.org>

Progressive Policy Institute. This is the home page of the Progressive Policy Institute of the Democratic Leadership Council. In addition to accessing information on the organization's history and ideology, visitors can access the institute's library, read current news articles about the DLC, and read current and back issues of the institute's "flagship magazine," *The New Democrat.* <www.ppionline.org>

Federal Reserve Board. In addition to explaining the structure and functions of the Federal Reserve Board, this site contains the famous "Beige Book" that reports on economic conditions in the nation eight times a year. It is an easy-to-read executive summary of business, manufacturing, and commercial activities in each of the system's twelve regional Federal Reserve banks. <www.bog.frb.fed.us>

Office of Management and Budget. The place to go to get recent versions of the federal budget. The site provides data as well as graphs and text. <www.whitehouse.gov/omb>

The Social Security Administration Home Page. Everything you always wanted to know about social security but were afraid to ask. <www.ssa.gov>

The General Accounting Office is the investigative arm of the Congress and is charged with examining all matters relating to the receipt and disbursement of public funds. This site recounts the history of the GAO and provides access to GAO reports and testimony, to the decisions and opinions of the comptroller general, and to "policy and guidance" materials. <www.gao.gov>

Bureau of the Census provides the current U.S. population count as well as current economic indicators. The Bureau's press releases can be accessed in the "newsroom," and the *Statistical Abstract of the United States* is available for viewing. <www.census.gov>

Readings

GEORGIA'S CONSTITUTION AND GOVERNMENT

4th edition
Arnold Fleischmann, University of Georgia
Carol Pierannunzi, KennesaW State University

Introduction

Courses providing an overview of American politics center around political institutions and processes at the national level. This occurs even though state and local governments affect the daily lives of most U.S. citizens in ways ranging from basic services such as streets, water, and fire protection to state support for public schools and universities. State and local governments spent $1.5 trillion in 1997, only slightly less than the federal government's $1.6 trillion. Moreover, state and local governments employed 17 million workers in 1998, including everything from police officers to college professors, while the federal government had 2.7 million civilian employees.[1]

Given the size and significance of state and local governments in the American federal system, a number of states require students to know something about these levels of government. In Georgia, the legislature has passed a law requiring graduates of public colleges and universities to demonstrate proficiency with both the United States and Georgia constitutions. This monograph is intended to assist students in satisfying that requirement.

This monograph is in its fourth edition and is divided into seven parts. The first covers Georgia's place within the American system of federalism. Part II traces constitutional development in Georgia, including a history of Georgia's ten constitutions and an overview of the current document, which took effect in 1983. Part III describes the political institutions established in the Constitution, namely, the three branches of government and Georgia's system of local governments. The fourth section covers constitutional provisions regarding elections. Part V examines citizens' basic rights and liberties. Part VI discusses policies included in the Constitution. Part VII offers some closing observations about the continuing significance and future of Georgia's Constitution.

I. Georgia and the American Federal System

Constitutions are important because they establish the basic "rules of the game" for any political system. They specify the authority of government, distribute power among participants in the political system, and establish fundamental procedures for conducting public business and protecting rights. Just as drawing up or changing the rules can affect the outcome of a game, individuals and groups battle over constitutions, which can help determine who wins or loses politically.

When it was ratified in 1789, the United States Constitution included federalism as one of its most important elements. Federalism is a type of political system that gives certain powers to the national government, others to the states, and some to both levels of government. This differs from a unitary system such as in Great Britain or France, where all authority rests with the national government, which can distribute it to local or regional governments. Federalism also stands in contrast to a confederation, where all power is in the hands of the individual states, and the national government has only as much power as the states give to it. The United States used such a system during 1781–1788 under the Articles of Confederation, as did the Confederate States of America. More recently, confederations were tried following the break-up of the former national governments in the Soviet Union and Yugoslavia.

National Supremacy

The U.S. Constitution's stability is due in large part to its broad grants of power and its reinterpretation in response to changing conditions. Article 1, section 8 grants Congress a series of "enumerated powers" such as taxing, spending, declaring war, and regulating interstate commerce. It also permits Congress to do whatever is "necessary and proper" to exercise the enumerated powers. This language is referred to as the "elastic clause" because of its flexible grant of authority. Article 6 reinforces the power of the national government by declaring that the Constitution and federal law are "the supreme law of the land." This so-called supremacy clause thus identifies the U.S. Constitution as the ultimate authority whenever there is a need to resolve a dispute between the federal government and the states. In an 1819 case, *McCulloch v. Maryland*, the U.S. Supreme Court adopted a broad view of the federal government's powers when it decided that the elastic clause allowed Congress to exercise "implied powers" not mentioned explicitly in the U.S. Constitution but that could be inferred from the enumerated powers. The supremacy clause and implied powers have been cornerstones for the expansion of the federal government's powers.

The 10th Amendment

The constitutions, laws, and policies of the 50 states cannot contradict the U.S. Constitution. Thus, federalism allows states many opportunities to develop in their own way, but it always holds out the possibility that the federal government may act to promote uniformity for the nation. Much of the debate over ratification of the U.S. Constitution focused on claims that the national government would be too powerful. This concern was reflected in proposals to add twelve amendments in 1789. Ten of the proposed changes were ratified by the states in 1791 and are commonly referred to as the Bill of Rights.

The 10th Amendment reads:

> The powers not delegated to the United States by the Constitution, nor prohibited by it to the States, are reserved to the States respectively, or to the people.

The amendment does grant the states "reserved powers," but it does not define them. As one might expect, this has produced conflicts between the national and state governments, many of which have had to be resolved by the U.S. Supreme Court. For much of the period from the 1890s through the mid-1930s, the Court did restrict efforts by Congress to enhance the power of the federal government. Since then, the power of the national government has grown, although some recent court cases have favored the states.

The 14th Amendment

The national government's power over the states was strengthened by the 1868 addition of the 14th Amendment to the U.S. Constitution. One of three amendments designed to end slavery and grant rights to blacks after the Civil War, the 14th states in part:

> No state shall make or enforce any law which shall abridge the privileges or immunities of citizens of the United States; nor shall any State deprive any person of life, liberty, or property without due process of law; nor deny to any person within its jurisdiction the equal protection of the laws.

This language essentially restates the fundamental principle of dual citizenship: Americans are citizens of both the nation and their state, and they are governed by the constitutions of both governments. The U.S. Constitution guarantees minimum rights to citizens that may not be violated by the states. The states, however, may grant broader rights to their citizens than are guaranteed by the U.S. Constitution.

The 14th Amendment has had an interesting and controversial history. The U.S. Supreme Court generally has defined the amendment's somewhat vague guarantees in terms of other provisions found in the U.S. Constitution. Since 1925, the Court has employed a process known as "selective incorporation" through which it incorporates into the meaning of the 14th Amendment's vague language the protections offered by the Bill of Rights. It does this selectively, that is, by applying these guarantees to the states on a case-by-case basis. Congress, too, has used the 14th Amendment in support of laws that restrict the power of state and local governments.

State Constitutions

States adopt their constitutions within the context of national supremacy; enumerated, implied, and reserved powers; dual citizenship; and the protections of the 14th Amendment. Many state constitutions are modeled after the U.S. Constitution. Because state constitutions generally do not include implied powers, they tend to be more detailed and restrictive in defining the powers of government. Thus, state constitutions often include policies that seemingly could be decided by passing laws, as with Georgia's lottery. Putting such decisions in constitutions makes it harder for opponents to change them.

States possess "police power," namely, the ability to promote public health, safety, morals, or general welfare. The police power is among the "reserved powers" in the 10th Amendment to the U.S. Constitution. Police powers are often delegated by states to local governments, which are covered in great detail in state constitutions, but are not mentioned in the U.S. Constitution.

Unlike the U.S. Constitution, which has been amended only 27 times, state constitutions are amended frequently, often to make narrow policy changes. Numerous amendments, along with provisions about local governments and the lack of implied powers, are major reasons that many state constitutions are so long, in contrast to the 8,700 words in the U.S. Constitution.

Table 1 indicates the number, length, and amendments for each state constitution. Georgia is noteworthy in two ways: it has had ten constitutions, second only to Louisiana, and its current constitution, which took effect in 1983, is the newest among the states.

A Brief Comparison of the U.S. and Georgia Constitutions

It is worth highlighting at the outset some of the basic similarities and differences between Georgia and the national government. These will be discussed in further detail throughout this monograph, as will comparisons between Georgia and the other 49 states.

Even though constitutions can be compared to one another, one should remember that Georgia's constitution is not static. The state has had ten constitutions, and the current one has been amended 58 times during its brief life. In addition, Georgia's constitutions have evolved because of the ways they have been interpreted by the courts.

Similarities The most obvious similarity between Georgia and the national government is the presence of a bill of rights in each constitution. These guarantees were added as the first ten amendments to the U.S. Constitution, but the bill of rights is included prominently in Georgia's constitution as the first article. Both governments adopt separation of powers with distinct legislative, executive, and judicial branches. The president and Georgia's governor have substantial power to appoint officials and veto bills, although there are some important differences discussed below. Both the U.S. Congress and the Georgia General Assembly are bicameral, and each calls its two chambers the Senate and House of Representatives. Both governments allow judicial review (the power of courts to declare acts unconstitutional). However, Georgia courts are given this power in the state constitution,[2] while this authority at the federal level was laid down in 1803 by the Supreme Court itself in the case of *Marbury v. Madison*.[3]

Differences Perhaps the most visible difference between the two constitutions is how much longer Georgia's is, mainly because it includes many detailed policies. These range from specific taxes to sections on retirement systems, local government services, the state lottery, and even nude dancing.

The two constitutions also include differences in both procedures and the structure of government. One procedural distinction deals with constitutional amendments. Georgia voters must approve all amendments to the state's constitution. There is no comparable role for citizens in amending the U.S. Constitution, where amendments require a two-thirds vote in each house of Congress and then must be ratified by three-fourths of the states, in either their legislature or conventions. Another procedural difference is that the Georgia Constitution requires the state to have a balanced budget, but the U.S. Constitution imposes no such limitation on the federal government. The Georgia Constitution also grants the governor a line-item veto (the ability to kill a specific item in a spending bill), but the U.S. Constitution grants the president no such power over legislation passed by Congress.[4]

There are striking structural differences among the three branches of governments. Unlike the national government, where judges are nominated by the president subject to

TABLE 1   State Constitutions as of January 1, 2000

State	Number of Constitutions	Estimated Number of Words	Number of Amendments
Alabama	6	310,296	664
Alaska	1	15,988	28
Arizona	1	28,876	125
Arkansas	5	40,720	85
California	2	54,645	500
Colorado	1	45,679	135
Connecticut	4	16,608	29
Delaware	4	19,000	132[a]
Florida	6	38,000	86
Georgia	10	37,849	58[b]
Hawaii	1	20,774	95
Idaho	1	23,442	115
Illinois	4	13,700	11
Indiana	2	10,315	42
Iowa	2	13,430	52
Kansas	1	12,616	91
Kentucky	4	23,911	36
Louisiana	11	54,112	107
Maine	1	13,500	168
Maryland	4	41,349	214
Massachusetts	1	36,700	118
Michigan	4	25,530	23
Minnesota	1	11,547	118
Mississippi	4	24,323	121
Missouri	4	42,000	99
Montana	2	13,726	23
Nebraska	2	20,048	213
Nevada	1	20,700	128
New Hampshire	2	9,200	143
New Jersey	3	17,800	52
New Mexico	1	27,200	139
New York	4	51,700	217
North Carolina	3	11,000	30
North Dakota	1	20,564	137
Ohio	2	36,900	159
Oklahoma	1	79,153	161
Oregon	1	49,326	220
Pennsylvania	5	27,503	26
Rhode Island	2	10,233	59
South Carolina	7	22,500	480
South Dakota	1	25,315	105
Tennessee	3	15,300	34
Texas	5	80,806	390
Utah	1	11,000	96
Vermont	3	8,295	52
Virginia	6	21,092	34
Washington	1	50,237	92
West Virginia	2	26,000	67
Wisconsin	1	14,392	133
Wyoming	1	31,800	68

[a] Amendments are not subject to voter approval.
[b] Six of the amendments included in this total were approved by Georgia voters in November 2000, after data for the rest of this table were published.

Source: *The Book of the States: 2000–01 Edition*, pp. 3–4.

Senate confirmation, Georgia elects almost all of its judges on a nonpartisan ballot. In addition, Georgia's attorney general issues advisory opinions, which generally have the force of law unless reversed by a court. There is no comparable process at the national level.

The legislative branches also exhibit some interesting differences. All legislators in Georgia (both the House and the Senate) serve two-year terms and are elected from districts based on population. This contrasts with the national government, where representatives serve two-year terms and senators are elected for six years. Moreover, while members of the U.S. House are elected from districts based on population, two senators are elected from each state–the same for California and Wyoming–which builds in a bias in favor of small states.

The most glaring difference in the two executive branches is the lack of a cabinet system in Georgia. The president has the authority to appoint and fire heads of almost all major federal agencies. In contrast, Georgia's constitution requires that voters elect six department heads. This "plural executive" can make life difficult for a governor, who has limited authority over these independently elected officials, who may not share the same views or political party as the governor. The constitution also requires that several other department heads be chosen by boards and commissions rather than by the governor or the voters.

Perhaps the most noticeable structural difference between Georgia and the national government deals with local government. Georgia's constitution is quite specific about the organization of local governments, the services they can provide, the ways they can raise and spend money, and similar matters. It even limits the maximum number of counties at 159.

II. Constitutional Development in Georgia[5]

Each of Georgia's constitutions can be considered a political response to some conflict, problem, or crisis (see Table 2). In addition to substantive differences, the documents also vary in the methods used to draft and approve them. Seven were written by conventions composed of elected delegates. Two were prepared by bodies whose members were either appointed or included because they held specific offices. The Constitution of 1976 resulted from a request by Governor Busbee to have the Office of Legislative Counsel prepare an article-by-article revision of the Constitution of 1945 for the General Assembly. Also, the 1861 constitution was the first to be ratified by voters.

Even before American independence in 1776, Georgians were exerting their independence from England. Colonial Georgia, dependent upon imports for most manufactured items, was hard hit by the various import taxes which had led to colonial protests. Public opinion in Georgia favored independence and citizens mobilized to break with England. The first self-government in Georgia was defined by the Rules and Regulations of 1776. This short and simple document was written hurriedly and adopted before the signing of the Declaration of Independence. All current laws were maintained except those in conflict with actions taken by the Continental Congress. It declared that governmental authority resided within the state, not with the British monarchy, and that power originated from the governed. While this document was not officially a state constitution, many have noted that it served as one. The Declaration of Independence prompted Georgians to adopt a more permanent government and constitution.

TABLE 2   Georgia's Ten Constitutions

Year Implemented	Revision Method[a]	Major Characteristics
1777[b]	convention	Separation of powers, with most in the hands of the unicameral legislature.
1789[b]	convention	Bicameral legislature, which chose the governor; no bill of rights.
1798[b]	convention	Popular election of governor; creation of Supreme Court; greater detail than predecessors.
1861	convention	Long bill of rights; first constitution submitted to voters.
1865	convention	Governor limited to two terms; slavery abolished; Ordinance of Secession repealed; war debt repudiated; some judges made elective.
1868	convention	Authorization of free schools; increased appointment power for governor; debtors' relief.
1877	convention	More restrictions on legislative power; two-year terms for legislators and governor; no gubernatorial succession; most judicial appointments by legislature.
1945	commission	Establishment of lieutenant governorship, new constitutional officers, new boards, state merit system; home rule granted to counties and cities.
1976	Office of Legislative Counsel[c]	Reorganization of much-amended 1945 constitution.
1983	select committee[d]	Streamlining of previous document, with elimination of authorization for local amendments.

[a] Group responsible for proposing new document.
[b] Not submitted to voters for ratification.
[c] State employees, attorneys.
[d] Almost exclusively leaders from the three branches of state government.
Source: Melvin B. Hill, Jr., *The Georgia State Constitution: A Reference Guide,* pp. 3–20.

Georgia's Nine Previous Constitutions

The Constitution of 1777   Georgia's first constitution included now familiar ideas such as separation of power among the legislative, executive, and judicial branches of government; proportional representation on the basis of population; and provisions for local self-government. This constitution, like the Rules and Regulations of 1776, included little expressed protection of individual liberties. Despite this omission, Georgia's political culture at the time was more liberal than other states, and the constitution was written to empower the "common man" (although only white males of 21 years who had paid property taxes in the previous year were permitted to vote). The Anglican Church was disestablished, and language in the document was easily understood. Local control of the judiciary was insured by the fact that no courts were established above the county courts.

The transition from the Rules and Regulations of 1776 to a new constitution in 1777 was little noted by citizens. This document governed the state until the downfall of the Articles of Confederation in 1788. Georgia ratified the U.S. Constitution in January 1788 (the fourth state to do so) and redrafted the state constitution to reflect this monumental change in national government.

The Constitution of 1789   The Constitution of 1789 provided for a bicameral legislature. Although there were some accommodations made for representation on the basis of population in the House of Representatives, all legislative districts were drawn within counties, which could have from two to five representatives and one senator. Slaves were counted as three-fifths of a person, in accord with the U.S. Constitution and to meet the demands of landowners seeking to enhance representation for areas with large plantations. The state capital was moved to Louisville from Augusta,[6] provisions were included to mandate public education at the county level, and new counties were created to be represented in the legislature. In addition, the constitution authorized the legislature to elect the governor and most other state elected officials except the legislature itself. Restrictions on voting included race, age, residence, and the payment of taxes in the previous year.

The Constitution of 1798   The short life of the Constitution of 1789 can be attributed to a scandal over land speculation by legislators. The Constitution of 1798 was written by a convention and retained much of the language of the previous document. However, it was much longer due to increased detail about the powers of the legislature. As time passed, this constitution was amended to permit more democratic requirements for voting, establish executive offices to handle some of the duties of the legislature, outlaw foreign slave trade, and establish local governments. This constitution proved to be more enduring than its predecessors and was in effect until the formation of the Confederacy in 1861.

The Constitution of 1861   Secessionist fever at the start of the Confederacy could hardly allow the state constitution to go untouched. T.R.R. Cobb, the main author of the Confederate Constitution, was also the author of the Georgia Constitution under the Confederacy. The size of the state legislature was reduced by permitting senators to represent more than one county, and the governor's power was increased significantly. Judicial review was institutionalized in this document, and state judgeships were established as elective offices.

The Constitution of 1861 was the first to be submitted to the voters for approval in a referendum. This also was the first Georgia constitution with an extensive list of personal liberties, including freedom of thought and opinion, speech, and the press. Citizens were warned, though, that they would be responsible for "abuses of the liberties" guaranteed to them. Naturally, the Georgia Constitution under the Confederacy included ideals of states' rights.

The Constitution of 1865   The Constitution of 1865 was drafted by reluctant Georgians in order to accommodate the demands of Congress for readmission to the Union. Only men who expressed moderate political beliefs before and after the war were permitted to work on the document, which included the abolition of slavery, repudiation of Civil War debt, and repeal of the acts of secession. This repeal was not met with great enthusiasm by the North, which had insisted that the ordinance of secession be declared void. Also absent was enfranchisement of the black population of the state, although this was not as likely to stir animosity in the North since blacks could only vote in six northern states at the time. These omissions put pressure on Georgia to rewrite the constitution just three years later in order to meet the requirements for reentry into the Union. The Constitution of 1865 was viewed largely as the work of northern "carpetbaggers" trying to make quick fortunes in the postwar South, or, worse yet in the eyes of many, "scalawags" (southerners willing to cooperate with Yankees).

The Constitution of 1868   When a constitutional convention was called in 1867, it was boycotted by most of Georgia's popular leaders. The state capital, at that time in Milledgeville, refused to accommodate many of the delegates, some of whom were black. Therefore, the convention was held in Atlanta, and the new constitution, perhaps in retaliation for the inhospitable treatment by the city of Milledgeville, specified Atlanta as the capital. The Constitution of 1868 met the requirements of Congress for readmission to the Union and eliminated all debts incurred prior to 1865. Public education was also provided for, to be funded by poll and liquor taxes, although it was some time before this policy actually was implemented. Black citizens were insured equal rights, at least on paper, and property rights for women were upheld. Moreover, some attempts were made to enhance the business climate in order to build a stronger tax base.

Due to the high representation of poor and black citizens at this convention, the Constitution of 1868 was a liberal document for the times, particularly after blacks were seated in the General Assembly in 1870. Overall, the new constitution was widely unpopular due to its compliance with northern demands, which were symbolized by the presence of northern troops until 1876. It remained a symbol of southern defeat until replaced in 1877.

The Constitution of 1877   Georgia's post-Reconstruction constitution was a return to more conservative ideals. It reduced the authority of state officials and shifted power to counties, most of which were rural. Most noteworthy was its not-so-subtle disenfranchisement of blacks and poor whites through the mandate that only those who had paid all back taxes would be eligible to vote. As the Constitution of 1877 was being drafted, factionalism within the ranks of the Democratic party erupted. Many who were sympathetic to old southern culture were reluctant to compromise with those who called for economic development and progressive policies. An agreement was reached to comply with northern demands for reconstruction, as well as demands from more industrialized northern states that the South continue to supply raw materials. This compromise stirred up a faction of the Democratic party labeled Bourbons, who were dedicated to pre-Civil War agrarian economic and social norms, white supremacy, and local and state self-determination. The Republicans found that the compromise left them with little power in Georgia, and it would be quite some time before the Republican party reasserted itself in the state.

The Constitution of 1877 was not well suited to changing conditions. For example, it forbade public borrowing, thereby eliminating the possibility of large-scale improvements in transportation or education financed by the state. The constitution eventually included 301 amendments, many of which were temporary or dealt with local rather than statewide issues. Others made Supreme Court justices elected officials, established juvenile courts and a court of appeals, empowered an elected Public Service Commission to regulate utilities, and modified the boards overseeing education.

This constitution also codified the system of representation under which the six counties with the largest population were to be represented in the lower house of the legislature by three persons each, the next 26 most populous counties by two each, and the remaining counties by one member. This 3-2-1 ratio became the basis for the Democratic party's use of the county-unit system to elect statewide candidates—a custom that became state law in 1917 with passage of the Neill Primary Act.

Under the county-unit system, Democratic candidates for statewide office were chosen in primaries based on county-unit votes, which were similar to the electoral votes used to elect the U.S. president. Each county had twice as many unit votes as it had seats in the Georgia House of Representatives under the 3-2-1 formula. Beginning in 1920, the eight largest counties had six unit votes, the next 30 counties had four unit votes, and the remaining counties had two unit votes. Thus, Fulton County, which had more than 6,000 voters go the polls in 1940, had 6 unit votes; Quitman and Chattahoochee Counties, which each had fewer than 250 votes cast the same year, had 2 unit votes each. A county's unit votes were awarded on a winner-take-all basis, which meant that the candidate finishing first got all the unit votes. Under this system, candidates could concentrate their campaigns in rural areas and could win a primary without getting a majority of the popular vote. In 1940, the 121 counties with 2 unit votes had 43.5 percent of Georgia's population, but 59 percent of the unit votes. In contrast, Georgia's eight most populous counties, with 6 unit votes each, had 30 percent of the state's population but a mere 12 percent of the unit votes. In 1946, Eugene Talmadge finished second in the primary for governor by about 6,000 popular votes. He won the Democratic nomination, however, by besting his opponent 242 to 146 in unit votes.[7] The county-unit system remained intact until 1963, when the U.S. Supreme Court held that this underrepresentation of urban areas violated the "equal protection" clause of the 14th Amendment (see Part IV).

The Constitution of 1945 The Constitution of 1877 lasted until 1945, albeit in much amended form. A 23-member commission appointed by the governor to draft a new constitution was finally created because of dissatisfaction with the 1877 constitution, a careful study of the document in the 1930s, and prodding by Governor Ellis Arnall. The use of a commission rather than an elected convention reflects the governor's wish to depoliticize the constitution and bring it up to date, as well as the General Assembly's previous failure to muster the two-thirds vote to call a convention.[8]

The new constitution included limited substantive changes. Its main effect was to condense its heavily amended predecessor. Perhaps the most notable changes were the creation of the office of lieutenant governor and new boards for corrections, state personnel, and veterans services. One contested issue was the ban against governors succeeding themselves, which the General Assembly retained in the draft submitted to the voters. The new constitution also authorized women to serve on juries and gave home rule to local governments, which increased their authority. The document also addressed the controversial issue of the poll tax.

With a turnout of less than 20 percent of those registered, voters approved the document by slightly more than a three-to-two margin following an active campaign on its behalf. Georgia thus became the first state to adopt a constitution proposed by commission rather than by an elected convention. The limits of this constitution emerged quickly. Within three years, the new constitution added its first amendments, with a total of 1,098 amendments proposed between 1946 and 1974. Voters ratified 826, of which 679 (82 percent) were local in nature.

The Constitution of 1976   An effort to revise the 1945 constitution occurred during the early 1960s, but a federal court ruling prevented voters from considering it during the 1964 general election. Another attempt died in 1970 when the House but not the Senate approved a document for submission to the electorate.

After assuming office in 1975, Governor George Busbee asked the Office of Legislative Counsel to draft a revision of the 1945 constitution in time for the 1976 election. The proposal included no real changes, but it did reorganize the constitution on an article-by-article basis so that it was easier to understand and interpret. After some revisions by the General Assembly, voters approved the document in November of that year. With no substantive changes in the new constitution, the General Assembly almost immediately set out to consider a more thorough revision, creating the Select Committee on Constitutional Revision during its 1977 session.

Georgia's Current Constitution

Adoption   Georgia's 1983 constitution was neither easily written nor quickly adopted. In fact, the Constitution of 1983 is a good example of how factionalism can play a role in state politics. Because the 1945 and 1976 constitutions so restricted the behavior of local governments, cities and counties often were forced to amend the constitution in order to make changes in taxation or municipal codes. Amendments were proposed by the legislature and approved through popular vote, with those proposals affecting the entire state appearing on the statewide ballot and those affecting only one county or city appearing on the ballot only in that jurisdiction. As a result, ballots were brimming with proposed amendments that often irritated voters.

Between 1946 and 1980, Georgians were asked to vote on 1,452 proposed amendments (1,177 of them purely local in nature) and ratified over 1,105. This created an unwieldy document understood by only the most diligent of constitutional students. Voters became so annoyed with the large number of proposals that they began to vote them down. In 1978, the statewide ballot included over 120 proposed changes in the state's constitution, one-third of which failed to pass.[9]

By the late 1970s, many were pleased when Governor George Busbee sought the rewriting of the constitution, although Busbee may not have realized the political difficulty of such a task. The proposed constitution was debated for three years by a Select Committee on Constitutional Revision whose members included the governor, lieutenant governor, speaker of the House, attorney general, and eight other elected officials. The Select Committee began work in May 1977 and appointed committees with broader citizen membership to revise individual articles of the constitution for consideration by the General Assembly and the electorate. In November 1978, two articles were submitted to voters, who rejected them.

Subsequent efforts by the Select Committee and the 1980 session of the legislature failed to produce a new constitution. During its 1981 session, though, the General Assembly created a Legislative Overview Committee on Constitutional Revision, with 31 members from each chamber, to work with the Select Committee. These efforts produced a document that was approved in a 1981 legislative special session and modified at the 1982 session before being submitted to the electorate.

Like constitutional revisions generally, this one was quite political. Lobbyists and others representing specific interests were quick to get involved in the process, which was a costly one, with one estimate of $30,000 per day for the 1981 special session of the General Assembly.[10] A confrontation occurred between the Speaker of the House of Representatives, Tom Murphy, and the governor over the powers to be granted to the legislature under the new constitution. This debate was fueled by the fact that governors had built up many informal powers under previous constitutions, including the naming of presiding officers of the House and Senate, as well as most legislative committee and subcommittee chairs. This practice ended with the 1966 election, when the legislature chose Lester Maddox as governor because no candidate got a majority of the popular vote. The General Assembly also organized itself without input from the governor and gained more power in subsequent years. Thus, by the early 1980s, legislators wanted to guard their political gains, but Governor Busbee favored the delegation of some powers to bureaucratic offices and state boards. The governor and the General Assembly also disagreed over taxes and gubernatorial term limits. At one point, Busbee asked legislators to forget the proposal and spend the remaining days of the session on other topics.[11] Agreement was eventually reached, and voters approved the new constitution in November of 1982 by a nearly three-to-one margin. It took effect in July of 1983.

Major Provisions of the 1983 Constitution   The new constitution included eleven articles, many of them detailed and complicated. Still, the document was indeed much shorter than its predecessor and was written in simpler and gender-neutral language, making it easier for the average citizen to read. Although it can be argued that the new constitution was one of evolution rather than revolution, it included many noteworthy changes:[12]

- eliminating the requirement that local governments place changes in taxation, municipal codes, and employee compensation on the state ballot;
- establishing a unified court system, consolidating the duties of justices of the peace and small claims courts into magistrate courts, and strengthening the state Supreme Court;
- requiring nonpartisan election of state court judges;
- enhancing the power of the General Assembly to enact laws and authorize the appropriation of taxes;
- giving the Board of Pardons and Paroles power to stay death sentences;
- establishing an equal protection clause;
- reducing the total amount of debt that the state may assume;
- providing more open-to-the-public committee and legislative meetings; and,
- incorporating more formal separation of powers between the legislative and executive branches.

It is worth noting, though, that the new constitution did not repeal the long list of local amendments in the old constitution. It simply allowed them to continue in force if approved by the General Assembly or the affected local government and "froze" them by prohibiting the addition of new local amendments.

TABLE 3   Procedures for Amending State Constitutions Through Their Legislatures

Procedure	Georgia	Number of States
Vote in Legislature:		
Majority		18
2/3	✓	19
3/5		9
Other		4[a]
Legislative Sessions:		
One	✓	35
Two		12
Other		3[a]
Voter Ratification:		
Majority Voting on Amendment	✓	42[b]
Majority Voting in Election		3
Other		5[c]

[a] Includes 3 states that require larger majorities if passed in one session, but only a majority if passed in two legislative sessions.

[b] Includes 3 states with different majorities for certain types of constitutional changes.

[c] Includes Delaware, whose constitution is amended by a two-thirds vote in two sessions of the legislature and does not require voter approval in a referendum.

Source: *The Book of the States: 2000–01 Edition*, pp. 5–6.

Constitutional Amendments   The fifty states vary in the methods used to amend their constitutions (see Table 3). The Georgia legislature can ask the state's voters to create a convention to amend or replace the constitution. The General Assembly also can propose amendments if they are approved by a two-thirds vote in each legislative chamber—a procedure like that at the national level. The governor has no formal role in this process, but may be influential in recommending amendments and mobilizing public opinion before voters go to the polls. The U.S. Constitution requires ratification of amendments by legislatures or conventions in three-fourths of the states. In contrast, the Georgia Constitution requires ratification by a majority of the voters casting ballots on the proposed amendment. Such proposals are voted upon in the next statewide general election after being submitted to the electorate by the General Assembly (November of even-numbered years).

Eighteen states require only a majority in their legislatures to submit a proposed amendment to voters; others are more restrictive. Georgia is among the 19 states requiring a two-thirds vote by its legislature. Some states face the obstacle of getting an amendment approved in two legislative sessions before it can be submitted to voters. A few states also require either more than a simple majority of people voting on an amendment or a majority of those voting in an election. The latter procedure can be especially difficult when people vote for highly visible offices like governor but skip proposed amendments. In such cases, not voting on the amendment is the same as voting "no." Four states, but not Georgia, also limit the number of amendments submitted to the voters at one election. It is also worth noting that Georgia is not among the 18 states whose constitutions allow amendments through the initiative process, in which voters circulate petitions to place proposed amendments on the ballot for voters to ratify or reject in a statewide referendum.

During 1997–1998, 46 states considered a total of 246 constitutional amendments, of which 229 (77 percent) were adopted. Sixty-seven of the proposed amendments dealt with government finance, taxation, and debt. Voters in 12 states considered 21 initiatives and approved eleven (52 percent).[13]

Despite the relatively young age of the Georgia Constitution, efforts to amend it have become somewhat common, although the number of proposals has not reached the dizzying heights of the previous constitution. There were 75 proposed general amendments on the ballot between 1984 and 2000, and voters approved 58 (77 percent). The total includes at least five proposals each year, with a high of 15 in 1988.

The November 2000 election included seven proposed amendments. The only proposal defeated by voters (52 percent opposed) would have allowed changes in the way marine vessels are taxed. Three amendments were approved to allow benefits for law enforcement officials, firefighters, public school employees, and state highway employees killed or disabled in the line of duty. One allowed members of the General Assembly to be removed from office after conviction for a felony rather than after exhausting all appeals. Another amendment raised from five to seven years the amount of time that state court judges must have been able to practice law before they can begin their judicial service. Finally, voters approved a measure related to property tax relief.[14]

III. Georgia's Governmental Institutions

Like most state constitutions, Georgia's mirrors the separation of powers adopted by the framers of the U.S. Constitution. Perhaps the most important aspect of the Georgia Constitution is what Melvin Hill calls its status as "a power-limiting document rather than a power-granting document."[15] Thus, many provisions specify things that the state of Georgia and its local governments *cannot* do.

The Georgia Constitution spells out the organization and authority of the legislative branch in Article 3 and the judicial branch in Article 6. Beyond that, the organization of governments looks a bit different than at the national level. Executive responsibilities are spread among provisions in Article 4, which covers six boards and commissions, and Article 5, which encompasses the governor, lieutenant governor, and the six elected department heads. Other provisions affecting administration and local government are found in Article 8, which considers Georgia's system of education. The framework for local government is in Article 9, which comprises almost 20 percent of the Constitution.

The Georgia General Assembly

Comparisons to Congress and Other State Legislatures[16]   On the surface, there are few differences between Congress and Georgia's legislature, which is officially named the Georgia General Assembly. Both are bicameral. The presiding officer of the house of representatives is called the speaker and is chosen by the members, but the leader of the senate (vice president of the United States and the lieutenant governor of Georgia) is elected independently of its members. Unlike Congress, where the entire House and one-third of the Senate are elected every two years, all 236 members of the General Assembly are up for election every two years. The General Assembly also meets for a very limited time each year and lacks the salary and staff support found in Congress.

The Georgia General Assembly has much in common with other state legislatures. Its members are charged with representing the people of their districts, reapportioning legislative seats following the census, enacting laws, adopting taxing and spending measures, overseeing enforcement of current laws, and interceding for constituents. Except for Nebraska, every state legislature is bicameral, elects its members on a partisan basis, and has an upper chamber called the senate. Forty-one states call their lower chamber the house of representatives, and Georgia and 41 other states convene regular legislative sessions annually. The fact that only eight state legislatures still meet biennially reflects the view that meeting once every two years may be too infrequent to keep up with problems in the modern world.

Differences do exist among legislatures, however. Size varies from a low of 49 in Nebraska's unicameral legislature to a high of 424 in the small state of New Hampshire. Georgia, with its 236 members, has the third-largest legislature. For the 49 bicameral legislatures, the average senate has 40 members, as compared to Georgia's 56. The average house of representatives has 111 members, much smaller than Georgia's 180 representatives.[17]

Qualifications such as minimum age, length of residence, and term limits vary. So do terms of office. Georgia is one of 11 states using only two-year terms. Members of Nebraska's unicameral legislature have terms of four years; four states have four-year terms for both chambers; the remaining 34 states elect their upper chamber to a four-year term and their lower chamber for two years. Regular legislative sessions range from off-year limits of 30 calendar days in New Mexico and Virginia and 20 legislative days in Wyoming to unlimited length for annual sessions in 13 states. Georgia is somewhere in the middle, with an annual session of 40 legislative days. Leadership, procedures, and compensation also vary widely among the states.

Size and Representation   Georgia's earliest legislatures were based on county representation, and the General Assembly initially had at least one representative for each county. One legacy of government based on counties is the size of the Georgia General Assembly, which has fluctuated over the years. During the 1960s, for example, the size of the House varied and was over 200 members at one point. As the number of counties grew to 159, the legislature became relatively large. Local population grew at different rates, however, and county-based representation soon proved problematic as small, sparsely populated counties were represented equally with larger ones. In addition, Senate districts were drawn to include three counties, and each seat rotated among its three counties at the end of each term. Thus, the real power in the legislative branch was concentrated in the House, where members could hold unlimited tenure.[18]

In the 1960s, federal courts ruled that all representation within state legislatures must be based on population rather than county. Multi-member House districts formerly provided for the election of several representatives within the same district, with candidates required to run for a designated seat. For example, someone running for District 72, Post 2 did not compete with candidates for District 72, Post 1, although the electorate consisted of the same voters. Multi-member House districts were eliminated in 1992, so Georgia citizens are now represented in single-member districts of equivalent population drawn across or within county lines. The power of the Senate increased with the elimination of seats rotating among counties, so senators are now able to run as incumbents.

With the adoption of the Constitution of 1983, the Senate has been restricted to *not more than* 56 members, while the House has been required to have *at least* 180 members. The legislature is able to enlarge the number of representatives in the House or decrease the number of members in the Senate, as long as the constitutional mandates on size are upheld. Reapportionment of districts occurs following the U.S. census held every ten years. With a 2000 census count of over 8.2 million residents, Georgia will have a state Senate with districts that average almost 147,000 people, and each state representative will have approximately 46,000 constituents.

Qualifications of Members   Article 3, section 2 of the Georgia Constitution requires that persons seeking office in the General Assembly be registered voters, U.S. citizens, and Georgia citizens for at least two years. It also requires that representatives live within their districts for at least one year. Those elected to the Senate must be at least 25 years old, while members of the House must be 21 or older. Persons may not simultaneously run for more than one office or in the primaries of two political parties. Also ineligible are persons on active military duty, those who hold other elected or civil offices within the state (unless they resign), and convicted felons.

Legislative Sessions   The Georgia General Assembly meets annually in a regular session that begins on the second Monday of January and lasts up to 40 legislative days. These are not calendar days, but days that the General Assembly is in session (not in recess or adjourned). The General Assembly may be called into special session by the governor, who sets the agenda, or by agreement of three-fifths of the membership of each chamber. Special sessions may be called to deal with unexpected crises, such as natural disasters, budgetary shortfalls, or other state emergencies. Special sessions may not last longer than 40 days and generally cannot be used for matters unrelated to the official agenda.[19]

Legislative Leadership   When members of the General Assembly arrive in Atlanta for the beginning of a new legislative session, their first priorities include selecting leaders and organizing committees. The Georgia Constitution provides for the selection of presiding officers in each chamber. In the Senate, the lieutenant governor serves as president, just as the vice president of the United States is formally the presiding officer of the U.S. Senate. Thus, the presiding officer of the Senate is chosen by Georgia's voters in a statewide election, although the winner is chosen independently from the governor. It is worth noting that 25 other states (including Nebraska's unicameral legislature) also make the popularly elected lieutenant governor presiding officer of the senate. In the remaining 24 states, the senate chooses its own presiding officer. The Georgia Senate also elects one of its members as president pro tempore should the need arise to replace the presiding officer.

In the House, the representatives elect a speaker from among their members, as do the lower houses in the other 48 bicameral legislatures and the U.S. House of Representatives. In Georgia, House members also elect a speaker pro tempore, as do 25 other states; the other 23 legislatures either have no such position or have their speaker appoint someone.[20] In the speaker's absence, the speaker pro tempore presides.

Types of Legislation Article 3 of the Georgia Constitution includes several sections detailing the General Assembly's procedures and powers for enacting laws, conducting impeachments, and spending public money. Bills before the General Assembly can be classified as resolutions, general legislation, and local legislation. All currently enforceable statutes are published in the *Official Code of Georgia Annotated*, which is updated periodically to include both new laws and legal opinions on implementation of current law.

Much of what passes through the General Assembly is not intended to be implemented as statute. Some of the items brought up for consideration are intended as statements of legislative opinion and may be enforceable only on the membership of the legislature itself. For example, the legislature may wish to recognize individuals or a sports team, in which case the General Assembly might pass a "resolution" describing their achievements. Resolutions also might be used to create special committees, to determine compensation for citizens who have been injured or suffered damages by state actions, or to set requirements for legislative staff. The resolution would therefore have little impact on other citizens of the state. It does, however, express the approval of the state government.

Resolutions might be passed to require the General Assembly itself to behave in a specific manner, as with rules of conduct, scheduling, or agreements on budgetary matters. In some cases, resolutions are passed by one chamber to establish rules only for the membership of that body, but joint resolutions require passage through both chambers. Resolutions generally do not require the signature of the governor because they do not require implementation outside the legislature itself. However, joint resolutions which are enforceable as law do require the governor's signature and may be vetoed.

General legislation has application statewide. Laws regarding election procedures or speed limits on state highways are examples. Local governments may not pass ordinances which contradict general law. Most general legislation intended to change existing law will specify exactly which statutes will be changed, but any new legislation supersedes past legislation.

Local legislation refers to those laws passed by the Georgia General Assembly which apply only to specific cities, counties, or special districts within the state. The General Assembly retains the power to govern localities through the passage of local legislation.[21] Local legislation may not contradict general legislation and may not be used to change the tenure of particular local officials. It can, however, be used to create or change political boundaries. The passage of local legislation differs in some ways from the passage of general law. Local bills must be preceded by a period of advertisement in which citizens of the jurisdiction concerned are notified of the potential law. This most often occurs in local newspapers.

Consideration of Bills Only members of the General Assembly may introduce legislation, although by custom governors have had members introduce bills on their behalf. Bills generally are written by several persons and may be sponsored by multiple legislators. Bills may be introduced in either chamber of the General Assembly or at the same time in both chambers. One exception is legislation dealing with public revenues or appropriation of public money, which the Constitution requires to begin in the House of Representatives.

Bills must adhere to a specific format dictated by the Constitution and the rules of each chamber. The title of the bill must relate directly to its content, and bills are constitutionally restricted to no more than one purpose. The Constitution mandates that all bills that are general legislation be read three times from the floor on three separate days. Because the title is required to be a summary of intent, reading the title only is substituted for the first reading of the entire bill. A second reading of the bill, which occurs on the second day after introduction, will also be of the title only. The Constitution forbids the introduction of bills which deal with specific individuals or which might limit the constitutional authority of the General Assembly. Population bills (those which apply to jurisdictions of a certain population) are also forbidden, as are bills that would have the effect of limiting business competition or creating monopolies within the state. Local legislation may be voted on after only one reading. The media may follow the passage of a bill, and according to the state Constitution, must be permitted entry into committee meetings.

Bills are passed by a simple majority of the entire membership of each chamber, although there are several exceptions to this rule. Tax legislation, proposed amendments to the constitution, veto overrides, punitive action taken against a member of the General Assembly, or motions to change the order of business require two-thirds majorities. Bills which have been rejected once in a legislative session also require a two-thirds majority to be reconsidered. Procedural changes may only require a majority of those members present. Once a bill has achieved a majority vote in one chamber, it must be passed in identical form by a majority vote in the other chamber in order to continue on the path to becoming a law.

The State Budget[22]   The budget is a special type of lawmaking. The Georgia Constitution directs the governor to prepare the state's annual budget and submit it to the General Assembly during the first five days of the regular legislative session. This leaves the governor with substantial authority in the early stages of budget formation. This is countered, however, by the legislature's virtually unlimited power to change the budget submitted by the governor. The Constitution also requires that the state adopt a balanced budget, something the federal government is not obligated to do. Georgia's governor can exercise a line-item veto in an attempt to remove specific spending without vetoing the entire budget. Like a regular veto, the line-item veto can be overridden by a two-thirds vote of the membership in each chamber of the General Assembly.[23]

The Executive Branch

One of the most striking differences between the U.S. and Georgia constitutions is the number of elected officials in the executive branch. The most visible in Georgia are the governor and the lieutenant governor. While they may be compared to the U.S. president and vice president, they are not elected together as a team and may represent different views and political parties.

Like the majority of states, Georgia has a plural executive, meaning that voters elect various department heads rather than having them picked by the governor like presidents choose the members of their cabinet. All but six states elect some executive branch officials in addition to a governor (see Table 4).[24] In fact, voters around the country choose over 500 officials in statewide elections (a number virtually unchanged since the mid-1950s). Some of these officials are required to be elected by state constitutions; others are provided for by law. Their tasks vary significantly. Financial monitoring, for instance, is assigned to elected auditors, comptrollers, and treasurers, as well as appointed officials. Education is also diverse: in addition to elected school superintendents and boards, seven states elect boards to govern public education, while Colorado and Nebraska voters elect the board of regents for their state universities.[25]

TABLE 4   Executive Branch Officials Elected by the Public

Office	Number of States	Georgia
Governor	50	Elected Statewide
Lieutenant Governor	42	Elected Statewide
Secretary of State	37	Elected Statewide
Attorney General	43	Elected Statewide
Agriculture Commissioner	10	Elected Statewide
Insurance Commissioner	11	Elected Statewide
Labor Commissioner	5	Elected Statewide
Education Superintendent	14[a]	Elected Statewide
Utilities	8	Elected Statewide[b]
Treasurer	39	Appointed by Governor[c]

[a] Another 7 states elect their boards of education.

[b] Georgia is not among the 8 states listed to the left. It has a Public Service Commission consisting of 5 board members elected to six-year terms.

[c] Tasks are performed by Director of Finance, who is appointed by the governor.

Source: *The Book of the States: 2000–01 Edition*, pp. 33–38.

The Governor   Governors are generally the most powerful political figures in their states. Their political clout is based on the formal authority granted in a state's constitution, as well as several other sources of power, including laws, the media, public opinion, ties to political parties and interest groups, and personal characteristics. Professor Thad Beyle has compared the formal power of governors in the fifty states, including their tenure potential, appointment powers, budgetary control, veto power, and the number of separately elected executive officials.[26]

The tenure potential (number of consecutive terms permitted for a governor) has been a contentious issue in Georgia's political history. The 1877 constitution limited the governor to two consecutive, two-year terms. A 1941 constitutional amendment provided for a four-year term, but prohibited governors from succeeding themselves in office. That was changed in 1976 to permit successive terms, but the lifetime limit for any governor was also two terms. The constitution implemented in 1983 permits two consecutive, four-year terms with no lifetime restriction on the time of a governor's service. That earned Georgia's governor a score of 4 on Beyle's 5-point scale for tenure potential. The most powerful tenure potential, which received a score of 5, exists in the nine states where governors face no limit on the number of four-year terms.[27] At the opposite pole is Virginia, which does not allow governors to succeed themselves. Unlike the governor, Georgia's other statewide elected officials face no constitutional limit on the number of consecutive terms they can serve. For example, Tommy Irvin was reelected in 1998 as Agriculture Commissioner, a post he first held in 1969.

In terms of appointment power, Beyle classifies Georgia's governor in the weakest category because of limited power in six key areas: health, education, transportation, corrections, public utilities regulation, and public welfare. In each of these cases, top administrators are chosen by voters (school superintendent and members of the Public Service Commission) or by boards. Gubernatorial control over boards and commissions is weakened because terms are long and staggered, which means that it can take some time before a governor's appointees are in control. In the case of one board (Transportation), the governor does not even appoint the members; the General Assembly chooses them.

Perhaps the most important appointment power of Georgia governors is their constitutional authority to fill vacancies in the executive and judicial branches without Senate confirmation.[28] In the case of elected positions, the governor picks someone who finishes an unexpired term, thus becoming the incumbent in the next campaign. By law, the governor also can fill vacancies at the local level when an official has been removed temporarily following an indictment.[29]

Beyle's 1–5 scale of budgetary power assigned a value of 1 to a governor who prepared the budget with other officials and faced unlimited legislative ability to amend, while 5 was for a budget prepared by a governor whose legislature was prohibited from increasing it. Like 42 other states, the Georgia governor rated a 3 on budgetary powers: the governor has full responsibility for preparing the budget and the legislature has unlimited ability to change it.

Using a similar 1–5 scale for veto power, Beyle rated Georgia's governorship a 5, meaning that the governor has both simple and line-item vetoes along with a requirement for a large majority of the legislature to override (two-thirds of the total membership of each chamber). Twenty-three states make it easier to override a gubernatorial veto: six require only a majority of legislators elected, five mandate three-fifths of those elected, and twelve specify three-fifths or two-thirds of those present for the override vote.[30]

The governor's veto power is included in the legislative, not the executive, article of the Georgia Constitution.[31] The governor has authority to act on legislation passed by the General Assembly that would have the effect of law, except for changes in the Constitution. If the governor signs a bill, it becomes law on a specified date, usually with the start of the fiscal year on July 1. The governor has six days to act on a bill while the General Assembly is in session. If the General Assembly has adjourned for the session or for more than forty days (like a recess), the governor has forty days after adjournment to act. When vetoing a bill, the governor is required to return it to the chamber where it originated within three days during the session or sixty days after adjournment. Once the General Assembly has received a veto message, the originating chamber may consider the vetoed bill immediately. Those bills vetoed during adjournment can be overridden during the next legislative session, as long as an election has not intervened.

A bill also becomes law if the governor does nothing (neither signs nor vetoes it). If the governor fails to act on a bill, it will become law following a six-day waiting period for bills passed during the first thirty-four days of the legislative session, or following a forty-day waiting period for bills passed during the final six days of the session. Thus, bills may sit on the governor's desk after adjournment of the legislature and become law even if the governor does not sign them.

Georgia is among the 43 states that provide for two types of vetoes, full and line-item. A full veto is a rejection of an entire bill. The governor transmits a vetoed bill back to the legislature with an explanation for the veto. The General Assembly is then free to either modify the bill to meet the expectations of the governor or try overriding the governor's veto. Line-item vetoes are rejections of specific passages in appropriations bills, which give the governor the power to kill spending for specific projects without having to veto an entire state budget. Reconsideration of bills in which specific funding has been line-item vetoed is not necessary, and the governor's actions officially reduce the appropriation if not over-ridden. A successful override allows a bill to become law in spite of the governor's veto. If an override fails in either chamber of the Georgia General Assembly, a bill is dead.

The Plural Executive   The Georgia Constitution requires voters to elect six department heads in addition to the governor and lieutenant governor. Together, these eight officials are referred to as the state's "elected constitutional officers."[32] Like a majority of states, Georgia elects an attorney general and secretary of state. Georgia is among the few states, however, letting voters pick a state school superintendent and individuals to head departments of agriculture, insurance, and labor.[33]

The six elected department heads possess power independent of the governor. They do so in part because of the prerogatives of their offices. The attorney general, for instance, exercises great discretion regarding the handling of litigation in which the state is a party and issues opinions on the legality or constitutionality of actions taken by the state.[34] The insurance and agriculture commissioners have substantial power to regulate certain types of businesses. In addition to the power they derive from being elected separately from the governor, the narrow focus of their offices also means that constitutional officers' natural constituencies (for votes and campaign money) are the interests affected most directly by their decisions. In fact, they are often seen as advocates of the industries they oversee.[35] Elected department heads may even be in conflict with one another. Thus, despite the image of the governor's power in Georgia, executive power in the state is dispersed.

Georgia's elected department heads must have reached the age of 25, been a U.S. citizen for at least ten years, and been a Georgia resident at least four years when they assume office. The attorney general also is required to have had seven years as an active-status member of the State Bar of Georgia, which supervises the legal profession in the state. The Constitution leaves it to the General Assembly to spell out the power and duties of these officers, to determine their salaries, and to fund their agencies.[36] There is also a procedure under which four of the eight constitutional officers can petition the Georgia Supreme Court to hold a hearing to determine if a constitutional officer is permanently disabled and should be replaced.[37]

Constitutional Boards and Commissions   States commonly assign decision making in certain policy areas to multi-member boards rather than departments headed by a single individual. Georgia is no exception. Eight boards have their authority spelled out in the Georgia Constitution; many others have been created by law or executive order (see Table 5).

The eight boards and commissions required by the Constitution are among the most powerful agencies in Georgia, in part because any changes in their basic authority and membership require a constitutional amendment rather than passage of a law by the General Assembly. Their power is also reflected in the resources they control. In fiscal year 2000, for instance, the University System Board of Regents received over $1.6 billion in state funds. Some funds are earmarked in the Constitution: Article 3 requires that state motor fuel taxes, which totaled more than $550 million in fiscal 1999, must be spent for "an adequate system of public roads and bridges." That provides substantial power to the Department of Transportation, whose revenues included another $632 million in federal money.[38]

TABLE 5   Constitutional Boards and Commissions in Georgia

Board/Commission	Members	Membership Selection
Public Service	5	Elected statewide on a partisan ballot for six-year terms.
Pardons and Paroles	5	Appointed by the governor to seven-year terms subject to Senate confirmation.
Personnel	5	Appointed by the governor to five-year terms subject to Senate confirmation.
Transportation	13[a]	One member per congressional district elected by majority vote of General Assembly members whose districts overlap any of the congressional district.
Veterans Services	7	Appointed by the governor to seven-year terms subject to Senate confirmation.
Natural Resources	18[a]	One member per congressional district and five at large (at least one of whom is from a coastal county) appointed by the governor to seven-year terms subject to Senate confirmation.
Education	13[a]	One member per congressional district appointed by the governor to seven-year terms subject to Senate confirmation.
Regents	18[a]	One member per congressional district and five at large appointed by the governor to seven-year terms subject to Senate confirmation.

[a] Membership can vary because it depends on the number of seats that Georgia has in the U.S. House of Representatives, which increased to 13 following the 2000 census and reapportionment. Totals reflect the new size following redistricting in 2001and appointment of new members.

Source: *Constitution of the State of Georgia*, art. 4 (for the first six boards); art. 8, sect. 2 (State Board of Education); art. 4, sect. 4 (Board of Regents).

The Constitution insulates these boards from political pressure to some degree by providing relatively long terms that are staggered. In the case of the State Board of Education and the University System Board of Regents, the governor is specifically prohibited from being a board member. Most constitutional boards and commissions use some geographical representation. Assigning one seat per congressional district has the effect of assuring South Georgia seats on boards that otherwise might be dominated by people from the Atlanta area. It also means that the size of a board can change as Georgia gets additional seats in the U.S. House of Representatives.

The Public Service Commission was originally created by statute in 1879 to regulate railroads. Today it is composed of five members who are elected statewide for staggered, six-year terms and regulates telephone services, utilities such as gas and electricity, communication networks, and transportation such as trucking and rail systems. The State Transportation Board may seem like the essence of pork-barrel politics, with one member chosen for each congressional district by the state legislators whose districts overlap it (and benefit from highway construction). Members of the remaining six boards are appointed by the governor, subject to confirmation by the Senate.

The Judicial Branch

There are essentially 51 legal systems in the United States, one at the federal level and a distinct system in each of the 50 states. Like the federal government and other states, Georgia has an elaborate system of trial and appellate courts (see Figure 1). Trial courts apply laws to the facts in specific cases, as when they render a verdict in a criminal or civil case. Appellate courts review the actions of trial courts to determine questions of law (whether statutes or constitutional questions were interpreted or applied correctly). Decisions in appellate courts are made by groups of judges with no witnesses or juries. The appellate courts rely on written and oral arguments by the parties in the case being appealed, although they can permit other parties to submit written briefs in support of either side in a case. Unlike Article 3 of the U.S. Constitution, which grants Congress broad authority regarding the legal system, Article 6 of the Georgia Constitution includes substantial detail about the operation of trial and appellate courts, the selection and conduct of judges, the election and performance of district attorneys, and a range of procedures.

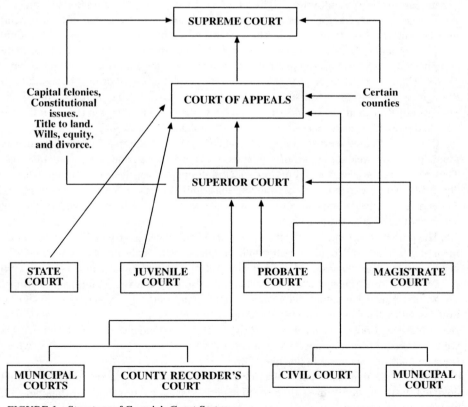

FIGURE 1   *Structure of Georgia's Court System*

Source: Judicial Council of Georgia and Administrative Office of the Courts *1998 Annual Report on the Work of the Georgia Courts*, p. 12.

The Georgia Constitution requires that state judges be elected, primarily on a nonpartisan ballot. Georgia's district attorneys, who are local officials responsible for criminal prosecutions, also are elected. This is quite different from the national level, where, subject to Senate confirmation, local prosecutors are presidential appointees under the authority of the U.S. Department of Justice, and judges are nominated by the president and can serve for life. There is some link between Georgia's executive and judicial branches, however, because the governor is permitted to appoint people to vacant or newly created judgeships.[39] One recent study calculated that 66 percent of superior court judgeships between 1968 and mid-1994 were filled by appointment.[40] Because judges are routinely reelected in Georgia and so many vacancies are filled by appointment, judicial selection in Georgia is often seen as a system of gubernatorial selection. Another practice not found at the national level is the ability of the attorney general to issue advisory opinions, which can have the force of law in Georgia unless overturned in court.

Trial Courts[41]   The Georgia Constitution requires that each county have at least one superior court, magistrate court, and probate court. Each county also can have a state court and juvenile court. Superior court is the court of general jurisdiction, hearing a broad range of serious cases (felonies and serious civil suits). There are also courts of limited jurisdiction, which hear specialized cases that are usually less serious than those in courts of general jurisdiction. The Constitution grants the General Assembly discretion over the creation, jurisdiction, and operation of courts.[42] Georgia is often characterized as one of the more complicated court systems, in large part because of the many trial courts of limited jurisdiction, some of which operate in only a few cities or counties rather than being uniform throughout the state. Juries in superior court generally have twelve members, but Georgia's Bill of Rights allows smaller juries (no fewer than six members) in courts of limited jurisdiction and for misdemeanor cases in superior court.[43]

Courts of limited jurisdiction include about 400 local courts. These are primarily municipal courts dealing with traffic matters, local ordinances, and other misdemeanors. They also process warrants and may conduct preliminary hearings to determine whether "probable cause" exists to charge someone in criminal cases. Local acts passed by the General Assembly determine courts' jurisdiction and the qualifications and method of selecting municipal court judges.

The probate court in each county deals with wills, estates, marriage licenses, appointment of guardians, and involuntary hospitalizations of individuals. Probate courts may also issue warrants in some cases. Magistrate courts deal with bail, misdemeanors, small civil complaints, and search and arrest warrants. They also may conduct preliminary hearings.

Some counties have state and juvenile courts. State courts are created by local legislation passed by the General Assembly and operate in 66 counties, hearing civil cases, traffic violations, or other misdemeanors. Only 54 of the 100 judgeships authorized in 1998 were full time. There may not be a separate juvenile court judge in small counties, where superior court judges serve in juvenile court.

The Constitution designates superior courts as Georgia's general jurisdiction trial courts. The state is divided for administrative purposes into circuits that vary in population and size. Each county has its own superior court, but judges may handle cases in more than one county within a circuit. As workloads change, the General Assembly has increased the number of circuits, as in 1998, when a forty-seventh circuit was created. Superior courts hear divorces, most cases involving civil disputes, land title cases, felonies, and equity cases. Jury trials are held in most cases. At the end of the 1998 fiscal year, there were 169 superior court judges.

Appellate Courts   Like most states, Georgia has two levels of appellate courts. Cases decided at lower levels may be appealed to the Court of Appeals, except in cases reserved for other courts, such as the Georgia Supreme Court's exclusive jurisdiction over election contests. The Court of Appeals, which was created in 1907 to relieve some of the burden on the Supreme Court, is elected statewide on a nonpartisan basis for staggered, six-year terms. The work of the Court of Appeals can be affected by state law, as when the General Assembly added a tenth judge in 1996 to help with the increased work load. The court often hears appeals on child custody, worker's compensation, and criminal cases that do not involve the death penalty. Cases appealed to the Court of Appeals are usually heard by a panel of three judges. If one of the judges on a panel dissents, however, a case may be heard by the full Court of Appeals.[44]

The Supreme Court is comprised of seven justices elected statewide on a nonpartisan basis to six-year terms. They choose whether to hear appeals from lower courts through the process of certiorari, or request for information from lower courts. The Court has exclusive appellate jurisdiction over all cases regarding the Georgia Constitution, the U.S. Constitution (as it applies to actions within the state), elections, and the constitutionality of laws. It also may hear cases on appeal from the Court of Appeals or may be called upon to decide questions of law from other state or local courts. It has authority to hear appeals for all cases in which a sentence of death may be given. The Supreme Court is also involved in administering the state court system and regulating the legal profession.[45]

Selection of Judges[46]   The 50 states employ five methods for choosing judges. Some states elect judges in partisan elections; others hold nonpartisan elections; others require that judges be appointed by the governor; three states have at least some judges elected by the legislature; still others allow for the selection of judges under a merit system of screening by nominating commissions that submit candidates to a state's governor for selection. Once in office, such judges stand periodically for election.

Georgia has a long-standing commitment to electing judges, although there are some qualifications regarding age, residence in counties or circuits, and membership in the state bar. Georgia's Constitution requires that members of the Supreme Court and Court of Appeals be elected in statewide nonpartisan elections for six-year terms. The justices of the Supreme Court choose a chief justice from among themselves. Superior court judges are also elected in nonpartisan elections, but serve four-year terms and are elected by voters who live within their circuits. State court judges are elected in nonpartisan, countywide elections for four years. Juvenile court judges are appointed, not elected, by the superior court judges of the counties they serve. The Georgia Constitution requires that all appellate and superior court judges shall have been admitted to practice law for seven years prior to assuming their judicial positions. Voters approved an amendment to the Constitution in 2000 imposing a similar seven-year requirement for state court judges (it had been five years).

The methods for choosing probate judges, magistrates, and municipal court judges are determined by law and can vary widely. In Athens-Clarke County, for instance, the probate judge and magistrate are elected on a partisan ballot, but municipal court judges are appointed. Unlike the rest of the judiciary, the Georgia Constitution does not require that probate judges, magistrates, or municipal court judges have been admitted to practice law for a minimum number of years. It leaves such matters for the General Assembly to specify by law, which means that non-lawyers could serve in such positions. This has often been a controversial issue. State law does require certain training for those assuming such positions, however.

The Constitution allows the Judicial Qualifications Commission to suspend, remove, or discipline judges who have been indicted or convicted of a crime, cannot perform the duties of their office, or "for conduct prejudicial to the administration of justice which brings the judicial office into disrepute." The Georgia Supreme Court must review the case before a judge is removed from office. Except in magistrate, probate, and juvenile courts, the Georgia Constitution authorizes the governor to appoint a replacement to serve the remainder of a judge's term when a position becomes vacant for any reason. The Judicial Nominating Commission assists the governor in making such appointments, although the selection process includes input from political leaders and members of the legal profession.

District Attorneys[47]   District attorneys are elected for four-year terms in each judicial circuit in Georgia. Qualifications for office include active membership in the State Bar of Georgia for three years. They represent the state as prosecutors in all criminal cases and in all cases heard by the Supreme Court and Courts of Appeals.

Juries[48]   The Georgia Constitution provides limited detail on juries, although it is significant that the matter is in Article 1 with the bill of rights rather than in the article on the judiciary, as it was in the Constitution of 1976. Citizens may be chosen to serve on grand juries or trial juries. While trial juries are the better known to the public because of media coverage of some criminal cases, grand juries are important in determining how and if a case will proceed against a defendant.

The Constitution specifies trial juries of 12 members, but allows the General Assembly to permit nonunanimous decisions and smaller juries in misdemeanor cases and in courts of limited jurisdiction. Juries are not required for all trials in Georgia, but the size of the jury is determined by the level of the court. Magistrate courts and juvenile courts never hold jury trials, and other lower courts are not likely to use juries. Superior courts have juries of 12 members. State courts have six-member juries. Juries in civil cases consist of six or 12 members, depending on the dollar amount of damages sought and whether either party requests a jury of 12 rather than six members in state court. Unanimous decisions are required in criminal cases, where the decision to use a jury rather than a judge for the verdict rests with the defendant.

Grand juries are used by over half the states to issue an indictment (a formal charge accusing someone of a crime). Four states (New Jersey, South Carolina, Tennessee, and Virginia) require grand juries for all indictments. Georgia is one of fifteen states that requires a grand jury for felony indictments. Six states require grand jury indictments for capital crimes, and the state of Pennsylvania does not empower the grand jury to indict. All other states make grand jury indictments optional, with the prosecutor filing an information in order to enter a formal charge against someone.

In deciding whether to issue an indictment, a grand jury must conclude that there is "probable cause" that the person committed the crime as charged. This a far less rigorous standard, however, than the "proof beyond a reasonable doubt" needed to convict the accused in a trial. Because the grand jury decides merely if sufficient evidence exists for an indictment, only the prosecution is heard, business is conducted in secret, and the defense has no right to cross-examine witnesses. Many have argued that this makes grand juries unnecessary and merely a "rubber stamp" for the prosecutor.

Grand juries in Georgia consist of 16–23 members. In addition to issuing indictments, grand juries have broad powers to study the records and activities of county governments, issue reports, and make certain decisions. For instance, grand juries in both counties had to review a request by some citizens to transfer the territory where they lived from Fulton County to Coweta County. Also, grand juries selected school boards in some counties until the Georgia Constitution was amended in 1992.

Local Government in Georgia[49]

In addition to allocating authority among the three branches of state government, the Georgia Constitution also establishes a framework for the operation of local government.[50] This is especially important since the U.S. Constitution says nothing about the matter. Local government in Georgia includes a range of counties, cities, and special districts (see Table 6).

Counties and Cities   The Georgia Constitution is very detailed regarding local government, although it is somewhat more specific regarding counties than cities and special districts. Article 9 even restricts the number of counties to no more than 159, although no such limit applies to other local governments. The Constitution also requires all counties to have certain elected officials. These local "constitutional officers" include a clerk of the superior court, judge of the probate court, sheriff, and tax commissioner (or tax collector and tax receiver), each of whom is elected to a four-year term. The Constitution leaves it to state law to spell out the characteristics of local legislative bodies such as county commissions and city councils.

TABLE 6   Number and Type of Local Governments in Georgia, 1952–1997

Year	Counties[a]	Municipalities[a]	School Districts	Special Districts
1952	159	475	187	154
1957	159	508	198	255
1962	159	561	197	301
1967	159	512	194	338
1972	159	529	189	366
1977	159	529	188	387
1982	159	532	187	390
1987	159	531	186	410
1992	159	534	183	421
1997	159	534	180	473

[a] Following the mergers between Columbus and Muscogee County in 1970, Athens and Clarke County in 1991, and Augusta and Richmond County in 1995, the U.S. Census Bureau counted the new governments as a municipality, not a county. This table, however, treats each merged government as a county because of its organization and functions.

Sources: U.S. Bureau of the Census, *Census of Governments*, selected years.

The Constitution goes to some length to prohibit counties from taking several types of actions, such as those affecting local school systems or any court. It also lists functions that cities and counties may perform, including public transportation, health services and facilities, libraries, and enforcement of building codes. This is especially important to counties, which were first authorized to provide urban services by a constitutional amendment ratified in 1972. Article 9 also allows counties and cities to use planning and zoning, take private property, make agreements with one another, and consolidate.

Special Districts   A wide range of special districts is permitted by the Georgia Constitution, but their characteristics are covered by general laws. Probably the most visible special districts are local school systems. Policy making for education at the local level is the responsibility of elected school boards, while a superintendent is hired as chief administrator. Prior to ratification of a constitutional amendment in November 1992, two-thirds of the county superintendents and 85 percent of the boards were elected. Elected superintendents in office on January 1, 1993 were allowed to serve out their terms.

Perhaps the most important characteristic of special districts is their relative independence from county and municipal governments. For instance, areas are setting up "community improvement districts" under state law to tax themselves extra for services beyond what their city or county provides. There are districts covering major malls in suburban Atlanta and one that collects $1.7 million annually for services in downtown Atlanta.[51] In addition to districts that cover only part of a local government's area, others have been established to deal with regional issues that a single city or county might not be able to address. MARTA, for example, provides bus and subway service in Fulton and DeKalb Counties. The Georgia Regional Transportation Authority (GRTA), which was created by the General Assembly at the request of the governor in 1999, has a say in transportation and major development decisions in areas not meeting federal clean air standards. Initially, GRTA had jurisdiction over 13 metropolitan Atlanta counties, but its reach could extend to other metropolitan areas of the state, such as Augusta and Macon, if they violate clean air standards.[52] In addition, the General Assembly created the North Georgia Metropolitan Water Planning District in 2001 to address water problems in 18 counties in the Atlanta area.[53] Overall, this system of special districts has evolved because of the state's constitutional power to establish local governments, with a recent trend toward multi-county districts to deal with growth and environmental concerns.

Home Rule   The Georgia Constitution provides "home rule" for cities and counties. In most states, this means that a local government is granted broad powers to write and amend its charter (the equivalent of a local government's constitution) and to take any action not prohibited by the state. Home rule has proven more limited in Georgia, however. One study found that Georgia was one of 25 states in 1990 without a general law providing optional forms of government for counties, and one of 26 that did not grant them some autonomy in choosing their form of government. The same was true regarding municipalities, where Georgia was one of 13 states that did not have a general law regarding optional forms, and one of only ten that did not give cities any choice in their organizational structure. Unlike 30 states, Georgia did not divide its cities into "classes" (usually based on population), with different levels of authority granted to each class. Like 27 states, Georgia grants broad flexibility to cities in carrying out local government functions; it also does so for counties, which only 20 other states do.[54]

Thus, Georgia grants its local governments some autonomy in day-to-day operations, but little author-ity to determine their own organizational structure.

A major reason for this limited local power is the Constitution itself, which places some restrictions directly on counties and cities. It also permits the legislature to adopt local acts, which are used to modify the workings of specific cities, counties, and special districts. Local acts were 51 percent of the bills passed between 1970 and 1996 and can cover a wide range of topics. For example, it took action by the General Assembly to estab-lish procedures for citizens to vote on merging governments in Athens-Clarke County in 1990 and in Augusta-Richmond County in 1995.[55] Many other state constitutions prohibit the adoption of local laws.

Local Government Finances[56]   The Constitution generally leaves the question of how local governments can raise and spend money to the General Assembly. In contrast, debt is covered in substantial detail. Georgia employs several restrictions common among the states. One is that debt cannot exceed ten percent of the assessed value of taxable property within the jurisdiction. Second, the Constitution places an annual limit on the amount that can be borrowed on a short-term basis.

A third requirement is that voters must approve the issuance of new debt by a simple majority in an election. However, this applies only to general obligation debt (borrowing in which the local government pledges tax revenues to pay off bonds sold to raise money, usually for major construction projects). The required voter approval and debt limitation do not apply to revenue bonds, which are not backed by taxes, but by revenues from proj-ects being financed by the bonds. Airport bonds, for example, are generally paid off with parking revenue, aircraft landing fees, rents from airlines and concessionaires, and the like. With all types of local government borrowing, though, the real limit is the willingness of investors to buy bonds issued by a local government. In addition, local governments are required by state law to adopt a balanced budget each year.[57]

Georgia, like most states, limits local tax rates, mainly through laws passed by the General Assembly. State law allows counties and municipalities to levy a one percent gen-eral sales tax in addition to the four percent state tax. They cannot levy the tax without the approval of their voters. Since 1985, counties have been permitted by law to use a one-per-cent special purpose local option sales tax (SPLOST). The SPLOST is temporary, must be approved in a referendum, and must finance specific projects. Two-thirds of the 116 coun-ties included in a 1994 survey by the Georgia Department of Community Affairs used SPLOST, with the most common uses of the funds being streets and roads, landfills, and solid waste.

In November of 1996, Georgia voters ratified a constitutional amendment to allow school districts to use a one-percent sales tax for construction. This tax is similar to the SPLOST used by counties and must be approved by a school district's voters in a referen-dum. This new revenue source could generate millions of dollars of funds, especially in rapidly growing school systems, and help school boards reduce their debt and dependence on property taxes. Despite the narrow statewide majority ratifying the amendment to authorize the tax, it quickly proved popular at the local level. Between March and Sep-tember of 1997, voters in 112 school districts approved a sales tax, while 12 districts defeated such measures. In most cases, turnout in these elections was extremely low, including less than ten percent of registered voters in several cases. The new sales tax revenues were expected to generate $4.6 billion for construction and the repayment of bonds sold previously to finance school district projects.[58]

IV. Elections

Just as constitutions specify the ways in which political institutions are organized, they also establish processes considered essential for a democracy. These include procedures for conducting elections, which are found in Article 2 of the Georgia Constitution.

Types of Elections

Voting may be the only political process in which many Georgians take part. The Georgia Constitution provides basic ground rules for elections, such as the use of secret ballots and establishment of 18 as the minimum voting age (Georgia adopted this minimum age in the 1940s and was the first state to do so). Runoff elections and recalls are constitutionally established, as are procedures for removing and/or suspending public officials. However, the Constitution leaves most of the specifics regarding voter registration and election procedures to the General Assembly to decide by passing laws.

Primary and General Elections   All states have general elections in which voters choose from a number of candidates to fill an office. In most states, including Georgia, voters select party nominees from a group of potential candidates in a primary election. Some states also use party conventions to nominate candidates for certain offices. Primaries are not specified in the Georgia Constitution, but procedures are provided for by political party rules or by law.

Runoffs   In most states, the individual who receives the most votes in an election is declared the winner, but others require that the winner of a primary or general election receive over a certain percentage of the votes cast. Seven states, including Georgia, hold runoffs if no single candidate is able to capture 50 percent of the vote. North Carolina also employs runoffs, but reduced the threshold from 50 percent to 40 percent in 1989. Georgia's runoff was originally adopted in 1917, but has changed somewhat since then.

The logic behind the runoff system is based, in part, on the assumption that elections should reflect the will of the majority of the electorate. In states where there is a tradition of one-party politics with little or no opposition in the general election, candidates have faced their strongest opposition in primaries. If only a plurality were required in such states, it would be possible to achieve elected office by finishing first in a primary with many candidates and receiving well under 50 percent of the vote. To prevent that from occurring, the top two finishers face each other in a subsequent runoff, where the winner would be the candidate getting a majority in this two-person race. Not surprisingly, the states currently using runoffs are southern states with a history of one-party domination.[59]

Traditionally, runoffs occurred after primaries, but in 1992 a runoff was held after a general election in Georgia between candidates for the U.S. Senate. In that instance, a third candidate prevented front-runner Wyche Fowler, the Democratic incumbent, from earning over 50 percent of the vote. His Republican opponent, Paul Coverdell, won the runoff. The General Assembly prevented this from occurring again when it adopted laws in 1994, 1996, 1997, and 1998 governing the use of such elections. A plurality (not a majority) is all that is needed to win a general election for a state office, except for the statewide constitutional officers, who still must achieve 50 percent. A majority remains required for party primaries and special elections, so runoffs could be common in such cases.[60] Runoff requirements also remain a requirement in many local elections.

Runoffs have been criticized as being biased against minority candidates, who might finish first in an election but not get a majority. A minority candidate could then be defeated in a runoff as whites voted in a bloc for the remaining white candidate. Runoffs have been the subject of litigation in Georgia. The U.S. Supreme Court permitted their continued use in 1999, however, when it refused to hear an appeal from a lower court, which had held that the law requiring primary runoffs was not racially discriminatory.[61]

Referendum and Recall Elections   States also conduct elections in which candidates are not running for office. The most common is a referendum, in which legislative bodies place issues on the ballot for public approval. Critics often complain, though, that asking people simply to vote "yes" or "no" on a question is not a good way to decide complex issues. Georgia voters are accustomed to referenda on whether to amend the state constitution. In their communities, they can be asked to decide whether local governments should levy sales taxes or be permitted to go into debt to by selling bonds to pay for public improvements such as roads and buildings.

Recalls are special types of elections that remove public officials from office before their terms have expired. Recall of state officials is allowed in Georgia and 15 other states; recall of local officeholders is more widely permitted. Some states exempt certain officeholders, usually judges, from the recall process. In Georgia, all persons who occupy elected state or local offices, even if they were appointed to fill unfinished terms, are subject to removal. Recalls are placed on the ballot through a petition process established by law. If an office becomes vacant through recall, a special election is held to fill the position.[62]

The Constitution allows other means for removing public officials. The House of Representatives may impeach any executive or judicial officer of the state, as well as members of the General Assembly. If the House votes in favor of impeachment charges, a two-thirds vote in the Senate is required to convict and remove the official from office.[63] The Constitution also includes procedures for the temporary suspension of the governor, the lieutenant governor, any of the other six constitutional officers, or a member of the General Assembly indicted for a felony by a grand jury.[64]

Timing of Elections[65]

The 1983 Constitution set the dates for the first general elections after its implementation; it also gave the General Assembly power to change the dates. This has not occurred, so elections for state offices are held the first Tuesday after the first Monday in November of even-numbered years. The members of the General Assembly are elected for two-year terms, which means that elections for these offices are at the same time as the U.S. House of Representatives. The governor and other statewide officeholders have four-year terms and are elected in years when the presidency is not on the ballot, which can protect Georgia candidates if their political party has an unpopular presidential candidate.

The Constitution sets length of terms for other elected officials, but leaves it to the General Assembly to determine by law when judges and most local officials will be elected.[66] County elections in Georgia are generally at the same time as major state and national races, but most city elections are held at different times, often in odd-numbered years.

Redistricting

Like other states, Georgia redraws district boundaries for its legislature and the U.S. House of Representatives every ten years following the U.S. census. A similar process occurs for city councils and county commissions whose members are elected from districts rather than at large. Gerrymandering (the practice of drawing districts in order to achieve political outcomes) is one method by which incumbents may protect their political careers, minority political parties may be prevented from gaining legislative seats, rural or urban districts may dominate, or the voting strength of minority groups may be diluted.

Although it did not originate in Georgia, the U.S. Supreme Court's 1962 decision in *Baker v. Carr*[67] affected Georgia profoundly. This landmark ruling and related decisions that followed forced states to draw legislative districts on the basis of population rather than political boundaries such as county lines. The "one person, one vote" standard required districts of equal population, although slight variation is tolerated. Based in part on crucial litigation in Georgia (see the discussion of *Miller v. Johnson* below), the U.S. Supreme Court has also limited the use of race in drawing legislative districts.

V. Rights and Liberties[68]

Just as constitutions establish governmental institutions and basic processes such as elections, they also guarantee rights to individuals and regulate government's ability to interfere with people's liberties. Amending a constitution is normally a very difficult process. Therefore, including rights and liberties in a constitution is designed to protect them better than if such guarantees could be reduced or eliminated simply by passing a law. State constitutions may not infringe upon liberties and rights protected by the U.S. Constitution. Because of dual citizenship and the 14th Amendment to the U.S. Constitution, these federal guarantees are minimum standards, however, and states may grant their citizens broader rights.

The Georgia Constitution allows state courts to determine whether laws or actions comply with the state or U.S. constitutions.[69] This process of judicial review is similar to that at the national level. Any law or administrative rule in Georgia, whether passed by the state or by local governments, may be challenged in court. In addition, some private practices may be challenged, such as activities of businesses or individuals. Unlike the U.S. Constitution, which specifies most rights in amendments, Georgia's constitutions since 1861 have included a bill of rights as an integral part of the document. Article 1 in the 1983 Constitution includes 28 paragraphs covering "Rights of Persons."

The discussion below covers some of the major provisions in Georgia's bill of rights. Under each heading, the first section describes how Georgia courts have applied these guarantees in specific cases. This is followed by a discussion of related federal court cases originating in Georgia. These cases are based on the U.S. Constitution and often brought about substantial changes not only in Georgia, but in the nation as a whole.

The first section covers civil rights, which are often thought of as the freedom to participate in the political system. It is generally linked to the guarantee of "equal protection" in the eyes of the law, which is the basis for much of the litigation on discrimination. The next three sections deal with civil liberties—the basic protection against unwarranted government intrusion into one's life. The fifth section deals with a protection not written explicitly into either the U.S. or Georgia constitutions, the right to privacy. Each section summarizes major federal court cases in a tables with full legal citations. Citations for decisions by Georgia courts are found in the endnotes.

Equal Protection[70]

Georgia Courts   The second paragraph in Georgia's bill of rights guarantees that, "No person shall be denied the equal protection of the laws." This language mirrors the 14th Amendment to the U.S. Constitution. While the Georgia Supreme Court has held that the federal and state equal protection guarantees "coexist," the justices have acknowledged that the state may interpret the Georgia Constitution to offer broader rights than are available under the U.S. Constitution.

A great deal of the controversy over equal protection involves government's classification of groups, with the courts being most vigilant regarding race and sex. In 1984, the Georgia Supreme Court found unconstitutional a law that provided benefits to children whose mothers were wrongfully killed but did not afford the same protection to children whose fathers were wrongfully killed. The Court also struck down Atlanta's program to set aside a share of contracts for minority- and female-owned businesses because the city failed to demonstrate the need for a race-conscious program.[71] Local governments have continued to adopt set-aside programs, however, after studies to determine the effects of prior discrimination. Such policies remain highly contentious, though, and must operate within guidelines laid out by the U.S. Supreme Court, which has become increasingly skeptical of such initiatives. Similar controversies have surrounded the use of affirmative action in admissions decisions at Georgia's public colleges and universities.[72]

Perhaps more contentious have been several Atlanta ordinances. In 1995, the Georgia Supreme Court held that Atlanta could create a registry of unmarried couples (both heterosexual and homosexual) and forbid discrimination based on sexual orientation. However, the Court concluded that the city exceeded its authority by extending insurance benefits to the domestic partners of city employees.[73]

Federal Courts and Racial Segregation   On the surface, the 14th Amendment would seem to prohibit discrimination based on race. Yet Georgia, like other southern states, used a number of strategies to disenfranchise black citizens from the 1870s to the 1960s. These included the poll tax, the white primary, and other restrictions eventually eliminated by federal legislation and court decisions.[74]

The poll tax required citizens to pay an annual levy to be eligible to vote, thereby making it harder for the poor to vote. Georgia had used a poll tax earlier in its history, but it became particularly restrictive when the 1877 constitution made it cumulative, which meant that anyone falling behind in the annual tax had to make back payments. The poll tax was not repealed until 1945, when Governor Ellis Arnall made it a major issue during the legislative session. In other southern states, it lasted until the 24th Amendment to the U.S. Constitution banned the poll tax in 1964.

Perhaps the most blatant attempt to disenfranchise blacks was the white primary, which restricted voting in party primaries to whites only. Blacks could participate in the general election, but their votes were inconsequential because there was seldom Republican opposition on the ballot. In a 1927 Texas case, the U.S. Supreme Court held that it was unconstitutional for state laws to restrict primary voting on the basis of race. Virtually the entire South was controlled by the Democratic party then, and party leaders thereafter used party rules to enforce the white primary. Unlike general elections, which are processes of government, primaries could be regarded as activities of political parties, which are "private" organizations.

White primaries in Georgia were adopted in some counties by the 1890s. The state Democratic party began using primaries rather than conventions to select statewide nominees in 1898, and beginning in 1900, only whites could vote in the party's primary elections. It was not until 1944 that the U.S. Supreme Court held in another case from Texas that party rules enforcing a white primary also abridged the right to vote based on race. Georgia's white primary was overturned the following year by a federal appeals court in *King v. Chapman*. Perhaps the most immediate effect of this decision was in Atlanta, where the city's business and political leaders began developing a coalition with the black middle class.[75]

Three other restrictions were included in the Disenfranchisement Act of 1908, which voters approved as an amendment to the Georgia Constitution by a two-to-one margin:

> The literacy test required that voters be able to read and explain any paragraph of the federal or state constitution; while the property qualification required ownership of 40 acres of land or property assessed at $500. The grandfather clause enfranchised men who had served in the United States or Confederate military forces and their descendants; no one could register under that provision after 1914.[76]

Implementation of the literacy test was in the hands of local election officials, who exercised great discretion, especially their power to purge voter registration rolls of those judged to be unqualified.

As the momentum grew to desegregate during the 1950s and 1960s, the Georgia General Assembly produced an array of legislation to forestall the process.[77] At one point, all state aid was removed from any public school that was integrated, and payments were authorized to parents of children who attended segregated private schools. In order to prevent blacks from attending college in the state, requirements for admission were set to include letters of recommendation from two former graduates of the institution to which a student was applying. Since no blacks had attended most of these institutions, such letters would be difficult to obtain. Although most actions by the Georgia General Assembly were struck down as unconstitutional, white parents were able to move to different school districts or to send their children to private academies which did not admit blacks. Segregation was largely maintained until Congress passed the 1964 Civil Rights Act, but it continued in many respects long after that date. Local school districts also tried to prevent or minimize desegregation, including the Chatham County school board's unsuccessful effort to claim that integration would heighten black children's feelings of inferiority.[78]

TABLE 7   Major Federal Cases on Discrimination and Representation

King v. Chapman 154 F.2d 450 (1946)	Building on a 1944 U.S. Supreme Court case covering Texas, the circuit court of appeals found that the rules of Georgia's Democratic party, which restricted voting in primary elections to whites only, violated the equal protection guarantee of the 14th Amendment.
Heart of Atlanta Motel v. United States 379 U.S. 241 (1964)	Upheld constitutionality of Title 2 of the Civil Rights Act of 1964, which prohibited racial discrimination in public accommodations.
Gray v. Sanders 372 U.S. 368 (1963)	Held that Georgia's county-unit system violated the 14th Amendment's equal protection guarantee because it malapportioned votes among the state's counties.
Fortson v. Toombs 379 U.S. 621 (1965)	Upheld a lower court's 1962 decision that the 14th Amendment required seats in the General Assembly to be apportioned with districts of roughly equal population rather than being based on county or other political boundaries.
Miller v. Johnson 515 U.S. 900 (1995)	Invalidated Georgia's congressional redistricting following the 1990 census as a violation of the 14th Amendment's equal protection clause because race was the predominant factor in drawing district boundaries. The General Assembly had created three black-majority districts, with the eleventh district having a very irregular shape.

The Civil Rights Act of 1964 was designed to end discrimination in public accommodations (hotels, restaurants, transportation, etc.). In *Heart of Atlanta Motel v. United States*, the U.S. Supreme Court upheld the Civil Rights Act as a valid exercise of Congress's authority to regulate interstate commerce. The Court rejected the motel's claim that it was a local business. Because the motel served interstate travelers, its practice of refusing lodging to blacks was held to obstruct commerce, and the motel would therefore have to serve blacks.

Federal Courts and Equal Representation   Since the early 1960s, the federal courts have become increasingly active in the process of drawing districts for legislative bodies. The courts have interpreted the equal protection guarantee of the 14th Amendment to mean that one person's vote should have the same weight in an election as another person's; to do this requires districts of roughly equal population. In *Toombs v. Fortson*, the Court ruled that reapportionment for the General Assembly must be made on the basis of the population of the state rather than by county or other political boundaries. Each district must have roughly the same number of inhabitants. After four earlier challenges had failed, in *Gray v. Sanders*, the U.S. Supreme Court struck down the county-unit system (see p. 10) as a violation of the 14th Amendment's equal protection guarantee because the system malapportioned votes by underrepresenting urban residents. Other litigation also forced the General Assembly to redraw congressional districts in the state.[79]

The last legal hurdles to enfranchising blacks were removed by the Voting Rights Act, which Congress passed in 1965 and has renewed four times since then. The law suspended use of literacy tests, allowed for federal election examiners and observers, and required affected state and local governments to receive approval from the federal government before making changes in their electoral systems. This "preclearance" by the U.S. Department of Justice is especially wary of changes which might dilute the voting strength of minorities. Most recently, the U.S. Department of Justice objected to congressional redistricting by the Georgia General Assembly following the 1990 census. After two unsuccessful attempts to redraw districts, state lawmakers finally satisfied the guidelines established by the federal government to protect minority voting strength in the 1992 elections.[80] Ironically, in 1995 those districts were ruled unconstitutional in *Miller v. Johnson* because race was a "predominant factor" used in drawing the district lines.[81]

Right to Life, Liberty, and Property[82]

Georgia Courts   Life, liberty, and property are the first rights listed in the Georgia Constitution. Like guarantees in the U.S. Constitution, they cannot be abridged "except by due process of law." State courts have found this guarantee to be broader than under the U.S. Constitution.[83] Georgia courts traditionally have found that the state has the power to regulate businesses so long as the regulation is applied equally to all who engage in the same types of businesses and has some "rational relationship" to a valid purpose. Only when litigants are able to show that their due process has been violated are they able to convince the courts that government regulation is "arbitrary" or "unreasonable." Thus, laws regulating the licensing and training of professionals have largely been upheld. The Georgia Supreme Court has held that a mandatory life sentence for a second drug conviction does not violate due process or equal protection despite statistical evidence that a larger percentage of blacks end up serving life sentences under the law.[84]

The Georgia Supreme Court has taken a broad view of government compensation owed to the owners of private property taken for public use. All states and the federal government have some power of eminent domain (the taking of private property for public use such as expanding a highway, constructing facilities, and laying water or sewer lines). While most Georgia court decisions have permitted government to determine the size and use of land taken, restrictions have been imposed on compensation for property. The courts also have applied the notion of "taking" to regulation of private property, i.e., government regulation may be so restrictive that it has the same effect as seizing someone's land. In this regard, the Georgia Supreme Court has reviewed a great many cases dealing with land-use regulation and has tended to favor property owners over cities and counties. There are no landmark federal cases from Georgia dealing directly with this issue, although the state has produced major cases dealing with the related question of privacy (see below).

Rights Related to Expression and Association

Georgia's bill of rights includes a number of provisions designed to allow people to hold and express opinions, to associate with others, and to participate in the political process. These include two paragraphs on religion, as well as one on freedom of speech and the press, another on the right to assemble and petition, and one on libel, which is not mentioned in the U.S. Constitution.

Georgia Courts and Freedom of Conscience and Religion[85]   Religious freedom was the earliest liberty to be addressed by Georgia's constitution drafters. Even the Rules and Regulations of 1776 included a provision for freedom of religion. The Georgia Constitution includes somewhat different language from the 1st Amendment to the U.S. Constitution. Perhaps the most striking difference is Georgia's limitation on religious practices: "but the right of freedom of religion shall not be so construed as to excuse acts of licentiousness or justify practices inconsistent with the peace and safety of the state."[86] Thus, Courts in Georgia have at times limited freedom of religion, as when the Georgia Supreme Court found that freedom of religion did not include the distribution of literature in public. Nor has the Court extended freedom of religion to the use of controlled substances.

Georgia Courts and Freedom of Speech and the Press[87] Georgia courts have adopted a broad interpretation of freedom of speech. For example, while the U.S. Constitution held that screening of movies was not in and of itself a violation of free speech, the Georgia Supreme Court found that an ordinance requiring approval of a censor before screening movies was unconstitutional in Georgia. The Court has held, however, that picketing was not protected free speech when the protest included an illegal strike.

Free speech, as interpreted by the Georgia courts, includes limits. Indeed, the Georgia Constitution says that people "shall be responsible for the abuse of that liberty," as in cases involving incorrect publication of delinquent debt, inaccurate information regarding criminal activity, or use of photographs for advertising without the subjects' permission. The Georgia Supreme Court has upheld an injunction against anti-abortion protesters on the ground that the protest was limited by reasonable restrictions regarding time, place, and manner. The Court also upheld the state's "Anti-Mask Act," which targets groups such as the Ku Klux Klan by prohibiting intimidating or threatening mask-wearing behavior, despite a claim that the law violates a person's freedom of speech.

The press does not have a constitutional right to withhold a confidential news source.[88] The media have been granted limited protection by a state law that allows reporters to be forced to turn over information from confidential sources when the evidence is material and relevant, is necessary for one of the parties to prepare a case, and cannot reasonably be gathered by other means.[89]

Controversies have swirled around language or behavior judged offensive by many people. For instance, the Georgia Supreme Court struck down a state law attempting to outlaw bumper stickers considered profane as being too vague and a violation of free speech. Even greater debates have involved sexually-oriented communication, particularly after the Georgia Supreme Court ruled that nude dancing was protected expression and overturned local regulations banning such entertainment as too broad or outside the authority granted to local governments. To reverse this action, Georgia voters approved a constitutional amendment in 1994 to increase local governments' control over nude dancing through their power to regulate alcoholic beverages. A number of local governments subsequently adopted ordinances to prevent clubs with nude dancing from serving alcohol. The Georgia Supreme Court has held that such local regulations do not violate the free speech rights associated with such entertainment.[90]

Federal Courts and Freedom of Speech and the Press The U.S. Supreme Court has considered many cases during the past 40 years dealing with the 1st Amendment's guarantees regarding religion, speech, the press, and association. Two major cases on obscenity originated in Georgia. In a 1969 decision, *Stanley v. Georgia*, the Court found that "the mere private possession of obscene matter cannot constitutionally be made a crime," which Georgia law had done. Police had a warrant to search Stanley's home for materials related

TABLE 8   Major Federal Cases on Freedom of Speech and the Press

Stanley v. Georgia 394 U.S. 557 (1969)	Overturned state law making private possession of obscene material a crime. The Georgia law was held to violate the 1st and 14th Amendments to the U.S. Constitution.
Paris Adult Theatre I v. Slaton 413 U.S. 49 (1973)	Banning the showing of allegedly obscene films to consenting adults in a commercial theater was held not to violate the 1st Amendment or the right to privacy.
Cox Broadcasting Corp v. Colin 420 U.S. 469 (1975)	Overturned the Georgia law prohibiting publication of the name of a rape victim obtained from public records.
Forsyth County, Georgia v. Nationalist Movement 505 U.S. 123 (1992)	Invalidated a local ordinance requiring participants to pay law enforcement costs for demonstrations and empowering the county administrator to determine how much to charge a group seeking a permit for a demonstration. The court found fault with the ordinance because it granted excessively broad discretion to the administrator, who was required to examine the content of a group's message in determining the fee to be charged for law enforcement protection.

to illegal gambling, but they found allegedly obscene material. The state claimed that certain types of materials should not be possessed or read, and that obscene materials may lead to sexual violence or other acts. The Court rejected these claims, holding that the state asserted the "right to control the moral content of a person's thoughts . . . but it is wholly inconsistent with the philosophy of the First Amendment."

In a 1973 case, *Paris Adult Theatre I v. Slaton*, the Supreme Court was asked to determine whether the state could ban a commercial theater from showing films considered obscene. Here the Court reached an opposite result from *Stanley*, holding that the state had an interest in "stemming the tide of commercialized obscenity." The Court held that it did not make a difference that the films in question were shown only to consenting adults and the business posted warnings of films' content and prohibited minors from entering. Instead, the Court held that the state had a valid interest in "the quality of life and the total community environment, the tone of commerce in the great city centers, and, possibly, the public safety itself."

Cox Broadcasting Corp. v. Colin dealt with Georgia's law prohibiting publication of a rape victim's name. Pitted against each other were the desire to protect the victim's privacy and the freedom of the press. The Court held that it would violate press freedom to prohibit the publication of crime victims' names obtained from public records.

Forsyth County was the scene of several marches by civil rights supporters and countermarches by the Ku Klux Klan during the 1980s. To manage these events, the county commission adopted an ordinance requiring those seeking a demonstration permit to pay a fee for law enforcement protection. The county administrator had discretion about the size of the fee, which could not exceed $1,000. One group refused to pay a $100 fee and sued the county. In *Forsyth County, Georgia v. Nationalist Movement*, the U.S. Supreme Court found that the county ordinance contained no standards for the administrator to follow and was thus unconstitutional because it "contains more than the possibility of censorship through uncontrolled discretion [and] the ordinance often requires that the fee be based on the content of the speech" of the group seeking the permit.

Rights of Those Accused and Convicted of Crimes[91]

The Georgia Constitution includes several provisions to protect people in dealing with the state's legal system. These include conditions regarding searches, seizures, and warrants by law enforcement officials; access to the courts and the use of juries; the right to an attorney and to cross-examine witnesses in criminal cases; the right against self-incrimination; protection against excessive bail and "cruel and unusual" punishment; and a prohibition against double jeopardy. Most of these guarantees parallel those in the U.S. Constitution's bill of rights, although Georgia has added other guarantees. For instance, the state bill of rights explicitly prohibits whipping and banishment from the state as punishment for crimes,[92] imprisonment for debt,[93] and being "abused in being arrested, while under arrest, or in prison."[94]

Georgia Courts   One of the most notable distinctions between the Georgia and U.S. constitutions is that the state offers greater protection to defendants against unreasonable searches and seizures by law enforcement authorities. In addition, Georgia has long recognized the right of indigents to have a lawyer appointed, although this right does not extend to civil cases.[95] A major problem with providing attorneys to poor criminal defendants has been in appropriating sufficient funds to make the guarantee work well.

Arguments often are made that certain punishments are "cruel and unusual." Georgia courts have held that punishment exceeding the crime is, in some cases, constitutional. For example, fines larger than amounts taken by theft have been permitted. In some instances, defendants have been banished from certain counties, but the Georgia Supreme Court has not upheld banishment from the state as a whole. Georgia's use of the death penalty was found to be unconstitutional in 1972 by the U.S. Supreme Court because the state did not have standards to protect against unequal application of capital punishment. Currently, Georgia law lists the conditions under which the death penalty may be sought and is in line with later U.S. Supreme Court rulings permitting executions. The Georgia Supreme Court, however, has considered it cruel and unusual punishment to execute someone who is mentally retarded,[96] but reached the opposite conclusion when considering life in prison for a second conviction for selling cocaine.[97]

Federal Courts and Search and Seizure   Georgia has not produced major federal cases related to the search and seizure rights of criminal defendants in the U.S. Constitution's 4th Amendment. In 1997, however, the U.S. Supreme Court overturned a Georgia law requiring candidates for state office to pass a drug test, which the General Assembly had passed as part of its anti-drug efforts during the 1980s. Walker Chandler filed to run as Libertarian party candidate for lieutenant governor in 1994 but refused to take the test. In *Chandler v. Miller*, the Court held that the drug tests did not fall within the category of constitutionally permissible suspicionless searches. Indeed, the Court found that the test was essentially "symbolic" rather than being directed at some identifiable problem that might demand such a search.

Federal Courts and the Rights of Criminal Defendants   The U.S. Constitution's 6th Amendment includes the right to a fair trial, which is not spelled out in detail. Therefore, the courts have had to define what that right means in practice. Some of these cases have dealt with the size of trial juries and whether they must reach a unanimous decision. In a

TABLE 9   Major Federal Cases Affecting Those Accused or Convicted of Crimes

Chandler v. Miller 520 U.S. 305 (1997)	Held that Georgia's requirement that candidates for state office pass a drug test violates the 4th and 14th Amendment protections against suspicionless searches.
Ballew v. Georgia 435 U.S. 223 (1978)	Held that a criminal trial using a jury of less than six members violated the 6th and 14th Amendment guarantees to a fair trial.
Furman v. Georgia 408 U.S. 238 (1972)	Held that Georgia's methods of administering the death penalty violated the 8th Amendment's guarantee against cruel and unusual punishment. The decision effectively ended executions in the United States for more than a decade.
Gregg v. Georgia 428 U.S. 153 (1976)	Upheld Georgia's revised law on capital punishment, which limited the crimes for which the death penalty could be imposed and specified the factors to be considered and procedures to be used in deciding when to impose capital punishment.
Coker v. Georgia 433 U.S. 584 (1977)	Found that Georgia's imposition of the death penalty for the crime of rape was grossly disproportionate and thus a violation of the 8th Amendment's ban on cruel and unusual punishment.
McCleskey v. Kemp 481 U.S. 279 (1987)	Rejected the claim that racial differences in the imposition of the death penalty violated the equal protection guarantee of the 14th Amendment and amounted to cruel and unusual punishment in violation of the 8th Amendment.

1973 Florida case, the U.S. Supreme Court had permitted six-member juries in civil cases. In *Ballew v. Georgia*, however, the Court ruled in 1978 that Georgia's use of five-person juries in misdemeanor cases violated the right to a fair trial, in part because of the reduced deliberation and bias in favor of the prosecution regarding hung juries. Georgia's current constitution allows the General Assembly to permit six-member juries in misdemeanor cases or in courts of limited jurisdiction.[98]

Federal Courts and the Death Penalty   Two appeals to the U.S. Supreme Court from Georgia during the 1970s became *the* landmark cases regarding the use of capital punishment in the United States. The first, *Furman v. Georgia* in 1972, effectively ended executions throughout the country. Four years later, *Gregg v. Georgia* allowed the state's rewritten capital punishment law to stand, thereby opening the door for states to resume executions.

What was different about these two cases? The members of the U.S. Supreme Court had a range of views regarding capital punishment, but the major concern was how the death penalty was applied. In *Furman*, the Court was concerned with both the lack of guidelines to use in deciding when to impose a death sentence and the wide variation in its use for similar crimes. The states then began revising their laws, and the Court decided several cases in 1976 based on the new statutes. In *Gregg*, the Court upheld Georgia's new capital punishment law, in part because it required specific findings by the jury regarding the facts of the crime and the character of the defendant; it also had a process for appellate courts to review death penalty cases.

Two other cases tested the constitutionality of the conditions under which Georgia imposed the death penalty. In *Coker v. Georgia*, the U.S. Supreme Court held that the death sentence for the crime of rape was grossly disproportionate to the offense and thus violated

TABLE 10   Major Federal Cases on the Right to Privacy

Doe v. Bolton 410 U.S. 179 (1973)	This is the less famous Georgia case decided along with *Roe v. Wade*. It overturned Georgia's ban on abortions as a violation of a woman's right to privacy.
Bowers v. Hardwick 478 U.S. 186 (1986)	Held that the right to privacy did not protect consensual homosexual sex from prosecution under Georgia's sodomy law.

the 8th Amendment ban on cruel and unusual punishment. In *McCleskey v. Kemp*, the Court confronted the issue of bias in imposing the death penalty. McCleskey presented a study showing that the use of the death sentence in Georgia was statistically related to the race of the murder victim and, to a lesser extent, the race of the defendant. This pattern, he argued, violated the 8th and 14th Amendments. The Supreme Court rejected these claims, citing appellate courts' review of cases with facts similar to McClesky's case.

The Right to Privacy

Georgia Courts   Like the U.S. Constitution, Georgia's does not mention a right to privacy. In 1904, though, Georgia became the first state to recognize a privacy right when the Georgia Supreme Court found this right in natural law and the guarantees of liberty found in the U.S. and state constitutions.[99] Privacy has been extended to the right of a prisoner to refuse to eat, even to the point of starvation, and a person's right to refuse medical treatment even if it was certain to lead to death.

Federal Courts   The U.S. Supreme Court first recognized a right to privacy in a 1965 Connecticut case dealing with government regulation of contraception. Since then, the courts have been forced to define the limits of privacy rights. These debates include two Georgia cases. *Doe v. Bolton* remains almost unnoticed today, but it was the challenge to Georgia's abortion law decided along with *Roe v. Wade*, the more widely known Texas case in which the Supreme Court held that the right to privacy included a woman's right to abortion.

The second Georgia case was *Bowers v. Hardwick*. In this case, Michael Hardwick challenged Georgia's sodomy law as a violation of the right to privacy in so far as it applied to consensual conduct. He also argued that as a homosexual he faced constant threat of arrest and prosecution. The Supreme Court rejected Hardwick's claim and upheld Georgia's sodomy law, which prohibited certain acts but did not specify the gender or sexual orientation of the participants.

Dual Citizenship and the Right to Privacy   Georgia's sodomy law provides a good example of the way in which dual citizenship can produce different rights under state and U.S. constitutions. The Georgia Supreme reinforced the *Hardwick* decision in 1996, when it ruled, in *Christensen v. State*,[100] that the state's sodomy law did not violate Georgia's right to privacy. That all changed in 1998, however. Based on facts involving a heterosexual couple, the Georgia Supreme Court, in *Powell v. State*, held, "insofar as it criminalizes the performance of private, non-commercial acts of sexual intimacy between persons legally able to consent, [the sodomy law] 'manifestly infringes upon a constitutional provision' . . . which guarantees to the citizens of Georgia the right to privacy."[101]

Thus, while any given state's sodomy law would not violate the federal right to privacy as applied in *Bowers v. Hardwick*, it might be a violation of broader rights guaranteed in its state constitution, as interpreted by state courts. This distinction may play out with other issues in the future, including the most recent battle over privacy rights—the question of doctor-assisted suicide, which is permitted in Oregon.[102]

VI. Public Policies and the Georgia Constitution

Unlike the U.S. Constitution, most state constitutions include a wide range of policies (government decisions in response to perceived problems). Of course, another way to enact policies is simply to pass laws. The inclusion of policy questions is a major reason that state constitutions are so long. Why do state constitutions include so many policy questions instead of being limited to more fundamental constitutional issues? At least three reasons stand out: politics, state court decisions, and the requirements of the federal government.

Politics and State Constitutions

One explanation for the many policies in state constitutions is straightforward—simple politics. If a group is able to get its position on an issue included in a state's constitution, its opponents will have a more difficult time trying to repeal or change the policy. This is really a matter of exercising power through the "rules of the game." Georgia's constitution is riddled with such provisions.

Earmarking Like many state constitutions, Georgia's "earmarks" certain funds (identifies revenue sources that must be spent for designated purposes). The most significant are motor fuel taxes, which Article 3 requires to be spent "for all activities incident to providing and maintaining an adequate system of public roads and bridges" and for grants to counties. Morever, this money goes for these purposes "regardless of whether the General Assembly enacts a general appropriations Act."[103] Thus, the Constitution provides those interested in highway construction with a guaranteed source of funds.

In other cases, the Constitution merely permits the earmarking of funds.[104] For instance, the General Assembly can use taxes on alcoholic beverages for programs related to alcohol and drug abuse. The legislature is also allowed to create a variety of trust funds for programs ranging from prevention of child abuse to promotion of certain crops. The 1992 amendment creating the state lottery requires that net proceeds (after expenses and prizes) go to "educational programs and purposes," with the governor's annual budget including recommendations for using these funds.[105] An amendment approved by voters in November 1998 further restricted the use of lottery funds.

Tax Breaks The Constitution provides special tax treatment to various groups and activities over and above what the General Assembly enacts through tax laws. An example is the taxation of timber, one of Georgia's major industries. An amendment approved by voters in 1990 requires that timber be taxed at fair market value only at the time of its harvest or sale.[106] Previously, it was taxed annually at market value. This change produced a major drop in property taxes for some counties and school districts.

The Constitution also requires that certain agricultural land be assessed at 75 percent of its value[107] and exempts part of the value of a disabled veteran's home from property taxes.[108] Other sections of the Constitution authorize rather than require the General Assembly to provide certain types of tax preferences, as with a 1988 amendment that applies to property on a historic register and a 1992 amendment that permits special treatment for heavy motor vehicles owned by nonresidents.[109]

"Morality" Issues   Various groups often attempt to use state constitutions to establish their position on controversial practices. This happened with the U.S. Constitution when the 18th Amendment was added in 1919 to ban the sale of alcohol. It was repealed, however, by the 21st Amendment in 1933. Similar provisions exist in the Georgia Constitution. The 1983 Constitution retained the prohibition against whipping as a punishment for a crime. While some of those drafting the new document saw this as outdated, it was retained out of fear that the General Assembly might pass bills permitting whipping in schools or prisons.[110] As noted above, a 1994 amendment permits local governments to prohibit alcohol sales at clubs with nude dancing.[111]

The 1983 Constitution, like all of its predecessors since 1868, prohibited lotteries. Interestingly, this prohibition was in Article 1, which covers the "Origin and Structure of Government" and the bill of rights. After being elected governor in 1990, Zell Miller convinced the General Assembly to submit a proposed amendment to voters to create state-run lotteries whose proceeds must be spent on education. That amendment was ratified by a narrow majority in November 1992 following a campaign that included major spending by its supporters.

Limits on Policy Making   Constitutions affect policies by deciding who makes decisions, limiting the discretion of government agencies, and allowing certain interests to be represented in the policy process. For example, Article 4 created six state boards and commissions, and Article 8 creates two more for education. As noted earlier, the Constitution establishes important political ties between the State Transportation Board and the General Assembly, thereby reducing the power of the executive branch over highways. An example of constitutional limits on the discretion of government agencies is the requirement that veterans be given a preference in state civil service employment.[112] Perhaps the most visible way the Georgia Constitution represents certain interests is through residency requirements, as with membership from each congressional district on certain boards and commissions and the requirement that at least one member of the Board of Natural Resources be from one of six coastal counties.[113]

State Court Decisions and Constitutions

A second reason for including policies in a constitution is to respond to a state court decision. For example, the Georgia Supreme Court might hold that a state law or an action by a local government violates the Georgia Constitution. Almost the only way to undo the court's action is to amend the state constitution, as with the above example regarding nude dancing. In addition, several decisions by the Georgia Supreme Court during the 1980s created confusion about sovereign immunity (the ability of citizens to sue the state or its local governments). As a result, an amendment was ratified in 1990 that attempted to clarify the matter.[114] Similarly, the 1983 Constitution added language to clarify a somewhat confusing series of cases regarding the authority of the state, cities, and counties regarding planning and zoning.[115]

The Federal Government and State Constitutions

A third way in which policies enter state constitutions is in order to satisfy some requirement of the federal government. For example, the constitution was amended in 1988 and 1992 to create a trust fund to provide medical services for the poor through the federal Medicaid program. Without the trust fund, money unspent at the end of the budgetary year would have to go to the state's general fund and could be used for any purpose, as specified elsewhere in the Constitution.[116] With the trust fund, the unspent money can be carried over to the next year to pay for medical care. Another example can be found in Article 3, which reflects federal court decisions about how legislative districts must be drawn.

VII. The Continuing Significance of Georgia's Constitution

A constitution is not some kind of sacred or unchanging blueprint for government. Constitutions are essentially political documents. That is why individuals, businesses, and interest groups often fight vigorously about interpreting and amending constitutions. For instance, lawsuits have attacked as racially biased the methods of selecting Georgia's judges and juries.[117] By approving an amendment to create a state-sponsored lottery in 1992, voters gave the governor, legislature, and bureaucracy millions of dollars to distribute to programs and individuals. They also paved the way for firms to profit from the production, sale, and marketing of lottery tickets. Another amendment granted a property tax break for growing timber,[118] although voters rejected a similar proposal for blueberries in 1994. The 1992 amendment requiring that local school board members be elected and superintendents be hired allows boards to recruit superintendents from anywhere. Under the old system of elected superintendents in some counties, only local residents could run for the office.[119]

As the preceding examples demonstrate, constitutions help distribute political and economic power. Constitutions also adopt policies that under other circumstances might be made simply by passing a law. Given the extensive detail in Georgia's Constitution, voters undoubtedly will face proposed amendments every even-numbered year as various interests try to modify the document to achieve their ends. If such attempts to enshrine policy in the Constitution continue, two outcomes seem possible. If proposed changes are ratified by voters, the Constitution might become so littered with amendments that it is unwieldy and difficult to interpret. The other possibility is that Georgians will become so annoyed with proposals on the ballot that they rebel by voting "no" on amendments. Neither scenario bodes well, however, for the durability or respectability of Georgia's 1983 Constitution.

Notes

Our thanks to Delmer Dunn, Thomas P. Lauth, Brad Lockerbie, and John A. Maltese for their advice on both the contents of this monograph and its use in the classroom.

1. U.S. Bureau of the Census, *Statistical Abstract of the United States: 2000* (Washington: Government Printing Office, 2000); http://www.census.gov/pub/govs/estimate/97sl00us.html.

2. *Constitution of the State of Georgia*, art. 1, sect. 2, para. 5.

3. 5 U.S. 137.

4. Congress passed a law in 1996 giving the president limited line-item veto authority. In June 1998, however, the U.S. Supreme Court ruled that this action was unconstitutional after President Clinton used it with 11 laws. See *Clinton v. City of New York*, no. 97–1374 (1998).

5. This section draws heavily from Melvin B. Hill, Jr., *The Georgia State Constitution: A Reference Guide* (Westport, Conn.: Greenwood Press, 1994).

6. On the changing location of the state capital, see Kenneth Coleman, editor, *A History of Georgia* 2d. ed. (Athens: University of Georgia Press, 1991), pp. 91, 96, 107, 208–9.

7. V.O. Key, Jr., *Southern Politics* (New York: Vintage, 1949), pp. 119–22; Hill, *The Georgia State Constitution*, pp. 224–25.

8. For a thorough account, see Harold P. Henderson, *The Politics of Change in Georgia: A Political Biography of Ellis Arnall* (Athens: University of Georgia Press, 1991), pp. 77–96.

9. Bill Montgomery, "New Constitution in Hands of Voters," *Atlanta Constitution*, November 2, 1982, p. 9A.

10. "A Constitutional Mess," *Atlanta Constitution*, August 28, 1981, p. 4A.

11. Bill Shipp, "Do the State a Favor: Forget the New Constitution," *Atlanta Constitution*, August 15, 1981, p. 2B. On the shifting power of governors and the General Assembly, see Harold P. Henderson and Gary L. Roberts, eds., *Georgia Governors in an Age of Change* (Athens: University of Georgia Press, 1988), pp. 199–207, 234–37, 267–69.

12. "Streamlined State Constitution," *Atlanta Constitution*, June 30, 1983, p. 22A; "New State Constitution Deserves Ratification" (editorial), *Atlanta Constitution*, October 24, 1982, p. 2C.

13. On procedures for amending state constitutions, see Council of State Governments, *The Book of the States: 2000–01 Edition* [hereafter cited as *The Book of the States*] (Lexington, Ky.: Council of State Governments, 2000), pp. 11–12.

14. For more information on these proposed amendments and elections more generally, see the Georgia Secretary of State's web site (www.sos.state.ga.us/elections).

15. Hill, *The Georgia State Constitution*, p. 70.

16. *Constitution of the State of Georgia*, art. 3. For comparisons to other states, see *The Book of the States*, chap. 3.

17. *The Book of the States*, p. 68.

18. See Edwin L. Jackson and Mary E. Stakes, *Handbook for Georgia Legislators* 10th ed. (Athens: Carl Vinson Institute of Government, University of Georgia, 1988), pp. 1–10.

19. *Constitution of the State of Georgia*, art. 5, sect. 2, para. 7.

20. *Constitution of the State of Georgia*, art. 3, sect. 3. Although the president pro tempore can become president of the Senate, the lieutenant governorship is left unfilled until the next general election should the position become vacant (see art. 5, sect. 1, para. 5). On other states, see *The Book of the States*, pp. 75–80.

21. *Constitution of the State of Georgia*, art. 3, sect. 5, para. 8.

22. *Constitution of the State of Georgia*, art. 3, sect. 9.

23. The line-item veto is not covered in the section dealing with appropriations, but in *Constitution of the State of Georgia*, art. 3, sect. 5, para. 13, which covers the place of the veto in the enactment of laws.

24. Table 4 excludes all judicial positions and some executive branch officials. Lieutenant governors are included despite their status as presiding officers in 27 legislatures because of their right to succeed governors and their executive responsibilities in several states.

25. *The Book of the States*, pp. 31–38.

26. Thad Beyle, "The Governors," in *Politics in the American States: A Comparative Analysis* 7th ed., edited by Virginia Gray, Russell L. Hanson, and Herbert Jacob (Washington: CQ Press, 1999), pp. 191–231.

27. See *Constitution of the State of Georgia*, art. 5, sect. 1; *The Book of the States*, pp. 15–16. For a brief history of the Georgia governor's office, see Edwin L. Jackson and Mary E. Stakes, *Handbook of Georgia State Agencies* 2d ed. (Athens: Carl Vinson Institute of Government, University of Georgia, 1988), pp. 38–39.

28. *Constitution of the State of Georgia*, art. 5, sect. 2, paras. 8 and 9; art. 6, sect. 7.

29. *Official Code of Georgia Annotated* [OCGA], title 45, chap. 5.

30. *The Book of the States*, pp. 98–100. Four states require larger majorities to override taxing, spending, or emergency measures.

31. *Constitution of the State of Georgia*, art. 3, sect. 5.

32. *Constitution of the State of Georgia*, art. 5, sect. 4, para. 1.

33. *Constitution of the State of Georgia*, art. 5, sect. 3.

34. OCGA, title 45, chapter 15; Jackson and Stakes, *Handbook of Georgia State Agencies*, pp. 63–69.

35. Rhonda Cook, "Oink If You Know the Secret Menu for Legislature's Wild Hog Supper," *Atlanta Journal and Constitution*, January 10, 1993, pp. A1, A12; and "Legislators Being Feted in Daytona," *Atlanta Journal and Constitution*, February 13, 1993, pp. A1, A6.

36. *Constitution of the State of Georgia*, art. 5, sect. 3.

37. *Constitution of the State of Georgia*, art. 5, sect. 4.

38. Governor's Office of Planning and Budget (www.opb.state.ga.us/FY01–BIB-Online.pdf); Georgia Department of Transportation (www.dot.state.ga.us/homeoffs/planning.www/question.htm).

39. *Constitution of the State of Georgia*, art. 6, sect. 7.

40. Georgia Supreme Court Commission on Racial and Ethnic Bias in the Court System, *Let Justice Be Done: Equally, Fairly, and Impartially* (final report, August 1995), p. 56.

41. Judicial Council of Georgia and Administrative Office of the Courts, *1998 Annual Report on the Work of the Georgia Courts* (available http://georgiacourts.org/aoc).

42. *Constitution of the State of Georgia*, art. 6, sects. 1–4.

43. *Constitution of the State of Georgia*, art. 1, sect. 1, para. 11(b).

44. *Constitution of the State of Georgia*, art. 6, sects. 5 and 7; *1998 Annual Report on the Work of the Georgia Courts*, p. 16.

45. *Constitution of the State of Georgia*, art. 6, sects. 6 and 7.

46. On differences in states' methods of selecting judges, see Henry R. Glick, "Courts: Politics and the Judicial Process," in *Politics in the American States: A Comparative Analysis* 7th ed., edited by Virginia Gray, Russell L. Hanson, and Herbert Jacob (Washington: CQ Press, 1999), pp. 241–246. On judicial selection in Georgia, see *1998 Annual Report on the Work of the Georgia Courts*, pp. 14–39; *Constitution of the State of Georgia*, art. 6, sect. 7.

47. *Constitution of the State of Georgia*, art. 6, sect. 8.

48. On jury selection in Georgia, see OCGA, title 15, chap. 12, art. 5; on juries generally, see Henry R. Glick, *Courts, Politics, and Justice* 3d ed (New York: McGraw-Hill, 1993), pp. 222–23.

49. For more detail, see Arnold Fleischmann and Carol Pierannunzi, *Politics in Georgia* (Athens: University of Georgia Press, 1997), chap. 9.

50. *Constitution of the State of Georgia*, art. 9, sects. 1 and 2; Hill, *The Georgia State Constitution*, pp. 184–200.

51. Steve Visser, "A Taxing Decision," *Atlanta Constitution*, June 14, 1999, p. E7.

52. David Goldberg and Kathey Pruitt, "GRTA Occupies Hot Seat," *Atlanta Constitution*, June 4, 1999, pp. A1, A8; Lucy Soto, "Public Still Skeptical About Transportation Board," *Atlanta Constitution*, June 7, 1999, pp. E1, E4.

53. Charles Seabrook, "Water Planning District" *Atlanta Constitution*, March 26, 2001, pp. E1, E6.

54. U.S. Advisory Commission on Intergovernmental Relations, *State Laws Governing Local Government Structure and Administration* report M-186 (Washington: Government Printing Office, 1993), pp. 7–9, 17–22.

55. On local acts in Georgia, see Fleischmann and Pierannunzi, *Politics in Georgia*, pp. 157–59, 233–38.

56. Taxation, debt limits, and revenue bonds are covered in *Constitution of the State of Georgia*, art. 9, sects. 4–6. Also see OCGA, title 36: chap. 5 on the property tax, chap. 7 on the income tax, and chap. 8 on the sales tax; Georgia Department of Community Affairs, *1994 Local Government Operations Survey: County Government Information Catalog* (December 1994).

57. OCGA, title 36, chap. 81, sect. 3(b).

58. For the amendment, see *Constitution of the State of Georgia*, art. 8, para. 4; also see James Salzer, "Georgia Voters Throw Weight Behind Desire for Better Schools with Sales Tax Approvals," *Athens Daily News and Banner-Herald*, October 19, 1997, p. 6A.

59. In addition to Georgia, runoffs are held in Alabama, Florida, Mississippi, North Carolina, Oklahoma, South Carolina, and Texas. Virginia repealed the runoff requirement in 1969, and Louisiana abandoned the runoff in favor of a nonpartisan primary in 1975. Arkansas, Kentucky, Maryland, and Utah have also used the runoff in the past. Arizona adopted a runoff for statewide general elections in 1988. See Key, *Southern Politics*, pp. 416–23; Charles S. Bullock III and Loch K. Johnson, *Runoff Elections in the United States* (Chapel Hill: University of North Carolina Press, 1992).

60. On recent changes in the requirements for winning elections, see OCGA, title 21, chap. 2, sect. 501; *Georgia Laws 1997*, no. 256, sect. 38 (pp. 645–47); *Georgia Laws 1998*, no. 826 (p. 825).

61. Kathey Pruitt, "Majority Vote Still Needed in Primaries," *Atlanta Constitution*, May 25, 1999, p. B3.

62. OCGA, title 21, chap. 4.

63. *Constitution of the State of Georgia*, art. 3, sect. 7.

64. *Constitution of the State of Georgia*, art. 2, sect. 3.

65. *Constitution of the State of Georgia*, art. 3, sect. 2, para. 5; art. 5, sect. 1, paras. 2 and 3; art. 5, sect. 3, para. 1.

66. *Constitution of the State of Georgia*, art. 6, sect. 7, para. 1; art. 8, sect. 5, para. 2; art. 9, sect. 1, para. 3.

67. 296 U.S. 186 (1962).

68. It does not seem necessary to include detailed citations to Georgia court cases in a general work such as this. Therefore, each section will include a citation to the appropriate location in Hill's definitive work on Georgia's Constitution, plus updates from the volume on the Constitution included in the *Official Code of Georgia Annotated*. These cases are discussed in more detail, with full citations in the endnotes, in Fleischmann and Pierannunzi, *Politics in Georgia*, pp. 62–67.

69. *Constitution of the State of Georgia*, art. 1, sect. 2, para. 5.

70. *Constitution of the State of Georgia*, art. 1, sect. 1, para. 2; Hill, *The Georgia State Constitution*, pp. 33–36.

71. *American Subcontractors Association v. City of Atlanta*, 259 Ga. 14, 376 S.E.2d 662 (1989).

72. Doug Cumming, "Applicants Nervously Await Decisions," *Atlanta Constitution*, March 25, 1998, p. C5.

73. Douglas A. Blackmon and Holly Morris, "Court Gives Split Ruling on Gay Rights," *Atlanta Constitution*, March 15, 1995, p. E1.

74. On the right to vote, see Laughlin McDonald, Michael B. Binford, and Ken Johnson, "Georgia," in *Quiet Revolution in the South: The Impact of the Vot-*

ing Rights Act, 1965–1990, edited by Chandler Davidson and Bernard Grofman (Princeton: Princeton University Press, 1994), pp. 67–102.

75. For a thorough discussion, see Clarence N. Stone, *Regime Politics: Governing Atlanta, 1946–1988* (Lawrence: University Press of Kansas, 1989).

76. William F. Holmes, "Part Five: 1890–1940," in *A History of Georgia* 2d ed., edited by Kenneth Coleman (Athens: University of Georgia Press, 1991), p. 280.

77. For a good synopsis of postwar racial change, see Numan V. Bartley, "Part Six: 1940 to the Present," in *A History of Georgia* 2d ed., edited by Kenneth Coleman (Athens: University of Georgia Press, 1991), pp. 361–74.

78. *Stell v. Savannah-Chatham County Board of Education,* 333 F.2d 55 (1964).

79. *Wesberry v. Sanders,* 376 U.S. 1 (1964).

80. See Hill, *The Georgia State Constitution,* p. 225.

81. Linda Greenhouse, "Justices, in 5–4 Vote, Reject Districts Drawn with Race the 'Predominant Factor'," *New York Times,* June 30, 1995, pp. A1, A13.

82. *Constitution of the State of Georgia,* art. 1, sect. 1, para. 1; Hill, *The Georgia State Constitution,* pp. 30–33.

83. *Suber v. Bulloch County Board of Education,* 722 F.Supp. 736 (S.D. Ga., 1989).

84. *Stephens v. State,* 265 Ga. 356, 456 S.E.2d 560, cert. denied 516 U.S. 849 (1995).

85. *Constitution of the State of Georgia,* art. 1, sect. 1, paras. 3 and 4; Hill, *The Georgia State Constitution,* pp. 36–38.

86. *Constitution of the State of Georgia,* art. 1, sect. 1, para. 4.

87. *Constitution of the State of Georgia,* art. 1, sect. 1, para. 5; Hill, *The Georgia State Constitution,* pp. 38–40.

88. *Vaughn v. State,* 259 Ga. 325 , 381 S.E.2d 30 (1989).

89. See OCGA, title 24, chap. 9, sect. 30.

90. *Goldrush II v. City of Marietta,* 267 Ga. 683, 482 S.E.2d 347 (1997).

91. *Constitution of the State of Georgia,* art. 1 sect. 1, paras. 11–24; Hill, *The Georgia State Constitution,* pp. 42–51.

92. *Constitution of the State of Georgia,* art. 1, sect. 1, para. 21.

93. *Constitution of the State of Georgia,* art. 1, sect. 1, para. 23.

94. *Constitution of the State of Georgia,* art. 1, sect. 1, para. 17.

95. *Bergman v. McCullough,* 218 Ga. App. 353, 461 S.E.2d 544 (1995), cert. denied 517 U.S. 1141 (1996).

96. *Fleming v. Zant,* 259 Ga. 687, 386 S.E.2d 339 (1989).

97. *Crutchfield v. State,* 218 Ga. App. 360, 461 S.E.2d 555 (1995).

98. *Constitution of the State of Georgia,* art. 1, sect.1, para. 1(b).

99. *Pavesich v. New England Life Insurance Co.,* 122 Ga. 190, 50 S.E. 68 (1904).

100. *Christensen v. State,* 266 Ga. 474, 464 S.E.2d 188 (1996).

101. *Powell v. State,* no. S98A0755 (November 23, 1998). A summary is available through the Georgia Supreme Court's web site (www.doas.state.ga.us/courts/supreme/op981123.htm).

102. For the U.S. Supreme Court's view of assisted suicide and the right to privacy, see *Washington v. Glucksberg,* 521 U.S. 702 (1997), and *Vacco v. Quill,* 521 U.S. 793 (1997).

103. *Constitution of the State of Georgia,* art. 3, sect. 9, para. 6(b).

104. *Constitution of the State of Georgia,* art. 3, sect. 9, para. 6(c-j).

105. *Constitution of the State of Georgia,* art. 1, sect. 2, para. 8(c).

106. *Constitution of the State of Georgia,* art. 7, sect. 2, para. 3(e).

107. *Constitution of the State of Georgia,* art. 7, sect. 1, para. 3(c).

108. *Constitution of the State of Georgia,* art. 7, sect. 2, para. 5.

109. *Constitution of the State of Georgia,* art. 7, sect. 1, para. 3(d). Also see Hill, *The Georgia State Constitution,* pp. 152–55.

110. Hill, *The Georgia State Constitution,* p. 49.

111. *Constitution of the State of Georgia,* art. 3, sect. 6, para. 7.

112. *Constitution of the State of Georgia,* art. 4, sect. 3, para. 2.

113. *Constitution of the State of Georgia,* art. 4; art. 8, sects. 2 and 4.

114. Hill, *The Georgia State Constitution,* pp. 56–59.

115. Hill, *The Georgia State Constitution,* pp. 194–95; *Constitution of the State of Georgia,* art. 9, sect. 2, para. 4.

116. Hill, *The Georgia State Constitution,* p. 99.

117. See Mark Curriden, "Is Naming Judges Serving Justice?" *Atlanta Journal and Constitution,* November 29, 1992, pp. G1, G3; Andrew Kull, "The Slow Death of Colorblind Justice," *Atlanta Journal and Constitution,* November 29, 1992, pp. H1, H5; Mark Curriden, "Road to a Judicial Appointment Not Clear—Even to State's Judges," *Atlanta Constitution,* December 21, 1992, p. C3.

118. *Constitution of the State of Georgia,* art. 7, sect. 1, para. 3(e).

119. *Constitution of the State of Georgia,* art. 8, sect. 5, paras. 2 and 3.

Appendices

DECLARATION OF INDEPENDENCE IN CONGRESS, JULY 4, 1776

The unanimous declaration of the thirteen
United States of America

When, in the course of human events, it becomes necessary for one people to dissolve the political bands which have connected them with another, and to assume, among the powers of the earth, the separate and equal station to which the laws of nature and of nature's God entitle them, a decent respect to the opinions of mankind requires that they should declare the causes which impel them to the separation.

We hold these truths to be self-evident: That all men are created equal; that they are endowed by their Creator with certain unalienable rights; that among these are life, liberty, and the pursuit of happiness; that, to secure these rights, governments are instituted among men, deriving their just powers from the consent of the governed; that whenever any form of government becomes destructive of these ends, it is the right of the people to alter or to abolish it, and to institute new government, laying its foundation on such principles, and organizing its power in such form, as to them shall seem most likely to effect their safety and happiness. Prudence, indeed, will dictate that governments long established should not be changed for light and transient causes; and accordingly all experience hath shown that mankind are more disposed to suffer, while evils are sufferable, than to right themselves by abolishing the forms to which they are accustomed. But when a long train of abuses and usurpations, pursuing invariably the same object, evinces a design to reduce them under absolute despotism, it is their right, it is their duty, to throw off such government, and to provide new guards for their future security. Such has been the patient sufferance of these colonies; and such is now the necessity which constrains them to alter their former systems of government. The history of the present King of Great Britain is a history of repeated injuries and usurpations, all having in direct object the establishment of an absolute tyranny over these states. To prove this, let facts be submitted to a candid world.

He has refused his assent to laws, the most wholesome and necessary for the public good.

He has forbidden his governors to pass laws of immediate and pressing importance, unless suspended in their operation till his assent should be obtained; and, when so suspended, he has utterly neglected to attend to them.

He has refused to pass other laws for the accommodation of large districts of people, unless those people would relinquish the right of representation in the legislature, a right inestimable to them, and formidable to tyrants only.

He has called together legislative bodies at places unusual, uncomfortable, and distant from the depository of their public records, for the sole purpose of fatiguing them into compliance with his measures.

He has dissolved representative houses repeatedly, for opposing, with manly firmness, his invasions on the rights of the people.

He has refused for a long time, after such dissolutions, to cause others to be elected; whereby the legislative powers, incapable of annihilation, have returned to the people at large for their exercise; the state remaining, in the mean time, exposed to all the dangers of invasions from without and convulsions within.

He has endeavored to prevent the population of these states; for that purpose obstructing the laws for naturalization of foreigners; refusing to pass others to encourage their migration hither, and raising the conditions of new appropriations of lands.

He has obstructed the administration of justice, by refusing his assent to laws for establishing judiciary powers.

He has made judges dependent on his will alone, for the tenure of their offices, and the amount and payment of their salaries.

He has erected a multitude of new offices, and sent hither swarms of officers to harass our people, and eat out their substance.

He has kept among us, in times of peace, standing armies, without the consent of our legislatures.

He has affected to render the military independent of, and superior to, the civil power.

He has combined with others to subject us to a jurisdiction foreign to our constitution, and unacknowledged by our laws, giving his assent to their acts of pretended legislation:

For quartering large bodies of armed troops among us;

For protecting them, by a mock trial, from punishment for any murders which they should commit on the inhabitants of these states;

For cutting off our trade with all parts of the world;

For imposing taxes on us without our consent;

For depriving us, in many cases, of the benefits of trial by jury;

For transporting us beyond seas, to be tried for pretended offenses;

For abolishing the free system of English laws in a neighboring province, establishing therein an arbitrary government, and enlarging its boundaries, so as to render it at once an example and fit instrument for introducing the same absolute rule into these colonies;

For taking away our charters, abolishing our most valuable laws, and altering fundamentally the forms of our governments;

For suspending our own legislatures, and declaring themselves invested with power to legislate for us in all cases whatsoever.

He has abdicated government here, by declaring us out of his protection and waging war against us.

He has plundered our seas, ravaged our coasts, burned our towns, and destroyed the lives of our people.

He is at this time transporting large armies of foreign mercenaries to complete the works of death, desolation, and tyranny already begun with circumstances of cruelty and perfidy scarcely paralleled in the most barbarous ages, and totally unworthy the head of a civilized nation.

He has constrained our fellow-citizens, taken captive on the high seas, to bear arms against their country, to become the executioners of their friends and brethren, or to fall themselves by their hands.

He has excited domestic insurrection among us, and has endeavored to bring on the inhabitants of our frontiers the merciless Indian savages, whose known rule of warfare is an undistinguished destruction of all ages, sexes, and conditions.

In every stage of these oppressions we have petitioned for redress in the most humble terms; our repeated petitions have been answered only by repeated injury. A prince, whose character is thus marked by every act which may define a tyrant, is unfit to be the ruler of a free people.

Nor have we been wanting in our attentions to our British brethren. We have warned them, from time to time, of attempts by their legislature to extend an unwarrantable jurisdiction over us. We have reminded them of the circumstances of our emigration and settlement here. We have appealed to their native justice and magnanimity; and we have conjured them, by the ties of our common kindred, to disavow these usurpations, which would inevitably interrupt our connections and correspondence. They, too, have been deaf to the voice of justice and of consanguinity. We must, therefore, acquiesce in the necessity which denounces our separation, and hold them, as we hold the rest of mankind, enemies in war, in peace friends.

We, therefore, the representatives of the United States of America, in General Congress assembled, appealing to the Supreme Judge of the world for the rectitude of our intentions, do, in the name, and by the authority of the good people of these colonies, solemnly publish and declare, that these United Colonies are, and of right ought to be, FREE AND INDEPENDENT STATES; that they are absolved from all allegiance to the British crown, and that all political connection between them and the state of Great Britain is, and ought to be, totally dissolved; and that, as free and independent states, they have full power to levy war, conclude peace, contract alliances, establish commerce, and do all other acts and things which independent states may of right do. And for the support of this declaration, with a firm reliance on the protection of Divine Providence, we mutually pledge to each other our lives, our fortunes, and our sacred honor.

JOHN HANCOCK
and fifty-five others

CONSTITUTION OF THE UNITED STATES OF AMERICA*

Preamble

We the people of the United States, in Order to form a more perfect Union, establish Justice, insure domestic Tranquility, provide for the common defense, promote the general Welfare, and secure the Blessings of Liberty to ourselves and our Posterity, do ordain and establish this Constitution for the United States of America.

Article I

Section 1 All legislative Powers herein granted shall be vested in a Congress of the United States, which shall consist of a Senate and a House of Representatives.

Section 2 The House of Representatives shall be composed of Members chosen every second Year by the people of the several States, and the Electors in each State shall have the Qualifications requisite for Electors of the most numerous Branch of the State Legislature.

No Person shall be a Representative who shall not have attained to the Age of twenty-five years, and been seven Years a Citizen of the United States, and who shall not, when elected, be an Inhabitant of that State in which he shall be chosen.

Representatives and direct Taxes shall be apportioned among the several States which may be included within this Union, according to their respective Numbers, *which shall be determined by adding to the whole Number of free persons, including those bound to Service for a Term of Years and excluding Indians not taxed, three-fifths of all other Persons.* The actual Enumeration shall be made within three Years after the first Meeting of the Congress of the United States, and within every subsequent Term of ten Years, in such Manner as they shall by Law direct. The Number of Representatives shall not exceed one for every thirty Thousand, but each State shall have at Least one Representative; *and until such enumeration shall be made, the State of New Hampshire shall be entitled to choose three, Massachusetts eight, Rhode-Island and Providence Plantations one, Connecticut five, New-York six, New Jersey four, Pennsylvania eight, Delaware one, Maryland six, Virginia ten, North Carolina five, South Carolina five, and Georgia three.*

When vacancies happen in the Representation from any State, the Executive Authority thereof shall issue Writs of Election to fill such Vacancies.

The House of Representatives shall choose their Speaker and other Officers; and shall have the sole Power of Impeachment.

Section 3 The Senate of the United States shall be composed of two Senators from each State, *chosen by the Legislature thereof,* for six Years; and each Senator shall have one Vote.

Immediately after they shall be assembled in Consequence of the first Election, they shall be divided as equally as may be into three Classes. The Seats of the Senators of the first Class

---

* Passages no longer in effect are printed in italic type.

shall be vacated at the Expiration of the second Year, of the second Class at the Expiration of the fourth Year, and of the third Class at the Expiration of the sixth Year, so that one-third may be chosen every second year; *and if Vacancies happen by Resignation or otherwise, during the Recess of the Legislature of any State, the Executive thereof may make temporary Appointments until the next meeting of the Legislature, which shall then fill such Vacancies.*

No Person shall be a Senator who shall not have attained to the Age of thirty Years, and been nine Years a Citizen of the United States, and who shall not, when elected, be an Inhabitant of that State for which he shall be chosen.

The Vice-President of the United States shall be President of the Senate, but shall have no Vote, unless they be equally divided.

The Senate shall choose their other Officers, and also a President *pro tempore,* in the absence of the Vice-President, or when he shall exercise the Office of President of the United States.

The Senate shall have the sole Power to try all Impeachments. When sitting for that purpose, they shall be on Oath or Affirmation. When the President of the United States is tried, the Chief Justice shall preside: And no person shall be convicted without the Concurrence of two-thirds of the Members present.

Judgment in Cases of Impeachment shall not extend further than to removal from Office, and disqualification to hold and enjoy any Office of honor, Trust, or profit under the United States: but the Party convicted shall nevertheless be liable and subject to Indictment, Trial, Judgment and punishment, according to Law.

Section 4   The Times, Places and Manner of holding Elections for Senators and Representatives, shall be prescribed in each state by the Legislature thereof; but the Congress may at any time by Law make or alter such Regulations, except as to the Places of choosing Senators.

The Congress shall assemble at least once in every Year, and such Meeting *shall be on the first Monday in December, unless they shall by Law appoint a different Day.*

Section 5   Each House shall be the Judge of the Elections, Returns and Qualifications of its own Members, and a Majority of each shall constitute a Quorum to do Business; but a smaller number may adjourn from day to day, and may be authorized to compel the Attendance of absent Members, in such Manner, and under such Penalties, as each House may provide.

Each House may determine the Rules of its Proceedings, punish its Members for disorderly Behaviour, and with the Concurrence of two-thirds, expel a Member.

Each House shall keep a Journal of its Proceedings, and from time to time publish the same, excepting such Parts as may in their Judgment require Secrecy; and the Yeas and Nays of the Members of either House on any question shall, at the Desire of one-fifth of those present, be entered on the journal.

Neither House, during the Session of Congress, shall, without the Consent of the other, adjourn for more than three days, nor to any other Place than that in which the two Houses shall be sitting.

Section 6   The Senators and Representatives shall receive a Compensation for their Services, to be ascertained by Law and paid out of the Treasury of the United States. They shall in all Cases except Treason, Felony and Breach of the Peace, be privileged from Arrest during their Attendance at the Session of their respective houses, and in going to and returning from the same; and for any Speech or Debate in either House, they shall not be questioned in any other place.

No Senator or Representative shall, during the Time for which he was elected, be appointed to any civil Office under the Authority of the United States, which shall have been created, or the Emoluments whereof shall have been increased, during such time; and no person holding any Office under the United States shall be a Member of either House during his continuance in Office.

Section 7   All Bills for raising Revenue shall originate in the House of Representatives; but the Senate may propose or concur with Amendments as on other bills.

Every Bill which shall have passed the House of Representatives and the Senate, shall, before it become a Law, be presented to the President of the United States; if he approve he shall sign it, but if not he shall return it with his Objections, to that House in which it originated, who shall enter the Objections at large on their Journal, and proceed to reconsider it. If after such reconsideration two-thirds of that House shall agree to pass the bill, it shall be sent, together with the objections, to the other House, by which it shall likewise be reconsidered, and, if approved by two-thirds of that House, it shall become a law. But in all such Cases the Votes of both Houses shall be determined by Yeas and Nays, and the Names of the Persons voting for and against the Bill shall be entered on the Journal of each House respectively. If any Bill shall not be returned by the President within ten Days (Sundays excepted) after it shall have been presented to him, the Same shall be a Law, in like Manner as if he had signed it, unless the Congress by their Adjournment prevent its Return, in which Case it shall not be a Law.

Every Order, Resolution, or Vote to which the Concurrence of the Senate and House of Representatives may be necessary (except on a question of Adjournment) shall be presented to the President of the United States; and before the Same shall take Effect, shall be approved by him, or being disapproved by him, shall be repassed by two-thirds of the Senate and House of Representatives, according to the Rules and Limitations prescribed in the Case of a Bill.

Section 8   The Congress shall have Power

To lay and collect Taxes, Duties, Imposts, and Excises, to pay the Debts and provide for the common Defence and general Welfare of the United States; but all Duties, Imposts and Excises shall be uniform throughout the United States;

To borrow money on the credit of the United States;

To regulate Commerce with foreign Nations, and among the several States, and with the Indian Tribes;

To establish an uniform Rule of Naturalization, and uniform Laws on the subject of Bankruptcies throughout the United States;

To coin Money, regulate the Value thereof, and of foreign Coin, and fix the Standard of Weights and Measures;

To provide for the Punishment of counterfeiting the Securities and current Coin of the United States;

To establish Post Offices and Post Roads;

To promote the Progress of Science and useful Arts by securing for limited times to Authors and Inventors the exclusive Right to their respective Writings and Discoveries;

To constitute Tribunals inferior to the Supreme Court;

To define and punish Piracies and Felonies committed on the high Seas and Offenses against the Law of Nations;

To declare War, grant Letters of Marque and Reprisal, and make rules concerning captures on land and water;

To raise and support Armies, but no Appropriation of Money to that Use shall be for a longer Term than two Years;

To provide and maintain a Navy;

To make rules for the Government and Regulation of the land and naval forces;

To provide for calling forth the Militia to execute the Laws of the Union, suppress Insurrections, and repel Invasions;

To provide for organizing, arming, and disciplining the Militia, and for governing such part of them as may be employed in the Service of the United States, reserving to the States respectively the Appointment of the Officers, and the Authority of training the Militia according to the discipline prescribed by Congress;

To exercise exclusive Legislation in all Cases whatsoever, over such District (not exceeding ten Miles square) as may, by Cession of particular States, and the acceptance of Congress, become the Seat of the Government of the United States, and to exercise like Authority over all places purchased by the Consent of the Legislature of the State, in which the same shall be, for Erection of Forts, Magazines, Arsenals, dock-Yards, and other needful Buildings;—And

To make all Laws which shall be necessary and proper for carrying into Execution the foregoing Powers, and all other powers vested by this Constitution in the Government of the United States, or in any Department or Officer thereof.

Section 9 *The Migration or Importation of such Persons as any of the States now existing shall think proper to admit shall not be prohibited by the Congress prior to the Year 1808; but a tax or duty may be imposed on such Importation, not exceeding ten dollars for each person.*

The privilege of the Writ of Habeas Corpus shall not be suspended, unless when in Cases of Rebellion or Invasion the public Safety may require it.

No Bill of Attainder or ex post facto Law shall be passed.

No capitation, or other direct, Tax shall be laid, unless in proportion to the Census or Enumeration herein before directed to be taken.

No Tax or Duty shall be laid on Articles exported from any State.

No Preference shall be given by any Regulation of Revenue to the ports of one State over those of another; nor shall Vessels bound to, or from, one State, be obliged to enter, clear, or pay Duties in another.

No Money shall be drawn from the Treasury, but in Consequence of Appropriations made by Law; and a regular Statement and Account of the Receipts and Expenditures of all public Money shall be published from time to time.

No Title of Nobility shall be granted by the United States: And no Person holding any Office or profit or Trust under them, shall, without the Consent of the Congress, accept of any present, Emolument, Office, or Title, of any kind whatever, from any King, Prince, or foreign state.

Section 10 No State shall enter into any Treaty, Alliance, or Confederation; grant Letters of Marque and Reprisal; coin Money; emit Bills of Credit; make any thing but gold and silver Coin a Tender in payment of Debts; pass any Bill of Attainder, ex post facto Law, or Law impairing the Obligation of Contracts, or grant any Title of Nobility.

No State shall, without the consent of Congress, lay any imposts or duties on imports or exports, except what may be absolutely necessary for executing its inspection laws: and the net produce of all duties and imposts, laid by any State on imports or exports, shall be for the use of the treasury of the United States; and all such laws shall be subject to the revision and control of the Congress.

No State shall, without the Consent of Congress, lay any duty of Tonnage, keep Troops or Ships of War in time of peace, enter into any Agreement or Compact with another State, or with a foreign power, or engage in War, unless actually invaded, or in such imminent Danger as will not admit of delay.

Article II

Section 1   The executive Power shall be vested in a President of the United States of America. He shall hold his Office during the Term of four years, and, together with the Vice-President, chosen for the same Term, be elected as follows:

Each State shall appoint, in such Manner as the Legislature thereof may direct, a Number of Electors, equal to the whole Number of Senators and Representatives to which the State may be entitled in the Congress; but no Senator or Representative, or person holding an Office of Trust or profit under the United States, shall be appointed an Elector.

The Electors shall meet in their respective States, and vote by Ballot for two persons, of whom one at least shall not be an Inhabitant of the same State with themselves. And they shall make a List of all the Persons voted for, and of the Number of Votes for each; which List they shall sign and certify, and transmit sealed to the Seat of Government of the United States, directed to the President of the Senate. The President of the Senate shall, in the presence of the Senate and House of Representatives, open all the Certificates, and the Votes shall then be counted. The person having the greatest Number of Votes shall be the President, if such Number be a Majority of the whole Number of Electors appointed; and if there be more than one who have such Majority, and have an equal number of Votes, then the House of Representatives shall immediately choose by Ballot one of them for President; and if no person have a Majority, then from the five highest on the List said House shall in like Manner choose the President. But in choosing the President the Votes shall be taken by States, the Representation from each State having one Vote; a quorum for this purpose shall consist of a Member or Members from two-thirds of the States, and a Majority of all the States shall be necessary to a Choice. In every Case, after the Choice of the President, the Person having the greatest Number of Votes of the Electors shall be the Vice-President. But if there should remain two or more who have equal votes, the Senate shall choose from them by Ballot the Vice-President.

The Congress may determine the Time of choosing the Electors and the Day on which they shall give their Votes; which Day shall be the same throughout the United States.

No person except a natural-born Citizen, *or a Citizen of the United States at the time of the Adoption of this Constitution,* shall be eligible to the Office of President; neither shall any Person be eligible to that Office who shall not have attained to the Age of thirty-five years, and been fourteen Years a Resident within the United States.

In Case of the Removal of the President from Office or of his Death, Resignation, or Inability to discharge the powers and Duties of the said Office, the same shall devolve on the Vice-President, and the Congress may by Law provide for the Case of Removal, Death, Resignation, or Inability, both of the President and Vice-President, declaring what Officer shall then act as President, and such

Officer shall act accordingly, until the disability be removed, or a President shall be elected.

The President shall, at stated Times, receive for his Services a Compensation, which shall neither be increased nor diminished during the period for which he shall have been elected, and he shall not receive within that Period any other Emolument from the United States, or any of them.

Before he enter on the execution of his Office, he shall take the following Oath or Affirmation:—"I do solemnly swear (or affirm) that I will faithfully execute the Office of the President of the United States, and will to the best of my Ability preserve, protect and defend the Constitution of the United States."

Section 2   The President shall be Commander in Chief of the Army and Navy of the United States, and of the Militia of the several States, when called into the actual Service of the United States; he may require the Opinion, in writing, of the principal Officer in each of the executive Departments, upon any subject relating to the Duties of their respective Offices, and he shall have Power to Grant Reprieves and Pardons for Offenses against the United States, except in Cases of Impeachment.

He shall have Power, by and with the Advice and Consent of the Senate, to make Treaties, provided two-thirds of the Senators present concur; and he shall nominate, and by and with the Advice and Consent of the Senate, shall appoint Ambassadors, other public Ministers and Consuls, Judges of the Supreme Court, and all other Officers of the United States, whose Appointments are not herein otherwise provided for, and which shall be established by Law: but Congress may by Law vest the Appointment of such inferior Officers, as they think proper, in the President alone, in the Courts of Law, or in the Heads of Departments.

The President shall have Power to fill up all Vacancies that may happen during the Recess of the Senate, by granting Commissions which shall expire at the End of their next Session.

Section 3   He shall from time to time give to the Congress Information of the State of the Union, and recommend to their Consideration such Measures as he shall judge necessary and expedient; he may, on extraordinary occasions, convene both Houses, or either of them, and in Case of Disagreement between them, with respect to the Time of Adjournment, he may adjourn them to such Time as he shall think proper; he shall receive Ambassadors and other public Ministers; he shall take Care that the Laws be faithfully executed, and shall Commission all the Officers of the United States.

Section 4   The President, Vice-President and all civil Officers of the United States shall be removed from Office on Impeachment for, and on Conviction of, Treason, Bribery, or other high Crimes and Misdemeanors.

Article III

Section 1   The judicial power of the United States shall be vested in one supreme Court, and in such inferior Courts as the Congress may from time to time ordain and establish. The Judges, both of the supreme and inferior Courts, shall hold their offices during good Behaviour, and shall, at stated Times, receive for their

Services a compensation which shall not be diminished during their Continuance in Office.

Section 2   The judicial Power shall extend to all Cases, in Law and Equity, arising under this Constitution, the Laws of the United States, and treaties made, or which shall be made, under their Authority;—to all cases affecting ambassadors, other public ministers and consuls;—to all cases of admiralty and maritime Jurisdiction;—to controversies to which the United States shall be a party;—to Controversies between two or more States;—*between a State and Citizens of another State;*—between Citizens of different States;—between Citizens of the same State claiming Lands under Grants of different States, and between a State, or the Citizens thereof, and foreign States, Citizens or Subjects.

In all Cases affecting Ambassadors, other public Ministers and Consuls, and those in which a State shall be Party, the supreme Court shall have original Jurisdiction. In all the other Cases before mentioned, the supreme Court shall have appellate Jurisdiction, both as to Law and Fact, with such Exceptions, and under such Regulations, as the Congress shall make.

The trial of all Crimes, except in Cases of Impeachment, shall be by Jury; and such Trial shall be held in the State where said Crimes shall have been committed; but when not committed within any State, the Trial shall be at such Place or Places as the Congress may by Law have directed.

Section 3   Treason against the United States shall consist only in levying War against them, or in adhering to their Enemies, giving them Aid and Comfort. No person shall be convicted of Treason unless on the Testimony of two Witnesses to the same overt Act, or on confession in open Court.

The Congress shall have power to declare the Punishment of Treason, but no Attainder of Treason shall work Corruption of Blood, or Forfeiture except during the Life of the Person attained.

Article IV

Section 1   Full Faith and Credit shall be given in each State to the public Acts, Records, and judicial Proceedings of every other State. And the Congress may by general Laws prescribe the Manner in which such Acts, Records, and Proceedings shall be proved, and the Effect thereof.

Section 2   The Citizens of each State shall be entitled to all Privileges and Immunities of Citizens in the several States.

A Person charged in any State with Treason, Felony, or other Crime, who shall flee from Justice, and be found in another State, shall on demand of the executive Authority of the State from which he fled, be delivered up, to be removed to the State having Jurisdiction of the crime.

No person held to Service or Labor in one State, under the Laws thereof, escaping into another, shall, in Consequence of any Law or Regulation therein, be discharged from such Service or Labor, but shall be delivered up on Claim of the party to whom such Service or Labor may be due.

Section 3 New States may be admitted by the Congress into this Union; but no new State shall be formed or erected within the Jurisdiction of any other State; nor any State be formed by the Junction of two or more States, or parts of States, without the Consent of the Legislatures of the States concerned as well as of the Congress.

The Congress shall have power to dispose of and make all needful Rules and regulations respecting the Territory or other property belonging to the United States; and nothing in this Constitution shall be so construed as to prejudice any Claims of the United States, or of any particular State.

Section 4 The United States shall guarantee to every State in this Union a Republican Form of Government, and shall protect each of them against Invasion; and on Application of the Legislature, or of the Executive (when the Legislature cannot be convened), against domestic Violence.

Article V

The Congress, whenever two-thirds of both Houses shall deem it necessary, shall propose Amendments to this Constitution, or, on the Application of the Legislatures of two-thirds of the several States, shall call a Convention for proposing Amendments, which, in either Case, shall be valid to all Intents and Purposes, as part of this Constitution, when ratified by the Legislatures of three-fourths of the several States, or by Conventions in three-fourths thereof, as the one or the other Mode of Ratification may be proposed by the Congress; provided *that no Amendment which may be made prior to the Year One thousand eight hundred and eight shall in any Manner affect the first and fourth Clauses in the Ninth Section of the first Article;* and that no State, without its Consent, shall be deprived of its equal suffrage in the Senate.

Article VI

All Debts contracted and Engagements entered into, before the Adoption of this Constitution, shall be as valid against the United States under this Constitution, as under the Confederation.

This Constitution, and the Laws of the United States which shall be made in Pursuance thereof; and all Treaties made, or which shall be made, under the Authority of the United States, shall be the supreme Law of the Land; and the Judges in every State shall be bound thereby, any thing in the Constitution or Laws of any State to the Contrary notwithstanding.

The Senators and Representatives before mentioned, and the Members of the several State Legislatures, and all executive and judicial Officers, both of the United States and of the several States, shall be bound by Oath or Affirmation to support this Constitution; but no religious Test shall ever be required as a qualification to any Office or public Trust under the United States.

Article VII

The Ratification of the Conventions of nine States shall be sufficient for the Establishment of this Constitution between the States so ratifying the same.

Done in Convention by the unanimous consent of the States present the Seventeenth day of September in the Year of our Lord one thousand seven hundred and Eighty-seven and of the Independence of the United States of America the Twelfth. In Witness whereof We have hereunto subscribed our Names.

GEORGE WASHINGTON
and thirty-seven others

Amendments to the Constitution*

Amendment I

Congress shall make no law respecting an establishment of religion, or prohibiting the free exercise thereof; or abridging the freedom of speech, or of the press; or the right of the people peaceably to assemble, and to petition the government for a redress of grievances.

Amendment II

A well-regulated militia being necessary to the security of a free State, the right of the people to keep and bear arms shall not be infringed.

Amendment III

No soldier shall, in time of peace, be quartered in any house without the consent of the owner, nor in time of war, but in a manner to be prescribed by law.

Amendment IV

The right of the people to be secure in their persons, houses, papers, and effects, against unreasonable searches and seizures, shall not be violated, and no warrants shall issue but upon probable cause, supported by oath or affirmation, and particularly describing the place to be searched, and the persons or things to be seized.

Amendment V

No person shall be held to answer for a capital, or otherwise infamous crime, unless on a presentment or indictment of a grand jury, except in cases arising in the land or naval forces, or in the militia, when in actual service in time of war or public danger; nor shall any person be subject for the same offense to be twice put in jeopardy of life or limb; nor shall be compelled in any criminal case to be a witness against himself, nor be deprived of life, liberty, or property, without due process of law; nor shall private property be taken for public use without just compensation.

---

*The first ten amendments (the Bill of Rights) were adopted in 1791.

Amendment VI

In all criminal prosecutions, the accused shall enjoy the right to a speedy and public trial, by an impartial jury of the State and district wherein the crime shall have been committed, which district shall have been previously ascertained by law, and to be informed of the nature and cause of the accusation; to be confronted with the witnesses against him; to have compulsory process for obtaining witnesses in his favor, and to have the assistance of counsel for his defense.

Amendment VII

In suits at common law, where the value in controversy shall exceed twenty dollars, the right of trial by jury shall be preserved, and no fact tried by a jury shall be otherwise reexamined in any court of the United States, than according to the rules of the common law.

Amendment VIII

Excessive bail shall not be required, nor excessive fines imposed, nor cruel and unusual punishments inflicted.

Amendment IX

The enumeration in the Constitution, of certain rights, shall not be construed to deny or disparage others retained by the people.

Amendment X

The powers not delegated to the United States by the Constitution, nor prohibited by it to the States, are reserved to the states respectively, or to the people.

Amendment XI [Adopted 1798]

The judicial power of the United States shall not be construed to extend to any suit in law or equity, commenced or prosecuted against one of the United States by citizens of another state, or by citizens or subjects of any foreign state.

Amendment XII [Adopted 1804]

The electors shall meet in their respective States, and vote by ballot for President and Vice-President, one of whom, at least, shall not be an inhabitant of the same State with themselves; they shall name in their ballots the person voted for as President, and in distinct ballots the person voted for as Vice-President, and they shall make distinct lists of all persons voted for as President, and of all persons voted for as Vice-President, and of the number of votes for each, which lists they shall sign and certify, and transmit sealed to the seat of government of the United States, directed to the President of the Senate;—the President of the Senate shall, in the presence of the Senate and House of representatives, open all the certificates and the votes shall then be counted;—the person having the greatest number of votes for President shall be the President, if such number be a majority of the whole number of electors appointed; and if no person have such majority, then from the persons having the highest numbers not exceeding three on the list of those voted for as President, the House of Representatives shall choose immediately, by ballot, the President. But in choosing the President, the votes shall be taken by States, the representation from each State having one vote; a quorum for this purpose shall consist of a member or members from two-thirds of the States, and a majority of all the States shall be necessary to a choice. And if the House of Representatives shall not choose a President whenever the right of choice shall devolve upon them, before *the fourth day of March* next following, then the Vice-President shall act as President, as in the case of the death or other constitutional disability of the President.

The person having the greatest number of votes as Vice-President shall be the Vice-President, if such number be a majority of the whole number of electors appointed; and if no person have a majority, then from the two highest numbers on the list the Senate shall choose the Vice-President; a quorum for the purpose shall consist of two-thirds of the whole number of Senators, and a majority of the whole number shall be necessary to a choice. But no person constitutionally ineligible to the office of President shall be eligible to that of Vice-President of the United States.

Amendment XIII [Adopted 1865]

Section 1 Neither slavery nor involuntary servitude, except as a punishment for crime whereof the party shall have been duly convicted, shall exist within the United States, or any place subject to their jurisdiction.

Section 2 Congress shall have power to enforce this article by appropriate legislation.

Amendment XIV [Adopted 1868]

Section 1 All persons born or naturalized in the United States, and subject to the jurisdiction thereof, are citizens of the United States and of the State wherein they reside. No State shall make or enforce any law which shall abridge the privileges or immunities of citizens of the United States; nor shall any State deprive any person of life, liberty, or property, without due process of law; nor deny to any person within its jurisdiction the equal protection of the laws.

Section 2 Representatives shall be apportioned among the several States according to their respective numbers, counting the whole number of persons in each State, excluding Indians not taxed. But when the right to vote at any election for the choice of Electors for President and Vice-President of the United States, Representatives in Congress, the executive and judicial officers of a State, or the members of the legislature thereof, is denied to any of the male inhabitants of such State, being twenty-one years of age and citizens of the United States, or in any way abridged, except for participation in rebellion, or other crime, the basis of representation therein shall be reduced in the proportion which the number of such male citizens shall bear to the whole number of male citizens twenty-one years of age in such State.

Section 3   No person shall be a Senator or Representative in Congress, or Elector of President and Vice-President, or hold any office, civil or military, under the United States, or under any State, who, having previously taken an oath, as a member of Congress, or as an officer of the United States, or as a member of any State legislature, or as an executive or judicial officer of any State, to support the Constitution of the United States, shall have engaged in insurrection or rebellion against the same, or given aid or comfort to the enemies thereof. Congress may, by a vote of two-thirds of each house, remove such disability.

Section 4   The validity of the public debt of the United States, authorized by law, including debts incurred for payment of pensions and bounties for services in suppressing insurrection or rebellion, shall not be questioned. But neither the United States nor any State shall assume or pay any debt or obligation incurred in aid of insurrection or rebellion against the United States, or any claim for the loss of emancipation of any slave; but all such debts, obligations, and claims shall be held illegal and void.

Section 5   The Congress shall have power to enforce, by appropriate legislation, the provisions of this article.

Amendment XV [Adopted 1870]

Section 1   The right of citizens of the United States to vote shall not be denied or abridged by the United States or by any State on account of race, color, or previous condition of servitude.

Section 2   The Congress shall have power to enforce this article by appropriate legislation.

Amendment XVI [Adopted 1913]

The Congress shall have power to lay and collect taxes on incomes, from whatever source derived, without apportionment among the several States, and without regard to any census or enumeration.

Amendment XVII [Adopted 1913]

Section 1   The Senate of the United States shall be composed of two Senators from each State, elected by the people thereof, for six years; and each Senator shall have one vote. The electors in each State shall have the qualifications requisite for electors of [voters for] the most numerous branch of the State legislatures.

Section 2   When vacancies happen in the representation of any State in the Senate, the executive authority of such State shall issue writs of election to fill such vacancies: *Provided,* that the Legislature of any State may empower the executive thereof to make temporary appointments until the people fill the vacancies by election as the Legislature may direct.

Section 3   This amendment shall not be so construed as to affect the election or term of any Senator chosen before it becomes valid as part of the Constitution.

Amendment XVIII [Adopted 1919, repealed 1933]

Section 1   After one year from the ratification of this article the manufacture, sale or transportation of intoxicating liquors within, the importation thereof into, or the exportation thereof from the United States and all territory subject to the jurisdiction thereof, for beverage purposes, is hereby prohibited.

Section 2   The Congress and the several States shall have concurrent power to enforce this article by appropriate legislation.

Section 3   This article shall be inoperative unless it shall have been ratified as an amendment to the Constitution by the legislatures of the several States, as provided by the Constitution, within seven years from the date of the submission thereof to the States by the Congress.

Amendment XIX [Adopted 1920]

Section 1   The right of citizens of the United States to vote shall not be denied or abridged by the United States or by any State on account of sex.

Section 2   The Congress shall have power to enforce this article by appropriate legislation.

Amendment XX [Adopted 1933]

Section 1   The terms of the President and Vice-President shall end at noon on the 20th day of January, and the terms of Senators and Representatives at noon on the 3d day of January, of the years in which such terms would have ended if this article had not been ratified; and the terms of their successors shall then begin.

Section 2   The Congress shall assemble at least once in every year, and such meetings shall begin at noon on the 3d day of January, unless they shall by law appoint a different day.

Section 3   If, at the time fixed for the beginning of the term of the President, the President-elect shall have died, the Vice-President-elect shall become President. If a President shall not have been chosen before the time fixed for the beginning of his term, or if the President-elect shall have failed to qualify, then the Vice-President-elect shall act as President until a President shall have qualified; and the Congress may by law provide for the case wherein neither a President-elect nor a

Vice-President-elect shall have qualified, declaring who shall then act as President, or the manner in which one who is to act shall be selected, and such persons shall act accordingly until a President or Vice-President shall have qualified.

Section 4 The Congress may by law provide for the case of the death of any of the persons from whom the House of Representatives may choose a President whenever the right of choice shall have devolved upon them, and for the case of the death of any of the persons from whom the Senate may choose a Vice-President whenever the right of choice shall have devolved upon them.

Section 5 Sections 1 and 2 shall take effect on the 15th day of October following the ratification of this article.

Section 6 This article shall be inoperative unless it shall have been ratified as an amendment to the Constitution by the Legislatures of three-fourths of the several States within seven years from the date of its submission.

Amendment XXI [Adopted 1933]

Section 1 The eighteenth article of amendment to the Constitution of the United States is hereby repealed.

Section 2 The transportation or importation into any State, Territory, or Possession of the United States for delivery or use therein of intoxicating liquors, in violation of the laws thereof, is hereby prohibited.

Section 3 This article shall be inoperative unless it shall have been ratified as an amendment to the Constitution by conventions in the several States, as provided in the Constitution, within seven years from the date of submission thereof to the States by the Congress.

Amendment XXII [Adopted 1951]

Section 1 No person shall be elected to the office of President more than twice, and no person who has held the office of President, or acted as President, for more than two years of a term to which some other person was elected President shall be elected to the office of President more than once. But this article shall not apply to any person holding the office of President when this article was proposed by the Congress, and shall not prevent any person who may be holding the office of President, or acting as President, during the term within which this article becomes operative from holding the office of President or acting as President during the remainder of such term.

Section 2 This article shall be inoperative unless it shall have been ratified as an amendment to the Constitution by the legislatures of three-fourths of the several States within seven years from the date of its submission to the States by the Congress.

Amendment XXIII [Adopted 1961]

Section 1   The District constituting the seat of Government of the United States shall appoint in such manner as the Congress may direct:

A number of electors of President and Vice-President equal to the whole number of Senators and Representatives in Congress to which the District would be entitled if it were a State, but in no event more than the least populous State; they shall be in addition to those appointed by the States, but they shall be considered for the purposes of the election of President and Vice-President, to be electors appointed by a State; and they shall meet in the District and perform such duties as provided by the twelfth article of amendment.

Section 2   The Congress shall have the power to enforce this article by appropriate legislation.

Amendment XXIV [Adopted 1964]

Section 1   The right of citizens of the United States to vote in any primary or other election for President or Vice-President, for electors for President or Vice-President, or for Senator or Representative in Congress, shall not be denied or abridged by the United States or any State by reason of failure to pay any poll tax or other tax.

Section 2   The Congress shall have the power to enforce this article by appropriate legislation.

Amendment XXV [Adopted 1967]

Section 1   In case of the removal of the President from office or of his death or resignation, the Vice-President shall become President.

Section 2   Whenever there is a vacancy in the office of the Vice-President, the President shall nominate a Vice-President who shall take office upon confirmation by a majority vote of both Houses of Congress.

Section 3   Whenever the President transmits to the President pro tempore of the Senate and the speaker of the House of Representatives his written declaration that he is unable to discharge the powers and duties of his office, and until he transmits to them a written declaration to the contrary, such powers and duties shall be discharged by the Vice-President as Acting President.

Section 4   Whenever the Vice-President and a majority of either the principal officers of the executive departments or of such other body as Congress may by law provide, transmit to the President pro tempore of the Senate and the Speaker of the House of Representatives their written declaration that the President is unable to discharge the powers and duties of his office, the Vice-President shall immediately assume the powers and duties of the office as Acting President.

Thereafter, when the President transmits to the President pro tempore of the Senate and the Speaker of the House of Representatives his written declaration that no inability exists, he shall resume the powers and duties of his office unless the Vice-President and a majority of either the principal officers of the executive department(s) or of such other body as Congress may by law provide, transmit within four days to the President pro tempore of the Senate and the Speaker of the House of Representatives their written declaration that the President is unable to discharge the powers and duties of his office. Thereupon Congress shall decide the issue, assembling within forty-eight hours for that purpose if not in session. If the Congress, within twenty-one days after receipt of the latter written declaration, or, if Congress is not in session, within twenty-one days after Congress is required to assemble, determines by two-thirds vote of both Houses that the President is unable to discharge the powers and duties of his office, the Vice-President shall continue to discharge the same as Acting President; otherwise, the President shall resume the powers and duties of his office.

Amendment XXVI [Adopted 1971]

Section 1   The right of citizens of the United States, who are eighteen years of age or older, to vote shall not be denied or abridged by the United States or by any State on account of age.

Section 2   The Congress shall have power to enforce this article by appropriate legislation.

Amendment XXVII [Adopted 1992]

No law, varying the compensation for the services of the senators and representatives shall take effect, until an election of representatives shall have intervened.

References

Chapter 1 / Dilemmas of Democracy
pp. 1–27

1. Associated Press, "Kevorkian Deaths Total 100," *New York Times,* 15 March 1998, p. 14.

2. Jack Lessenberry, "In Tactical Change, Kevorkian Promises to Halt Suicide Aid," *New York Times,* 26 December 1993, p. 1.

3. Dirk Johnson, "Kevorkian Sentenced to 10 to 25 Years in Prison," *New York Times,* 14 April 1999, p. 1.

4. Center for Political Studies of the Institute for Social Research, *American National Election Study 1996* (Ann Arbor: University of Michigan).

5. 1977 Constitution of the Union of Soviet Socialist Republics, Article 11, in *Constitutions of Countries of the World,* ed. A. P. Blaustein and G. H. Flanz (Dobbs Ferry, N.Y.: Oceana, 1971).

6. Karl Marx and Friedrich Engels, *Critique of the Gotha Programme* (New York: International Publishers, 1938), p. 10. Originally written in 1875 but published in 1891.

7. See the argument in Amy Gutman, *Liberal Equality* (Cambridge: Cambridge University Press, 1980), pp. 9–10.

8. See John H. Schaar, "Equality of Opportunity and Beyond," in *Equality,* NOMOS IX, ed. J. Roland Pennock and John W. Chapman (New York: Atherton Press, 1967), pp. 228–249.

9. Sam Vincent Meddis, "Crime's No Worse, but USA's Fear Grows," *USA Today* (International Edition), 28 October 1993, p. 1. See also Wesley G. Skogan, *Disorder and Decline: Crime and the Spiral of Decay in American Neighborhoods* (New York: Free Press, 1990), Chap. 2.

10. See generally Milton Friedman, *Capitalism and Freedom* (Chicago: University of Chicago Press, 1962).

11. Various interpretations of what *populist* really means could be seen in the spirited debate that occurred on H-POL (the Internet daily discussion group on American political history) in the spring and summer of 1995. For a discussion of definitions in print, see Michael Kazin, *The Populist Persuasion: An American History* (New York: Basic Books, 1995).

12. The communitarian movement was founded by a group of ethicists and social scientists who met in Washington, D.C., in 1990 at the invitation of sociologist Amitai Etzioni and political theorist William Galston to discuss the declining state of morality and values in the United States. Etzioni became the leading spokesperson for the movement. See his *Rights and the Common Good: The Communitarian Perspective* (New York: St. Martin's Press, 1995), pp. iii–iv. The communitarian political movement should be distinguished from communitarian thought in political philosophy, which is associated with theorists such as Alasdair MacIntyre, Michael Sandel, and Charles Taylor, who wrote in the late 1970s and early 1980s. In essence, communitarian theorists criticized liberalism, which stressed freedom and individualism, as excessively individualistic. Their fundamental critique was that liberalism slights the values of community life. See Allen E. Buchanan, "Assessing the Communitarian Critique of Liberalism," *Ethics,* 99 (July 1989),

pp. 852–882, and Patrick Neal and David Paris, "Liberalism and the Communitarian Critique: A Guide for the Perplexed," *Canadian Journal of Political Science,* 23 (September 1990), pp. 419–439. Communitarian philosophers attacked liberalism over the inviolability of civil liberties. In our framework, such issues involve the tradeoff between freedom and order. Communitarian and liberal theorists differ less concerning the tradeoff between freedom and equality. See William R. Lund, "Communitarian Politics and the Problem of Equality," *Political Research Quarterly,* 46 (September 1993), pp. 577–600. But see also Susan Hekman, "The Embodiment of the Subject: Feminism and the Communitarian Critique of Liberalism," *Journal of Politics,* 54 (November 1992), pp. 1098–1119.

13. Etzioni, *Rights and the Common Good,* p. iv, and Etzioni, "Communitarian Solutions/What Communitarians Think," *The Journal of State Government,* 65 (January–March), pp. 9–11. For a critical review of the communitarian program, see Jeremiah Creedon, "Communitarian Manifesto," *Utne Reader* (July–August 1992), pp. 38–40.

14. Etzioni, "Communitarian Solutions/What Communitarians Think," p. 10. See also Lester Thurow, "Communitarian vs. Individualistic Capitalism," in Etzioni, *Rights and the Common Good,* pp. 277–282. Note, however, that government's role in dealing with issues of social and economic inequality is far less developed in communitarian writings than is its role in dealing with issues of order. In the same volume, an article by David Osborne, "Beyond Left and Right: A New Political Paradigm" (pp. 283–290), downplays the role of government in guaranteeing entitlements.

15. Etzioni, *Rights and the Common Good,* p. 17.

16. See James A. Stimson, Michael B. MacKuen, and Robert S. Erikson, "Dynamic Representation," *American Political Science Review,* 89 (September 1995), pp. 543–565.

17. See C. B. Macpherson, *The Real World of Democracy* (New York: Oxford University Press, 1975), pp. 58–59.

18. Thomas E. Cronin, *Direct Democracy* (Cambridge, Mass.: Harvard University Press, 1989), p. 47.

19. Jack Citrin, "Who's the Boss? Direct Democracy and Popular Control of Government," in *Broken Contract?,* ed. Stephen C. Craig (Boulder, Colo.: Westview, 1996), p. 271.

20. Lawrence K. Grossman, *The Electronic Republic* (New York: Viking, 1995).

21. M. Margaret Conway, *Political Participation in the United States,* 2d ed. (Washington, D.C.: Congressional Quarterly, 1991), p. 44.

22. Benjamin I. Page and Robert Y. Shapiro, *The Rational Public* (Chicago: University of Chicago Press, 1992), p. 387.

23. See Robert A. Dahl, *Dilemmas of Pluralist Democracy* (New Haven, Conn.: Yale University Press, 1982), p. 5.

24. The classic statement on elite theory is C. Wright Mills, *The Power Elite* (New York: Oxford University Press, 1956).

25. See Robert A. Dahl, *Who Governs?* (New Haven, Conn.: Yale University Press, 1961). See also Clarence N. Stone, *Regime Politics* (Lawrence: University of Kansas Press, 1989); and John P. Heinz, Edward O. Laumann, Robert L. Nelson, and Robert H. Salisbury, *The Hollow Core* (Cambridge, Mass.: Harvard University Press, 1993).

26. Peter Bachrach and Morton S. Baratz, "Two Faces of Power," *American Political Science Review,* 56 (December 1962), pp. 947–952; and John Gaventa, *Power and Powerlessness* (Urbana: University of Illinois Press, 1980).

27. See, for example, Dan Clawson, Alan Neustadtl, and Denise Scott, *Money Talks* (New York: Basic Books, 1992).

28. Kay Lehman Schlozman and John T. Tierney, *Organized Interests and American Politics* (New York: Harper & Row, 1986).

29. E. E. Schattschneider, *The Semi-Sovereign People* (New York: Holt, Rinehart, & Winston, 1960), p. 35.

Chapter 2 / The Constitution
pp. 28–56

1. Laurence H. Tribe, "And the Winner is . . . ," *New York Times*, 12 February 1999, p. A27.

2. Gallup Organization, *Gallup Poll Monthly* (June 1992), pp. 2–3.

3. Samuel Eliot Morison, *Oxford History of the American People* (New York: Oxford University Press, 1965), p. 172.

4. John Plamentz (rev. ed. by M. E. Plamentz and Robert Wokler), *Man and Society*, Vol. 1: *From the Middle Ages to Locke* (New York: Longman, 1992), pp. 216–218.

5. Extrapolated from U.S. Department of Defense, *Selected Manpower Statistics, FY 1982* (Washington, D.C.: U.S. Government Printing Office, 1983), Table 2-30, p. 130; and U.S. Bureau of the Census, *1985 Statistical Abstract of the United States* (Washington, D.C.: U.S. Government Printing Office, 1985), Tables 1 and 2, p. 6.

6. Joseph T. Keenan, *The Constitution of the United States* (Homewood, Ill.: Dow-Jones-Irwin, 1975).

7. David P. Szatmary, *Shays' Rebellion: The Making of an Agrarian Insurrection* (Amherst: University of Massachusetts Press, 1980), pp. 82–102.

8. Robert H. Jackson, *The Struggle for Judicial Supremacy* (New York: Alfred A. Knopf, 1941), p. 8.

9. Forrest McDonald, *Novus Ordo Seclorum: The Intellectual Origins of the Constitution* (Lawrence: University Press of Kansas, 1985), pp. 205–209.

10. Donald S. Lutz, "The Preamble to the Constitution of the United States," *This Constitution*, 1 (September 1983), pp. 23–30.

11. Richard E. Neustadt, *Presidential Power: The Politics of Leadership* (New York: Wiley, 1960), p. 33.

12. Robert A. Goldwin, Letter to the Editor, *Wall Street Journal*, 30 August 1993, p. A11.

13. Herbert J. Storing, ed., *The Complete Anti-Federalist*, 7 vols. (Chicago: University of Chicago Press, 1981).

14. Alexis de Tocqueville, *Democracy in America, 1835–1839*, Reprint, ed. J. P. Mayer and Max Lerner (New York: Harper & Row, 1966), p. 102.

15. Jerold L. Waltman, *Political Origins of the U.S. Income Tax* (Jackson: University Press of Mississippi, 1985), p. 10.

Chapter 3 / Federalism   pp. 57–78

1. Rick Bragg, "Louisiana Stands Alone on Drinking at 18," *New York Times*, 23 March 1996, p. 1; "Louisiana Court Upholds Drinking Age of 21," *New York Times*, 3 July 1996, p. A17.

2. Ronald Reagan, "National Minimum Drinking Age: Remarks on Signing HR4616 into Law (17 July 1984)," *Weekly Compilation of Presidential Documents*, 23 July 1984, p. 1036.

3. *South Dakota v. Dole*, 483 U.S. 203 (1987).

4. Daniel J. Elazar, "Opening the Third Century of American Federalism: Issues and Prospects," *Annals of the American Academy of Political and Social Sciences*, 509 (May 1990), p. 14.

5. William H. Stewart, *Concepts of Federalism* (Lanham, Md.: University Press of America, 1984).

6. Edward Corwin, "The Passing of Dual Federalism," 36 *University of Virginia Law Review* 4 (1950).

7. See Daniel J. Elazar, *The American Partnership* (Chicago: University of Chicago Press, 1962); and Morton Grodzins, *The American System* (Chicago: Rand McNally, 1966).

8. Martha Derthick, "The Enduring Features of American Federalism," *The Brookings Review*, Summer 1989, p. 35.

9. *Seminole Tribe of Florida v. Florida*, 116 S. Ct. 1114 (1996).

10. *Printz v. United States*, 521 U.S. 98 (1997).

11. *McCulloch v. Maryland*, 4 Wheat. 316 (1819).

12. James T. Patterson, *The New Deal and the States: Federalism in Transition* (Princeton, N.J.: Princeton University Press, 1969).

13. Ronald Reagan, "Statement on Signing Executive Order Establishing the Presidential Advisory Committee on Federalism," 1981 Pub. Papers 341, 8 April 1981.

14. *Alden v. Maine* (98-436), *Florida v. College Savings Bank* (98-531), and *College Savings Bank v. Florida* (98-149).

15. Joseph F. Zimmerman, *Contemporary American Federalism: The Growth of National Power* (New York: Praeger, 1992), Chap. 4.

16. Council of State Governments, *The Book of the States, 1994–95*, Vol. 30 (Lexington, Ky.: Council of State Governments, 1994), pp. 580–581.

17. "Unfunded Federal Mandates," *Congressional Digest,* March 1995, p. 68.

18. U.S. Bureau of the Census, *Statistical Abstract of the United States: 1993* (Washington, D.C.: U.S. Government Printing Office, 1993), Table 466, p. 291.

19. Alice Rivlin, *Reviving the American Dream: The Economy, the States, and the Federal Government* (Washington, D.C.: Brookings Institution, 1992).

20. Michael A. Pagano and Ann O'M. Bowman, "The State of American Federalism, 1992–93" *Publius* 23 (Summer 1993), pp. 1–22.

Chapter 4 / Public Opinion, Political Socialization, and the Media
pp. 79–111

1. Gallup Organization, "Slim Majority of Americans Think Death Penalty Applied Fairly in This Country," *Gallup Poll Releases,* June 30, 2000.

2. Warren Weaver, Jr., "Death Penalty a Three Hundred–Year Issue in America," *New York Times,* 3 July 1976.

3. *Furman v. Georgia,* 408 U.S. 238 (1972).

4. *Gregg v. Georgia,* 248 U.S. 153 (1976).

5. Tracy L. Snell, *Bureau of Justice Statistics Bulletin: Capital Punishment 1998* (Washington, D.C.: Office of Justice Programs, U.S. Department of Justice, 1999), pp. 11–12. Revised online 6 January 2000 at <www.ojp. usdoj.gov/bjs/pub/pdf/cp98.pdf>.

6. See Roberta S. Sigel, ed., *Political Learning in Adulthood: A Sourcebook of Theory and Research* (Chicago: University of Chicago Press, 1989).

7. Times Mirror Center for the People and the Press, *The New Political Landscape* (Washington, D.C.: 1994), p. 144; The Pew Center for the People and the Press, News Release, 29 February 1996, p. 28.

8. The wording of this question is criticized by R. Michael Alvarez and John Brehm in "When Core Beliefs Collide: Conflict, Complexity, or Just Plain Confusion?," a paper prepared for delivery at the annual meeting of the American Political Science Association, Washington, D.C., September 1993, p. 9. They argue that using the phrase "personal choice" (which they call a core value) triggers the psychological effect of reactance, or the feeling that a freedom has been removed. But this core value is precisely our focus in this analysis. Alvarez and Brehm favor using instead the battery of six questions on abortion that have been used in the General Social Survey. Those six questions are also used in Elizabeth Adell Cook, Ted G. Jelen, and Clyde Wilcox, *Between Two Absolutes: Public Opinion and the Politics of Abortion* (Boulder, Colo.: Westview Press, 1992). Those interested primarily in analyzing various attitudes toward abortion probably should use data from the General Social Survey.

9. Although some people view the politics of abortion as "single-issue" politics, the issue has broader political significance. In their book on the subject, Cook, Jelen, and Wilcox say, "Although embryonic life is one important value in the abortion debate, it is not the only value at stake." They contend that the politics is tied to alternative sexual relationships and traditional roles of women in the home, which are "social order" issues. See *Between Two Absolutes,* pp. 8–9.

10. Ibid., p. 50.

11. The increasing wealth in industrialized societies may or may not be replacing class conflict with conflict over values. See the exchange between Ronald

Inglehart and Scott C. Flanagan, "Value Change in Industrial Societies," *American Political Science Review* 81 (December 1987), pp. 1289–1319.

12. Nathan Glazer, "The Structure of Ethnicity," *Public Opinion* 7 (October/November 1984), p. 4.

13. For a review of these studies, see Robert S. Erikson, Norman R. Luttbeg, and Kent L. Tedin, *American Public Opinion,* 3d ed. (New York: Macmillan, 1988).

14. Steven A. Holmes, "Census Sees a Profound Ethnic Shift in U.S.," *New York Times,* 14 March 1996, p. A8.

15. Glazer, "Structure of Ethnicity," p. 5.

16. National Election Study for 1994, an election survey conducted by the Center for Political Studies at the University of Michigan.

17. See David C. Leege and Lyman A. Kellstedt, eds., *Rediscovering the Religious Factor in American Politics* (Armonk, N.Y.: Sharpe, 1993), for a comprehensive examination of religion in political life that goes far beyond the analysis here.

18. John Robinson, "The Ups and Downs and Ins and Outs of Ideology," *Public Opinion* 7 (February/March 1984), p. 12.

19. For a more positive interpretation of ideological attitudes within the public, see William G. Jacoby, "The Structure of Ideological Thinking in the American Electorate," paper presented at the Annual Meeting of the American Political Science Association, Washington, D.C., September 1993. Jacoby applies a new method to survey data for the 1984 and 1988 elections and concludes "that there is a systematic, cumulative structure underlying liberal-conservative thinking in the American public" (p. 1).

20. Angus Campbell, Philip E. Converse, Warren E. Miller, and Donald E. Stokes, *The American Voter* (New York: Wiley, 1960), Chap. 10.

21. Marjorie Connelly, "A 'Conservative' Is (Fill in the Blank)," *New York Times,* 3 November 1996, sec. 4, p. 5

22. Ibid.

23. A relationship between liberalism and political tolerance was found by John L. Sullivan et al., "The Sources of Political Tolerance: A Multivariate Analysis," *American Political Science Review* 75 (March 1981), p. 102. See also Robinson, "Ups and Downs," pp. 13–15.

24. Herbert Asher, *Presidential Elections and American Politics* (Homewood, Ill.: Dorsey, 1980), pp. 14–20. Asher also constructs a two-dimensional framework, distinguishing between "traditional New Deal" issues and "new lifestyle" issues.

25. John E. Jackson, "The Systematic Beliefs of the Mass Public: Estimating Policy Preferences with Survey Data," *Journal of Politics* 45 (November 1983), pp. 840–865.

26. Milton Rokeach also proposed a two-dimensional model of political ideology grounded in the terminal values of freedom and equality. See *The Nature of Human Values* (New York: Free Press, 1973), especially Chap. 6. Rokeach found that positive and negative references to the two values permeate the writings of socialists, communists, fascists, and conservatives and clearly differentiate the four bodies of writing from one another (pp. 173–174). However, Rokeach built his two-dimensional model around only the values of freedom and equality; he did not deal with the question of freedom versus order.

27. In our framework, opposition to abortion is classified as a communitarian position. However, the Communitarian movement led by Amitai Etzioni adopted no position on abortion. (Personal communication from Vanessa Hoffman by e-mail, in reply to my query of 5 February 1996.)

28. But a significant literature is developing on the limitations of self-interest in explaining political life. See Jane J. Mansbridge, ed., *Beyond Self-Interest* (Chicago: University of Chicago Press, 1990).

29. Aaron Wildavsky, "Choosing Preferences by Constructing Institutions: A Cultural Theory of Preference

Formation," *American Political Science Review* 81 (March 1987), pp. 3–21.

30. David O. Sears and Carolyn L. Funk, "Self-Interest in Americans' Political Opinions," in Mansbridge, *Beyond Self-Interest,* pp. 147–170.

31. Two researchers who compared the public's knowledge on various topics in 1989 with its knowledge of the same topics in the 1940s and 1950s found similar levels of knowledge across the years. They point out, however, "that knowledge has been stable during a period of rapid changes in education, communication, and the public role of women seems paradoxical." They suspect, but cannot demonstrate, that the expected increase in knowledge did not materialize because of a decline in the public's interest in politics over time. See Michael X. Delli Carpini and Scott Keeter, "Stability and Change in the U.S. Public's Knowledge of Politics," *Public Opinion Quarterly* 55 (Winter 1991), p. 607.

32. Michael X. Delli Carpini and Scott Keeter, *What Americans Know About Politics and Why It Matters* (New Haven, Conn.: Yale University Press, 1996).

33. Ibid., p. 269.

34. There is evidence that the educational system and parental practices hamper the ability of women to develop their political knowledge. See Linda L. M. Bennett and Stephen Earl Bennett, "Enduring Gender Differences in Political Interests," *American Politics Quarterly* 17 (January 1989), pp. 105–122.

35. W. Russell Neuman, *The Paradox of Mass Politics: Knowledge and Opinion in the American Electorate* (Cambridge, Mass.: Harvard University Press, 1986), p. 81.

36. Pamela Johnston Conover and Stanley Feldman, "How People Organize the Political World: A Schematic Model," *American Journal of Political Science* 28 (February 1984), p. 96. For an excellent review of schema structures in contemporary psychology—especially as they relate to political science—see Reid Hastie, "A Primer of Information-Processing Theory for the Political Scientist," in *Political Cognition,* ed. Richard R. Lau and David O. Sears (Hillsdale, N.J.: Erlbaum, 1986), pp. 11–39.

37. John Hurwitz and Mark Peffley, "How Are Foreign Policy Attitudes Structured? A Hierarchical Model," *American Political Science Review* 81 (December 1987), pp. 1099–1220.

38. See Milton Lodge and Ruth Hamill, "A Partisan Schema for Political Information Processing," *American Political Science Review* 80 (June 1986), pp. 505–519.

39. Arthur Sanders, *Making Sense Out of Politics* (Ames: Iowa State University Press, 1990).

40. Lee Sigelman, "Disarming the Opposition: The President, the Public, and the INF Treaty," *Public Opinion Quarterly* 54 (Spring 1990), p. 46.

41. Benjamin I. Page, Robert Y. Shapiro, and Glenn R. Dempsey, "What Moves Public Opinion?," *American Political Science Review* 81 (March 1987), pp. 23–43.

42. Michael Margolis and Gary A. Mauser, *Manipulating Public Opinion: Essays on Public Opinion as a Dependent Variable* (Pacific Grove, Calif.: Brooks/Cole, 1989).

43. Daily fax assaults against the Clinton campaign in the 1992 election season are discussed in Jacob Weisberg, "True Fax: Mary Matalin, Vindicated," *New Republic,* 5 June 1993, pp. 11–12.

44. Robin Wright, "Hyper Democracy: Washington Isn't Dangerously Disconnected from the People; the Trouble May Be It's Too Plugged In," *Time,* 23 January 1995, pp. 14–31.

45. Rich Lowry, "Fax Populi: Armed with Computers and Fax Machines, Grass-Roots Organizations Are Shaking Up the Liberal Establishment," *National Review,* 7 November 1994, pp. 50–54. *Fax Congress Now* is a computer program designed to facilitate faxing government officials; see *Macworld,* May 1995, p. 48. The percentage of homes with fax machines comes from Steve Lohr, "The Great Unplugged Masses Confront the Future," *New York Times,* 21 January 1996, sec. 4, p. 1.

46. John December, Neil Randall, and Wes Tatters, *Discover the World Wide Web with Your Sportster* (Indianapolis, Ind.: Sams.net Publishing, 1995), pp. 11–12.

47. Janny Scott, "A Media Race Enters Waters Still Uncharted," *New York Times,* 1 February 1998, pp. 1, 17.

48. Jon Bigness, "Clinton's Crisis, Internet's Boom," *Chicago Tribune,* 30 January 1998, sec. 3, pp. 1, 4.

49. Doris A. Graber, *Mass Media and American Politics* (Washington, D.C.: Congressional Quarterly Press, 1984), pp. 78–79. See also W. Lance Bennett, *News: The Politics of Illusion,* 3d ed. (White Plains, N.Y.: Longman, 1996), Chap. 2.

50. Steven Lipin and Elizabeth Jensen, "Westinghouse, Infinity Deal Sets Stage for Other Radio Groups Seeking Mergers," *Wall Street Journal,* 21 June 1996, p. A3.

51. S. Robert Lichter and Richard E. Noyes, *Good Intentions Make Bad News* (Lanham, Md.: Rowman & Littlefield, 1995), p. 26, n. 9.

52. Michael Nelson (ed.), *Guide to the Presidency* (Washington, D.C.: Congressional Quarterly Press, 1989), p. 729.

53. Graber, *Mass Media,* p. 241.

54. W. Lance Bennett, *News: The Politics of Illusion,* 3d ed. (White Plains, N.Y.: Longman, 1996), p. 26.

55. "America's Watching: Public Attitudes Toward Television," pamphlet published in New York by the Network Television Association and the National Association of Broadcasters, 1995, pp. 17–18.

56. Pew Research Center for the People and the Press, "TV News Viewership Declines," press release, 13 May 1996, p. 1.

57. Pew Research Center for the People and the Press, *Scene 96: Take 2* (Washington, D.C.: Pew Charitable Trusts, 1996), p. 6.

58. Debra Gersh Hernandez, "Profile of the News Consumer," *Editor & Publisher,* 18 January 1997, p. 6.

59. Times Mirror Center for the People and the Press, "The American Media," 15 July 1990. This fits with findings of Stephen Earl Bennett in "Trends in Americans' Political Information, 1967–1987," *American Politics Quarterly* 17 (October 1989), pp. 422–435. Bennett found that race was significantly related to level of political information in a 1967 survey but not in a 1987 survey.

60. Pew Research Center for the People and the Press, "Americans Only a Little Better Off, but Much Less Anxious," *Press Release,* 23 May 1997, p. 5.

61. One seasoned journalist argues instead that the technology of minicams and satellites has set back the quality of news coverage. Now a television crew can fly to the scene of a crisis and immediately televise information without knowing much about the local politics or culture, which was not true of the old foreign correspondents. See David R. Gergen, "Diplomacy in a Television Age: The Dangers of Teledemocracy," in *The Media and Foreign Policy,* ed. Simon Serfaty (New York: St. Martin's Press, 1990), p. 51.

62. Stephen Earl Bennett in "Trends in Americans' Political Information, 1967–1987," *American Politics Quarterly* 17 (October 1989), pp. 422–435. Bennett's findings are supported by a national poll in 1990 that found only 40 percent of the sample had read a newspaper "yesterday," compared with 71 percent in 1965. Times-Mirror Center for the People and the Press, "The American Media," 15 July 1990, p. 100. Two researchers who compared the public's level of knowledge in 1989 with answers to the same questions in the 1940s and 1950s found similar levels of knowledge across the years but added, "that knowledge has been stable during a period of rapid changes in education, communication, and the public role of women seems paradoxical." They suspect, but cannot demonstrate, that the lack of expected increase is because of a decline in political interest over time. See Michael X. Delli Carpini and Scott Keeter, "Stability and Change in the U.S. Public's Knowledge of Politics,"

Public Opinion Quarterly 55 (Winter 1991), pp. 583–612.

63. The Times-Mirror Center for the People and the Press, Report dated 13 January 1993.

64. W. Russell Neuman, Marion R. Just, and Ann N. Crigler, *Common Knowledge: News and the Construction of Political Meaning* (Chicago: University of Chicago Press, 1992), p. 10.

65. Ibid., p. 113.

66. Laurence Parisot, "Attitudes About the Media: A Five-Country Comparison," *Public Opinion* 10 (January/February 1988), p. 60.

67. The statistical difficulties in determining media effects owing to measurement error are discussed in Larry M. Bartels, "Messages Received: The Political Impact of Media Exposure," paper prepared for delivery at the annual meeting of the American Political Science Association, Washington, D.C., September 1993. According to Bartels, "More direct and convincing demonstrations of significant opinion changes due to media exposure will require data collections spanning considerably longer periods of time" (p. 27).

68. "Clinton Gets a Bounce: Most People Who Watched Give His State of Union Speech High Marks," 27 January 1998, CNN/Time All-Politics Web site <www.allpolitics.com>. The Nielsen estimates of total number of viewers was 53.1 million, reported in the anonymous news item "Clinton's Troubles Built TV Ratings," *New York Times*, 29 January 1998, p. A19.

69. Benjamin I. Page, Robert Y. Shapiro, and Glenn R. Dempsey, "What Moves Public Opinion?" *American Political Science Review* 81 (March 1987), p. 31.

70. Shanto Iyengar and Donald R. Kinder, *News That Matters: Television and American Opinion* (Chicago: University of Chicago Press, 1987), p. 33.

71. Ibid., p. 60.

72. W. Russell Neuman, "The Threshold of Public Attention," *Public Opinion Quarterly* 54 (Summer 1990), pp. 159–176.

73. Robert Entman, *Democracy Without Citizens: Media and the Decay of American Politics* (New York: Oxford University Press, 1989), p. 86.

74. A panel study of ten- to seventeen-year-olds during the 1988 presidential campaign found that the campaign helped these young people crystallize their party identifications and their attitudes toward the candidates but had little effect on their political ideology and views on central campaign issues. See David O. Sears, Nicholas A. Valentino, and Rick Kosterman, "Domain Specificity in the Effects of Political Events on Preadult Socialization," paper prepared for delivery at the annual meeting of the American Political Science Association, Washington, D.C., September 1993.

75. John J. O'Connor, "Soothing Bromides? Not on TV," *New York Times*, 28 October 1990, Arts and Leisure section, pp. 1, 35.

76. James Fallows, *Breaking the News: How the Media Undermine American Democracy* (New York: Pantheon Books, 1996).

77. These facts from "ASNE Survey: Journalists Say They're Liberal," at <www.asne.org/kiosk/editor/97.jan-feb/dennis4.htm>. The research project is described in American Society of Editors, "Newspaper Journalists Examined in Major Study," *News Release*, 10 April 1997. Available at <www.asne.org/kiosk/newsworkforc.htm>.

78. Markle Presidential Election Watch, "Networks Yawned, Public Shrugged at Campaign '96," press release data, November 1996, found at <www.markle.org/J95327pr3.html>.

79. *The People, The Press, and Their Leaders* (Washington, D.C.: Times-Mirror Center for the People and the Press, 1995).

80. Dorothy Giobbe, "Dole Wins . . . in Endorsements," *Editor & Publisher*, 26 October 1996, p. 7.

81. Michael Robinson and Margaret Sheehan, *Over the Wire and on TV: CBS and UPI in Campaign '80* (New York: Russell Sage Foundation, 1983).

82. Michael J. Robinson, "The Media in Campaign '84: Part II; Wingless, Toothless, and Hopeless," *Public Opinion* 8 (February/March 1985), p. 48.

83. Maura Clancey and Michael J. Robinson, "General Election Coverage: Part I," *Public Opinion* 7 (December/January 1985), p. 54.

84. Schneider and Lewis, "Views on the News," p. 11. For similar findings from a 1994 study, see Times-Mirror Center for the People and the Press, "Mixed Message About Press Freedom on Both Sides of the Atlantic," press release of 16 March 1994, p. 65. See also Patterson, "News Decisions," p. 21.

85. Charles M. Madigan and Bob Secter, "Second Thoughts on Free Speech," *Chicago Tribune*, 4 July 1997, pp. 1, 18, 20.

Chapter 5 / Participation and Voting
pp. 112–137

1. V. Dion Haynes, " 'Normal' Folks Held in Arizona Militia Plot," *Chicago Tribune*, 4 July 1996, p. 1.

2. Patricia King, " 'Vipers' in the 'Burbs," *Newsweek*, 15 July 1996, p. 23.

3. Haynes, " 'Normal' Folks Held," p. 1.

4. This information is taken from the Link section of "The Militia Watchdog" at <www.greyware.com/authors/pitman/militia.htm>, updated June 16, 1996.

5. Cited in "Minuteman Press Online," obtained at <www.afn.org/~mpress/page1.html> on July 6, 1996. The "Restoring America" militia site can be found at <www.techmgmt.com/restore/restore.html>.

6. Lester W. Milbrath and M. L. Goel, *Political Participation* (Chicago: Rand McNally, 1977), p. 2.

7. See Sidney Verba, Kay Lehman Scholzman, and Henry E. Brady, *Voice and Equality: Civic Voluntarism in American Politics* (Cambridge, Mass.: Harvard University Press, 1995), pp. 40–42. In a highly publicized article, Robert D. Putnam argued that partici-pation in politics in the United States has suffered because our nation is losing the "social capital" that is based on active participation in community life. For example, Americans are "bowling alone"–that is, they are still bowling, but not in organized leagues. See his "Bowling Alone: America's Declining Social Capital," *Journal of Democracy* 6 (January 1995), pp. 65–78. Putnam's analysis inspired related critical observations on contemporary society, but it also sparked criticism of his data and his argument. For an empirical rebuttal, see Everett C. Ladd, "The Data Just Don't Show Erosion of America's 'Social Capital,' " *Public Perspective* 7 (June–July 1996), pp. 1, 5–22.

8. Michael Lipsky, "Protest as a Political Resource," *American Political Science Review* 62 (December 1968), p. 1145.

9. William E. Schmidt, "Selma Marchers Mark 1965 Clash," *New York Times*, 4 March 1985.

10. See Sidney Verba and Norman H. Nie, *Participation in America: Political Democracy and Social Equality* (New York: Harper & Row, 1972), p. 3.

11. Russell J. Dalton, *Citizen Politics*, 2d ed. (Chatham, N.J.: Chatham House, 1996).

12. Stephen C. Craig and Michael A. Magiotto, "Political Discontent and Political Action," *Journal of Politics* 43 (May 1981), pp. 514–522. But see Mitchell A. Seligson, "Trust Efficacy and Modes of Political Participation: A Study of Costa Rican Peasants," *British Journal of Political Science* 10 (January 1980), pp. 75–98, for a review of studies that came to different conclusions.

13. Philip H. Pollock III, "Organizations as Agents of Mobilization: How Does Group Activity Affect Political Participation?" *American Journal of Political Science* 26 (August 1982), pp. 485–503. Also see Jan E. Leighley, "Social Interaction and Contextual Influence on Political Participation," *American Politics Quarterly* 18 (October 1990), pp. 459–475.

14. Arthur H. Miller et al., "Group Consciousness and Political

Participation," *American Journal of Political Science* 25 (August 1981), p. 495. See also Susan J. Carroll, "Gender Politics and the Socializing Impact of the Women's Movement," in *Political Learning in Adulthood: A Sourcebook of Theory and Research,* ed. Roberta S. Sigel (Chicago: University of Chicago Press, 1989), p. 307.

15. Dalton, *Citizen Politics,* p. 65.

16. M. Kent Jennings, Jan W. van Deth, et al., *Continuities in Political Action: A Longitudinal Study of Political Orientations in Three Western Democracies* (New York: Walter de Gruyter, 1990).

17. See James L. Gibson, "The Policy Consequences of Political Intolerance: Political Repression During the Vietnam War Era," *Journal of Politics* 51 (February 1989), pp. 13–35. Gibson found that individual state legislatures reacted quite differently in response to antiwar demonstrations on college campuses, but the laws passed to discourage dissent were not related directly to public opinion within the state.

18. See Verba and Nie, *Participation in America,* p. 69. See also John Clayton Thomas, "Citizen-Initiated Contacts with Government Agencies: A Test of Three Theories," *American Journal of Political Science* 26 (August 1982), pp. 504–522; and Elaine B. Sharp, "Citizen-Initiated Contacting of Government Officials and Socioeconomic Status: Determining the Relationship and Accounting for It," *American Political Science Review* 76 (March 1982), pp. 109–115.

19. Elaine B. Sharp, "Citizen Demand Making in the Urban Context," *American Journal of Political Science* 28 (November 1984), pp. 654–670, especially pp. 654 and 665.

20. Verba and Nie, *Participation in America,* p. 67; and Sharp, "Citizen Demand Making," p. 660.

21. See Joel B. Grossman et al., "Dimensions of Institutional Participation: Who Uses the Courts and How?," *Journal of Politics* 44 (February 1982), pp. 86–114; and Frances Kahn Zemans, "Legal Mobilization: The Neglected Role of the Law in the Political System," *American Political Science Review* 77 (September 1983), pp. 690–703.

22. *Brown v. Board of Education,* 347 U.S. 483 (1954).

23. Max Kaase and Alan Marsh, "Political Action: A Theoretical Perspective," in *Political Action: Mass Participation in Five Western Democracies,* ed. Samuel H. Barnes and Max Kaase (Beverly Hills, Calif.: Sage, 1979), p. 168.

24. *Smith v. Allwright,* 321 U.S. 649 (1944).

25. *Harper v. Virginia State Board of Elections,* 383 U.S. 663 (1966).

26. Everett Carll Ladd, *The American Polity* (New York: Norton, 1985), p. 392.

27. Ivor Crewe, "Electoral Participation," in *Democracy at the Polls: A Comparative Study of Competitive National Elections,* ed. David Butler, Howard R. Penniman, and Austin Ranney (Washington, D.C.: American Enterprise Institute, 1981), pp. 219–223.

28. Thomas E. Cronin, *Direct Democracy: The Politics of Initiative, Referendum, and Recall* (Cambridge, Mass.: Harvard University Press, 1989), p. 197; David B. Magleby, "Direct Legislation in the American States," in *Referendums Around the World,* ed. David Butler and Austin Ranney (Washington, D.C.: American Enterprise Press, 1994), p. 232.

29. David B. Magleby, *Direct Legislation: Voting on Ballot Propositions in the United States* (Baltimore: Johns Hopkins University Press, 1984), p. 59. See also Ernest Tollerson, "In 90's Ritual, Hired Hands Carry Democracy's Petitions," *New York Times,* 9 July 1996, p. 1.

30. "Fears on Economy Doom Environment Issues, Tax Cuts," *Chicago Tribune,* 8 November 1990, sec. 1, p. 22.

31. Heather Abel, "Has Big Money Doomed Direct Democracy?" *High Country News,* 28 October 1996 (Vol. 28, No. 20). Available at <www.hcn.org/1996/oct28/dir/Feature_Has-big-mo.html>.

32. *The Book of the States 1996–97,* vol. 28 (Lexington, Ky.: Council of State Governments, 1996), p. 150.

33. *Chicago Tribune,* 10 March 1985.

34. Crewe, "Electoral Participation," p. 232. Several scholars have successfully explained variations in voting turnout across nations with only a few institutional and contextual variables. (See G. Bingham Powell, Jr., "American Voter Turnout in Comparative Perspective," *American Political Science Review* 80 [March 1986], pp. 17–43; and Robert W. Jackman, "Political Institutions and Voter Turnout in the Industrial Democracies," *American Political Science Review* 81 [June 1987], pp. 405–423.) However, this work has been criticized on methodological grounds and also for failing to successfully explain two deviant cases, the United States and Switzerland, both of which have low voter turnout. (See Wolfgang Hirczy, "Comparative Turnout: Beyond Cross-National Regression Models," paper prepared for presentation at the annual meeting of the American Political Science Association, Chicago, September 1992.)

35. Verba and Nie, *Participation in America,* p. 13.

36. Max Kaase and Alan Marsh, "Distribution of Political Action," in *Political Action,* p. 186; Dalton, *Citizen Politics,* p. 80.

37. Milbrath and Goel, *Political Participation,* pp. 95–96; Dalton, *Citizen Politics,* p. 80.

38. Verba and Nie, *Participation in America,* p. 148. For a concise summary of the effect of age on voting turnout, see Michael M. Gant and Norman R. Luttbeg, *American Electoral Behavior* (Itasca, Ill.: Peacock, 1991), pp. 103–104.

39. Richard Murray and Arnold Vedlitz, "Race, Socioeconomic Status, and Voting Participation in Large Southern Cities," *Journal of Politics* 39 (November 1977), pp. 1064–1072; and Verba and Nie, *Participation in America,* p. 157. See also Bobo and Gilliam, "Race, Sociopolitical Participation, and Black Empowerment," *American Political Science Review* 84, 2 (June 1990), pp. 377–393. Their study of 1987 national survey data with a black oversample found that African Americans participated more than whites of comparable socioeconomic status in cities in which the mayor's office was held by an African American.

40. William H. Flanigan and Nancy H. Zingale, *Political Behavior of the American Electorate,* 8th ed. (Washington, D.C.: Congressional Quarterly Press, 1994), pp. 41–43.

41. Ronald B. Rapoport, "The Sex Gap in Political Persuading: Where the 'Structuring Principle' Works," *American Journal of Political Science* 25 (February 1981), pp. 32–48.

42. Bruce C. Straits, "The Social Context of Voter Turnout," *Public Opinion Quarterly* 54 (Spring 1990), pp. 64–73.

43. See Sidney Verba, Kay Lehman Scholzman, and Henry E. Brady, *Voice and Equality: Civic Voluntarism in American Politics* (Cambridge, Mass.: Harvard University Press, 1995), p. 433.

44. Stephen D. Shaffer, "A Multivariate Explanation of Decreasing Turnout in Presidential Elections, 1960–1976," *American Journal of Political Science* 25 (February 1981), pp. 68–95; and Paul R. Abramson and John H. Aldrich, "The Decline of Electoral Participation in America," *American Political Science Review* 76 (September 1981), pp. 603–620. However, one scholar argues that this research suffers because it looks only at voters and nonvoters in a single election. When the focus shifts to people who vote sometimes but not at other times, the models do not fit so well. See M. Margaret Conway and John E. Hughes, "Political Mobilization and Patterns of Voter Turnout," paper prepared for delivery at the annual meeting of the American Political Science Association, Washington, D.C., September 1993.

45. Apparently, Richard A. Brody was the first scholar to pose this problem as a puzzle. See his "The Puzzle of Political Participation in America," in *The New American Political System,* ed. Anthony

King (Washington, D.C.: American Enterprise Institute, 1978), pp. 287–324. Since then, a sizable literature has attempted to explain the decline in voter turnout in the United States. Some authors have claimed to account for the decline with just a few variables, but their work has been criticized for being too simplistic. See Carol A. Cassel and Robert C. Luskin, "Simple Explanations of Turnout Decline," *American Political Science Review* 82 (December 1988), pp. 1321–1330. They contend that most of the post-1960 decline is still unexplained. If it is any comfort, voter turnout in Western European elections has seen a somewhat milder decline, and scholars have not been very successful at explaining it, either. See Richard S. Flickinger and Donley T. Studlar, "The Disappearing Voters? Exploring Declining Turnout in Western European Elections," *West European Politics* 15 (April 1992), pp. 1–16.

46. Abramson and Aldrich, "Decline of Electoral Participation," p. 519; and Shaffer, "Multivariate Explanation," pp. 78, 90.

47. The negative effect of registration laws on voter turnout is argued in Frances Fox Piven and Richard Cloward, "Government Statistics and Conflicting Explanations of Nonvoting," *PS: Political Science and Politics* 22 (September 1989), pp. 580–588. Their analysis was hotly contested in Stephen Earl Bennett, "The Uses and Abuses of Registration and Turnout Data: An Analysis of Piven and Cloward's Studies of Nonvoting in America," *PS: Political Science and Politics* 23 (June 1990), pp. 166–171. Bennett showed that turnout declined 10 to 13 percent after 1960, despite efforts to remove or lower legal hurdles to registration. For their reply, see Frances Fox Piven and Richard Cloward, "A Reply to Bennett," *PS: Political Science and Politics* 23 (June 1990), pp. 172–173. You can see that reasonable people can disagree on this matter.

48. David Glass, Peverill Squire, and Raymond Wolfinger, "Voter Turnout: An International Comparison," *Public Opinion* 6 (December/January 1984), p. 52. Wolfinger says that because of the strong effect of registration on turnout, most rational choice analyses of voting would be better suited to analyzing turnout of only registered voters. See Raymond E. Wolfinger, "The Rational Citizen Faces Election Day," *Public Affairs Report* 6 (November 1992), p. 12.

49. Data from a League of Women Voters Study published on the NBC News Web site at <www.decision96>.msn. com/vote/motor.htm> and dated 16 May 96.

50. "Motor Voters Didn't Vote, Study Finds," *Los Angeles Times,* 21 June 1997, p. A18.

51. Recent research finds that "party contact is clearly a statistically and substantively important factor in predicting and explaining political behavior." See Peter W. Wielhouwer and Brad Lockerbie, "Party Contacting and Political Participation, 1952–1990," paper prepared for delivery at the annual meeting of the American Political Science Association, Chicago, 1992, p. 14. Of course, parties strategically target the groups that they want to see vote in elections. See Peter W. Wielhouwer, "Strategic Canvassing by Political Parties, 1952–1990," *American Review of Politics* 16 (Fall 1995), pp. 213–238.

52. See Charles Krauthammer, "In Praise of Low Voter Turnout," *Time,* 21 May 1990, p. 88. Krauthammer says, "Low voter turnout means that people see politics as quite marginal to their lives, as neither salvation nor ruin. . . . Low voter turnout is a leading indicator of contentment." A major study in 1996 that compared 1,000 likely *non*-voters with 2,300 likely voters found that 24 percent of the non-voters said they "hardly ever" followed public affairs, versus 5 percent of likely voters. See Dwight Morris, "No-Show '96: Americans Who Don't Vote," Summary Report to the Medill News Service and WTTW Television, Northwestern University School of Journalism, 1996.

53. Crewe, "Electoral Participation," p. 262.

54. Samuel H. Barnes and Max Kaase, *Political Action*, p. 532.

55. *1971 Congressional Quarterly Almanac* (Washington, D.C.: Congressional Quarterly Press, 1972), p. 475.

56. Benjamin Ginsberg, *The Consequences of Consent: Elections, Citizen Control, and Popular Acquiescence* (Reading, Mass.: Addison-Wesley, 1982), pp. 13–14.

57. Ginsberg, *Consequences of Consent*, pp. 6–7.

58. Some people have argued that the decline in voter turnout during the 1980s served to increase the class bias in the electorate because people of lower socioeconomic status stayed home. But recent research has concluded that "class bias has not increased since 1964" (p. 734, Jan E. Leighley and Jonathan Nagler, "Socioeconomic Class Bias in Turnout, 1964–1988: The Voters Remain the Same," *American Political Science Review* 86 [September 1992], pp. 725–736). Nevertheless, Rosenstone and Hansen say, "the economic inequalities in political participation that prevail in the United States today are as large as the racial disparities in political participation that prevailed in the 1950s. America's leaders today face few incentives to attend to the needs of the disadvantaged," in *Mobilization, Participation, and Democracy in America.* See Steven J. Rosenstone and John Mark Hansen, *Mobilization, Participation, and Democracy in America* (New York: Macmillan, 1993), p. 248.

Chapter 6 / Political Parties, Campaigns, and Elections pp. 138–172

1. "Voter Anxiety Dividing GOP; Energized Democrats Backing Clinton," news release, 14 November 1995 (Washington, D.C.: Times-Mirror Center for the People and the Press), p. 101; and "Democratic Congressional Prospects Improve," news release, 5 April 1996 (Washington, D.C.: Pew Research Center for the People and the Press), p. 32.

2. Center for Political Studies of the Institute for Social Research, *American National Election Study 1996* (Ann Arbor: University of Michigan, 1996).

3. David W. Moore, "Perot Supporters: For the Man, Not a Third Party," *Gallup Organization Newsletter Archive* 60, 17 August 1995; the Gallup Organization's Web page at <www.gallup.com/newsletter/aug95>.

4. See Jerome M. Clubb, William H. Flanigan, and Nancy H. Zingale, *Partisan Realignment: Voters, Parties, and Government in American History,* vol. 108 (Beverly Hills, Calif.: Sage, 1980), p. 163.

5. See Gerald M. Pomper, "Classification of Presidential Elections," *Journal of Politics* 29 (August 1967), pp. 535–566.

6. The discussion that follows draws heavily on Austin Ranney and Willmoore Kendall, *Democracy and the American Party System* (New York: Harcourt, Brace, 1956), Chaps. 18 and 19.

7. See Steven J. Rosenstone, Roy L. Behr, and Edward H. Lazarus, *Third Parties in America: Citizen Response to Major Party Failure* (Princeton, N.J.: Princeton University Press, 1984), pp. 5–6.

8. Of these topics, reducing the deficit seems to be the most popular with American voters (although it attracts the attention of only about 50 percent of the electorate). See David W. Moore and Lydia Saad, "Americans Still Favor Independent and Third-Party Candidates," *Gallup Organization Newsletter Archive* 60, 7 July 1995; see also the Gallup Organization's Web page at <www.gallup.com/newsletter/july95>.

9. Perot activists were mainly well-off, highly educated white males, mostly self-styled independents. See Randall W. Partin, Lori M. Weber, Ronald B. Rapoport, and Walter J. Stone, "Sources of Activism in the 1992 Perot Campaign," in *The State of the Parties: The Changing Role of Contemporary American Parties,* ed. Daniel M. Shea and John C. Green (Lanham, Md.: Rowman and Littlefield, 1994), pp. 147–162.

10. Rosenstone, Behr, and Lazarus, *Third Parties in America*, p. 8.

11. See James Gimpel, *National Elections and the Autonomy of American State Party Systems* (Pittsburgh, Pa.: University of Pittsburgh Press, 1996).

12. Measuring the concept of party identification has had its problems. For recent insights into the issues, see R. Michael Alvarez, "The Puzzle of Party Identification," *American Politics Quarterly* 18 (October 1990), pp. 476–491; and Donald Philip Green and Bradley Palmquist, "Of Artifacts and Partisan Instability," *American Journal of Political Science* 34 (August 1990), pp. 872–902.

13. Rhodes Cook, "GOP Shows Dramatic Growth, Especially in the South," *Congressional Quarterly Weekly Report,* 13 January 1996, pp. 97–100.

14. There is some dispute over how stable party identification really is, when the same respondents are asked about their party identification over a period of several months during an election campaign. The research literature is reviewed in Brad Lockerbie, "Change in Party Identification: The Role of Prospective Economic Evaluations," *American Politics Quarterly* 17 (July 1989), pp. 291–311. Lockerbie argues that respondents change their party identification according to whether they think a party will help them personally in the future. But also see Green and Palmquist, "Of Artifacts and Partisan Instability."

15. Bill Keller, "As Arms Buildup Eases, U.S. Tries to Take Stock," *New York Times,* 14 May 1985; Ed Gillespie and Bob Schellhas, *Contract with America* (New York: Times Books, 1994), p. 107.

16. The Republican data came from "Delegates, Party Voters Sometimes at Odds," *Washington Post National Weekly Edition,* 12–18 August 1996, p. A8; the Democratic data were provided by Mario Brossard of the *Washington Post* via e-mail on 21 August 1996. The *Post* surveyed 505 Republican and 508 Democratic delegates. Data for registered voters came from a national survey of approximately 1,500 respondents.

17. See, for example, Gerald M. Pomper, *Elections in America* (New York: Dodd, Mead, 1968); Benjamin Ginsberg, "Election and Public Policy," *American Political Science Review* 70 (March 1976), pp. 41–50; and Jeff Fishel, *Presidents and Promises* (Washington, D.C.: Congressional Quarterly Press, 1985).

18. Robert Harmel and Kenneth Janda, *Parties and Their Environments: Limits to Reform?* (New York: Longman, 1982), pp. 27–29. See also John Huber and Ronald Inglehart, "Expert Interpretations of Party Space and Party Locations in 42 Societies," *Party Politics* 1 (January 1995), pp. 73–111; and Alan Ware, *Political Parties and Party Systems* (New York: Oxford University Press, 1996), Chap. 1.

19. Personal communication with DNC and RNC staff, 24 January 1994, and information updated from the national committees' home pages on the Web (see "World Wide Web Resources" for this chapter).

20. See Ralph M. Goldman, *The National Party Chairmen and Committees: Factionalism at the Top* (Armonk, N.Y.: Sharpe, 1990). The subtitle is revealing.

21. William Crotty and John S. Jackson III, *Presidential Primaries and Nominations* (Washington, D.C.: Congressional Quarterly Press, 1985), p. 33.

22. Phillip A. Klinkner, "Party Culture and Party Behavior," in Shea and Green, *The State of the Parties*, pp. 275–287; and Philip A. Klinkner, *The Losing Parties: Out-Party National Committees, 1956–1993* (New Haven, Conn.: Yale University Press, 1994).

23. The Federal Election Commission, "FEC Reports on Political Party Activity for 1997–98," press release of 9 April 1999, pp. 1–2.

24. John Frendreis, Alan R. Gitelson, Gregory Flemming, and Anne Layzell, "Local Political Parties and Legislative Races in 1992," in Shea and Green, *The State of the Parties,* p. 139.

25. Robert Biersack, "Hard Facts and Soft Money: State Party Finance in the 1992 Federal Elections," in Shea and Green, *The State of the Parties,* p. 114.

26. Martin P. Wattenberg, *The Decline of American Political Parties, 1952–1994* (Cambridge, Mass.: Harvard University Press, 1996).

27. In 1996, the Democratic National Committee mounted an unprecedented drive to organize up to sixty thousand precinct captains in twenty states, while the new Republican candidate for U.S. senator from Illinois, Al Salvi, fired his own campaign manager and replaced him with someone from the National Republican Senatorial Campaign Committee. See Sue Ellen Christian, "Democrats Will Focus on Precincts," *Chicago Tribune,* 29 June 1996, p. 5; and Michael Dizon, "Salvi Fires Top Senate Race Aides," *Chicago Tribune,* 24 May 1996, sec. 2, p. 3.

28. Barbara Sinclair, "The Congressional Party: Evolving Organizational, Agenda-Setting, and Policy Roles," in L. Sandy Maisel, ed., *The Parties Respond* (Boulder, Colo.: Westview Press, 1990), p. 227.

29. The model is articulated most clearly in a report by the American Political Science Association, "Toward a More Responsible Two-Party System," *American Political Science Review* 44 (September 1950), Part II. See also Gerald M. Pomper, "Toward a More Responsible Party System? What, Again?," *Journal of Politics* 33 (November 1971), pp. 916–940. See also the seven essays in the symposium, "Divided Government and the Politics of Constitutional Reform," *PS: Political Science & Politics,* 24 (December 1991), pp. 634–657.

30. This is essentially the framework for studying campaigns set forth in Barbara G. Salmore and Stephen A. Salmore, *Candidates, Parties, and Campaigns: Electoral Politics in America,* 2d ed. (Washington, D.C.: Congressional Quarterly Press, 1989).

31. Martin P. Wattenberg, *The Rise of Candidate-Centered Politics: Presidential Elections of the 1980s* (Cambridge, Mass.: Harvard University Press, 1991).

32. Michael Gallagher, "Conclusion," in *Candidate Selection in Comparative Perspective: The Secret Garden of Politics,* ed. Michael Gallagher and Michael Marsh (London: Sage, 1988), p. 238.

33. *The Book of the States, 1996–97,* vol. 31 (Lexington, Ky.: Council of State Governments, 1996), pp. 157–158. See also Federal Election Commission, "Party Affiliation and Primary Voting 2000," on-line at <www.fec.gov/votregis/primaryvoting.htm>.

34. Rhodes Cook, "Earlier Voting in 1996 Forecasts Fast and Furious Campaigns," *Congressional Quarterly Weekly Report,* 19 August 1995, p. 2485.

35. Ibid., pp. 2485–2487, and Federal Election Commission, "2000 Presidential Primary Dates and Candidate Filing Deadlines for Ballot Access (Data as of 2/24/2000)." Document on-line at <http://www.fec.gov/pages/2kdates.htm>. For a description of how caucuses operate and how differently they work in the two parties, see William G. Mayer, "Caucuses: How They Work, What Difference They Make," in William G. Mayer, ed., *In Pursuit of the White House: How We Choose Our Presidential Nominees* (Chatham, N.J.: Chatham House, 1995), pp. 105–157.

36. Gary R. Orren and Nelson W. Polsby (eds.), *Media and Momentum: The New Hampshire Primary and Nomination Politics* (Chatham, N.J.: Chatham House, 1987), p. 23.

37. See James R. Beniger, "Winning the Presidential Nomination: National Polls and State Primary Elections, 1936–1972," *Public Opinion Quarterly* 40 (Spring 1976), pp. 22–38.

38. In 2000, one elector refused to vote. For other exceptions, see Michael Nelson (ed.), *Congressional Quarterly Guide to the Presidency* (Washington, D.C.: Congressional Quarterly Press, 1989).

39. Harold W. Stanley and Richard G. Niemi, *Vital Statistics on American Politics,* 2d ed. (Washington, D.C.: Congressional Quarterly Press, 1990), p. 132; and the 1992 and 1996 National Election Study, Center for Political Studies, University of Michigan.

40. Rhodes Cook, "House Republicans Scored a Quiet Victory in '92,"

Congressional Quarterly Weekly Report, 17 April 1993, p. 966.

41. Quoted in E. J. Dionne, Jr., "On the Trail of Corporation Donations," *New York Times,* 6 October 1980.

42. Salmore and Salmore, *Candidates, Parties, and Campaigns,* p. 11. See also David Himes, "Strategy and Tactics for Campaign Fund-Raising," in *Campaigns and Elections: American Style,* ed. James A. Thurber and Candice J. Nelson (Boulder, Colo.: Westview Press, 1995), pp. 62–77.

43. "FEC Announces 1996 Presidential Spending Limits," Federal Election Commission press release of 15 March 1996; "If the Presidential Election Were Held in 1999," Federal Election Commission press release of 7 July 1999.

44. Paul S. Herrnson, "Party Strategies and Campaign Activities in the 1992 Congressional Elections," in Shea and Green, *The State of the Parties,* pp. 83–106; and Robert Biersack, "Hard Facts and Soft Money: State Party Finance in the 1992 Federal Elections," ibid., pp. 107–132.

45. Adam Clymer, "System to Limit Election Spending Found in Shambles," *New York Times,* 16 June 1996, p. 1.

46. Salmore and Salmore, *Candidates, Parties, and Campaigns,* p. 11.

47. David Moon, "What You Use Depends on What You Have: Information Effects on the Determinants of Electoral Choice," *American Politics Quarterly* 18 (January 1990), pp. 3–24.

48. See the "Marketplace" section in monthly issues of the magazine *Campaigns & Elections,* which contains more than a hundred names, addresses, and telephone numbers of people who supply "political products and services"—from "campaign schools" to "voter files and mailing lists."

49. Stephen Ansolabehere, Roy L. Behr, and Shanto Iyengar, "Mass Media and Elections: An Overview," *American Politics Quarterly* 19 (January 1991), pp. 109–139.

50. See Darrell M. West, *Air Wars: Television Advertising in Election*

Campaigns, 1952–1992 (Washington, D.C.: Congressional Quarterly Press, 1993), p. 7.

51. Phil Kuntz, "Dole Is Lifted by the Selection of Kemp, Convention That Avoided Divisiveness," *Wall Street Journal,* 19 August 1996, p. A14.

52. Pamela Johnston Conover and Stanley Feldman, "Candidate Perception in an Ambiguous World: Campaigns, Cues, and Inference Processes," *American Journal of Political Science* 33 (November 1989), pp. 912–940.

53. Michael M. Gant and Norman R. Luttbeg, *American Electoral Behavior* (Itasca, Ill.: Peacock, 1991), pp. 63–64. The literature on the joint effects of party, issues, and candidates is quite involved. See also David W. Romero, "The Changing American Voter Revisited: Candidate Evaluations in Presidential Elections, 1952–1984," *American Politics Quarterly* 17 (October 1989), pp. 409–421. Romero contends that research that finds a "new" American voter who votes according to issues is incorrectly looking at standardized rather than unstandardized regression coefficients.

54. Conover and Feldman, "Candidate Perception," p. 938.

55. Party identification has been assumed to be relatively resistant to short-term campaign effects, but see Dee Allsop and Herbert F. Weisberg, "Measuring Change in Party Identification in an Election Campaign," *American Journal of Political Science* 32 (November 1988), pp. 996–1017. They conclude that partisanship is more volatile than we have thought.

56. For an analysis of the Republicans' problem, see Russell L. Riley, "Party Government and the Contract With America," *PS: Political Science and Politics,* 28 (December 1995), pp. 703–707.

Chapter 7 / Interest Groups
pp. 173–193

1. Saundra Torry, "Powerful Pack Got Settlement Talks Rolling with Big Tobacco," *Washington Post,* 20 April

1997, p. A7; Jonathan Weisman, "Tobacco Foes Smell a Victory in Coming Court Battles," *Congressional Quarterly Weekly Report,* 10 May 1997, p. 1060; John Schwartz, "In Tobacco Suits, States Find Strength in Numbers, Mississippi Attorney General Rallies Coalition of Colleagues in Landmark Legal Battle," *Washington Post,* 18 May 1997, p. A6.

2. Juliana Gruenwald, "President Punts Tobacco Issue Toward Campaign '98," *Congressional Quarterly Weekly Report,* 20 September 1997, p. 2214.

3. Jonathan Weisman, "Tobacco's Survivalism," *Congressional Quarterly Weekly Report,* 10 May 1997, p. 1065.

4. Pam Belluck, "Tobacco Companies Settle a Suit with Minnesota for $6.5 Billion," *New York Times,* 9 May 1998, p. 1.

5. Alexis de Tocqueville, *Democracy in America, 1835–1839,* reprint, ed. Richard D. Heffner (New York: Mentor Books, 1956), p. 79.

6. *The Federalist Papers* (New York: Mentor Books, 1961), p. 79.

7. Ibid., p. 78.

8. See Robert A. Dahl, *A Preface to Democratic Theory* (Chicago: University of Chicago Press, 1956), pp. 4–33.

9. Alan Rosenthal, *The Third House* (Washington, D.C.: Congressional Quarterly, 1993), p. 7.

10. This discussion follows from Jeffrey M. Berry, *The Interest Group Society* (New York: Longman, 1997), pp. 6–8.

11. John Mark Hansen, *Gaining Access* (Chicago: University of Chicago Press, 1991), pp. 11–17.

12. William H. Honan, "With Money Threatened, Colleges Are Moving on All Lobbying Fronts," *New York Times,* 28 June 1995, p. B7.

13. Anne N. Costain, *Inviting Women's Rebellion* (Baltimore: Johns Hopkins University Press, 1992).

14. David B. Truman, *The Governmental Process* (New York: Alfred A. Knopf, 1951).

15. Herbert Gans, *The Urban Villagers* (New York: Free Press, 1962).

16. Robert H. Salisbury, "An Exchange Theory of Interest Groups," *Midwest Journal of Political Science* 13 (February 1969), pp. 1–32.

17. See Mancur Olson, Jr., *The Logic of Collective Action* (New York: Schocken, 1968).

18. See ibid.

19. See, for example, Edward O. Laumann and David Knoke, *The Organizational State* (Madison: University of Wisconsin Press, 1987), p. 3. Cited in Robert H. Salisbury, "The Paradox of Interest Groups in Washington—More Groups, Less Clout," in *The New American Political System,* 2d ed., ed. Anthony King (Washington, D.C.: American Enterprise Institute, 1990), p. 226.

20. Dan Clawson, Alan Neustadtl, and Denise Scott, *Money Talks* (New York: Basic Books, 1992), p. 1.

21. "PAC Activity in 1994 Remains at 1992 Levels," Federal Election Commission, 31 March 1995, p. 5.

22. John R. Wright, "Contributions, Lobbying, and Committee Voting in the U.S. House of Representatives," *American Political Science Review* 84 (June 1990), pp. 417–438; and Richard L. Hall and Frank W. Wayman, "Buying Time: Money Interests and the Mobilization of Bias in Congressional Committees," *American Political Science Review,* 84 (September 1990), pp. 797–820.

23. Kay Lehman Schlozman and John T. Tierney, *Organized Interests and American Democracy* (New York: Harper & Row, 1986), p. 150.

24. Berry, *The Interest Group Society,* p. 166.

25. Yumiko Ono, "Tobacco Firms Rush to Counterattack Despite Signs of Dissension in Ranks," *Wall Street Journal,* 14 August 1995, p. A3.

26. Dirk Johnson, "Weed Killers in Tap Water in Corn Belt," *New York Times,* 18 August 1995, p. A10.

27. Berry, *The Interest Group Society,* pp. 135–137.

28. Marc K. Landy and Mary Hague, "Private Interests and Superfund," *Public Interest* 108 (Summer 1992), pp. 97–115.

29. Sidney Verba, Kay Lehman Schlozman, Henry Brady, and Norman H. Nie, "Citizen Activity: Who Participates? What Do They Say?," *American Political Science Review* 87 (June 1993), p. 311.

30. Jeffrey M. Berry, *Lobbying for the People* (Princeton, N.J.: Princeton University Press, 1977), pp. 6–10.

31. Schlozman and Tierney, *Organized Interests,* pp. 58–87.

32. Jonathan Rauch, *Demosclerosis* (New York: Times Books, 1994), p. 91.

33. Adam Clymer, "Congress Passes Bill to Disclose Lobbyists' Roles," *New York Times,* 30 November 1995, p. A1.

34. Eric Schmitt, "Order for Lobbyists: Hold the Gravy," *New York Times,* 11 February 1996, p. 30.

35. See Jonathan Rauch, *Demosclerosis.*

Chapter 8 / Congress   pp. 194–222

1. These events are recent, and a well-researched history of the Clinton impeachment has yet to be written. Useful, however, is *Uncovering Clinton* (New York: Crown Publishers, 1999), by Michael Isikoff, the *Newsweek* reporter who was a key figure in breaking the story about Lewinsky and the president. For Lewinsky's account of her affair with Clinton, see Andrew Morton, *Monica's Story* (New York: St. Martin's Press, 1999). Solid analysis from a judicial perspective is found in Richard A. Posner, *An Affair of State: The Investigation, Impeachment, and Trial of President Clinton* (Cambridge, Mass.: Harvard University Press, 1999).

2. "The Articles of Impeachment," *CQ Weekly,* 9 January 1999, p. 47.

3. Jeffrey L. Katz, "Shakeup in the House," *CQ Weekly,* 7 November 1998, pp. 2989–2992.

4. See Dan Carney, "Hyde Leads Impeachment Drive in Growing Isolation," *CQ Weekly,* 5 December 1998, pp. 3247–3249.

5. Richard L. Berke with Janet Elder, "Damaged by Trial, Senate's Standing Sinks in New Poll," *New York Times,* 3 February 1999, p. A1; and James Bennet with Janet Elder, "Despite Intern, President Stays in Good Graces," *New York Times,* 24 February 1999, p. A1.

6. Clinton was later found to be in contempt of court for providing false testimony in a deposition in the Paula Jones lawsuit. John M. Broder and Neil A. Lewis, "Clinton Is Found to Be in Contempt in Jones Lawsuit," *New York Times,* 13 April 1999, p. A1.

7. Clinton Rossiter, *1787: The Grand Convention* (New York: Mentor, 1968), p. 158.

8. James M. Lindsay and Randall B. Ripley, "How Congress Influences Foreign and Defense Policy," in *Congress Resurgent,* ed. Randall B. Ripley and James M. Lindsay (Ann Arbor: University of Michigan Press, 1993), pp. 25–28.

9. Norman J. Ornstein, Thomas E. Mann, and Michael J. Malbin, *Vital Statistics on Congress, 1995–1996* (Washington, D.C.: Congressional Quarterly Press, 1996), pp. 56–58.

10. Albert R. Hunt, "In Congress, Some Things Never Change," *Wall Street Journal,* 28 March 1996, p. A15.

11. "The Critique of Congress," *American Enterprise* 3 (May–June 1992), p. 101.

12. Karlyn Bowman and Everett Carll Ladd, "Public Opinion Toward Congress: A Historical Look," in *Congress, the Press, and the Public,* ed. Thomas E. Mann and Norman J. Ornstein (Washington, D.C.: American Enterprise Institute and the Brookings Institution, 1994), p. 55.

13. "Ethics," *American Enterprise* 3 (November–December 1992), p. 84.

14. Timothy E. Cook, *Making Laws and Making News* (Washington, D.C.: Brookings Institution, 1989), p. 83.

15. Jonathan S. Krasno, *Challengers, Competition, and Reelection* (New Haven, Conn.: Yale University Press, 1994).

16. The final election report for 1998 is on-line at <www.fec.gov/pubrec/fe98/cover.htm>.

17. John Harwood and Jeanne Cummings, "Congressional Democrats Improve

Election Chances," *Wall Street Journal,* 29 October 1998, p. A24.

18. Ornstein, Mann, and Malbin, *Vital Statistics,* pp. 22–23, 28–29.

19. Hanna Fenichel Ptikin, *The Concept of Representation* (Berkeley: University of California Press, 1967), pp. 60–91.

20. Carol M. Swain, *Black Faces, Black Interests* (Cambridge, Mass.: Harvard University Press, 1993), p. 197.

21. *Miller v. Johnson,* 115 S. Ct. 2475 (1995).

22. *Abrams v. Johnson,* 117 S. Ct. 1925 (1997).

23. Walter J. Oleszek, *Congressional Procedures and the Policy Process* (Washington, D.C.: Congressional Quarterly Press, 1996), p. 91.

24. Roger W. Cobb and Charles D. Elder, *Participation in American Politics,* 2d ed. (Baltimore: Johns Hopkins University Press, 1983), pp. 64–65.

25. Andrew Taylor, "Congress Hands President a Budgetary Scalpel," *Congressional Quarterly Weekly Report,* 30 March 1996, pp. 864–867.

26. It was Woodrow Wilson who described the legislative process as the "dance of legislation." Eric Redman used the phrase for the title of his case study, *The Dance of Legislation* (New York: Touchstone, 1973).

27. Woodrow Wilson, *Congressional Government* (Boston: Houghton Mifflin, 1885), p. 79.

28. Lawrence D. Longley and Walter J. Oleszek, *Bicameral Politics* (New Haven, Conn.: Yale University Press, 1989), p. 4.

29. Karen Foerstal, "Gingrich Flexes His Power in Picking Panel Chiefs," *Congressional Quarterly Weekly Report,* 7 January 1995, p. 3326.

30. Joel D. Aberbach, *Keeping a Watchful Eye* (Washington, D.C.: Brookings Institution, 1990), p. 44.

31. Ornstein, Mann, and Malbin, *Vital Statistics,* pp. 131–137.

32. Gary W. Cox and Mathew D. McCubbins, *Legislative Leviathan* (Berkeley: University of California Press, 1993); and Keith Krehbiel,

Information and Legislative Organization (Ann Arbor: University of Michigan Press, 1992).

33. Andy Plattner, "Dole on the Job," *Congressional Quarterly Weekly Report,* 29 June 1985, p. 1270.

34. Janet Hook, "Leaders Jockey Within Gingrich Power Vacuum," *Los Angeles Times,* 17 January 1997, p. A1.

35. Jackie Koszczuk, "Hastert Gently Gavels in an Era of 'Order' in the House," *CQ Weekly,* 27 February 1999, pp. 458–465.

36. Charles O. Jones, *The United States Congress* (Homewood, Ill.: Dorsey Press, 1982), p. 322.

37. See Jerry Gray, "Freshmen Challenge G.O.P. Elders," *New York Times,* 21 October 1995, p. 1; and Jackie Calmes, "Militancy of GOP Freshmen May Leave Gingrich Little Room to Compromise," *Wall Street Journal,* 22 December 1995, p. A3.

38. Cox and McCubbins, *Legislative Leviathan;* D. Roderick Kiewiet and Mathew D. McCubbins, *The Logic of Delegation* (Chicago: University of Chicago Press, 1991); and Krehbiel, *Information and Legislative Organization.*

39. Dan Carney, "As Hostilities Rage on the Hill, Partisan-Vote Rate Soars," *Congressional Quarterly Weekly Report,* 27 January 1996, pp. 199–201; and Martin P. Wattenberg, *The Decline of American Political Parties, 1994* (Cambridge, Mass.: Harvard University Press, 1996), Chap. 11.

40. See Mark A. Peterson, *Legislating Together* (Cambridge, Mass.: Harvard University Press, 1990).

41. James Sterling Young, *The Washington Community* (New York: Harcourt, Brace, 1964).

42. Richard F. Fenno, Jr., *Home Style* (Boston: Little, Brown, 1978), p. 32.

43. Louis I. Bredvold and Ralph G. Ross (eds.), *The Philosophy of Edmund Burke* (Ann Arbor: University of Michigan Press, 1960), p. 148.

44. Warren E. Miller and Donald E. Stokes, "Constituency Influence in Congress," *American Political Science Review* 57 (March 1963), pp. 45–57. On

minority legislators, see James B. Johnson and Philip E. Secret, "Focus and Style: Representational Roles of Congressional Black and Hispanic Caucus Members," *Journal of Black Studies* 26 (January 1996), pp. 245–273.

45. George Hager, "Clinton, GOP Congress Strike Historic Budget Agreement," *Congressional Quarterly Weekly Report,* 3 May 1997, pp. 993, 996–997.

46. Robert Weissberg, "Collective vs. Dyadic Representation in Congress," *American Political Science Review* 72 (June 1978), pp. 535–547.

47. Jeffrey M. Berry, *The Interest Group Society,* 3d ed. (New York: Longman, 1997).

Chapter 9 / The Presidency
pp. 223–245

1. Miles A. Pomper and Chuck McCutcheon, "As Kosovo Crisis Escalates, Calls Increase to Reconsider Use of Ground Troops," *CQ Weekly,* 3 April 1999, pp. 809–811.

2. Carla Anne Robbins and Charles Goldsmith, "Politicians Fret but Public Stands by Kosovo Conflict," *Wall Street Journal,* 13 May 1999, p. A32.

3. Pat Towell, "Congress Set to Provide Money, but No Guidance for Kosovo Mission," *CQ Weekly,* 1 May 1999, pp. 1036–1040.

4. R. W. Apple, Jr., "Clinton Tailors Legacy but Kosovo Isn't Fabric," *New York Times,* 10 June 1999, p. A18.

5. See Louis Fisher, *Presidential War Power* (Lawrence: University Press of Kansas, 1995).

6. Wilfred E. Binkley, *President and Congress,* 3d ed. (New York: Vintage, 1962), p. 155.

7. Richard E. Neustadt, *Presidential Power,* rev. ed. (New York: John Wiley, 1980), p. 10.

8. Ibid., p. 9.

9. George C. Edwards III, *At the Margins* (New Haven, Conn.: Yale University Press, 1989). See also Jon R. Bond and Richard Fleisher, *The President in the Legislative Arena* (Chicago: University of Chicago Press, 1990).

10. See Edwards, *At the Margins,* pp. 101–125.

11. Theodore J. Lowi, *The Personal President* (Ithaca, N.Y.: Cornell University Press, 1985).

12. Richard A. Brody, *Assessing the President* (Stanford, Calif.: Stanford University Press, 1991), pp. 27–44.

13. Paul Brace and Barbara Hinckley, *Follow the Leader* (New York: Basic Books, 1992).

14. Charles W. Ostrom and Dennis M. Simon, "Promise and Performance: A Dynamic Model of Presidential Popularity," *American Political Science Review* 79 (June 1985), pp. 334–358.

15. "Prepared Text of Carter's Farewell Address," *New York Times,* 15 January 1981, p. B10.

16. "Two Cheers for United Government," *American Enterprise* 4 (January–February 1993), pp. 107–108.

17. Morris Fiorina, *Divided Government,* 2d ed. (Needham Heights, Mass.: Allyn & Bacon, 1996), p. 153.

18. See generally, Charles O. Jones, *The Presidency in a Separated System* (Washington, D.C.: Brookings Institution, 1994).

19. David R. Mayhew, *Divided We Govern* (New Haven, Conn.: Yale University Press, 1991); and David R. Mayhew, "The Return to Unified Government Under Clinton: How Much of a Difference in Lawmaking," in *The New American Politics,* ed. Bryan D. Jones (Boulder, Colo.: Westview Press, 1995), pp. 111–121.

20. See Sean Kelley, "Divided We Govern: A Reassessment," *Polity* 25 (Spring 1993), pp. 475–484; and George Edwards, Andrew Barrett, and Jeffrey Peake, "The Legislative Impact of Divided Government: What *Failed* to Pass in Congress," n.d., Center for Presidential Studies, Texas A&M University.

21. For an overview of the gridlock argument, see James L. Sundquist (ed.), *Back to Gridlock?* (Washington, D.C.: Brookings Institution, 1995).

22. U.S. Bureau of the Census, U.S. Department of Commerce, *Statistical Abstract of the United States, 1995* (Washington, D.C.: U.S. Government Printing Office, 1995), p. 350; and U.S. Office of Management and Budget, *Budget of the United States Government, Fiscal Year 2001* (Washington, D.C.: 2000), p. 368.

23. Jeffrey H. Birnbaum, *Madhouse: The Private Turmoil of Working for the President* (New York: Times Books, 1996).

24. Edward Weisband and Thomas M. Franck, *Resignation in Protest* (New York: Penguin, 1975), p. 139, quoted in Thomas E. Cronin, *The State of the Presidency,* 2d ed. (Boston: Little, Brown, 1980), p. 253.

25. See Richard W. Waterman, "Combining Political Resources: The Internalization of the President's Appointment Power," in *The Presidency Reconsidered,* ed. Richard W. Waterman (Itasca, Ill.: Peacock, 1993), pp. 172–210.

26. *Public Papers of the President, Lyndon B. Johnson, 1965,* vol. 1 (Washington, D.C.: Government Printing Office, 1966), p. 72.

27. Kevin Phillips, *The Politics of Rich and Poor* (New York: Random House, 1990), p. 88.

28. John W. Kingdon, *Agendas, Alternatives, and Public Policies* (Boston: Little, Brown, 1984), p. 25.

29. Richard E. Neustadt, "Presidency and Legislation: The Growth of Central Clearance," *American Political Science Review* 48 (September 1954), pp. 641–671.

30. Seth King, "Reagan, in Bid for Budget Votes, Reported to Yield on Sugar Prices," *New York Times,* 27 June 1981, p. A1.

31. Jeffrey M. Berry and Kent E. Portney, "Centralizing Regulatory Control and Interest Group Access: The Quayle Council on Competitiveness," in *Interest Group Politics,* 4th ed., ed. Allan J. Cigler and Burdett A. Loomis (Washington, D.C.: Congressional Quarterly Press, 1994), pp. 319–347.

32. The extent to which popularity affects presidential influence in Congress is difficult to determine with any precision. For an overview of this issue, see Jon R. Bond, Richard Fleisher, and Glen S. Katz, "An Overview of the Empirical Findings on Presidential-Congressional Relations," in *Rivals for Power,* ed. James A. Thurber (Washington, D.C.: Congressional Quarterly Press, 1996), pp. 103–139.

33. Sidney M. Milkis, *The President and the Parties* (New York: Oxford University Press, 1993), pp. 189–191.

34. John Aloysius Farrell, "A Loyal Standard Bearer," *Boston Globe,* 7 June 1996, p. A1.

35. Fred Barnes, "Hour of Power," *New Republic,* 3 September 1990, p. 12.

36. Alexander George, "The Case for Multiple Advocacy in Foreign Policy," *American Political Science Review* (September 1972), pp. 751–782.

37. John P. Burke and Fred I. Greenstein, *How Presidents Test Reality* (New York: Russell Sage Foundation, 1989); Richard E. Neustadt and Ernest R. May, *Thinking in Time* (New York: Free Press, 1986).

38. Dan Balz, "Clinton Concedes Marital Wrongdoing," *Washington Post,* 27 January 1992, p. A1.

Chapter 10 / The Bureaucracy
pp. 246–263

1. Adam Bryant, "F.A.A. Struggles as Airlines Turn to Subcontracts," *New York Times,* 2 June 1996, p. 1.

2. James Q. Wilson, *Bureaucracy* (New York: Basic Books, 1989), p. 25.

3. Bruce D. Porter, "Parkinson's Law Revisited: War and the Growth of American Government," *Public Interest* 60 (Summer 1980), p. 50.

4. See generally Ballard C. Campbell, *The Growth of American Government* (Bloomington: Indiana University Press, 1995).

5. See Anne Schneider and Helen Ingram, "Social Construction of Target Populations: Implications for Politics and Policy," *American Political Science Review* 87 (June 1993), pp. 334–347.

6. Theda Skocpol, *Protecting Soldiers and Mothers: The Political Origins of Social Policy in the United States* (Cambridge, Mass.: Harvard University Press, 1992).

7. Linda L. M. Bennett and Stephen Earl Bennett, "Looking at Leviathan: Dimensions of Opinion About Big Government," in *Broken Contract*, ed. Stephen C. Craig (Boulder, Colo.: Westview Press, 1996), pp. 23–45.

8. John T. Tierney, "Government Corporations and Managing the Public's Business," *Political Science Quarterly* 99 (Spring 1984), pp. 73–92.

9. U.S. Bureau of the Census, *Statistical Abstract of the United States, 1999* (Washington, D.C.: U.S. Governmental Printing Office, 1999), pp. 364, 411.

10. U.S. Bureau of the Census, *Statistical Abstract of the United States, 1992* (Washington, D.C.: U.S. Government Printing Office, 1992), pp. 332–333.

11. Patricia Wallace Ingraham, *The Foundation of Merit* (Baltimore: Johns Hopkins University Press, 1995), p. 9.

12. Doris A. Graber, *Mass Media and American Politics*, 3d ed. (Washington, D.C.: Congressional Quarterly Press, 1989), p. 51.

13. Jeffrey M. Berry, *Feeding Hungry People* (New Brunswick, N.J.: Rutgers University Press, 1984).

14. Charles E. Lindblom, "The Science of Muddling Through," *Public Administration Review* 19 (Spring 1959), pp. 79–88.

15. See Michael T. Hayes, *Incrementalism and Public Policy* (White Plains, N.Y.: Longman, 1992).

16. Andrew Weiss and Edward Woodhouse, "Reframing Incrementalism: A Constructive Response to the Critics," *Policy Sciences* 25 (August 1992), pp. 255–273.

17. John Frohnmeyer, *Leaving Town Alive* (Boston: Houghton Mifflin, 1993), pp. 213, 262.

18. Thomas W. Church and Robert T. Nakamura, *Cleaning Up the Mess* (Washington, D.C.: Brookings Institution, 1993).

19. See generally Terry M. Moe, "The Politics of Bureaucratic Structure," in *Can the Government Govern?*, ed. John E. Chubb and Paul E. Peterson (Washington, D.C.: Brookings Institution, 1989), pp. 267–329.

20. See generally John J. DiIulio, Jr., Gerald Garvey, and Donald F. Kettl, *Improving Government Performance: An Owner's Manual* (Washington, D.C.: Brookings Institution, 1993).

21. David Vogel, "AIDS and the Politics of Drug Lag," *Public Interest* 96 (Summer 1989), pp. 73–85.

22. A good short introduction to TQM in government is James E. Swiss, "Adapting Total Quality Management to Government," *Public Administration Review* 52 (July–August 1992), pp. 356–362.

23. See Donald F. Kettl and John J. DiIulio, Jr. (eds.), *Inside the Reinvention Machine* (Washington, D.C.: Brookings Institution, 1995); and Ronald Moe, "The 'Reinventing Government' Exercise: Misinterpreting the Problem, Misjudging the Consequences," *Public Administration Review* 54 (March–April 1994), pp. 111–122.

Chapter 11 / The Courts
pp. 264–289

1. Keith White, "Danforth Says Court Nominee Is Making His Own Case," Gannett News Service, 19 July 1991 (LEXIS).

2. David Brock, *The Real Anita Hill* (New York: Free Press, 1992), p. 61; Jane Mayer and Jill Abramson, *Strange Justice: The Selling of Clarence Thomas* (Boston: Houghton Mifflin, 1994).

3. Jeffrey Rosen, "Annals of Law: Moving On," *The New Yorker*, 29 April and 6 May 1996, p. 73.

4. Ibid., pp. 66–67.

5. *Missouri v. Jenkins*, 515 U.S. (1995); *Adarand Constructors, Inc. v. Peña*, 515 U.S. (1995).

6. Felix Frankfurter and James M. Landis, *The Business of the Supreme Court* (New York: Macmillan, 1928), pp. 5–14; and Julius Goebel, Jr., *Antecedents and Beginnings to 1801*, vol. 1 of *The History*

of the Supreme Court of the United States (New York: Macmillan, 1971).

7. Maeva Marcus (ed.), *The Justices on Circuit, 1795–1800,* vol. 3 of *The Documentary History of the Supreme Court of the United States, 1789–1800* (New York: Columbia University Press, 1990).

8. Robert G. McCloskey, *The United States Supreme Court* (Chicago: University of Chicago Press, 1960), p. 31.

9. *Marbury v. Madison,* 1 Cranch 137 at 177, 178 (1803).

10. Interestingly, the term *judicial review* dates only to 1910; it was apparently unknown to Marshall and his contemporaries. Robert Lowry Clinton, *Marbury v. Madison and Judicial Review* (Lawrence: University Press of Kansas, 1989), p. 7.

11. Henry J. Abraham, *The Judicial Process,* 6th ed. (New York: Oxford University Press, 1993), pp. 274–279; Lee Epstein et al., *The Supreme Court Compendium* (Washington, D.C.: Congressional Quarterly Press, 1994), Table 2-12.

12. *Ware v. Hylton,* 3 Dallas 199 (1796).

13. *Martin v. Hunter's Lessee,* 1 Wheat. 304 (1816).

14. *Constitution of the United States of America: Annotated and Interpreted* (Washington, D.C.: U.S. Government Printing Office, 1987) and supplements.

15. Garry Wills, *Explaining America: The Federalist* (Garden City, N.Y.: Doubleday, 1981), pp. 127–136.

16. *State Justice Institute News,* 4 (Spring 1993), p. 1.

17. Charles Alan Wright, *Handbook on the Law of Federal Courts,* 3d ed. (St. Paul, Minn.: West, 1976), p. 7.

18. William H. Rehnquist, "The 1999 Year-End Report on the Federal Judiciary," *The Third Branch* 32, 1 (January 2000), on-line at <www.uscourts. gov/ttb/jan00ttb/jan2000.html>.

19. Ibid.

20. Linda Greenhouse, "Precedent for Lower Courts: Tyrant or Teacher?" *New York Times,* 29 January 1988, p. B7.

21. *Texas v. Johnson,* 491 U.S. 397 (1989); *United States v. Eichman,* 496 U.S. 310 (1990).

22. *Regents of the University of California v. Bakke,* 438 U.S. 265 (1978).

23. *Adarand Constructors, Inc. v. Peña,* 515 U.S. (1995); *Miller v. Johnson,* 515 U.S. (1995).

24. "Reading Petitions Is for Clerks Only at High Court Now," *Wall Street Journal,* 11 October 1990, p. B7.

25. H. W. Perry, Jr., *Deciding to Decide: Agenda Setting in the United States Supreme Court* (Cambridge, Mass.: Harvard University Press, 1991); Gregory A. Caldiera and John R. Wright, "The Discuss List: Agenda Building in the Supreme Court," 24 *Law & Society Review* 807 (1990).

26. Doris M. Provine, *Case Selection in the United States Supreme Court* (Chicago: University of Chicago Press, 1980), pp. 74–102.

27. Perry, *Deciding to Decide,* p. 286.

28. "Rising Fixed Opinions," *New York Times,* 22 February 1988, p. 14. See also Linda Greenhouse, "At the Bar," *New York Times,* 28 July 1989, p. 21.

29. Jeffrey A. Segal and Harold J. Spaeth, *The Supreme Court and the Attitudinal Model* (Cambridge: Cambridge University Press, 1993).

30. Thomas G. Walker, Lee Epstein, and William J. Dixon, "On the Mysterious Demise of Consensual Norms in the United States Supreme Court," *Journal of Politics* 50 (1988), pp. 361–389.

31. See, for example, Walter F. Murphy, *Elements of Judicial Strategy* (Chicago: University of Chicago Press, 1964); and Bob Woodward and Scott Armstrong, *The Brethren* (New York: Simon & Schuster, 1979).

32. Greenhouse, "At the Bar," p. 21.

33. Stephen L. Wasby, *The Supreme Court in the Federal Judicial System,* 3d ed. (Chicago: Nelson-Hall, 1988), pp. 107–110.

34. Sheldon Goldman and Elliott Slotnick, "Clinton's First Term Judiciary: Many Bridges to Cross," *Judicature* 80 (1997), pp. 254–273.

35. *Congressional Quarterly's Guide to the U.S. Supreme Court,* 2d ed. (Washington, D.C.: Congressional Quarterly Press, 1990), pp. 878–890.

36. Maureen Dowd, "The Supreme Court: Conservative Black Judge, Clarence Thomas, Named to Marshall's Court Seat," *New York Times,* 2 July 1991, pp. A1, A16.

37. *Brown v. Board of Education II,* 349 U.S. 294 (1955).

38. Alexander M. Bickel, *The Least Dangerous Branch* (Indianapolis: Bobbs-Merrill, 1962); and Robert A. Dahl, "Decision-Making in a Democracy: The Supreme Court as a National Policy-Maker," 6 *Journal of Public Law* 279 (1962).

39. William Mishler and Reginal S. Sheehan, "The Supreme Court as a Countermajoritarian Institution? The Impact of Public Opinion on Supreme Court Decisions," *American Political Science Review* 87 (1993), pp. 87–101.

40. Thomas R. Marshall, *Public Opinion and the Supreme Court* (Boston: Unwin Hyman, 1989).

41. Ibid., pp. 192–193; Gerald N. Rosenberg, *The Hollow Hope: Can Courts Bring About Social Change?* (Chicago: University of Chicago Press, 1991).

42. William J. Brennan, Jr., "State Supreme Court Judge Versus United States Supreme Court Justice: A Change in Function and Perspective," 19 *University of Florida Law Review* 225 (1966).

Chapter 12 / Civil Liberties and Civil Rights   pp. 290–333

1. *United States v. Baker and Gonda,* 890 F. Supp. 1375 (1995).

2. Charles Platt, *Anarchy Online* (New York: HarperPrism, 1997.)

3. *United States v. Baker and Gonda,* 890 F. Supp. 1375 (1995).

4. *Adarand Constructors, Inc. v. Peña,* 518 U.S. (1995); Seth Mydans, "Challenging the Concept of 'Disadvantaged,'" *New York Times,* 18 June 1995, sec. 1, p. 8.

5. Learned Hand, *The Bill of Rights* (Boston: Atheneum, 1958), p. 1.

6. Leonard W. Levy, *The Establishment Clause: Religion and the First Amendment* (New York: Macmillan, 1986); Leo Pfeffer, *Church, State, and Freedom* (Boston: Beacon, 1953); and Leonard W. Levy, "The Original Meaning of the Establishment Clause of the First Amendment," in *Religion and the State,* ed. James E. Wood, Jr. (Waco, Tex.: Baylor University Press, 1985), pp. 43–83.

7. *Reynolds v. United States,* 98 U.S. 145 (1879).

8. *Everson v. Board of Education,* 330 U.S. 1 (1947).

9. *Board of Education v. Allen,* 392 U.S. 236 (1968).

10. *Lemon v. Kurtzman,* 403 U.S. 602 (1971).

11. *Agostini v. Felton,* 96 U.S. 552 (1997).

12. *Engle v. Vitale,* 370 U.S. 421 (1962).

13. *Wallace v. Jaffree,* 472 U.S. 38 (1985).

14. *Lee v. Weisman,* 505 U.S. (1992).

15. Michael W. McConnell, "The Origins and Historical Understanding of the Free Exercise of Religion," 103 *Harvard Law Review* 1409 (1990).

16. *Sherbert v. Verner,* 374 U.S. 398 (1963).

17. *Employment Division v. Smith,* 494 U.S. 872 (1990).

18. *Boerne v. Flores,* 95 U.S. 2074 (1997).

19. Laurence Tribe, *Treatise on American Constitutional Law,* 2d ed. (St. Paul, Minn.: West, 1988), p. 566.

20. Zechariah Chafee, *Free Speech in the United States* (Cambridge, Mass.: Harvard University Press, 1941).

21. Leonard W. Levy, *The Emergence of a Free Press* (New York: Oxford University Press, 1985).

22. *Schenck v. United States,* 249 U.S. 47 (1919).

23. *Gitlow v. New York,* 268 U.S. 652 (1925).

24. *Dennis v. United States,* 341 U.S. 494 (1951).

25. *Brandenburg v. Ohio,* 395 U.S. 444 (1969).

26. *Tinker v. Des Moines Independent County School District,* 393 U.S. 503 at 508 (1969).

27. *United States v. Eichman,* 496 U.S. 310 (1990).

28. Linda Greenhouse, "Supreme Court Voids Flag Law," *New York Times,* 12 June 1990, p. A1.

29. *Miller v. California,* 413 U.S. 15 (1973).

30. *ACLU v. Reno* (1996 U.S. Dist. LEXIS) (June 12, 1996).

31. *Reno v. ACLU,* 96 U.S. 511 (1997).

32. Donald Alexander Downs, *The New Politics of Pornography* (Chicago: University of Chicago Press, 1989), pp. 95–143.

33. *American Booksellers Ass'n v. Hudnut,* 598 F. Supp. 1316 (1984).

34. *New York Times v. Sullivan,* 376 U.S. 254 (1964).

35. *Near v. Minnesota,* 283 U.S. 697 (1931).

36. For a detailed account of *Near,* see Fred W. Friendly, *Minnesota Rag* (New York: Random House, 1981).

37. *New York Times v. United States,* 403 U.S. 713 (1971).

38. *Branzburg v. Hayes,* 408 U.S. 665 (1972).

39. *Hazelwood School District v. Kuhlmeier,* 484 U.S. 260 (1988).

40. *United States v. Cruikshank,* 92 U.S. 542 (1876); *Constitution of the United States of America: Annotated and Interpreted* (Washington, D.C.: U.S. Government Printing Office, 1973), p. 1031.

41. *DeJonge v. Oregon,* 299 U.S. 353 (1937).

42. *United States v. Miller,* 307 U.S. 174 (1939).

43. *Barron v. Baltimore,* 32 U.S. (7 Pet.) 243 (1833).

44. *Chicago B. & Q. R. v. Chicago,* 166 U.S. 226 (1897).

45. *Gitlow v. New York,* 268 U.S. at 666 (1925).

46. *Palko v. Connecticut,* 302 U.S. 319 (1937).

47. *Duncan v. Louisiana,* 391 U.S. 145 (1968).

48. *McNabb v. United States,* 318 U.S. 332 (1943).

49. *Baldwin v. New York,* 399 U.S. 66 (1970).

50. Anthony Lewis, *Gideon's Trumpet* (New York: Random House, 1964).

51. *Gideon v. Wainwright,* 372 U.S. 335 (1963).

52. *Miranda v. Arizona,* 384 U.S. 436 (1966).

53. *Wolf v. Colorado,* 338 U.S. 25 (1949).

54. *Mapp v. Ohio,* 367 U.S. 643 (1961).

55. *United States v. Leon,* 468 U.S. 897 (1984).

56. *James v. Illinois,* 493 U.S. 307 (1990).

57. Paul Brest, *Processes of Constitutional Decision-Making* (Boston: Little, Brown, 1975), p. 708.

58. *Griswold v. Connecticut,* 381 U.S. 479 (1965).

59. *Roe v. Wade,* 410 U.S. 113 (1973).

60. See John Hart Ely, "The Wages of Crying Wolf: A Comment on *Roe v. Wade,"* 82 *Yale Law Journal* 920 (1973).

61. *Webster v. Reproductive Health Services,* 492 U.S. 490 (1989).

62. *Planned Parenthood v. Casey,* 505 U.S. (1992).

63. *Bowers v. Hardwick,* 478 U.S. 186 (1986).

64. *The Gallup Poll Monthly* (August 1991), p. 56; Paul M. Sniderman and Thomas Piazza, *The Scar of Race* (Cambridge, Mass.: Belknap Press of Harvard University Press, 1993), pp. 133–134; Jack Citrin, "Affirmative Action in the People's Court," *The Public Interest* 122 (1996), pp. 40–41.

65. *The Slaughterhouse Cases,* 83 U.S. 36 (1873).

66. *Civil Rights Cases,* 109 U.S. 3 (1883).

67. Mary Beth Norton et al., *A People and a Nation: A History of the United States,* 3d ed. (Boston: Houghton Mifflin, 1990), p. 490.

68. *Plessy v. Ferguson,* 163 U.S. 537 (1896).

69. *Plessy,* 163 U.S. at 562 (Harlan, J., dissenting).

70. *Cummings v. County Board of Education,* 175 U.S. 528 (1899).

71. *Brown v. Board of Education,* 347 U.S. 483 (1954).

72. *Brown v. Board of Education,* 347 U.S. 483, 495 (1954).

73. *Brown v. Board of Education,* 347 U.S. 483, 494 (1954).

74. *Brown v. Board of Education II,* 349 U.S. 294 (1955).

75. Jack W. Peltason, *Fifty-eight Lonely Men,* rev. ed. (Urbana: University of Illinois Press, 1971).

76. *Alexander v. Holmes County Board of Education,* 396 U.S. 19 (1969).

77. *Milliken v. Bradley,* 418 U.S. 717 (1974).

78. Norton et al., *People and a Nation,* p. 943.

79. But see Abigail M. Thernstrom, *Whose Vote Counts? Affirmative Action and Minority Voting Rights* (Cambridge, Mass.: Harvard University Press, 1987).

80. *Richmond v. J. A. Croson Co.,* 488 U.S. 469 (1989).

81. *Martin v. Wilks,* 490 U.S. 755 (1989); *Wards Cove Packing Co. v. Atonio,* 490 U.S. 642 (1989); *Patterson v. McLean Credit Union,* 491 U.S. 164 (1989); *Price Waterhouse v. Hopkins,* 490 U.S. 228 (1989); *Lorance v. AT&T Technologies,* 490 U.S. 900 (1989); and *EEOC v. Arabian American Oil Co.,* 499 U.S. 244 (1991).

82. *Saint Francis College v. Al-Khazraji,* 481 U.S. 604 (1987).

83. Dee Brown, *Bury My Heart at Wounded Knee: An Indian History of the American West* (New York: Holt, Rinehart & Winston, 1971).

84. *Muller v. Oregon,* 208 U.S. 412 (1908).

85. *International Union, United Automobile, Aerospace & Agricultural Implement Workers of America v. Johnson Controls,* 499 U.S. 187 (1991).

86. *Reed v. Reed,* 404 U.S. 71 (1971).

87. *Frontiero v. Richardson,* 411 U.S. 677 (1973).

88. *Craig v. Boren,* 429 U.S. 190 (1976).

89. *J.E.B. v. Alabama ex rel. T.B.,* 508 U.S. (1994).

90. *United States v. Virginia,* slip op. 94-1941 & 94-2107 (decided June 26, 1996).

91. Melvin I. Urofsky, *A March of Liberty* (New York: Knopf, 1988), p. 902.

92. *Harris v. Forklift Systems,* 510 U.S. (1993).

93. *Facts on File* 206B2 (4 June 1965).

94. As quoted in Melvin I. Urofsky, *A Conflict of Rights: The Supreme Court and Affirmative Action* (New York: Scribner's, 1991), p. 29.

95. *Regents of the University of California v. Bakke,* 438 U.S. 265 (1978).

96. *United Steelworkers of America, AFL-CIO v. Weber,* 443 U.S. 193 (1979).

97. *Firefighters v. Stotts,* 467 U.S. 561 (1984).

98. *Adarand Constructors, Inc. v. Peña,* 518 U.S. (1995).

99. William H. Honan, "Moves to End Affirmative Action Gain Support Nationwide," *New York Times,* 31 March 1996, p. 30; James Brooke, "Colorado Bases College Aid on Need Rather Than Race," *New York Times,* 16 January 1996, p. A8.

100. Stephen Earl Bennett et al., *Americans' Opinions About Affirmative Action* (Cincinnati: University of Cincinnati, Institute for Policy Research, 1995), p. 4.

Chapter 13 / Policymaking and the Budget pp. 334–355

1. Allen Verhey, "Theology After Dolly: Cloning and the Human Family," *Christian Century,* 19 March 1997, p. 285.

2. "Clinton Urges Ban on Cloning of Humans," *Christian Century,* 18 June 1997, p. 583.

3. Brian McGrory, "President Asks for Human Clone Ban," *Boston Sunday Globe,* 11 January 1998, p. 1.

4. These Time/CNN poll results by Yankelovitch Partners, Inc., from 26–27 February 1997, were published in Jeffrey Kluger, "Will We Follow the Sheep?" *Time,* 10 March 1997, p. 71.

5. The policymaking process can be depicted in many ways. Another approach, a bit more elaborate than this, is described in James E. Anderson, *Public Policymaking,* 2d ed. (Boston: Houghton Mifflin, 1994), p. 37.

6. See Christopher J. Bosso, "The Contextual Bases of Problem Definition," in *The Politics of Problem Definition,* ed. David A. Rochefort and Roger W. Cobb (Lawrence: University Press of Kansas, 1994), pp. 182–203.

7. Jeffrey M. Berry, *The Interest Group Society,* 3d ed. (New York: Longman, 1997), p. 187.

8. For a brief overview of the evolution of AT&T and government regulation, see Robert W. Crandell, *After the Breakup* (Washington, D.C.: Brookings Institution, 1991), pp. 16–42.

9. See Martha Derthick and Paul J. Quirk, *The Politics of Deregulation* (Washington, D.C.: Brookings Institution, 1985); and Robert Britt Horowitz, *The Irony of Regulatory Reform* (New York: Oxford University Press, 1989).

10. Edmund L. Andrews, "Congress Votes To Reshape Communications Industry, Ending a 4-Year Struggle," *New York Times,* 2 February 1996, p. A1.

11. Jeffrey M. Berry, "The Dynamic Qualities of Issue Networks," paper delivered at the annual meeting of the American Political Science Association, New York, September 1994.

12. Jeffrey M. Berry, "Subgovernments, Issue Networks, and Political Conflict," in *Remaking American Politics,* ed. Richard A. Harris and Sidney M. Milkis (Boulder, Colo.: Westview Press, 1989), pp. 239–260.

13. N. Gregory Mankiw, "Symposium on Keynesian Economics Today," *Journal of Economic Perspectives* 7 (Winter 1993), pp. 3–4. In his preface to four articles in the symposium, Mankiw says, "The literature that bears the label 'Keynesian' is broad, and it does not offer a single vision of how the economy behaves."

14. For a concise discussion of the 1990 budget reforms, see James A. Thurber, "Congressional-Presidential Battles to Balance the Budget," in James A. Thurber (ed.), *Rivals for Power: Presidential-Congressional Relations* (Washington, D.C.: Congressional Quarterly Press, 1996), pp. 196–202.

15. *A Citizen's Guide to the Federal Budget,* <http://www.access.gpo. gov/su_docs?budget99/guide/ guide04.html>.

16. Ronald D. Elving and Andrew Taylor, "A Balanced-Budget Deal Won, a Defining Issue Lost," *Congressional Quarterly Weekly Report,* 2 August 1996, pp. 1831–1836.

17. Richard A. Musgrave and Peggy B. Musgrave, *Public Finance in Theory and Practice,* 2d ed. (New York: McGraw-Hill, 1976), p. 42.

18. Mark T. Kehoe, "Clinton Veto Tally: Up to 11," *Congressional Quarterly Weekly Report,* 6 January 1996, p. 10.

19. George Hager, "Congress, Clinton Yield Enough to Close the Book on Fiscal '96," *Congressional Quarterly Weekly Report,* 27 April 1996, p. 1155.

20. Elizabeth Kolbert, "Public Opinion Polls Swerve with the Turns of a Phrase," *New York Times,* 5 June 1995, p. 1; and Adam Clymer, "Of Touching Third Rails and Tackling Medicare," *New York Times,* 27 October 1995, p. A11.

21. Times-Mirror Center for the People and the Press, "Voter Anxiety Dividing GOP: Energized Democrats Backing Clinton," press release of 14 November 1995, p. 88.

22. Fay Lomax Cook et al., *Convergent Perspectives on Social Welfare Policy: The Views from the General Public, Members of Congress, and AFDC Recipients* (Evanston, Ill.: Center for Urban Affairs and Policy Research, Northwestern University, 1988), Table 4-1.

23. U.S. Bureau of the Census, U.S. Department of Commerce, *Statistical Abstract of the United States, 1995* (Washington, D.C.: U.S. Government Printing Office, 1995), p. 289.

Index

Credits *(continued from the copyright page)*

Photos
Chapter 1: p. 1, Michael Dwyer/Stock Boston; p. 8, Jim Wilson/NYT Pictures; p. 19, Bob Daemmrich/The Image Works; *Chapter 2:* p. 28, Camerique/Index Stock Imagery; p. 29, Ron Edmonds/AP-Wide World Photos; p. 32, Courtesy of the John Carter Brown Library at Brown University; p. 45, Daguerreotype of Isaac Jefferson, by Plumbe, ca. 1845 (MSS 2041), Special Collections Department, University of Virginia Library; p. 52, Corbis Images; *Chapter 3:* p. 57, Bob Daemmrich/Stock Boston; p. 61, Liss/Liaison International; p. 62, left, Michelle Bridwell/Photo Edit, right, Benali/Liaison International; p. 70, Library of Congress; p. 76, Eastcott/Momatiuk/Woodfin Camp and Associates; *Chapter 4:* p. 79, J.L. Atlan/SYGMA; p. 84, Corbis Images; p. 100, AP-Wide World Photos; *Chapter 5:* p. 112, Bruce Kliewe/Index Stock Imagery; p. 114, left, Division of Rare and Manuscript Collections, Cornell University, Carl A. Kroch Library; right, Bachrach Photography; p. 115, Eugene Richards/Magnum Photos; p. 122, left, National Archives, right, Brown Brothers; p. 133, left, right, David Maialetti/Philadelphia Daily News; *Chapter 6:* p. 138, Joe Traver/Liaison International; p. 139, Dan Wagner; p. 147, Craig Lassig, © AFP/Corbis; p. 159, Jim Cole/AP-Wide World Photos; *Chapter 7:* p. 173, Mark Burnett/ Photo Researchers; p. 186, Charles Moore/Black Star; *Chapter 8:* p. 194, Mark Reinstein/The Image Works; p. 213, Reuters/Larry Downing/Archive Photos; *Chapter 9:* p. 223, Robert Llewellyn; p. 243, AP/Wide World Photos; *Chapter 10:* p. 246, P.F. Bentley; p. 247, Rick Bowner/Wide World Photos; p. 256, J. Scott Applewhite/Wide World Photos; p. 260, Ron Watts/Black Star; *Chapter 11:* p. 264, Camerique/Index Stock Imagery; p. 265, left, Brad Markel/Liaison International, right, F. Lee Corkran/Corbis-Sygma; p. 273, Liaison International; p. 277, The Supreme Court Historical Society; p. 280, Ken Heinen; *Chapter 12:* p. 290, Paul Conklin/Photo Edit; p. 317, Leonard Freed/Magnum Photos; p. 320, Brown Brothers; p. 325, AP-Wide World Photos; *Chapter 13:* p. 334, Myrleen Ferguson Cate/Photo Edit; p. 349, Pool Photo/Newsmakers/Liason Agency.

Text and Art
Figure 4.3: 1996 National Election Study. 1996 Center for Political Studies, University of Michigan Press. Used with permission.

Figure 5.2: Reprinted by permission of the publisher from *American National Election Studies Data Sourcebook, 1952-1978* by Warren E. Miller, Arthur H. Miller, and Edward J. Schneider, Cambridge, Mass.: Harvard University Press. Copyright © 1980 by the President and Fellows of Harvard College.

Figure 7.1: Based on Jeffrey M. Berry, Kent E. Portney, and Ken Thomson, *The Rebirth of Urban Democracy.* Copyright © 1993. Used by permission of Brookings Institution.

Figure 9.1: Samuel Kernell, *Going Public,* 3rd ed. (Washington D.C.: Congressional Quarterly Press, 1997), fig. 4.2. Copyright © 1997 by Congressional Quarterly Press. Used with permission.

Figure 9.2: NYT Graphics/NYT Pictures. New York Times/CBS News Poll, *New York Times,* March 1, 1998. Reprinted by permission.

Table 9.1: "An Introduction to Presidential-Congressional Rivalry," in *Rivals for Power*, ed. James A. Thurber, pp. 8, 9. Copyright © 1996 CQ Press.

Figure 13.2: From Jeffrey M. Berry, "The Dynamic Qualities of Issue Networks, " paper delivered at the annual meeting of the American Political Science Association, New York City, September 1994.